two key acc
stead, the sa
gies, learn t
proc

SALES MANAGEMENT: A CAREER PATH APPROACH

G. David Hughes
The University of North Caroli

Library of Congres
Hughes, G. David (G
Sales management
McKee, Charles H. Sing
P. cm.
Includes bibliographical ref
ISBN 0-538-87866-5
1. Sales management—Vocatio
guidance. I. McKee, Daryl O. II.
HF5438.4.H825 1998
658.81002373—dc21

Printed in the United States of America

International Thomson Publishing
South-Western College Publishing
The ITP trademark is used under license.

ITP®
International Thomson Publishing is an ITP Company.

Cincinnati • Albany • B
New York • Pac

Exhibit I.2

Strategy Level	
Business strategy	All
Marketing strategy	One p One ma
Sales strategy	Sell to su
Failure to reinvent sales force leads to	Insufficient s customer cove

Adapted from the consulting brochure of The Alexander

5. Identify the criteria you would use in selecting a job in selling.

6. Who could help evaluate your fit for a sales career?

ENDNOTES

1. *Statistical Abstract of the United States,* issues from 1984 to 1990.
2. *U.S. Occupational Outlook,* Fall, 1991.
3. Wilton Woods, The Jobs Americans Hold, *Fortune,* July 12, 1993, p. 54.
4. Professional Management Foundation, A National Survey on Hiring Projections for the First Half of 1997, Report #38, prepared for Management Recruiters International, Inc., December, 1996, pp. 16–21.
5. Rob Prazmark Goes for the Gold, *Sales & Marketing Management,* December, 1990, pp. 24–25.
6. The name is disguised, but the case is real. The student graduated from an undergraduate program in business in 1990.
7. Jaclyn Fierman, The Death and Rebirth of the Salesman, *Fortune,* July 25, 1994, pp. 80–91.
8. Fierman, 1994.
9. Mack Hanan, James Cribbin, and Herman Heiser, *Consultative Selling,* New York: American Management Association, Inc., 1970.
10. Buyers Choice, *Sales & Marketing Management,* August 20, 1979, pp. 38–40.
11. Scott Paper is on a Roll, *Sales & Marketing Management,* September, 1991, p. 50.
12. Interview by G. David Hughes with Alston Gardner, President and co-founder of Target Market Systems and Tim Sullivan, vice president of marketing, March 25, 1997.
13. William Keenan, Jr., Death of the Sales Manager, *Sales & Marketing Management,* October, 1994, pp. 66–74.
14. Based in part on *Sales & Marketing Management,* Are Your Reps Ready for the Year 2000?, February, 1997, p. 36.
15. Fierman, 1994.
16. Fierman, 1994, p. 80.
17. Ibid.
18. Fierman, 1994.
19. Ibid.
20. Ibid.
21. *Reinventing the Sales Organization,* The conference Board Report Number 1102-95-CH which summarized a conference held June 23, 1994 at the Fairmont Hotel, Chicago, IL.
22. David J. Cichelli, Is it time to re-invent your organization, presentation at The Conference Board conference on The Reinvented Sales Organization, *ibid.*
23. James W. Cortada, Reading the tea leaves: The future of sales management, presentation at The Conference Board conference on The Reinvented Sales Organization, *ibid.*
24. Gardner interview, March 25, 1997.
25. Salespeople's Average Annual Compensation, *Sales & Marketing Management,* June 17, 1991, p. 73.
26. Personal communication from Janet C. Prill, Organization Consultant, Organization & Management Systems, IBM United States, June 26, 1992.
27. Prill.
28. Information about the Sales and Marketing Executives International and its college-administered certification program can be obtained at its home page on the world wide web (http://www.smei.org).
29. Laurie Hays, IBM's Gerstner Holds Back From Sales Force Shake-up, *The Wall Street Journal,* July 7, 1993, B1, B6.
30. Gerhard Gschwandtner, Fran Tarkenton, *Personal Selling Power,* May/June, 1991, p. 14.
31. National Association of Colleges and Employers, *Salary Survey,* April, 1997, Bethlehem, PA.
32. http://www.dartnellcorp.com/pressl.html, All Levels of Sales Reps Post Impressive Earnings Gains, Aug. 1, 1997.
33. Michele Marchetti, Enough Money? *Sales & Marketing Management,* October, 1996, pp. 51–60.
34. Based on David Whitford, This Year's Model, *INC.,* February, 1995, pp. 45–52.

2

WHAT SALESPEOPLE DO

LEARNING GOALS

1. To examine the activities of a salesperson
2. To identify aspects of the salesperson's job that are undergoing change
3. To explore sales and sales management as a potential career

No two days are alike in the life of a salesperson, and no two salespeople's jobs are alike. This makes it difficult to describe precisely what salespeople do. In this chapter we will examine the activities and job descriptions for representatives in a variety of industries and companies, and then present some generalizations that will help the reader to decide whether to consider a selling career further and if so, which industry to choose. Assignments at the end of the chapter will provide personal experiences and insights into specific industries and companies.

SELLING IN THE INFORMATION AGE

A person entering sales now begins his or her selling career at a special time. Two historical forces have merged to change the selling process. The first historical force was dispersion of productive capacity worldwide. Sales in the United States during the 1960s and 1970s were driven by its domination of world production. The United States dominated in part because its manufacturing facilities were undamaged during World War II. Anyone could sell anything anywhere. As Japanese manufacturers began to intrude on the world market in the 1980s with high quality products, economic domination began to shift. The new production facilities used efficient cost-reducing processes that were difficult to imitate. Buyers began to focus on value, and selling became more challenging.

The second historical force was driven by the development of low-cost computing and communications technology. In the words of Robert J. Hershock, 3M Corporate Vice Pres-

Title: Salesperson, Food Sales Division

I. Objectives: To provide primary contact with established and potential customers within an assigned territory with the objective of achieving optimal sales volume.

II. Key Responsibilities: Selling, sales planning, promotion, and market research while constantly striving to offer superior customer service.

III. Specific Responsibilities

A. Selling
1. Sell personal advice, availability, the reputation of the company, and finally the food products.
2. Advise established customers on pertinent business issues.
3. Make cold calls to establish new accounts.
4. Establish rapport and confidence with customers.

B. Sales planning
1. Anticipate customer needs by analyzing patterns of past orders.
2. Create specific selling tactics for each call.
3. Prioritize calls according to volume, future value, profitability, and needs.

C. Promotion
1. Effectively integrate promotions, such as samples, with selling effort.
2. Evaluate the effectiveness of samples.

D. Market research
1. Identify trends in the wholesale food industry and include them in the sales strategy.
2. Follow beef market prices to be able to explain reasons for wholesale price changes to customers.
3. Keep abreast of pertinent information in local merchant magazines.

E. Customer service
1. Work closely with current and potential customers to determine their needs.
2. Follow each order through to delivery and check on customer satisfaction.
3. Stress your accessibility to the customer, giving numbers for your cellular and home phones.
4. Remedy problems and complaints as quickly as possible.

IV. Organizational Relationships

A. Reporting relationships
1. Report directly to the general sales manager.
2. Communicate with credit and collection managers regarding past due accounts.
3. Supervise and coordinate the daily calling activities of the telephone salesperson for a team effort.

B. Authority
1. Exercise complete authority over pricing, within a range.
2. Exercise complete authority for delivery dates.

C. Accountability
1. Maintain accountability for prices to the customer.
2. Maintain accountability for prices to the general sales manager.

V. Personal Behavioral Attributes

A. Job-related behaviors
1. Flexibility
2. Resourcefulness
3. Self-motivation
4. Decisiveness
5. Good oral/written communication skills

B. Time and expense control
1. Excellent time management under stressful situations
2. Conscientious use of company vehicle, telephone, and other expenses to generate maximum sales at minimum costs

Exhibit **2.5**   THE SALESPERSON'S BOUNDARY

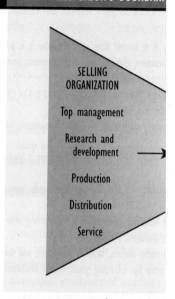

SELLING
ORGANIZATION

Top management

Research and
development

Production

Distribution

Service

Another study, focusing on
tail. Based on a survey of sale
tencies, out of 82 that were ider
people alike.[13] These were an a

- Listen.
- Communicate effectivel
- Communicate courteou:
- Establish a time manage
- Develop continuing pro
- Field questions courteo\u0274

The successful salesperson
be less than half of the work wee
person for Northwestern Mut
prospects and clients, 20% sche
5% on education and training.[14]

A separate study examined
success in salespeople.[15] The st\u1d64
results identified six "failure fa\u1d04

Poor listening skills

Lack of focus on priorities

Insufficient effort

Inability to determine cust\u1d0f

Lack of sales presentation p

Inadequate product knowle\u1d04

A sales career basically cons
services. It may take a long time

Exhibit **2.2**   JOB DESCRIPTION FOR A SALESPERSON FROM A MANUFACTURER OF CONSUMER ELECTRONICS

Title: Salesperson

I. Objectives: To achieve his/her assigned quotas within the assigned territory.

II. Responsibilities: To serve as a liaison between the store and the factory. To handle any problems that may arise.

   A. Activities

   1. Advise on products that will sell well in a particular store. Recommend advertising campaigns, promotions, and displays.

   2. Evaluate the strengths and weaknesses of the retailer.

   B. Planning

   1. Analyze market conditions to detect trends.

   2. Develop account sales strategies to maximize opportunities.

   3. Develop training sessions for retailers' salespeople.

   4. Prioritize accounts, calling on those with high potential first.

   5. Organize territory records.

   6. Complete reports accurately and in a timely manner.

   C. Personal Development

   1. Develop skills in selling, planning, communication, and customer relations.

   2. Know product attributes and benefits.

   3. Know competition.

   4. Establish rapport with wholesaler and retailer.

   5. Actively support independent stores.

   D. Qualifications

   1. A good planner

   2. Good oral and written communication skills

   3. Positive mental attitude

   4. Creative

   5. Enthusiastic

   6. Flexible

specialize in internal medicine, but not heart surgeons. The representative groups calls according to their location, to minimize travel time. The plan schedules call-backs on accounts with high sales potential. This territory plan, also known as a *working order,* is translated by the representative into a schedule of calls, known as the *forward itinerary.* This itinerary provides structure for the representative. It includes the phone numbers of hotels so that managers can locate the representative in case of emergencies. Any changes in the itinerary must be approved by the manager. The district manager uses these forward itineraries to schedule visits with each representative. The general manager and the sales administrative staff use the itinerary to contact representatives in case of an urgent need to call on an account.

The plan for the next week begins with the forward itinerary. The representative consults his or her records about the best time to call on an account, the results from previous calls, appointments that have been made, plans for cold calls, and assignments from the home office such as market surveys or recruiting assignments. The representative then creates a schedule for each day that includes extra calls to allow for broken appointments, accounts who are away, or those who are too busy. With all of this preplanning in hand, the detail person plans for the next day.

| Exhibit **2.4** | THE INTEGRATED SOFTWAI |

Title: Industry Salesperson

Grade Level: Senior Salespe

Reports To: Industry Manag

Major Purpose:

To generate maximum revenue \
Responsible for account strategie
satisfaction

Primary Responsibilities:

1. Attain or exceed software lic
2. Complete monthly reports.
3. Manage all assigned resource:
4. Develop accounts.
5. Negotiate licenses.

Requirements:

- Bachelor's degree in comp
- Five years in software sale
- Extensive software knowled
- Superior presentation and
- Excellent interpersonal skill
- Self-motivation

GENERALIZATIONS ABOUT

What are the common activi
sically, the salesperson span
as illustrated in Exhibit 2.5.
pabilities of the selling firr
buyer may be using the purc
for final consumption.

To examine the role of tl
scriptions from the following
lishing, chemicals, telecom
The following five common

1. Sell products or serv
   amounts that equal o
2. Service accounts in a
3. Maintain appropriate
4. Maintain a current l
   grams, selling skills,
5. Manage time and cor

Boy Scouts of America, Rhone-Poulenc Rorer (pharmaceutical sales), and Syncsort (software).[9]

Checking a few entries provides interesting information. For example, what would a salesperson at Great American Opportunities do? What does the company do? A few clicks reveal that it is a fundraising organization to help schools and youth organizations reach their goals. In addition, it teaches students the value of setting goals, teamwork, and money management. It describes itself as, ". . . customer-satisfaction driven, employee-oriented, high in integrity, striving for excellence, growth motivated, innovative and responsive to change, and good stewards of our resources."[10] The company is 100% employee-owned. Salary is $27,000 plus commission and bonus. Benefits are attractive, including stock options and a 401(k) program. The locations of open territories are listed. One to three years of sales experience are needed in addition to a BA or AA degree. If it fits your profile you may contact the company using its e-mail address.

Monsterboard.com lists 50,000 jobs worldwide, helps build a resume, and provides employer profiles. Careermosaic.com lists jobs, employers, on-line job fairs, and permits

| Exhibit **3.1** | HOW DO YOU MEASURE UP? |

(Use a scale of 1 = very poor to 10 = excellent)

	As rated by:	
	Self	Other
Communication Skills		
Ability to convincingly express an idea to individuals and groups	_____	_____
Energy		
Ability to maintain a high activity level for extended periods to sustain an effective performance level	_____	_____
Initiative		
Assertiveness, energy, and aptitude in getting the job done	_____	_____
Integrity		
High degree of ethical and moral standards and conduct	_____	_____
Intelligence		
Ability to learn and apply knowledge in a logical and rational manner	_____	_____
Interpersonal Skills		
Ability to present a positive impression	_____	_____
Job Interest		
Sincere interest in company products (Identify a company that interests you)	_____	_____
Motivation		
Desire to succeed by one's own efforts	_____	_____
Planning/Organization		
Ability to efficiently plan and implement a program designed to achieve an agreed upon goal	_____	_____
Resilience		
Ability to maintain effectiveness after objections, rejections, and disappointments	_____	_____

Timothy J. Trow, How to Recruit, Interview & Select Productive Sales Representatives, The National Society of Sales Training Executives, 1981, and other private sources

the posting of a resume. Thus without leaving your computer you are on your way to getting an interview.

The food industry can be a good place to get sales and merchandising experience. Hormel Foods' web site shows that the qualified candidate must have a bachelor's degree in marketing, business, management, or sales with demonstrated leadership and persuasive skills, work ethic, and an entrepreneurial spirit, and the ability to relocate. Compensation includes a company car and benefits. Available locations are listed.[11] Clicking on the web site gives information about the company and reveals four screening questions. If you fit this profile you can reply by fax.

Having seen the power of recruiting on the Internet you may decide to create your own web page. This activity would certainly convince a company that you are computer-literate. You can get help in creating a web page on the Internet. By typing www.ypn.com and clicking on a button you will see simple steps for creating an electronic resume. Another electronic resume site is www.occ.com/occ/JLK/HowToEResume.html.

The more traditional means for getting an interview include the materials at a university career services office. This office and the alumni office may have a database on alumni in industries and companies that interest you. Some alumni volunteer to be mentors to new graduates. Friends, people who work for the company, customers of the company, and professors can provide leads.

The next step in developing your strategy is planning for the interview. Using the selling steps approach, you have identified a prospect, and made an appointment. Now you must make a presentation that demonstrates, with proof, that you can meet the needs of the company.

. . . .

THE RECRUITING PROCESS

Steps in the Process

Understanding the steps in the recruiting process and their functions can reduce anxiety. The steps vary with each company. To reduce anxiety the candidate may want to ask about the steps in a particular company's recruitment process and how long they take. Here are some examples:

- **Procter & Gamble** has the following four progressive stages: (1) Resume and testing (application form, sales career interest, and problem solving), (2) Initial 30-minute interview; (3) Comprehensive interview (60 minutes), and (4) Panel interview/offer.[12]
- **Northwestern Mutual Life Insurance** uses the following steps to select candidates for an internship: (1) Interview with a top sales manager, (2) Learning how insurance works, (3) A sales aptitude test, (4) A survey of markets to see the potential, and (5) Meeting and shadowing current interns and career agents.
- **Grocery, Inc.** uses pre-selection, initial interview, second interview, a day in the field, and a final offer.
- **Wallace Company** uses an on-campus interview, an office visit that includes tests to examine logical thinking and communication skills, a small social pizza night, a day in the field, and a college day. The Wallace process takes 6 to 8 weeks.[13]

5. Take advantage of opportunities. Don't take advantage of the recruiter. Days are long and schedules are tight. It's the recruiter's responsibility to "call time," but interviewees should also be careful about the length of their responses. It's OK to give a relatively short answer and ask if the recruiter would like elaboration or another example. If the recruiter is enthralled, he or she will say yes. If the particular Q&A *is not* going right, the recruiter can rephrase, redirect, clarify, or ask a new question.

6. Make your case. If your work experience has been in a *very* different field and the recruiter is struggling to "connect," offer an explanation of how what you learned, liked, or hated makes you a better or wiser person and candidate for the job at hand.

7. It is very important to be yourself. It helps you stand out.

8. Conservative, hardworking, creative, and "people persons" are surprisingly common. Be prepared to explain how or why you are *more* creative (give examples), or what happens when *you* work with people who are not so people-oriented. How does your creativity and interest in people manifest itself in your marketing efforts?[24]

SOME FINAL QUESTIONS BY THE APPLICANT

The final decision by the applicant will require answers to a few more questions. What are the values and career patterns of the person who will be my manager? Ask to see his or her resume. If a manager has moved extensively among companies, be suspicious. Is the manager more concerned with scoreboards showing sales than with developing customers and salespeople? Do the promotional materials talk only about the company or do they emphasize the benefits of its products to customers and society? Unfavorable answers may tip the decision toward rejecting the offer.[25]

The question of compensation will require some calculations to reflect differences in cost of living. For example, assume that a person was considering an offer of $25,000 in New Orleans and one in Seattle. How much should the compensation be in Seattle to equal the New Orleans offer? To answer this question, we need to know the relative cost of living in both cities, information provided by the *ACCRA Cost of Living Index*. Values for selected cities are shown in Exhibit 3.2.

The cost of living index for New Orleans is 93.5, whereas the index for Seattle is 111.9. Using New Orleans as the denominator, because this is the basis for comparison, we multiply 111.9/93.5 times $25,000 and find that the Seattle offer must be $29,920. Going in the reverse direction, a Seattle offer of $25,000 would require only $20,889 in New Orleans.[26]

If after all of this evaluation process you are still eager to have the job, keep yourself fresh in their memory. A follow-up letter thanking the recruiter for the interview is a start. You could also send a copy of an article about the company or a competitor that appeared in *The Wall Street Journal, Business Week,* or *Fortune,* to show your continued interest in the company.

Exhibit 3.2 | CITY COST OF LIVING INDEXES

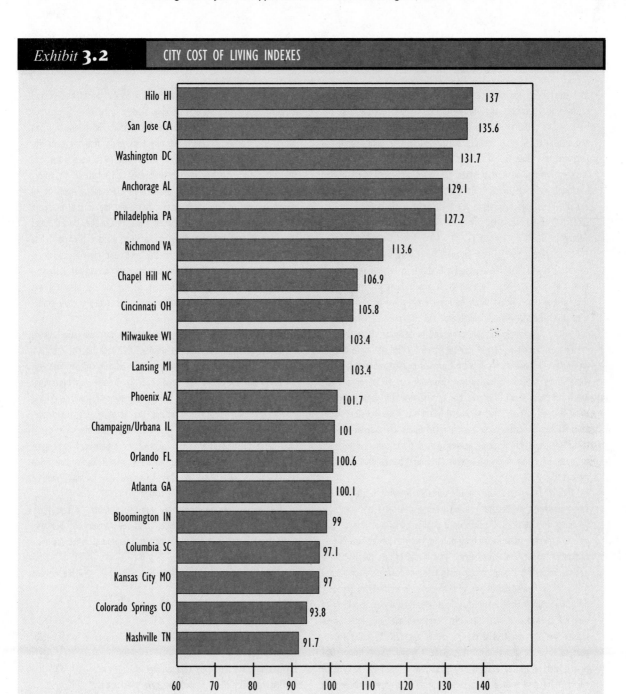

Hilo HI	137
San Jose CA	135.6
Washington DC	131.7
Anchorage AL	129.1
Philadelphia PA	127.2
Richmond VA	113.6
Chapel Hill NC	106.9
Cincinnati OH	105.8
Milwaukee WI	103.4
Lansing MI	103.4
Phoenix AZ	101.7
Champaign/Urbana IL	101
Orlando FL	100.6
Atlanta GA	100.1
Bloomington IN	99
Columbia SC	97.1
Kansas City MO	97
Colorado Springs CO	93.8
Nashville TN	91.7

Case 3.1   INTERVIEWING IN A FOREIGN CULTURE: A JAPANESE EXPERIENCE

As I stepped off the plane at Narita Airport in Japan, my mind was racing with excitement and anticipation, as I knew that the next two weeks would somehow drastically change my future. I had spent about two months sending out resumes and cover letters, in both English and Japanese, to various Japanese firms. I had already attended a Japanese Business Symposium in Washington, D.C., through which I was offered a second interview, to take place in Japan. In my mind, I had done everything possible to prepare for a job interview—research, making contacts—and I was even told to call and set up an interview when visiting Japan.

I had read stories of how Japanese firms were trying to globalize; the demand was high for bilingual individuals to help bridge the cultural and language gaps. So, with great expectations plus reassurance from people that I would surely be hired, I embarked on my trip with a positive attitude. What I hadn't expected was the way I found myself with a near-blank schedule book and no seeming alternative.

On the second jet-lagged day in Japan, I called all those companies that had told me to call when I arrived in their country. The only thing wrong with the situation was that with one excuse or another, nearly all those I called refused me an interview. The Japanese rarely come out and just say "No," so what I heard was the usual story about Japanese hiring practices and recruiting schedules. I wondered whether I had somehow miscalculated, misinterpreted their invitation to come to Japan, or if this might be a form of cultural barrier that I was up against.

Utterly discouraged and equally confused by what I felt was unfair treatment, I decided to give job hunting one more try, thanks to prodding from relatives. I picked up a publication of job listings available to Japanese students studying abroad, though I myself was not an exchange student, and *forced* myself to call and inquire (beg) about a possible interview. The surprising thing I found, despite the opinions I had recently formed about the general closed-mindedness of Japanese firms, was that in fact, many companies were actually quite willing to give me a chance. It was then that I realized that this little bit of victory was the result of a change in my approach. In order to appeal to these companies over the phone, I found myself using steps that I later recognized as cold calling; only now I had to readjust my approach to deal with a foreign company and an interviewer with a different background and language.

The actual interviews—11 in two weeks—were just as surprising as my first dilemma. Not only did I find my previous interviewing experiences from the United States inadequate preparation, but the preconceived notions I had about what an interview should be like had somehow become my major stumbling block.

In contrast with interviews in the United States, interviews in Japan include entrance exams and personality tests. Aside from the basic difference in interviewing technique, I found that there were other cultural differences that one must be aware of and adjust to for a successful outcome. For example, Japanese firms place more emphasis on a candidate fitting into a corporate culture, and the amount of desire and vitality communicated to the interviewer. This implies United States firms do not look at these things. So at first, when I tried to relate my qualifications based on my university major and my job experience, I faced a somewhat indifferent reaction from my interviewer. Moreover, when I tried to sell myself by focusing on the job description, I was treated to an even grimmer reaction and a "what can a mere graduate do?" sort of skepticism.

Despite the painful mistakes and letdowns, I found myself slowly but surely learning some valuable lessons. With each interview, I came to realize the importance of considering the company's needs first. This is true to any interview, here or abroad. My mistake was in concentrating too much on my needs. Though understanding my needs was a very important factor, concentrating too hard on this aspect prevented me from communicating the most important message: how I could serve their needs with my qualities and experiences. My biggest lesson was in realizing that though I knew what I wanted and what my capabilities were, none of these mattered if I couldn't translate them into what would benefit the company.

Thus to sum up my experiences with two proverbs, I'd say: "Hindsight is 20/20" and "When in Rome, do as the Romans do." But also, a job is a job and is it really worth it to compromise what you truly want?

Akiko Nakano

CASE QUESTIONS

1. What else could Ms. Nakano have done to ensure a better reception in Japan?
2. What does she mean by cold calling?
3. What company needs should she have considered?
4. Did the job meet her needs?
5. How can you benefit from her experience?

Case 3.2   TO DO OR NOT TO DO

Merrie Samuels graduated from Ohio State four years ago with a double major in business administration and philosophy, which reflected her divided interests at that time. Her grade point average showed a steady improvement, from a C-, through a C, then a B, and an A in her senior year. Her parents paid her room and tuition, but she earned spending money by working in the kitchen and conducting campus tours. During her last two years she was an announcer and disc jockey for the college radio station. On vacations she worked at McDonald's in her home town in Ohio. She was vivacious, energetic, well-liked, and thoroughly enjoyed her college experience.

Lacking focus, Merrie took a job as a stock picker at a wholesale drug company. After a year she convinced her boss to recommend her for a sales position that was open. She got the job and called on drugstores and hospitals for 3 years before deciding to move on to better opportunities.

During her calls on drugstores she had encountered salespeople and field managers for drug manufacturers. In discussing their job responsibilities with them, she became aware of the differences between their job and hers. One person represented a manufacturer and called on only physicians and hospitals, selling prescription products. Another represented a manufacturer who advertised to consumers through television and print media and distributed the products over the counter (OTC) at drugstores and supermarkets. The latter salesperson performed important merchandising roles that linked the company's advertising to the promotions in the stores.

Merrie decided to stay in the healthcare field, but she was torn between representing prescription products and selling over-the-counter products. Reflecting on the fact that she enjoyed merchandising activities and that she lacked a technical background, she decided to go the OTC route.

A few days later she shared this decision with a friend who represented a leading manufacturer of prescription products. At first he hesitated to give advice. Then he blurted out, "You've got it all wrong. I don't have a scientific background. The company discovered many years ago that it could train people in the technical knowledge, but it could not train them to communicate effectively. So it hires communicators and trains them in the product knowledge. Merrie, I think there are better career opportunities on the prescription side of the business. There, I've said it. But you have to make up your own mind."

CASE QUESTIONS

1. How could Merrie use the critical questions at the beginning of the chapter to help her decide? What would be her sources of information?
2. Would Exhibit 3.1 have helped her?
3. What advice would you have given her at various points in her decision processes?

Case 3.3   KAREN'S FIRST INTERVIEW

Karen Elder sat in anticipation of her first job interview, which was to be with the Alaskan Oil Company. She had done her homework by studying the annual reports of the company and preparing responses to anticipated questions. Her tension mounted as the time for the interview passed and the interviewer had not finished with the previous candidate.

Finally the door opened and Sharon, a friend of Karen's, walked out with a disturbed look on her face. "Good luck," she said with a tone of sarcasm in her voice. Sharon seemed eager to leave, so there was no time to ask about the interview before the door opened for Karen. Mr. Andrews introduced himself and apologized for being behind schedule. He explained that his plane was late. Perhaps that also explained his reserved manner and the appearance of being upset.

Mr. Andrews began the interviewing process by saying that he was not going to go through Karen's resume and ask questions per the customary interviewing procedure. Instead, he said that Karen would have a minute to think back on her academic, work, and extracurricular experiences. Then she was to speak for 15 minutes about them, highlighting her personal involvement in each area.

Karen took a minute to write down a few notes. She then spoke for 3 minutes about her involvement with a fund raising project for her professional business fraternity until Mr. Andrews interrupted her. "I want to know what *you* did, not what *we* did," he said. After a few more minutes he interrupted again and said, "What did you do? What was your decision?"

(continued)

Case 3.3 KAREN'S FIRST INTERVIEW—CONTINUED

While Karen was detailing some of her current work experience, Mr. Andrews constantly glanced out of the window behind her. She felt that he was just waiting for the 30 minutes to pass. Karen kept talking until she had covered the three areas, but Mr. Andrews took no notes on the paper in front of him.

Mr. Andrews then described Alaskan Oil's policy of starting everyone as a foreman in an oil field. He paused, looked closely at Karen, and said, "You'd get dirty." Karen was dressed in the prescribed blue business suit, professional blouse, and pearls. She thought that she should probably have worn overalls. Karen responded, "I am aware of that." He continued with, "You would have to tell men your father's age what to do and they probably would not like it. Do you think you could do that?" Karen was offended, given her work experience and business degree from a top school. She assured him that this would be no problem.

Mr. Andrews described the training program. "You'd be in a different city each week for a few months—from Boston, to Dallas, to St. Louis, to Los Angeles. You would move so much you would not even know what city you were in most of the time." The implication was clear. The message was negative. Karen responded, "I have traveled a lot and I enjoy the challenge. I have studied for 4 years so I am ready to apply my knowledge and skills. I would be happy to get on a plane now. I am by no means geographically bound."

He then pulled out a diagram showing a triangle and explained that every employee begins at the bottom, level 1, as a foreman and rises through the ranks on either the production or staff side. He then added, "I just got the word that by 1998, over 60% of upper management will be women and minorities, so you would be guaranteed to rise through the ranks quickly. For example, I am here at level 5. Two women who entered with me are now off the page and are making more bucks than I'll ever see."

When Mr. Andrews asked if she had any questions, Karen asked, "What is the culture of Alaskan Oil Company? Why do you enjoy working there?" He responded that it was not a progressive company. It generally waited for other companies to innovate and then followed. "Take day care. I'm sure that eventually we will have to get it because of the changes, but it will take a while. The benefits are good. The company covered my $40,000 surgery bill."

Karen felt that her first interview was a failure.[27]

CASE QUESTIONS

1. What did Karen do right? What could she have done better?
2. What was the problem here?
3. What could Karen do now if she really wanted to work for the Alaskan Oil Company?

SUMMARY

The recruiting process from the applicant's viewpoint mirrors steps in the selling process. The candidate must know his or her product (self- assessment), identify prospects (match personal profile with company requirements), and get an interview. In addition to the usual printed sources the Internet provides an ideal place to begin to develop a strategy for a recruiting experience that will launch a career.

ASSIGNMENTS/DISCUSSION QUESTIONS

1. Prepare for an interview with McNeil. Visit your local pharmacy and look at the McNeil products. Ask the staff what they think of the products and the McNeil salespeople. What questions would you ask during the interview?

2. Using the web site www.jobweb.org compare the job descriptions for five selling jobs. What generalizations can you make? Rank them as a fit for your profile and explain your ranking.

3. How have you used networking to further your career? Explain.

4. Exchange your resume with a classmate and practice interviewing each other. Have a third classmate evaluate the process.

5. Based on your readings in this course, identify the type of sales-related job that appeals the most to you. Conduct a search for that type of job, using the Internet and secondary sources in the library. Identify the features that employers are looking for in candidates for that job. Evaluate your own qualifications with respect to each feature sought.

ENDNOTES

1. Letter to Professor G. David Hughes from Jeff Schomburger, UNC Recruiting Team Leader, January 9, 1997.
2. Personal communication to G. David Hughes from Marcus Davis, of Nationwide Insurance, April 10, 1997.
3. This company supplied the information with the understanding that it would not be revealed.
4. Personal communication from Scott Menger, District Manager, Marion, Merrell, Dow Pharmaceutical, March 20, 1992.
5. Personal communication from G. David Hughes.
6. www.adm.uwaterloo.ca:80/infocecs/CRC/step1-skills.html (May 6, 1997, p. 1.)
7. www.adm.uwaterloo.ca:80/infocecs/CRC/step1-interest&values.html (May 6, 1997, pp. 2–7.)
8. www.adm.uwaterloo.ca:80/infocecs/CRC/step1-achievements.html (May 6, 1997, p. 1.)
9. www.jobweb.org/search/jobs/list.cfn?Search = Jobs&keywords = sales (May 6, 1997, pp. 1–2.)
10. www.jobweb.org/employer/greatam.htm (May 6, 1997, pp. 1–3.)
11. www.jobweb.org/search/jobs/view.CFM/72639 (May 6, 1997, p. 1.)
12. Letter to Professor G. David Hughes from Jeff Schomburger, January 9, 1997.
13. Personal communication from Rich Campbell, District Manager, May 14, 1997.
14. *Sales & Marketing Management,* Matchmaking Made Easy, October, 1996, p. 46.
15. Richard Nelson, Maybe It's Time to Take Another Look at Tests as a Sales Selection Tool?, *Journal of Personal Selling & Sales Management,* 7 August, 1987, pp. 33–38.
16. George B. Glisan and Jon M. Hawes, Selecting Creative People for Sales Positions, *Industrial Marketing Management,* 19 (4), November, 1990, pp. 331–37.
17. Arthur Bragg, Are Good Salespeople Born or Made? *Sales & Marketing Management,* September, 1998, p. 76.
18. Richard Kern, IQ Tests for Salesmen Make a Comeback, *Sales & Marketing Management,* April, 1988, pp. 42–45.
19. Richard Nelson, Maybe It's Time to Take Another Look at Tests as a Sales Selection Tool?, *Journal of Personal Selling & Sales Management,* 7 August, 1987, pp. 33–38.
20. E. James Randall, Ernest F. Cooke, and Lois Smith, A Successful Application of the Assessment Center Concept to the Salesperson Selection Process, *Journal of Personal Selling & Sales Management,* May, 1985, pp. 53–61.
21. Barry J. Farber, Fired Anyone Lately? Smart Sales Managers Know When to Let Salespeople Go, *Sales & Marketing Management,* 148, (1), January, 1996, pp. 20–22.
22. *Sales & Marketing Management,* Where to Find the Next Top Performer, December, 1996, p. 30.
23. McNeil Interview Record.
24. Adapted from a letter from Trash Davis, General Manager, Everyday Center, Ambassador Cards, a Division of Hallmark Cards, Inc., to a college placement director, January 21, 1992.
25. John R. Graham, If You Don't Get the Right Answers, Don't Take the Job, *Marketing News,* 24 (6) March 19, 1990, pp. 8, 26.
26. Cost-of-Living Comparisons, *National Business Employment Weekly, Managing Your Career,* Spring, 1992, p. 35.
27. Written by Katarina Oldenburg, BSBA, University of North Carolina, 1992.

4

THE SELLING PROCESS AND BEYOND

1. To learn and apply the basic steps in the selling process
2. To understand the different needs of a prospect
3. To appreciate the difference between needs, benefits, and product attributes
4. To learn how today's salespeople must have knowledge and skills beyond just those of the selling process

THE BASIC SELLING PROCESS

Although many modern sales organizations have replaced traditional title of salespeople with titles such as territory manager, account manager, and business development manager, skills in the basic selling process are still necessary. In this chapter, we first look at the theory behind selling: What basic laws of human behavior does selling use? Next, we outline the steps in the selling process. Then we examine how some companies have adapted these steps to their needs by combining them and using different labels that fit their industry. Finally, we examine the skills and knowledge required of a territory manager, an account manager, and a business development manager to effectively implement the selling process.

BEHAVIORAL MODELS BEHIND THE SELLING PROCESSES

A few key behavioral science models form the foundation of the selling process. The AIDA model instructs the salesperson to gain *Attention*, stimulate *Interest*, create *Desire*, and move the prospect to *Action*. The second model is the stimulus-response model that is common to many communication and learning theories: the prospect will respond, given proper stimuli by the salesperson. The third model is the need-satisfaction model, which stresses the importance of identifying the needs and wants that exist in the mind of the prospect. An extension of the need-satisfaction model is problem-solution theory. Finally, trait theories focus on characteristics of effective sellers. Sales strategists must consider different theories of selling for different products, customers, and salespeople.

The AIDA theory assumes that the prospect goes through a series of mental states from attention, to interest, to desire, and, finally, to action. This strategy is useful in industrial sales where the sale is complicated and repeat calls are necessary. The AIDA model gives the new salesperson a structure for learning the selling process and encourages salespeople to plan their sales calls in advance. The model has two limitations. First, it is difficult to identify these mental states at a particular moment in time. Second, the selling process is dominated by the salesperson, with little consideration for feedback from the prospect.

Stimulus-response theory may be the appropriate strategy for low-priced products, when the product is uncomplicated, and when time is a factor so that only a short presentation may be made. This strategy requires the salesperson to use a memorized or canned presentation, which simplifies the selection and training of salespeople, but has the disadvantage of eliminating two-way communication between the salesperson and the prospect.

Need-satisfaction theory shifts attention to the prospect because it assumes that purchases are made to satisfy needs. This selling strategy is used by salespeople selling household goods, insurance, automobiles, and some industrial products. The salesperson attempts to avoid persuasion and concentrate on identifying the needs of prospects by encouraging them to do most of the talking. The disadvantage of this approach is that it requires a more highly trained salesperson who has an understanding of the psychology of communication, has empathy for the prospect, and is willing to spend an appropriate amount of time with the prospect. Recruiting and training this type of salesperson is an expensive process.

The **problem-solution theory** is a logical extension of the need-satisfaction theory because it helps the prospect to identify his or her needs. Furthermore, it helps prospects to identify and analyze alternative solutions to their problems, solutions that may not include the products and services of the seller. At this point the salesperson becomes a true consultant to the prospect, as discussed in Chapter 1. This strategy is appropriate in highly technical sales or perhaps when selling to a buyer for a chain store, but it would be used rarely in direct sales to consumers. The disadvantage of this approach is that it requires a highly trained salesperson who is willing to make a long-term commitment to working with a prospect with the goal of turning it into a long-term account.

Trait theory addresses the question of "What are the characteristics of a successful salesperson?" For example, Weitz reviewed 21 studies of successful salespeople's profiles. He found inconsistent relationships between salespeople's sales productivity and their age, knowledge, educational level, empathy for customers' needs, sociability, and forcefulness.[1] On the other hand, Evans found that salespeople were more successful when their age, education, height, and politics matched those of their prospects, although evidence on this issue has been mixed.[2] Certainly the salesperson makes a difference: Biong and Selnes found that the salesperson had a significant influence on the buyer's commitment to a future relationship with the supplier.[3]

Each company will want to train its salespeople in its own procedure, but the following discussion provides a summary of steps common to many company training programs. Exhibit 4.1 summarizes nine steps common to most selling situations. This condensation may give the incorrect impression that selling is a mechanical, highly structured process.

Exhibit **4.1**	THE SALESPERSON'S ACTIVITIES IN THE SELLING PROCESS

1. PROSPECT FOR LEADS

    Identify potential customers with unmet needs.

2. CLASSIFY LEADS

    Rank the leads by their expected value, which is their profit potential times the probability of making the sale.

3. DEVELOP A SELLING STRATEGY AND CALL OBJECTIVES

    Set the objective of the first call by matching a key need to a product benefit.

4. MAKE THE APPROACH

    Gain the attention and interest of the prospect using the need-benefit match selected above.

5. MAKE THE PRESENTATION

    Expand on the product benefits to satisfy needs, checking for indifference, objections, authority, and ability to buy.

6. TRIAL CLOSE

    Test close on a minor point to see if the prospect is accepting the benefits and is ready to buy.

7. HANDLING OBJECTIONS

    Accept objections as a form of feedback. Clarify needs and provide proof that the product benefits will meet the needs.

8. CONCLUDE PRESENTATION AND CLOSE

    When a sufficient number of benefits have been accepted, the salesperson will move to close on the goal of the call, which may be a demonstration or the order.

9. FOLLOW-UP

    Prepare for a demonstration, complete the order forms, analyze the call, and complete the customer records.

The communication may be verbal or nonverbal, as with body language. Listening can be as important as talking for a salesperson. Asking questions can be a key skill in the selling process. Each selling situation requires consideration of the complex needs of the buyer and his or her buying style. The dynamics of the situation require a unique strategy for each account, and this strategy will have to be modified as the selling process evolves.

APPLYING THE CONCEPTS

As you read the details of the selling process in the next section, keep in mind the questions in the following case.

Brad Ferguson had called on Peter Vasquez, purchasing agent for Electro Manufacturing, each month for a year, with no sale. Brad had been warned by noncompeting salespeople that Peter was a tough buyer. The potential for a large, continuous sales volume and the challenge of cracking a tough account kept him hanging in. He had contacted Bob Spencer, Electro's chief engineer, who promised to speak to Peter about his company's line. Peter, however, had a stream of objections. First it was the design, then the price, and most recently the service agreement. After each objection Brad would gather more information about his products and company's policies. He would revise his strategy and return prepared to answer objections. After a year he still had not received an order. What did he do right? What could he have done better? Should he continue to call? Did Brad understand Peter's needs?

THE BASIC SELLING PROCESS

The selling process that is used in many companies consists of the following nine steps: (1) prospecting, (2) classifying leads, (3) developing a selling strategy, (4) making the approach, (5) presenting, (6) trial closing, (7) handling objections, (8) concluding the presentation and closing, and (9) handling details after the close, including a post-case analysis. These steps are commonly used by industrial salespeople, pharmaceutical salespeople calling on physicians and hospitals, grocery products salespeople calling on supermarket chains, and other industries in which the nature of the sale is relatively complex. Each of these steps will be discussed in detail and linked to Exhibit 4.1.

This exhibit may be used by sales managers to train new salespeople and to counsel present salespeople. It may also be used by salespeople to prepare their sales interviews and to evaluate their effort. Although each sale will include these common elements, it may be necessary to change the order in which they occur.

Step #1. Prospecting

Prospecting is the identification of potential new customers. In the same way that a gold prospector searches the hills for a rich lode of gold, the salesperson searches for individuals with unmet needs or needs that are not fully met by their present suppliers. A salesperson must never stop prospecting because present customers may move, go out of business, have changes in needs, or have their needs met by competition. A successful salesperson will allocate time to the process of generating quality prospects.

Sources of new prospects can include present satisfied customers, or a salesperson may find out about a new company coming to town through a newspaper announcement or the issuing of a building permit for a new factory or store. Industrial salespeople often use sources such as the *Thomas Register*, which lists companies according to the types of products they sell, thereby identifying needs for raw materials and component parts.

County Business Patterns, which is published by the U.S. Department of Commerce, reports for each county in the United States the number of companies and employees according to standard industrial classifications. A company may supply salespeople with leads that are generated from a direct mail campaign. The mailing lists for these campaigns can be purchased from companies that have the names and addresses of over 10 million businesses and 94 million households.[4] The Northwestern Mutual Life Insurance Company suggests the following sources for leads: friends and acquaintances, referrals, networks of professional organizations, existing policyholders, cold calls, referrals from new clients, Welcome Wagon lists, newspaper stories of new companies arriving, and mailing lists.[5]

Territory records, suggestions from other salespeople in other territories, and the company selling plan are all sources of stimulating ideas for generating prospects. The company selling plan will reflect the company's forecast for certain industries, its estimate of competitive activity, and the comparative advantages of its product. The plan will also reflect those products that are scheduled for promotional and advertising support, thereby making the salesperson's prospecting job easier.

Step #2. Classifying Leads

If sales prospecting is like prospecting in gold mining then salespeople must rank leads according to the greatest payoff. For the gold prospector payoff is the combination of the percent chance of finding gold and the size of the nuggets found. In selling, the payoff, or expected value, is the probability of the prospect buying times the magnitude of the sale. The process of prospecting in selling has therefore become one of estimating probabilities of buying and sales potential. The salesperson will want to classify the prospect as early in the process as possible to prevent wasting time—the major resource in selling.

Low cost sources for sales prospects, such as library directories and asking other businesspeople in town, will give a rough estimate of the side of the business and the magnitude of its need for the products. But a prospect must have more than a need in order to qualify as a potential customer. Prospects must have the *ability* and the *authority to buy.* The ability to buy is reflected in measures such as income and credit rating. The authority to buy is more difficult to define. Many salespeople have been frustrated to learn at the end of a presentation that they were not dealing with the person who had the authority to buy, but who, in effect, had only the authority to turn down the proposal. Many times the customer contact was simply gathering information for someone else, or was simply a member of a buying committee, meaning that the salesperson had to go through the process of selling again. In small companies, it is frequently difficult to gain access to those individuals who make buying decisions because they are busy running the company. New salespeople sometimes make the mistake of calling on prospects who are not *eligible to buy* from the company directly because the prospect must buy through a buying cooperative. Many companies will have at least three decision-makers—the ultimate authority who holds the purse strings, the worker who will use the product or service, and the technical expert who specifies the features.[6]

The salesperson classifies a lead as a prospect when the lead had a reasonable probability of buying, had sufficient needs to justify a profitable sale, had the financial resources to buy, and was classified as eligible to buy. During an initial call, a prospect may reveal information that changes his or her classification to "unqualified." Listening can be the most important skill during prospecting.

Are you a good listener? Using a scale of 1 to 100, with 100 as outstanding, rate your associates' skills in the first column in the following table and then have them rate themselves.

	I Rate Them	They Rate Me
Your best friend		
Your boss		
A subordinate		
Your spouse or significant other		
Your parents		
Your favorite teacher		
Your least favorite teacher		

What did this comparison tell you about your listening skills? Generally being a good listener is part of being a good friend. Failing to listen can strain relationships, including marriages, and cause accidents. To practice good listening we must listen to the content and not be distracted by delivery styles, constant judging of the content, and preparing a response before the person has finished, thereby tuning them out.

Communication is not limited to the logic of the spoken word. Nonverbal communications can be important. Body language can be very important. Try an experiment with a friend. While he or she is talking pretend to be distracted. Look away or page through a magazine. What is their response? How would it make you feel?

Have a friend guess what mood you are conveying when you use body language to convey that you are excited, angry, confused, interested, or disinterested. How many of them did the friend describe correctly?

Step #3. Developing a Selling Strategy

A selling strategy for each prospect requires a clear understanding of his or her needs and how the salesperson's products will meet these needs.

Need-Benefit Match   The salesperson uses the information from prospecting to develop a rough selling strategy. Strategy development consists of identifying a general need of the prospect and matching a product benefit to that need. This need–benefit match will be used for the initial approach.

The salesperson will contact the prospect and use the generalized need that has been identified and the matched benefit as an inducement to gain favorable attention and an interview. This generalized need and matching benefit may also be used in the approach, which is the critical first 30 seconds in the sales interview.

The prospect's perceived needs can be driven by the prospect's adoption cycle and where the product being sold is in its product life cycle. An innovator or early adopter prospect will be motivated to learn about new products, whereas a laggard will want to know who uses the product. The selling strategy must focus on these different needs.

A product that is late in its product life cycle may be viewed as a commodity by the prospect, who will concentrate on the terms of trade—price, delivery date, and billing arrangements. It is now possible to have the computer search for the best deal and order the product on the computer network, thereby bypassing the salesperson completely. In contrast, a prospect for a new product will want to know the unique attributes that will meet his or her needs better than a competitive product. Thus, old and new products will require a different need–benefit match strategy.

Company Selling Plan   The company selling plan will help the salesperson to develop an effective selling strategy because it will give call objectives, opening benefits, additional benefits to stress, and suggested closes. Selling plans may vary throughout the year. For example, a pharmaceutical salesperson may have a plan that stresses a nasal decongestant during the flu season and a product to treat swimmers' ear infections during the summer.

Identifying prospects' needs and meeting these needs with product or service benefits are central to the selling process. Therefore we must examine the different kinds of needs that a prospect experiences.

Professional Needs   A prospect will constantly be seeking ways to meet his or her professional needs, the needs of the organization, and personal needs. Professional needs, which may be defined as on-the-job needs, are created by the role that the individual plays within an organization. Problem-solving consists of meeting a collection of needs. For instance, the manager of the automobile fleet for salespeople has the problem of choosing among a wide variety of automobiles to meet the multiple needs of transportation, comfort, efficiency, economy, and corporate prestige. The salesperson who can best meet all these needs with the benefits of his or her automobile will solve the fleet manager's problem and make a sale.

Organizational Needs   The organizational needs of a prospect are linked closely to the needs of the organization. Organizational needs may include growth; better utilization of resources, as reflected in financial ratios; more effective use of personnel, as reflected in productivity measures; and enhancement of the company's prestige and credibility among its customers, suppliers, and the public at large.

Michael Dell founded a $2 billion computer business by understanding the changing needs of buyers of microcomputers. He looked at systems developed by others in a fresh way, analyzed what customers wanted, cut margins, streamlined production, cut out the middleman, and made telemarketing an art form.[7] Dell turned the telephone order taker into a computing specialist who developed long-term relationships with customers. Dell even completes multimillion dollar deals over the phone by sending a proposal and then walking the decision makers through the proposal using a speaker phone.[8]

A sophisticated salesperson understands the professional and organizational needs of a prospect and includes them in a statement of benefits. For example, a sales trainer in the grocery products industry instructs his or her salesperson to identify the criteria used for promoting to a chain store buyer. Is the buyer evaluated according to profit, turnover, margin, or return on investment? A salesperson who can appeal to these criteria will create a win-win selling situation—the buyer looks good in his or her organization and the salesperson makes a sale.

Think Like the Prospect   Try to think like a buyer by imagining that you are sitting where he or she is. A study of purchasing agents has shown what they think as the salesperson arrives.

- Time is short. I get 20 calls per day. Don't come without an appointment.
- Make certain that I am the buyer for your product.
- Learn all you can about our needs before you come in. Jump at the chance to be shown around the plant.
- If you don't know your product inside and out, know where to get quick answers and be ready to set up a meeting between your engineers and ours.
- Have some benefits that justify my changing suppliers.
- Forget the old-boy network. The link is how your company can help mine.
- Convince me that you can help me to trim my supplier base.[9]

Hierarchy of Personal Needs   Personal needs have been classified by many authors, but the most widely used classification, and one that is familiar to most readers, is the one provided by Maslow: physiological, safety, belonging and love, esteem, and self-actualization.[10] Building on these familiar concepts will shorten the time required to understand the buyer's needs.

Physiological needs are an individual's need for food, shelter, and clothing. When these basic needs are met, the individual may move to the next need in the hierarchy, that of safety. A prospect with a high need for safety avoids risks and seeks certainty or security. To meet these needs, the salesperson should match benefits such as the long and successful reputation of the company for delivery of a reliable product, the technical support that will be supplied, and the fact that the product has been used by many other companies known to the prospect. This same prospect may also want an organized selling proposal with a definite structure and clear definitions of benefits.

Belonging and love needs may take several forms in the selling situation. An insecure prospect with a high need for belonging will want to have others in on the buying decision, or to be assured that other successful companies use the product or service. Conversely, a power-oriented prospect will want self-esteem. In this case, the salesperson will want to stress how the purchase of the equipment will enhance the prospect's power and prestige within the organization. For example, a larger computer system may require everyone in the organization to come to the prospect for information, thereby enhancing his or her power and prestige in the company.

A prospect's esteem will be enhanced in the organization when he or she makes the right decision in buying a product or service. Prospects who feel that their esteem is at risk will often buy products from only the leading manufacturers, thereby minimizing later criticism. Salespeople from other companies will have to supply many additional benefits to offset this perceived possible risk to esteem.

Self-actualization is a philosophical, internal experience that is usually achieved only by a few persons, and therefore cannot be central to many selling situations. For some individuals, it may be realized with a sense of achievement for having effected change within the organization by making a wise purchase. For others, achievement may be simply the physical one of increased productivity.

The skillful salesperson will identify these complex need patterns early in the selling interview by probing with careful questions, listening carefully, and observing nonverbal communications, such as body language and the decor of the prospect's environment. An understanding of these need patterns will help the salesperson to tailor the presentation to include benefits that will meet these three types of needs. Some observers think that women are often above average salespeople because of their natural empathy. They picture how the buyer will react; they are skilled in identifying needs; they are more socially inclined; and, they are more attuned to details.[11]

The development of a selling strategy for a present customer is simplified by the fact that the salesperson can review territory records and past selling plans, and will have information about the customer's business objectives, competition, previous objections, and needs–benefit matches that were successful in the past.

Benefits Defined   By now it should be apparent that people do not buy products or services; instead, they buy a bundle of benefits to meet their needs, thereby solving a problem. Physicians do not want a drug; they want to heal their patients. We do not buy automobiles; we buy transportation, comfort, and prestige, subject to the constraints of our budget. A manufacturer does not buy a numerically-controlled lathe; he or she buys higher productivity and lower set-up costs. Thus, a benefit occurs when a product or service attribute satisfies a customer's need.

(Now try to answer the questions facing Brad in the case given earlier)

Call Objective   The next step in the development of this initial strategy is to set the objective for the first sales interview. This objective is the action that the salesperson wants the prospect to take. Does he or she want to make a sale on the first call, or to get agreement for a demonstration, survey, or proposal? The objectives may change as the selling process develops. A salesperson who had planned to get permission for a survey may be pleasantly surprised to learn that the prospect is ready to buy on the first call.

Step #4. Making the Approach

When the prospect is **classified** (Step #2) and the **selling strategy** has developed an objective to satisfy a prospect's need (Step #3), the salesperson turns to the approach (Step #4). This is the crucial step in the selling process when the salesperson must gain the attention and interest of the prospect so he or she may move to the presentation stage (Step #5).

The goals of the approach may be summarized as follows: (1) Get the prospect's attention, (2) Relax any defenses, (3) Obtain the prospect's respect and confidence, (4) Probe for the benefits wanted most, and (5) Arouse interest in hearing the presentation.[12]

Types of Approaches A variety of approaches may be used, including the *benefit approach* (focusing on customer benefits), the *referral approach* (focusing on a third party's recommendation), the *introductory approach* (focusing on the selling company and/or the salesperson), and the *product approach* (focusing on the physical product).

The strongest is the *benefit approach*. The salesperson opens with a statement of general need, such as, "Would you like to increase productivity in your production line? Would you like to save money? Would you like to make money? Would you like some enjoyment in your life?" Having gained the attention of the prospect, the salesperson turns to the benefits of his or her offer that will meet these general needs. If the prospect shows interest, the salesperson may proceed with the presentation phase. If interest is insufficient, the salesperson will want to probe for a better understanding of the prospect's needs (Step #3).

The *referral approach* may be a strong approach if the reference person is highly regarded by the prospect. Less strong approaches are the *introductory approach*, in which the salesperson introduces himself or herself and the company, and the *product approach*, in which the salesperson hands the product to the customer to gain interest and attention. The product approach may be effective when the product is portable, when customer relationships are well established, when there is little time for a presentation, or when the customer needs to dominate the buying process. A salesperson selling high-fashion clothing to a department store buyer may use this approach by simply bringing the latest fashion item and placing it on the desk of the buyer.

Probing during the Approach Tactical probing will occur at many points in the selling process. Shortly after the approach is completed, the salesperson will probe to learn additional needs of the buyer in order to earn the right to continue the interview. Probing at this stage amounts to the gathering of primary data that could not be collected before the interview. Later in the presentation when a prospect does not accept a stated benefit, the salesperson will use probing to confirm the prospect's needs and gain acceptance of the benefit.

Probing amounts to asking the right question at the right time. Open-ended questions, such as how, what, where, when, why, and who, yield the maximum amount of information. Closed-ended questions that can be answered with a yes or a no are used to clarify a point, reach agreement, or get a response from a non-talkative prospect. A chemical manufacturer's salesperson would be asking a closed question by asking, "Did your present supplier meet delivery schedules during the petroleum shortage?" A salesperson for word-processing equipment could ask, "Does your secretarial staff spend a lot of time retyping a page to correct a minor error?"

Asking the right question at the right time is only half of successful probing. The other half is careful, effective listening. One must listen for what the prospect does not say as well as what he or she does say.

Before moving to the next stage, the salesperson will want to reconfirm who the decision makers are, thereby avoiding presenting to the wrong person or to only one member of the buying committee. In selling, as in tennis, the winner is generally the person who makes the fewest unforced errors. At this point in the process, the salesperson will want to review some of the frequently made mistakes, which are:

- disregarding the importance of the first impression
- forgetting that the goal is to get the order
- selling the company instead of the product's benefits
- lacking responsiveness to needs and objections
- over complicating with technical jargon
- relying on product literature for product knowledge
- talking instead of listening
- brushing off questions and objections and
- failing to ask for the order[13]

Step #5. Making The Presentation

Two-way communication between the salesperson and the prospect is the heart of the presentation.

Presenting Benefits   The salesperson presents benefits and the prospect responds by accepting the benefits, by objecting, by doubting that the product can produce the benefits, with indifference, or with no clear reaction. The salesperson must analyze these reactions and decide how to respond. If the prospect agrees with the opening benefit, the salesperson may proceed to a trial close or a presentation of additional benefits. If the prospect is indifferent or if the response cannot be classified, the salesperson should probe for more information. To reconfirm a need, the seller should get agreement on a statement of the buyer's objectives and needs. If the prospect expresses doubt that the product has the benefits, proof should be offered. Objections must be classified as minor or major. It is important for the salesperson to wait for the prospect's reaction before proceeding to the next benefit.

Probing Customer Needs   Probing may be necessary in order to classify the prospect's response or to confirm the need to which the benefit had been matched. This probing stage should be a natural part of the conversation. It requires careful listening.

Presentation Styles   Each company will want to develop its own style of presentation. A grocery products manufacturer instructs its salespeople in the following steps: (1) summarize the situation, (2) state the idea, (3) describe how the idea works, (4) state the benefits, and (5) recommend action. To aid in the presentation, companies provide salespeople with sales aids that include brochures and visual aids, such as charts, slides, and movies, to emphasize features that produce the benefits claimed for their products. Some companies prefer highly structured or "canned" presentations. These presentations may be useful to simplify the training of new salespeople who sell simple or standardized products.

Step #6. Trial Closing

When several benefits have been accepted or objections have been handled successfully, a trial close may be used to see if the prospect is ready to buy. A trial close consists of an early attempt to gain a commitment by the prospect on details of the order or a minor point such as the color, the delivery date, or the payment method that will be used. If the prospect is ready to make a decision on a minor point, then he or she is close to making the major decision of buying the product or service.

Step #7. Handling Objections

Objections may take the form of *doubts, minor objections,* or *major objections.* A doubting prospect is asking for proof that a product or company has features that provide the stated benefits. The salesperson may provide this proof with a demonstration, samples, additional information such as research results, or by quoting authorities in the field.

Minor Objections   A minor objection is an objection that is based on incomplete facts. For example, "Your price is too high," may mean that the prospect has not been shown sufficient benefits, quality, and service to create a total value that more than justifies the price. To overcome this type of objection, the salesperson should paraphrase the objection as a question and answer it with facts. The salesperson should not lower the price unless the prospect is willing to concede on a point.

In meeting objections it will often be necessary to concede, so you must do it strategically. Smith suggests the following steps:

1. Start with your highest expectations.
2. Avoid conceding first.
3. Be sure the customer understands the value of a concession.
4. Make concessions in small amounts.
5. Admit mistakes and make corrections willingly.
6. Be prepared to withdraw a concession.
7. Avoid split-the-difference strategies.
8. Don't advertise a willingness to concede.[11]

Major Objections   A major objection is based on the fact that there is some disadvantage in the product when applied to the prospect's need. If the need is a minor one, in comparison with other needs that will be met by the product, the salesperson may offset this objection by summarizing the many other benefits of the product. If, however, the need is central to the prospect's problem, then it may be necessary to terminate the presentation at this point.

Objections Provide Feedback   Objections provide the salesperson with feedback for those points where the prospect does not agree with either the definition of the needs or the stated benefits that will meet these needs. Objections require backing up in the selling process to confirm needs, to provide features that produce agreed-upon benefits, or to summarize benefits. It may also be necessary to reclassify the prospect. Are the needs, ability to buy, and authority to buy really there? An objection may be the prospect's way of asking for more reasons for buying. Perhaps the seller has not dealt with the buyer's personal or organizational needs, such as the risks associated with making a wrong buying decision.

The seller must listen carefully to minor objections because they may be major objections in disguise. A prospect may choose to hide the real objection. For example, a prospect may complain about the price of a new computer, when the real objection is that he or she is unwilling to invest the time and energy in learning a new computer system. Once the salesperson identifies this hidden objection, it is possible to deal with it directly by showing how the benefits more than offset the need to learn the new system. Procrastination can also be a hidden objection. The procrastinating prospect may be moved to a buying decision by pointing out the costs of foregoing the benefits.

At this point in the selling process the salesperson will need to use negotiating skills. The goal of negotiation is to increase the areas of agreement and reduce the areas of disagreement. Negotiation is an exchange of perceived values. An exchange takes place when both parties perceive that the values gained are greater than those given. The salesperson must identify those benefits of the proposition that have high perceived value for the buyer.

Experienced salespeople welcome objections as an important part of feedback in the selling process. They anticipate objections and prepare their responses as part of their selling strategy.

Step #8. Concluding the Presentation and Closing

Many new salespeople are comfortable discussing product benefits with customers, but are reluctant to ask for the order. Discussing benefits does not close the sale. There are a number of closing techniques that are useful at this stage of the selling process.

Achievement of Objective   When the prospect has agreed to a sufficient number of benefits, the salesperson should close the presentation and seek the goal of the call. How many benefits are sufficient? There is no general answer to this question; the number will depend on the nature of the product and each selling situation. Trial closes will help the salesperson decide when to make the final close.

Types of Closes   Some salespeople are afraid to *ask directly,* "Will you buy?" because they fear that they will be rejected and they have a strong need to be accepted by the prospect. Rather than use a direct closing strategy, these salespeople may want to use another closing strategy.

The *assumptive close* assumes that the sale is made, so the seller proceeds to questions such as the spelling of names, proper address, quantity desired, size, and color. An assumptive close may concern the details of where and when the demonstration should be held. If the call objective is a survey of needs, an assumptive close may be a request for the names of the persons who would be involved in such a survey and an introduction to these individuals. Handing the prospect a pen to sign the order or handing him or her the car keys represents a *physical action close.* A *negative close* occurs when the salesperson urges the need to buy now because the product is in short supply or a price increase will occur shortly. *Special concession closes* are used commonly in the grocery products industry: the seller may agree to give a special advertising or promotional allowance for buying now. If the close is not successful, the salesperson should summarize needs and benefits and try a different close. In some cases, these closes may boomerang because the prospect feels manipulated. When the objective of the call is a demonstration, survey, or presentation, the closing strategy will differ only slightly.

Termination Short of the Objective   An impasse may be reached in the selling process when the prospect's needs do not justify a purchase, or when a major objection reveals that the product's benefits will not meet a central need. At this point the salesperson must remain calm, thank the prospect for his or her time and attention, and leave the door open for another call in case the prospect's needs change or the product is redesigned. The salesperson should analyze the reasons for the call being unsuccessful.

(At this point what advice do you have for Brad?)

Step #9. After the Presentation

Arrange for the Next Call   Several important selling activities are required after the interview is terminated. If the interview results in a sale, it will be necessary to complete the appropriate order forms. If the goal of the interview was a demonstration, it may be necessary to make arrangements for the equipment that will be demonstrated.

Administrative Tasks   The salesperson should complete the territory records for this account, showing needs, benefits, and objections that occurred during this interview so that he or she will be well prepared for the next interview. Completion of the weekly call report may include an evaluation of the product when it was impossible to overcome objections. If other salespeople share these problems, it may be necessary to redesign the product.

Post-Call Analysis   The seller will want to do a self-evaluation of the call to identify personal strengths and weaknesses in product knowledge and selling skills that need improvement. Many post-call analysis questions will need to be answered. Was the call successful? Why? What benefits triggered the sale? Are there other customers with similar needs who might respond to the same presentation? Was the presentation unsuccessful? Why? Why was the sale postponed? What proof or selling material will enable you to reclose the sale successfully? How long should you wait to call again?

This self-analysis could include measures of the successful managing of accounts, such as sales volume, market share, contribution, expenses, and perhaps return on investment, compared with last year or with the district or regional averages.

Follow-up   Service after the sale is an important part of account and territory management. Sales follow-up assures that the order will not be canceled, and it paves the way for future orders by building confidence in the customer that the salesperson will deliver as promised. Keeping the customer happy is an important ingredient in profitable selling. It costs five times as much to get a new customer as it does to keep a present one.[14] It can also be a good source for new leads.

SELLING TO AN ORGANIZATION

Selling to an organization requires a broader application of the nine steps just outlined. It requires a thorough understanding of the complexities of the buying organization. Hanan, Cribbin, and Donis suggest a *systems selling strategy*.[15] They note that a buying organization has four structures—the power structure, the group structure, the role structure, and the status structure. Each of these structures has a life of its own, complete with behavioral codes, performance standards, vocabulary, objectives, and criteria for entry. The system seller must identify these structures and their leaders so that he or she may help them meet their personal and group objectives. Negotiation is the process by which a seller penetrates these four organizational structures.

Negotiation is a vital component in the selling process when the product, associated services, delivery arrangements, and the price can be adapted to meet a prospect's needs. Many purchasing managers have been trained to negotiate, so sales managers are finding it necessary to train their salespeople in the art of negotiation.

What Is Negotiable?

Dow Corning created a two-day negotiation course for its salespeople based on the principles developed by Chester L. Karrass.[16] The Dow Corning program uses a negotiation worksheet that includes items that may be subject to negotiation, such as characteristics of the product, special features, packaging, inventory, delivery, price, technical support, and safety factors. Each of these negotiable dimensions is then analyzed according to the customer's requirements, the value of that dimension to the customer, whether Dow Corning meets the requirements, which competitors meet the requirements, which items are not negotiable for Dow Corning and which are not negotiable for the customer, and, finally, the limits beyond which Dow Corning and the customer will not go on negotiable dimensions. Salespeople are trained to know the limits of their authority, to be patient, and to concede slowly.

Telephone Negotiations

The danger of negotiating on the telephone is that the initiative lies with the caller and mistakes are made often under the pressure of a phone call. The negotiator must know the power structure of his or her organization and the power structure of the customer's organization. An appreciation of hidden personal values becomes an important component in negotiating. These subtleties cannot be perceived on the telephone.

Team Negotiation

Team negotiation has many advantages. In addition to providing greater expertise and moral support, it provides better listening, better planning, and a show of strength. Its principal disadvantage is a lack of unanimity among team members, thereby making it difficult to make a counterproposal.

Greater competition in the marketplace, more than any other single factor, will require that many industrial salespeople be trained in the art of negotiation. But negotiation must be built on a sound understanding of the selling process because negotiation requires an understanding of the prospect's needs and the product benefits that will meet these needs. The major difference between selling and negotiating is that in negotiating many product attributes are variable, whereas in selling they are fixed.

It is important in negotiating to avoid creating an adversarial relationship, and to focus on achieving a win-win outcome (where both the seller and buyer are better off after the sale is completed). According to Hanan, Cribbin, and Donis, systems selling requires turning a customer into a partner, not an adversary.[17] There is a need to develop common objectives, common strategies for achieving the objectives, common risks, and common defenses against outside threats. Systems selling is an extension of consultative selling, discussed in Chapter 1. These authors stress the need to know the motives of prospect partners in the selling–buying partnership.

EXAMPLES OF BENEFIT SELLING STEPS

Each company will develop a set of benefit selling steps that will be appropriate to its needs. Grocery Products, Inc. (disguised) identifies five steps, as follows: state the circumstances, present your plan, describe your plan, stress the benefits, and close. Prospecting and classifying leads are not included because the salespeople call on established accounts that currently sell their products. The sales call will have as an objective the acceptance of a new product or promotion. In each of these steps the company stresses communication skills, the handling of objections, and understanding account benefits.

Wallace is a company that specializes in supplies and systems to help companies manage their information systems. Thus, they are a business-to-business type of selling. Rich Campbell, a district manager, described their selling steps as follows:

> We use the theories of Jack Carew-*Dimensions of Professional Selling.* It is a needs-based selling approach with a strong focus on relationship building. We teach salespeople many skills, including: how to make cold calls, use the telephone, talk to the gatekeeper, use voice mail, how to handle objections, how to make a sales call, a formal presentation, and how to close. We use the LAER process (Listen, Acknowledge, Explore, Respond) for handling objections and overcoming them. We also teach the salespeople how to develop and sell the entire account versus selling orders. The salespeople are trained extensively by their District Manager and are reinforced by three, week-long training schools in our corporate headquarters. We also use role playing extensively as a training and development tool.[18]

The Nationwide Insurance sales agents process is as follows: have a list of qualified prospects, identify prospects' needs, study relevant Nationwide products and services, and satisfy their needs with Nationwide products. Their sales presentation process consists of the following four steps: establish rapport with the customer, explore their needs, present Nationwide products as solutions, and close. At each step in this process the Nationwide salesperson asks questions, listens to the goals and needs of the customer, reviews current insurance programs, helps discover gaps in protection, and provides recommendations to solve the client's needs. These techniques are applied in all forms of selling—personal, telephone, seminar, direct mail, and follow-up programs.[19]

Northwestern Mutual Life Insurance describes the following requirements and responsibilities for its college interns: establish clientele, meet with clients, analyze client's situation, make recommendations, close the sale, and provide ongoing service beyond the sale.[20] Although these steps are presented as responsibilities they are also the steps in the selling process.

The selling steps are also used by the salesperson to manage a territory and forecast sales. For example, a company that sells computer software requires its salespeople to report by product and industry the estimated sales potential at each stage of the selling process. An industry table could look like the following:

Industry	Estimated Sales ($000)			
	Qualified Prospects	Presentation	Closing	Total
Education	30	20	50	$100
Financial	70	30	20	120
Government	90	50	10	150
Totals	190	100	80	$370

Similar tables could be made by product category. These tables would help the salesperson to identify where he or she was having difficulty in the selling process in certain industries or with specified products.

Selling to the high-technology industry can be a fast-paced process because of the short life cycle of the products and the intense global competition. Target Market Systems, a consulting firm that specializes in consulting to high-tech sales forces that sell to high-level executives, trains these high-tech salespeople using its Target Account Selling plan. It includes steps to identify customer demographics, markets, products, size, and competition. It identifies prospect's needs, problems, and decision criteria. It also forces the seller to ask some critical questions. Can we win? Is it worth winning?[21] This plan is a high-level selling process.

....

BEYOND BASIC SELLING SKILLS

To see how the role of the salesperson has grown beyond the basics of selling we turn to a company that will be known as Grocery, Inc., to protect its confidentiality. The three position descriptions that follow, however, are actual, with only the references to the company removed.[22]

Exhibits 4.2, 4.3, and 4.4 show the principle duties and responsibilities for the territory manager, the account executive, and business development manager. It should be noted that these are separate career paths in this company. Thus, there is no hierarchal relationship. Instead each is expected to cooperate with the other to effectively implement the Grocery, Inc. selling plan. Compare these position descriptions with those shown in Chapter 2 to see how the salespeople's roles have expanded because of competition and technology. Which of these three career paths would you prefer and why?

Exhibit **4.2**	GROCERY, INC. TERRITORY MANAGER POSITION DESCRIPTION

Name _____   Title _____

Team _____   Reports to _____

KEY RESULTS AREA

The Territory Manager is responsible for building and maintaining business in all assigned formats including direct, indirect, and retail business within an assigned geographical territory.

INTERNAL PRINCIPAL DUTIES AND RESPONSIBILITIES

Develop a business plan for profitable volume at all assigned formats, including direct, indirect, and retail.

Principal Duties and Responsibilities

INTERNAL:

Develop business plan for profitable volume at all assigned formats, including direct, indirect, and retail.

- Develop strategies at direct and indirect to achieve financial contribution and volume goals through a six month planning process.
- Develop retail presentations to achieve financial contribution and volume goals.

Responsible for communication of market conditions, including key account and retail information to all appropriate team personnel.

- Identify and communicate competitive activity to all team members.
- Monitor and provide communication feedback on PIA (a retail merchandising company) activities via DRIVE evaluations, store audits, PIA 1-800 calls, input to response log and follow-up letters regarding training issues.
- Identify and manage pricing opportunities within assigned territory or as requested by Retail Operation Manager.
- Respond to special assignments as requested by Retail Operation Manager.

Exhibit **4.2** GROCERY, INC. TERRITORY MANAGER POSITION DESCRIPTION—CONTINUED

Adhere to required administrative policies.

- Responsible for proper execution and distribution of CPP contracts, retail drafts, and reclamation procedures on a timely and accurate basis.
- Timely submission of expense reports.

Maintain required administrative procedures.

- Document expenditures on an accurate and timely basis where it applies.
- Complete weekly plans and accomplishments in agreement with established schedule.
- Store call cards kept up-to-date with all pertinent information.
- Develop pre-call plans to accomplish strategic objectives. Complete special administrative requests as directed by Retail Operations Manager.
- Maintain sales binder to support all aspects of sales calls, (i.e. benefit selling presentations, code lists, ranking reports, etc.).
- Maintain/utilize computer technology for administrative procedures.

Develop category Management Plan where appropriate.

- Identify potential category management partners.
- Develop strategies to achieve mutual financial goals.

EXTERNAL:

Sell profitable volume to all formats.

- Implement strategic plans to meet financial goals.
- Prioritize sales efforts on high financial contributors during presentations.
- Responsible for selling profitable distribution to exceed "by account" goals where authorized.
- All distribution and merchandising functions *are the responsibility of our contracted companies.* Monitoring, directing, training, and appropriately assisting in the achievement of these acceptable standards may be directed by the Retail Operations Manager.
- Any shelf tags replaced or new tags placed to close a void will be initialed by the Territory Managers.
- Sell and monitor to enhance distribution, share of shelf, (**50%** or greater) and profitable volume.

Implement Category Management Plan where applicable.

- Establish top-to-top communications to implement category plan.
- Present category management capabilities to potential category management partners.
- Present and initiate category management plan to meet mutual strategic financial goals. Request assistance from appropriate Business Development Manager as needed.

Participate in food shows and special events.

- Participate in selling at scheduled food shows.
- Coordinate demos and other special events as authorized by Retail Operations Manager.
- Participate in requested Blitz store activity to enhance financial contributions.
- Participate in reset activity as requested in all formats with Retail Operation Manager approval. (Reset activity is the responsibility of our contracted companies. ROM approval will be granted for training purposes or very exceptional business reasons.)

Personal Development

- Commit to continuous self-development. Continue to upgrade computer automation skills.
- Participate in training seminars to improve personal selling skills.
- Effective utilization of time management to maximize company volume and profits.

Working Relationships

Reports to: Retail Operations Manager
Work with: All Company Associates
               Appropriate Associate Company Personnel
               Penetration of all assigned customers to highest level

Exhibit **4.3**	GROCERY, INC. CUSTOMER ACCOUNT EXECUTIVE POSITION DESCRIPTION

Name _____   Title _____

Team _____   Reports to _____

KEY RESULTS AREA:

The Account Executive is responsible for developing, executing, and communicating key account action plans to achieve financial contribution goals. Emphasis to be placed on achieving a mutually beneficial category management plan.

INTERNAL:

Responsible for planning and developing direct/indirect activities.

- Responsible for recapping and evaluating previous account action plans.
- Determine and prioritize account opportunities including innovative ideas to increase business.
- Review product mix to determine "established" new item distribution opportunities.
- Establish volume and financial contribution goals by direct/indirect account.
- Identify shared opportunities at direct/indirect accounts.

Responsible for developing a mutually beneficial category management plan with direct/indirect accounts.

- Prepare account capabilities presentation to determine direct/indirect account's level of interest in category management.
- Coordinate with multi-functional resources and team members to analyze market data and trends and develop key category opportunities.
- Develop strategies and tactics as they relate to the targeted areas of opportunity for category management.
- Refine strategies and tactics as they relate to the targeted areas of opportunity after category management presentation.
- Develop category management action plan.

Responsible for managing key account direct/indirect activities.

- Responsible for set up and management of direct/indirect promotional funding.
- Maintain all price lists, code lists, account activity database, and customer mailing list database.
- Develop surveys, ad promotions, special promotions, telemarketing programs, food shows, etc.
- Use multi-functional resources for promotional results analysis and advertising tracking (ours and competition).
- Source and utilize all multi-functional resources to aid in the development of all account business reviews.
- Responsible for developing "new" item presentations with the use of multi-functional resources.
- Coordinate and utilize multi-functional resources for the purpose of shelf management, schematic development, and retail store solutions.
- Coordinate demonstrations, kiosks, etc.

Participate in developing Team's strategic direction and action plans.

- Provide input when developing the team's strategic direction and overall action plan.
- Coordinate personal action plans in conjunction with the team's strategic direction and overall action plan.

Maintain open communication with team members.

- Communicate in a timely manner all key account information to all team members.
- Responsible for providing information in such a manner for effective and consistent execution.
- Responsible for communicating with the Continuous Replenishment Analyst, the Order Revenue Manager, the plant, etc.
- Provide positive reinforcement of key account programs and initiatives to team members.
- Responsible for maintaining an open line of communication for gaining feedback from other team members.

Maintain timely and effective administrative procedures.

- Responsible for prompt and accurate payment of account billings.
- Monitor and balance account accrual fund ledger.
- Timely submission of store audits.
- Practice cost effective administrative procedures.
- Timely submission of expense reports.

Exhibit 4.3   GROCERY, INC. CUSTOMER ACCOUNT EXECUTIVE POSITION DESCRIPTION—CONTINUED

EXTERNAL:

Maintain open and timely communication with third party associates.

- Attend coverage meetings of retail merchandising company to disseminate key account information and strategies, where appropriate.
- Meet with retail merchandising company to review progress, develop strategies, and reinforce objectives.
- Conduct store audits to monitor progress of retail merchandising company.

Develop and maintain key account contacts at all levels.

- Develop relations with account key decision makers.
- Coordinate and execute key account presentations for all major initiatives.
- Schedule account calls and act as the primary contact.

Execute account action plan.

- Present and gain approval of account action plan.
- Utilize multi-functional resources as part of the action plan presentation.
- Negotiate, update, and modify action plan as necessary to meet financial objectives.

Execute a mutually beneficial category management plan.

- Present company capabilities to direct/indirect account's key decision makers.
- Utilize multi-functional resources as part of the capabilities presentation.
- Gain an agreement to mutually develop a category management plan.
- Implement the category management plan.
- Update and modify the category plan as necessary to meet mutually agreed upon objectives.

Personal Development:
Commit to continuous self-development.

- Stay abreast of industry trends through customer visits, industry meetings, literature, etc.
- Continuous pursuit of internal training.
- Continued external education, including workshops, seminars, etc.

Working Relationships:
Reports to: Customer Team Leader
Works with: Customer Development Group

Exhibit 4.4   GROCERY, INC. CUSTOMER TEAM BUSINESS DEVELOPMENT MANAGER POSITION DESCRIPTION

Name _____   Title _____

Team _____   Reports to _____

KEY RESULTS AREA:

The Customer Team Business Development Manager provides support in data acquisition and analysis for the Customer Team, for the purpose of developing category plans and enhancing business development.

Principal Duties and Responsibilities

INTERNAL

Use state-of-the-art tools to support the development of Category Management plans.

- Access and analyze business data including internal, syndicated, market, consumer and customer provided data, space management software, and participate in current developments.
- Make recommendations for business improvements based upon analysis results, account, and Team strategies.
- Combine information to assist in the development of Category Management presentations.

(continued)

Exhibit 4.4   GROCERY, INC. CUSTOMER TEAM BUSINESS DEVELOPMENT MANAGER POSITION—CONTINUED

Develop category space management plans with input from accounts and Account Handlers.

- Use space management software to analyze space utilization.
- Develop plan-o-grams with input from the Team.
- Utilize Spaceman/Apollo software where applicable.

Interface with Core Team and the Home Office personnel to provide on-going support for key action plans.

- Identify data, information, and availability of resources needed for analysis.
- Work with appropriate representatives to develop and use models to analyze the impact of recommendations.

Assist in evaluating the performance of key promotions and action plans.

- Use models and ad volume tracking to analyze the impact of key promotions.
- Use pricing models to analyze the effectiveness of price promotions.
- Use models to evaluate the effectiveness of special projects, such as Kiosk, shelf hangers, Category Management plans, etc.

Develop and maintain business tracking formats for the Team, with Account Handler's input.

- Key account code list, retail pricing survey, ad tracking, volume tracking, monthly retail audits for pricing, shelving, and merchandising.

Assist in the development of Customer Team.

- Assist in the on-going computer training of Team members.
- Participate in the identification and implementation of business/process improvements within and between Region Teams.
- Coach and encourage Team members.
- Provide feedback on Team performance.
- Participate in Team Action plan development, problem solving, and decision making.

EXTERNAL

Work with the account Team, associate companies and the region's Finance, Marketing, or Systems Manager, to assist the account in the development of action plans and special projects.

- Maintain working relationships with appropriate account personnel (Category Manager, Category Analyst, Marketing, Information Systems, and Space Management personnel, etc.), and associate companies.
- Communicate local market information through information systems and Team personnel.
- Develop an understanding of account category strategies.

Work with the account to assess data needed for analysis.

- Determine and obtain account data as needed for analysis and planning.
- Serve as an information resource for appropriate account personnel.

Support category plan development and presentation.

- Participate in account meetings to help define and gather information required for Category Management planning.
- Provide support for the presentation of Category Management plans.

PERSONAL DEVELOPMENT

Participate in the development of self and other Region business development personnel.

- Stay abreast of industry trends through customer visits, industry meetings, literature, etc.
- Receive internal training in financial management, SKU Rationalization, Category Management, computer, space management, and data analysis.
- Continue external education, including advanced degrees, workshops, seminars, etc.
- Share personal operational improvements with Region business development personnel.
- Conduct/participate in monthly Business Development Manager teleconference to enhance training.
- Provide a monthly status letter to the Team.

Exhibit 4•4	GROCERY, INC. CUSTOMER TEAM BUSINESS DEVELOPMENT MANAGER POSITION—CONTINUED

Working Relationships
Reports to: Team Leader
Work with: Region BDM
                      Team Accounts
                      Account Executives
                      Logistics Manager
                      Headquarters Personnel
                      Region Core Team Members
                      Associate Companies

A review of these job descriptions illustrates several critical points. First, the selling functions become complex as the marketing strategy moves from selling, through consulting, and finally to partnering with the account. It will be noted that there is a sharing of data and strategies between Grocery, Inc. and its accounts. Secondly, there is a need for a variety of knowledge and skills. The Territory Manager requires teaming skills. The Account Executive requires merchandising skills. The Business Development Manager requires analytical skills. Grocery, Inc. is developing a new kind of selling organization that has specialization pulled together with teaming. Third, it will be noted that computers play a role in analysis, data management, and presentation. Which of these three management roles would you like to fill? Why?

Case 4•1	ANALYZING THE SELLING PROCESS: HERMAN MILLER, THE PERIODICALS SALESPERSON

"Mr. Winkler, on my last call we were discussing periodicals that you send regularly to your field sales staff and you commented that your company might be looking for something new to re-stimulate the enthusiasm of salespeople. Are you still in the market for such a product?"

"Yes, I suppose so." (Somewhat disinterested.)

"I didn't follow up your lead at that time because you had just contracted for our *Sales Manager Quarterly Bulletin* and I wanted you to see the benefits it provides your field sales managers before discussing a new publication we're in the process of releasing. In selecting a periodical for your field sales staff, what objectives do you have in mind? What do you want it to provide?"

"Well . . . we think it should give some tips on selling, some success stories, some material from a different point of view than the usual company material."

"I'm certainly glad to confirm that these are your objectives, Mr. Winkler, because our new *Suggestions for Successful Selling* publication will give you just what you're looking for. Here's a mock-up of our first issue scheduled for September. The Selling Tips are practical, field-tested contributions from members of sales and marketing executives with whom we've contracted. In addition, there's a regular column by a marketing professor from a School of Business Administration. And to provide some good background information, every other issue will include a commentary on current business trends. In combination, these articles should provide considerable information to your field staff and make them appreciate the company's concern for keeping them. How does this sound to you?"

"Well . . . that sounds pretty good."

"Mr. Winkler, *Suggestions for Successful Selling* will be mailed monthly at a cost of $28 for twelve issues. There's a 10% discount for all original subscribers before July 1. Could I sign you up?"

"Well . . . let me think about it. We really haven't made up our minds about changing. We're still just looking."

"I can understand your hesitation. The subscription rate for your staff of 500 would be $9,000 less 10 percent, or $8,100. This could be made in quarterly payments. Would that arrangement be attractive to you?"

"Well, that's interesting, but I believe we'll wait. I've got another appointment in a few minutes. Thanks for coming by."

CASE QUESTION

What went wrong and why? If you were the sales manager observing this selling process, what coaching would you give?

Case 4.2 — ANALYZING THE SELLING PROCESS: SELLING TO A PURCHASING AGENT

"Mr. Franklin, your company has established a well-earned reputation for high-quality products that provide predictable and dependable results. As a result, your salespeople have had to continually prove the value of your products against cheaper competitive products by showing the benefits when compared with the higher price you charge. Wouldn't you agree with that analysis?"

"I sure would. I hear our sales manager discussing this with our salespeople all the time, constantly hammering home the benefits our products bring to the user compared with cheaper competitors."

"That's my point, Mr. Franklin. Quality costs more but it pays off. We feel the same way about the products we've sold you. Admittedly they cost more than the line you are now considering, but the dependability of performance is certainly worth something in comparing our prices with our competition."

"Well, I understand that, Joe, but headquarters says I have to make some savings in my purchases and this is the largest expenditure we'll make this year. As you know, this recession has hit everybody and we have to make some cuts."

"OK, that's a fact I can't refute, but the service we've given you over the past three years has provided longer wear, fewer replacements, and less down time on your production line."

"I'm not so sure I can agree with you on that, Joe. How can you measure what didn't happen? These are only a lot of sales claims and you know it."

"Come on, Mr. Franklin, you know we've worked closely with your production people and had our engineers in here on emergency calls at night and on weekends to help get some important orders out on schedule. Are you saying that didn't save your company some penalties they would have had to pay if you hadn't met your contract dates?"

"No, I'm not saying that, Joe, and I don't want you twisting what I'm saying, but anyway, that's Production's problem. I'm in charge of Purchasing and I've been told to trim my purchases by 10%. Since you can't give me a lower price, I've decided to go with your competitor. Their specifications seem OK to me. If their products and service don't live up to their claims, we'll find out soon enough, and you'll have another crack at it the next time."

CASE QUESTION

What went wrong and why? If you were the sales manager observing this selling process, what coaching would you give?

Case 4.3 — ROLE PLAYING THE SELLING PROCESS

To help students practice analysis, decision making, and communication skills of selling, divide the class into teams with three persons in each team. Each person will play the role of the salesperson, the prospect, or the field sales manager who is observing and coaching.

The Selling Process, Part A

Linda (or Larry) Walter, The New Office Equipment Salesperson

In August, 1991, Linda Walter was completing her second month as a new salesperson for the Edwards Office Equipment Company. Edwards grossed about $6.1 million per year, selling office furniture, adding machines, office supplies, typewriters, and small hand-held calculators. Most of their customers were small businesses and professionals such as lawyers and doctors. Some of their biggest customers were insurance agencies, real estate brokers, and banks.

Linda had become fascinated by the new hand-held Business Organizer. It was small enough to fit in a shirt pocket and sold for less than $85. She had taken one of these machines home along with the instruction manual and played with it several evenings, much to her fascination. It seemed perfect for the businessperson because it would handle all the functions needed for business analysis. It would perform the standard arithmetic functions of addition, subtraction, multiplication, and division, but it did much more. In one of its three calculating modes it could compute the cost, selling price, and margins that

are calculated by retailers. The financial mode could calculate compound interest, annuities, amortization, bonds, and mortgage payments. With this organizer it would not be necessary for a loan officer or a real estate agent to carry a book of mortgage rates. A loan officer could quickly calculate different payments for varying interest rates and terms of a mortgage. Linda worked through the many examples in the instruction book that accompanied the organizer. She was amazed at how clearly the book explained financial calculations; it was practically a financial mini-course. The third mode of the organizer was a statistical one. This mode permitted the calculation of means, standard deviation, linear regression, and trend-line analysis. Following the simple examples in the manual, a businessperson could easily analyze and project sales.

The Business Organizer had a calendar feature that showed appointments for each day, with an alarm feature so appointments would not be missed. Finally, it could store 290 frequently used telephone numbers. It showed the number and would dial it when the unit was held close to the mouthpiece of the phone.

Reflecting on the various prospects in her territory, Linda decided that bank loan departments would be the place to begin to try selling the units. She decided to start with Metropolitan Bank and Trust, a medium-sized bank in her territory. This bank had four

Case 4.3 — ROLE PLAYING THE SELLING PROCESS—CONTINUED

retail loan officers who arranged loans for the public to purchase large items such as homes, automobiles, and boats. Metropolitan had seven commercial loan officers who arranged loans for business, such as expansions, inventories and purchase of new equipment. Mr. Charles Monet was the Vice President in charge of the Commercial Loan Department. The bank had recently purchased from Edwards office furniture for a branch.

The economic outlook for the summer was not good. An economic recovery had not occurred. The mutual funds and money market funds had siphoned funds out of savings accounts, thereby reducing the funds available for loans. There were indications that a recession would occur during the summer. Economic issues were clouded by the politics of a presidential election year. Metropolitan Bank had recently introduced a new promotional campaign to commercial accounts titled "Creative Banking," in which it claimed it took its customers' needs to heart.

Linda began to map out her strategy for selling some of these organizers to Monet.

The Buying Process, Part B

Charles (Or Claudette) Monet, Vice President, Metropolitan Bank and Trust Company

Charles Monet, Vice President of the Commercial Loan Department, had been in banking for 12 years, but he had never seen anything like this year. Large retail chains and airlines were filing for bankruptcy. The sales of some loan customers, such as automobile dealers, had dropped 25%. This was really a period for creative banking and identifying new market opportunities. A major dimension of the present job was keeping old customers happy when there was no money to lend. Mr. Monet reasoned that if there was a recession the situation could reverse quickly—the demand for commercial loans could drop quickly and the supply of money for lending could increase.

"Creative Banking" had become the theme of Metropolitan's Commercial Department during these difficult times. Commercial loan officers became more involved in the daily business of old customers and

new prospects. They helped them with their financial decisions and showed them ways to make their investments work harder by such techniques as faster turnovers, and taking discounts on invoices. Thus these loan officers were engaging in the consultative selling of the bank's services.

During a recent board meeting, Mr. Monet had explained the strategies of creative banking and consultative selling. Other bank officials explained some of their strategies for solving their problems. For example, there was a promotional drive to increase deposits so there would be money to lend. Some of the strategies included certificates of deposit for the larger customers and premiums for the smaller customer.

One morning shortly after the bank opened, Mr. Monet received a call from Linda Walter, a salesperson of the Edwards Office Equipment Company, asking for an opportunity to present some ideas on how a new organizer might be helpful in Mr. Monet's daily operations. Metropolitan Bank had bought some office equipment from Edwards when the bank opened a new branch office, so Mr. Monet decided to grant this salesperson an interview.

CASE QUESTIONS

1. How should Linda go about making an appointment with Monet?
2. What must she do to prepare for this interview?
3. Assume you are Linda. How would you proceed when you walk into Monet's office?
4. If you were Charles Monet, what would be some of the problems at the top of your mind?
5. What benefits would you be looking for in a hand-held organizer?
6. How many of these organizers would you buy and how would you distribute them?
7. Could these organizers be a useful part of programs for creative banking and consultative selling?

SUMMARY

This chapter summarizes the selling process as presented in many training programs and textbooks on personal selling. The material may be used by new salespeople to learn how to sell, by experienced salespeople to sharpen their skills, and by sales managers while counseling salespeople. Examples of the selling processes in the grocery products industry, in insurance companies, and in business-to-business companies that sell information systems and high-technology systems illustrate how these basic concepts are adapted to each situation. Job descriptions that are typical of the changing roles in the grocery products industry illustrate how technology and competition are expanding the role of the salesperson.

A discussion of systems selling is viewed as an application of organizational behavioral science. The seller must recognize that each buying organization has four structures: a power structure, a group structure, a role structure, and a status structure. The salesperson must first identify these structures and their leaders and then develop selling strategies accordingly. To penetrate these structures, the salesperson must be able to negotiate.

ASSIGNMENTS/DISCUSSION QUESTIONS

1. What are the purposes of having a structured selling process?
2. Distinguish between product features and user benefits. Give examples of each.
3. What are the advantages and disadvantages of a "canned" selling process?
4. Give three examples of a "need–benefit match."
5. If a rifle manufacturer were to claim that the rifle is "perfectly balanced," list five benefits that this feature would provide the buyer or user.

ENDNOTES

1. B. A. Weitz, A Critical Review of Personal Selling Research: The Need for Contingency Approaches, in *Critical Issues in Sales Management: State-of-the-Art and Future Research Needs,* G. Albaum and G. A. Churchill, Jr., editors, Eugene, Oregon: Division of Research, College of Business Administration, University of Oregon, 1979, p. 83.
2. F. B. Evans, Selling as a Dyadic Relationship—A New Approach, *American Behavioral Scientist 6,* May, 1963, pp. 76–79.
3. Harold Biong and Fred Selnes, The Strategic Role of the Salesperson in Established Buyer-Seller Relationships, *Working Paper No. 96-118,* Marketing Science Institute, December, 1996.
4. For example, American Business Lists, *A Catalog of Sales Leads,* Omaha, Nebraska.
5. www.Northwesternmutual.com
6. Dorothy Leeds, Where are the Real Decision Makers? *Personal Selling Power,* March, 1993, pp. 62–63.
7. L. B. Gschwandtner, Michael Who? *Personal Selling Power,* March, 1993, pp. 14–21.
8. Gehard Gschwandtner, Direct Relationship Marketing, *Personal Selling Power,* March, 1993, pp. 22–27.
9. Editte Cohen, A View From the Other Side, *Sales & Marketing Management,* June, 1990, pp. 15–16.
10. A. H. Maslow, *Motivation and Personality,* New York, Harper & Row, 1954.
11. Alan W. Farrant. Saleswomen Sales Skills, *American Salesman,* 35 (10), October, 1990, pp. 9–12.
12. Bill Palmroth, The Creative Approach in Selling, *American Salesman,* 35 (2), April, 1990, pp. 7–9.
13. The Nine Biggest Mistakes Salespeople Make on a Sales Call, *Profit-Building Strategies for Business Owners,* 21 (4), April, 1991, pp. 23–24.
14. Tom Reilly, The Best Offense is a Great Defense, *Personal Selling Power,* March, 1993, p. 56.
15. Mack Hanan, James Cribbin, and Jack Donis, *Systems Selling Strategies,* New York, American Management Association, 1978, pp. 50–64.
16. C. L. Karrass, *Give and Take: The Complete Guide to Negotiating Strategies and Tactics,* New York, Crowell, 1974.
17. Hannan, Cribbin, and Donis, Chapter 8.
18. Personal correspondence from Rich Campbell, District Manager, Greensboro, NC, dated May 14, 1997.
19. *Nationwide Selling System,* March, 1994, p. 11.
20. www.northwesternmutual.com/sales/intern/req-mail.htm (April 30, 1997).
21. Personal communication with Alston Gardner, CEO, and Tim Sullivan, VP, Target Market Systems, Inc., Atlanta, GA, March 25, 1997.
22. The outstanding cooperation and contribution of this company to this and subsequent chapters is acknowledged.

5

THE SALESPERSON
AS A BUSINESS MANAGER

···

LEARNING GOALS

1. To learn how basic business concepts and skills are practiced by a salesperson
2. To appreciate the pressures on salespeople to be more productive
3. To learn how to organize for the effective use of time
4. To learn the importance of analytical and computer skills in personal selling

···

PERSONAL SELLING REQUIRES NEW SKILLS

As we saw in Chapter 4 the role of a salesperson has changed dramatically because of the strategies of the trend toward establishing partnerships with clients, greater domestic and global competition, automated data systems, notebook computers for salespeople, downsizing sales staffs, demands for increased productivity, and telemarketing. These changes are reflected in new titles such as key account sales support representative, national account manager, sales support representative, customer service representative, business development manager, and telemarketing salesperson. Not all companies have made this transition, so we still have the older titles of territory salesperson, district manager, regional manager, sales trainer, and administrator. Linking all of these salespeople together requires clear objectives and a means for measuring whether these objectives are achieved.

Computer and communication technologies have provided the data and the means for making these links. Territory goals can be defined more clearly thanks to computers. Thus instead of goals such as "increase overall sales volume 10% next year," we see goals of "increase dollar contribution from your hospital accounts by 10% next year by stressing your new inventory control system and reducing your shipping costs by 2%." Such goals use basic business concepts. These concepts and how they can be applied by the territory salesperson are the focus of this chapter. It will also become apparent from these discussions that the young salesperson has an excellent opportunity to demonstrate his or her basic business skills and readiness for promotion to management.

Assume that you were assigned the task of developing measures for evaluating the productivity of salespeople. What basic concepts from your business and economics courses would you apply? What objectives should the salesperson have?

. . . .

TERRITORY OBJECTIVES

Territory objectives are part of the salesperson's quota, which is derived from the company's marketing strategy. Territory objectives should be specified in terms of measurable activities and measurable results. Examples of measurable activities include the number of calls, needs assessments, presentations, and closes. Examples of measurable results include growth in sales volume, market share, share of an account's business, account profit, and customer satisfaction. The salesperson must develop strategies so that the activities maximize the results. We will examine several planning systems for companies in different industries.

The highly productive salesperson must manage the territory as though it were a business. The company supplies the salesperson with a portfolio of products, a portfolio of potential customers, and assets, such as brands, goodwill, an automobile, and samples. The salesperson supplies the most important asset—time. The highly productive salesperson will allocate his or her time to selling a profitable mix of products to accounts with growth potential. A real example will illustrate this point.

Bill Currens is a salesperson for Somerville Packaging. His 1998 sales goals and objectives (disguised) are as follows:

1. Exceed 1997 sales with existing accounts by 5%.
   a. Strengthen customer relationships by meeting regularly with their purchasing, package development, quality assurance, and marketing departments.
   b. Promote plant visits and seminars.
   c. Demonstrate creative pricing and planning.
2. Tighten inventories and track orders more closely.
3. Monitor receivables weekly and follow up on accounts over 30 days.
4. Increase total contribution of accounts by 3%.
5. Follow specific account strategies.
   a. A grocery manufacturer
      (1) Complete print trial by 6/98
      (2) Ship in production quantities by 9/98
   b. A pharmaceutical manufacturer
      (1) Produce a successful production run on carton by 4/98
      (2) Present to marketing/purchasing by 6/98
      (3) Have management meet by 7/98
      (4) Present computer graphics by 8/98
      (5) Have customer service staff visit plant by 9/98
   c. Pursue and develop strategies for the following high-potential accounts:
      (1) Country Style Jellies and Jams
      (2) Daytona Remanufactured Auto Parts

Another example is Wallace, which sells information systems supplies to companies, and requires its salespeople to have a daily, weekly, and monthly plan. The salesperson prepares a plan for the next month showing the major account goals, plans for presentations and entertainment, anticipated sales, and an overall synopsis of activities. This plan is reduced to a weekly plan which considers the geographic location of accounts, their size, and their potential. The plans are reviewed by the district manager who gives feedback on time and account management to assure that time is being used wisely. The salesperson then reduces the weekly plan to a daily one.[1]

The Nationwide Insurance agent is required to submit a weekly report. A company that sells durable goods to grocery chains and hardware stores has a computerized system for planning that is part of its system for evaluation. The Grocery, Inc., salesperson, whose job descriptions we saw in the previous chapter, has a monthly calendar and a daily plan that shows the projected number of cases for each store. These data are on a database in the salesperson's notebook computer. The Daily Schedule appears in Exhibit 5.1. These plans must be translated into call strategies, so that time is used productively.

Exhibit 5.1   **GROCERY, INC. DAILY SCHEDULE REGION: 23**

Territory Manager: Romando Alvarez

Friday, March 17, 1997

Comments: Called on Publix in Brooksville, which is not on my list, working on a sale.

Store Number and Name	Wholesaler	Call Made	Product Name	Goal	Sales
6301 U Save 36 Lutz, FL	3423	Yes	A	20	50
6401 Winn Dixie 611 Lutz, FL	3262	Yes	C D E	20 10 10	30 10 8
9601 Winn Dixie 847 Wesley Chapel, FL	3262	Yes	F B G	20 20	20 20 12
4201 Publix 523 Brooksville, FL	8804	Yes	A F	15 15	15 15
1051 Hitchcocks Hqr. Alachua, FL	Affil.	Yes	A B C G H Q	35 35 35 450 490 7	35 35 35 450 490 7

Note: Romando made 7 store calls and a headquarters call that had been planned, plus an extra call. Not all calls are shown in this abstracted report.

....

CALL STRATEGIES

Several rules have been developed over the years to help salespeople allocate calls productively. The *80/20 rule* has been validated by many companies in many industries. It states that in general, 80% of a company's sales will come from 20% of its accounts. Surveys have produced refinements in the rule, such that 50% of sales come from 10% of the accounts and 90% comes from 50% of the accounts.[2] When a few accounts produce a large share of the business, personal relationships are important. These relationships can be changed by an account's moving to just-in-time inventory control or computer-based purchases. The salespeople must detect and adapt to these changes in an account's needs.

Another rule is the *ABC rule* of account classification. This rule advises salespeople to classify all accounts into three categories and to spend most of their time in the top category. The A category includes the first 15% of the accounts that typically produce 65% of the territory sales. The B category includes the next 20% of the accounts that produce 20% of the sales. The C category includes the last 65% of the accounts, which produce only 15% of the sales. The salesperson will concentrate on the A accounts until their potential is realized before moving on to the B accounts. Perhaps the C accounts will be contacted by direct mail or telephone, which is a cheaper call than a personal sales call. The company may decide to turn the C accounts over to a local distributor. The salesperson will want to track the growth potential for C and B accounts, because they can quickly grow into A accounts.

The ABC rule has its roots in microeconomics. In economics we would say, "Call on the A accounts until the marginal revenue from the additional call equals the marginal cost of that call, then move to the B accounts." Avon found that it could make more money by terminating the least productive salespeople because they were costing more money than they brought in.[3]

A bad call strategy is to call on all accounts an equal number of times, as may be seen in Exhibit 5.2. In this example the salesperson has 1000 calls per year to allocate over 200 accounts. If each account received five calls, the A accounts would generate $8667 per call, the B accounts would generate $2000 per call, and the C accounts only $462 per call. By taking one call from a C account and instead calling on an A account, the salesperson can increase sales by $8205 ($8667 − $462). This is microeconomic theory in practice.

Implementing this theory requires data and the salespersons' intuition. Sales call allocation models have been built that combine sales data and the salesperson's intuition to de-

Exhibit **5.2**	**ABC ACCOUNT CLASSIFICATION**					
					If Equal Calls Per Customer:	
Classification	No. of Accts. (1)	% of Total Accts. (2)	Sales ($000) (3)	% of Total Sales (4)	Total Calls Per Classif. (5)	Sales ($) Per Call (6) (3/5)
A	30	15%	$1,300	65%	150	$8,667
B	40	20	400	20	200	2,000
C	130	65	300	15	650	462
TOTALS	200	100%	$2,000	100%	1,000	$2,000

termine the number of calls that a salesperson should make on each account.[4] Companies that do not have the data or the resources to build a model will improve productivity just by requiring the salespeople to go through the exercise of ABC classification and to assign calls to accounts.

Exhibit 5.3 illustrates a card system that a salesperson could use to help classify accounts. It shows critical data such as past sales, growth rates, account share, account ranking, and the assigned number of calls, based on the experience of the salesperson. It also summarizes account addresses, competition, and account benefits sought. The salesperson

---

Exhibit 5.3 ACCOUNT RECORDS FOR TERRITORY MANAGEMENT

A	Northern Engineering	$713	0.95	$677	30	30	$203	3	20
A	Western Tool	$1,200	1.05	$1,312	10	20	$262	2	10
A	Central Mfg.	$500	1.20	$600	40	47.5	$285	1	11
Class	Acct. Name	Buying Req. Last Year ($000)	Growth Rate	Buying Req. This Year ($000)	Percent Share Last Year	Planned Share	Exp. Potential This Year ($000)	Rank	Calls This Year

Address:
Their
Products:

Their
Competitors:

Buying Influences (Name, Title):
1.
2.
3.
4.

Benefits Emphasized Previously:

Our Products:

Our Competitors:

Our Strengths:

Our Weaknesses:

Strategies to Increase Share
→ Quantity Discount
→ Promotional Support
→ Lower Delivery Costs
→ More Technical Support
→ Custom Design
→ Product Benefits _____
→ Service Benefits _____
→ Price/Value Benefits _____
→ Other _____

Strategies to Increase Buying Requirements
→ More Intensive Use of Products_____
→ Sales to Other Depts. _____
→ New Uses for Products_____
→ New Products _____
→ Other _____

Factors That Influence Account's Growth Rate
→ Population Size and Age Distribution _____
→ Economic Factors 1._____
       2._____
→ Competition _____
→ Govt._____
→ Other _____

can note factors that will affect account growth and he or she can record strategies to increase buying requirements and share.

Target Marketing Systems, a sales force consulting firm, has an organized Sales Plan to focus salespeople who are selling high-tech products to senior persons in the company. It stresses the important point that the benefit of the plan is to identify what is known about the account. It is not just a recording device for known facts. After gathering information about the account and its competitors the Sales Plan asks some critical questions, such as: Is there an opportunity? Can we compete? Can we win? Is it worth winning?[5]

Microcomputer programs are now available to track key data for each account. An example of how such a program can increase sales force productivity is demonstrated by James George, who is co-founder and sales vice president of Rocky Mountain Sof-Trak, which produces microcomputer software. He found that his stack of looseleaf pages was frustrating because he had 130 customers and 1000 prospects. It was especially a problem when he was on the road. He purchased an account management program for $70 and loaded his database in less than an hour. Rather than spend 70% of his work day updating paper files, he spends the time contacting accounts. His gross revenue increased over 40%. His next goal is networking, so he can access the files of his salespeople.[6]

· ·

OBJECTIVES DETERMINE RANK

What measures should be used to track the productivity of the salesperson? There are no general answers to this question. The answer depends on many factors such as the product life cycle, the corporate strategy, and the relationships with the account. The company that sells hard goods to grocery chains and hardware stores uses three measures for each account—return on assets, account contribution, and account growth. Grocery, Inc., assists its accounts in activity-based costing, which leads to account-based profit and loss. Wallace measures gross profit margins in three categories—product, account, and salesperson. These tend to be bottom-line measures, but they tell us little about how the salesperson is contributing to the variables that drive the value added. Furthermore, companies should be ready to change the criteria as life cycles and strategies change.[7]

The rank of an account depends on the objective used. An account that ranks high on past sales can rank low on future sales if it is in a declining market. Furthermore, an account that produces a high sales volume could rank low in profit contribution if it buys only the company's low margin products. Similarly, if it pays its bills slowly or demands additional technical services, it will have high account costs, which lower its overall contribution.

Exhibit 5.4 illustrates the need to consider growth rates when ranking accounts according to sales per call. The Central account ranks second, but with a growth rate of 1.20, in a few time periods it will exceed Western, the highest ranked account. Northern has a declining rate, 0.95; in future periods it will drop in rank. The sales per call ratio suggests that many of the "Other" accounts do not deserve a direct call and should be covered by other means, such as telemarketing or local distributors.

Ranking accounts according to sales volume fails to consider the fact that customers buy a mix of products and that not all products have the same margins. A customer who buys only low margin products could easily produce a high volume but be an unprofitable account. Exhibit 5.5 illustrates this point. One-half of the sales of Central Manufacturing are for axles (column 3), which have a 10% margin (column 2). Its contribution as a percent of sales is only 18%, which ranks it third in percent contribution.

Exhibit **5.4**	SALES FORECAST FOR 1 PERIOD(S)

	Accounts ($000)				
	Central Mfg. Co.	Western Tool Inc	Northern Eng. Ltd	Other Accts.	Totals
REQUIREMENTS LAST PERIOD*	$500	$1,250	$713	$6,245	$8,708
ESTIMATED GROWTH/PERIOD*	1.20	1.05	0.95	1.00	1.01
FORCSTD. TOTAL REQRMTS./PER.	$600	$1,313	$677	$6,245	$8,835
OUR SALES LAST PERIOD*	$200	$125	$214	$1,249	$1,788
OUR SHARE POINTS LAST PER.	40.00	10.00	30.01	20.00	20.24
FORECASTS					
SHARE POINTS*	47.50	20.00	30.00	20.00	22.63
SALES ($000)	$285	$263	$203	$1,249	$2,000
CALLS/PERIOD*	11	10	20	839	880
SALES/CALL ($000)	$25.91	$26.25	$10.16	$1.49	$2.27
RANK*	2	1	3		

*THESE ITEMS INSERTED BY PLANNER

Exhibit **5.5**	CONTRIBUTION FROM ACCOUNT-PRODUCT MIX FOR 1 PERIOD(S)

Sales Forecast ($000)		Central Mfg. 285		Western Tool 263		Northern Eng. 203		Other Accounts 1249		Totals 2000	
Product	Product Margin*	Product Mix*	Contrib ($000)	Product Mix*	Contrib ($000)	Product Mix*	Contrib ($000)	Product Mix*	Contrib ($000)	Product Mix*	Contrib ($000)
AXLES	10%	50%	$14.25	30%	$7.88	10%	$2.03	30%	$37.47	31%	$61.63
BARS	20%	30%	$17.10	30%	$15.75	10%	$4.06	30%	$74.94	28%	$111.85
CLUTCHES	30%	10%	$8.55	30%	$23.63	50%	$30.48	20%	$74.94	23%	$137.60
DRUMS	40%	10%	$11.40	10%	$10.50	30%	$24.38	20%	$99.92	18%	$146.20
TOTAL CONTRIBUT		100%	$51.30	100%	$57.75	100%	$60.96	100%	$287.27	100%	$457.28
CONTB. % OF SALES		18.00%		22.00%		30.00%		23.00%		22.87	
RANK		3		2		1					
CALLS/PERIOD		11		10		20		839		880	
CONTB/CALL ($000)		$4.66		$5.78		$3.05		$0.34		$0.52	
RANK		2		1		3					

*INSERTED BY PLANNER

Using Exhibit 5.5, how much would the contribution increase if the salesperson could increase sales of clutches and drums to 20% each, reducing the axles and bars by 10% each? As a salesperson how would you accomplish this goal? What kind of compensation method would you need to be motivated toward this end?

Accounts also use a company's services to different degrees. If they are slow in paying bills, the company is, in effect, giving them a loan, and the profitability of that account depends on the current loan rates. If they are a just-in-time inventory account with special needs, the company has inventory and warehousing costs to consider. Perhaps they demand more than their share of technical services and advertising support. If they order in small quantities, they greatly increase the company's handling and freight costs. Exhibit 5.6 illustrates these costs and makes it possible to develop an account strategy to make the accounts more profitable.

Northern Engineering has the highest account costs, but it still makes the largest contribution in terms of both percent of sales and absolute dollars. It could be even more profitable if its direct freight percent (6%) and its accounts receivable costs (4%) could be lowered. Perhaps it is buying in small quantities.

What are some possible reasons for Northern Engineering buying in small quantities? If you were the salesperson, how would you make this account even more profitable?

If you were the salesperson in this example and your territory objectives were defined in terms of account profitability, you now must develop a set of strategies for making these accounts more profitable. If your income is based on the profit contribution of each account, you will be highly motivated to develop such strategies. Your task now is to translate your strategy into the number of calls that you plan to make, and then schedule these calls to use your time most effectively.

Creating this kind of analysis requires that salespeople keep activity statistics. Exhibit 5.7 shows how the Nationwide Agent keeps statistics according to four lines of business—auto, homeowners, commercial, and life.

Exhibit 5.6 — ACCOUNT COSTS AND NET CONTRIBUTION FOR 1 PERIOD(S)

	Central Mfg. %Sales	$(000)	Western Tool %Sales	$(000)	Northern Eng. %Sales	$(000)	Other Accounts %Sales	$(000)	Totals %Sales	$(000)
SALES FCST. ($000)	100.00%	$285.00	100.00%	$262.50	100.00%	$203.21	100.00%	$1,249	100.00%	$2,000
ACCT-PROD CONTRIB.	18.00	$51.30	22.00	$57.75	30.00	$60.96	23.00	287.27	22.87	457
ACCOUNT COSTS										
FREIGHT (DIRECT)	1.00	$2.85	3.00	$7.88	6.00	$12.19	3.00	$37.47	3.02	60
INVENT. (IMPUTED)	3.00	$8.55	4.00	$10.50	2.00	$4.06	1.30	$16.24	1.97	39
ACT REC (IMPUTED)	3.00	$8.55	2.00	$5.25	4.00	$8.13	3.00	$37.47	2.97	59
TEC SVC (DIRECT)	1.00	$2.85	0.00	$0.00	1.00	$2.03	1.00	$12.49	0.87	17
ADV/PRO (DIRECT)	0.00	$0.00	0.00	$0.00	2.00	$4.06	1.00	$12.49	0.83	17
TOTAL ACCOUNT COST	8.00	$22.80	9.00	$23.63	15.00	$30.48	9.30	$116.16	9.65	$193.06
PERSONAL SELLING										
COST/CALL ($000)		0.053		0.053		0.053		0.053		
CALLS/ACCOUNT		11		10		20		839		880
SALES COST/ACCT.	0.20	0.583	0.20	0.53	0.52	$1.06	3.56	$44.47	2.33	47
TOTAL MKTG. COSTS	8.20	$23.38	9.20	$24.16	15.52	$31.54	12.86	$160.62	11.99	240
NET CONTRIBUTION	9.80%	$27.92	12.80%	$33.60	14.48%	$29.42	10.14%	$126.65	10.88%	218
% OF TOTAL CONTRB.	12.83		15.44		13.52		58.21		100.00	
% OF TOTAL CALLS	1.25		1.14		2.27		95.34		100.00	
NET CONTB/CALL $000		$2.54		$3.36		$1.47		$0.15		$0.25
RANK		2		1		3				

Exhibit 5.7 FINANCED AGENT WEEKLY REPORT—NATIONWIDE INSURANCE

Agent Name/Number: _____

AM Name/District: _____

Week Ending: _____

Weeks on Plan: _____

Prospect X-date		Appointments		Closing Interviews		Current Sales		New Annual Commissions		Previous Week		Prior 2 Weeks		Prior 3 Weeks	
Plan	Actual	Plan	Actual	Plan	Actual	Plan	Actual	Plan	Actual	Plan	Actual	Plan	Actual	Plan	Actual

Line: Auto

HO

Referred Leads — Comm'

Plan | Actual — Life

Totals:

Agent Analysis of Activity/Request for Assistance

Agency Manager Observation

Activity Requiring Assistance

Actions to be Taken

Agent Signature: _____

AM Signature: _____

HIGH-TECH MANAGEMENT

Twenty years ago high-tech territory management consisted of a hand-held calculator and a telephone credit card. Today high-tech territory management can include notebook computers with modems for downloading electronic mail, account profitability analysis, order tracking, inventory status, and competitive analysis. The computer can have FAX capabilities and be linked to a cellular phone or a private short wave radio corporate network. Will all of this technology result in greater sales force productivity? In some cases it may have increased sales and profitability and in other cases it may have stopped a decline in sales.

The latter would be the case when systems were introduced as a defensive strategy rather than an offensive one. For example, in the grocery products industry, chain stores had more information than manufacturers because the chain had all of the information generated at the store level by Uniform Product Code (UPC) scanners. Grocery manufacturers have been playing catch up by developing microcomputer systems that will give salespeople better information for presentations. Thus the quality of sales calls may be improved through more sophisticated account analysis. In many fields the microcomputer has reduced paperwork, speeded proposals, eliminated telephone tag with the home office, and generally made more time available to work with accounts. A few examples will illustrate these points.

Jerry Whitlock sold seals and gaskets the old-fashioned way, walking and talking. Today he does $1 million of business a year using e-mail, fax, and the World Wide Web from his home.[8]

J. B. Wampler, Jr., a 15-year veteran salesman with IJ Companies, a Knoxville, TN, food service distributor, credits his laptop computer with sending business through the roof. IJ Companies spent $300,000 equipping its 100-person sales force with laptops as part of a program to strengthen customer loyalty by filling orders 100%, that is, no backorders. Here is how the system works. After the buyer agrees on the order, the salesperson types it in the computer, plugs the computer into the phone line in the buyer's office, and dials the warehouse computer. In 87 seconds the salesperson learns if the order can be filled 100%. If not, alternatives are suggested along with expected arrivals of out-of-stock items. Buyers like to know before the delivery truck arrives that a product is out of stock. The IJ Companies estimate that the new system has helped increase sales by $2.7 million without any increase in salespeople, trucks, drivers, or decreasing prices.[9]

Some benefits are difficult to reduce to a dollar figure. A survey of 285 sales and marketing executives who use computer sales support (CSS) systems found that the major benefit was better sales management through control and feedback from the field.[10] The five most important applications were customer account management, database inquiries, word processing, checking orders, and forecasting. When a company such as Xerox cuts its suppliers from 5000 to 300, it expects the account manager to have full information at his or her fingertips.

General Foods USA found that its CSS system lowered communication costs (phone, postage, mailing, and copier). The system also had psychological advantages for the sales force: they had a higher level of confidence in their information and they felt more professional, which led to more analysis and more presentations.[11]

Early forecasts in the fashion clothing industry are critical because commitments for materials and designs must be made at least six months before the products are sold. There is little room for error. Overestimating demand results in closeouts and distress sales, whereas underestimating demand means a loss of sales because the production cycle is often longer than the days left in the selling season. For the salesperson, forecasting errors translate into lost commissions because the salespeople are paid on products finally delivered, not on products sold. Orders often are not filled because of a lack of sizes or colors. The company and the salesperson share the same goal—an accurate and early forecast of demand. To achieve this common goal, the order cycle must be shortened. This shortened cycle gives the company a more accurate forecast and it gives the salesperson a claim on inventory, thereby assuring delivery and commissions. The Wrangler Female and Children's Apparel Division of Blue Bell created an information network system that reduced the order cycle from 3 weeks to 3 days.[12] It increased company sales by 10% and, of course, salesperson's commissions as well.

The Wrangler system gave each salesperson a friendly, bullet-proof system that could call up a toll-free 800 number to place an order. Every time the salesperson called the home office computer, the laptop was updated for the status of 2,000 items in inventory in the warehouse. The salesperson then entered the order and the window of availability (the first and last date of availability) appeared. The computer then completed and sent the order to the home office computer. Wrangler estimated that its investment in the system was paid back in less than one year. It used a turnkey vendor of sales support systems to develop the system. Advertisements for these vendors appear regularly in *Sales & Marketing Management*.

Hewlett Packard, a computer manufacturer, estimated that it could realize a return of $6 to $8 million if the sales force could increase customer contact time by 25%. In a pilot test 100 salespeople were given portable computers. Available selling time increased 35%. It then gave all 2000 salespeople a computer.[13]

Marion Merrell Dow, a pharmaceutical firm, used a small hand-held computer for its call reporting system. At the end of each day, the salespeople downloaded all of their call data for the day. The next morning call reports were available for the marketing and sales managers. For their second generation they used the GRiDPAD, which has a screen with an electronic pen, thereby eliminating the need to learn to type. Input is just like writing on a form. It also accepts physicians' signatures on orders for samples. The signature goes into the computer at the home office and the samples are shipped from there. This system has two benefits: it meets the requirement of the Food and Drug Administration for greater accountability of samples and it eliminates the need for the salespeople to carry samples, saving time and reducing the inventory of samples in the field.[14] Software for the GRiDPAD includes electronic mail, tools for managing leads, territory management, forecasting, client profiles, and sales order history.

Baxter International supplies hospitals with a range of products from bedpans to surgical supplies. It developed systems for each salesperson that analyze and organize complex proposals for major hospitals. It is an important part of Baxter's close working relationship with hospitals that includes a just-in-time inventory system and surgical instrument packs that are unique to a specific surgeon. A program was also developed to aid district sales managers to manage the district.

Salespeople in the finance and insurance industries were among the earliest users of computers because of the need to analyze data and change proposals quickly. Salespeople in the Employee Benefits Department of Travelers Insurance found that laptops could better demonstrate their health, dental and other group benefit products than flipcharts, slides, and transparencies.[15] The Travelers' software includes a computerized animated slide show that can be customized for a specific client. The computer plugs into a television projector for group presentations.

The Frito-Lay division of PepsiCo equips its route salespersons with hand-held computers that are linked into a data network. It is estimated that the system saves the salespeople 5 hours per week. They then added a trade development system to help account executives pinpoint Frito-Lay profit opportunities for supermarket managers. In preparation for the presentation, the computer analyzes 200 different Frito-Lay products and completes the presentation in 15 minutes. Formerly it took 10 days or more.[16] The time saved can be spent with customers instead of in the office.

Sales force software is now a major industry. Each December *Sales & Marketing Management* reviews the available software. Hundreds of programs in 37 categories range from account management to zip code tracking. Some of the most extensive categories include direct marketing, hiring and training, lead tracking, geographic mapping, market analysis, market research, telemarketing, and territory management.

FUTURE HIGH-TECH DEVELOPMENTS

While the grocery manufacturers have been playing catch-up in marketing information systems, retailers have taken advantage of even newer technologies. For routine reorders, salespeople and route persons have been replaced by Electronic Data Interchange (EDI) systems that translate the scanned Uniform Product Code (UPC) at the checkout counter into a Uniform Communication Standard (UCS) that allows computers to talk to each other. Thus the UPC not only automates checkout, it automates inventory control and re-ordering. The product order is generated by the computer at the store level, goes into the customer's purchase order system, is translated into a UCS, which then goes to the supplier who ships it to the store. The supplier's computer transmits the invoice to the customer's computer, which compares it with the order and processes the payment. The advantages to the buyers are reduced lead times, lower backup inventories, improved service levels, improved cash flow, and freeing buyers to deal with more productive activities, such as promotional buys.

Retailers are going the next step in generating market information by getting information about their customers in specific stores, thereby enabling a microsegmentation. Products, brands, sizes, and colors can be unique to each store. This is accomplished by customer SMART cards that, when scanned, give the store computer demographic data. This customer information will further strengthen retailers' bargaining power over manufacturers. Previously the manufacturer had all of the market information and therefore the bargaining power. The incentive to the shopper for carrying the scannable membership card is cash rebates or merchandise awards for buying specific products, automatic coupon credits, and newsletters.

SUMMARY

The young salesperson should manage a territory as though it were a business, making maximum use of assets that the company supplies—products, brands, goodwill, potential accounts, car, and samples—along with the salesperson's most important asset—time. The territory management process begins by translating corporate and territory objectives into personal objectives. Then the salesperson must develop account strategies and allocate sales calls appropriately so as to increase the territory contribution to profit. To accomplish this end the salesperson must develop strategies to increase the share of the account's business, sell products with a higher margin, reduce territory costs, identify new accounts, and find more efficient ways to serve small accounts. The 80/20 rule or the ABC rule will get the salesperson started in this allocation, but these rules are generally based on sales volume. To maximize profitability, the salesperson will need to analyze the product mix and the services for each account.

The microcomputer has made salespeople more productive by reducing paperwork, thereby making more time available to sell. Sales have increased because of better forecasts, shorter order cycles, more complete order fulfillment, better analysis, easier proposal preparation, and increased control over samples. Continued development in retail computer systems will reduce the need for order takers, thereby requiring only a more sophisticated salesperson who has a close client relationship with accounts.

ASSIGNMENTS/DISCUSSION QUESTIONS

1. Name five business concepts that a salesperson can use to run the territory as a business.

2. Develop a selling strategy to improve the account-product mix for Central Manufacturing.

3. Develop some creative ways that a microcomputer can be used to manage the territory for a salesperson for General Foods and also for Bill Currens, whose objectives are described in the chapter.

4. Create a spreadsheet for Exhibit 5.4.

   a. Change the number of planning periods from 1 to 5. How does the ranking of these accounts change? What is driving this change?

   b. In Exhibit 5.5, experiment with a change in product mix for Central Manufacturing. What would happen to the net contribution if the salesperson were able to sell the account on buying more drums with a higher margin, if the mix of drums shifted from .1 to .3, and there was a corresponding drop in axles from .5 to .3? What would the salesperson need to do to cause this shift?

ADDITIONAL READINGS

Hughes, G. David. Computerized Sales Management, *Harvard Business Review* (March–April 1983): 102–112.

Moriarty, Rowland T., and Gordon S. Swartz, Automation to Boost Sales and Marketing, *Harvard Business Review* (January–February 1989): 100–109.

Wedell, Al, and Dale Hempeck, Sales Force Automation—Here and Now, *Journal of Personal Selling & Sales Management* 7:2 (August 1987).

ENDNOTES

1. Personal communication from Rich Campbell, District Manager, Wallace, May 14, 1997.
2. The Shape of Things to Come, *Sales & Marketing Management,* January, 1990, pp. 36–41.
3. Tara Parker-Pope, Ding-Dong: Fewer Salespeople Will Help Avon Come Out Ahead, *The Wall Street Journal,* Tuesday, April 22, 1997, p. B1.
4. Leonard M. Lodish, A User-Oriented Model for Sales Force Size, Product, and Market Allocation Decisions, *Journal of Marketing* 44, Summer, 1980, pp. 70–78; A.A. Zoltners, P. Sinha, and P.S.C. Chong, An Optimal Algorithm for Sales Representative Time Management, *Management Science* 25 (12) December, 1979, pp. 1197–1207.
5. *Target Account Selling*[R] Sales Plan, Atlanta, GA: Target Marketing International, Inc., 1994.
6. Thayer C. Taylor, Databases Save Time and Customers, *Sales & Marketing Management,* March,

1990, p. 105.

7. David James, Keeping Track: Knowing What to Measure, and Why, *Business Review Weekly,* June 3, 1996, pp. 68–70.

8. Thomas Petzinger, Jr., Gasket Salesman Uses e-mail, fax, the Web- and Shoe Leather, *The Wall Street Journal,* April 4, 1997, p. B1.

9. William Stack, Getting 2% More Business from Every Customer, *Sales & Marketing Management,* September, 1989, pp. 80–81.

10. Louis A. Wallis, *Computer-Based Sales Force Support,* New York: The Conference Board, Report No. 953, 1990.

11. Wallis, p. 14.

12. Louis A. Wallis, *Computers and the Sales Effort,* New York: The Conference Board, Research Report No. 884, 1986, pp. 16–17.

13. Allen J. Wedell and Dale Hempeck, What If We Automated Our Sales Reps to Show the Value of Our Automation? *Marketing News,* May 8, 1987, p. 11.

14. Thayer C. Taylor, The PC Evolution . . . , *Sales & Marketing Management,* February, 1991, p. 54.

15. The Travelers' Salespeople Hit the Road Big with Laptops, *Personal Selling Power,* March, 1991, p. 46.

16. Arthur Bragg, Getting Face-to-Face with Customers, *Sales & Marketing Management,* February, 1991, p. 46.

6

ETHICAL AND LEGAL ISSUES IN PERSONAL SELLING AND SALES MANAGEMENT

LEARNING GOALS

1. To understand the role of ethical sales practices in supporting business strategy and building long-term customer relationships
2. To clarify the ethical and legal decisions facing a sales manager and field salesperson
3. To develop a working knowledge of the marketing laws that apply to sales
4. To know when to seek advice regarding legal questions

THE LEGAL–ETHICAL CONTINUUM

The 1980s, with its junk bond and savings and loans scandals, was described by some as the decade of greed. This period of scandal led to a new search for ethical behavior in the 1990s. Corporations introduced codes of ethics and training programs and business schools introduced new courses on ethics. As the world moves into a new century, many companies are working to develop long-term relationships with their customers, which requires high ethical standards. Yet the basic questions remain: What does it mean to be ethical? What does it mean to be legal?

To gain insight into these questions, it may help to think of a continuum of behavior ranging from individual free choice on the left to legal constraints on the right. In the middle of this continuum is a vague area known as ethical behavior, which is guided by values formed by social institutions such as the family, the church, and schools.

Laws codify behavior that is required by society. Failure to obey the law results in a loss of wealth or freedom. Individual free choice, on the left end of the continuum for example, permits individuals to decide where to live, whom to marry, and what to believe.[1] In recent decades both laws and individual free choice have expanded, squeezing and sometimes eliminating the middle, ethical area of behavior. Defendants in the junk bond and savings and loan scandals of the 1980s were quick to argue that they did nothing illegal, but they ignored the middle ground of ethical behavior that is driven by social values to achieve social goals.

There are many reasons for unethical behavior, but often the problem results from increasing pressure to perform—often under conditions of diminishing resources. Sometimes the result is fudged sales figures, abused competitors, or shortchanged customers.[2] Whatever the internal pressures for performance shortcuts, firms are often left to repair the damages caused in public. Citicorp fired a president and senior executives of a credit-card-processing division for allegedly overstating revenues. American Express fired executives for failing to write off accounts of customers who had filed for bankruptcy. Alamo Rent-A-Car agreed to refund $3 million to customers who were overcharged for repairs to damaged vehicles.[3] Thus layoffs may improve the balance sheet ratios in the short term, but in the long run permanent damage to the customer base may result.

Performance pressures cause ethical dilemmas for sales managers as well as salespeople. A survey conducted by researchers Joseph Bellizzi and Robert Hite among more than 500 sales managers found evidence that sales managers may be less than uniform in dealing with unethical sales force behavior. Specifically, the researchers found that sales managers were less likely to discipline salespeople for unethical behavior when the situation had led to negative consequences for the firm or when the salesperson involved performed poorly.[4] Gender also plays a role. The researchers found that managers discipline male salespeople more severely for ethical violations than they do female salespeople. Similarly, other research suggests that sales managers are reluctant to enforce codes of ethics with long-time employees or "star" employees.[5]

To do their jobs well, sales managers and salespeople must understand both marketing laws and ethical guidelines. The legal and regulatory environment requires each salesperson to have sufficient knowledge of marketing laws and regulations to know when he or she should consult the legal department of the company. Firms also have a stake in assuring that salespeople, who represent the business to the outside world, understand ethical behavior as set by the company and its customers.

The first part of this chapter will examine how companies are responding to the need for codes of ethics. The second half of the chapter will discuss regulations that apply directly to field sales. Discussion of the legal considerations when recruiting, evaluating, and terminating salespeople will appear in later chapters.

....

ETHICS, LAW, AND RELATIONSHIP-BASED SELLING

As the business world moves into the new millenium at Internet speed, the fundamental nature of customer relationships is changing. The creed of the past was *caveat emptor* ("let the buyer beware"). Firms often focused on turning a short-term profit, sometimes at the expense of ethical or even legal business practices. On-the-spot bidding for products in one-time exchanges created pressure to cut price, cut costs, and cut corners.

Competitive pressure continues to grow, but sellers increasingly understand that long-term performance requires a customer orientation. There is hard evidence that a customer orientation on the part of the firm—and loyalty on the part of customers—lead to improved financial performance. Firms with a customer orientation focus on building buyer relationships and loyalty. Loyal customers are more likely to increase their future purchases, to make purchases across the firm's different product/service lines, and to refer other customers to the firm. Such loyal and long-term relationships with customers are built on trust. Ethical and legal behavior is the foundation for that trust. One study showed that firms following more ethical practices grew at a higher rate between 1950 and 1990 than other companies.[6]

One example of the increasing importance of ethics and trust in sales relationships is the growth of just-in-time (JIT) purchasing. When firms move from purchasing on a bid basis to a long-term JIT arrangement, the nature of the sale changes. As research by Gary Frazier and his colleagues demonstrated,[7] strong buyer-seller relationships are necessary if JIT arrangements are to work well. Both parties must be ready to invest resources in building one another's commitment to the relationship and mutual trust. Creative selling that cuts corners is inappropriate here, and will not work in JIT exchanges.

Relationships with customers reflect relationships with employees. Firms that provide a "higher" purpose for their employees, in addition to financial rewards, develop a special kind of employee involvement. Results from a survey of more than 900 members of the American Marketing Association, conducted by Shelby Hunt and his colleagues, found that emphasizing corporate ethical values increases marketers' commitment to their organizations.[8] Hunt and his fellow researchers suggested that managers who use more formal approaches to building ethical values in organizations are more apt to influence employee behavior and win their commitment.

Building ethics into the organization begins at the top of the business. A sales manager can build ethics into his group by a four-step process developed by Donald Robin and Eric Reidenbach.[9] This process includes (1) creating an ethical profile consistent with the firm or unit's mission statement; (2) identifying groups that are affected by the sales group; (3) developing ethical core values that can be acted upon; and (4) integrating those values into the sales department's culture.

Ethical Profile   The firm's mission statement not only drives its marketing and sales planning, it also drives the ethical profile that the firm presents to outside groups, including customers. Robin and Reidenbach suggest that managers who prepare an ethical profile for their unit begin by reviewing their unit's internal strengths and weaknesses, as well as external opportunities and threats. A classic and powerful example of an ethical opportunity are the Ronald McDonald Houses. These facilities allow families of chronically or terminally ill children to stay together during their treatment. They tap into a powerful ethical opportunity with a prime McDonald's target market (families with children).

Affected Groups   Sales affects groups other than customers, including those inside the firm (such as manufacturing and distribution) and those outside the firm (such as competitors and stockholders). Identifying the affected groups enables the sales manager to clarify specific core values that can be used in training salespeople. Each group must be examined in terms of the potential impact of sales actions. For example, a commitment to realistic delivery schedules (that is, not to stretch the truth to make a sale) may cost short-term sales, but it maintains credibility within the firm—and the long-term customer.

Ethical Core Values   The unit's ethical profile and its affected groups lead directly to the creation of a set of actional core values, the ethical guidelines for salespeople to follow. A guideline for consumer goods salespeople might state that they should "present products in the way that you would like them sold to your family." One advantage of this guideline is that it provides a reasonably clear direction for behavior, even in diverse situations. Another advantage is that it may engender organizational pride that leads to salespeople's commitment to the firm.

Statements of ethics help guide unsupervised decisions during crises. Johnson & Johnson relied on ethics to guide decisions during the recall of Tylenol that had been tampered with. In the absence of a direct policy, Merck employees are guided by the statement, "profit derived from work that is beneficial to society."[10]

Enculturation Process   The training and mentoring programs that will be discussed in Chapter 10 apply to ethical behavior, as well as selling techniques and organizational strategy. Enculturating ethical values can include training, mentoring, and a variety of ongoing communications programs. For example, Rexnord chairman Robert V. Krikorian distributed a videotape shown to all employees in which he instructed them to "walk away from business when it means doing anything unethical or illegal".[11]

Bringing salespeople into a firm's particular culture, a process called enculturation, requires effective communication of corporate values. The media for communicating corporate values vary greatly. For example, Westvaco developed a programmed learning text on the subject of legal pitfalls in selling.[12] Citicorp developed an ethics board game in which employees solve hypothetical quandaries. General Electric employees can use their personal computers to get answers to ethical questions. Texas Instruments employees have a weekly ethics column on their electronic news service. Some companies have a hotline where employees can have ethical questions answered and report ethical violations. The need to communicate corporate ethics clearly is heightened by the ethics of the emerging managers. A recent survey of Americans 18 to 30 years old revealed that about 75% cheated in high school, 45% cheated in college, and 18% included false information on their resumes.[13]

Business schools have introduced ethics in a variety of ways. The Harvard Business School requires applicants to write an essay on how they managed and resolved an ethical dilemma. It requires all MBAs to take a nongraded, nine-session course on ethics. It encourages the faculty to integrate ethics in the core courses and to develop ethics cases. Finally, Harvard offers three ethics electives.[14] Other schools are developing role play sessions in which the students assume the different roles of the stakeholders. They also use videotapes and cases that require students to struggle with ethical dilemmas.[15]

Ethics in the Sales Force

Salespeople are subject to ethical criticism because of their high visibility, their competitive environment, and their isolation from the corporate environment. The public is inclined to generalize from a few bad experiences with high-pressure salespeople in highly competitive industries such as home repair, autos, and insurance. The ethics of marketing executives and salespeople have been studied extensively.[16]

The public may regard some selling behavior as merely unethical when, in fact, it is illegal. Puffery, overstatement of product attributes for promotional purposes, may violate the law. For example, a salesperson overstated a chemical product's capabilities and cost his company $6,000. The salesperson who told clients that warnings in the securities prospectus were unimportant triggered class action suits that were settled for amounts from $260,000 to $3 million. Detail representatives failed to mention warnings, resulting in a wrongful death claim for $400,000.[17] The authors have heard salespeople complain of unethical behavior when a competitor required a customer to buy a bundle of products or gave special discounts to selected customers. This was more than unethical behavior. It was illegal. If the salesperson had known the law, these cases could have been reported to superiors for appropriate legal action.

Unethical behavior such as product puffery, making promises that cannot be met, or selling more features than are needed just to increase the sale all are against the customer's best interest. But considerable unethical behavior also hurts the salesperson's company. For example, falsified trip reports that claim calls that were not made, inflated expense accounts, and over-optimistic forecasts of future sales can jeopardize the future of the company.

Ethics problems can also occur in the form of sexual harassment by a manager who abuses his power. In 1996 the president and CEO of the pharmaceutical firm Astra was relieved of his duties after a Business Week investigation exposed his advances toward female salespeople. In this case a former female salesperson obtained an out-of-court settlement.[18]

However, all is not bleak. Several factors suggest a move toward improved ethics, including increased involvement of women in the workforce and increasingly open competition. Some research suggests that women have higher ethical standards, and because they now represent one-third of the sales force, their presence could be expected to improve ethics in the field.[19] In addition, open competition can improve ethics. A study of ethics in the trucking industry before and after deregulation concluded that ethics improved. Salespeople now compete on rate and services differences to solve needs, rather than on perks and bribes.[20]

THE REGULATION OF MARKETING ACTIVITIES

Understanding the laws that relate to personal selling may not seem as important as learning about the company, its products, and its customers, until the new salesperson is informed of the consequences of violating the laws. For example, engaging in price fixing or bid rigging with a competitor could result in a $100,000 fine for the salesperson and a $1 million fine for the company. A pharmaceutical representative who promotes a drug for a use that has not been approved by the Food and Drug Administration could be liable, along with the company, for compensatory and punitive damages if the patient dies as a result. Many insurance companies are now adding compliance officers to assure that salespeople do not engage in deceptive practices.[21] The result of ethical vigilance can be a long-term improvement in the bottom line. Companies that have been convicted of corporate crime have been found to lag behind their peers in sales growth and returns on sales and on assets.[22]

Public policy in the United States has been designed to preserve competition, protect the consumer, and conserve national resources and the environment. The salesperson will be concerned largely with policies for preserving competition. A salesperson is the representative of the company and has many legal responsibilities to the company, such as protecting company secrets and not making unauthorized contractual arrangements on behalf of the company. The salesperson must be careful not to leak competitive information when discussing the development of new products. Letters must be written carefully and checked by the legal department to ensure that an informal proposal does not become a binding contract. The salesperson must adhere to approved claims for products and services. This chapter will attempt to alert the salesperson to some of the subtleties of the regulatory environment, such as price fixing, price discrimination, controlling distribution, and unfair selling practices.

THE NEW SALESPERSON'S DILEMMA: WHETHER TO TAKE THE DEAL

To understand legal and ethical situations facing a salesperson consider the following example. *To meet the contest goal of 100 cases of peanut butter, Lisa Dunn needed to sell 50 more cases. The buyer for a small supermarket chain said that he would buy 75 cases if she would give him a 6% discount on the price and $10 per case to advertise the product* *in the local newspaper. Lisa was excited because the sale would put her in first place in her district. Are there any problems with her accepting the deal?*

Understanding the legal and ethical environment of the times will illustrate the complexity of the decision and why Lisa may want to seek the opinion of her manager. Corporate values, which should have been made clear in her early training, and personal values will also frame her ethical behavior.

COLLUSION TO FIX PRICES

The Law

The Sherman Antitrust Act of 1890 is the basic law in the United States that outlaws monopolies and collaboration. Section 1, as interpreted by the courts, makes entering into a contract, combination, or conspiracy that unreasonably restrains trade illegal. Section 2 makes monopolizing, attempting to monopolize, or combining or conspiring to monopolize trade illegal. The courts have interpreted price fixing as illegal *per se* under Section 1 of the Sherman Act. A *per se* violation means that proving that the activity restrained trade or created a monopoly is not necessary, thereby eliminating the need for costly court trials.

Antitrust pressure has carried over to professionals, such as lawyers, doctors, stockbrokers, druggists, architects, engineers, and others, who failed to announce their prices or follow a fee schedule that was suggested by their association. Large price-fixing cases are not only historical—they still happen. In 1996 Archer Daniels Midland (ADM) admitted that it conspired with two Japanese companies and a Korean company to fix the prices on two agricultural commodities. ADM agreed to pay a record-breaking $100 million fine.[23] Other current price-fixing and bid-rigging charges have been leveled against a variety of companies, such as the following: 24 major Nasdaq securities firms; two disposable plastic dinnerware companies; a South Dakota dairy company for a conspiracy involving publicly bid contracts; and a saleswoman and the two companies that she represented for bid-rigging in supplying advertising display materials to Philip Morris.[24]

Charges of price fixing are not limited to large companies. The Federal Trade Commission (FTC) found that American Art Clay, Binney & Smith, and Milton Bradley had engaged in a price fixing conspiracy when selling art supplies to public school systems. The $1.2 million refund was allocated by State Attorneys General according to the number of students in each state in grades kindergarten through 12.[25]

Conditions That Create Collusion

A summary of price-fixing cases identifies the conditions that lead to collusion. The concept of the product life cycle reminds us that competition becomes severe as products become mature and there is little product differentiation among sellers. High fixed costs increase the break-even level of a firm; they put pressure on the selling function to maintain high levels of sales, which, in turn, is an inducement to fix prices with competitors. Similar cost structures among manufacturers help to support collusion to avoid a price cut by a low-cost rival.

Barriers to entry, such as licensing requirements, large investments in production equipment, or a lack of access to raw materials, may lead to collusive pricing because it is difficult for new firms to enter the industry. The fewer the number of sellers in a market, the easier it is to implement collusion because a firm that acts as a price cutter can be found and penalized quickly by other members of the collusion.

PRICE DISCRIMINATION

A seller need not engage in collusion with other sellers to reduce competition. A seller may build a monopolistic position through price discrimination. Price discrimination occurs when a seller offers different price terms to different buyers within the same trade group. Section 2a of the Clayton Act (1914), as amended by the Robinson-Patman Act (1936), makes it illegal to discriminate among purchasers of goods of like grade and quality when the effect of price discrimination may substantially lessen competition or create a monopoly. An exception to this rule can occur when the discrimination reflects a difference in costs or an attempt to meet the price of a competitor.

Price discrimination can result from buyer pressure. For example, chain stores have used a variety of techniques to induce their suppliers to give them a better price. In addition to seeking direct differential discounts, they have set up phantom brokerage firms and required a brokerage allowance, required special cooperative advertising allowances, secured quantity discounts available to only a few buyers, and induced a lower price by claiming that a competitive seller had offered such a price.

Price discrimination occurs when one party is put at a disadvantage that results in a lessening of competition. A weak competitor may claim price discrimination when in fact the alleged price discriminator was lowering prices to reflect lower costs, quantity discounts, functional discounts, the clearance of perishable or obsolete goods, or in a good faith meeting of competition. Thus the law provides for these defenses against a charge of price discrimination.

Costs   Price differentials are permitted when there is only due allowance for differences in the cost of manufacture, sale, or delivery resulting from differing methods or quantities in which commodities are sold or delivered. This defense is not as popular as it once was because of the difficulty of establishing costs for a specific product when a company sells a large number of products and the allocation of joint production and marketing costs is difficult, if not impossible.

Quantity Discounts   Quantity discounts are permitted as long as they reflect a true cost saving in the manufacture, sale, or delivery of the product. The Federal Trade Commission placed upper limits on the quantities that must be purchased to get a discount.

Functional Discounts   A functional discount is a means for paying a member of a channel of distribution for performing certain functions, such as storing, financing, advertising, or shipping. A functional discount could be a suitable defense, but problems are created when this discount is passed along the channel of distribution and a subsequent competitor is at a price disadvantage.

Although functional discounts raise questions of cost allocation and meeting competition, the Act is clear on the matter of brokerage discounts. It is illegal for a seller to pay any broker's fee or to allow a discount in lieu of a broker's fee to a buyer. This provision was intended to stop large firms such as A&P from setting up phantom brokerage firms simply to get a larger discount.

Functional discounts may become discriminatory if they are not given proportionally to all buyers. For example, if a chain store is given an advertising allowance equal to $.20 per case for a cooperative newspaper advertisement, the little family-owned corner grocery store must be given the same allowance to enable it to distribute handbills to its customers.

Perishable or Obsolete Goods   A seller of a perishable good, such as vegetables, a fashionable product, such as clothing, or a technologically obsolete product, such as a computer, may give a discount to move the product quickly. Such a discount is not price discrimination.

Meeting Competition   The Robinson-Patman Act makes provision for charging a lower price to a customer in good faith to *meet* an equally low price of a competitor. In this case, price discrimination is not illegal, even if competition was reduced as a result. The burden of proving good faith falls upon the seller, which introduces two issues. First, was there a genuine offer by a competitor or was this just a negotiation tactic? Second, how does one determine a competitive price without appearing to engage in price fixing? These questions will be addressed in the following sections.

EXCHANGING PRICE INFORMATION

There are at least two legal ways for a salesperson to meet a competitive offer in good faith without engaging in an activity that could be interpreted as price fixing. One approach is to have the prospective buyer supply a copy of the competitor's offer or price list. Such documents should be clearly marked by the buyer and the salesperson as having come from the buyer, not the competitor. If a competitor's written quotation is not available, a seller may decide to include a statement on the invoice to the effect that the seller's price is given on reliance of the buyer's representation of the competitor's offer and that the buyer will cooperate in any later investigation regarding charges of price discrimination.

Many companies instruct their salespeople to refuse to discuss prices with competitors. Some companies even advise that their salespeople should be dramatic, even to the point of knocking over a chair, to emphasize the fact that they will not discuss prices. These instructions are to help the competitor to recall correctly the fact that this company will not discuss prices should the competitor ever be called on the witness stand in a grand jury investigation of price fixing.

PREDATORY PRICING

Predatory pricing is selling below cost with the intention of destroying competitors. The provision of the Robinson-Patman Act that makes predatory pricing illegal is often criticized for limiting effective competition by limiting price cutting. A seller is afraid to use price as a competitive tool for fear of being charged with price discrimination. This concern is real because a variety of industries have been represented in predatory pricing cases.

BUYER LIABILITY

The Robinson-Patman Act also places responsibility on the buyer, as well as the seller. In particular, it is also unlawful to knowingly induce or receive a price that is discriminating. This provision protects the salesperson from being drawn into an illegal act by a hard-bargaining buyer. It also protects the seller from competing with a nonexistent competitor or meeting, not beating, an offer that was not bona fide. It is difficult, however, to distinguish between discrimination and competition.

CONTROLLING DISTRIBUTION

The price mechanism is not the only way to create a monopoly. Many contractual arrangements can limit the vertical freedom of a buyer, restricting a buyer's alternative sources of supply or the conditions under which the buyer may resell the product. These arrangements may reduce competition directly or indirectly through vertical price fixing, which is illegal under the Sherman Act.

Vertical Price Fixing

Vertical price fixing, like horizontal price fixing, is illegal. For example, Nintendo fixed the price to consumers of its video game consoles at $99.95 by reducing the supply or terminating dealers who advertised or sold below this price and by asking other dealers to report offenders. New York, along with 38 other states and the Federal Trade Commission, filed suit against Nintendo. The courts ruled in favor of New York. Nintendo was ordered to advise its dealers that they were free to set their own prices. Nintendo was then required to provide up to $25 million in coupons to those who purchased the console in 1989–1990 and to pay the 39 states that participated in the action a total of $5 million.[26]

Tying Arrangements

Several forms of tying arrangements are possible. A tying arrangement occurs when a buyer is required to purchase one product before another can be purchased. For example, a tying arrangement would exist when the buyer is required to buy Product B in order to get the desired product, Product A. This condition exists when the seller has a comparative advantage for Product A because it is a new product that is selling well or has a patent advantage. In order to move a slower moving product such as B, the seller links this inferior product to Product A. When the seller forces the buyer to purchase a whole line of products, the arrangement is known as full-line forcing. Tying arrangements may violate the Clayton Act or the Sherman Act because other sellers are prevented from competing for this buyer's business.

Tying contracts may be a subtle form of price discrimination. A seller could bundle a group of products and sell it at a total price that was discriminating, claiming a savings in the cost of distribution. If the discounts cannot be justified on the basis of a cost saving, the bundled price may be a discriminatory one.

Exclusive Distribution

The job description for a salesperson often includes establishing new dealerships to handle the company's products. The question of exclusive dealing generally enters these negotiations. In some instances, the seller wants to require the dealer to handle his or her products exclusively, although the dealer may want to handle competing lines. Conversely, there will be occasions when a manufacturer wants to have several dealers in a territory, but a new dealer refuses to purchase unless given an exclusive coverage of the territory. Exclusive dealing can be very complex and has become the subject of many court cases. A review of some of these cases will help the young salesperson or sales manager to recognize the complexities of the issue and seek legal counsel early.

Cases in Exclusive Dealing

The trend in court decisions on exclusive dealing is that *contractual* requirements by a seller to exclude others from competing or supplying a buyer do have anticompetitive effects and are illegal. Whether persuasive methods are illegal is less clear, as has been seen in some cases of franchising. The key test in exclusive dealing cases is the market share of the seller, but the courts have not established the percent of market share that constitutes anticompetitive behavior.

Reciprocity

"If you buy from me, I will buy from you" constitutes reciprocity, which may be anti-competitive. The salesperson must be careful not to enter inadvertently into reciprocity. For example, supplying one's purchasing department with the sales figures for particular customers will be interpreted as an attempt to engage in reciprocity. Conversely, if a customer indicates that it wishes to become a supplier of the salesperson's company, the salesperson should refer it to the purchasing department with the understanding that it must bid for the business on the basis of its own merits, without reference to its status as a customer.

UNFAIR PRACTICES

The Law

Unfair trade practices—such as television commercials that use trick photography to make the product look better—are regarded as illegal under the Federal Trade Commission Act (1914), Section 5, as amended by the Wheeler-Lea Act (1938). This set of laws is used to stop deceptive door-to-door selling, such as salespeople claiming that they were doing a market survey, not selling books, or salespeople for heating contractors stating that they were conducting fire inspections. Unfair trade practices can occur even when the salesperson does not intend it. The salesperson, in his or her enthusiasm for the product, may unintentionally promise more than the product can deliver or may imply a warranty that the company does not wish to support. Salespeople should make guarantees with great care and within the bounds of corporate policy.

Bribery

Giving money or other valuables to influence a buyer's employee to decide in favor of the seller can constitute bribery, which is a violation of Section 5 of the Federal Trade Commission Act. The Foreign Corrupt Practices Act (1977) makes it a criminal offense to pay a foreign official for help in selling to a foreign government.

EMPLOYEE ISSUES: DISCRIMINATION AND HARASSMENT

In the past, sales managers may have felt that most of the legal and ethical issues they had to contend with focused outside the firm on trade practices. Avoiding charges of price fixing, price discrimination, or other unfair trade practices have been, and remain, a major concern for sales managers. But now sales managers face a variety of legal and ethical issues that are increasingly important and are focused inside the firm. These issues reflect growth in the diversity of the work force, the legal rights of minorities, and the ethical responsibilities of managers toward those they manage.

For example, only about 3 of every 100 salespeople in the United States is African-American.[27] Further, 60% of sales executives responding to a recent survey indicated that African-Americans are either underrepresented or not represented at all on their sales force.[28] Yet 75% say that they think whether a salesperson is African-American makes no difference in a purchasing manager's decision to buy the firm's products (another 6% said purchasing managers are more likely to buy if the salesperson is African-American and 11% said they are less likely to buy).[29] The fact that African Americans are underrepresented on the sales force, and that most sales managers say race won't affect a sale, suggests that integration of the sales force will become an increasingly prominent issue. Among the trends that make these issues increasingly important are the following:

- **Diversity.**   The work environment is becoming more diverse and the sales force is under increasing pressure to reflect that diversity. Women, racial and ethnic minorities, gays, the disabled, and other groups are growing in power as markets, as organized political interests, and as self-support networks. The growing legal rights of these minority groups require that the sales manager become familiar with, and act within, a complicated and sometimes ambiguous set of laws and legal interpretations. Growth in the diversity of the sales force adds a complicating ethical dimension, in that the sales manager must assure fairness while working with people with different viewpoints and concerns.
- **Self-supervision.**   The sales manager is the person primarily responsible for directing the employees who fill boundary spanning roles. Salespeople typically interact with more outsiders than anyone else in the firm. They represent the organization. It is the sales manager's job to see that they typify the firm's understanding of legal and ethical behavior in dealing with others. It is also part of the sales manager's job to see that salespeople are dealt with legally by others. Although the sales manager is responsible, both ethically and legally, for directing the behavior of the sales force, the sales force is increasingly outside of the direct supervision of the sales manager. In part, this reflects the increasing efficiency of sales managers at moving the sales force out of the office and into the field. Beyond this, more and more salespeople telecommute from their homes or even their cars and do not keep an office at the company.
- **Relationship selling.**   The shift in marketing paradigms from an exchange to a relationship orientation may complicate the problems of assuring ethical and legal sales behaviors. Whereas the exchange orientation focused on making the immediate sale, the relationship orientation focuses on building a long-term relationship. Often the one-to-one relationship between a salesperson and a buyer has real economic value to the firm. Attempting to build the relational selling approach within a firm can lead to ethical and legal concerns. For example, the sales manager may make false assumptions about buyers, believing that they cannot develop effective long-term business relationships with members of certain minority groups. Or the salesperson may feel that she is under pressure to establish too close a relationship with male buyers in order to make the sale.
- **Globalization.**   The growth of international commerce has magnified differences in social customs. Behavior is interpreted differently in different cultures. For example, a smile and direct eye contact from a woman salesperson may be seen as pleasant behavior in some cultures, but in others it may be seen as a sexual invitation. Legal requirements may complicate the impact of intercultural differences. The customs of some countries (for example, Islamic countries) may forbid women

from having supervisory roles over men. U.S. firms may be liable for refusing to send a female manager to these locations, or for any sexual harassment of a female employee who is sent there.[30]

The internal legal and ethical responsibilities of sales managers reflects these changes in the external environment. These changes are ongoing, and imply that guidelines for managing are continuously changing as well.

Discrimination

The Equal Employment Opportunity Commission (EEOC) interprets and enforces several laws that affect how employees can be selected, managed, and terminated. Among these laws are the:

- **Age Discrimination Act**—prohibits discrimination against employees over 40 based on age.[31]
- **Americans with Disabilities Act (ADA) of 1992**—prohibits discrimination in employment practices against "qualified individuals with disabilities," which means someone who meets "legitimate skill, experience, education, or other requirements of an employment position that s/he holds or seeks, and who can perform 'essential functions' of the position with or without reasonable accommodation."[32]
- **Equal Pay Act**—an amendment to the Fair Labor Standards Act of 1963 that prohibits paying wages based on gender.[33]
- **Title VII of the Civil Rights Act of 1964**—prohibits hiring or firing employees, offering them pay or privileges, or making terms or conditions of employment, based on race, color, religion, sex, or national origin.[34]

Legal and corporate guidelines are less clear about managing gay salespeople than they are about other minorities. Yet in all likelihood, the sales manager will be supervising openly gay salespeople. About 16% of sales executives surveyed by *Sales & Marketing Management* magazine reported that there were openly gay members on their sales forces.[35] About 37% believe that purchasing managers are less likely to buy from an openly gay or lesbian salesperson.[36]

While federal and state laws are evolving on this issue, many major firms like AT&T, Disney, and Levi Strauss have added sexual orientation as a component of their diversity programs.[37] Companies like Lotus, Ziff-Davis, MCA-Universal, Viacom, and American Express offer gay and lesbian employees health insurance and insurance benefits for domestic partners.[38] Sales managers are advised not to assume that everyone on their force is heterosexual and to examine their own company's policy.[39]

Sexual Harassment

Sexual harassment is a pervasive problem in organizations. A survey of 9000 women found that 88 percent said they had been victims of sexual harassment and 52% said they had been fired or forced to quit a job because of sexual harassment.[40] In a 1991 survey by the National Association of Female Executives, 53% of the 1300 women responding said they had been sexually harassed or knew someone who had been.[41] Similarly, results of a survey conducted by *INC.* magazine found that 59% of business respondents believed that sexual harassment was a major problem in the United States.[42]

Sexual harassment costs money, time, and emotional devastation. A survey of Fortune 500 firms found that the average cost of sexual harassment is about $6.7 million per firm.[43] That average is attributed to turnover, absenteeism, and reduced productivity. It does not include legal expenses.

Employment discrimination on the basis of sex, race, color, religion, or national origin is prohibited under Title VII of the Civil Rights Act of 1964. Although the courts initially did not believe that sexual harassment was actionable under this act, in 1980 the Equal Employment Opportunity Commission (EEOC) issued guidelines interpreting sexual harassment as a type of discrimination.[44]

The EEOC identified sexual harassment as follows: "Unwelcome sexual advances, requests for sexual favors, and other verbal or physical conduct of a sexual nature constitute sexual harassment when any of the following criteria are met: (1) submission to such conduct is made either explicitly or implicitly a term or condition of an individual's employment, (2) submission to or rejection of such conduct by an individual is used as the basis for employment decisions affecting that individual, or (3) such conduct has the purpose or effect of unreasonably interfering with an individual's work performance or creating an intimidating, hostile, or offensive work environment." [45]

Sales managers are advised to focus on several key issues pertaining to sexual harassment:[46]

- **"Quid pro quo" ("this for that") harassment** refers to cases in which employee hiring, pay, promotion, or termination were based on sexual favors from the employee. This type can be committed only by an individual in the organization with control over another's job.[47]
- **"Hostile work environment" harassment** involves cases in which a sexually hostile work environment was created by discussing sexual activities, unnecessary touching, comments on physical attributes, displaying sexually suggestive pictures, using demeaning or inappropriate terms, using obscene gestures, granting job favors to those who participate in consensual sexual activity, or using crude or offensive language.[48] This form of sexual harassment can exist even when there is no actual or threatened injury to the employee, but that alters the terms of employment and creates a hostile work environment.[49]
- **"Unwelcome" sexual conduct** is defined by the person subjected to it. The 1986 Supreme Court ruling in Meritor Savings Bank v Vinson found that the victim's consent is not a defense against a sexual harassment claim.[50]
- **The "Reasonable Woman Doctrine"** replaces the "reasonable man" as a benchmark for determining a sexually harassing work environment, based on a 1991 U.S. Circuit Court of Appeals decision.[51]

Guidelines for Managing a Diverse Workforce

The increasing diversity of the sales force requires that the manager become proactive in preventing incidents of discrimination or sexual harassment. Steps he or she can take include the following:[52]

- **Learn company policies and procedures.** Examine the company's policies on diversity, non-discrimination, and sexual harassment in detail.
- **Offer a rationale for diversity.** Existing salespeople should be instructed that, given an increasingly diverse population of buyers, a diverse sales force can be a competitive advantage.
- **Communicate company policy to subordinates.** Let subordinates know the company's diversity, non-discrimination, and sexual harassment policies by posting them in the office and distributing a copy for review. Include procedures for reporting incidents.
- **Train subordinates in how to handle sexual harassment situations.** Provide ongoing training for dealing with such situations. Cathy Owens Swift and Russell

Kent suggest offering assertiveness training relating to stopping offensive behavior and gender awareness training to facilitate open communications among male and female salespeople about how they want to be treated at work.[56] Encourage employees to discuss behaviors that they might consider harassment.

- **Openly discuss sexual harassment issues during sales meetings.** Use the sales meeting to clarify sexual harassment issues and to sensitize salespeople to the other gender's viewpoint.
- **Ensure that codes of conduct are established and enforced.** Guidelines on dress codes, language, and behavior can help to discourage incidents of sexual harassment.
- **Protect subordinates against work-related harassment outside the firm.** The sales manager is responsible for protecting his or her salespeople from harassment both inside and outside of the firm. Subordinates should be informed that protecting them from sexual harassment is more important than making the sale.
- **Become familiar with discrimination and sexual harassment issues.** Videotaped training programs on discrimination and sexual harassment may be available

---

Case 6.1 — COMPANY VERSUS COMMUNITY INTERESTS

In May, 1997, when Greg Huntley took over as manager in the Western Pennsylvania district, he didn't realize the importance of high school football to the surrounding communities. During the fall, Friday evenings and Saturdays vibrated with excitement and competition. The 1998 season looked like a championship year for Jefferson High School because of its outstanding quarterback, Byron Prichard. Greg thought that it would be an exciting year for his son, Greg, Jr., who had just transferred to Jefferson High as a freshman.

When Greg, Sr., reviewed the personnel files of his salespeople, he noted that there was a Byron Prichard, Sr., who had been on probation for six months. The note in the file simply said, "A major problem with substance abuse resulted in failure to meet quotas and complaints from customers. If the problem is not corrected, he should be taken out of selling and moved to the home office in New York no later than July 1, 1997." The report had been signed by the previous manager and Byron, Sr.

CASE QUESTIONS

1. Who stands to gain or lose by moving Byron, Sr.?
2. Should Greg, Sr. bend the corporate rules so that Byron, Jr. can remain in school?
3. What do you recommend?
4. Do you think the previous manager made a good decision in recommending transferring Byron, Sr., or should he have just fired him at the end of the probation?

Case 6.2 — PERSONAL NEEDS IN THE OFFICE

How do you think a regional sales manager should handle the following situations?[54]

1. The full-time baby-sitter became ill so the service manager brought a 12-month-old baby to work. This is the third time it has happened in the last three months. (In answering this question would the manager's gender make a difference? Would you have a different response if the manager has a private office? Suppose the employee was a part-time telephone clerk?)

2. A star salesperson works from home and customers call him there. When customers call they can hear a baby cry in the background.
3. Should a woman promise to return from maternity leave even though she is not sure that she will?
4. A divorced father sees his eight-year-old daughter infrequently. He would like to have her come to the office on Wednesday afternoon and do her school work.
5. Should a manager let her daughter visit the office to sell Girl Scout cookies?

through the firm's Human Resources Department. These should be viewed by the sales manager. In addition, it is important that the sales manager watch for and read new articles and books on the issue to monitor changes in laws and regulations. The sales manager should reflect on his or her own views about discrimination and sexual harassment to detect and eliminate any bias or resentment.[55]

- **Keep high personal standards of conduct.** Sales managers have a responsibility for setting an example of non-discrimination and sensitivity to minority issues. This includes keeping their conversations free of innuendo or jokes, respecting the rights of other employees, and ensuring that they do not engage in stereotyping based on gender, race, or other characteristics.

SUMMARY

The legal dimensions of personal selling primarily involve preserving competition so that the marketplace will be the means for allocating resources according to the demands of the public. The purpose of this chapter is to alert salespeople and sales managers to those laws and court decisions regarding price fixing, price discrimination, controlling distribution, and unfair practices that may, in the eyes of the courts, result in a reduction of competition. After learning these laws and court cases, the salesperson will be better prepared to know when to turn to the legal department for advice. The general rule, of course, is, "If in doubt, seek advice."

Meanwhile, the increased emphasis on relationship marketing has led to most corporations developing codes of ethics, training programs, and information systems to communicate what they regard as ethical behavior.

ASSIGNMENTS/DISCUSSION QUESTIONS

1. Develop a table of relevant law and cases to train salespeople in the following industries:
   a. Folding boxes
   b. Grocery packaged goods
   c. Door-to-door books.
2. Distinguish between illegal and unethical behavior of sales representatives.
3. How can a company determine if a candidate will be an ethical representative?
4. How can a company determine if a salesperson is behaving ethically?
5. As sales manager, how should you react to the following situations?
   a. A female salesperson says that one of the male salespeople has been making unwelcome advances but that she doesn't want to make a big deal of the incidents for fear of not being included as a member of the sales team.
   b. You overhear one salesperson making disparaging remarks about the sexual habits of a salesperson who is openly gay.
   c. You practice team interviewing, in which new job applicants interview with members of the team they will be assigned to and hiring decisions are made jointly with the team. After a recent round of interviews that included an African-American applicant, two members of the all-white sales team suggested that the applicant wouldn't fit in with the group. They didn't specifically allude to race.

d. A female salesperson says that she is being pressured by an important customer to go out with him.

INTERNET ASSIGNMENTS

1. Prepare an overview of key discrimination law issues that would affect the sales manager, using sites such as the Employment Discrimination Law Materials posting at the Cornell Legal Information Institute (www.law.cornell.edu/employment_discrimination.html).

2. Two applicants have applied to you for a job as a salesperson. Both appear equally qualified in all respects, but one uses a wheelchair. As sales manager, you are concerned that this applicant's situation will pose a constraint on her potential performance, because the job involves travel to small business clients whose offices are not equipped to accommodate wheelchairs. Research the Americans with Disabilities Act to determine whether you would be illegally discriminating by not hiring her. Start with the U.S. Department of Justice's ADA Home Page (www.usdoj.gov/crt/ada/adahom1.html). As an additional consideration: What are the ethical issues involved here?

3. Based on a web search, identify the codes of conduct at five major companies. In each case, evaluate the implications of the code of conduct for the sales manager and salespeople of that company.

4. Examine back issues of the Newsletter of DePaul University's Institute for Business & Professional Ethics (www.depaul.edu/ethics/newslet.htm). What issues are identified in these newsletters that pertain to sales management and selling? What are the implications for the sales manager and the salesperson?

5. Search the web for nonprofit associations that have programs relating to ethics. Examples are the Association for Practical and Professional Ethics (http://php.ucs.indiana.edu/~appe/home.htm) and the National Association of Sales Professionals (www.nasp.com). Identify the practical benefits to a sales manager from participation in such an organization.

Appendix 6.1 HANDLING SEXUAL HARASSMENT COMPLAINTS: A CHECKLIST FOR SALES MANAGERS[56]

Taking the Complaint

- Assure the complainant that you take them seriously and will take action quickly.
- Do NOT express an opinion or display emotion about the alleged incident.
- Do NOT make promises about any outcomes.
- Determine—and document—all facts in the case, including:

  - Who was the harasser?
  - Where and when did the alleged incident(s) take place?
  - Who said what to whom?
  - Was this a continuing practice or a single incident?
  - Were there any witnesses to the incident? Who are they?
  - Did the complainant talk to anyone else about the incident? Who?
  - Is there any documentary evidence of the incident?

- Exactly how did the complainant communicate that the behavior was unwelcome?
- How was the complainant affected by the incident?

- Ask the complainant to sign the written statement.
- Assure the complainant that:

  - A prompt and thorough investigation will be conducted.
  - The investigation will be kept as confidential as possible.
  - There will be no retaliation against the complainant for filing a complaint.

Interviewing the Alleged Harasser

- Interview the alleged harasser immediately.
- Advise the alleged harasser of the accusation and the purpose of the meeting.
- Encourage the alleged harasser to respond to the accusations. If he or she says that the conduct was welcome, obtain all relevant facts.
- Ask the alleged harasser to disclose the times, places, and circumstances relating to each incident.
- Ask the alleged harasser to provide names of witnesses.
- If the alleged harasser denies that the incident occurred, or says that it did not occur in the way alleged by the complainant:

  - Assure the alleged harasser that you have reached no conclusion about the incident.
  - Assure the alleged harasser that you will maintain confidentiality as much as possible.
  - Inform the alleged harasser that retaliation against complainants or witnesses is forbidden.
  - Document the alleged harasser's statement, including a summary of which facts are agreed upon and which are contested, and ask him or her to sign it.
  - Begin an investigation of the incident(s).

Investigating the Incident(s)

- Make sure that any harassment has ended. This might include keeping the parties separated, monitoring them closely, or providing paid time off during the investigation.
- Do NOT significantly alter the responsibilities of the complainant.
- Contact an expert on sexual harassment complaints (perhaps in the Human Resource Department).
- Check company policy about who should conduct the investigation.
- If you must conduct the investigation:

  - Decide whom to interview and the information needed.
  - Document all interviews.
  - Conduct final interviews with the alleged harasser.

Taking Appropriate Action

- If you determine that the alleged harassment did occur:

  - Check organizational policy on sexual harassment.
  - Take disciplinary action against the harasser.
  - Be prepared to explain the outcome and actions taken.
  - Advise the harasser that they have the right to appeal the decision to a higher level.

- Follow up with the complainant to ascertain:

  - Whether the harassment has stopped.

- That there have been—and will be—no reprisals.
- That the complainant is working well with and accepted by co-workers.
- That the complainant and harasser are separated, if this can be done without adversely affecting the complainant.

Document the Investigation

- Develop a thorough and exact record of the investigation.
- Include the documentation in the personnel file of the harasser.

Source: Cathy Owens Swift and Russell L. Kent, Sexual Harassment: Ramifications for Sales Managers, *Journal of Personal Selling & Sales Management* 14(1), Winter 1994, pp. 77–87.)

ENDNOTES

1. Lord (John Fletcher) Moulton of Bank, Law and Manners, *The Atlantic Monthly,* 134(1), July, 1924, pp. 1–5.
2. Kenneth Labich, The New Crisis in Business Ethics, *Fortune,* April 20, 1992, p. 167.
3. Labich, p. 168.
4. Joseph A. Bellizzi and Robert E. Hite, Supervising Unethical Salesforce Behavior, *Journal of Marketing,* 53, April, 1989, pp. 36–47.
5. Clarke L. Caywood and Gene R. Laczniak, Ethics and Personal Selling: Death of a Salesman as an Ethical Primer, *Journal of Personal Selling and Sales Management,* 6, August 1986, pp. 81–88.
6. Labich, p. 172.
7. Gary L. Frazier, Robert E. Spekman, and Charles R. O'Neal, Just-In-Time Exchange Relationships in Industrial Markets, *Journal of Marketing,* 52, October 1988, pp. 52–67.
8. Shelby D. Hunt, Van R. Wood, and Lawrence B. Chonko, Corporate Ethical Values and Organizational Commitment in Marketing, *Journal of Marketing,* 53, July, 1989, pp. 79–90.
9. Donald P. Robin and R. Eric Reidenbach, Social Responsibility, Ethics, and Marketing Strategy: Closing the Gap Between Concept and Application, *Journal of Marketing,* 51, January 1987, pp. 44–58.
10. Susan J. Harrington, What Corporate America is Teaching About Ethics, *Academy of Management Executive* 5:1, 1991 p. 22.
11. Daniel B. Moskowitz and John A. Bryne, Where Business Goes to Stock Up on Ethics, *Business Week,* October 14, 1985, pp. 63, 66.
12. Westvaco Corporation, *Legal Pitfalls in Selling,* New York: Westvaco Corporation, 1977.
13. Labich, 176.
14. John A. Byrne, Can Ethics Be Taught? Harvard Gives it the Old College Try, *Business Week,* April 6, 1992, p. 34.
15. Mary L. Nicastro, Infuse Business Ethics into Marketing Curriculum, *Marketing Educator* 11(1), Winter, 1992, p. 1.
16. For research and an excellent bibliography see Anusorn Singhapakdi and Scott J. Vitell, Marketing Ethics: Sales Professionals Versus Other Marketing Professionals, *Journal of Personal Selling & Sales Management* 12(2), Spring, 1992, pp. 27–37.
17. Karl A. Boedecker, Fred W. Morgan, and Jeffrey J. Stoltman, Legal Dimensions of Salespersons' Statements: A Review and Managerial Suggestions, *Journal of Marketing,* 55, January, 1991, p. 71.
18. Mark Maremont, Abuse of Power, *Business Week,* May 13, 1996, pp. 86–98.
19. Leslie M. Dawson, Will Feminization Change the Ethics of the Sales Profession? *Journal of Personal Selling & Sales Management,* 12(1), Winter, 1992, pp. 21–31.
20. Kenneth C. Schneider and James C. Johnson, Professionalism and Ethical Standards Among Salespeople in a Deregulated Environment: A Case Study of the Trucking Industry, *Journal of Personal Selling & Sales Management,* 12(1), Winter, 1992, pp. 40–43.
21. Marketing Scandals, *The Wall Street Journal,* March 18, 1997, p. 1, col. 5.
22. Does Corporate Crime Pay? *Business Week,* April 14, 1997, p. 30.

23. R. A. Melcher, All roads lead to ADM, *Business Week,* September 23, 1996, pp. 42, 44; R. Henkoff, Betrayal, *Fortune,* February 3, 1997, pp. 82–86.
24. www.antitrust.org/news/pricefixing.html (February 7, 1997, p. 1).
25. *FTC News Summary,* vol. 39–80, July 4, 1980, p. 2.
26. In re Nintendo of America, Inc., FTC File No. 901-0028, New York v. Nintendo of America (DC S NY, Apr. 1991); BNA ATRR No. 1511 (Apr. 11, 1991), 505, abstracted in *Journal of Marketing,* October, 1991, p. 96.
27. Allison Lucas, Race Matters, *Sales & Marketing Management,* September, 1996.
28. *Ibid.*
29. *Ibid.*
30. Robert K. Robinson, Billie Morgan Allen, David E. Terpstra, and Ercan G. Nasif, Equal Employment Requirements for Employers: A Closer Review of the Effects of the Civil Rights Act of 1991, *Labor Law Journal,* November 1992, pp. 725–734.
31. *Ibid.*
32. U.S. Department of Justice, 1997, *The Americans with Disabilities Act: Questions and Answers,* www.usdoj.gov/crt/ada/ada.html (July 18, 1997).
33. Employment Discrimination Law Materials, www.law.cornell.edu/topics/employment_discrimination.html (July 18, 1997).
34. *Ibid.*
35. Michael Adams, Selling Out, *Sales & Marketing Management,* October, 1996, pp. 78–87.
36. *Ibid.,* p. 79.
37. Michael Adams, Selling Out, *Sales & Marketing Management,* October, 1996, pp. 78–87.
38. *Ibid.*
39. *Ibid.,* p. 86.
40. Claire Safran, What Men Do to Women on the Job: A Shocking Look at Sexual Harassment, *Redbook,* November, 1976, pp. 123–128.
41. Chris Lee, Sexual Harassment: After the Headlines, *Training,* March, 1992, pp. 23–31.
42. What Are You Doing About Sexual Harassment? *INC.,* August, 1992, p. 16.
43. Ronni Sandroff, Sexual Harassment in the Fortune 500, *Working Woman,* December, 1980, pp. 46–52.
44. Lloyd R. Cohen, Sexual Harassment and the Law, *Society,* May–June, 1991, p. 8.
45. Code of Federal Regulations, V. 29, Ch. XIV, Section 1604.11, July, 1990.
46. Cathy Owens Swift and Russell L. Kent, Sexual Harassment: Ramifications for Sales Managers, *Journal of Personal Selling & Sales Management,* 14(1), Winter, 1994, pp. 77–87.
47. Bureau of National Affairs, Preventing Sexual Harassment: A Fact Sheet for Employers, *Bulletin to Management,* p. 43.
48. Swift and Kent, p. 78.
49. *Ibid.,* p. 78.
50. Sandroff.
51. Howard Simon, Ellison v. Brady: A 'Reasonable Woman' Standard for Sexual Harassment, *Employee Relations Law Journal,* Summer, 1991, pp. 71–80.
52. *Ibid.*
53. Brigid Moynaham, Creating Harassment-Free Work Zones, *Training and Development,* May, 1993, pp. 67–70.
54. Adapted from Work & Family, *Wall Street Journal,* June 21, 1993, p. R3.
55. Swift and Kent, p. 85.
56. Based on Cathy Owens Swift and Russell L. Kent, Sexual Harassment: Ramifications for Sales Managers, *Journal of Personal Selling & Sales Management,* 14(1), Winter, 1994.

7

THE SALES MANAGEMENT PROCESS

··

LEARNING GOALS

1. To review the management functions and activities common to management in all organizations and to see how they apply to sales management
2. To appreciate that the youngest sales manager performs the same functions as top management, but with different areas of emphasis
3. To establish the framework for the remainder of the text
4. To understand how quality management skills apply to sales management

··

A TYPICAL SALES MANAGEMENT PROBLEM

To appreciate the importance of understanding the management process consider the following case. Jim Hightower started Highline Communications just six years ago in an area that was enjoying an industrial boom. Initially he didn't have to solicit business after his opening announcement because customers came looking for his services. The growth continued until his sales volume exceeded his capacity. He expanded by buying out a small competitor. He then hired three sales representatives who responded to his newspaper ads. Sally Sharp was one of these reps.

His current problem surfaced three years later after he expanded to the tri-state area, added three more reps, and promoted Sally to supervise the sales staff. After three months with her new responsibilities she came to Jim, outlined her problems, threw up her hands, and said excitedly, "We've got to get organized." Jim paused, thought for a moment, and said, "OK, where do we begin?" This chapter will enable students to answer Jim's question by explaining basic management processes.

After decades of examining what managers do, most management scholars agree that there is an identifiable set of skills, functions, and activities that are performed by all managers, whether they are in production, finance, accounting, marketing, or sales.[1] This chapter will illustrate how these basic management skills, functions, and activities apply to

103

sales management and will emphasize the fact that even young sales managers have the opportunity to practice them. This opportunity explains why so many chief executives started in sales.

Later in the chapter recent developments in Total Quality Management (TQM) will be examined. TQM is a particular approach to the general management process. It focuses on anticipating and meeting customer needs.

A definition of management seems in order at this point. Mackenzie defines management as "achieving objectives through others."[2] The manner by which objectives are established and achieved becomes the *management process*.

THE MANAGEMENT PROCESS

The management process consists of the coordination of three elements—ideas, things (tangible resources), and people. This process is outlined in Exhibit 7.1, which provides the structure for the remainder of this text.[3]

The management process may be described at three different levels. At the lowest level, we find management activities. Clusters of similar activities form a management function. In order to perform these functions and activities, the manager must possess the basic management skills for analyzing the environment to identify opportunities and problems, to make decisions, and to communicate effectively.

MANAGEMENT SKILLS

At this point in our discussion we will simply define management skills. Later in the text there will be an opportunity to develop these skills through case analysis. These skills are necessary to perform each of the management activities.

Analyzing the Problem

The analysis of a sales problem or opportunity requires skills in gathering and analyzing the facts, identifying opportunities or problems, and determining the cause of a problem or opportunity. For example, a common sales management problem is the creation of territories to assure adequate coverage of a market. The sales manager will need to analyze the market potential, the workload, travel time, expenses, and the abilities of the salespeople before developing alternative territory designs.

Making Decisions

To make a decision, a manager must first create alternative courses of action, such as several different territory designs, and then evaluate the gains and losses associated with each alternative. One of these alternatives must then be selected. Until this selection is made, we have no decision; we have only studies and analyses.[4]

The salesperson engages in decision making when he or she sets priorities, decides which products to promote, chooses which product features to emphasize, or selects a sales strategy to overcome competition. Field sales managers make decisions when they structure territories, solve account problems, and choose salespeople for promotion. General sales managers make decisions when they choose a promotional strategy, select field sales

Exhibit 7.1 THE MANAGEMENT PROCESS

Elements

Ideas	Things		People

Tasks

Conceptual Thinking Formulate change.	**Administration** Managed tasks and roles.	**Leadership** Influence people to accomplish agreed-upon goals.

Continuous Functions

Analyze Problems: Facts, causes, and alternative courses of action.
Make Decisions: Choose an alternative.

Communicate Ensure understanding.

Sequential Functions

Plan Predetermine a course of action.	**Organize** Arrange and relate work for effective accomplishment of objectives.	**Staff** Choose competent people for positions in organization.	**Direct** Bring about purposeful action toward desired objectives.	**Control** Ensure progress toward objective according to plan.

Activities

Forecast Where will the present course lead?	**Create Position Descriptions** Define scope, relationships, responsibilities, and authority.	**Select** Recruit qualifiable people for each position.	**Delegate** Assign responsibility and exact accountablity for results.	**Establish Reporting System** Determine critical data needed, how and when to measure.
Set Objectives Determine desired end results.	**Delineate Relationships** Define liaison lines to facilitate coordination.	**Orient** Familiarize new people with the situation.	**Motivate** Persuade and inspire people to take desired action.	**Develop Performance Standards** Set conditions that will exist when key duties are done well.
Develop Strategies Decide how and when to achieve goals.	**Establish Position Qualifications** Define qualifications for persons in each position.	**Train** Make proficient by instruction and practice.	**Coordinate** Relate efforts in most effective combination.	**Measure Results** Ascertain extent of deviation from goals and standards.
Develop Policies Make standing decisions on strategies.	**Establish Organizational Structure** Draw organizational chart.	**Develop** Help improve knowledge, attitude, and skill.	**Manage Differences** Encourage independent thought and resolve conflict.	**Take Corrective Action** Adjust plans, counsel to attain standards, replan, and repeat cycle.
Program Establish priority, sequence, and timing of steps.			**Manage Change** Stimulate creativity and innovation in achieving goals.	**Reward** Praise, remunerate, and discipline.
Set Procedures Standardize methods.				
Budget Allocate resources.				

©1991 G. David Hughes and Charles H. Singler.
Adapted from R. Alec Mackenzie, The Management Process in 3-D, *Harvard Business Review*, November–December, 1969, pp. 80–87; Louis A. Allen, *The Professional Manager's Guide*, ed 4, Louis A. Allen Associates, 1969; R. L. Ackoff, *A Concept of Corporate Planning*, New York: Wiley/Interscience, 1970; Harold Koontz and Cyril O'Donnell, *Management: A Systems and Contingency Analysis of Managerial Functions*, ed 6, New York: McGraw-Hill Book Co., 1976.

managers for promotion, and determine the size and organizational structure of the sales force. Because all of these decisions are made in a state of uncertainty, the decision maker must assess the probabilities of outcomes that are associated with each decision. Multiplying the probability of an alternative producing a desired result times the estimated profit resulting from that outcome produces the *expected value* of that alternative. Expected values can then be used to choose among different alternatives.

Communicating Effectively

Communication is the effective transfer of information from a sender to a receiver. The information is communicated effectively when the receiver gains understanding from the message, not just its content. Communication is a critical skill for sales and sales management. It is obvious that salespeople must be effective communicators with prospects and buyers, but it is less obvious that they must be effective communicators with contact persons within their company. Effective communication with peers, superiors, credit personnel, the billing office, shipping clerks, engineers, production-scheduling personnel, and research and development personnel will make the salesperson more effective in his or her assigned area of responsibility and more promotable to the next level of management. The means by which salespeople communicate include reports, itineraries, telephone calls, voice and computer mail, and memos to managers and company departments regarding the success of sales promotions, customer complaints, and recommendations.

Field sales managers communicate upward with reports, itineraries, and memos. They communicate downward with staff bulletins, individual memoranda, training sessions, sales meetings, and personal counseling. They communicate in both directions when they evaluate salespeople's past performances and report these evaluations to the salesperson and to the next level of sales management.

General sales managers monitor communications at the lower levels. They communicate to lower levels regarding new plans, policies, procedures, and overall company sales performance. They communicate upward with regard to goal accomplishment and recommendations for changes. Their ability to communicate well helps them achieve current goals and be promoted.

MANAGEMENT FUNCTIONS

Management is a continuous process that begins with the function of planning, moves sequentially through the functions of organizing, staffing, directing, and controlling, and then returns to planning. The management process, therefore, is circular. It never ends because feedback loops will reveal that objectives were not fully met and refinements will be necessary. The management functions and the activities within each function are summarized in Exhibit 7.1.

Strategic Planning

Strategic planning is *not* predicting and preparing for the future; it is the marshalling of resources to make the future happen in your favor.[5] To make the future happen in your favor, you must control those events that are controllable and adapt to those that are uncontrollable. Wisdom and experience are required to distinguish between controllable and uncontrollable events.

Organizing

Organizing consists of combining roles that must be performed to accomplish specific objectives. These roles become the basis for an individual's job description. Departments are formed by grouping together persons who perform similar roles. This grouping of role specialties expands the number of subordinates who can be managed, thereby making the organization more efficient and controllable. Line and staff relationships are established by the *kind* of authority that is allocated to subordinates. The degree of decentralization of authority is determined by *how much* authority will be allocated to subordinates. Physical location can also affect the degree of delegation. A salesperson who is far from the office may have more authority delegated.

Staffing

Staffing consists of choosing qualified people for each position in the organization. We must recognize that it is not always possible to recruit people who are qualified for a position; thus we must identify characteristics that make them qualified, after additional training. We will see later in the text that this distinction is important in conforming with federal regulations regarding equal employment opportunities.

Directing

Directing guides people through appropriate actions to achieve the desired objectives of the organization. *Directing* is a broader term than *leading* because the concept of directing includes delegating, motivating, coordinating, and managing change and conflict.

Controlling

Controlling ensures that the system progresses toward the objectives of the organization according to the plan. When a system is out of control, minor adjustments may bring it back. This out-of-control state of the system may also reveal that the objectives and the plan were not realistic. Thus it may be necessary to cycle back through the planning stage and repeat the whole sequence of functions.

As can be seen in Exhibit 7.1, each of the management functions may be further subdivided into a sequence of activities. A brief discussion of each of these activities will help us to see how they are incorporated into sales management. Later in this chapter we will see how these definitions may be translated into the excitement of consulting by using them to make a "sales management audit." (How can Jim Hightower, in the opening management problem, convert planning activities concepts into action?)

MANAGEMENT FUNCTIONS

Planning Activities

The seven planning activities shown in Exhibit 7.1, column 1, determine a course of action that will lead the company toward its mission. Planning involves a seven step process: information gathering, setting objectives, developing strategies, developing policies, developing programs, setting procedures, and budgeting.

Information Gathering The first step in planning is to gather information about the problem under consideration. Useful information can come from both subjective and objective sources. Subjective sources (such as informal conversations, structured interviews, observation, and other means) can help to identify the significant issues inherent in a problem. Objective sources (such as formal surveys of employees, customers, and other groups) can provide reliable measures relating to the problem.

Developing an appropriate framework for understanding a problem is an important management skill. Experts on decision-making recommend looking at problems from multiple perspectives, using different types of measures.[6] Studies of successful managers in dynamic industries suggest that they gather more "real time" data than do unsuccessful managers.[7]

In addition to monitoring the present, managers must anticipate the future. Changes in technology, competitor strategy, legislation, customer demand, and other factors can all affect a company. Managers use techniques like scenario planning to identify—and plan for—events that could impact their company.

Because future sales are critically important to the entire organization, sales managers also work extensively with forecasts. Developing accurate estimates of future sales has implications for an organization's personnel needs, production planning, distribution requirements, and more. They also affect the sales area itself in terms of staffing, training, and other resource allocations.

Setting Objectives   When we determine the desired end results of an organization, we are setting its objectives. There may be a hierarchy of objectives in which a lower objective must be met in order to achieve a higher one. For example, to achieve a selling objective, a salesperson may have objectives for the number of calls per day, the number of presentations made, and the number of new accounts established. Corporate objectives must be translated into sales force objectives and individual objectives.

The five characteristics of an objective can be remembered easily by the letters SMART—*S*pecific, *M*easurable, *A*greed, *R*ealistic, and *T*ime-related. *Specific* objectives must be expressed in terms of quantity. "Increase sales 10%" is specific. Objectives must be *measurable.* For example, sales dollars and number of cases are measurable. "Make the company a leader in its field" is not measurable and therefore is not a good objective. An objective must be *agreed upon.* If a person does not help to set the objective there is no ownership, so there is less motivation to perform. Objectives that are not *realistic* can be demotivating if they are out of reach. Objectives must be specified in *time.* For instance, "increase sales 10% next year" specifies a precise time period for achievement.

Developing Strategies   In its most basic form, strategy development is deciding what to do, how, and when. *Stratagem,* from ancient Greek, means a trick for deceiving an enemy. Hence strategies are what generals and admirals formulate. In an organizational context, *strategy* takes on a less belligerent meaning. It is simply *the means by which an organization will achieve its objectives, given a set of environmental constraints and organizational policies.* Salespeople and sales managers develop strategies for tapping opportunities and meeting competition. For example, a selling strategy for a pharmaceutical product would be to position it as the best therapy for an illness. The strategy would be implemented by communicating to physicians the basic research that demonstrates the superiority of the product.

Developing Policies   Policies are standing decisions regarding recurring strategic matters. Policies place limits on the kinds of strategies that are acceptable for achieving objectives. For example, a pharmaceutical firm could have a policy of making only products that promote health in humans. This policy would provide an automatic rejection of product ideas for veterinary products. An understanding of a policy keeps the planner from developing a plan that would not be acceptable to top management. A policy is an automatic decision maker. It provides uniformity, fairness, control, efficiency, and simplified communication.

Policies that affect salespeople include corporate policies regarding ethics, returned goods, dress codes, pricing, and trade-ins. The field sales manager will follow corporate policies regarding recruiting, selecting, evaluating, promoting, and separating salespeople. These policies must comply with federal policies regarding equal employment opportunities.

Developing Programs   Programs break objectives and strategies into manageable action steps that can be identified, delegated, and implemented, and the results measured. These action steps are also known as *tactics,* another term of Greek warfare meaning the science or art of maneuvering troops or ships in the presence of the enemy. A *schedule* is that part of a program that places a priority on the completion of action steps and specifies the time sequence in which these steps will be performed. Sales managers create selling programs that schedule salespeoples' activities to achieve sales objectives.

Setting Procedures   Procedures are standardized programs of action regarding recurring tactical matters. Procedures are often the most efficient way for performing a task. They also provide uniformity for completing the task. The recording of an order may require conforming with standard procedures. Selling procedures will include detailed descriptions for completing order forms, handling expenses or accident reports, and so on.

Budgeting   Budgeting is the allocation of resources to programs. Resources include people, working capital, and information. Information about the market and competitors is becoming an increasingly important and costly resource in sales management. Salespeople and sales managers must budget their time, expenses, and promotional materials.

Organizing Activities

Organizing activities (Exhibit 7.1, Column 2) arrange work for the effective accomplishment of the objectives that were specified during the planning phase.

Creating Position Descriptions   The position or job description defines the scope, relationships, responsibilities, and authority assigned to a specific position within an organization. In sales management, the salesperson's job description is the basic document for recruiting, selecting, training, evaluating, and rewarding the salesperson. Examples of job descriptions for salespeople, district sales managers, and general sales managers will appear in later chapters.

Establishing Position Qualifications   The position qualifications are the criteria by which people will be selected and evaluated if hired. Defining the qualifications for people in each position therefore becomes an important part of organizing. Qualifications should be defined in terms of candidates' behavioral traits, such as motivation, work habits, job interest, initiative, integrity, and communication skills. If the candidates have good behavioral traits, they can be trained in specifics such as product knowledge, attitudes toward selling, selling skills, and habits in managing their territories.

Establishing Organizational Structure   When roles have been identified and similar ones grouped together into departments, liaison lines must be established to facilitate communication and coordinate activities. It is now possible to draw an organizational chart. This chart should reflect the strategy of the organization. Unfortunately, strategies change faster than organizations can change. Many times organizational designs remain the same because of vested interests in old organizational structures. Strategies may fail because the old organizational structure may be incapable of implementing a new strategy.

The lines on an organizational chart reflect more than communication links; they convey the kind and magnitude of authority appropriate for each role. In addition to internal communication, these links contact the boundaries of the organization to identify opportunities and threats facing the organization. Communication links may become overloaded, thereby confusing role relationships and reducing the effectiveness of an organization.

Sales force organizational designs may specialize the sales force by product, customer type, product application, account management, or geography. They must specify how many field managers to use at each level of management. Exhibit 7.2 illustrates various sales force organizations. (Jim Hightower seems to have outgrown his present organizational design. If you were advising him, which organizing activity should he do first, second, and so on? Why?)

Staffing Activities

After the position descriptions and qualifications are established during the organizing phase, the next function requires staffing activities (Exhibit 7.1, column 3).

Recruiting/Selecting   The initial stage of staffing includes the recruiting, screening, and final selection of qualifiable people for each position in the organization. All of these steps consist of identifying those people who have a high potential for performing the roles required by the job description.

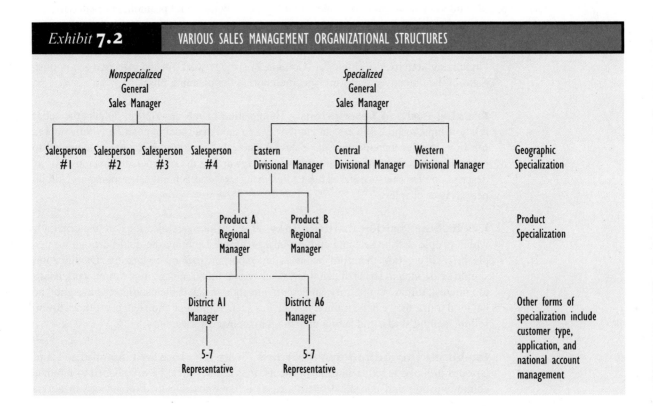

Exhibit 7.2   VARIOUS SALES MANAGEMENT ORGANIZATIONAL STRUCTURES

Some companies have current salespeople participate in the process of recruiting and selecting by asking them to recommend prospects from social contacts, customers, and competitors, and by recruiting at schools and universities in their territories. The screening function may be performed in part by the salesperson, if the company requires prospects to ride with a salesperson for a day. The salesperson then files a report on the potential of the prospect, which becomes part of the final screening process.

The role of the field sales manager in recruiting is the identification of sources for recruiting, screening applicants, complying with company recruiting procedures, contacting references, conducting a hiring interview, and recommending candidates to the regional manager.

The general sales manager monitors the field managers' recruiting and selecting activities to be certain that they comply with company and federal policies. The general sales manager must also select the field managers.

Selection includes not only bringing individuals into the organization, but also selecting those out of the organization who did not perform as required. Terms such as *separation, termination,* and *dehiring* are used to describe this process. Federal regulations regarding equal opportunities during hiring apply also to equal opportunities at the time of separation. Reasons for termination must be carefully documented to give a salesperson opportunities to correct deficiencies and to make certain that the company is not discriminating in its hiring, training, and promotional activities. It is unfortunate that it has taken a federal regulation to bring about the good management procedure of giving careful consideration to why people fail to perform well in a given job.

Orientation/Training   Familiarizing the new salesperson with the company, the environment, and the territory becomes the responsibility of the field sales manager. A good orientation prevents later misunderstandings, unhappiness on the job, and demotivation.

Training makes a qualified candidate proficient through instruction and practice. We will see later that there is great variance among training programs for salespeople because of differences in the characteristics of the products they sell and the selling tasks that are assigned to them.

Developing Individuals   Salespeople and managers are expected to improve their knowledge, skills, and attitudes by using self-development techniques and company programs to ultimately qualify for positions of greater responsibility.

Development for the salesperson requires gaining knowledge about company products, processes, procedures, programs, and people as well as about customers and competitors. The skills of analysis, decision making, and communication must be developed. Field sales managers provide training programs and informal on-the-job training that help salespeople gain this knowledge.

Field managers also engage in their own personal development to make themselves promotable. Part of the latter activity is developing a replacement for himself or herself. The general sales manager provides field managers with opportunities for training and development, establishes career counseling, and monitors compliance with policies for development. Because selling and sales management require a high level of energy, some companies encourage health development and physical fitness programs.

A critical management activity is the counseling and coaching of subordinates so that they improve their knowledge, skills, and attitudes.

Developing Teams   Team-building skills are emerging as another important staffing activity for managers. Teams seem to improve results in organizations when multiple skills, backgrounds, and viewpoints are required.[8] Managing teams requires learning to develop group skills, accountability, and commitment.[9] Managers of teams must learn how to assemble the correct mix of technical skills—and personalities—to get the job done, as well as to train the teams in effective group problem-solving techniques. Managers of teams must also learn how to hold teams accountable and how to engender individual commitment to the team effort.

Directing Activities

The next function in the management process is the directing (Exhibit 7.1, column 4) of the staff toward the objectives that were selected during the planning phase.

Delegating   Delegating consists of assigning responsibility and authority to a subordinate and holding him or her accountable for the results.

The salesperson is largely on the receiving end of delegation. The field sales manager may delegate to the salesperson certain activities for the short term, such as training new salespeople. The field sales manager has line responsibility delegated to him or her for the field sales staff. The general sales manager may be responsible for warehousing, service personnel, brokers, manufacturers' salespeople, the selection of distributors, and the training of distributors' salespeople.

Motivating   Motivating salespeople is the most important activity of the sales manager. It involves creating conditions on the job that persuade and inspire people to take the action necessary to achieve the objectives of the organization. The motivating process will include removing factors that are demotivating and creating environments to help the individual motivate himself or herself.

Coordinating   Coordination of efforts is required so that all individuals are working toward a common goal. The selling plan coordinates the advertising and personal selling efforts within the marketing mix. It also coordinates sales management activities such as staffing and training.

Managing Change/Managing Conflict   Change and conflict are inevitable in any dynamic, innovative organization. Some companies build conflict into the planning process to assure that planners will be challenged to develop the best plan possible. An organization that encourages creative and independent thinking must expect conflict and must learn how to channel this conflict for the good of the organization. Organizational theorists who previously thought in terms of resolving conflict now think in terms of managing it. Thus an organization that does not have some conflict may be an organization that lacks innovation and dynamic growth. The Japanese culture emphasizes cooperation among people at the same level of an organization. Perhaps this cultural difference helps to explain why Japanese companies often find it difficult to be creative.

Controlling Activities

The final step in the management process is control (Exhibit 7.1, column 5). Controlling activities ensure that the direction of the staff moves the organization toward the objectives of the plan.

Establishing Reporting Systems   Reporting systems ensure that the organization is moving toward its objectives. To establish these systems, it is necessary to determine what critical data are needed, and how and when they will be reported. We saw in Chapter 6 that the microcomputer is playing a major role in reporting systems.

Developing Performance Standards Performance standards specify how well activities in the job description must be performed. For example, a salesperson who does not make 10 calls per day may not be performing adequately, if such is the standard of the company. All levels of sales management will have similar standards. For example, the field sales manager may be required to recruit and train salespeople so that no territory is without a salesperson for more than 5% of the year.

Measuring Performance The control system must include procedures for measuring results, such as dollar sales or market share, to see if the salesperson is meeting his or her goals. Control is automatic when the salesperson is supplied with these data. Sales quotas and sales results enable the salesperson to evaluate his or her performance without waiting for evaluations from a manager.

Taking Corrective Action When results deviate from performance standards, it is necessary to counsel personnel to help them attain standards. Replanning and repeating the management process is necessary when the original plan is not realistic, or when unexpected environmental changes occur. Sales management corrective action includes retraining, reassignment, demotion, and termination.

Rewarding Rewards for superior performance include the obvious financial awards, but also include social-psychological rewards, such as praise from a manager, recognition in a newsletter or at a sales meeting, or winning a contest. This activity must also include negative action such as probation, demotion, or firing. (If you were a consultant to Jim Hightower in the opening case, what would you say at this point?)

· ·

COMPARING FUNCTIONS AND ACTIVITIES AT SEVERAL LEVELS OF SALES MANAGEMENT

The organization of a sales force can include several levels: a district manager, a regional manager, and a general manager. To determine how management functions and activities are assigned to the different levels of sales management, the authors conducted a survey of 700 sales managers, at three levels, in 25 companies representing five different industries. The results of this survey are summarized in Exhibits 7.3 and 7.4. These findings clearly support the statement that young field managers perform all of the management functions of a top manager.

Exhibit 7.3 compares the management functions and activities at different levels of sales management. The findings for functions are consistent with expectations. As managers move to higher levels, they regard the functions of planning and organizing as more important and staffing as less important. Directing and controlling are of equal importance across all levels. This similarity suggests that a young sales manager gains good experience in the entire management process for use later, when he or she is promoted.

The seven planning activities illustrate how planning becomes more important as one moves up the administrative ladder. In each activity, the second-line manager weighted

Exhibit 7.3	THE PERCENT IMPORTANCE OF MANAGEMENT FUNCTIONS AND ACTIVITIES TO OWN JOB AS PERCEIVED BY FIRST-LINE, SECOND-LINE, AND GENERAL SALES/MARKETING MANAGERS (RESPONDENTS ALLOCATED 100 POINTS AMONG 22 ACTIVITIES)

| | Importance to Own Job | | | |
Functions/Activities	First-Line Managers %	Second-Line Managers %	General Sales/Marketing Managers %	Probability of Nonsignificant Differences across Management Levels
PLAN	17.6	24.7	36.5	
Forecast	2.2	3.5	7.1	.01*
Self Objectives	3.8	5.0	5.9	.01
Develop Strategies	3.4	5.1	5.6	.01
Develop Policies	1.6	2.7	4.0	.01
Develop Programs	3.5	4.6	6.5	.01
Set Procedures	1.8	2.1	4.2	.01
Budget	1.3	1.8	3.1	.01
ORGANIZE	4.2	5.2	7.9	
Establish Organizational Structure	1.9	2.3	3.5	.01
Create Position Descriptions	1.1	1.3	2.3	.01
Establish Position Qualifications	1.2	1.5	2.1	.01
STAFF	34.7	22.7	10.1	
Recruit/Select	8.7	6.0	1.9	.01
Orient/Train	9.2	5.4	3.6	.01
Develop Personnel	16.8	11.3	4.7	.01
DIRECT	21.1	23.0	21.4	
Delegate	4.3	5.9	5.3	.01
Motivate	9.6	8.5	7.9	.17
Coordinate	3.3	4.0	4.1	.07
Manage Change	3.8	4.7	4.0	.09
CONTROL	22.4	24.4	24.1	
Establish Report Systems	2.5	3.3	4.5	.01
Develop Standards	3.3	4.0	4.3	.02
Measure Performance	5.8	6.0	7.0	.32
Take Corrective Action	5.5	6.0	4.5	.16
Reward	5.4	5.2	3.8	.05
Totals (subject to rounding error)	100.0%	100.0%	100.0%	
Total No. of Managers	600	86	24	

*To be read as follows: There is 1 chance in 100 that the difference in the perception of the importance of forecasting across these management levels is the result of chance. Respondents were asked to allocate 100 points to reflect the importance of each activity in their job.

these activities as more important than did the first-line manager. Similarly, in each case, top management considered them more important than did second-line managers. This pattern held true also for each of the organizing activities.

Staffing is clearly the responsibility of first-line management. Thus a young sales manager who may be out of college only three years will be responsible for recruiting, selecting, orienting, training, and developing personnel. Such can be the challenge of sales management.

COMPARING FIRST-LINE FUNCTIONS AND ACTIVITIES ACROSS INDUSTRIES

Exhibit 7.4 compares the perceived importance of functions and activities across five industries. Each industry is compared with the perceptions of all respondents who are not in that industry.

The activities in the planning function indicate that first-line managers in the petroleum/rubber and office supplies/equipment industries regard planning activities as more important than average, and the first-line managers in pharmaceutical companies regard them as less important. These findings may be explained by the role of the salesperson in these industries. The pharmaceutical salesperson performs a communication-persuasion role, whereas salespeople in the other two industries perform a more consultative role.

Staffing functions tend to be more important in the pharmaceutical and office supplies/equipment companies and less important in the petroleum/rubber companies. Such dissimilarities may be explained by differences in turnover rates and growth rates among industries. These differences in importance of management activities among industries raise doubts about the wisdom of hiring sales managers from other industries. Furthermore, an additional analysis of the 16 pharmaceutical companies revealed significant differences within one industry, thereby raising doubts about hiring managers from other companies within the industry. The pirated manager may not perceive the subtle differences in the importance of activities in the strategies of the new company, which could create organizational conflicts.

SALES MANAGEMENT APPLICATION OF THESE FINDINGS

Job Clarification

The data in the survey were collected to help sales managers and trainers. All cooperating companies were supplied with their averages, the 95% confidence intervals for their company and industry, and instructions for applying the results to their organization. Some companies made the results part of the training sessions for managers. Managers were asked to complete questionnaires that required them to record their perception of the importance of the various activities by allocating 100 points among them. The survey results were then presented and differences were discussed. This use of survey data in training sessions can clarify errors in job perceptions that occur among persons at different levels of management.

A Sales Management Audit

These management functions and activities may be used to evaluate individual managers, levels of management, or the corporate management process. Exhibit 7.5, an audit form, illustrates how this may be accomplished.

The pattern in Exhibit 7.5 suggests several management problems. The manager in this case seems to be dealing with short-term problems such as developing programs, procedures, and budgets, but does not take care of the longer-range activities such as forecasting, setting objectives, and developing strategies and policies. Further probing will reveal possible causes of the problem: this manager does not think that these steps are important, does not have the time to do them, or does not know how to do them.

Exhibit **7.4**	THE PERCENT IMPORTANCE OF MANAGEMENT FUNCTIONS AND ACTIVITIES AS PERCEIVED BY FIRST-LINE FIELD SALES MANAGERS IN FIVE INDUSTRIES (RESPONDENTS ALLOCATED 100 POINTS AMONG 22 ACTIVITIES)

	Industries					
Functions/Activities	**All First-Line Managers** %	**Pharma-ceutical** %	**Other Medical** %	**Office Supplies/ Equipment** %	**Petroleum/ Rubber** %	**Clothing Manufr.** %
PLAN	17.6	15.2	23.8	23.6	26.5	21.2
Forecast	2.2	1.7**	3.8	3.2**	4.7*	2.8**
Set Objectives	3.8	3.4**	4.2	5.2**	4.3	4.4**
Develop Strategies	3.4	3.1**	4.4	4.3*	4.1	4.0**
Develop Policies	1.6	1.3**	2.1	2.3	2.5	2.9**
Develop Programs	3.5	3.2**	3.9	4.5**	5.2	3.6**
Set Procedures	1.8	1.6**	2.5	2.4*	2.6	2.2**
Budget	1.3	1.0**	2.9**	1.8**	3.1**	1.3**
ORGANIZE	4.2	3.2	8.8	5.9	7.6	6.1
Establish Organizational Structure	1.9	1.5**	4.3**	2.5	3.6	2.4**
Create Position Descriptions	1.1	0.8**	2.3	1.7*	2.0	1.8**
Establish Position Qualifications	1.2	0.9**	2.2	1.6	2.0	1.9**
STAFF	34.7	37.2	23.4	32.8	17.6	27.2
Recruit/Select	8.7	8.9	5.7	10.2*	3.0	7.8
Orient/Train	9.2	9.4	5.8	10.7**	6.6	7.6
Develop Personnel	16.8	19.0**	11.9	12.0*	8.0	11.9**
DIRECT	21.0	21.3	21.9	18.8	23.4	22.3
Delegate	4.3	4.1*	5.2	3.7**	6.8	5.7*
Motivate	9.6	10.2**	8.7	8.2	7.4	8.6**
Coordinate	3.3	3.2*	3.6	3.4	4.2	4.4*
Manage Change	3.8	3.8	4.4	3.6	5.0	3.7
CONTROL	22.4	23.0	22.2	19.0	24.9	23.2
Establish Report Systems	2.5	2.2**	4.0	2.7	3.9	3.5**
Develop Standards	3.3	3.2	4.0	2.6**	5.4	4.1
Measure Performance	5.8	6.3**	4.6	4.1**	5.5	5.3**
Take Corrective Action	5.5	5.7*	5.0	4.9	5.3	5.2*
Reward	5.4	5.7	5.0	4.8	4.8	5.2*
Totals (subject to rounding error)	100.0%	100.0%	100.0%	100.0%	100.0%	100.0%
Total No. of Companies	25	16	3	3	2	1
Total No. of First-Line Managers	600	428	31	93	21	27

* 5 0.05; ** 5 0.01: Probability of the industry average activity percent differing from the percent of all other first-line managers. Respondents were asked to allocate 100 points to reflect the importance of each activity in their job.

Some of the reasons for preoccupation with short-term planning are found in the other functions. The position descriptions are poorly done and there are no position qualifications. These deficiencies may increase the time required to recruit, select, orient, and train new salespeople and evaluate existing ones, leaving little time for long-range planning. This hypothesis could be tested by having the manager indicate the percent of time spent

Exhibit 7.5	AN AUDIT OF A SALES MANAGER'S PERFORMANCE

Evaluation

Functions/Activities	Not Done	Poorly Done			Outstanding			Weight	Evaluation × Weight (3)
PLAN					(1)			(2)	(1) × (2)
Forecast	⓪	1	2	3	4	5	6	2.2	0.0
Set Objectives	0	①	2	3	4	5	6	3.8	3.8
Develop Strategies	0	1	2	③	4	5	6	3.4	10.2
Develop Policies	0	1	②	3	4	5	6	1.6	3.2
Develop Programs	0	1	2	3	④	5	6	3.5	14.0
Set Procedures	0	1	2	3	④	5	6	1.8	7.2
Budget	0	1	2	3	④	5	6	1.3	5.2
ORGANIZE									
Establish Organizational Structure	0	1	2	③	4	5	6	1.9	5.7
Create Position Descriptions	0	①	2	3	4	5	6	1.1	1.1
Establish Position Qualifications	⓪	1	2	3	4	5	6	1.2	0.0
STAFF									
Recruit/Select	0	1	2	3	4	⑤	6	8.7	43.5
Orient/Train	0	1	2	③	4	5	6	9.2	27.6
Develop Personnel	0	1	②	3	4	5	6	16.8	33.6
DIRECT									
Delegate	0	1	②	3	4	5	6	4.3	8.6
Motivate	0	①	2	3	4	5	6	9.6	9.6
Coordinate	0	1	②	3	4	5	6	3.3	6.6
Manage Change	⓪	1	2	3	4	5	6	3.8	0.0
CONTROL									
Establish Report Systems	0	①	2	3	4	5	6	2.5	2.5
Develop Standards	0	①	2	3	4	5	6	3.3	3.3
Measure Performance	0	1	2	③	4	5	6	5.8	17.4
Take Corrective Action	0	1	2	③	4	5	6	5.5	16.5
Reward	0	1	2	③	4	5	6	5.4	16.2
Totals								100.0	235.8

The weighted total in this case of 235.8 may be compared with an average of 350 or with the scores of other managers, and it may be used as a benchmark from which to set goals for improvement in the management of the sales force.

on each activity and then compare these percentages with the percentages of more successful managers.

The directing and controlling activities show similar weaknesses. Additional probing will be necessary to identify alternative means for correcting the situation. At one extreme, it may be necessary to redesign the entire sales management organization. At the other extreme, some management training may be all that is necessary. Between these two extremes are the alternatives of firing or demoting the manager.

By adding a column of importance weights (column 2, Exhibit 7.5) and multiplying the evaluation scores by these weights, we reflect both the importance and performance of each management activity (column 3). The sum of these weighted evaluations may be compared with those of other managers and may serve as a benchmark for establishing goals to improve a manager's performance.

....

TRANSITION TO A NEW ORGANIZATIONAL DESIGN

Grocery, Inc. provides an example of a company that is moving away from the district management design to a team design. Its job description for the Customer Team Leader Position is Exhibit 7.6.

Compare this job description with the theoretical model of the management process in Exhibit 7.1. Are any points missing in the Grocery, Inc. description for the Team Leader?

Exhibit **7.6**	GROCERY, INC. CUSTOMER TEAM LEADER POSITION DESCRIPTION

Name _____   Title _____

Team _____   Reports to _____

Key Results Areas:

The Team Leader is responsible for creating a supportive team environment that encourages the achievement of Individual Action Plans and Team Goals. These include achievement of financial Contribution Objectives and managing to an established Team Budget.

PRINCIPAL DUTIES AND RESPONSIBILITIES

INTERNAL:

Responsible for recruiting, training, and developing a multi-functional team, including office personnel, where applicable

- Responsible for recruitment of candidates from internal and external sources.
- Establish training schedule with team Development Manager for new hire and provide training opportunities for team and individual growth.
- Coach and counsel all team members.
- Evaluate performance of all team members via a formalized review process.
- Responsible for the development and achievement of personal action plans for all team members.
- Develop a succession plan for all team positions.

Create and manage Team Financial Budget

- Manage team budget—not to exceed the bottom line.
- Accountable for approving team expense reports.

Manage and lead Category Management/Strategic Planning in a proactive business environment

- Develop strategies to achieve financial contribution and volume goals through customer action plans.
- Forecast financial contribution and volume to meet team objectives.
- Identify and make use of outside resources to achieve team objectives, utilizing core team and headquarters staff.

Maintain timely and effective administrative procedures

- Submit quarterly pricing reports to Regional Managing Director.
- Maintain monthly store audits by all team members—consistent with regional procedures.
- Write consistent work-with letters identifying accomplishments and areas of opportunity.
- Ensure accurate and regular updating of all Retail Informational Databases.

| Exhibit **7.6** | GROCERY, INC. CUSTOMER TEAM LEADER POSITION DESCRIPTION—CONTINUED |

Provide a positive environment that encourages Teamwork

- Provide short- and long-term vision to promote a positive team environment.
- Facilitate regular team meetings.
- Develop and maintain a "back-up system" through cross-training of all team members.
- Identify and pursue outside learning opportunities and training.

Encourage open communication by all team members throughout the company

- Identify and communicate competitive activity to all team members.
- Utilize all internal communication systems in a timely and effective manner.
- Incorporate Retail Operations in a day-to-day management of retail priorities.

Assist in determining the strategic direction of the regional team

- Take an active role in Regional Board meetings to help facilitate decisions.
- Provide input to Regional Board regarding regional operations.
- Identify opportunities for process improvements within the team and region.

EXTERNAL:

Provide support to enhance customer development

- Facilitate "Top-to-Top" discussion with customers.
- Pursue a pro-active role in Apollo/Spaceman program to achieve shelf management objectives.
- Provide input for implementation of region consumer fund.
- Monitor the system to manage the customer fund to achieve financial contribution objectives.
- Manage the team leader personal account.

Provide accurate and timely information to our associate company to enable execution of account priorities

- Ensure team members' attendance of monthly meetings.
- Assist in the establishment of Gold and Acceptable standards.

Lead category plan development and implementation

- Facilitate account meetings to help define and gather information required for Category Management Planning.
- Utilize all resources in development of Category Management Plan.

Personal Development:

Commit to continuous self-development

- Stay abreast of industry trends through customer visits, industry meetings, literature, etc.
- Continuous pursuit of internal training.
- Continued external education, including workshops, seminars, etc.

Working Relationships

Report to:	Regional Managing Director
Work with:	Team Accounts
	Account Executives
	Logistics Manager
	Business Development Manager
	Retail Operations Manager
	Associate Company Personnel
	Headquarters Personnel
	Region Core Team Members

....

MINICASES

Training Managers

Fast-growing companies often fail to provide adequate training for their first-line field sales managers. A survey of companies that sell computer software found that the median budget for training a manager was $8,000 whereas the budget for training a new salesperson was $20,000. Fifty percent of respondents reported receiving no management training in the last year. They rated the quality of the training a 5 or 6 on a 9-point scale.[10]

Triad Systems is an exception in the software industry. It offers nine workshops, which in order of priority, are as follows:

1. Interviewing and hiring
2. Problem solving—approaches and skill development
3. Applying the management process:
   • Establishing a performance improvement program
   • Career counseling
   • Giving performance evaluations
4. Time management and delegation
5. Leadership and personal style
6. Team building
7. Coaching
8. Communicating up and down the organization
9. Negotiating for a win/win solution[11]

Given your knowledge of the management process, what would you add to this list?

Sales Systems Integration at Diagraph Corporation

James Brigham faced a problem.[12] As owner of Diagraph, a St. Louis manufacturer of industrial labeling, coding, and marking equipment, he had watched profits decline for four years, despite increasing sales. The sales process that the company had used for years, based on cold calls, trade shows, and passive referrals, wasn't working any more. The label-printing division, Diagraph's fastest-growing unit, had the lowest margins. And the marking-equipment division, its cash cow, was beginning to run dry.

Investigation of the problems showed inefficiencies in the sales process. Marking-equipment salespeople would go out on calls—which experts estimate to cost an average of $250 each—and return with only a $200 order for heavy-duty pens, inks for stencil machines, and similar supplies.

Brigham solved his problem by redesigning the sales process. He added a telemarketing program and created a catalog, which he mailed to all customers and prospects. Customers could now place routine orders themselves by calling a toll-free number, which cut Brigham's cost-per-order from $250 to $10.

To remotivate the salespeople, Brigham restructured his commission program to focus on generating new business. He cut the commission on his traditional marking-equipment line from 10% to 3.5%, but boosted the commission on newer company lines up to 10%.

Diagraph also uses the telemarketing subsystem for lead qualification. When prospects respond to company ads, telemarketers call for more information, including buying intentions and qualifications. Prioritized leads are then routed to the salespeople.

The resulting sales system redesign has brought sales up and the cost of selling down.

Sales Process Redesign at Comcast Cable

As senior vice president of advertising sales at Comcast Cable, Filemon Lopez saw that he needed control.[13] The sales process was not consistent. Salespeople were developing leads and closing sales in a hodgepodge of different ways.

Lopez's first step was to survey his 330 salespeople. He asked them in what areas they needed help, how they used their time, whether they received enough of the right kinds of training, and more. His most troubling finding: salespeople were passively waiting for customers to come to them.

Based on the input from his salespeople, Lopez established territories so salespeople did not run into one another's accounts. A systematic lead-generation program was also developed, with telemarketing support, to identify and qualify prospects within the territories.

In order to assure that leads were pursued systematically—and using appropriate sales techniques—an ongoing training program was instituted. New salespeople went through a two-week course on a consultative approach to value-focused selling. Once a month, veteran salespeople attended training classes on special topics like needs-analysis and closing.

Training was followed up with a skills assessment review. Managers observed salespeople in the field to verify that they were conforming to the company's sales techniques, including finding out about customers' needs and problems.

The result: a substantial increase in Comcast sales.

Case 7.1 — I-30 TRUCK CENTER

Sharon O'Kelly, six months a district sales manager for Marshall Motors, a medium- and heavy-duty truck manufacturer, couldn't help laughing to herself as she drove to her call on the I-30 Truck Center, Marshall's Jamestown truck dealer. The characters who ran the dealership had always been a source of jokes among the Marshall personnel assigned to District 110. Unfortunately, the problems with this large dealer were no laughing matter. I-30 suffered from inadequate inventory and orders in process, no working prospect system, and failing market penetration percentages, which were not only serious problems, but continuous.

Sharon's stated job accountabilities were to meet a sales quota of 1700 units, to maintain adequate dealer inventory and a three-times inventory turnover, to train dealer salespersons, to call on large customers of dealers, to promote company programs, and to enforce company sales policies. Since starting with Marshall Motors as a sales trainee, Sharon had sold trucks at a company-owned dealership for a year and had worked for the regional marketing staff for six months. As a district sales manager, she managed a sales force of 18 dealers in a territory 300 miles wide and almost that long. Although she had the authority to terminate dealers and to recommend new ones, this was an alternative used very infrequently. Her overriding objective was to increase sales of Marshall Trucks through the franchised dealers.

After a brief time in the district, Sharon realized that very little of her time and effort were spent selling trucks. Instead, she found she was most effective in improving the dealers' inventory and order systems, setting up prospect listings, sales planning, sales department organization, and overall sales efficiency. Currently, industry sales were booming, and lead time at the factory was eight to ten months for most of the truck models. The district sales managers were being pressed by the company's regional management to get their dealers to reserve production time at the factory by submitting orders to meet their sales for the next 12 months. In response, Sharon developed sales projections and a simple order planning, tracking, and control system that several of her dealers had successfully adopted. Problems had arisen in implementing the plan at the I-30 Truck Center.

I-30 was founded by three brothers who had moved from the mountains in the western part of the state in the 1950s to start a dairy farm in the eastern Piedmont. Their success in farming led them to start an agricultural implements business, which, in turn, led them into truck sales, parts and service, and a contract with Marshall Motors in the early 1960s. The truck operation expanded into a small trucking company and a truck leasing business. As the area grew, the farm land they owned became increasingly valuable, so the brothers opened a real estate company and began some speculative building.

continued

These many overlapping businesses were master-minded by the older brother, H.V. By default, he was overseer of the financial affairs and general manager of every business except the dairy business. William, the second brother, ran the dairy farm, but occasionally stepped in to help with any other businesses where he thought he was needed. In theory, Max, the youngest, ran the truck dealership. A friendly, gregarious, likeable fellow, Max loved to sell.

Sharon's boss had described Max as "a good ol' boy who just wants to be left alone to sell trucks." Max spent most of his time on the dealership floor or on the telephone with customers. He sold trucks to people all over the eastern United States. The salaried salesmen he hired acted mainly as Max's assistants, completing paperwork, delivering trucks, and covering the floor when Max was out.

On one of her early sales calls at the I-30 Truck Center, Sharon reviewed her customer inventory and order printout and realized that I-30 did not have enough units on hand or on order to begin to meet forecasted sales. After lengthy discussions with Max, in which he raised all the typical dealer objections—high cost of inventory, risk of ordering so far in advance, and the difficulty of stocking units to meet customer specifications—he agreed to order eight units with staggered production dates and to implement the order control system. The next month, under pressure from the regional sales manager, Sharon called the factory to see if the orders had been received. None had been submitted.

With fire in her eyes, Sharon made a special call on the I-30 Truck Center. When she asked Max why he hadn't ordered the units after agreeing to do so, he responded, "Oh, H.V. wouldn't let me order them because he said we didn't need them and the dealership couldn't stand the inventory interest expense." H.V. was out, but Sharon waited for his return. She met with him in his office, explained her sales and order system, and asked why the orders had not been submitted after Max had agreed to do so. H.V. answered, "Max doesn't think we can sell those trucks, and, anyway, William went to a used truck broker in Columbus last week and loaded us up with enough used trucks to last at least a couple of months. Right now we have $750,000 in used units, $200,000 in new units, and our credit line is for $1,000,000. It will take six months, if we're lucky, to get out from under all this used

junk. If we find a customer for a new piece we don't have in stock, we'll just have to buy it from another dealer since your lead times are so ridiculously long."

"H.V., Max gave me a different story," Sharon responded. "I need to know who makes the ordering and inventory decisions here. Let's get Max in here and decide what to order *today!*" Max came in, and a little later William wandered through on his way to the feed store. The discussion got heated, with each brother accusing the other of meddling in his business and making poor inventory decisions. Max walked out, using the excuse that he had a customer to meet. William left to take care of some purchases. H.V. closed his office door and said, "Sharon, the dealership is supposed to be Max's, but he won't take the responsibility for running it; he doesn't even manage the sales department. We hired a general manager one time, but he quit because Max owns the business and is too pigheaded to take orders from anybody else. What do you think we should do?"

CASE QUESTIONS

1. How many business operations are the three brothers involved in?
2. What are the management problems at the I-30 Truck Center?
3. What are the specific sales management problems that Sharon O'Kelly and I-30 have?
4. In addition to the lack of leadership or sales organization, what other causes are responsible for their falling sales penetration?
5. Should Sharon seriously consider recommending that Marshall Motors terminate the dealership with I-30 Truck Center? Why?
6. How should Sharon answer H.V.?
7. How should Sharon answer H.V. if he presses her for some solution?
8. What recommendations should Sharon make to her regional sales manager?
9. What legal complications could arise from actions taken as a result of Question #8?
10. What are the five prerequisites for the survival of the I-30 Truck Center?
11. How would you rate the long-term chances of survival of the I-30 Truck Center?

SUMMARY

The goal of this chapter is to present a brief overview of the skills, functions, and activities of management, thereby providing a framework for the remainder of the book. The findings of the survey reported in this chapter reveal that although all levels of sales management engage in all of the management activities, differences exist in how managers at different levels weight the importance of each activity. The higher levels of sales management engage more heavily in planning and organizing, whereas the lower levels are more involved with staffing. All levels of management engage equally in the functions of directing and control. The findings of this study reveal that even the most junior sales manager can begin to develop management skills.

These management functions and activities may appear to be simply an academic exercise, but they can be used to clarify the roles of managers and to audit sales managers at different levels. Such audits require measures of perceived importance, time spent, and evaluations of how well the activities are performed.

ASSIGNMENTS/DISCUSSION QUESTIONS

1. Discuss which of the management skills and activities a salesperson will have an opportunity to practice.

2. Evaluate the completeness of the following objectives:
    a. Increase sales.
    b. Double the sales of the three major products within the next 6 months.
    c. Increase the number of calls on new accounts in each territory by 25% without reducing the number of calls on active accounts.
    d. Maintain the sales of product X in each territory at or near quota for this fiscal year after the introduction of product Y.

3. What is the relationship between job qualifications and a job description?

4. Why do you think the three levels of managers shown in the survey in Exhibit 7.3 agree that recruiting and selecting are clearly the responsibility of first-line management?

5. Why do you think the first-line managers in the survey in Exhibit 7.3 believe overwhelmingly that to "develop personnel" is their most important management activity?

6. If a survey of the first-line and second-line managers of a company were to show a statistically significant lower rating by the first-line managers of the relative importance of setting objectives, what could possibly explain this?

7. Develop a sales management audit for a local company. The class should form teams to reduce the workload.

8. Working in teams, brainstorm the items that should be included in a quality-control pre-call checklist for salespeople working in a pharmaceutical firm.

9. Identify specific instances you have seen of how technology has changed the sales process. In each instance, note the impact on the quality of the sales encounter.

10. Identify the types of barriers you believe a sales manager might encounter in trying to use total quality management tools with his sales force. Then note ways he or she might overcome those barriers.

ENDNOTES

1. See Henry Mintzberg, The Manager's Job: Folklore and Fact, *Harvard Business Review,* July–August, 1975, pp. 49–61.
2. R. Alec Mackenzie, The Management Process in 3-D, *Harvard Business Review,* November–December, 1969, pp. 80–87.

3. Mackensie 80; Louis A. Allen, *The Professional Manager's Guide,* ed 4, Palo Alto, CA: Louis A. Allen Associates, 1969; R.L. Ackoff, *A Concept of Corporate Planning,* New York: Wiley/Interscience, 1970; Harold Koontz and Cyril O'Donnell, *Management: A Systems and Contingency Analysis of Managerial Functions,* ed 6, New York: McGraw-Hill, 1976.

4. Koontz and O'Donnell, p. 196.

5. Ackoff, p. 6.

6. J. Edward Russo and Paul J.H. Shoemaker, *Decision Traps: Ten Barriers to Brilliant Decision-Making and How to Overcome Them,* New York: Simon & Schuster, 1989.

7. Kathleen Eisenhardt, Speed and Strategic Choice: How Managers Accelerate Decision Making, *California Management Review,* Spring, 1990, pp. 39–55.

8. Jon R. Katzenbach and Douglas K. Smith, *The Wisdom of Teams: Creating the High-Performance Organization,* Boston: Harvard Business School Press, 1993.

9. *Ibid,* p. 8.

10. Brian Pope, Sink or Swim: How companies train their sales managers, in *The Sales Manager's Survival Guide,* J. Brian Pope, editor, Atlanta, GA: Culpepper and Associates, 1991, pp. 6–7.

11. Jim Hess, How Triad Systems Corporation Develops Regional Sales Managers, In *The Sales Manager's Survival Guide,* J. Brian Pope, editor, Atlanta, GA: Culpepper and Associates, 1991, p. 12.

12. Adapted from Paul B. Brown, Opportunity Rings Once, *INC.,* November, 1990, p. 152.

13. Adapted from Andy Cohen, Starting Over: Redesigning the Process, *Sales & Marketing Management,* 147(9), September 1995, p. 40.

8

DEVELOPING SALES STRATEGY

....

LEARNING GOALS

1. To see how a first-line sales manager shares the same planning activities as a CEO
2. To understand how the firm's overall business strategy relates to field-level sales strategy
3. To learn how to apply planning and organizing activities at the field level
4. To experience the excitement and responsibility of a first-line manager

....

THE FIRST EXPOSURE TO MANAGEMENT

A first-line sales manager faces difficult problems in district planning, strategy development, and organizational design with little training or experience. The manager manages processes, not people.[1] And these processes can be complicated, as we saw in the Team Leader job description for Grocery, Inc., in Chapter 7. This chapter illustrates such problems. The cases provide opportunities for developing skills in problem identification and decision making, so that these new functions do not come as a shock.

A sales manager must develop skills in managing processes to meet company goals, salespeople's goals, and his or her own goals. For example, the field manager helps each salesperson develop territory plans and strategies to meet the salespeople's assigned goals, which, in turn, meet district and corporate goals. Territory resources, such as salespeople's time, expense accounts, samples, promotional materials, and, perhaps, district expenses, must be planned and allocated in the most advantageous 27manner possible. The young manager must also look upward to evaluate company sales strategies and make recommendations for change. The new field sales manager suddenly realizes that planning is now for a longer term than the planning practiced by a salesperson. To be an effective manager, he or she will need training to develop these skills.

This chapter will expand on the planning activities that are listed in Exhibit 7.1 in Chapter 7, so the first column in that exhibit should be reviewed before reading further.

THE FIELD SALES MANAGER'S ROLE IN PLANNING

Planning lacks the excitement and the immediate fulfillment of selling. Some new managers would rather spend time sharing their selling expertise by engaging in activities such as training, counseling, and coaching, which are closely related to selling. This early period may disillusion the new manager who thought a sales manager was simply a super salesperson. He or she will need training, coaching, and counseling to develop planning skills.

Which functions are the most important for the first-line sales manager? By reading across the rows of Exhibit 8.1, we see that planning becomes a more important function as one moves up the sales management hierarchy. General sales managers regard planning as more than twice as important for their jobs as do first-line managers (36.5 versus 17.6). Conversely, implementation functions decline as one moves from first-line to general management (from 78.2 to 55.6). Thus the first-line manager will be concerned primarily with implementing the plans of superiors, but she or he will have opportunities to practice planning and organizing skills in preparation for promotion.

INFORMATION GATHERING AND FORECASTING

In their role as executives responsible primarily for spanning the boundary between the company and its outside environment, sales managers continuously scan a wide variety of data. These data come in many forms, ranging from published documents to syndicated data on the sale of competing products to the latest rumors from the field. Obviously, such

Exhibit **8.1**	MANAGEMENT FUNCTIONS AT THREE LEVELS (IMPORTANCE WEIGHTS)		
	Sales Management Levels		
Functions	**First Line**	**Second Line**	**General**
Create Change:			
Plan	17.6	24.7	36.5
Organize	4.2	5.2	7.9
Total Plan and Organize	21.8	29.9	44.4
Implement:			
Staff	34.7	22.7	10.1
Direct	21.1	23.0	21.4
Control	22.4	24.4	24.1
Total Implementation	78.2	70.1	55.6
Total Importance	100.0	100.0	100.0

Adapted from Exhibit 7.3, Chapter 7.

data will vary in reliability. Yet the increasingly rapid pace of business activity often requires managers to make decisions with imperfect information.

An important responsibility of the sales manager is to develop an information system that allows him or her to detect changes in the environment that are important to the firm. The sales manager must then translate this information into intelligence and decisions that help the firm adapt to change. In this context, intelligence is analyzed information that has action implications for the firm.[2]

In order to successfully complete this role, the sales manager must continuously be responsive to "weak signals" in the operating environment that could have unexpectedly strong impacts on the firm. In addition, he or she must produce concrete information—including quantitative forecasts—which others in the firm can use to plan their own operations.

Advances in information technology have only amplified the difference between data and information. The sales manager is continuously confronted by an external environment rich with sources of data, as shown in Exhibit 8.2. An important part of the sales manager's job is to actively manage the flow of data into information useful to the firm.

Informal sources of information can be critical, because data usually follows a flow from "rumor" to "event" to "record".[3] For example, initial warning about a competitor's forthcoming new product introduction may come from salespersons' discussions with customers. Sensitizing salespeople to the need for this information, and training them to probe for it in routine sales encounters, is the responsibility of sales management.

The competitor's new product may not become a public event until it is actually offered on the market, perhaps accompanied by public announcements. It is not available in the documented record until it reaches the trade news and sales are recorded in syndicated databases. By then, the firm's strategic response options may be severely limited and the competitor's advantage firmly established.

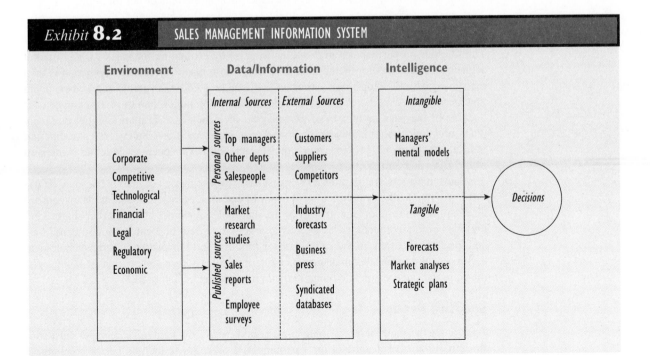

Exhibit 8.2   SALES MANAGEMENT INFORMATION SYSTEM

The sales manager has a responsibility for producing two types of intelligence from the data and information that pass through his or her position. One type of intelligence consists of the "mental model" of the firm's competitive position that he or she forms with other managers and with salespeople in the firm. This strategic perspective can be formalized through planning processes. For example, Royal Dutch Shell pioneered the use of scenario planning to allow its managers to develop shared perspectives on the firm and its options under different strategic situations.[4]

More concrete forms of intelligence are documented reports such as market analyses and forecasts. A market analysis is a report that examines the factors driving change within a product market. These factors include financial, managerial, process, technological, legal, political, and other issues. The market analysis is useful in emerging product markets, where long-term change must be interpreted based on an understanding of changes in underlying market structures. There is also evidence that a fresh market analysis may be useful in mature markets, where the complacency of established firms can create openings for new competitors.[5]

Because sales drives the planning for other areas of the firm, the sales manager is often instrumental in the preparation of forecasts. A forecast is an estimate of how future events will affect the selling environment and an estimate of the outcomes of alternative strategies in this environment. For example, a company making videocamcorders may want to estimate such future events as the state of the economy and technological developments. First, people are more likely to buy camcorders in a rising economy than in a declining one. Second, if they know that a new model camcorder will be produced shortly, they may decide to postpone their purchase.

Forecasting is not predicting and preparing for the future, but an attempt to understand and influence the future in favor of the forecaster. The forecasting responsibilities of the field sales manager tend to be for a one-year time horizon and include the following variables: market conditions, staffing needs, compensation and expense needs, and management activities. This time horizon is longer than that of the salesperson whose longest plan horizon is one month. Hence the new manager must stretch his or her thinking.

Market Conditions

The salesperson participates in the sales forecast by estimating the sales for key market segments or accounts for the coming year. This "bottom-up" forecasting approach is then reconciled with the "top-down" forecast that is generated by corporate economists using macroeconomic data. Forecasts by salespeople are often larger than those of management because of the basic optimism of salespeople, their lack of information about company plans, and their lack of knowledge of broad economic conditions. Sales force participation in forecasting not only provides marketplace data, but it also generates a greater ownership of the goals and quotas.

Sales managers are required to forecast sales by key market segments that may be defined geographically, by product, by industry of end user, or by key accounts. Managers are also required to estimate the growth of the market by customer class, market shares, and the sales of key competitors, as well as to assess the effect of local economic conditions and local competition on the sale of major products in their districts. The psychological tug-of-war the field sales manager encounters in sales forecasting is that of being optimistic to the salesperson and being realistic in what can be achieved.

Staffing Needs

To estimate the need for salespeople in the coming years, the field sales manager must consider the growth or decline in the customer base, changes in the number of competitive salespersons, the effect of the company selling plan, any redesign of the organization's selling processes, the time to train replacements to a productive level, and the capacity of the sales staff as it will be affected by loss of personnel because of resignations, terminations, promotions, transfers, rotations, and retirements. The manager must also consider the effect of new products, new competitors, new markets, and the company's Affirmative Action Program (AAP). This program sets requirements for applicant flow, hiring, and other fair employment practices that will determine the size and composition of the sales force relative to the agreed-upon AAP hiring goal.

Some companies hire only to fill existing vacancies; this may require several days or months in order to locate qualified applicants, interview them, check references, hire, and then train them. Other companies avoid this delay and the lost sales from an open territory by hiring a "floating" representative in anticipation of a vacancy occurring. The latter procedure increases the number of salespeople on the staff, thereby increasing the expenses for salaries and fringe benefits. Because the "floater's" ultimate assignment is unknown, there will be additional relocation costs when the final assignment is made. The manager must balance these costs against the losses from an open territory.

The strategic impact of the structure of sales staffing must also be considered. For example, the highly contested computer workstation market requires that salespeople be able to talk knowledgeably about specific applications. Given the size of the market, the use of a specialized direct sales force gave companies like Sun Microsystems, Digital Equipment, and Hewlett-Packard a competitive advantage. Other computer companies, working with a sales force of dealers and resellers, had less direct control of sales.[6]

Compensation and Expense Needs

Once the decision has been made to increase the sales force, it is necessary to forecast compensation and selling expenses. In forecasting the budget for compensation, the sales manager must anticipate applicant qualifications, changes in job descriptions because of new products or technology, and competition. It may be necessary to pay more for the more qualified applicant. It may also be necessary to increase the compensation package for present salespeople to prevent competitors from pirating the best ones. Expenses that must be forecasted include automobile and other forms of travel, lodging, meals, entertainment, equipment, activity fees, telephone, postage, selling materials (such as samples and literature), sales meetings, and training expenses. Travel and lodging expenses have been especially sensitive to inflation, so inflation rates must be estimated. Thus the young first-line sales manager must apply all of his or her skills in economics, accounting, and financial analysis. Few sales training programs include training in budgeting and forecasting.

The strategic impact of the compensation system must also be considered. For example, at Digital Equipment, selling strategy in general and sales force compensation in particular were criticized by some as leading to problems.[7] For a long time, Digital's products were the only ones available that offered companies an alternative to mainframe computers. Under these circumstances, Digital computers seemed to sell themselves. In addition, top management wanted to create a consultative atmosphere with clients, not a "strong sale" orientation. So salespeople were on straight salary. But the lack of a commission structure was also seen as driving away good salespeople, and led to calls for a commission-based—and stronger selling—orientation.

Forecasting Sales Management Activities

After the field sales manager has forecasted the needs of the sales district, he or she must forecast personal management activities such as recruiting, hiring, training, trips with salespeople, evaluation, counseling, and coaching. When allocating scarce management time, the sales manager must allocate his or her effort to those activities that will yield the greatest productivity of the sales force. The manager must also forecast the need for changes in staff support, such as secretaries, systems engineers, and repair personnel. He or she will also need to consider the logistical problems associated with producing and distributing sales literature and promotional materials such as samples, display materials, selling aids (audio tapes, records, and slides) and reporting devices such as laptop computers and FAX machines. Many of these estimates are continuous through the year.

SETTING OBJECTIVES

For the first-line manager, setting objectives means establishing the end results to be achieved by the sales district. A sales organization may have a hierarchy of annual objectives. For example, the company may have as its objective increasing its profit by 25% before taxes. This company goal may be translated into a sales management goal such as, "Increase sales of the three most profitable items by 15% and reduce expenses by 5%." This sales management objective may be translated into a district objective such as, "Increase the sales of products A, B, and C by 15%; make one more call per day; and reduce the cost per sales call by 10%."

Management by Objectives

The field sales manager will probably be implementing a corporate MBO (Management By Objectives) program. MBO programs integrate the company's need for achieving sales growth and profit with the needs of the salespeople for income, recognition, and development. An effective MBO program channels the energies of each salesperson within the district toward mutually established and agreed-upon goals. The salesperson and the sales manager gain an understanding of the work to be done, the costs and the deadlines to be met, and how the results will be measured. MBO programs provide greater control within the sales organization, but they also permit greater freedom for self-expression once the objectives have been established. MBO systems are flexible because objectives are renegotiated on a regular basis, thereby permitting modifications to reflect changes in the environment and in strategies.

MBO programs have many benefits. A manager and a salesperson define responsibilities in terms of results, not work, thereby giving the salesperson the freedom to work out his or her own strategies. *Performance standards, controls, evaluation, and feedback are made easier by MBO programs because objectives must be stated in terms that are specific, measurable, agreed-upon, realistic, and time-related.* These five characteristics of an objective must be further refined for implementation at the district level. In order to be measurable, the objective must be observable and expressed in quantified terms. For example, we cannot directly measure "customer satisfaction," but we can infer satisfaction by measuring the number of complaints or returned goods.

Objectives must be specific to a particular area of performance, rather than overall performance. The number of calls on prospects is a specific objective. If the salesperson is not achieving this objective, specific training can be used. If, in contrast, the objective is expressed in overall terms, such as increased market share, it is impossible to know why it was not achieved and what course of action to take. The *objectives must be traceable to the efforts of an individual* rather than a group, so the individual feels responsibility and ownership. When possible, *express the costs of reaching an objective* so that the costs of the activities to reach the objective can be related to the benefits from achieving it.

The output of the manager-salesperson interchange is a document that reflects the results the salesperson is committed to achieve. The MBO process can save management time because it encourages self-commitment, self-analysis, and self-supervision by the salesperson.

The process for implementing an MBO program often begins with the president of the company, who defines his or her objectives and passes them along to the next level of management. The process cascades through various levels of management until it finally reaches the salespeople. Each individual in the MBO process should be encouraged to take some risks and stretch his or her abilities. Each individual should be motivated to prepare for greater responsibility. This process should develop a cohesive relationship between a superior and a subordinate.

What should be included in an MBO program? Any objective that contributes to the end result of helping the salesperson meet the sales quota can be considered. Thus MBO could include adding 10 more prospects per month, making one more needs assessment per week, reducing by 30% the time required to make a proposal by using a microcomputer program, and reducing the average account outstanding by 5 days during the next six months. Accomplishing these objectives will help to achieve a sales quota.

Salesperson's Objectives

Exhibit 8.3 illustrates objectives of a salesperson for a soap manufacturer. These objectives are in four activity classifications—sales closing, product distribution, self-development, and territory management. The time frame for accomplishment has been established as the next fiscal year. The objectives for three of the four activities have been expressed in precise quantitative terms—the orders-to-call ratio, percent distribution, and days in a territory. Each of these objectives may be evaluated against existing data sources, such as invoices, daily reports, account analysis, and expense reports. The self-development objective is more difficult because it involves skill improvement, which is difficult to measure. Perhaps the training department has tests for measuring skills in overcoming objections. Generally, such measures are based on the subjective observations of field managers during field trips.

Exhibit 8.3 — OBJECTIVES FOR A SOAP SALESPERSON FOR NEXT FISCAL YEAR

Activity	Objective	Data Source for Evaluation
Sales Closing	Increase orders-to-call ratio from 63% to 72% in accounts to which we ship direct.	Invoices and daily call reports
Product Distribution	Achieve distribution of new Family Size Detergent in 70% of key accounts, with no loss of distribution for other sizes.	Quarterly analysis of key accounts
Self-Development	Improve skills in overcoming objections, with no reduction in calls.	Training Department test and field manager's observations
Territory Management	Revise my route plan so that I spend 3 more days in the western part of my territory where potential is untapped.	Call report, Expense report

Field Manager's Objectives

The first-line field sales manager will also have a set of objectives. These objectives may be stated in terms of improving the total district performance or improving the performance in certain product groups. Many of this manager's objectives will be focused toward the development of personnel. Thus the manager may have objectives for developing team spirit, improving or replacing the least productive salespeople, getting a good salesperson promoted, and making MBO programs work. She or he will also have administrative objectives, such as taking appropriate action on delinquent reports or maintaining optimum inventory levels. Exhibit 8.4 illustrates a sales manager's action plan for maintaining optimum inventory levels by reducing stock-out conditions without increasing inventory carrying costs.

MBO procedures are not limited to managers who are selling tangible products. Commercial banks have lending officers who are really salespeople for the bank. These lending officers have managers who perform first-line sales management functions. They analyze current industry characteristics, competitive factors, and the bank's current industry position. They develop industry objectives and set a division plan for profitability. They work with individual calling officers in setting personal goals and objectives for specific accounts and then monitor the performance of lending officers according to mutually agreed-upon objectives.

Preventing Problems with MBO

MBO systems, like all planning systems, can become an end in themselves so that too much time is spent planning and too little time implementing. Furthermore, it is often difficult to evaluate their effect on morale or productivity because MBO programs may be only a part of several management changes that were implemented.

If the salespeople have managed their territories as a business, complete with income and productivity statements (Chapter 5), the groundwork will have been established for

---

Exhibit **8.4**	A SALES MANAGER'S ACTION PLAN

Key Activity: Maintaining Optimum Inventory Levels
Objective: To reduce stock-out conditions from 10% to 3% with no increase in inventory carrying costs.

Action Plan Steps	Completion Date
1. Identify stock-out items during the previous six months.	10/15
2. Classify frequency of out-of-stock by stock number and customer type.	10/16
3. Analyze usage pattern and profitability of customer types.	11/01
4. Examine customer purchasing procedures and analyze our purchasing/manufacturing procedures.	11/14
5. Discuss and review findings with persons who impact inventory levels.	11/17
6. Define the problem and create alternative solutions.	11/22
7. Evaluate the alternatives and recommend one.	12/01
8. Gain management approval, agreement, and support at each level.	12/07
9. Implement recommended changes.	12/31
10. Evaluate the recommendation by determining stock-out conditions.	03/31
11. Review, monitor, and modify the system as needed.	

Adapted from a presentation to the National Society of Sales Training Executives by R. V. Lippincott, Director, Training and Management Development, Sterling Drug Incorporated, December 6, 1976.

management by objectives. By comparing these income and productivity statements for all salespeople in the district, the sales manager can quickly identify those who have weaknesses; he or she can then negotiate objectives with them to improve their performance on activities that will improve their productivity.

DEVELOPING STRATEGIES

Strategies may be defined briefly as deciding how and when to achieve objectives. The field sales manager begins with the company selling plan and then adapts the plan and its objectives to his or her district by helping the salespeople develop objectives and strategies that are appropriate for each salesperson and for local conditions. Local conditions may include a regional brand that is selling at a lower price, a high unemployment level, or an out-of-stock condition for very popular products. The manager must work with the salespeople to develop benefit statements that will overcome local problems by building on the company's strengths and avoiding competition against the primary strengths of the competitor. By working with each salesperson, the manager will assure that territory strategies are consistent with the corporate selling plan.

At the level of general strategy, firms develop one of four strategies around a product: build, hold, harvest, or divest.

A **build strategy** involves an attempt to increase the product's market share. This strategy tends to be used when the product is in the early stages of its life cycle; that is, after it has been introduced or while the market is still growing rapidly. Research on new products indicates that a strong, well-targeted sales effort is a key to their success.[8] A firm might also pursue a build strategy if it feels it has a strong competitive position in an attractive market.

A **hold strategy** involves an attempt to maintain market share. This is likely to be the strategy when the product is in the maturity stage of its life cycle. Because the market has ceased growing, market share must come by attracting rivals' customers, so substantial gains are unlikely, or may be prohibitively expensive. The firm may turn to a defensive strategy of preventing competitors from attracting its own customers.

A **harvest strategy** involves an attempt to maximize cash flow from the product. This strategy is common when the product is in the late maturity to early decline stage of its life cycle, or when the firm feels that it lacks a sufficiently strong competitive position to continue with the product-market for the long term. Because the firm may have residual brand awareness and customer goodwill, it may continue to sell for some time—but without further investment in the product, its advertising, or other support.

A **divest strategy** involves attempts to actually withdraw the product from the market. This strategy is usually used when the product is in the decline stage of its life cycle or if the firm feels that the market has otherwise become unattractive. Here the sales manager finds himself or herself backing a product that upper management has decided to drop as soon as it can be sold off.

In order to translate the corporate selling plan to the salespeople, the sales manager must have a clear understanding of the corporate plan. A study by Booz, Allen, and Hamilton found that 96% of senior executives felt that middle managers did not have a full understanding of new business goals and about 50% felt that middle managers complied with new strategies only partially or not at all.[9]

A study among the top U.S. firms confirms that this is a problem in marketing and sales.[10] The study surveyed both the top marketing executive of the corporations and the same firm's first-line field sales managers. The researchers found that sales managers matched the top marketing managers' classification of products reasonably well on more aggressive strategies—particularly on build strategies—but poorly on the less aggressive strategies.

In particular, most sales managers were not inclined to classify their products under harvest or divest strategies, even though top marketing management had classified them in those categories. In follow-up interviews, sales managers noted several problems in aligning with top managements' idea of product strategy. These included: short product life cycles, top management ambivalence about whether to discontinue or relaunch a product, rapid turnover among marketing managers, and a tendency of both marketing and sales managers to stress sales volume regardless of formal company policy.[11]

IMPLEMENTING POLICIES

Implementing policies is a major part of the first-line manager's job, but because of the distance between the home office and the salespeople, some errors in interpretations occur. As a result, the manager is often involved in arbitrating conflicts that grow out of a policy conflict. The manager will also make recommendations for changes in policy and, in emergencies, find ways to operate outside policies.

Policies may be defined as standardized answers for recurring **strategic** *questions.* Policies are boundaries on acceptable alternatives for achieving objectives. For example, a pharmaceutical company may have a policy of focusing only on the healthcare problems of humans. If it developed a product that solved a problem in animals, it would sell or license the product because the company policy is to deal only with human problems. Policies aid an administrator in a complex organization. They are automatic decision makers that free managers to focus on infrequent problems. They also provide uniformity across the company and simplify the control of salespeople and communications with them. Some common sales management policies include dress codes, ethics, a return goods policy, pricing and trade-in policies, antitrust policies, and adherence to affirmative action programs when hiring, promoting, compensating, or separating salespeople.

DEVELOPING PROGRAMS

What Are Sales Programs?

A program is a series of **tactical** *action steps to achieve an objective. Programs become* **schedules** *when they assign times for completion.* The dates for completion reflect the priorities of the steps. Exhibit 8.4, seen earlier, illustrates a sales manager's action plan for maintaining optimum inventory levels. It includes a schedule because each step is assigned a completion date.

Managers will become involved with programs at many different levels within the company; they even need to evaluate competitive programs so they can estimate their effect on company sales. Managers must translate the company's national programs into their districts. They must work with salespeople to develop programs to achieve each of their key objectives. Finally, managers must develop programs that can help them achieve their management objectives and their self-development objectives.

When implementing the national selling program, the manager's principal role is to make certain that the program is understood, supported, introduced, and implemented with vigor. He or she must make certain that tools, such as samples, are available and used for implementing the program. Implementing a program includes spotting and correcting pitfalls early, generating and sustaining enthusiasm for the program, coaching where skills need improvement, and finally, providing feedback to the regional manager with recommendations for improving the program.

Establishing Priorities

Priorities are necessary because salespeople and managers have multiple objectives with activities that compete for the scarcest resource, that of time. By establishing priorities, the manager can distinguish between important activities and emergency ones. Emergencies may not necessarily be important, but when they are, the establishment of priorities provides a basis for returning to normal activities.

Salespeople establish priorities when they allocate the length of time and frequency of their calls according to the potential for each account. They also create daily and long-term itineraries to carry out the programs and meet their specified objectives. Prioritizing activities is an important part of time and territory management, as was seen in Chapter 6.

A field sales manager has an itinerary for making trips with salespeople, meeting important customers, training, market planning, appraising, counseling, coaching, staffing, and self-development. An important management task is ensuring that salespeople comply with their scheduled itineraries, product promotion schedules, appointments, and regularly scheduled call-backs on major accounts.

Priorities must be reevaluated continuously because environmental changes occur. The manager must distinguish between "must do" and "could do" actions. The short-term "could do" activities have a way of crowding out the long-term "must do" ones. Samples of a manager's activity schedule appear in Chapter 9, Exhibit 9.3.

SETTING PROCEDURES

What Are Procedures?

Procedures are standardized tactics for implementing a strategy. Sales management procedures include many elements, such as how to complete an order form, an expense report, and an automobile accident report. Procedures also exist for classifying prospects, call-reporting, sampling, complaint handling, relocation and moving, and recruiting. A procedure manual with such procedures eliminates the need for managers to make decisions in these areas, thereby freeing them to develop programs for nonrecurring events. Procedures, like policies, provide control, fairness throughout the sales force, and simplified communication.

Field managers must be certain that salespeople understand procedures, their non-negotiability, and the futility of fighting them. Noncompliance with procedures is a major problem for managers, especially in nonselling activities such as gathering market research data and processing memos, orders, returns, credits, and correspondence.

Procedures for Managers

The new manager's job can be made easier if the company provides a field sales manager's procedures manual. It helps the new manager to anticipate standard implementation problems and find ways to solve them. These manuals cover such topics as product promotions, recruiting procedures, warning and probation procedures, separation routines, spouse information sessions, territory redesign, salary review, bonus procedures, performance review, and procedures for the promotion of salespeople.

BUDGETING

Budgeting translates a program of action into the resources that are necessary to implement it. A budget is not limited to tangible resources such as investments and expenditures. It should also consider management capacities, staffing, and information needs, such as market research. These resource estimates may require the planner to develop a new program if the existing one will not meet profit goals. Once the program and the associated budget are adopted, the budget becomes a control device for measuring results in financial terms and taking appropriate corrective action.

The sales manager must become familiar with concepts such as controllable and uncontrollable expenses, account codes, sales and expense quotas, break-even analysis, marketing cost analysis, and promotional costs (conventions, seminars, etc.), as well as resources including time, expenses, equipment, and promotional materials. A budget is an important management tool, which a new manager must learn how to use effectively. The availability of microcomputers with standard programs can greatly simplify the young manager's budgeting process. These computers can also make it possible to do "what if" planning and determine the effect on the budget of a change in strategy.

In addition to technical budgeting skills, the sales manager must also have the interpersonal skills to work with other department managers in the budgeting process. For example, the sales management mix can have a significant impact on the success or failure of a new product launch. But the sales manager must anticipate the cost implications of these changes, including whether the costs should be allocated to the new product project rather than the sales organization.[12]

THE FIELD SALES MANAGER'S ROLE IN ORGANIZING

The key to implementing a program is the assigning of people to roles to perform given tasks. *The organizing function structures the roles of individuals for the effective accomplishment of objectives.* Of the five management functions—planning, organizing, staffing, directing, and controlling—first-line sales managers reported that organizing was the least important of their responsibilities (Exhibit 7.3, Chapter 7). Although these managers do not create organizational designs they do have input into implementation of the design by contributing to elements for the job description, position qualifications, evaluation criteria, territory alignment, and promotion recommendations.

The major direct organizational links for the field sales manager are downward to the salesperson and upward to a regional or general manager. The manager can have many dotted-line links with other areas, such as credit and collections, marketing research, product management, advertising, and promotion.

The primary organizational activity of the field sales manager is reorganizing. He or she will generally be promoted into an existing district, but changes in the market and the needs of the company may require the addition or deletion of territories. As a result, the field sales manager's ongoing organizational responsibility is to remain flexible to organizational change and to participate by recommending changes in territories.

···

TARGET MARKET ANALYSIS

Market analysis involves two key activities: (1) prioritizing sub-markets based on their attractiveness and (2) examining market dynamics so as to take advantage of opportunities and eliminate (or minimize) potential threats.

Case 8.1   LELAND PUBLICATIONS

Mike Branden, the Southeastern District Supervisor for Leland Publications, wasn't certain he agreed with the company's policy that allowed transfers of salespeople, but in this case he felt he had more to gain than to lose when his regional manager, Paul Hancock, approved the transfer of Ken Adams to fill the open territory in Atlanta. Mike wasn't convinced that the advantage of getting an experienced salesperson whom he didn't know was better than hiring an applicant of his own selection. His current experiences with Ken Adams confirmed his judgment.

The company's thinking was that if salespeople were unhappy in their present assignments, or for other reasons wanted to live elsewhere, then a transfer would provide extra motivation that would make them more productive. This logic resulted in Leland's transfer policy that allowed salespeople with more than 2 years' experience to transfer to any open territory at their own expense if their last performance review was at least satisfactory and their present manager approved the request.

Ken Adams, a seasoned salesperson with six years of experience in a territory headquartered in Charleston, West Virginia, and a sales record of above-average productivity, had requested the transfer because his wife, Nancy, had been raised in Birmingham, Alabama, and wanted to get back to the south. Ken, who had graduated from the University of West Virginia, had been happy to have been assigned initially to Charleston, his hometown. Although he traveled extensively into adjacent parts of Ohio, Kentucky, and Virginia, he liked the area and felt at home with the people.

It had taken Ken and his family some time to find a home in an Atlanta suburb. The difference in the cost of living between Charleston and Atlanta was a bit of a shock to them, but they seemed to have adjusted well, and the reduced time on the road for Ken pleased Nancy and the kids. Allowing for the differences in Charleston and Atlanta, and the time for Ken to learn his way around, Mike expected Ken to be performing at least at an acceptable level eight months after his move. In fact, Mike had expected Ken to become one of his top people because he had been given what he wanted. The problem was that it hadn't worked out that way. Call averages in Mike's district were slightly less than 14 per day, above the company standard of 10. Ken Adams's average had been eight initially, and for two of the last three months had increased to nine. When Mike told Ken about the district

average, and that nine was unsatisfactory, Ken was surprised. He intimated that this was an acceptable level in his previous district. Because Mike was not familiar with Ken's previous district or its manager, he felt reluctant to make any comparisons. But, to make matters worse, Ken's dollar sales were only in the marginally satisfactory range for the district. Mike's preliminary analysis was that Ken was not getting the sales return he should from the metropolitan sections of his territory where the potential was considerably greater. By contrast, he was doing better in Columbus, Macon, and Augusta, which have smaller sales potentials. A brief review of Ken's call pattern indicated to Mike that Ken was not allocating the proper amount of time to the metropolitan Atlanta sections. Three months before, Mike and Ken had reviewed the daily and weekly planning guide used by the other salespeople, after which Ken's call average picked up for a while. Unfortunately, a corresponding increase in sales was not forthcoming and last month, Ken's call average was down to its previous level. Mike also suspected that Ken was not using the specific call objectives kind of planning used by the others. During his last review with Paul Hancock, Mike was asked what he planned to do about the situation.

CASE QUESTIONS

1. What is the problem?
2. What are the possible causes of the problem?
3. Is the evaluation of Ken's dollar sales productivity as marginally satisfactory valid criticism of his performance? Why?
4. What are the possible reasons for Ken's low call average?
5. How could Mike Branden confirm whether Ken Adams's problem is poor planning?
6. If Ken's problem is poor call planning, how could Mike attempt to correct the problem?
7. What is the possible reason Ken was doing better in Columbus, Macon, and Augusta, which had smaller potentials?
8. Could a call average of nine have been acceptable in Ken's previous territory? Why?
9. What are the advantages and disadvantages of a transfer policy as used by Leland Publishing?
10. Discuss the reasons for each of the conditions in the transfer policy.

Case 8.2   TRIDENT AUTOMOTIVE SUPPLIES

Two years ago Sandy Kremer was hired and assigned to a new territory that included Pennsylvania and Ohio. The first year, his sales exceeded his quota by 26%; last year the increase was 38%. Although these numbers were very good, his manager thought that he should spend more time developing the key accounts that determined the bulk of his sales. Sandy had plotted the number of call-backs against his percentage increase in sales and had found a strong positive relationship. Thus he could expect proportional increases in sales by calling on the accounts more frequently. He wondered if at some point there would be diminishing returns for an account. He also noted that he was covering only about half the potential customers in his territory. Increasing call-backs to present customers left even fewer calls for potential customers.

Sandy's manager suggested two strategies. First, he could do a survey of key accounts in both states and work out a program to call on only the best accounts and ignore all others. Second, he could call on all potential customers in one state, make the optimum call-backs on key accounts, and make less frequent calls on the remainder of the accounts in that state.

CASE QUESTIONS

1. What other strategies could Sandy consider?
2. What organizational changes should the manager consider?
3. How could Sandy apply concepts from Chapter 6?

Case 8.3   PETE CERVANTES'S PROBLEM

I've been the sales manager of seven sales representatives and three telephone order representatives. My problem is that they don't always report to me. Instead, they bypass me and go directly to the owner, to whom they used to report. This situation is undermining my authority and my ego. I discussed the problem with the owner, who understands the problem, but nothing has changed. Although my ego may be part of the problem, I am more concerned with finding solutions to their problems. Going to the boss delays solutions. We need to change the organization to solve this problem.

CASE QUESTIONS

1. Why isn't the problem being solved?
2. Whose behavior does the sales manager control?
3. Whose behavior can be changed?
4. Even if the boss cooperated, would the problem cease?
5. How should the problem be solved?

Nationwide Insurance has a planning process to help it to decide the number and placement of agents in a territory. It consists of a market summary, agency strength planning, and a decision tree.[13]

Market Summary

The market summary assesses the potential of the market by examining five-year projections for the number of households, household incomes, property values, the percent of owner-occupied housing, percent of renter-occupied housing, percent of mobile homes, the percent of homes built between 1960 and 1990, number of nationwide and competitive agencies in the territory, and the market share. By analyzing these data it can decide on the placement of new and existing agents.

Agency Strength Planning

This planning phase focuses on the number of agents required to meet the sales plan for the local market. The total agency force required to meet this potential for the year and the next five years less the number of planned terminations sets the recruiting goal for hiring and training new agents. This analysis is used to establish the agents' five year gross commission goal. These documents are updated annually.

Decision Tree

The decision tree analysis uses the new agent hiring plan and the market summary to identify the best alternative for selecting present and new agents in local markets.

....

SUMMARY

The new field sales manager will have an opportunity to develop further those planning and strategy skills that he or she learned as a salesperson. The domain and time horizon of the field manager are considerably greater than that of the salesperson. This expansion of skills in planning and strategy formation provides good training for promotion to higher levels of management.

At first the new sales manager may miss the excitement of selling and the more immediate response to his or her efforts. Although the new manager is involved in planning, most of his or her efforts will be spent in implementing the plans of others through functions such as staffing, directing, and controlling.

Forecasting can be an important activity for sales managers who must forecast market conditions, competition, staffing needs, compensation, and expenses. The time horizon of the young manager moves from a few weeks or months to a year. The manager must also forecast what management activities should be accomplished during the year.

Field sales managers must translate the selling objectives in the company selling plan into objectives for the district and for each territory. These objectives must strike a balance between being achievable and challenging. The manager and the salesperson will work together to establish personal objectives so that the salesperson is committed to them. This process may be part of a company MBO (Management By Objectives) program. Objectives become more precise and involve a shorter time horizon as one moves down the organization.

National account managers may have a separate set of objectives that reflect their total responsibility for the account. These objectives will reflect the need to work effectively with people at all levels in the client firm and in the account manager's firm.

Field sales managers implement strategies that have been developed at higher levels, provide feedback about these strategies, and make strategy recommendations in both directions—to salespeople and to superiors. In preparation for promotion, the young manager will want to begin to think in terms of growth strategies.

The first-line sales manager rarely produces policy, but sometimes influences policy-making through recommendations. This manager will be called upon to interpret policies and settle conflicts that such policies may create. Sales programs and procedures must be translated into local environments. They must also be evaluated. First-line managers are given early opportunities to develop skills in evaluating and, to some extent, developing programs and procedures.

ASSIGNMENTS/DISCUSSION QUESTIONS

1. Explain why the following are good or bad objective statements:
   a. To do better.
   b. To turn in reports on time.

    c. To triple sales of product X within the next quarter.

    d. To triple sales in your territory within the next fiscal year while maintaining complete coverage of your territory.

    e. To maintain a 10% increase in sales on products X and Y in your territory during the next fiscal year while improving the coverage of all major customers to meet the minimum call standard.

    f. To submit your daily call reports by the first of the following week without fail for the next six months.

2. Write an objective for your first job after graduation. Include all necessary criteria.

3. Write a sample procedure to be used by salespeople in the case of sickness or accident.

4. How can a field sales manager convince a salesperson that his or her sales forecast is overly optimistic?

5. Because the cost of a "floater" is considerable, what are the disadvantages of leaving a territory vacant until a suitable applicant can be found?

6. Why would a general sales manager have a lower quota for a district than the district manager would have for the same district?

7. Create two alternative solutions to Action Step #6 in the program outlined in Exhibit 8.9.

8. Carlos Marco became the new Detroit district manager for North Central Hospital Supply Company five years after he finished college. He was excited about the growth in outpatient clinics in his district. His experiences in southern California suggested that although salespeople would need to spend more time with these clinics, the payoff was big. He proposed to his regional manager that his Detroit district be expanded from five to eight salespeople. The regional manager thought that this was a good idea and asked for a detailed proposal with input from the current group. What should this proposal include? How do you think the salesforce will react to this proposed change?

9. As a veteran sales manager for a firm that markets office furnishings to major businesses and governmental institutions, you have been told by the vice president for marketing to discontinue pushing the company's traditional line in favor of a new ergonomic line. The traditional line has generated 90% of sales and is strongly favored by your customers. What would you do?

10. Working in teams, brainstorm the factors in the company or its environment that might cause a sales manager to question historically-based forecasts. Then list the sources of information that might have led to the identification of those factors.

ENDNOTES

1. Alston Gardner, President of Target Marketing Systems, personal communication, March 25, 1997.

2. Adapted from Leonard M. Fuld (1995), *The New Competitor Intelligence,* New York: Wiley.

3. Ibid., p. 28.

4. J. Edward Russo and Paul J.H. Shoemaker (1990). *Decision Traps: Ten Barriers to Brillian Decision-Making and How to Overcome Them,* New York: Simon & Schuster.

5. George G. Gordon, Industry Determinants of Organizational Culture, *Academy of Management Review,* 16(2), pp. 396–415.

6. Evan Ramstad, Ambitious Compaq Invades the Market for Workstations, *Wall Street Journal,* October 29, 1996.

7. John R. Wilke, At Digital Equipment, A Resignation Reveals Key Problem: Selling, *Wall Street Journal,* April 26, 1994, p. A1.

8. Robert G. Cooper and Elko J. Kleinschmidt, Resource Allocation in the New Product Process, *Industrial Marketing Management,* 17, August, pp. 249–262.

9. *Wall Street Journal,* May 1, 1990.

10. William M. Strahle, Rosann L. Spiro, and Frank Acito, Marketing and Sales: Strategic Alignment and Functional Implementation, *Journal of Personal Selling and Sales Management,* 16(1), Winter, 1996, pp. 1–20.

11. Ibid., pp. 13–14.

12. Linda Rochford and Thomas R. Wotruba, The Impact of Sales Management Changes on New Product Success, *Journal of the Academy of Marketing Science,* 24(3); pp. 263–270.

13. Nationwide Insurance Office of Agency Development, *Agency Planning and Placement,* October 24, 1996, p. 1–1.

9

STAFFING BY FIELD MANAGERS

LEARNING GOALS

1. To understand the recruiting and selection process from the company's viewpoint
2. To learn the processes for recruiting and selecting salespeople
3. To learn the forces that determine the number of people to recruit
4. To be able to apply the concept of behavioral traits in real-world situations
5. To understand the legal and ethical dimensions of staffing
6. To expand on the staffing functions and activities outlined in Exhibit 7.1. (Refer to the Staff column in this exhibit.)

A TYPICAL PROBLEM FOR A YOUNG MANAGER

A newly appointed sales manager who is out of college only three or four years will immediately be faced with major staffing decisions. An understanding of the types of decisions is accomplished through the examination of the following case.

Lois McDermott was a new pharmaceutical field sales manager facing her first hiring decision. She had been through the company's recruiting training program, had followed all the guidelines and, in fact, had interviewed the applicant twice. Now Lois faced the decision of recommending to her regional sales manager to hire the applicant, or turning him down.

The applicant, John Chang, in his mid 20s, graduated last month with a B.S. in Business Administration, majoring in marketing and sales management, with a GPA of 2.95. He earned 100% of his college expenses by working at the following jobs:

- Cashier and office assistant, Market Fair Supermarkets (Spring semester, senior year).
  - Supervised 10 persons in absence of manager.
  - Trained new employees.

143

- Teller, Fidelity Bank & Trust (Summer, junior year).
  - Completed transactions on customers' accounts.
  - Sold bank services.
- Organizational Manager, Western Distributing (Summer, sophomore year).
  - Recruited, interviewed and selected students for summer sales jobs.
  - Taught and directed 19 students.
- Marketing Intern, Rockwell Financial Services (Summer, freshman year).
  - Designed sales literature.
  - Trained on products from Professional Development Program.
- Waiter, O'Rourke's Restaurant (During school year, all four years).

John impressed Lois as being hard-working, intelligent, goal-oriented, organized, but reserved. His heavy work schedule seemed to leave little time for campus activities. Lois called his last three employers to confirm his references. Their comments were similar—diligent, energetic, decisive, but a loner. During his two days in the field with two different salespersons, the applicant was described as being "very observant; lots of questions after each call about the selling process and what the company expected; hesitant to enter into 'small talk' with accounts; very willing to stay the full day and even beyond; a bit on the reserved side."

As Lois analyzed her reservations about the applicant's suitability for sales, she realized they revolved around his persuasiveness, congeniality, and communications skills. There seemed to be no question about his suitability for a career in business, but she honestly doubted his ability to sell.

Keep Lois' decision in mind as you read this chapter. At the end you will be asked if you think she should recommend hiring John.

STAFFING IS THE CRITICAL ROLE OF FIELD MANAGERS

Staffing is the most important function of first-line sales managers, as was seen in Chapter 7, Exhibit 7.3. For many customers, particularly in service industries, the salesperson is almost synonymous with the firm.[1] Recruiting and selecting salespeople can have a long-term effect on the district, the company, and how the manager spends his or her future time. A bad recruiting decision is like a bad tee shot in golf: you can waste a lot of time looking for ways to get out of a bad situation. A poor recruiting decision can create the need for more training, motivating, and developing of a salesperson than the system permits, thereby taking a manager's time away from good salespeople.

The success of every other sales management activity depends on the success of recruiting and selecting salespersons; successful recruitment determines the quality and quantity of the sales force. The field sales manager must strike a balance between two conflicting goals—finding the perfect candidate and keeping every territory filled. The cost of an open territory is more obvious than the cost of long-term administrative problems from hiring the wrong candidate. Hence probably more errors are made in hiring than in not hiring.

PLANNING SALES FORCE REQUIREMENTS

Planning for staffing the sales force takes place at two levels—general sales management and field sales management. In this chapter we will examine how the field manager decides the number and characteristics of the people to recruit. The field sales manager's plan requires three inputs—the job description, district personnel forecasts, and the company selling plan.

The Job Description

The activities to be performed by a salesperson appear in the job description, as seen in Chapter 2. A good job description should include the behavior required to perform these activities, the education and experience of the applicant, and the links with supporting staff members, such as systems engineers, product managers, installation clerks, service persons, and customer relations persons. The existence of such supporting staff members simplifies the selling process and therefore simplifies recruiting. The level of supervision will also determine the minimum qualifications of an applicant; a less qualified applicant may be hired if there is close supervision. Recruiting and selecting quality salespersons is made more difficult by the fact that few field sales managers have received specific training for these activities.

Personnel Forecasts

The number of persons to recruit depends on the district sales forecast and anticipated departures from the present sales staff. Sales forecasts identify changes in demand and competition that affect the size and location of the sales force. For example, some companies are reducing the size of their staff in the northeastern United States and increasing it in the sunbelt areas, thereby reflecting population and industrial shifts. These forecasts also estimate competitors' share of the market and of the sales force, enabling us to estimate if we are falling behind in our share of selling effort.

We must also estimate the turnover of the sales force, which requires separate estimates of promotions, retirements, and voluntary or involuntary separations. With these turnovers in mind, the sales manager must recruit in advance of needs. Some managers have a policy of recruiting to replace the poorest performer on the staff. The length of a training program will determine how far in advance a forecast must be made; a long training program requires an early identification of sales force staffing requirements.

The personnel forecast must include predictions of new product introductions by our firm and our competitors. These introductions can greatly affect the quality and quantity of salespersons required, as well as lengthen training programs.

Sales force organizational strategies must be anticipated. For example, a company that splits its sales force into an industrial and a consumer sales force will have different processes for recruiting salespersons and managers. Candidates for the consumer products will need to have skills in mass merchandising. Candidates for the industrial products will need to be applications-oriented.

Personnel requirements are influenced by changes in the marketing strategy that, when translated into a selling plan, will require an increase or decrease in the number of salespeople needed.

The Selling Plan

The selling plan reflects the objectives of the company, its marketing strategies, the role of personal selling in these strategies, and, finally, the selling strategies of the sales force. The plan gives the field sales manager a means for assigning the tasks to be performed with the staff available to perform them. This selling plan and the manager's forecast for his or her district will reveal any gaps that must be filled through recruiting.

· ·

METHODS FOR DETERMINING SALES FORCE SIZE

Whereas the general manager may have sophisticated computer models for estimating the size of the sales force in broad terms, the field manager must estimate very specific situations by answering questions such as the following. Will Lisa be ready for promotion this year? Eric is on probation. Will he survive in the next three months? Will the planned expansion of my major account occur this year? Can competition correct its problems and therefore be a major factor again?

Assume that Lisa will be promoted and Eric will be terminated. Those events seem just about certain. But there is about a 50% chance that Lindsey will retire this year. There is also a 50% chance that Angie will be transferred to a job as assistant trainer. Although the chances of competition changing are low, our new products will require some additional capacity. Based on this information, a minimum of three new recruits are needed for this district this year.

Before deciding to hire additional salespeople, the general manager needs to explore ways to make the salespeople already on staff more productive. Perhaps direct mail, telemarketing, e-mail, FAX, and the Internet can generate leads, saving time for later steps in the selling process. But if new hires are necessary, the manager should determine the number by some rational means. The following is a hypothetical example of determining the number of salespeople required.

Estimating the Size of the Candidate Pool

How many people should you recruit to fill three positions? If the regional manager likes to have some choice you must recruit more than three, maybe five. If we advertise widely we will receive many resumes but according to past experience, only 20% will pass the initial screening. The initial interview and references will reject half of those who passed the initial screening. Because of competition for good salespeople in the territory, only 70% have accepted our offers in the past. Based on this information, use the following formula to calculate the number of resumes you need and how many interviews you need to conduct. An equation will show the relationships among these variables.

Let R = Total resumes needed
  C = Number of candidates passed to regional manager
  F = First screen ratio to continue to next phase
  I = Interview reference check ratio to continue
  P = Probability that candidate will accept an offer

Then,

$$R = C/(F \times I \times P)$$

Using the example above, how many resumes must you collect?

$$R = 5/(0.2 \times 0.5 \times 0.7)$$
$$= 5/.07$$
$$= 71.4 \text{ or } 72 \text{ resumes must be collected to generate 5 good candidates.}$$

How many interviews must you conduct? If only 20% of the 72 resumes are good, you must plan on conducting 14 or 15 interviews.

Given all of your other duties as a field manager, collecting 72 resumes and conducting 15 interviews can be very time-consuming. What can you do to cut down on that workload? Assume that you find that one or two candidate sources always produced a first-screen ratio of 0.4. What would this ratio do to your workload? Using the above equation but changing F, we have the following estimate:

R = 5/(0.4 × 0.5 × 0.7)
  = 35.7 or 36 resumes are needed from the quality source.

You must still conduct 14 or 15 interviews (0.4 × 36) because although you have reduced the number of resumes to collect, you have more of them passing the first screen.

This equation can be put into a spreadsheet such as Lotus 1-2-3. Calculations can be made to address what if situations. What if the regional manager wanted two candidates for each opening? What if the economy moves into a recession and the acceptance ratio moves from 0.7 to 0.8? Or you could ask how we could improve our recruiting program to improve all of these ratios.

....

RECRUITING

Who Recruits?

The answer to this question will vary among companies. Some companies make recruiting part of a salesperson's job description because these salespeople are located throughout the country which can add to the diversity of the applicant pool. Recruiting is almost always part of the job description for a district sales manager, if only to screen applicants identified by others. Sales recruiting may be handled also by a team from headquarters and, to a lesser degree, by the recruiting staff from the personnel department. These teams may travel to regular recruiting sites or areas where territories are vacant. Universities that have supplied successful candidates over past years will be targeted for special attention.

Sources of Candidates

Sources of applicants for sales positions are numerous. The initiative may come from the applicant who writes to the company or contacts one of its employees. Additional sources include social contacts; college placement offices for students and alumni; private, state, and federal employment agencies; customers; competitors; company personnel in other departments (service, production, or office staff); noncompeting companies; persons calling on the company; clubs; high schools; newspapers; trade associations; and university faculty. Salespeople may call on some of these sources as part of their routine job activities. Computer web sites, as noted in Chapter 3, are becoming an important source of quality candidates, especially when computer skills are required for the job.

Over the years, companies will identify certain sources that provide the most productive applicants. Companies may use a college as a prescreening device when they find that students in previous years have been successful in selling careers. Successful graduates employed by a company will attract other student applicants.

The level of candidates' experience and their corresponding level of placement within the sales force is a key issue in recruiting salespeople. In sophisticated customer markets where long-term relationships are an asset, some experts suggest that it is important to hire salespeople with industry knowledge and an existing client base.[2] Because of their experience and contacts, they may command higher levels of pay and more job perks than some salespeople already with the firm.

On the other hand, a study conducted among sales managers and sales vice presidents found that firms that tend to hire salespeople for entry-level positions—and then promote from within—have a more trusting relationship with their salespeople.[3]

This approach has its own benefits, because salespeople who trust the firm are more likely to make extra efforts to help it succeed. They are also less likely to look for jobs elsewhere, saving the firm the costs of replacing them, and the lost customers that a salesperson may take with them.

The hire-new-and-promote-from-within philosophy can be extended to include the idea of hiring salespeople from among the support staff.[4] Support staff such as administrative assistants, customer service workers, and account coordinators are often eager to enter the field. They are likely to know the industry, the company, and its customers, and may need only training and on-the-job coaching to be converted into excellent salespeople.

Legal Considerations

Some companies with federal contracts must have written Affirmative Action Compliance Programs that comply with the *Federal Contract Compliance Manual.* Presidential Executive Orders might exempt companies with fewer than 100 employees and with governmental contracts of less than $50,000. These Executive Orders tend to be political and change with elections.

The *Compliance Manual* is designed to assure minorities of equal treatment with regard to recruiting, selecting, training, compensation, and promotion. Sales managers must have active programs for recruiting minorities and other protected groups (women, veterans, handicapped, and protected age groups) from minority colleges; women's colleges; minority referrals from college placement officers or alumni placement officers; state employment agencies; private employment agencies; private agencies specializing in minorities, females, and handicapped; protected age groups; and organizations that represent minorities (such as the Urban League, the Urban Coalition, and NAACP).

One of the factors in recruiting that must be carefully monitored in the process of selection is the number of applicants from potentially affected groups (African-American, American Indian, Asian/Pacific, disabled, female, and Hispanic). Federal regulations state that, "A selection rate for any race, sex, or ethnic group which is less than four-fifths (or eighty percent) of the rate for the group with the highest rate will generally be regarded by the federal enforcement agencies as evidence of adverse impact, while a greater than four-fifths rate will generally not be regarded by federal enforcement agencies as evidence of adverse impact."[5] If a selection process causes adverse impact, the process must be modified to eliminate the adverse impact or the employer must validate that this process is justified by business necessity or that a less onerous procedure is not available.

To determine if there is an adverse impact, the recruiter must compute the "impact ratio" for each race, sex, or ethnic group. Assume, for example, that 40 people are hired from 100 Caucasian applicants, 15 are hired out of 50 African-American applicants, and five are hired out of 25 Hispanic applicants. The relevant percentages and ratios are summarized in Exhibit 9.1. The Caucasian acceptance rate is 40% (40/100), the African-American acceptance rate is 30% (15/50), and the Hispanic acceptance rate is 20% (5/25). Because the 40% Caucasian acceptance rate is the largest number, it becomes the base for computing the impact ratio of other applicant categories. The impact ratio for African-Americans then is .75 (.3/.4), and the Hispanic acceptance rate is .5 (.2/.4). The recruiting and selection process in this case would be deemed to have a negative impact on African-Americans and Hispanics because both ratios are below the guideline of 0.80. Additional legal considerations will be discussed in the next section, which examines the selection process.

| Exhibit 9.1 | COMPUTING IMPACT RATIOS FOR AFFIRMATIVE ACTION PROGRAMS |

Race	Number of Applicants (1)	Number of Hires (2)	Percent of Applicants (3)	Impact Rate (4)
			$((2/1) \times 100)$	$((3)/(40) \times 100)$
White	100	40	40%	
African-American	50	15	30%	$(30/40) \times 100 = 75\%$
Hispanic	25	5	20%	$(20/40) \times 100 = 50\%$

An affirmative action program that results in selection levels less than 80% is a clear violation of the guidelines, but programs that meet this 80% test are not necessarily free of biases in their hiring. For example, screening devices such as tests might still bias against minorities but not in sufficient numbers to be detected by the four-fifths rule. In such a case, an individual could bring suit. Furthermore, the four-fifths rule does not assure that the test is valid, that is, that there is a verified relationship between the items in the test and the types of behavior that are required to be a sales representative. The EEOC rulings accept standard psychological procedures for the validation of this relationship.

THE SELECTION PROCESS

The selection process requires a careful consideration of all important dimensions for hiring and, where possible, standardization of these dimensions. This process should minimize overemphasizing one dimension and personal biases, such as the tendency to hire a person similar to one's own image. It should minimize the tendency to jump to a decision simply to fill the territory. Because the selection process is expensive in terms of managers' time for interviewing, interview guides should be designed to minimize duplication of coverage of topics by several interviewers, unless such duplication is planned. The selection process includes criteria for selection, selection procedures, and legal dimensions.

Criteria for Selection

The following criteria are important to consider when evaluating candidates.

Personality   Personalities are individual styles for dealing with one's environment. Thus we may think of a person as sociable, forceful, or having empathy for others. Numerous studies have used personality variables as predictors of sales productivity, with very mixed results. Early research indicated that **empathy** and **ego** are predictors of sales success.[6] Empathy is the ability to sense the reactions of another person. Ego-drive is the inner need to persuade another individual as a means for gaining one's own gratification. It is easy to see how these two personality traits could combine to produce a forceful sales presentation.

More recent research supports the importance of empathy as a predictor of a salesperson's performance, and adds an additional dimension: professionalism.[7] In the sales context, professionalism refers to having favorable and appropriate conduct and presentation skills. Interestingly, researchers Pilling and Eroglu, in a survey of retail buyers from across the United States, found evidence that professionalism has a positive impact on a buyer's intention to listen to future sales presentations—but only if the salesperson showed high levels of empathy. As the researchers noted, "buyers may be distrustful of high 'professionalism' in the absence of a caring attitude."[8]

Although tests that include intelligence, personality, and aptitude/skills do have a higher correlation with later performance in nonselling occupations than do application forms, reference checks, experience, and personal interviews,[9] personal interview results were found to have a high correlation with later sales performance of new retail sales personnel.[10] This finding is probably explained by the fact that the interview of a sales candidate is very similar to the selling process that will be used by the salesperson. Thus good performance in the personal interview should be a good predictor of later selling performance.

Additional reasons why companies prefer personal interviews three to one over testing[11] include the cost of testing, delays in getting results, doubts that the test is specific to the job, the fact that tests turn off some applicants, and a legal concern. The company must be ready to demonstrate that the test has been validated for the job requirements and does not discriminate against a protected group. Perhaps one group finds it easier to take tests than another group because of differences in educational opportunities or backgrounds. In that case, all tests could be discriminatory. The validity and reliability of personality tests, therefore, is controversial when selecting salespeople. Companies that use validated tests use them to examine the candidate's ability to reason clearly, communicate effectively, and have personality traits that match those of successful candidates. These companies stress the fact that the test is one of many sources of information to make a decision to hire or not.

Personal interviews have their own limitations. Individual managers have biases that can flavor their evaluation of a job candidate. Team-based interviewing may help avoid this problem. In team-based interviews, a series of one-on-one interviews with the same candidate is followed by a meeting of the interviewers to consolidate their evaluations. Such a process helps to cancel out individual biases.

One personality trait has been shown to lead to success in school, politics, work, and sales. That trait is **optimism.**[12] The need to find a better predictor of success in sales was explained by John Creedon, president of Metropolitan Life Insurance. Each year 60,000 applicants were screened down to 5,000, using an insurance industry standard profile, testing, and interviewing techniques. Even with this extensive screening, half quit in the first year and 80% quit after four years. Because training costs were $30,000 per sales agent, he figured that Metropolitan lost $75 million per year in hiring costs and that thousands of persons became discouraged—a high social cost. Seligman, a professor of psychology, conducted experiments with Metropolitan in which it hired as agents persons who scored high on his optimism tests, but low on the insurance industry standard tests. He was able to demonstrate that optimism is an excellent predictor of success.[13] Seligman has also demonstrated that it is possible to turn pessimists into optimists, so that existing salespeople and executives can become more productive.[14]

Related to personality are the values that an individual holds as important. Research among industrial salespeople indicates that those who value personal achievement are more likely to be top performers.[15] These individuals value a sense of accomplishment, self-respect, self-fulfillment, and being well respected. The study found no relationship between a "fun and excitement" value structure and sales performance.

Managers must guard against stereotyping selling personalities. People do change. For example, in college Kathryn Braun was so shy her friends called her "the mouse." She was a computer field salesperson until she joined Western Digital, a supplier of disk controller boards, as an application engineer. She became vice president and general manager of storage products operations four years later. Her friends now regard her as aggressive. Thus shyness can be overcome.[16]

Job-Related Behavioral Traits   Many companies are turning to job-related behavioral traits because demographics, such as age or gender, have not been good predictors of sales performance, according to a study that examined 350,000 cases.[17] The limitations of personality and demographic variables became a legal matter when the Equal Employment Opportunity Commission required that companies have an Affirmative Action Program for hiring minorities, women, and other protected groups that validate all measurement techniques used for screening applicants. For these reasons, many sales managers are returning to measuring job-related behavioral traits on the assumption that past behavior, both successful and unsuccessful, is the best predictor of future behavior on the job.

Some job-related behavioral traits were discussed in Chapter 3. Additional ones that appear often in interview guides and are used by sales recruiters appear in Exhibit 9.2. Reading through the list, it is easy to see how some of these apply to selling activities. The salesperson must have a high level of physical and mental energy, be ambitious, have analytical abilities, seek challenges, and not be easily depressed. These behavioral traits are often built into managers' interviewing guides where they are ranked according to their importance to the job.

The ability to work on a team is a behavioral trait that is becoming increasingly important for salespeople. A study conducted by the Hay Group among 26 leading corpora-

---

Exhibit **9.2**	BEHAVIORAL TRAITS USED FOR SELECTING SALESPEOPLE

Decisiveness	Analytical abilities, problem analysis
History of successfully overcoming obstacles	Adaptability
Aggressiveness	Ambitiousness
Individualism	Average or above-average intelligence
People- and results-oriented	Communication skills, oral and written
Realistic ego drive	Breadth
Objective view of abilities and potentials for achievement	Average creative ability
Healthy maturity level	High energy level, physical/mental
Self-confidence	Deals with failure realistically
Requires less outside enforcement	Competitiveness
Decisions not affected by emotions	Self-motivation
Not easily depressed	Stress tolerance
Seeks challenges	Sensitivity
High degree of perceived self-worth	Tenacity
Trusts others only to a realistic degree	Planning and organizing abilities
Not really affected by peer or societal pressures	Resilience
Learning abilities	Integrity
Sales ability	Judgment

Sources consist of various screening documents for sales recruiting.

tions like General Electric and AT&T found that the ability to work on a team was a job requirement at all of the firms surveyed.[18]

When evaluating the candidate along behavioral traits, the manager must decide whether a person could correct a trait deficiency after proper training. For example, if a person is hired with only average skills in an area that cannot be learned easily, such as communications skills, that person is likely never to rise above a mediocre performance level. But some skills, such as planning, organizing, and persuading, can be learned with proper training and supervision. Thus selection depends on a judgment call regarding the candidate's ability to improve behavior along weak traits.

A perceptive sales manager should be able to identify these behavioral traits by studying the applicant's resume and asking questions. Exhibit 9.3 can help the manager prepare to ask probing questions during the interview. Some companies build a profile of people who have succeeded and those who have not to aid them in their hiring process.[19]

Assessment Centers   Some companies evaluate salespeople with assessment centers. These centers are intense testing environments that place candidates in problem settings where they must make realistic decisions and act upon their decisions. Origi-

---

Exhibit **9.3**   SAMPLE BEHAVIORAL TRAIT QUESTIONS

Adaptability: Look for geographic mobility and a variety of organization memberships. "How did you feel about the shift from a small (large) high school to a large (small) college? What kinds of problems did you face after your last move?"

Analytical Abilities: Courses (e.g., case courses) and jobs that required analysis and problem solving. "Describe how you have analyzed a recent problem and solved it."

Breadth: Hobbies, clubs, organizations, vacations, concerts, plays, lectures, reading habits. "What interesting books have you read in the last year? How do you spend your spare time?"

Oral Communication Skills: Courses, roles in clubs, speeches, public speaking courses. "What presentations have you made? How effective do you think you were?"

Written Communication Skills: Reports, newspaper articles, poetry, short stories, jobs requiring memos. "What reports have you written? How were they received? Do you make a major contribution to team reports?"

Creativity: Check resume for art, music, writing, photography, creative alternative solutions to problems. "Describe a situation where your creative solution solved a problem. Describe how you did something better than your predecessor on a job."

Energy Level: Look at history of previous employment, extracurricular activities, community service. "How do you spend your leisure time? What sports have you played during the last month?"

Learning Ability: Look beyond GPA to specific course performance. "What subjects come easy? Which were the hard ones?"

Motivation: Look in resume for evidence of goal setting, previous accomplishments, career focus, number of career changes.

Persuasiveness: Look for previous leadership or selling roles, course selection, hobbies, and previous employment. "Describe the most recent time that you persuaded someone to accept your point of view. If you have sold, describe your most satisfying sale."

Planning Abilities: Examine the educational plan, work, and extracurricular activities for evidence of using time effectively. "How do you establish your personal priorities? How do you organize your day?"

Sensitivity: Look for evidence of openness, willingness to listen, and awareness of the needs of others. "Describe the last time that someone came to you with a personal problem."

Stress Tolerance: Assess responses to high stress situations in previous jobs, physical activities, college experiences, and recreational activities. "Under what conditions are you most productive? When do you feel under pressure? How do you handle it? How do you handle interpersonal conflicts?"

Tenacity: Search for evidence that reflects striving for goals with a distant payoff. "Why did you change your college major? Describe a major obstacle that you overcame during the last year."

nally used by the government to recruit spies, assessment centers have been successful in selecting managers and salespeople. Developing a center requires a clear job analysis, the development and validation of exercises to measure critical job skills, assessor training, candidate evaluation procedures, and feedback to the candidate and the organization.[20]

(Referring to the case that opens this chapter, do you think Lois should recommend John Chang?)

Selection Procedures

Selection procedures are screens designed to eliminate candidates who have the lowest probability of success in selling from the pool of applicants. The tools used should begin with the lowest-cost and most valid tools and proceed to the higher-cost tools that are more difficult to validate. Using these criteria, Nelson suggested that the order of tools for recruiting salespeople should be: (1) resumes, (2) application forms, (3) reference checks, (4) personal interviews, and (5) tests.[21] Most companies use multiple interviews. The first one is a screening interview to decide whether to continue the candidate in the process. The brief screening interview would come before step 2, when the application form is given to the candidate. The outcome of this process should be a pool of applicants who have the highest probability of successfully fulfilling the activities in the job description.

Steps in the Selection Process   Each company will have its own selection process. Many firms use some variation on a written application followed by two sets of interviews. Firms can reduce turnover and increase employees' job satisfaction if they clarify work requirements to candidates.

For example, Russ Reed, general manager of W.S. Reed Co., an office products manufacturer in Grand Rapids, Michigan, gives sales candidates a written job description. Requirements include producing 100% or more of full quota, demonstrating effective work habits, continuing self-education on selling skills and product knowledge, maintaining a comprehensive account card on each client, and making 12 to 15 new account presentations a month.[22]

Research indicates that it is important for sales managers to look for candidates with a positive attitude toward the firm and the job. A study among salespeople with direct selling firms found that employees' intentions to quit were formed *before* their feelings about the organization's climate, rather than the other way around.[23] This suggests that it is important to build techniques into the recruitment process that detect the applicant's predisposition toward the position.

Exhibit 9.4 describes the steps that are used by field sales managers in a pharmaceutical company. The first contact with a candidate is often at a slide presentation, showing the typical day of a pharmaceutical salesperson, or an interview with a present detail salesperson. After a preliminary interview with a candidate, the district sales manager completes his or her screening interview notes. At this point, the manager decides whether to continue the process or send a turndown letter to the applicant. The second screening stage occurs when the applicant sends a completed application and a college transcript. The application is screened by the district sales manager who then interviews the candidate and either sends a turndown letter or arranges for the candidate to spend two days in the field with salespeople for a first-hand view of the job.

If the decision is to continue the screening process, the field sales manager obtains a motor vehicle report from the state in which the applicant is licensed, conducts a spouse information session with the applicant and spouse (if applicable), and contacts the applicant's references and previous employers. On the approval of the field sales manager the

Exhibit **9.4**	THE SELECTION PROCESS BY A PHARMACEUTICAL COMPANY

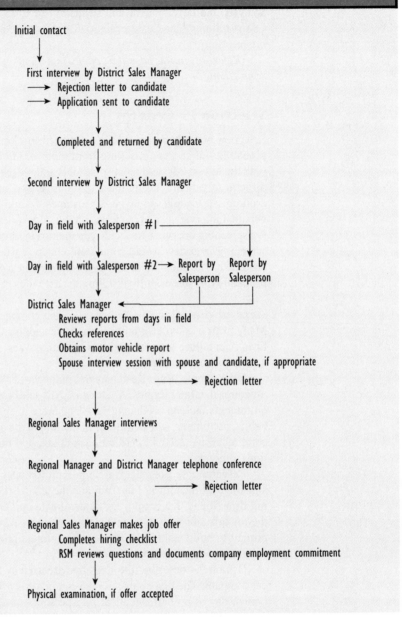

candidate is interviewed by the regional sales manager at the regional office. If hired, the necessary documents are completed and arrangements are made to have the applicant receive a physical examination.

Some sales managers process all of the paper and promise to hire an applicant as soon as there is an open territory. This procedure reduces uncertainty for the applicant and reduces the number of days of open territory for the company.

Exhibit **9.5**	RECRUIT'S QUESTIONS AND SOURCES OF ANSWERS

"How much will I make and how will I be rewarded?"
  Hiring contract, compensation ranges at entry level, commission rate, bonus programs, and fringe benefits.

"What are my job responsibilities?"
  Job description and current sales quotas.

"How well must I perform them?"
  Performance standards.

"How will I be evaluated?"
  Performance review, evaluation form, trip reports.

"How will I learn what is expected of me?"
  Training program, policies, procedures.

"To whom do I report?"
  Job description and organization chart.

"With whom will I work?"
  Orientation and organization chart.

"How do I get promoted?"
  Development program.

REFERENCE CHECKS

Most employers either skip reference checks or do them so poorly that they are useless. Reference checks do have limitations. One assumes that a candidate will not give as a reference a person who would not give a favorable report. Respondents to a reference check usually limit their responses to avoid personal or company liability.

Some steps that can be taken to improve the value of reference checks as a hiring tool include the following:

- Use former customer checks as primary sources, former employer checks as secondary ones.
- Prepare an opening statement and follow-up questions before you make your first contact.
- Listen carefully to responses—what isn't said is often just as important as what is said.[24] Some respondents can be very creative in not giving unfavorable information, to protect themselves from a possible law suit.

Before conducting reference checks, a manager should be certain to have witnessed, signed releases from the applicants that allow contacting previous employers and educational institutions.[25] Reference checks can make the manager and the company liable for invasion of privacy.

A Final Step in the Selection Process   The final interview with the regional manager can be a tense experience for the candidate so that many of the questions asked and the manager's answers will not be remembered by the candidate. To help the new recruit, some experienced companies have reduced the common questions and sources of answers to a document like Exhibit 9.5.

To assure that sales management personnel policies do not have adverse impacts on protected groups, the sales manager must apply the four-fifths rule to all personnel decisions from recruiting through promoting or firing. This rule, as previously described, when applied to the selection decision, states that the selection rate for minorities must not be less than four-fifths, or 80 percent, of the majority group selection rate. Procedures and criteria for validating tests for selection should conform to the professional standards of educational and testing associations.

Recruiting Documentation   Keeping extensive records regarding selection and rejection of sales applicants is good for many reasons. The most obvious is the need to document a decision in case the company faces a suit regarding adverse impact on a minority group or a complaint by the applicant. But the documentation can also be positive. A company should identify those sources of candidates and selection procedures that generate candidates who have the highest probability of success on the job.

To assure proper documentation and to assure uniformity across all interviews some companies have forms for the interviewer. Confidentiality prevents reporting these forms for specific companies, but we can outline the kinds of items that are found in the interview guides used by companies that sell to grocery and hardware stores.

First Interview, for Initial Screening

1. Instructions to the Interviewer: Put the candidate at ease, explain the purpose of the first interview, and note points in the application or resume that need clarification.
2. Clarify gaps in education, employment history, job hopping, and specific interests in the company.
3. Determine if candidate should have an in-depth interview by having him/her discuss education, career goals, accomplishments, and interest in company.
4. At this point the interviewer gives literature and describes the opportunities, including products, responsibilities, location, training, compensation, and benefits.
5. The candidate is asked what he or she thinks of and expects from the job and whether he or she feels qualified. The candidate is evaluated on behavioral traits such as goals, interpersonal skills, problem-solving ability, communication skills, individual characteristics, and leadership. After the candidate leaves, the interviewer rates him or her along these dimensions and makes a recommendation for an in-depth interview or a rejection.

Second, In-Depth, Interview

This interview covers the same items as step 5 in the first interview, but in more depth. The interviewer is provided with specific questions for each item. The form has ample space for writing replies from the candidate. Summary scores are again given for these traits and a recommendation is made to advance or reject the candidate.

Recruiting by Consulting Firms

Because recruiting has become expensive in terms of managers' time and because it requires special skills and screening instruments, many companies are turning to consulting firms that specialize in recruiting. We will examine the procedures used by two companies, The Gallup Organization and Selecting Winners.

The Gallup Organization, formerly known as Selection Research Incorporated, has a five-step process to develop interviewing instruments for clients. They then use this instrument to screen candidates that they have recruited though advertisements, web sites, and other sources.

1. Have the client identify the best salespeople, those who they would like to clone. Ask why these persons were put in the best category. Typical answers include "best with customers," "highest sales volume," "she has a tough territory but sales are up," or "he knows how to sell new accounts."

2. A job analysis is conducted using six or eight of the best salespersons in each of several focus-group interviews. The goal of these sessions is to identify the culture, knowledge, skills, attitudes, abilities, and perceptions that are needed to succeed. The qualities identified in these sessions are converted into questions for future testing. First they are sorted into similar construct categories and compared with 7500 questions in the SRI-Gallup database which has been developed in over 20 years of this research. Questions are now evaluated to be consistent with EEOC requirements.

   Questions are mostly behavioral and job-related. The respondent will give a top-of-mind awareness response by drawing on his or her own behavioral patterns for a response. No clues are given to indicate a correct answer because there is no correct answer. But the analysts who review the responses search for a *listen-for*. The *listen-for* is the kind of response that is given by successful representatives.

   The same question can be used to screen candidates for different positions, but the *listen-for* will be different. For example, "How do you feel when someone doubts what you say?" will get a negative emotional response from an excellent salesperson. They say, "I don't like it, it bothers me that people don't trust me." In screening teachers the response is positive. "I like it when someone doubts what I have to say because it shows that the student is learning."

3. The next stage is a pilot interview using persons in the company who have been outstanding salespeople and a contrasting group that has been less successful. The interviewers and the analysts do not know how management has classified these pilot individuals. These interviews are often conducted by telephone because Gallup has found that there is no significant difference between telephone and personal interviews.

4. At this stage a trained analyst reviews a transcript of the interview and scores the *listen-fors*. A statistical analysis of these scores with managements' rating of the success level of the pilot respondents reduces a question pool of 150 to 40 to 80 questions for the final version.

5. The instrument is now ready to be used, along with other information, for the employment decision. A predictive validity study is conducted when enough candidates have been hired and their performance evaluated.[26]

Barry Shamis, Managing Partner of Selecting Winners, a division of Target Market Systems, describes a six-step process that they use.

1. Write a profile of successful persons, noting the behavioral traits that indicate that they do the right things in the right way.

2. Recruit qualified candidates using innovative approaches and working hard. Work backwards. Where are these people today? The successful ones are not reading want ads. Use computer on-line sources. Focus on technical or professional journals. Use present successful employees, who are the best sources.

3. Initial screening is to determine if the consultant wants to spend more time on the candidate. Shamis screens the resume and then uses a telephone interview to advance or reject the candidate. Read the resume in chronological order to

understand what brought them to where they are. Look for patterns, trends, and gaps.

4. The personal interview should start with easy, direct questions and then move to ones that have only one answer, have a planned purpose, and are job-related. Probing questions should follow answers to previous questions. Ask for examples, and then more examples.

5. Data verification requires reference checks to verify behavioral traits that were identified earlier. Put the burden on the candidate to find references who are willing to talk about the quality of work that she or he has done.

6. Evaluation of the candidate uses a simple matrix that has the requirements in the rows and the candidates in the columns. Each candidate is evaluated along each requirement one at a time. These evaluations must be supported with data gathered during the process.

Shamis has found that when companies use this process they quickly converge on the candidate to hire.[27]

Legal Dimensions of Selection

There are two legal dimensions to consider when hiring a salesperson. First, every step in the recruiting and selecting processes must be consistent with the company's Affirmative Action Compliance Program (AACP) in order to implement Title VII of the Civil Rights Act of 1964. The Equal Employment Opportunity Commission (EEOC) was created to administer Title VII and has direct access to the courts.

A sales manager's affirmative action compliance program should include a guide on preemployment inquiries so that recruitment does not discriminate. This guide should indicate what questions regarding gender, marital status, and physical data may be asked without violating federal regulations. The guide must identify criteria that are "bona fide occupational qualifications (BFOQ)." Age and gender may be BFOQs when hiring a fashion model, but may be illegal when hiring a salesperson. Exhibit 9.6 provides an interview guide to the types of inquiries that are discriminatory and those that are acceptable. Such lists can never be complete because they are continuously affected by court decisions. A company should prepare such a list by consulting current publications of the Equal Employment Opportunity Commission.

The second legal concern is common in computer hardware, software, and other high-tech companies. Some employees know trade secrets. It could be difficult for the new company to prove that it did not use these secrets. The potential new employee may have signed a contract with the former employer precluding employment with a competitor for a specified period of time. Be certain to ask and get appropriate answers in writing.[28]

EVALUATING THE RECRUITING AND SELECTION PROCESS

Recruiting and selecting, like other sales management activities, must be evaluated continuously. Two procedures for such an evaluation are measuring turnover rates and staffing productivity measures.

Turnover rates may be computed by dividing the number of salespeople who left in a given time period by the average size of the sales force during that time period. For example, if 22 salespeople left or were terminated, and if there were 200 salespeople at the beginning of the year and 240 at the end of the year, the average sales force size would be

| Exhibit **9.6** | AN INTERVIEW GUIDE FOR AFFIRMATIVE ACTION COMPLIANCE PROGRAMS |

Name: Ask if the applicant used another name during work or educational experiences to verify qualifications, but do not ask for a father's surname or if a name has been changed.

Gender: Notice appearance, but don't make comments unless gender is a bona fide occupational qualification.

Creed or Religion: Although you cannot ask affiliations, holidays observed, or the name of a spiritual leader, you can ask whether special arrangements need to be made for working on Saturdays or Sundays.

Race or Color: Questions of race, color of skin/eyes/hair may not be used and photographs are not permitted.

Marital Status: After the candidate is hired you may ask, for insurance purposes, if a person is married, single, divorced, has children and if so, their ages.

Age: Minimum age questions, such as, "Are you 18?" are acceptable and you may ask age questions after hiring, as required for insurance purposes. Before hiring you may not observe or guess age.

Physical Data: Asking height or weight could have an adverse impact on Spanish-surnamed and Asian-Americans. If the job involves manual labor, describe the requirements. You may require a physical examination.

Criminal Record: You may not ask if a person has been arrested, convicted, or spent time in jail unless it is related to a job. You would not hire a convicted bank robber as a bank teller or a drug addict as a pharmaceutical salesperson.

Military Experience: You may ask about job-related military experiences but not whether the person was in the service, type of discharge, or draft status.

Housing: You cannot ask about present housing (e.g., apartment, live with parents, etc.) because these are economic status questions that reflect unfavorably on minorities. You can ask for ways to contact a person if he or she does not have a telephone.

Citizenship: The law protects lawfully immigrated aliens, so you cannot ask about citizenship. You can ask if a person's visa prevents working in this country.

Education: Educational questions are acceptable only when job related.

Organizations: Memberships in professional groups are appropriate, but not social organizations.

Language: Job-related language questions are appropriate, but the language spoken at home or by parents is not an appropriate inquiry.

National Origin: One's national origin or that of one's spouse may not be asked.

Relatives: Names and addresses of relatives may be asked only as persons to be notified in case of an emergency.

Sources: Collected corporate screening documents.

220 and the turnover rate would be 0.10, or 10%. The computations are as follows:

$$22 / ((200 + 240) / 2) = 22/220 = 0.10, \text{ or } 10\%$$

Employee turnover has many associated costs. One is the cost of lost business; others include termination costs, such as severance pay and storage of idle equipment. Hiring costs include agency fees, advertising expenses, interviewing time for all persons involved, travel costs for the applicants and interviewers, relocation expenses, and screening expenses such as medical and psychological examinations. Additional training costs may include fees at training centers and by field trainers, training materials, and travel associated with training. Additional supervision is required by field sales managers. A rough estimate of all of these figures gives a total monthly impact per salesperson who left the company. Multiplying this expense by the number of terminations will give the total expense of salesperson turnover. An examination of the total cost of turnover suggests that spending more on recruiting and selection would be a good investment.

Staffing productivity measures are the number of candidates generated; their quality, as measured by the number who make it through to the final screen; the proportion who stay with the company; and the number who move to higher management.

Case 9.1   THE CASE OF SALLY SIMPSON

Sally Simpson was hired by National Business Forms, in June, three weeks after graduating from St. David's College with a B.A. in history. St. David's is a liberal arts college with an enrollment of approximately 4000 undergraduates, located in Schenectady, New York, 35 miles from Amsterdam, where Sally's family has lived for two generations. Sally is the youngest of six children. While at St. David's, Sally was a member of the drama club, a cheerleader, a member of the honor society, and graduated *cum laude*. She spent her junior year in France in a language program and worked each of the past three summers at a prep school in New England.

National Business Forms, headquartered in Baltimore, was expanding its sales force in the midwest, and in recruiting at St. David's had hired three graduates, including Sally. The initial screening interview was conducted by a recruiting team from National's personnel department, with the final interview by the personnel manager in Baltimore. Along with two other applicants recruited from Kansas City and Chicago, Sally was assigned to Scott Johnson's district and given a territory radiating out of St. Louis into parts of Illinois and Missouri, which required her to be away from her St. Louis home base a total of 15 working days out of a nine-week cycle. National Business Forms relocated about two-thirds of all new salespeople they hired. They paid for a trip to St. Louis for Sally to locate an apartment and all of the expenses of Sally's move. They provided a car, base salary, a bonus, and reasonable expenses.

Sally's District Sales Manager, Scott Johnson, headquartered in Chicago, supervised eleven salespeople in Illinois, Indiana, Missouri (four in St. Louis), Wisconsin, and Iowa, including two other women salespeople in Chicago and Milwaukee.

Sally got off to a good start in the training class in Baltimore and worked with two salespeople in their territories for two weeks before returning to St. Louis, where John Faircloth, the senior salesperson in St. Louis, helped her get started. For the four months following her field training, Sally had been very busy. She made a full trip around her territory, including the three weeks of travel, set up her records, prepared the required reports, and expanded her knowledge of the industry and the company's products via the correspondence courses sent to her by the sales training department.

Scott Johnson had spent two days with Sally in field training activities during each of the past four months, as he did with all of his trainees. In his last trip report on Sally, he had expressed his approval of her sustained effort and the progress she was making. He complimented her on her positive attitude, the way customers responded to her personality and friendly approach, the improvement he had noted in her knowledge and skills on each of the past three trips, and her general understanding of the job.

Sally had mentioned several times the heavy volume of the work and the fact that the job was tougher and took more of her personal time than she had expected, but that she thought she was gradually getting on top of it. She complained somewhat that the training assignments, study time, reports, and travel had so limited her free time that she hadn't had the opportunity to make any friends.

Scott did his best to put her immediate concerns in perspective and to make Sally realize that, although field sales was tough at first, as she became more knowledgeable she would be able to accomplish the required reporting and planning more quickly. He also assured her that as she worked her territory repeatedly she would establish friendships with many of her customers' employees. He tried to make her realize that the period of training required more concentration and effort on everyone's part to enable her to achieve the required level of competence, and that her progress to date was ahead of that of the average trainee.

Sally was pleased to receive his evaluation and reassurances, and reaffirmed her determination to qualify for the next advanced training class. As a result, Scott was surprised and disappointed on his return from working with the Cedar Rapids representative to receive a telephone call from Sally saying she had just returned from an out-of-town swing and was so discouraged that she was resigning and wanted to be checked out as quickly as possible. When pressed for an explanation, Sally said she had tried her best but she felt that she just wasn't suited for the work. Scott reluctantly accepted her decision and planned to fly to St. Louis on Monday.

CASE QUESTIONS

1. What major job-related behavioral characteristics are required for a job as a field salesperson?

2. How would these behavioral characteristics differ from those required for an in-plant salesperson?

3. Would any different behavioral characteristics be required for a salesperson with a territory where a significant amount of traveling (up to 50%) is required?

4. What qualifications does Sally Simpson have that match the behavioral characteristics for the job for which she was hired?

5. For what business reasons might an interviewer hire an applicant whose qualifications did not reasonably match the required job-related behavioral characteristics?

6. Who should conduct the final hiring interview: (a) a member of the personnel department, (b) the field sales manager to whom the applicant will report, (c) any field sales manager? List the advantages and disadvantages of each.

7. Should Sally Simpson have been hired? Was this a mistake in interviewing and hiring or in orientation and training?

Case **9.2**	THE SCREENING INTERVIEW

With another classmate, role play Lois and John in the opening case. What questions would you ask him in the in-depth interview?

Would you hire him?

Case **9.3**	STORM CLOUDS

Although emphasis at National Hardware Products had always been on current dollar and product group sales versus forecasts and on an analysis of the calling activities of salespeople, recently pressure had come from management for salespeople to increase their recruiting activities and to follow through on account col-lection. A heated discussion occurred at the last sales meeting about these added activities.

Why? What are likely to be some of the key issues for the sales-people? What are likely issues for management? What should be done to resolve the two viewpoints?

HIRING FOR FOREIGN ASSIGNMENTS

Many salespeople have foreign assignments or work with foreign nationals. Initial hiring screening for these salespeople should include questions that probe their behavior in dif-ferent cultures. Are they patient with cultures that are not as time-driven as the United States? Can they accept the fact that the way things are done in the United States may not be the best way in another country? Many companies provide training for the candidate and his or her family before a move abroad. This training is similar to multicultural train-ing within the United States to sensitize managers to the need to draw on the strengths of diversity. A salesperson returning from a foreign assignment also needs training.

FIRING SALESPEOPLE

The other end of the staffing process is employee termination. Richard Deems, a career management consultant, believes that many sales managers are reluctant or unable to fire salespeople, but it goes with the territory. Deems suggests a five-step process for effec-tively firing a salesperson:[29]

- Identify the problem. Be clear and specific.
- Discuss the problem with the salesperson. Outline expectations and consequences in a written memo. Sign the memo and have the salesperson sign as well.
- Offer assistance.
- Allow time for improvement. Deems recommends allowing two-to-six weeks for the salesperson to demonstrate improvement.
- Fire the salesperson if the agreed-upon improvement is not forthcoming. Deems recommends firing at the beginning of the day, allowing the sales manager enough time to communicate the decision to the rest of the team. These discussions can fo-cus on the firm's performance values. Outplacement counseling as well as a sever-ance package can help the terminated salesperson find a new position.

··

SUMMARY

Subsequent sales management tasks are made easier by a good system for recruiting and selecting candidates. This system begins with planning the sales force requirements with regard to the quantity and quality of salespeople needed. The job description, the selling plan, and the sales forecasts help the sales manager to determine the sales force requirements. In recruiting candidates, the sales manager must make certain that sources used will not adversely impact minority persons. The selection process begins with criteria for selection that are job related. It represents a tradeoff between the immediate need to fill a territory and finding the ideal candidate. The Civil Rights Act adds many new dimensions to the process of recruiting and selecting. Interviewers must phrase their questions carefully and keep complete records.

Evaluations of the recruiting and selection process use measures such as the number of candidates produced and the turnover costs after recruitment.

ASSIGNMENTS/DISCUSSION QUESTIONS

1. Students should exchange resumes before a class session and prepare questions for interviewing each other. During the class session, students will be called upon to serve as the interviewer and the candidate. Use the exhibits in this chapter. The class will be required to evaluate the process.

2. What are the objectives of the selection interview?

3. What is the value to the interviewer of a written application?

4. What are selection criteria and what is their importance?

5. Where are selection criteria derived from?

6. Which subject should be covered first in the selection interview—information about the job or about the applicant? Why?

7. What are the relative advantages of turning the applicant down in person and in writing?

8. What rewards or benefits can be expected from recruiting and selecting qualified applicants?

9. What costs can be expected from poor personnel selection?

10. What is the purpose of checking references, previous employers, resume information, professors, etc.?

11. Working with a team, brainstorm the advantages to the firm—and to the affected salesperson—when a sales manager fires him or her for just cause.

ENDNOTES

1. L.A. Crosby, K.R. Evans, and D. Cowles, Relationship Quality in Services Selling: An Interpersonal Influence Approach, *Journal of Marketing,* 54, July 1990, pp. 68–81.
2. Geoffrey Brewer, Brain Power, *Sales & Marketing Management,* May 1997, pp. 39–48.
3. Shankar Ganesan, Barton A. Weitz, and George John, Hiring and Promotion Policies in Sales Force Management: Some Antecedents and Consequences, *Journal of Personal Selling & Sales Management,* 13(2), Spring 1993, pp. 15–25.
4. Michele Marchetti, Toasting Sales Support Staff, *Sales & Marketing Management,* April 1996, pp. 33–34.

5. Testing and Selecting Employees' Guidelines, *Employment Practice Guide 11* (1978) Chicago: Commerce Clearing House, pp. 2223–2224.

6. J. Greenberg and H. M. Greenberg, Predicting Sales Success—Myths and Reality, *Personnel Journal* 55:12, December 1976, pp. 621–627.

7. Bruce K. Pilling and Sevo Eroglu, An Empirical Investigation of the Impact of Salesperson Empathy and Professionalism and Merchandise Salability on Retail Buyers' Evaluations, *Journal of Personal Selling & Sales Management,* 14, Winter, 1994, pp. 45–58.

8. Ibid., p. 56.

9. John E. Hunter and R.F. Hunter, Validity and Utility of Alternative Predictors of Job Performance, *Psychological Bulletin* 96, 1984, pp. 72–98.

10. Richard D. Arvey and J.E. Campion, The Employment Interview: A Summary and Review of Recent Research, *Personnel Psychology* 35, 1982, pp. 736–65.

11. Alan J. Dubinsky and Thomas E. Barry, A Survey of Sales Management Practices, *Industrial Marketing Management* 11, 1982, p. 136.

12. Martin E.P. Seligman (1991), *Learned Optimism,* New York: Alfred A. Knopf.

13. Seligman, pp. 97–101.

14. Seligman, pp. 207–292.

15. Michael J. Swenson and Joel Herche, Social Values and Salesperson Performance: An Empirical Examination, *Journal of the Academy of Marketing Science,* 22(3), Summer, 1994, pp. 283–289.

16. Sue Kapp, The Mouse that Roared, *Business Marketing* 72:10, October, 1987, pp. 9, 12.

17. Greenberg and Greenberg, pp. 621–22.

18. Geoffrey Brewer, Brain Power, *Sales & Marketing Management,* May, 1997, pp. 39–48.

19. Andy Anderson, S&MM Roundtable, *Sales & Marketing Management,* September, 1991, p. 70.

20. C. Patrick Fleenor, Selling & Sales Management in Action: Assessment Center Selection of Sales Representatives, *Journal of Personal Selling & Sales Management* 7:1, May, 1987, pp. 57–59.

21. Richard Nelson, Maybe It's Time to Take Another Look at Tests as a Sales Selection Tool? *Journal of Personal Selling & Sales Management* 7:2, August, 1987, pp. 33–38.

22. Barry J. Farber, Start at the Beginning: Managers Must Groom Sales Stars Even Before They Get in the Door, *Sales & Marketing Management,* 148(3), March, 1996, p. 24.

23. Predeep K. Tyagi and Thomas R. Wotruba, An Exploratory Study of Reverse Causality Relationships Among Sales Force Turnover Variables, *Journal of the Academy of Marketing Science,* 21(2) Spring 1993, pp. 143–153.

24. Robert G. Head, Systematizing Salesperson Selection, *Sales & Marketing Management,* February, 1992, pp. 66–67.

25. Arthur Bragg, Checking References, *Sales & Marketing Management* 142(13), November, 1990, pp. 68–73.

26. Dr. Richard E. Harding, Vice President, Research, SRI Gallup, personal correspondence, August 11, 1992.

27. Barry Shamis, Managing Partner, Selecting Winners, a division of Target Market Systems, personal correspondence, March 28, 1997.

28. John C. Yates, Recruiting: Can you keep a secret? *The Culpepper Letter,* Number 152, October, 1996.

29. Geoffrey Brewer, The Fine Art of Firing, *Sales & Marketing Management,* April, 1997, p. 67.

10

TRAINING, COACHING, AND DEVELOPING SALESPEOPLE

LEARNING GOALS

1. To expand on the staffing functions and activities introduced in Chapter 9
2. To understand the differences between training, coaching, and counseling, and to develop skills that can be applied to case problems
3. To be able to design a training program

AN OPENING CASE

One of your new salespeople is being badly beaten by the competition. You first noted the problem through lost-order reports. Later he asked for help. You made some sales calls with him and assisted him in closing three orders. You have also worked with him on sales techniques and proposal writing skills. He is scheduled for a training session to improve his product knowledge. Although you would like to spend more time with him, given his high potential, your workload is massive at this time. In addition to your managerial duties, you have been covering two territories vacated by salespeople who resigned. You can't afford to spend any more time with him, but you know that the company can't continue to lose business to competitors.

How do you define the problem? What are some alternative solutions? You should be able to answer these questions after reading this chapter.

THE MANAGERS' TRAINING TASKS

Mark Twain told the story of a man who spent his life in search of the greatest general of all time. When the man died and went to heaven, St. Peter met him and said,

"I know of your quest. The greatest general died before you did. Come, I will introduce you." When the man was introduced he was shocked. "I know this man. He was the cobbler in my hometown." St. Peter replied, "Yes, but had he been a general, he would have been the greatest general of all time." This story was told by Dr. Donald O. Clifton, the founder of Selection Research (now The Gallup Organization), a consulting company that helps clients select and develop salespersons, managers, and executives. Clearly the cobbler was never in an environment that would allow him to develop his potential.

Clifton went on to say, "After my 30 years of studying successful, productive executives, managers, athletes, salespersons, and organizations, I have come to the conclusion that productivity more than anything else is a matter of helping people become, not what they might have been, but becoming more of what they already are."[1] He turns the definition of management around. Instead of "management is getting work done through people," he sees management as "getting people done through work."[2] The inference is clear: people who are developed properly will be productive. *Selecting qualifiable people,* putting them in a *self-motivating environment,* and *providing focused training experiences* will make the organization successful. If a general sales manager can accomplish both of these tasks the sales force will be productive. To accomplish these tasks the general sales manager must understand present organizational designs, the forces that demand change, the successes in new designs, the limitations of some of the new designs, and finally, how to select and train sales managers.

A young sales trainer may need the advice that a newspaper editor gave a young cub reporter who was told to find the story; the editor said to answer the questions who, what, when, where, why, and how. The sales trainer must also answer these questions, but in a slightly different order. Why is sales training necessary? Who should be trained? What should be the content of the training program? When should the training be given? How should the training be done? Who should the trainers be? Where should the training take place? How should the training programs be evaluated?

Field sales managers play three important roles in orienting and training salespeople. First, they must orient and train people in selling. Second, they must identify on-going training needs of existing salespeople. And third, they must identify salespeople who are candidates for management positions and help prepare them for these new roles. Thus the sales manager is helping to develop the future management capabilities of the company. The importance of such development has been expressed by the Chinese philosopher Kuan Teu who, in 300 BC, said, "If you are going to plan for a year, plant corn; if you are going to plan for a decade, plant trees; if you are going to plan for a lifetime, train and develop people."

Training is one of the key predictors of selling success.[3] The ability of the sales manager to identify training needs, focus the training program on those needs, and continuously revise the training program as training needs change will be an important determinant of the sales force's performance. The training factor becomes particularly crucial in selling environments where products and services rapidly become obsolete.[4]

The relationship between training and other sales management activities may be seen in the flow chart in Exhibit 10.1. The job description helps identify the desired qualifications for the recruiting and selection efforts. Some companies prefer to recruit applicants with no previous sales experience who have similar backgrounds so that they may use a standardized orientation and training program. Other companies adjust their training programs to the diversity of the recruits. The trainee's qualifications and the company's orientation and training program produce knowledge, attitudes, skills, and habits that will lead to results. Performance appraisals are used to evaluate these results and to identify the need for more training. This appraisal also determines compensation levels.

Exhibit 10.1 THE RELATIONSHIP BETWEEN TRAINING AND OTHER SALES MANAGEMENT FUNCTIONS

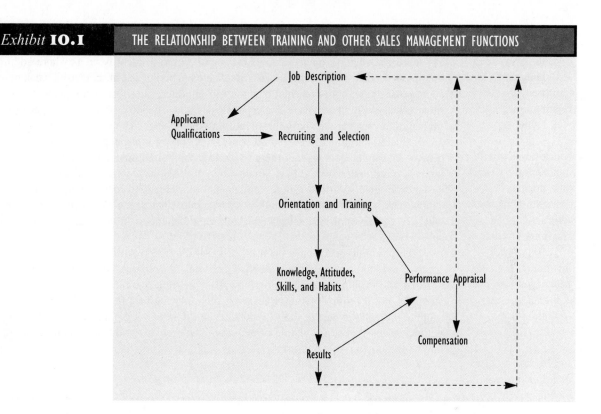

WHY TRAIN?

A training program for salespeople is critical because they operate with minimum supervision. The goal of training is not just to communicate information, but also to change the individual's behavior. The goals for a new salesperson may be to create positive attitudes; to orient him or her toward the company, its products, and the territory and community; and to help the salesperson satisfy his or her personal needs. The training goal from the company viewpoint may be to lower the cost of new recruits by speeding their personal development. The company will also have goals for expanding the sales force or providing a flow of qualified persons to meet future needs.

Training programs for current, experienced salespeople may have goals of improving morale, motivation, or customer relations. Experienced salespeople need training when there are new products, new markets, new competition, new technology, and new marketing strategies. Special training programs may exist for older salespeople with declining performance who have been resisting changes in the selling environment, or whose skills have not kept pace with the changing environment. Increases in productivity may be sought by improving skills in territory management, time utilization, negotiation, closing and other elements of the selling process, consultative selling, and knowledge of the entire marketing process. Better training may also have as its goal reducing necessary supervision and reducing the turnover of the sales force. Some companies have goals of improving territory reports, forecasts, and recordkeeping in general. Finally, salespeople with a potential for management may be given training in management.

The broad objective of sales training is an improvement in an individual's job-related behaviors that translates into superior job performance. This objective is shared by motivation programs (Chapter 11), better evaluations and feedback (Chapter 13), and compensation plans (Chapter 14).

A variety of performance deficiencies can be used to identify areas where additional training is needed. These deficiencies are reflected in poor sales, absenteeism, weak new account prospecting, poor presentations, low closing rates, sales lost to competitors, high territory costs, and high turnover of salespeople per year. The job description and performance evaluation reviews are the basis for identifying the deficiencies in these productivity rates.

To identify training needs some companies survey salespeople, field managers, and general sales managers, asking them to identify their strengths, their weaknesses, and the kinds of training they would like. Small-group discussions are used to identify problem areas and possible solutions. Some companies hold telephone focus groups (a conference call with about eight people) with their salespeople. Customer surveys are used to identify what customers want in a salesperson and the deficiencies in company and competitive salespeople.

When training needs have been identified and agreed upon by all concerned, the person in charge of training should establish priorities for training with management and then proceed to develop a training program. The program should build on an individual's strengths, not try to make him or her over into a new person. It should be made clear that training is a routine part of the salesperson's job. The training plan should include a clear outline of objectives, a schedule of activities, the methods and materials to be used, and how the results will be measured.

WHO SHOULD BE TRAINED?

Because training is a continuous process, the question, "Who should be trained?" can be answered very simply: everyone. Training for the new salesperson must be heavy in orientation and selling skills. The experienced salesperson will need training in marketing, new products, and management. Problem salespeople will need training or retraining that is specific to their particular needs. The older salesperson will need encouragement to learn new products and methods. The sales manager will also want to tap the knowledge of these older people by using them as field sales trainers.

WHAT SHOULD BE THE CONTENT OF THE TRAINING PROGRAM?

Expenditures on training do not lead directly to training-based performance. The sales manager's role is to translate the training budget into the proper mix of training content. For example, research conducted by Adel El-Ansary on the training practices of sales forces in the paper and plastics industry found no significant difference among the training budgets of more-successful and less-successful firms.[5] Instead, he found that training content was more strategy-focused among top-performance firms, and more knowledge-focused among lower-performing firms. Overall, the content of training programs can be divided into four parts—orientation, organizational strategy, selling activities, and follow-through.

Orientation

The orientation program requires an understanding of the needs of the new employee. The new college graduate entering a sales career, for example, faces uncertainty, anxiety, and discomfort as he or she leaves the familiar surroundings of the college campus. The orientation program should be designed to reduce these uncertainties and reassure the candidate that the right career decision was made. It should be a very positive experience because of new friends, a new environment, learning new skills, and the excitement of being part of a dynamic industry and company. Complete orientation programs include materials about the industry, the company, the role of personal selling in the marketing mix, the channels of distribution, the territory, the community, and the informal social structure of which the applicant will be a part.

Company orientation includes its history, its products, corporate policies, and procedures for accomplishing routine tasks. The new applicant's position in the organization is identified with organizational charts that clearly define reporting relationships. The role of personal selling in the marketing mix is also described in the discussion of company policies and procedures. At this point the new salesperson learns whether a salesperson in this company is a communicator or a consultant.

Orientation into the territory includes details such as trading areas, streets, travel routes, parking facilities, and territory records that include customer and prospect names, past strategies, and buying patterns. Much of this type of training takes place on the job. When the job requires out-of-town travel, the training includes procedures for lodging, additional supplies of samples, and a forward itinerary that informs the field sales manager and home office where the salesperson will be in case of an emergency.

It is important that the salesperson feels at home in a new environment, so community orientation is important. Community orientation includes social and athletic facilities available, churches, banking, and housing details such as telephone, gas, and electricity. Of particular importance is the introduction of the new salesperson to other company salespeople living nearby. Field sales managers who take this phase of orientation seriously help the new trainee overcome many initial anxieties.

The informal company social structure can help the new salesperson bridge the gap between college life and corporate life. This structure provides opportunities for meeting people individually as well as at social gatherings and recreational activities. A company with high turnover among young salespeople will want to examine its orientation program carefully.

Organizational Strategy

Salespeople work within the larger context of business-to-business competition. They must make day-to-day decisions within this context, consistent with their understanding of their firm's strategy. Providing insight into the firm's strategy allows firms to become more involved in helping to make that strategy succeed. It also helps guide the salespeople in the many small decisions—about pricing, product allocation priorities, positioning of the firm in sales presentations, and the like—that must be made in the field with little or no supervision.

Strategic training includes information about strategic markets, product strategies, and company and competitor strategies. Research indicates that this type of information may account for much of the differences between successful sales forces and those that are less successful.[6]

Selling Activities

The content of training programs in selling skills may be divided into four categories—*k*nowledge, *a*ttitudes, *s*kills, and *h*abits (KASH). Some trainers feel that attitudes are most important, habits are second in importance, followed by skills, and then knowledge.[7] The salesperson must have extensive **knowledge,** not only about his or her company and products, but also about industry trends, customer organizational structures and decision makers, competitors' activities, and economic conditions that influence customers' buying decisions. In industrial selling, the salesperson must understand the production process of prospects in order to make proper product applications. He or she also needs to know technical details of the product, pricing, production scheduling, warehousing and shipping details, servicing, and corporate credit policies. All of these subject areas may be included in initial and continuing training programs.

Knowledge is particularly important in the pharmaceutical industry where a misstatement about a drug can be fatal. Merck, Sharp & Dohme is regarded by some observers as having the best sales force in the pharmaceutical industry. Its training program first covers medical basics such as anatomy and physiology before moving into the second phase: up to 1 year on company products. Phase three covers diseases and indications treated by its products. Every 2 years each salesperson attends a 1 week medical school update on diseases. Individual training is provided by a mentor in a hospital to learn the practical elements of drugs. Bimonthly district meetings review the latest developments in treatments.[8]

A customer-oriented **attitude** is another key ingredient in the sales training mix. As Ed Mello, vice president of marketing and client development at CSC Consulting in Dallas notes of the training program for his 250-person sales force: "We're really trying to drive empathy in our salespeople . . . All solutions have to be expressed in the currency of the client."[9] Similarly, Boston-based Fidelity Investments Institutional Services uses role-playing and classroom work to teach salespeople to ask questions that probe customers' problems from their viewpoint.

Another additudinal issue is the use of problem-focused coping—rather than emotional coping—to deal with the stress of selling.[10] Salespeople face a lot of stress in their work roles. They may tend to cope with this stress by avoidance or other emotional strategies. A more successful approach seems to be problem-focused coping: analyzing the situation, taking responsibility, using self-control, and attempting to improve themselves. Researchers David Strutton and James Lumpkin suggest that training emphasizing the value of problem-focused coping approaches—and the negative consequences of emotional coping—may be beneficial.[11]

A successful salesperson must also have a positive mental attitude; he or she must be sold on the product and company in order to sell these to others. Personal pride in the company, its products, its industry, and in the career as a salesperson creates confidence and enthusiasm for everything the salesperson does. The new applicant must understand the importance of personal selling to the company and to the industry, and that without this function, all other functions in the company come to a halt.

Training in developing good habits includes self-discipline, effective use of time, adequate planning, proper travel routing, and good recordkeeping. In short, this is managing the territory as a business (Chapter 5). Training also emphasizes the links between the job-related behaviors identified during the recruiting process and the behaviors of successful salespeople.

Research indicates that most sales training executives and sales managers think that more time should be allocated to developing selling skills.[12] Skill development training is required in all phases of the selling process, from prospecting through needs identification, probing, presentation, meeting objections, and closing. Salespeople also need training in effective listening.

Training salespeople in adaptive selling is particularly important. Adaptive selling involves changing the sales presentation to fit the situation. Research by Ronald Marks and his colleagues indicated that adaptive selling is a significant driver of sales performance.[13] They also conclude that it is likely that salespeople must believe that adaptive selling works before they will begin to practice it. This research implies that salespeople may need to be trained on the importance of adaptive selling, and how to recognize different types of sales situations and the corresponding types of sales presentations to use.

The concept of account management requires new forms of training. The salesperson now must develop skills in estimating account potential, developing selling strategies, negotiating, demonstrating to buying teams, persevering, and handling turndowns.

Sales trainers can learn from the Japanese. Although Japanese salespeople will have attractive brochures, like their western counterparts, there are important differences. The product claims are carefully documented so that promises can be delivered. The Japanese salesperson is trained to be responsible immediately for any product difficulty. After the seller has worked with key client departments to correct the problem, a followup report to the client is required explaining why the product failed and what has been done to prevent it ever recurring. Partnering with the client comes easier for Japanese salespeople because their culture is team-oriented, as contrasted with the western salesperson who is trained to operate independently.[14]

Follow-Through

Follow-through is receiving increased attention among sales trainers. A failure to make the sale requires analysis by the salesperson and the trainer to determine where the salesperson needs skill development. The salesperson may be weak in diagnosing the problems of the prospect. Problem-solving skills should be examined also when the sale is made so that the salesperson recognizes his or her strengths, as well as reasons for failure.

Customer satisfaction requires follow-through on the order with the effective management of delivery, installation, payment, and customer complaints. Satisfaction makes subsequent sales easier.

THE LEARNING PROCESS

A training program must reflect five steps that are necessary to learn to sell and manage.

1. Awareness-acquisition. The awareness and acquisition of information is achieved with such materials as texts, videotapes, programmed learning, and lectures.
2. Understanding. Understanding goes beyond acquiring information. Too often a person can know but not understand the information. Role playing and the case method can give the trainee an opportunity to demonstrate an understanding of the material.
3. Agreement-acceptance. Often a person can acquire and understand the concepts but not agree with them. The trainer must find why this is so. A learning environment must be established to understand and remove acceptance barriers.
4. On-the-job application. A golfer will often say, "It's a long distance between the driving range and the first tee." We can understand and accept the concepts but find that using them in a real-world environment can be difficult.
5. Habit-comfort zone. The individual must achieve a level of learning so that a desired behavior is a comfortable habit. This zone is achieved through practice.

These steps are cumulative. Failure to progress through any stage satisfactorily terminates learning. It is impossible to proceed until that stage is learned.

It is also important to create a favorable learning environment for the salesperson. Notes Larry Laws, president of Tech Resource Group: "The hardest thing about training is to get salespeople actually to want to be there. The training has to be pertinent to their business, and it must be fun, or you'll lose them after the first 15 minutes."[15]

WHEN SHOULD THE TRAINING BE GIVEN?

Timing will depends on many circumstances, such as the stage in the salesperson's career, the complexity of the material being sold, and special occasions such as new products, new markets, new strategies, new promotional campaigns, and new competition. Special occasions may be precipitated by problems identified during a salesperson's performance appraisal. Training philosophies differ among companies within the same industry. Some companies prefer to give initial training at a centralized location before sending a new salesperson into the field, whereas other companies prefer on-the-job training and therefore send new employees into the field immediately to work with experienced salespeople. Some companies have a combination of initial training after hiring, on-the-job training, and advanced training at the home office.

Training programs vary across industries and companies. For example, a program in a company with a high pyramid structure with many levels of managers would begin with a 20-week structured on-the-job training program. The recruit works with the unit manager, who explains each step in the sales call, demonstrates it, and then lets the recruit try it. Then the trainee makes sales calls with the trainer who observes and makes suggestions for improvements. The new salesperson next attends a training program at corporate headquarters where small, problem-solving discussion groups are used to study the business in depth and to learn advanced selling techniques. On-the-job training continues with regular sales meetings, organized reading programs, district bulletins, company and trade publications, and interactions with other salespeople. When the young salesperson has demonstrated the maturity and ability to handle additional responsibilities, he or she is promoted to district field salesperson, which presents the opportunity to work with district managers and unit managers calling on major accounts, recruiting, training, and performing other marketing operations at the district level. The next step is to attend the Sales Management Training School. Successful completion of this phase earns the salesperson a promotion to Unit Manager, the first level of field sales force management.

Many companies, such as Procter & Gamble, have flattened their organizations by eliminating these layers of management. The recruit is expected to get sales training during a summer internship program with them and move quickly into account management. The reasons for this organizational flattening are discussed in Chapter 17. It takes away the sales training function of these layers of management, requiring such training to be done by outside consultants.

Training for a high-tech product such as a computer system can take as long as one year. The program begins with training in computers and their applications. About six months into the program, the trainee and the company must decide whether the best career path is being a salesperson or a systems engineer. The salesperson will attend company courses in large systems marketing (8 weeks), industry applications (1 week), large systems implementation (12 weeks), and marketing school (3 months). These courses are held at the branch office and the corporate educational center.

A typical training program for a chemical company will use on-the-job training. It will begin at the home office with an explanation of employee benefits and the signing of an intention agreement. The trainee sees a slide show of the history of the company, receives cash advances, and is given instructions regarding expense account procedures and progress reports. He or she then spends 15 to 30 minutes each interviewing persons in functional areas such as marketing, manufacturing, planning, and product development. The trainee is subsequently sent to his or her first field training assignment to spend one-half day each with regional managers. The trainee observes a technical salesperson on a regular sales call. At the completion of this call, the trainee must complete an observer's checklist of what took place in the selling process, which sensitizes him or her to the important steps in the chemical sales process. The individual then proceeds to about eight weeks of product and technical training, and attends plant training modules that include tours of production facilities, laboratory operations, and administrative operations. Topics include plant safety, transportation activities, and plant engineering. The trainee now returns to the headquarters for instruction in the sales manual, regional office administration, sales forecasting, contract logs, customer files, and progress reporting. At this point, the trainee is instructed in supply and distribution systems, customer service, and credit activities. These steps take about eight months.

The sales training for a Hallmark Cards salesperson must be longer than a year so that he or she can see how actions in April can affect December sales. Hallmark sales training consists of seven phases with the training divided between the field and the home office at Kansas City (KC).

Hallmark Sales Training Program

Phase I	1 week	Orientation in the field and retail experience.
Phase II	2 weeks	Classroom in KC. Selling skills, math, merchandising, channels of distribution, and reports.
Phase III	7 weeks	Field training in territory organization and planning, call scheduling, competitive surveys, order book, fixture installations, hiring casual labor, sales call alone, business profit plan for an account, and retail experience.
Phase IV	1 week	Classroom in KC. Market development, merchandising, retail support programs, selling skills, seasons, and company benefits.
Phase V	6 to 9 months	Field training including a mentor program, territory orientation, introduction to top volume retailers, a day with a sales development specialist, and development of seasonal marketing skills. At the end of this period there will be a review of skills in sales calls, territory management, awareness of retailers' needs, and a 6-month evaluation.
Phase VI	1 week	Classroom training in KC to begin full implementation of advanced sales programs and career development.[16]

HOW SHOULD THE TRAINING BE DONE?

Sales training, like any training process, carries responsibilities for the teacher and the learner. These responsibilities may be summarized as follows: relevance, benefits, experience, feedback, classroom application, self-evaluation, and on-the-job application. These responsibilities and the teaching process as viewed by the teacher and the learner are summarized in Exhibit 10.2. Reading down the columns of this exhibit reveals that the process provides opportunities for active involvement, which enhances learning.

Exhibit **10.2**	ADULT TEACHING AND LEARNING RESPONSIBILITIES AND PROCESSES	

Responsibility	Teaching Process	Learning Process
1. Relevance	1. Define why it is necessary to learn the subject.	1. Recognize the need to learn.
2. Benefits	2. Specify gains to learners.	2. Perceive the training goals as my goals.
3. Experience	3. Offer learning through participation.	3. Learn the subject matter in a way that makes use of my experience and allows me to participate.
4. Feedback	4. Test the learner's understanding.	4. Test my understanding of the material.
5. Classroom application	5. Allow learners to use their new knowledge to produce some result.	5. Practice using the new knowledge.
6. Self-evaluation	6. Help the learner to evaluate himself or herself without fear.	6. Evaluate my practice in a supportive climate.
7. On-the-job application	7. Provide supportive climate on the job.	7. Apply my learning on the job.

Training Methods

Sales training methods may be classified by the degree of involvement permitted the trainee. The *lecture method* has minimum involvement and should be used only to convey factual information, such as the history of the company, its products, policies, and procedures. *Demonstrations* provide some visual involvement by trainees and maximum involvement when they are permitted to practice demonstrating. *Conference and small-group discussion methods* permit a high level of involvement; the trainees may introduce personal experiences and try out ideas on other members of the group. Small-group discussions of case material represent one of the best means by which trainees can develop and sharpen their problem-solving skills. *Role playing* is perhaps the most often used method for developing selling skills. (The instructor or trainee plays the role of the buyer and another trainee plays the role of the salesperson.) While watching a videotape replay, the trainee may be surprised to learn what he or she said in the presentation. Such experiences can be frightening, but they make the real world experience seem less difficult.

Some training methods can be individual and personal. For example, some tutorial methods, known as "curbstone conferences," involve the field sales manager giving immediate advice after having observed the salesperson in action. Correspondence courses are another form of individual, high-involvement learning methods. Computerized training, described in more detail later, provides an opportunity for the salesperson to learn at his or her own pace, often in the field.

Good training programs recognize the strengths and weaknesses of each of these techniques by using a combination of them. Many trainers use the old selling dictum of, "Tell them, show them, let them do it, and review it." Confucius said, "I hear and I forget. I see and I remember. I do and I understand." Sales trainers will want to follow the advice of Confucius by involving trainees in the learning process.

Training is more formal and is often in groups. Coaching includes diagnostics and is generally a one-on-one activity performed by a trainer or supervisor. Learner-controlled instruction (LCI) is an individualized training approach. LCI begins with a needs assessment. The trainer or sales manager and the salesperson then agree on areas in which additional training is needed. The trainer provides the salesperson with materials or identifies resource persons and turns the trainee loose to proceed at his or her own speed. The trainer and the salesperson make a contract that states what is to be learned and the time period for learning it. Such approaches work well with highly motivated individuals.

Coaching

Coaching consists of observing skill performance, helping individuals gain insights into their behavior, demonstrating means for improving these skills, providing an opportunity to practice the skills, and giving feedback. Any trainee who has taken a golf or tennis lesson will recognize this procedure. The professional says, "Hit a few." Then he or she says a few kind things about the swing and demonstrates ways to improve it. The next coaching step is practice shots and feedback from the professional. The sales manager will want to keep this sports coaching sequence in mind as he or she prepares for a coaching session with a salesperson.

Coaching sustains, develops, and improves skills to levels of performance that have been agreed upon by the trainer and trainee. The steps in coaching are as follows:

1. *Discuss and agree on the skill to be developed and the level of proficiency to be achieved.* A person has no motivation for learning unless the importance of developing the skill and the necessary level of proficiency have been agreed on. There may be many ways to develop the skills, so it may be necessary to negotiate the best methods for each salesperson, thereby recognizing each person's needs.

2. *Observe the performer in action on the job.* The observation phase should focus on having the performer do a self-evaluation. What was the objective? What was achieved? What do you think you did well? What needs improvement? How could this improvement be achieved? These and similar questions encourage a self-evaluation by the salesperson. Most people learn better through self-discovery than by being told. The self-evaluation approach has the additional advantage of continuing after the coach has left.

3. *Demonstrate the desired method of performance in a non-threatening manner.* Greater learning takes place when the salesperson is involved in this demonstration. It is important to maintain a non-threatening environment during this step.

4. *Transfer the skill to the job.* Performance will not improve unless classroom skills are transferred to the job. The coach must again observe the salesperson in the field and ask self-evaluation questions. It may be necessary to repeat steps 3 and 4 until the desired level of proficiency is achieved.

5. *Practice to develop confidence, proficiency, and habit.* Classroom skills often are lost on the job because insufficient time for practice resulted in insufficient levels of confidence, competency, and habit.

During the early training of a salesperson, coaching takes place in the classroom and in role-play situations. Later field sales managers use curbstone coaching. Curbstone coaching occurs after the manager has observed the salesperson in an actual situation. It can occur in the walk to the car or over a drink. It is important to conduct the coaching session as soon as possible, while all events are fresh in the salesperson's mind.

The coaching process involves more than developing immediate skills. It has the longer-term goal of training the salesperson in self-discovery that leads to self-evaluation and improvement without the need for close supervision. Thus after each call the salesperson will be able to determine what went well, what went poorly, and how to do better next time.

Training Coaches

Many companies have found that sales managers do not actively engage in coaching because they don't know how, it is time consuming, and it lacks the personal rewards of other management activities. Coaching can also be a threatening experience for the manager and the salesperson because reputations and interpersonal skills are on the line. When a young manager coaches an older salesperson there are additional discomforts. These negative dimensions of coaching often blind the manager to the fact that this process can provide positive and motivating feedback to salespeople.

Few companies train sales managers in coaching. Some companies provide a coaching document to record the object of the call, statements of needs, benefits and proofs, the handling of objections, and post-call review. Role playing is the most appropriate method to teach coaching. Switching roles between the manager and the salesperson gives each party new insights into the process. Efforts to improve the coaching process and even create a field coach can greatly improve selling skills in the sales force. Kraft-General Foods is an exception. The steps in its coaching process are summarized in Exhibit 10.3. They are identical to the sports model used earlier—observation of behavior, joint-call coaching, post-call coaching, and modified behavior. *(Use the Kraft-General Foods coaching model in Exhibit 10.3 to develop a program for improving the productivity of the salesperson in the opening case.)*

Training Materials

Training materials reflect a wide range of technologies from such basics as books and blackboards to the electronics of recordings, television, computers, and the Internet. Programmed learning is one teaching procedure that has used a range of techniques. Perhaps the earliest form of programmed learning, and one that is still commonly used, is training salespeople in a "canned" presentation. A canned presentation follows an assigned script with memorized responses. This type of programmed learning is appropriate in industries that have a high turnover among salespeople and a relatively uncomplicated product.

The materials used most often for sales force training are printed manuals, followed by video and audio tapes, respectively, as shown in Exhibit 10.4.[17]

Printed materials, such as workbooks or training manuals, provide another means for programmed learning. Printed materials offer the advantage of relatively low cost, and ease of distribution. They also provide a document that salespeople can return to for clarification or when questions arise.

Audio and video resources are an important part of training. Use of videos has been shown to increase comprehension and retention of material by more than 50% over printed material alone.[18] The availability and ease of using video camcorders makes it easy for the salesperson to analyze his or her presentation skills. Audio tapes can describe new product information and strategies; the salesperson may listen to them at home or while driving to customers.

Motorola uses videos to train salespeople about products, company, marketing information, and selling techniques.[19] The videos are produced for the company by professional film studios at a cost of $700 to $1,200 per minute. Once they are completed, the videos are mailed to as many as 1,000 Motorola salespeople at a time. The salespeople use the videos with their printed self-study guides, which include multiple-choice tests. They take the exams open-book, sending their answers to Motorola. If they fail the exam twice, their sales manager is notified.

Business simulations have been created to help salespeople learn about business in general and marketing in particular, to develop sales strategies, and to develop a skill for

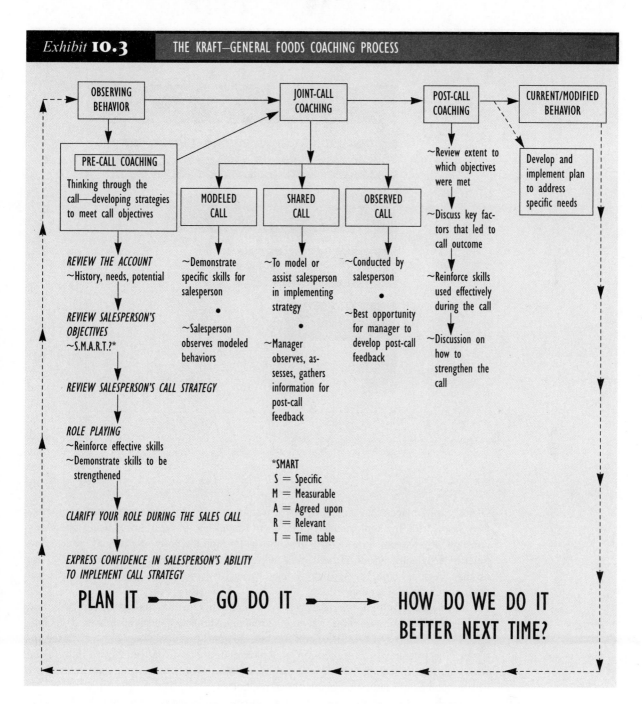

Exhibit 10.3 THE KRAFT—GENERAL FOODS COACHING PROCESS

PLAN IT ➤ GO DO IT ➤ HOW DO WE DO IT BETTER NEXT TIME?

routing their time through the territory. These games may be hand-scored or may use a computer.

Computerized Training

Advances in computer and communications technology are opening a variety of sales training options.

Computer-assisted learning programs permit branched learning experiences in which correct decisions are reinforced and incorrect choices result in additional information.

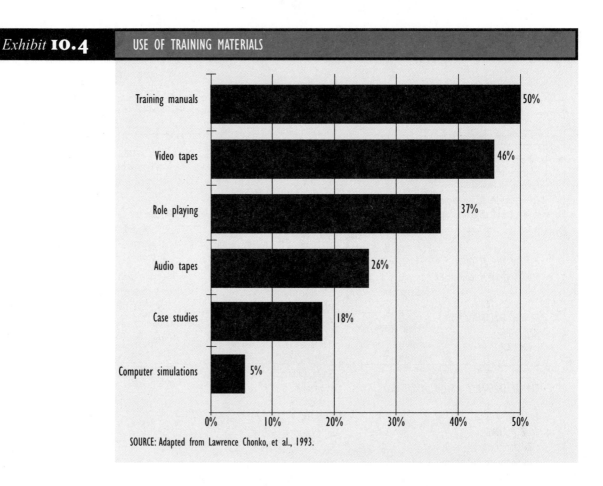

Exhibit 10.4   USE OF TRAINING MATERIALS

SOURCE: Adapted from Lawrence Chonko, et al., 1993.

Glaxo, a pharmaceutical company, has a training center containing personal computers with laser discs for sophisticated graphic presentations. In addition to using branching questions, the system shows how a drug moves through the body of a patient. Some computer training applications include discs and manuals that can be sent to salespeople to use on their personal computers. Such systems can greatly reduce the cost of training by reducing the cost of traveling.

Multi-media training programs can involve action, question-and-answer formats, and graphics custom-tailored to the individual company. Multi-media can be delivered on compact disks, using CD-ROM drives on the salesperson's personal computer, or via the Internet. The Interactive Multimedia Association claims that using interactive multimedia with traditional training methods like lecture and video leads to learning gains up to 56% greater than using traditional instructional methods.[20]

Internet-delivered training may offer companies a lower-cost and quicker alternative for delivering computer instruction. International Data Corp. estimates that U.S. Internet-based training, which amounted to $19 million in 1995, will grow to $1.7 billion by the year 2000. Using an intranet system, companies can offer their salespeople training that includes audio and video content. This format can be widely distributed, centrally controlled, and can include an assessment feature.[21]

For example, Sun Microsystems in Mountain View, California, distributes training to its salespeople via the Internet. Sun has 5000 distributors and 2000 direct salespeople. The company figures the Internet-distributed training will allow it to complete the training cycle more rapidly at a lower cost. Sun expects to cut its training costs by 50% and shorten sales training time 75% using the Internet.

Advanced technologies, like all media, offer advantages and disadvantages. Among the advantages are potentially lower distribution costs and central control of content. Among disadvantages are limited interpersonal contact. The development of newer techniques should not blind us to the fact that basic sales training materials, such as outlines, bulletins, letters,and flip-charts, are very effective, low cost, and frequently used.

WHO IS THE TRAINER?

Who is the sales trainer? Broadly speaking, anyone and everyone can be a sales trainer for a salesperson. It could be a person outside the company who is not generally in a training role, such as a smart buyer or a sharp competitor who has just taught a salesperson a lesson that he or she will never forget. It could be a football coach or a politician who is particularly inspiring. But generally when we think of sales trainers we are focusing on formal sales training programs that use company or outside personnel in structured training situations. Company personnel are not limited to those in marketing, as we saw earlier in the Conoco example. Persons in engineering, production, research and development, and finance all play important roles in training salespersons.

Marketing people who are involved in sales training include trainers and managers at headquarters, field personnel such as the field sales manager, and special salespeople who have been trained to assist in instructing new salespeople and who are sometimes given compensation to assist in training recruits. These salesperson/trainers are also learning new skills in preparation for management responsibilities.

Deciding who will conduct the training involves a series of tradeoffs. Line personnel at headquarters have extensive experience and introduce substantial authority into the training process, but they lack time and may lack teaching ability. The cost of moving trainees to the headquarters location must also be considered. Staff trainers, at headquarters or regional offices, are trained in teaching methodology and are aware of the latest in teaching aids, but they lack the authority that goes with line control over trainees and their department adds a fixed cost to the selling function. On the other hand, field sales managers know the personal needs of the salespeople, as well as unique features of the territory, and have authority, but, unfortunately, few field sales managers have received any instruction in training.

Outside training personnel may be used by companies with small sales forces and low turnover rates, thereby not requiring a fixed investment in training departments, and by companies that have flattened their organizations and eliminated the training component of the manager's job. These outside personnel include sales training consultants; trade associations; sales clubs; continuing education programs through local colleges, the American Management Association, or the Sales and Marketing Executives Club; correspondence courses; and rented materials such as videotapes and teleconferences. The quality and appropriateness of these training sources vary greatly.

Some evidence exists that top-performing sales forces use a wider variety of training sources than low-performing sale forces.[22] These included specification salespeople, company-based trainers, trade association personnel, representatives from vendor sales forces, department managers, and vendor training schools.

Some industry-specific training may be provided by consultants who specialize in an industry or by trade associations that provide sales training for their members. For example, The Jack Morton Company developed a CD-ROM training program for Coldwell Banker sales associates and for the securities industry to make certain that brokerage firms complied with Securities and Exchange Commission regulations.[23]

Relatively little empirical research has been conducted about the effectiveness of various training sources. One recent study, conducted among 42 companies in 15 industries, found no evidence that staff sales trainers provide more effective training than other sources.[24]

MENTORING PROGRAMS

Mentoring provides a young salesperson with a confidential advisor who provides insights beyond training and coaching. This individual can provide useful insights about organizational behavior and the unwritten policy manual. They can also provide social support as well as specific vocational or task training.[25] Among the vocational/task functions mentors can help with are coaching (such as help in developing selling scripts), protection (advice on avoiding violations of sales force behavioral norms, for example), exposure (such as assignment to projects that engage new skills), and visibility (telling others of the salesperson's capabilities).[26]

It is estimated that one-third of major companies have formal mentoring programs.[27] More formalized programs may offer certain advantages, such as careful selection and placement of mentors, and management of the mentor-salesperson relationship.

Some veteran salespeople may make better mentors than others. Characteristics to look for seem to include:

- strong interpersonal skills
- a supportive attitude
- willingness to share time and information
- involvement in the job and the company
- a favorable attitude toward the particular salesperson

Mentor-salesperson relationships also appear to have a life cycle, including initiation, cultivation, and separation.[28] During the initiation phase, the mentor helps the salesperson develop an occupational identity. During the cultivation phase, the mentor and salesperson test their mutual expectations and form an interpersonal bond. Eventually, they face a separation phase as one or the other moves on, advances beyond the need for the mentor, or otherwise separates from the relationship.

WHERE SHOULD THE TRAINING TAKE PLACE?

Sales training is a continuing process. Every time a manager checks a salesperson's report, sends a note, discusses business on the phone, passes along something to read, criticizes or compliments, it is a training experience. Training, therefore, is not limited to classroom experiences.

Formal training programs may be held at the home office, a training center, university facilities, a conference center, or a motel. Centralized locations have the advantages of better facilities, equipment, and materials, and they provide an *esprit de corps* when sales-people from many regions are brought together. These centralized locations can be expensive in terms of time, money, and administrative problems, but may be less costly than repeating the training individually in numerous locations.

Communication problems can arise between the field sales manager and the trainer at headquarters regarding training goals and methods. The trainee is caught in the middle when, upon returning to the field, the manager says, "Yes, I know what you were told at headquarters, but now let me show you how it is done in the real world." To prevent this conflict, agreement must exist on the goals and methods before the training begins and the trainer must report the trainee's progress to the field sales manager during the training at headquarters.

Decentralized locations can be a local motel, the branch office, or traveling clinics. Decentralized procedures are less expensive in terms of trainees' time and travel expenses. Local programs also tend to receive more support from the local manager. Decentralized programs have disadvantages, however, in that there may not be time or capacity for training at the local level.

The most effective form of training takes place in front of the customer. The classroom is only the prelude to the ultimate sales training experience—the uncertainty of the customer and the buying environment. Selling is an interactive skill that must be acquired through the interaction of the salesperson and the buyer. Just as in sports, real learning takes place when the competition gets tough.

For field sales training, Falvey advocates a buddy system that pairs a trainee with a salesperson who has had less than two years' experience.[29] This approach assures that skills will be current and realistic at the entry level. It is also recommended that the training take place in the trainee's territory where the trainer is at a disadvantage and is likely to make honest mistakes. This approach has many benefits for the trainee. It forces the trainer to rely on basic selling skills and not rely on friendship selling, which is not yet available to the trainee. The trainee sees how an experienced salesperson plans in an unfamiliar territory and uses territory records. It enables the trainee to become productive more quickly because there is no need to translate skills into a new environment.

EVALUATING TRAINING PROGRAMS

Target Marketing Systems (TMS), stated that "The broad purpose of any training program is to change attitudes, behaviors or skills in a way that positively impacts business results."[30] But how to evaluate the training program has long been a problem for sales trainers. If clear and measurable goals were established before training, this step becomes simpler, but not easy. If the goal of sales training is to improve statistics such as the **size of the sale, increased profit, lower expenses, sales forecasting accuracy, a higher closing rate, or sales of a more balanced product mix,** then the success of the training effort should be measured in these terms. **Before-and-after measures** of these variables must be made in a control group and an experimental group, such that the experimental group receives the training and the control group does not. But such a controlled experiment is difficult to implement in the real world. If salespeople are paid on a commission no one will want to be in the control group.

If the training goal is to increase salespeople's knowledge of product benefits, applications, or competitors, then the effectiveness of training may be measured by giving salespeople objective tests covering these topics. Most sales training, however, focuses on job-related behaviors dealing with attitudes, skills, and habits that are extremely difficult to measure because they are subjective rather than objective. Changes in sales skills fall in the subjective category, so they must be evaluated by subjective observation by the field manager. Results may be measured by statistical analysis of changes in sales, profits, expenses, and other measures.[31] McGraw-Hill videotaped presentations by salespeople before and after training and then content-analyzed the tapes to detect improvements that could be traced to training.[32] The company also did a survey of prospects before and after training to detect strengths and weaknesses in the training program. For example, they found that the training improved probing but that salespeople were not equipped to handle the resulting objections. Some significant portion of the growth in sales three years after the training program was attributed to the program.

TMS developed a means for training program evaluation based on the model developed by Professor Donald Kirkpatrick. This model considers four levels of training effectiveness as follows:

Effect	Question	Measurement Method
Reaction	Did they like it?	Surveys
Learning	Did they learn?	Pre/post tests Cases Exercises
Behavior	Are they using it?	Surveys/interviews with participants, managers, customers
Business Results	Is it working and yielding value for the organization?	Increased close rates Increased sales or profit contribution[33]

When budgets are tight the training program is one of the first items to be cut. Such a program will help to justify the training budget and provide feedback for improving the training.

Perhaps the difficulty in evaluating training programs concerns the philosophical difference in accounting procedures between expenditures on equipment and expenditures on humans. Expenditures on equipment are generally treated as an investment, whereas expenditures on humans are expensed. Accountants would probably change this philosophy if sales trainers could demonstrate more clearly the fact that expenditures on sales training have positive effects that last many years, so that training expenditures should be amortized over many years.

DEVELOPING SALESPEOPLE

A survey of sales managers (Chapter 7, Exhibit 7.3) revealed that the most important activity of first- and second-line managers is developing personnel. Developing personnel may be defined as helping a subordinate develop goals, knowledge, attitudes, skills, and habits beyond those that are necessary to perform the present job. This process is sometimes known as developing a "life plan."

It is in the best interest of a company to develop as fully as possible the capabilities of its employees in order to maximize its return on investment in recruiting, hiring, and training. Many companies develop compensation plans, benefit programs, and promotion policies that stress promotion from within. Benefit programs may include programs of continuing education and reimbursement of the costs of advanced studies. Some companies evaluate supervisors on their ability to develop subordinates. As career counseling becomes an important part of a sales manager's job, companies are developing coaching and counseling programs for managers and prospective managers. The programs focus not only on the managers' present jobs, but also on the activities at the next higher management level.

Career Counseling

The first-line field sales manager's primary task in developing salespeople is to help them gain a realistic understanding of the process for "getting ahead." Many salespeople express a strong desire to get ahead without realizing that the first step is to be successful in their present assignment. Hence the first step is for the manager and the salesperson to work on the knowledge, attitudes, habits, and skills that are necessary to succeed as a salesperson. After this, the manager turns to helping the salesperson develop plans for the next step in his or her career.

In order for a career planning system to work, the company must reward a manager for moving his or her salespeople along to the next higher position. Without such rewards, the manager has a natural incentive to keep a good salesperson.

Life Planning

Several steps have been identified by some sales managers to help a salesperson develop a life plan after he or she expresses a desire to get ahead. These steps are:

1. Identify a Career Objective
   a. Have the individual rank-order several jobs that he or she finds most attractive.
   b. Beginning with the top-ranked job, help the salesperson identify the knowledge, attitudes, habits, and skills that are necessary to qualify for that job.
2. Match the job requirements to a realistic self-assessment
   a. The salesperson should list his or her assets and liabilities in terms of this job.
   b. The job qualifications are matched against the salesperson's qualifications to determine what is necessary to become qualified.
3. Plan a course of action for the first objective
   a. The manager helps the individual determine how he or she will be able to acquire the necessary qualifications, by when, and at what cost.
   b. The manager identifies what the company can provide to help the individual qualify.
   c. The manager and the salesperson develop a realistic program of self-development, with resources, checkpoints, and realistic outcomes.
   d. If all indications are positive, the salesperson begins to implement the career planning program.
4. Or face reality and move on to the next objective
   a. Perhaps the most sobering step is the assessment of the chances of the individual getting the first choice job after becoming qualified. Perhaps such opportunities rarely occur.
   b. Move to the next choice and cycle through again.

Although this process can require a lot of the manager's time and emotional energy, helping young people in their career development can be emotionally rewarding.

In the next chapter, which discusses motivation, we will see that a major demotivator is a dead-end job. A job situation may become unbearable when an individual senses that a job is not only a dead end, but no one cares and there is no effort made to correct the situation.

SUMMARY

Orientation and training provide qualifiable applicants with the knowledge, attitudes, skills, and habits necessary to produce sales results. The performance appraisal conducted by the sales manager evaluates these results and, with the concurrence of the salesperson, determines what additional training is necessary.

To develop a training program, the sales manager or training specialist must answer a series of questions. Why train? The answer to this question will identify the training goals and express them in terms that are measurable, thereby facilitating the evaluation of the training program. A training needs assessment may be necessary to identify these training goals. Who should be trained? Because training is a continuous process, the answer is simple—all salespeople must be trained. But the type of training that they receive will differ according to their position in their career path development. What should be the content of the training program? The new salesperson has to be oriented into the company and must understand the role of personal selling in the marketing mix, the territory, the community, and the social structure of the company. All salespeople need training in selling activities, new markets, new products, new competition, new market strategies, and territory management. Training in following through is also becoming an important part of sales training. When should the training be given? The point at which training is given will vary among industries and companies. Some companies prefer to give training before sending the salesperson into the field, whereas other companies prefer initial on-the-job training. Training programs are offered also on special occasions, such as the introduction of new products and when problems are identified during performance appraisals of salespeople. How should the training be done? Most training programs combine lectures, demonstrations, group discussions, role playing, on-the-job training, and tutorials to create an optimal learning experience. Training materials range from elementary devices, such as blackboards, to electronic equipment, such as videotape recorders and computers. Who is the trainer? Trainers may be staff personnel from a training department, line sales managers, or outside consultants and associations. Where should the training take place? The training planner must balance the advantages and disadvantages of centralized and decentralized locations. How can training programs be evaluated? The answer to this question is simplified somewhat by a clear statement of training goals, but some goals are easier to measure than others. For example, if the goal is to communicate knowledge about products and markets, trainees may be given a simple objective test to evaluate training effectiveness. If, however, the training is to develop behavioral changes, such as selling skills, it may be necessary to develop elaborate before-and-after measures. Programs may be evaluated also by changes in statistics, such as sales and profits, closing rates, and reduced expenses.

Developing salespeople is the most important single activity performed by field sales managers. The development begins by qualifying them first as salespeople and then helping them to develop a realistic life plan for their career.

Case 10.1   SALLY SIMPSON, REVISITED

Reread the Sally Simpson Case, 9.1, in Chapter 9.

CASE QUESTIONS

1. What is the problem from the standpoint of orienting and training?

2. What advance indications were there of the development of the problem?
3. Could the problem have been prevented? If so, how? If not, why not?
4. Should Scott try to dissuade Sally?

Case 10.2   SHELBY BUILDING SUPPLIES

Shelby Building Supplies was a typical, successful member of the industrial community in the Southwest. Established in Los Angeles in 1960 by Jim Shelby, the company took advantage of the explosive growth in southern California before expanding its distribution to northern California, Oregon, and Washington, and ultimately to 11 western states. With sales representatives and warehouses in the major metropolitan and growth areas, Shelby Building Supplies provided numerous opportunities for career advancement for its employees by following a policy of promotion from within. All of its division sales managers and most of its warehouse managers came from the ranks of the salespeople. Although Jim Shelby's two sons, John and Sam, expected to inherit the major share of the business, it was common knowledge that long-time employees, particularly among the senior managers, were given the opportunity to buy into the company. In a recent announcement to all employees, Mr. Shelby told of expansion plans and the opportunity to participate in a profit-sharing plan that would be offered when these plans were implemented next April at the beginning of the new fiscal year.

Tim Brush started with Shelby Building Supplies as a salesman in Sacramento four years ago, after graduation from Sacramento State College. Tim developed into an aggressive, hardworking salesman, ambitious, imaginative, and with a friendly ability to get along with customers and peers. Tim worked northern California and western Nevada in addition to the Sacramento and San Joaquin Valley areas. This required him to be on the road more than 50% of the time, which didn't please his wife, Mary, whom he had married soon after graduation. However, Tim convinced Mary that this assignment enabled him to prove his abilities in a variety of working conditions. His predictions were borne out in an excellent sales record that attracted the attention of Doug Webster, the Vice President of Sales.

Two years ago, Tim was offered a transfer to Oakland, which he promptly accepted. Although Tim had no added responsibilities, Oakland was a boom market for building supplies. It offered the opportunity for greater income and his travel was cut by 75% which pleased Mary greatly. The transfer proved advantageous for Tim, and he continued his above-average performance. The metropolitan Oakland area provided him with a new set of insights into the sales of Shelby Building Sup-

plies and the added income from his increased sales enabled Tim and Mary to buy their first home. However, as pleased as Tim was with his prosperity, he wanted more responsibility. Specifically, Tim wanted a promotion to division sales manager.

Although Tim knew this would get him back on the travel circuit, Mary had reluctantly agreed. In addition, he discussed it with Don Goodman, his division sales manager. In fact, he talked with Don about it during his annual counseling session immediately following his transfer, which was just about the time the company instituted a career planning program. Tim believed that the only way to get ahead was to keep bringing up the subject, and on each working trip with Don, Tim would figure out some way to press the issue as to when he could expect to be promoted.

Don Goodman recognized Tim's talents and considered him to be one of the most productive salespeople in his division. Don also recognized Tim's impatience and desire to be promoted, which sometimes clouded his judgment. When Tim first voiced his interest in additional responsibilities, Don asked him what he was doing to prepare himself for these added responsibilities. He reminded Tim of the company's educational program that provided 75% reimbursement of tuition for job-related courses taken during time off. Also offered was a variety of packaged programs, some of which were programmed learning and other correspondence forms. Don also suggested that Tim would benefit from further training in verbal and written skills. It wasn't that Tim couldn't express himself effectively, for he had demonstrated his ability for the past four years as a salesman. Tim's grammar and vocabulary were a bit unpolished and Don was concerned about Tim's ability to express himself properly at division sales meetings, managers' conferences, and before large groups at building supplies meetings and conventions, which was part of the responsibility of a division manager, but not of a salesperson.

In addition, Don had some reservations about Tim's commitment to handling all the paperwork that came across a division manager's desk. Tim's attention to paperwork was not up to the level of his other skills as a salesman, and Don wasn't sure how Tim would react when the volume of correspondence increased. Tim wasn't necessarily tardy, but he was rarely first in sending his reports, and he almost never

continued

Case 10.2   SHELBY BUILDING SUPPLIES—CONTINUED

submitted more than was required. In contrast to the initiative he displayed in the field in search of new sales opportunities, Tim's unsolicited written feedback was almost nonexistent. Don had kidded him about it, commenting that he couldn't understand how anyone with Tim's sales record and nose for business never had any information to share about the marketplace or the competition. Tim's response was that he was too busy selling to take time to write. Don's analysis was that Tim was less confident expressing himself in writing and avoided doing so whenever possible.

To Tim's credit, he took Don's advice and enrolled in an advanced public speaking course at the University Extension Division. This wasn't exactly what Don had in mind, but it was a start. Tim's initial reaction to the class was somewhat hesitant, but he soon learned to enjoy the challenge, and, after completing the course, joined the local Toastmasters Club. At the end of a 10-day field trip that Don made with several salespeople, culminating with two days with Tim on Thursday and Friday, they discussed Tim's continuing lack of interest in paperwork while professing a strong ambition to be promoted. To make a point, Don asked Tim to be at Don's office in San Francisco promptly at 9:00 AM the following Monday. He wanted Tim to see the volume of mail that had accumulated during his absence and to impress upon him the absolute need to be able to handle that volume of correspondence if he wanted to become a division sales manager. Tim knew that Don had no way of knowing what correspondence was waiting for him on his return, and Tim was impressed with the quantity and variety of mail and the amount of work that would go into replying. Tim's reaction was that this was something he would have to learn to do if the job demanded it. From that point on, Tim's reporting and correspondence began to show some improvement.

Following the last division sales managers' conference in Los Angeles at the Shelby headquarters, Don discussed with Doug Webster Tim's performance and interest in moving up. Their conversation was lengthy; every phase of Tim's performance and qualifications was reviewed. Doug Webster's feeling seemed to be that although Tim's sales ability was well recognized, his administrative skills and ability to manage people were unknowns. It was for these reasons that Don decided against making a formal recommendation that Tim be promoted to Division Sales Manager. He knew that if he pushed Doug Webster, he would get a definite "NO," and he didn't want to have Mr. Webster go on record as having turned Tim down.

It was with a clear memory of that conversation that Don met with Tim on their next working trip. Don had completed the review of the quarterly product sales when Tim asked to change the subject.

When Don inquired about what he had on his mind, Tim replied, "Don, I've been with the company for a little over four years as a salesperson. Judging by what you've said about my performance and my own estimation, I think I've done a better than average job. I've had a variety of sales experiences, both rural and metropolitan, and I think I'm ready for a promotion. I'd like to stay with Shelby and make a career out of it. It's a great company, they've treated me well, the new expansion plans sound exciting, and I can see myself in a top management spot someday down the road. The problem is that I've been offered a job with a big increase by a competitor. Although I would still be a salesman for a while, they promised to make me a division sales manager. I'd like to stay with Shelby, but the competitive offer is very attractive, particularly the promise of becoming a division manager. Can you make the same promise if I stay with the company?"

Don thought for a long time, to the point that Tim became a little uncomfortable. Finally, Don responded, "Tim, let me make it perfectly clear. You've done a great job as a salesperson, one of the best in the division, and I want you to know that. I know you are ambitious and want to be a division sales manager so badly you can almost taste it. Moreover, you are convinced you are qualified right now! Let me ask you a theoretical, but a very real, question. If you were a division sales manager right now, and one of your salespeople were to ask you, 'Will you promise me that I will become a division sales manager?', how would you answer him?"

CASE QUESTIONS

1. How would you answer Don Goodman's question?
2. How do you think Tim Brush will answer Don Goodman's question?
3. Why do you think Don Goodman phrased the question the way he did?
4. How can you assure an employee who may be qualified and who asks the same question Tim Brush asked?
5. How would you evaluate Tim Brush's qualifications for division sales manager?
6. What qualifications are required for the job of a division sales manager?
7. What management development has Don Goodman provided Tim Brush?
8. If Tim Brush decides to stay, how could Don Goodman help Tim develop the needs identified by Doug Webster?
9. Should Don Goodman ask questions about the competitive offer? If so, what question could he ask?

Case **10.3**	COACHING AN OLDER SALESPERSON

You have been a unit manager for Kraft Foods for two years and have just taken over a new sales group. One of the salespeople, Michael Higgins, has 15 years of experience, but he gives you the impression that he is just "riding the waves" and not producing up to his potential. On your first two trips with him you noticed that he seemed to be disorganized and had passive sales presentations. You are about to make a third trip with him. You think that he could become a model salesperson with the proper direction and support, but you are somewhat apprehensive because 10 years ago he helped to train you as a new salesperson.[34]

Using the Kraft coaching model, Exhibit 10.4, as a process template, how would you plan your next trip?

Case **10.4**	COACHING THE AMBITIOUS SALESPERSON

Susan Gustafson was just made a Kraft Foods account manager after three successful years as a salesperson. She had won several awards, was organized, knew her business, and made aggressive sales presentations. She was fired-up to take over the Market Fair chain account because it represented considerable business.

After two visits to Market Fair with Susan you were fairly comfortable that she was catching on quickly. (She knew she was catching on quickly and let everyone know it.) She felt confident that she could make the presentation for a new product by herself and insisted on doing so. After some hesitation you agreed to let her go alone.

When she finished the presentation, she came to you visibly upset. She made her usually aggressive presentation of the new product but was thrown out of the account. She is discouraged. She is concerned about returning to the account and about what other account managers will say when they find out what happened.

Susan is wondering if she should have taken the promotion. She can't understand why her "proven" successful selling techniques for calling on individual stores are not working at headquarters.[35]

CASE QUESTIONS

1. Did you make a mistake in letting Susan go alone?
2. What could you have done differently?
3. Plan for a coaching session using Exhibit 10.3 as a guide.

Case **10.5**	TRAINING FOR SALES PROCESS REDESIGN

As senior vice president of advertising sales at Comcast Cable, Filemon Lopez saw that he needed control.[36] There was no consistency in the sales process. Salespeople were developing leads and closing sales in a hodgepodge of different ways.

Lopez's first step was to survey his 330 salespeople. He asked them in what areas they needed help, how they used their time, whether they received enough of the right kinds of training, and more. His most troubling finding: salespeople were passively waiting for customers to come to them.

Based on the input from his salespeople, Lopez established territories so salespeople did not run into one another's accounts. A systematic lead-generation program was also developed, with telemarketing support, to identify and qualify prospects within the territories.

In order to assure that leads were pursued systematically—and using appropriate sales techniques—an ongoing training program was instituted. New salespeople went through a two-week course on a consultative approach to value-focused selling. Once a month, veteran salespeople attended training classes on special topics like needs-analysis and closing.

Training was followed up with a skills assessment review. Managers observed salespeople in the field to verify that they were conforming to the company's sales techniques, including finding out about customer's needs and problems.

The result: A substantial increase in Comcast sales.

CASE QUESTIONS

1. What would you identify as the keys to the success of Comcast's selling process redesign effort?
2. Based on the information provided, what types of training content and delivery media would you expect might be appropriate?

ASSIGNMENTS/DISCUSSION QUESTIONS

1. On what should the content of a training program be based?

2. If orientation is a training process of acquainting the trainee with the existing situation or environment, to whom and to what should a trainee be oriented, in addition to those items listed in the text?

3. Briefly define sales training.

4. In periods of depressed economic conditions and reduced budget expenditures, should training be increased or decreased and why?

5. At what point does the training process begin? At what point does it end?

6. Compare the advantages and disadvantages of training inexperienced versus experienced salespeople.

7. Who is fundamentally responsible for the training of a field salesperson? Explain.

8. What are the benefits to the individual of an effective company program of personnel development?

9. Compare the training responsibilities of the organization and the individual participants.

10. In some companies the sales training manager reports to the sales general manager, whereas in other companies the trainer reports to the director of human resources. Where do you think the trainer should report? Should the training manager at the home office report the trainee's performance to the trainee's field sales manager? Discuss both sides of these questions.

11. What reasons would explain why the training and development of sales managers have been neglected?

12. Discuss the relative importance of the need for sales management training and sales management development.

13. How might a company with a policy of promotion from within avoid the problem of inbreeding?

14. If a salesperson who was recently promoted to first-line field sales management was successful as a salesperson primarily because of his or her drive and ability to get results, identify at least two sales management activities in which the individual will probably need training.

ENDNOTES

1. Donald O. Clifton (1980), Varsity Management, Lincoln, NE: Selection Research, p. 3.
2. *Ibid.*
3. C. David Shepherd and Rick E. Ridnour, The Training of Sales Managers: An Exploratory Study of Sales Management Training Practices, *Journal of Personal Selling & Sales Management,* 15(1), Winter 1995, pp. 69–74.
4. Alan J. Dubinsky, Some Assumptions about the Effectiveness of Sales Training, *Journal of Personal Selling & Sales Management,* 15(3), Summer, 1996, pp. 67–76.
5. Adel I. El-Ansary, Selling and Sales Management in Action: Sales Force Effectiveness Research Reveals New Insights and Reward-Penalty Patterns in Sales Force Training, *Journal of Personal Selling & Sales Management,* 13(2), Spring, 1993, pp. 83–90.
6. El-Ansary, 1993.
7. T.D. Fallon (1967), *Sales Training Program Content,* The New Handbook of Sales Training, Robert F. Vizza, editor, Englewood Cliffs, N.J.: Prentice-Hall, pp. 127–133.

8. Merck's Grand Obsession, *Sales & Marketing Management* 65, June, 1987; America's Best Sales Forces, *Sales & Marketing Management,* June, 1989, pp. 47–68.

9. Geoffrey Brewer, Brain Power, *Sales & Marketing Management,* May, 1997, pp. 39–48.

10. David Strutton and James R. Lumpkin, Problem- and Emotion-Focused Coping Dimensions and Sales Presentation Effectiveness, *Journal of the Academy of Marketing Science,* 22(1), Winter 1994, pp. 28–37.

11. Strutton and Lumpkin 1994.

12. Alan J. Dubinsky, Some Assumptions about the Effectiveness of Sales Training, *Journal of Personal Selling & Sales Management,* 16(3), Summer, 1996, pp. 67–76.

13. Ronald Marks, Douglas W. Vorhies, and Gordon J. Badovick, A Psychometric Evaluation of the ADAPTS Scale: A Critique and Recommendations, *Journal of Personal Selling & Sales Management,* 16(4), Fall, 1996, 53–65.

14. George Leslie, U.S. Reps Should Learn to Sell 'Japanese Style,' *Marketing News* 24, October 29, 1990, p. 6.

15. Andy Cohen, Tin Man Training: Not Paying Proper Attention to Automation Training Can be Hazardous to a Company's Health, *Sales & Marketing Management,* 147(10), October, 1995, pp. 128–129.

16. David Pylipow, Human Resources Director, Hallmark Marketing Corporation, personal correspondence, August 12, 1992.

17. Based on Lawrence B. Chonko, John F. Tanner, Jr., and William A. Weeks, Sales Training: Status and Needs, *Journal of Personal Selling & Sales Management,* 13(4), Fall 1993, pp. 81–86.

18. Bristol Voss, Video Revelations and Reviews, *Sales & Marketing Management,* April, 1992, pp. 64–79.

19. Earl D. Honeycutt, Jr., Tom McCarthy, and Vince Howe, Sales Technology Applications: Self-Paced Video Enhanced Training: A Case Study, *Journal of Personal Selling & Sales Management,* 13(1), Winter 1993, pp. 73–77.

20. Ann Boland, Multimedia Fortifies Learning, *Advertising Age—Business Marketing,* 81(1), February, 1996, p. 20.

21. Robert M. Kahn, (1991) 21st Century Training, *Sales & Marketing Management,* Special Technology Supplement, pp. 81–88.

22. Adel I. El-Ansary, Selling and Sales Management in Action: Sales Force Effectiveness Research Reveals New Insights and Reward-Penalty Patterns in Sales Force Training, *Journal of Personal Selling & Sales Management,* 13(2), Spring 1993, pp. 83–90.

23. The Jack Morton Company brochure, 1997.

24. Alan J. Dubinsky, Some Assumptions about the Effectiveness of Sales Training, *Journal of Personal Selling & Sales Management,* 16(3), Summer 1996, pp. 67–76.

25. Raymond A. Noe, An Investigation of the Determinants of Successful Assigned Mentoring Relationships, *Personnel Psychology,* 41, 1989, pp. 457–479.

26. Ellen Bolman Pullins, Leslie M. Fine, and Wendy L. Warren, Identifying Peer Mentors in the Sales Force: An Exploratory Investigation of Willingness and Ability, *Journal of the Academy of Marketing Science,* 24(2), Spring 1996, pp. 125–136.

27. Arthur Bragg, Is a Mentor Program in Your Future? *Sales & Marketing Management,* September, 1989, pp. 54–63.

28. Kathy Kram, Phases of the Mentoring Relationship, *Academy of Management Journal,* 24(2), 1983, pp. 608–625.

29. Jack Falvey, Forget the Sharks; Swim with your Salespeople, *Sales & Marketing Management,* November, 1990, pp. 8–10.

30. Stephen J. Bistritz, Evaluating Sales Training Programs, *A White Paper,* Target Marketing Systems, Inc., Atlanta, GA, 1996, p. 1.

31. Earl D. Honeycutt and Thomas H. Stevenson, Evaluating Sales Training Programs, *Industrial Marketing Management* 18, August, 1989, p. 217.

32. B.A. Johnson and J. Pierce, Research Brings Proof of Value, Future Direction to Sales Training, *Training and Development Journal* 28, November, 1974, pp. 25–32.

33. Donald Kirkpatrick (1996), *Evaluating Training Programs: Four Levels,* San Francisco: Berrett-Koehler.

34. Adapted from Kraft-General Foods' training materials developed by Jay Hernandez. Used by permission.
35. *Ibid.*
36. Adapted from Andy Cohen, Starting Over: Redesigning the Process, *Sales & Marketing Management,* 147(9) September, 1995, p. 40.

HELPING SALESPEOPLE TO MOTIVATE THEMSELVES

LEARNING GOALS

1. To learn what demotivators must be removed to create a motivating environment
2. To be able to identify environments that motivate
3. To understand why you cannot motivate people
4. To learn how to help people motivate themselves
5. To identify methods that should be used to motivate salespeople based on their experience with the company and with selling

MANAGING SUCCESS

As you read this chapter think about the following situation. What is the problem?

Charlene was ranked among the top producers in the company for four years. Her reputation, which was widely recognized throughout the field sales force, was of an intelligent, personable, persistent, imaginative, and hard working salesperson. Jim Snow, her district sales manager, worked with her only every four to six months, in contrast to his monthly or bi-monthly field trips with his average-producing salespeople. His philosophy was, "If it ain't broke, don't fix it." He repeatedly said of his highly successful sellers, "Stay out of their way," and "Let them have their heads." He saw his responsibility as helping underproducers become more productive by spending more field time with them.

If management is defined as the process of getting work completed through people, then *motivation is the process of creating job environments that will inspire, persuade, encourage, or challenge individuals to manage themselves.* Managing through motivation is no easy task because it requires a change in management philosophy from direct control to indirect control by creating job circumstances in which individuals will direct themselves.

191

Defining motivation as an individual process differs from more popular definitions that characterize motivation as a process of inspiring or persuading employees to want to work. Although the importance of the leader's charismatic influence cannot be discounted, behavioral scientists have shown that motivation is an individual process of meeting one's own needs. The manager who wants to motivate his or her salespeople must therefore understand their individual needs and arrange for reinforcers that will satisfy these needs.

The major role of field sales managers is directing and leading the efforts of salespeople to achieve company goals as expressed in quotas. These managers must recognize that territory and company success depend in a very large part on their ability to enable salespeople to use the knowledge and skills that they acquired through orientation and training. The sales manager often hears, "You need the salespeople a lot more then they need you because you get paid for what they do, not what you do."

THEORIES AND RESEARCH ON JOB MOTIVATION

Needs Hierarchy

Abraham Maslow[1] theorized that motivation is an internal drive that stimulates an individual to action in order to satisfy personal needs. This hierarchy provides the basis for self-motivation theory. A need may be defined as a perceived deficiency that will influence a person to adjust optimally to his or her environment. Exhibit 11.1 shows the levels in the needs hierarchy and how they may be met in a sales context.

In most cases primary needs, the physiological and safety ones, must be met before a person can focus on the secondary social, esteem, and self-actualization needs. Physiological needs are for survival, so they include needs for air, water, food, shelter, and other elements necessary to maintain life. At some basic level, the sales job allows an individual to obtain these resources necessary for life.

When these needs are met, the next important category is safety needs, which include physical and emotional security. Companies may help to satisfy these needs through various forms of job security, retirement benefits, and health and accident benefits.

When these primary physiological and safety needs are met, social needs emerge as the next most important category. Social needs include being loved, the desire to belong, and to be accepted or cared for. The sales manager must provide a context that provides for the salesperson's social needs—through creation of formal and informal support programs—while avoiding problems that can arise from these same needs. For example, a salesperson who wants to be liked by customers may have difficulty asking for the order

Exhibit **11.1**	SATISFYING MASLOW'S HIERARCHY OF NEEDS THROUGH SALES
Need Level	**Sales Management Issue**
Self-actualization	Using best personal skills to sell socially valued benefits
Esteem	Recognition for performance; feeling of success
Social	Peer social support; mentoring
Safety	Retirement, health, other insurance benefits
Physiological	Means to pay for life necessities (food, shelter)

for fear of being rejected. Similarly, a field sales manager who wants to be liked by his or her salespeople will unreasonably support them against the company.

Esteem includes the dual needs for self-esteem and the esteem of others. Self-esteem is reflected in self-confidence, efforts to be in control, a sense of independence, and in being "your own person." The need for the esteem of others leads to high achievement, prestige, recognition, and status. In selling, satisfying these needs results in competitive achievements, recognition, promotion, and overall high levels of performance.

Self-actualization needs are often identified as self-realization and self-fulfillment. These are the needs to realize an individual's full potential, not for esteem or social acceptance, but rather for the purpose of meeting one's life objectives or contributing to the good of society. This highest level of need satisfaction is realized when a salesperson becomes "absorbed" in the sales process and believes that the product he or she is selling contributes to values and outcomes that he or she holds as important. *(Describe some parts of a job that gave you great satisfaction.)*

Self Motivation Environment

Frederick Herzberg conducted a series of studies about motivation in industry and the importance of work and working conditions. His research team measured workers' attitudes toward specific tasks and job surroundings. Elements of the job that provided satisfaction were called *motivators*. He used the term *hygiene factors* to describe the context of the job that was dissatisfying or demotivating. He concluded that satisfying the hygiene factors is a prerequisite for effective motivation. Thus the demotivators must be removed before motivation can begin. Demotivators included company policies and administration, supervision, interpersonal relations, working conditions, salary, status, and security. *(Can you give personal examples of how these factors demotivated?)*

Herzberg concluded that one does not motivate people to succeed but instead provides people with an opportunity to succeed, and they will motivate themselves. The motivating environment includes responsibility for doing the work, the feeling of achievement for doing the work well, the recognition that is received, and the advancement that derives from this accomplishment. In this context, job enrichment is the opportunity for an employee to grow psychologically through challenging work. Work enlargement is only the process of making the job bigger.[2]

The Open Management System

Kafka and Schaefer stated three motivational principles for managers: (1) see a situation from the other person's point of view, (2) identify and build on an individual's strengths rather than concentrating on how to correct weaknesses, and (3) understand and satisfy the individual's human needs.[3]

The Other Person's Point of View   Because an individual's point of view is the result of his or her total experiences, and because no two individuals have the same experiences, no two individuals can have the same point of view on all matters. The best that can be achieved is areas of understanding or agreement. If a manager wishes to see the situation from an employee's point of view, the manager must express a sincere desire to be understanding, to be willing to listen, to be a good observer of nonverbal communications, to communicate well, to generate similar interests if necessary, and to achieve clearly defined, mutually agreed-upon common goals.

Build on Strengths   Our contemporary value structure emphasizes correcting weaknesses rather than building on individuals' strengths. Emphasizing a person's weaknesses is demotivating; emphasizing his or her strengths is motivating. The management challenge, therefore, is to achieve superior performance by identifying people's special talents and arranging circumstances that allow them to use these talents to achieve mutually agreed-upon goals. Activities that are enjoyed most are usually done best. Therefore, developing areas of strength should produce happier and more productive individuals by satisfying their needs.

Individual Needs   The Open Management System focuses on five basic human needs—the need for economic security, the need for recognition or prestige, the need to dominate or control, the need for emotional security or personal self-worth, and the need to belong. These needs are very similar to those that have been identified by Maslow and Herzberg.

Applying Open Management Principles   The Open Management System is directed more toward implementation than are the theories of Maslow and Herzberg. This system begins with the individual's point of view by understanding his or her self-image, human symbols, strengths, and individual needs.

Individuals' *self-images* are reflections of how they see themselves and how they want others to see them. These images are composites of the many roles the individual plays—adult, parent, spouse, employee, community member, church member, organization member, and others. It is important to understand how the individual sees himself or herself because he or she will be receptive to anything that reinforces a self-image and will resist anything that threatens this image. To work effectively with an individual, we must understand and reinforce the self-image by satisfying the related needs, building on strengths, and not emphasizing weaknesses.

Human *symbols* are a way of telling others what is important to us. Our symbols include physical possessions like automobiles and houses; topics of personal interest, such as ideas and philosophies; and activities, such as sports, vacations, schools, and occupations. By observing these human symbols, the manager can identify persons' self-images and begin to identify their needs. The manager must look for a pattern of symbols that identifies an individual's needs and the importance of these needs to the individual. The manager must avoid making judgments regarding the values of these symbols and needs, thereby projecting his or her value system on the value system of the salesperson. Such judgments cause the manager to lose the perspective of the salesperson.

A manager who uses symbols to identify *individual needs* must consider several important points regarding the relationships between symbols and needs. First, one symbol may reflect different needs to different individuals. Second, it is the needs that must be satisfied, not the symbols. For example, a salesperson who wins a contest is satisfying a need for recognition, not the need for a color television set. Third, it is the use of a person's *strengths* on the job that provides consequences that satisfy the individual's needs. The manager, therefore, must understand the present needs of salespeople and anticipate their future ones. The Open Management System of motivation requires considerable empathy on the part of the manager.

Intrinsic versus Extrinsic Motivators   Maslow, Herzberg, Kafka, and Schaifer focus on intrinsic needs, but most motivation systems in sales management use external rewards, such as bonuses and trips. Kohn reviews over 500 articles on the topic of rewards and concludes that most rewards are punishment for those who did not receive the reward and that extrinsic rewards have only short-run benefits for trivial, repetitive tasks.[4] He concludes that the stimulus-response model that B. F. Skinner developed by studying rats does not apply to humans, but this model has dominated reward systems in homes, schools, and companies. Furthermore, the stimulus-response model reduces interpersonal relationships to a marketplace exchange model, which does not explain intrinsic motivation. Even the person receiving the rewards can feel punished if they feel controlled by the process.

According to Kohn, incentives impede performance for five reasons. First, incentives imply a threatened punitive dimension for the receiver as well as those who do not receive the reward. Second, incentive contests strain relationships between peers and across levels in the hierarchy of the organization. Third, incentives fail to uncover the underlying causes for poor performance—the demotivators noted above. It becomes easier to give rewards than to fix the system. Fourth, rewards discourage innovation and risk taking, yet pushing the frontier and learning by mistakes are necessary for competitive leadership.[5] Fifth, and most critical, is that extrinsic rewards destroy intrinsic motivation, which include the pleasure from doing a job well.[6] The feeling of contributing to the advancement of the organization and society can be a strong motivator. The process, according to Evans, should be like the excitement of a slot machine, not the certainty of a vending machine.[7]

In a study of salespeople, Greenberg and Greenberg found that "increased compensation was the least commonly cited reason" for switching to another company.[8] Similarly, David Shipley and Julia Kiely found in a survey of industrial salespeople that making more money was the fifth-rated motivating factor.[9] Ahead of money, in order of importance, were self satisfaction from doing a good job, satisfying customers' needs, meeting family responsibilities, and increasing the chance for promotion. A study of software salespeople found that the drive for the dollar was only one of six motivators. The other five were the drives for power, uniqueness, knowledge, to serve others, and the rare person who likes to follow the rules. Most software salespeople think rules are to be broken.[10]

Although money is not a primary motivator for many people, failure to be paid fairly is a demotivator. Kohn said that people should be paid generously and equitably and then be helped to put money out of their minds.[11]

Individual Performance Determinants   Churchill, Ford, and Walker have conducted extensive research on the individual differences that may contribute to a salesperson's performance. They apply findings from psychological research on job performance by considering the following variables: motivation; aptitude; skill level; role perception; and personal, organizational, and environmental variables. To explain the psychological process of motivation, they have chosen the expectancies model, which attempts to explain the amount of effort that a salesperson wishes to expend on each selling activity.

These researchers define expectancy as the salesperson's estimate of the probability that effort expended on a specific activity will improve performance. For example, "If I increase my calls on potential new accounts by 10% (effort), then there is a 50% chance that my volume of new account sales will increase by 10 percent during the next six months (performance level)." The total motivation to perform this activity is the expectancies associated with these activities times the importance of performance outcome to the salesperson.[12]

The researchers tested this model by surveying 227 salespersons in two industrial companies. They examined the relationships among age, job tenure, marital status, family size, and educational level and the importance of each of the following needs: pay, job security, recognition, promotion, liking and respect, sense of accomplishment, and personal growth. The findings indicate that in these companies financial rewards were most highly valued by older salespeople with long job tenure and by married individuals with large families. Promotion and opportunities for accomplishment and growth were more valued by younger, less experienced salespersons who were single or had small families, and those with relatively high levels of formal education.[13]

Ross notes that many researchers assume that salespeople are profit maximizers, like corporations. Other researchers assume that they are quota achievers; motivation is then assumed to decline as quota is achieved. Expectancy theory, as applied to sales, predicts that motivation is determined by the attractiveness of the reward, how much the reward is determined by the salesperson's task, and the achievability of the task. Expected utility risk choice models consider the utility and the probability of the outcomes.

After considering these models, Ross conducted several experiments to study the effect of the level of quotas on subjects' call selection decisions. He concluded that they take few risks if they are far below their quota, but more risks once the quota is met.[14] Badovick found that failure to meet quota had a substantial influence on subsequent salesperson motivation.[15] Setting of quotas requires a critical balance between being high enough to be challenging but not so high as to be discouraging, thereby reducing the chances that the salesperson will try for that really big sale.

This brief summary of the theories of motivation as they relate to salespeople suggests that what is needed is a theory that integrates all of these concepts. The motivational procedures that are recommended in the earlier parts of this chapter combine the humanistic and behavioral theories. The cognitive theories have not received wide application in sales management.

Role Conflict and Ambiguity   Research confirms the point made above that a clear job description is an important motivating factor. Donnelly and Ivancevich concluded that greater role clarity may play an important part in a salesperson's job performance.[16] Doyle and Shapiro concluded that the nature of the sales task has more to do with motivation than with personality, compensation, or the quality of management.[17] They studied the sales systems of four companies—two with clearly defined sales tasks and two without. They found that salespeople worked longer hours on the job when the tasks were clearly defined and when they saw a positive relationship between their efforts and results.

Direction of Causality in Job Satisfaction   There have been numerous attempts to measure job satisfaction of salespeople. Churchill, Ford, and Walker developed a satisfaction scale that included items regarding the job, peer relationships, supervision, company policies, compensation, promotion, and customer types.[18] Researchers and practitioners, however, often question the direction of causality between job satisfaction and productivity. Practitioners argue strongly that highly productive salespeople will be highly satisfied and that the management task is to make them productive, not to make them satisfied.

Recent research by Bagozzi supports this position. He states, "Apparently salespeople are motivated by the anticipated satisfaction that comes with performance more than they are by the performance itself."[19] Bagozzi concludes that self-esteem is the key determinant of motivation. He recommends that, "Management should enhance self-esteem by regularly providing positive reinforcement in the form of personal recognition and monetary rewards, as well as socially visible acknowledgments of good performance."[20] In another study, Bagozzi reported that role ambiguity has its greatest adverse effect on self-esteem because this ambiguity weakens self-regard and self-competence on the job. He concluded further that role ambiguity and motivation appear to have about equal but opposite effects on performance, so that the optimum sales management action would be to reduce this ambiguity and increase motivation simultaneously.[21]

Motivation in a Changing Culture   Because motivation programs are built on individual needs and values, they must reflect changes in these values and needs as they occur in a changing culture. Yankelovich, an authority on national values, concludes that the productivity problem with the American work force is the growing mismatch between incentives and motivation.[22] Motivations have changed but incentives have not. He notes further that one of the problems is the fact that many top managers are trained to deal with only the tangibles in business—finance, engineering, or production—so that they are uncomfortable in dealing with the intangibles of human behavior. He points out that these technology and capital investment decisions were once the key factors in productivity, but that the human dimension is becoming relatively more important.

Rapid changes in cultural values can produce generation gaps. Dunn provides an interesting case about a sales manager of one generation who is unhappy about the lifestyle and values of one of his outstanding salespeople.[23] This case raises serious questions about motivating salespeople to produce or to conform to established procedures.

One final ingredient in creating a self-motivating environment is to be an enthusiastic manager and create enthusiasm in others. "Management experts agree that enthusiastic people work better. Being fired up can sell ideas and make profits. Enthusiastic managers inspire workers. Enthusiastic workers inspire each other."[24]

WHY IS MOTIVATION THEORY RARELY APPLIED?

Although Maslow's motivational theory was first published in 1943, this and subsequent theories have found little systematic application in industry. This lack of application is explained largely by the fact that the systems for motivating individuals run counter to society's and industry's preference for dealing with groups by setting up systems, methods, and procedures that apply equally to all members of the group. Organized society finds it easier and cheaper to deal with groups than with individuals. Furthermore, governments and unions mandate that everyone be treated equally. The aforementioned theories of motivation, however, strongly suggest that group motivation schemes will be only marginally effective.

To motivate individuals to the maximum of their abilities, it is necessary to identify their individual needs and then arrange consequences in the environment to enable them to use their strengths to meet their needs. This identification is difficult, time-consuming, and could appear to be prying into the private affairs of individuals. Programs for individual motivation may also run into legal opposition from industry, institutions, government, and unions, all of which support standardized job categories and job descriptions, but for different reasons. Industry and institutions seek efficient assignment, evaluation, and compensation; governments want standardization for regulatory purposes and equal treatment; unions favor standardization because it facilitates organizing and controlling. It appears, therefore, that the gains in efficiency derived from standardized job descriptions and reward systems are offset by less than optimal individual productivity. Anyone who is concerned with the effects of motivation on productivity must consider the tradeoffs between organizational efficiency and increased individual productivity.

A second reason for not implementing individual motivation systems is that they require eliminating demotivators, which is a costly and time-consuming process. Some managers would prefer the short-range incentive systems that give immediate results, but they must be supplemented with other incentives as the short-run effect wears off.

MOTIVATION IN THE SALES ENVIRONMENT

Motivation differs from the other activities of sales management (Chapter 7) because it must be applied indirectly. The action-oriented field sales manager must accept that it is not possible to command a salesperson to be motivated. It is possible, however, to create environments that encourage salespeople to motivate themselves. Because all motivation is self-motivation, the first step in a motivation program is to create an environment in which self-motivation is possible. This process must begin with the removal of demotivators, which may be defined as those conditions that discourage positive efforts. Thus the successful sales manager must generate an early awareness of the causes of demotivation and their effects on productivity.

Job Demotivators

Hundreds of sales managers were asked in one study to identify demotivators, which were classified as follows: uncertain job requirements, misapplied qualifications, inadequate development, poor working environment, and poor reward systems. *Which ones have you experienced?*

Uncertain Job Requirements   People may not know what they are supposed to do, the limits of their responsibilities, their interrelationships with others who have related responsibilities, and where they fit into the organization. Statements such as, "I didn't know I was supposed to do that, too" and "That's not my responsibility" reflect poor job descriptions, inadequate orientation, poor training, or all three.

If the job requirements are uncertain, it follows that the performance standards are uncertain. Replies like, "How well am I supposed to do the job?" "How do I know when I'm doing the job the way you want it done?" "Yes, I know you'll tell me, but I'd like to know, too, so I can evaluate my own performance" and "The other supervisor said he wanted it done a different way" by a salesperson reflect a system of inadequate performance standards. A clear definition of job responsibilities does not remove uncertainty unless the salesperson knows the level of performance that is expected. Academic research has supported this demotivator when it found that role ambiguity and role conflict are negatively related to job satisfaction.[25] Role ambiguity—not knowing what one is supposed to do—also appears to be the main factor in lack of commitment to the company.[26]

Poor Person–Job Fit   An individual may be unsuited psychologically, temperamentally, or even physically for a career in personal selling. A manager who recognizes that a salesperson is in the wrong job might be doing the person a favor by terminating an unsatisfactory relationship and suggesting other career opportunities that might be more suitable. One study points out that improving promotion opportunities is a key to reducing turnover among high performers.[27] Improving job satisfaction also helped reduce turnover, but more among low-performing salespeople than high-performing ones. The bottom line is that it is important to manage turnover selectively.

Underqualified people often become discouraged or frustrated because of their inability to acquire the necessary knowledge and skills within a requisite time, to perform within the job standards, or to compete successfully with their associates. In contrast, the overqualified individual may become bored or bitter because of the lack of opportunity to use his or her talents.

Related to the overqualified case is the individual who perceives the present job as a dead end with no opportunity to develop personally and be promoted to higher responsibilities and recognition within the organization.

Inadequate Personal Development   Inadequate development of a salesperson can be caused by inadequate training, poor supervision, or poor communications. To those individuals with a potential for development and a willingness to learn, the lack of proper training is frustrating and discouraging. This discouragement is particularly pertinent to new entrants into the field of selling. To the average or above-average performer, supervision that is thought to be unfair or incompetent is highly demotivating. "Is anybody listening?" A new salesperson will, at times, feel frustrated and lonely in the sales territory. A manager who is a good listener can help prevent small problems from becoming major demotivators. It helps to ask people what motivates them, as illustrated in Exhibit 11.2.

Poor Working Environment   The environment in which some jobs are performed may be depressing or unacceptable to some people, particularly for extended employment. A comfortable and well equipped automobile may be important for a salesperson who spends many hours on the road. Creative individuals tend to be more sensitive to their environment and therefore find an unsatisfactory environment more demotivating. An individual with a metropolitan background may become demotivated if assigned to a rural territory that requires travel, and vice versa.

Relationships with one's peers can be an important part of the working environment. The demotivator of poor peer relationships is one of the less important ones for field salespersons because they do not interact with their peers frequently. Nevertheless, it is disturbing and demotivating to some individuals who may require a close working relationship with others.

Poor Reward Systems   Unfair or inadequate compensation is viewed as lack of appreciation for efforts expended or results produced, and can be a strong demotivator. Pay equity can be more important than pay levels. Research results indicate that salespeople compare themselves with others—inside and outside of the organization—to determine whether they are paid fairly.[28] Based on their research among salespeople in 80 industries, James Roberts and Lawrence Chonko suggest that managers consider both internal and external comparisons. They also suggest that thorough job evaluations, objective industry salary surveys, interviews with individuals and small groups about standards of comparison, and use of compensation consultants may help avoid perceived pay inequity.[29]

An increase in pay will have only a temporary effect if other demotivators are not corrected. "It isn't the hard work that gets me, it's the lack of appreciation." Recognition can be a stronger reward than compensation for employees who have a strong need for social rewards. The highly visible acknowledgment of a salesperson at a sales meeting for having made an important sale or the winning of an incentive, such as a television set, may provide a stronger reward than the commission associated with the sale.

Work–Family Conflict   The increasing number of dual-worker and single-family households has increased the extent to which work-family conflict is a demotivator for salespeople. As difficulties from family responsibilities flow into the workplace, and difficulties from work flow into the home, employees face emotional exhaustion and job dissatisfaction.[30] Researchers who have studied this issue suggest that it "may not be productive in the long run to make heroes of the '80 hour a week' superstar salesperson" and advise focusing salespeople's attention on working smarter, not longer hours.[31] Flexible and realistic scheduling, training on effective time management, development of daycare facilities on site, and other methods can also help reduce the drain on salespeople caused by conflicts between work and family responsibilities.

It should also be noted that a number of demotivators that lead to salesperson turnover may be external to the firm—such as general economic conditions, job opportunities, and competitor actions that affect within-firm conditions.[32]

Exhibit **II.2**	CLASS STUDY OF SALES DEMOTIVATORS

An easy way to identify motivators is to ask the salespeople. To demonstrate this ease, 29 students were assigned the task of interviewing a salesperson. The companies represented included two food wholesalers, four grocery manufacturers, three pharmaceutical companies, two companies in the computer industry, two companies in the furniture industry, and one company each in clothing manufacturing, insurance, music, medical equipment, coffee, packaging, financial services, and hair care. A total of 34 salespeople were asked to describe those activities that demotivated and motivated them. The responses were grouped into the following categories, including the percent of mentions:

Company Demotivators:

1. Not knowing what to do (51%). No job description, no quotas, vague performance standards, and not knowing the territory, the accounts, and their needs.
2. Compensation unfair (24%).
3. Poor work environment (24%). Wrong territory, weak peers, and problem accounts.
4. Management weaknesses (18%). Negative, few positive comments, supervision too close, disorganized, incompetent.
5. Poor communications (15%).
6. Poor logistics (12%). Delivery problems resulting in loss of commission and heavy paperwork that seems unnecessary.
7. Dead-end job (12%). Family business, no openings above for outsiders; boring after job mastered.

Selling Demotivators:

1. Rejection (15%). Several philosophical and optimistic salespeople had the following observations about rejection: "Use rejection to motivate and prepare more thoroughly for the next time." "Set sights on what you can do in the future, rather than dwell on what you did not do in the past." "Persistence breaks down resistance." "Success is a journey, not a destination."
2. Loneliness (12%).
3. Travel (12%).
4. Prospecting (6%).
5. Competition (6%).

Company Motivators:

1. Positive supervision (27%). Recognizes salespeople's needs and changes in their needs; gives positive feedback.
2. Recognition (21%). Letters, memos, bulletins, sales meetings, prizes, trips, things others can see, and a sense of being a winner.
3. Good communications with manager (15%). Phone calls, field trips, monthly bulletins, and district meetings.
4. Opportunities to learn (12%).

Selling Motivators:

1. Autonomy (24%). Self control and low supervision.
2. Self motivation (21%).
3. Immediate feedback from reaching goals (15%).

(How does this list from salespeople compare with the list of demotivators given by managers earlier? What are some reasons for their being different? What questions did these demotivators and motivators suggest to you when you have an interview and when you ride with a salesperson for a day?)

Job Motivators

Recognition   Recognition programs are effective when they reinforce performance. Properly managed recognition programs clearly identify the behaviors or outcomes desired and recognize only those individuals who have attained them. Effective recognition programs help the successful salesperson feel successful. They also help the sales force in general anticipate the recognition they will receive from success.

Converting job performance into work satisfaction, involvement in the job, and commitment to the organization requires a catalyst: the feeling of success. It is not enough that a salesperson is successful, she or he must feel successful. A study among 466 industrial equipment and supply salespeople from six companies found that feelings of success had a much more powerful effect on job satisfaction than did actual job performance.[33] Through recognition programs, the sales manager may be able to enhance the feeling of success among his or her high-performing salespeople. Notes one sales manager, who provides vacation trips for top performers: "People are motivated to earn the trip more for the bragging rights than the trip itself."[34]

Based on research conducted among medical supplies salespeople, Steven Brown and his colleagues concluded that emotional experiences—and the anticipation of those experiences—are a critical driving force in salesperson motivation.[35] They suggested that sales managers can build anticipated emotional rewards by clarifying what is at stake for the salesperson. Anticipated emotions were stronger drivers of motivation than actual outcome emotions in their study, so the researchers suggest that sales managers emphasize goal-directed emotions. For example, they suggest ending an awards ceremony with an announcement of the rewards to come during the next selling cycle.

Communications   Communicating with salespeople involves the two-way exchange of information; it includes listening to them and providing them with information. Communicating with salespeople is important at two levels: functional and symbolic.

At one level, communicating with the salesperson has a functional value: it provides both the sales manager and the salesperson with the information that each needs to make better decisions. Salespeople typically operate outside of direct supervision. To be successful, salespeople must be largely self-directed. But in order to make decisions that are consistent with the organization's strategy and goals, they must share in its information system. Correspondingly, the salesperson can provide the sales manager with information that he or she needs to keep tabs on the competition, to understand the conditions facing the salesperson, and other issues.

At another level, communicating with the salesperson has a symbolic value: it acknowledges his or her importance to the manager and the organization. Asking the salesperson's opinion and keeping him or her informed is a way of letting the individual know that he or she is a valuable member of the organization. It sends the message that the salesperson is included within the organizational community.

A sales manager can use a variety of mechanisms to communicate with salespeople: face-to-face discussions, videotapes, electronic mail, interactive computer information systems, physical or electronic bulletin boards, attitude surveys, team visits to customers, and more. Different media can be used for different purposes. For example, Boeing sends a half-hour videotape with a briefing by the company president—on sales, new product announcements, future plans—to each employee's home every quarter.[36] More than 80% of employees reportedly watch the tape, and it provides them with an opportunity to share their work with their families.

Learning Opportunity   Effective salespeople respond to challenge, including the challenge of learning relevant skills. Effective sales managers, in turn, build a path of learning opportunities for each salesperson. The learning path for a particular salesperson will vary with his or her background, area of sales responsibilities, and future career goals. The elements that the sales manager uses to build this "learning path" for the salesperson can include both tasks—such as a new product or territory assignments or the opportunity to lead a sales team—and training.

Training can help salespeople to clarify their job responsibilities and open the way to opportunities for advancement. The type of training needed depends on the "learning path" of the individual salesperson. Training is itself a motivator. The amount of training provided to salespeople is a strong predictor of job satisfaction, according to a study conducted by Emin Babakus and his colleagues among the sales force of an international service organization.[37]

Socialization and Social Support Organizational socialization is the process through which people learn the values, attitudes, interests, skills, and knowledge needed to become a functioning member of a particular group.[38] Based on their study of socialization practices among sales forces in 22 Canadian and U.S. companies, Stephen Grant and Al Bush recommend that sales managers focus on:

- clarifying exactly what salespeople should expect in their new jobs
- building a quality relationship between new salespeople and "all significant others who will have a role to play in their initiation into the organization"[39]

One method the researchers note for accomplishing the latter goal is to establish a "buddy" or mentoring system to match a new salesperson with a veteran. Research indicates that veteran salespeople who have more job experience, who are more satisfied in their jobs, and who are better at dealing with interpersonal relations, tend to be more willing to serve as mentors. Interpersonal competence is also important in their *ability* to serve as mentors.[40]

The effort required to gain entry into a sales force, or an elite unit of the sales force, can also be a motivating factor. Research among salespeople throughout the world led researchers to conclude that a challenging or "effortful" initiation enhances the salesperson's appreciation of group membership.[41] They conclude that salespeople value membership in a sales group more when more effort is required for initiation, and they value membership less if less effort is required for initiation. The researchers suggest that this same principle can be applied to veteran salespeople through the creation of elite sub-groups, such as "honor clubs" for those who have achieved 100% of quota.

Organizational Culture An organization's culture is the shared values and beliefs of its members. It has been referred to as "the way we do things around here." Usually there are subcultures within organizations, representing professional disciplines like sales. A unique sales force culture can be a competitive advantage for the firm if it is valuable (in that it leads to increased sales revenue, reduced operating costs, or both), rare in the industry, and difficult for competitors to imitate.[42] One way that sales force culture can be a competitive advantage is through its motivating effect on employees toward higher levels of sales and more customer-oriented behavior.[43]

Sales force culture may become more important as a source of competitive advantage—and a motivational technique—as increasing numbers of salespeople spend an increasing amount of time in the field. Advances in information technology have allowed salespeople to spend more time with customers and less in the office. Some sales departments have placed salespeople permanently in the field, officing in their homes or cars, or operating without a fixed office. Although this has the potential for increasing revenue and decreasing costs, it places a new burden on the sales manager to maintain a distinct culture in his or her group.

Sales force culture is developed and maintained through a variety of methods, including objects (such as symbols and heroes), communications (language, jargon, stories), and behaviors (rites and rituals, socialization processes, rewards).[44] An example of most of these devices is seen in the Mary Kay sales organization and particularly in its annual

"Seminar" event. Mary Kay has a salesforce of 300,000 people, selling cosmetics person-to-person throughout the world.

A recent Seminar, attended by 36,000 Mary Kay saleswomen, illustrates the enculturation process.[45] Symbols of achievement seen at Seminar included color-coded suits, sashes, badges, crowns, pins, and other devices. One sales director wore a gold band with "$1,000,000"—the amount she and her group sold that year—spelled out in diamonds. They also included the heroes of the company culture, including the top performing salespeople and Mary Kay herself. Communications used to maintain the culture included stories about the heroes, and particularly how Mary Kay got her start, building her organization from nothing into a $613 million business. The stories—such as how Mary Kay telephoned twice to visit with a salesperson's sick daughter—also convey the values of the firm. The sales "consultants" remember customers' birthdays, send them short notes, and show them the level of personal interest that is part of the firm's cultural value system. Behaviors also reinforce the Mary Kay culture at Seminar, such as when Mary Kay crowned four Queens of Seminar.

Sales managers have been trained to identify the needs of buyers and to sell the benefits of their products that will meet these needs. But many managers fail to see the analogy between buyers with needs and salespeople who have needs to be met on the job. Managers must continually sell the benefits of being a company salesperson.

If we ask, "Why do people work?" the most common answer will be, "To acquire the means to satisfy their needs off the job." We earn money to buy goods and services that we need and want. Although this answer recognizes the role of money as our exchange medium, it fails to identify the important role of job motivation in our industrial society.

Would the individual who works for money to satisfy needs off the job continue to work if he or she inherited a large sum of money? There are innumerable volunteers who work hard, enjoy what they are doing, and receive no compensation. This leads to the conclusion that most needs are job-related and can be satisfied on the job. It is important to emphasize that the individual is working to satisfy his or her needs, not the needs of the employer. Just as a mistaken purchase that fails to satisfy the buyer's needs results in buyer dissatisfaction, a job that does not meet the employee's needs on and off the job leads to demotivation that appears as loss of productivity, unrealized potential, requests for transfer, resignation, termination, or worst of all, retirement on the job. Behavior is a function of consequences that satisfy the individual's human needs.

If people buy to satisfy their needs, if people work to satisfy their needs on and off the job, and if management is the process of getting results through people, then how should managers manage? Clearly, their management style should encourage employees to meet their needs. Douglas MacGregor noted that we can improve our ability to control people only if we adapt to human nature, rather than attempting to make human nature conform to our wishes.[46]

There is a selling dictum that states, "If you would sell what John Brown buys, you must see John Brown's needs through John Brown's eyes." A management version of this saying could be, "If you would motivate how John Brown sells, you must see John Brown's needs through John Brown's eyes."

A MOTIVATION PLAN

A motivation plan begins with identifying the demotivators and motivators of the salespeople from their own perspective.

Eliminating Job Demotivators

A study of salespeople leaving their jobs suggested that turnover is a result of lack of management support.[47] Thus eliminating demotivators begins with the field sales manager. Failing to satisfy hygienic factors is like flipping the light switch when the wiring is defective: no matter how often one turns on the switch, it's still dark. Similarly, no amount of job enrichment will produce a motivated employee if there are demotivators, such as unfair compensation. It is essential to clean up the negative job environment before initiating positive motivational efforts. Although this may appear to be a formidable task, current management practices provide the means to eliminate most demotivators.

Identify the Job Clearly   Unclear job responsibilities and conflicting job standards are the most important job demotivators. Academic studies of job satisfaction among salespeople have revealed that dissatisfaction is caused by role ambiguity and conflict.[48] A job description that clearly defines the responsibilities of salespeople and their position in the organization will remove this demotivator. The organizational linkage becomes increasingly important as the organization grows. Field sales personnel who are separated from the home office for extended periods need to be reminded of their important function in the company.

Hire Qualified or Qualifiable Candidates   Properly designed hiring standards based on qualifications that will produce the required job behavior will go far toward minimizing the hiring of overqualified or underqualified applicants. In certain types of selling, qualified applicants may not be available. Then it becomes necessary to identify and hire qualifiable applicants. This type of hiring requires identification of job-related *behavioral* qualifications that predict a high probability of success after proper orientation and training. These job-related behavioral qualifications are essential to reducing the turnover of newly hired underqualified individuals and minimizing the hiring of persons for the wrong job.

Orient and Train Candidates   Programs will be necessary to orient and train entry-level sales personnel so that they can develop the required knowledge and skills to become productive. Some flexibility will be necessary in these programs to reflect the varying needs of the applicants. The recent college graduate, the experienced salesperson who is changing companies or industries, and the experienced individual who is changing career paths all have different training needs.

Refresher training programs are necessary for the present sales force because of rapid changes in products, competition, market conditions, and channels of distribution.

Provide Proper Supervision   Poor supervision is clearly one of the most serious demotivators, resulting in immediate as well as long-term loss of sales, underdevelopment of salespersons with potential, unresolved personnel problems which become magnified, and turnover through resignation of salespersons with management potential. Proper supervision is critically tied to a strong sales management training and retraining program that produces managers who are evaluated on their supervisory skills, as well as on the sales results produced by their district. Good supervision requires agreed-upon job definitions and standards for salespersons and field sales managers. If performance cannot be measured, it cannot be controlled. If it cannot be controlled, it cannot be managed.

Reward Equitably   Compensation and benefit programs can motivate salespeople, but if they are perceived as inadequate or unfair, they are a strong demotivator. Constant reviews of compensation plans are necessary to be as fair as possible, given the variability of territories, market conditions, and competitive salespersons. A company will want to compare its compensation plan with those of competitive companies, using data provided by research firms that exist solely for this purpose.

Develop Personnel   A lack of advancement opportunities and a lack of opportunities for personal growth are serious demotivators. Many companies fail to recognize that demotivators are costing them those individuals on whom the company depends to fill its management positions. Evaluation programs should identify persons with management potential. Many companies fund advanced training for these persons. The apparent expense of such a management training program should be more than offset by the short-term benefit of motivating sales personnel, the long-term benefit of providing a pool of management personnel for future growth, and the retention of present employees who would seek growth opportunities elsewhere.

Monitor Continuously   Eliminating job demotivators is a continuous process. Changes in market conditions, corporate marketing strategies, domestic and foreign competition, and federal regulations will require a continuous reexamination of job descriptions, evaluation systems, and training programs. Age distributions, economic conditions, and college students' images of sales careers will alter the supply of candidates available for hiring. These dynamics require a continuous reexamination of the sales environment in order to identify and reduce demotivators.

Creating a Self-Motivating Environment

When the demotivators have been eliminated from the job environment, positive motivational efforts may take effect. Now the manager can turn to the question, "How can individuals be motivated?" Individuals must be motivated individually rather than collectively if they are to achieve their maximum potential. A commitment to individual motivation is mandatory if a serious attempt is to be made to motivate sales personnel.

Individual Supervision   The single most effective positive motivator that the field sales manager has is the ability to apply personalized supervision. This supervision includes individual needs identification, job restructuring for motivation opportunities, and need-satisfying supervision. Individualized supervision recognizes that management is the process of getting the job done through people; that motivation is the process of creating job circumstances that will inspire, persuade, encourage, or challenge individuals to manage themselves; that job-motivated individuals work to satisfy their needs on the job; and that managers should manage not in the style that satisfies their needs but in the style that satisfies the needs of their employees.

Individual Needs Identification   It is clear from the preceding discussion that the important needs are those of the employee, not the manager. But how should the manager identify the employee's individual needs? Methods range from casual observation, through a case-study method, to highly structured recordkeeping. One company uses the case method in an unusual way to identify the needs, symbols, self-images, and strengths of salespeople. In this company, a sales manager and a salesperson jointly write a case about the salesperson that includes the following kinds of information: personal history, activities, interests, hobbies, job histories, job performance, career goals, strengths and deficiencies, and behavioral characteristics (such as, "aggressive," "takes charge," "quiet," or "a loner"). These cases are used to help the manager understand motivations and are used in training programs for managers. Surveys have shown that increased compensation is the least common reason for salespeople changing companies.[49]

Job Restructuring for Motivational Opportunities   After identifying the salesperson's individual needs, the manager must confirm that the job does in fact possess the means for this person to be motivated on the job.[50] If it does not, the manager faces the options of terminating the salesperson, transferring him or her to a job that will be more satisfying, restructuring the job to provide individual opportunities to satisfy needs or living with the realization that the job will not satisfy the individual's needs and performance will suffer. Restructuring requires job enrichment that will provide opportunities for psychological growth.

To restructure the job, the manager must know clearly the present job requirements of a salesperson and requirements that may be expected in the future. The individual's needs must be related to these job requirements to determine if the job can be transformed into a motivating opportunity. The manager must then create need-satisfying opportunities. For example, a salesperson with a need for self-esteem may be asked to organize a presentation for the next sales meeting.

Need-Satisfying Supervision   Individualized supervision requires the continuous application of need-satisfying supervision. This supervision is the process of working with a salesperson to set his or her objectives and evaluating his or her performance in achieving these objectives.

Technical Resources   Salespeople develop a sense of pride in being part of a modern, progressive organization. They like to feel that their company has developed the best products, strategies, selling programs, and promotional support materials to help them sell effectively. These technical competitive advantages are referred to as technical resources. The presentation of a new strategy, selling program, or support material to the sales force at a sales meeting can provide considerable motivation.

Leadership Styles   Few sales managers would claim to have the charismatic leadership style of John Kennedy, Vince Lombardi, or Dr. Martin Luther King Jr., but managers will have qualities such as warmth, integrity, fairness, realism, and decisiveness that will generate trust and respect, thereby making salespeople want to work for them. Such leadership styles generate a positive atmosphere that produces teamwork and identification with the company's objectives. Managers will possess these qualities in varying degrees and should learn how to use them well.

Motivational Resources   Major sales meetings will often include a keynote speaker, such as an athlete or coach, who inspires salespeople to do their best as if they were in the NCAA basketball finals or the Olympics. Many examples from competitive sports can be applied to selling. Albert E. N. Gray was an official of the Prudential Insurance Company of America and a motivational speaker for the insurance. He stressed the common denominator of every person who has ever been successful—"the habit of doing things that failures don't like to do."[51] Successful people succeed because their purpose is strong enough to form a habit of doing what they don't like to do, such as prospecting for new clients. Habit is retaining the momentum. Once stopped, it takes a lot of energy to overcome inertia.

There are many books, audiovideo tapes, audio tapes, and seminars on self improvement. The Reverend Norman Vincent Peale stressed positive thinking. Sales consultant Zig Ziglar stresses following through and maintaining motivation.[52] Anthony Robbins, an author, speaker, and trainer, stresses knowing what you want and taking control of your life to achieve your goals.[53] Stephen Covey, a professor and consultant, stresses the need to study the habits of successful people. He defines habit as the intersection of knowledge, skill, and desire.[54] The seven habits that he identifies are: (1) be proactive, (2) begin with the end in mind, (3) put first things first, (4) think win/win, (5) seek first to understand, then to be understood, (6) synergize and (7) sharpen the saw. Martin Seligman, a professor of psychology and a researcher, has found that optimistic people are more successful and that optimism is a trait that can be learned.[55]

Financial Motivators   Financial motivators, such as bonuses and contests, are an important part of the motivation systems in many companies. In some companies the only motivational schemes are financial ones. A financial incentive that is used without considering the human needs of the employee tends to have short-term effects. After a while, salespeople tend to ask, "What have you done for me lately?" Financial schemes can be effective over the long term only when the basic human dimensions of motivation have been cared for.

Implementing the Plan

When studying the needs of salespeople, the manager finds that their needs differ based on their sales experience, company experience, and productivity. Some of these differences among salespeople—and the corresponding differences in needs—are summarized in Exhibit 11.3.

External New Recruits   New salespeople who are in their first selling job, and are also new to the company, tend to be bundles of uncertainty regarding company policies, their own selling abilities, specific responsibilities, performance standards, and the field sales

Exhibit **11.3**	MOTIVATIONAL ISSUES BY LEVEL OF EXPERIENCE IN COMPANY AND IN THE SALES PROFESSION

	Company	
	New	Experienced
New (Sales Field)	**External New Recruits** • Enculturate into company. • Socialize into sales force. • Clarify sales role responsibilities.	**Internal Recruits** • Socialize into sales force. • Clarify sales role responsibilities.
Experienced	**Hired Guns** • Enculturate into company. • Socialize into sales force. • Clarify sales role responsibilities.	**Old Hands** Unsuccessful • Review person-job fit. • Supervise and coach. • Improve working environment. Successful • Recognize achievement. • Develop new skills.

manager's leadership style. This uncertainty provides the field sales manager with an excellent motivational opportunity to help new salespeople identify with the company and thereby build trust, loyalty, and self-confidence. To establish this motivational foundation, the sales manager may proceed as follows:

1. Enculturate them into the company through orientation about company history, benefits, and other issues.
2. Socialize them into the sales force by training in products, skills, planning, programs, policies, procedures, and establishment of a mentor.
3. Orient them in the territory (including housing, banks, etc.), and introduce them to associates.
4. Clarify role responsibilities by establishing a job description, performance standards, performance appraisal forms, the compensation plan, and promotional tracks.
5. Minimize the effect of trauma by arranging early failures during training.
6. Identify early strengths, human needs, areas in which special training is needed.
7. Arrange and guide them through early opportunities for achieving success.

Internal Recruits   Salespeople who move into their first selling job from elsewhere in the company—such as service representatives who have transferred into sales or management-track employees who are rotating throughout the organization—probably already identify with the company culture. It is important in these cases for the sales manager to socialize the internal recruit into the sales force and clarify the sales role; in other words, to treat him or her as a new recruit from the perspective of sales.

Hired Guns   The experienced salesperson who is new to the company moves rapidly along the learning curve, adapting company and sales experience from elsewhere to the context of the new firm. As with the internal recruit, the sales manager may be tempted to skip the enculturation/socialization processes for "hired guns." This would be a mistake.

Culture is company-specific. Cultures that generate high levels of sales, low turnover, and other favorable outcomes are the result of specific value-based social structures within firms. The hired gun brought into the firm because of his or her experience may have gained that experience in a different type of organization and sales force. If the company and sales force are to retain their cultural advantages, these experienced newcomers must be enculturated into their new environment. Otherwise, the firm will eventually begin to drift culturally toward the average of its new hires.

Old Hands   The experienced salesperson category can be divided into those who are successful and those who are having difficulties. With successful salespeople the field sales manager has the ideal situation for providing continuing opportunities to use their strengths, to be successful, and to satisfy their needs for achievement, control, and self-worth. This case provides an opportunity to apply Herzberg's "You don't motivate people to succeed; instead, you provide people with opportunities to succeed, and they will be motivated."

In the case study at the beginning of this chapter, Charlene's manager fell prey to the belief that top producers are independent loners and that their self-confidence is such that they don't welcome comments and suggestions from their managers.

Several authors have focused on this problem. Quick recommends that top performers should be managed as follows: (1) maintain close contact with the stars, perhaps even closer than problem salespeople; (2) look for new, nonmonetary ways to reward these high performers; and (3) always have some feedback for the top producers because growth and improvement are necessary for a sense of well being and satisfaction.[56]

Falvey introduces a variation on the 80-20 rule that is used in the allocation of a salesperson's time to customers.[57] He suggests 80% of the resources for motivation—compensation, recognition, management time, and support—be allocated to the top 30% of the salespeople. He notes that people should be treated according to their performance, not equally regardless of performance. He concludes that the single most damaging sales management mistake is to assume that the high producers don't need you. Greenberg and Greenberg concluded that top sales people need appreciation more than anyone else.[58]

The need for different types of motivation at different career stages was reinforced by research findings of William Cron and his colleagues.[59] They suggested that new recruits in the exploration stage of their careers do not tend to feel that they will be rewarded for effective performance. Sales managers may need to confront that skepticism directly. Salespeople in mid-career, on the other hand, are looking for the ladder to success. In this case, visible and challenging specialized positions may be helpful. Finally, older salespeople in the late stages of their careers—often without a realistic chance of promotion—pose particularly challenging motivational problems for the sales manager.

Although many jobs cannot be restructured to capitalize on a salesperson's strengths, every manager can create ways to satisfy their individual needs. For example, the salesperson who has a strong need for recognition and prestige may be assigned a special session at a district sales meeting. The individual who needs to dominate a situation should be reminded that personal selling permits running one's territory as a business. Reviewing the fringe benefits will aid the salesperson who has a strong need for economic security. A strong need to belong can be met by keeping in close contact with salespeople and making sure that they are included in all business and recreational activities. By recognizing a salesperson's strengths and achievements, a manager can help meet this individual's need for emotional security.

When an experienced salesperson has difficulty, the field sales manager has the opportunity to convince the person that a deficiency exists and to help him or her identify the reasons for the failure to meet mutually agreed-upon performance standards. The manager and salesperson together may then develop a program and schedule for improving performance. The manager can then work with the salesperson to achieve these goals and enjoy the consequences derived from improving selling skills.

Older salespeople who are less successful than they once were sometimes pose special motivational problems. These problems may be the result of:

- Declining performance resulting from a lack of interest, effort, self-discipline, a failure to keep current on new job requirements, or deteriorating selling skills
- Self-doubts because of growing seniority and the increasing number of younger associates who are moving ahead quickly
- Declining health or family problems
- Missed opportunities for promotion, real or imagined
- Unequal time with the field sales manager because of the manager's need to spend time with new salespeople

Such problems provide the field sales manager with a real test of his or her motivational abilities. It will be necessary to put the deficiencies in their proper perspective relative to the older salesperson's contribution to the total selling effort. The manager will need to get agreement on the variations between standards and performance. It will be necessary to correct time discrepancies between the efforts of younger and older salespeople. The manager could use the older salesperson to solve this problem by having him or her act as a trainer for younger salespeople.

In almost all motivational problems, whether they are with new, experienced, or older salespeople, the field sales manager has the means for converting these problems into motivational opportunities that will inspire, encourage, persuade, or challenge the salespeople to manage themselves productively. Specific actions that can be taken to motivate salespeople are shown in Exhibit 11.4.

Keeping the Field Sales Manager Motivated

Although field sales managers may have started their new assignments with high motivation, they will also have lows. The task of the general sales manager is to keep them motivated.

During the transition from a salesperson to management, the new field sales manager suffers a letdown that requires support and encouragement. The new manager quickly ex-

| *Exhibit* **11.4** | ACTIONS FOR MEETING THE NEEDS OF SALESPEOPLE |

Need: Recognition, Prestige, and Approval

1. Acknowledge achievements in district bulletins, personal memos, at district sales meetings, in front of spouse, in person.
2. Assign responsibility for session at district sales meeting and work with the salesperson on it to assure success.
3. Assign attendance at convention, or responsibility as "Salesperson in Charge" at convention.
4. Arrange for the individual to be recognized as the district authority on a product, procedure, or skill and assign her to help others.
5. Assign him to help screen promising applicants.
6. Help her qualify for promotion.
7. Assign him responsibility to head a selling team.

Need: Domination or Control

1. Assign responsibility as workshop leader or for market surveys.
2. Solicit her suggestions for better territory management of time, effort, needs, and goals.
3. Teach him better planning to achieve better territory and customer control.
4. Find ways to demonstrate the concept that salespeople are managers of their own territories.
5. Reassign to more challenging territory.

Need: Economic Security

1. Spell out performance standards to qualify for annual salary review and bonus.
2. Review the fringe benefits, such as life and health insurance, pension plan, automobile selection, and the employees' education fund.
3. Work closely with her to develop more productive working habits and territory management by objectives.
4. Help the salesperson plan his personal activities to maximize benefits from optional fringe benefits.
5. Emphasize the policy of salary and incentive bonus based on performance and productivity instead of seniority, and advise her of her relative standing in the group.

Need: To Belong

1. Maintain closer contact by mail, telephone, or in person to build confidence and provide reassurance.
2. Reassure him as a person, with birthday card, employment anniversary, etc. Inquire about and know her family, community activities, church, or other organizations. Praise his efforts to the group.
3. Emphasize the interdependence of all activities within the company, the district and region; encourage feedback.
4. Be sure she is included in all district activities, business or recreational, and arrange to have her invited by peers.
5. Encourage close working relationship with salespeople in bordering territories.
6. Encourage him to join outside community or business-related groups.

Need: Personal or Emotional Security, Self-Worthiness

1. At appraisal and counseling interview, review progress and achievements.
2. Assign her a series of reasonable projects and maintain close contact either personally or through trainer to emphasize their importance. Help her attain the objective so that she becomes accustomed to success.
3. Recognize his personal as well as business achievements, hobbies, customer rapport, and other areas of interest, and let him know you care.
4. Solicit her opinions and suggestions on promotion, marketing surveys, special assignments. Emphasize strengths.

Case II.1   TRI-STAR CHEMICAL COMPANY

Tri-Star Chemical Company enjoyed excellent growth over the past four years, doubling its sales of $48 million and exceeding the chemical industry growth trend by 37%. This growth resulted primarily from its expansion in the Texas, Oklahoma, and Louisiana markets where Tri-Star increased its sales coverage from six to eighteen salespeople, with six having been added in the last 12 months.

Randy Johnson, the current regional sales manager in this area, was 52 years old, having started as a salesman with Tri-Star 27 years ago, covering half the state of Texas and part of Oklahoma. Randy's philosophy was that hard work produces results, and when people produce results you pay them accordingly. Recently, Tri-Star hired a new personnel manager, Jim Solomon, who added some voluntary management training, including a course on the application of behavioral science theories on the job. Whereas two of the four other regional sales managers enrolled in the program and sent several of their DSMs, Randy has not. Instead, he commented, "These kinds of programs may have their place, but if you pay your people what they're worth you won't have any major problems. Money is what salespeople work for. That's their security."

Tom Hartman, who retired a year ago as district sales manager in Texas, trained both Randy Johnson and Gary Holmes, a salesman five years Randy's senior and who started with Randy. Tom grew up with Tri-Star and was a major influence in its growth in Texas, where he hired and trained a number of salespeople who transferred to other areas. Some were promoted to DSM, and two, like Randy Johnson, were promoted to regional sales manager as the company grew and the RSM level of management was added. Even though Tom hired and trained Randy and eventually worked for him, there was no resentment between them. In fact, Tom was Randy's biggest booster, even though his management style was considerably different. As Tom always said, "Randy is interested in results, and that's what the company hired him for. The strategies of how you get salespeople to produce the results is the responsibility of the district sales manager." Although Tom as a salesman had personally covered most of the district his salespeople had and knew most of the top management of the customers they sold to, his approach to management was to let his salespeople make the sale and be the heroes and he'd applaud their achievements. He provided technical support when it was needed and moral support when they failed. Tom was proud of his team and they worked together very productively, usually being at or near the top when the sales results were analyzed.

As the district expanded in personnel and ultimately was split, Tom recruited most of the new salespeople, including Judy Sampson three years ago, their first female salesperson. In the chemical sales field, where salespeople dealt with sales engineers and production managers in the plants and in the oil fields, there weren't many female applicants, and hiring Judy raised some eyebrows among the other salespeople. Tom had to defend his actions to several other DSMs. Randy,

however, never commented. Because Judy was a slow starter due to her lack of background in chemical sales, Tom had assigned two experienced salespeople to work with her in addition to the time he worked with her each month. Judy was 26 years old, had been divorced for 2 years, and had a 3-year-old daughter at the time she was hired. Initially she had some difficulties making arrangements for her daughter when she worked out of town, but eventually she solved the problem with the regular help of an older neighbor woman as a temporary live-in babysitter. At present she was about an average salesperson.

When Tom Hartman retired a year ago, Skip Petersen was promoted to DSM from an adjoining region. Skip had been with Tri-Star 6 years, had moved laterally into two different territories, each more important than the last. He had built a reputation for being an innovative, hard-working salesman who outsold the competition and attracted attention for the results he got. He invariably placed in the top five of every sales contest and enjoyed the publicity his successes rated in the regional and national sales bulletins. He was a natural athlete and was very active in participative sports. Skip was an achiever. When Tom came up for retirement and Randy Johnson had the opportunity to select Skip from two other candidates, Randy identified Skip as the kind of manager he wanted.

In the year since his promotion, Skip became increasingly concerned and impatient. Initially he tried to get to know his new district, the customers, their potential, the decision makers, who the major competition was in the area and how they were doing, and where the best sales opportunities existed for increased sales. Skip spent many evenings and weekends reviewing the records, analyzing the data, and making plans for the kinds of programs he wanted to introduce. In fact, he spent so much time that his wife began to make comments about whether his promotion was worth the price she and their young son were having to pay.

The problem Skip was encountering was hard for him to define. Sales had continued to grow at about the same rate as before he took over, but not in proportion to the sales opportunities that he saw. Although his nine salespeople were friendly enough, they weren't adopting his suggestions for improving their prospecting, planning, and selling skills the way he had suggested and expected. And then there were the problems with Judy Sampson and Gary Holmes, which he wasn't certain how to handle.

Judy was doing OK in her sales performance, even though he was sure that with more effort she could do better, but that wasn't the problem. Judy called him at home about one thing or another just about every other night. He realized she couldn't reach him during the day when he was out working with one of the other salespeople and she was on her own territory. The difficulty was the frequency of her calls and the subject matter. If it wasn't some problem with one of her accounts, it was about some sale she had made that she wanted

continued

Case II.I   TRI-STAR CHEMICAL COMPANY—CONTINUED

to hash over. And if that weren't enough, she'd tell him about some of the things her daughter Sally was doing. Skip's wife was becoming increasingly annoyed. She even went so far as to ask sarcastically what was going on between them. At that point, Skip became angry and ended up in a minor row with his wife. Skip remembered that Tom Hartman had said something about Judy's calls. Skip couldn't remember what it was, but he sure didn't appreciate Tom's allowing Judy to continue that practice.

The problem with Gary Holmes was quite different; in fact, it was almost the opposite of Judy's problem. Gary had been with Tri-Star a long time. Compared with Skip, he was an old-timer even though he was in his mid-50s. In addition, he and Randy Johnson, the regional sales manager, were salespeople together and were still good friends. Gary was the independent type and rarely contacted Skip. He was one of the most productive salespeople in the district, and had his own way of selling, which didn't match the methods Skip liked to see used, particularly by the new salespeople. Because Gary was one of the most productive salespeople, Skip wanted to have him help in the training of the new salespeople, but he didn't want them trained in the unorthodox way that Gary sold. Skip talked with Gary on the last two field trips he made with him about the methods he used, but without

success. In fact, Gary seemed to resent Skip's comments about his methods, and kept referring to the results he was getting. The situation became acute as a result of a telephone call Skip received from Randy Johnson. It seems that Gary told Randy that he wished Randy would "get Skip off my back. I don't need some young kid telling me how to sell. I've been getting top-notch results since before he was born." Randy told Skip he didn't want personnel problems to get in the way of productivity and he wanted the problem with Gary resolved promptly.

CASE QUESTIONS

Assign each of the characters in this case to a student or group of students, and determine the answers to the following:

1. Specify the predominant leadership style or needs of each of the persons in the case by identifying the pattern of actions (symbols) as they relate to the theories of Maslow, Herzberg, Open Management, and/or others.

2. Identify and explain the major problems with each individual.

3. How could the problem(s) be resolved? How could Skip Petersen motivate Judy Sampson and Gary Holmes?

periences that it is more difficult to satisfy personal needs through the work of others than through direct efforts as a salesperson. The general sales manager must identify and provide circumstances in which the motivational needs of the field sales manager can be satisfied. Because needs are generalizable, Exhibit 11.1 applies to a manager as well as a salesperson. The regional or general manager can use these actions with the field sales manager, but apply them at a higher level. Of course, the field sales manager who recognizes his or own problem can apply some of the actions on his or her own behalf.

Conger notes that, "The era of managing by dictate is ending and is being replaced by an era of managing by inspiration. Foremost among the new leadership skills demanded of this era will be the ability to craft and articulate a message that is highly motivational. . . . To create a meaningful frame for an organizational mission, values and beliefs are an essential component—especially those that reinforce commitment and provide guidance for daily action."[60]

(If you were Charlene's manager, what would you do today? Next week? Six months from now?)

SUMMARY

Motivation is based on the concept that all behavior is motivated behavior and each of us, without exception, plays, works, and does all the things that we do to meet personal needs. Resourceful sales managers realize that the best that can be done is to arrange job circumstances so that these needs can be met on the job.

To develop the proper environment for motivating, a sales manager must first identify job demotivators—uncertain job requirements, misapplied qualifications, inadequate personal development, poor working environment, and poor reward systems. A logical approach for individualized motivation begins with an understanding of why people work. To gain insights into behavior on the job, we may begin with the question, "Why do people buy?" This logical process leads us to the conclusion that sales managers should manage in a way that enables each salesperson to meet his or her needs on the job.

The development of a program of motivation begins with eliminating job demotivators. To do this, a manager must identify the job clearly, hire qualifiable candidates, train these candidates, provide proper supervision, reward equitably, develop personnel, and monitor them continuously. To motivate individuals, the manager must develop appropriate leadership styles, use all available resources, and supervise salespeople individually. This individual supervision requires the need to identify each individual's needs, to restructure the job for motivational opportunities, and then to use a management style of individualized need-satisfying supervision. The field sales manager must deal with motivating new salespeople, experienced salespeople, and older salespeople who may have retired on the job. The general sales manager must motivate the field sales managers directly and the salespeople indirectly.

Financial motivators have been relegated to a minor role in this discussion because they have only short-term effects if the proper environment for motivating has not been created. The salesperson quickly forgets having won a contest if the total job environment is unsatisfactory.

Theories of motivation include approaches that may be described as humanistic, cognitive, and behavioral psychology. The humanistic and behavioral approaches have been used in sales management more than the cognitive models, which are still in a state of development.

The complexity of motivating a sales force is increased by the fact that younger salespersons' personal values may differ widely from those of managers. The manager must work hard to understand the needs of the salesperson through that person's eyes.

ASSIGNMENTS/DISCUSSION QUESTIONS

1. Discuss the components of good supervision.
2. Discuss the relationships among symbols, strengths, human needs, self-image, and point of view, as stated in the Open Management System. Give an example of how this theory might apply.
3. What is the relationship between motivators and demotivators?
4. Discuss the application of motivational theory to a career development program.
5. Discuss the motivational needs of a young salesperson.
6. Discuss the motivational needs of the older salesperson.
7. Discuss a program a field sales manager could implement with an older salesperson whose performance deteriorated because he or she did not keep pace with technological changes in the product line.
8. Interview a salesperson and ask what demotivates and what motivates them.

ENDNOTES

1. A. H. Maslow (1954), *Motivation and Personality,* New York: Harper & Row.
2. Frederick Herzberg, One More Time: How Do You Motivate Employees? *Harvard Business Review,* January-February, 1968, pp. 53–62.

3. Vincent W. Kafka and John H. Schaefer (1990), *Working Relationships,* Morgan, CA: Effective Learning Systems Press.

4. Alfie Kohn (1993), *Punished by Rewards,* New York: Houghton Mifflin.

5. *Ibid.,* Chapter 4.

6. *Ibid.,* Chapter 5.

7. Jeanette Evans, "Operant Conditioning," *SAR Dog Alert,* 17(2), March–April, 1997, pp. 1–6.

8. Jeanne Greenberg and Herb Greenberg, Money Isn't Everything, *Sales & Marketing Management,* May, 1991, pp. 10–14.

9. David E. Shipley and Julia A. Kiely, Industrial Sales Force Motivation and Herzberg's Dual Factor Theory: A UK Perspective, *Journal of Personal Selling & Sales Management,* 6, 1986, pp. 9–16.

10. Russ Watson (1991), What Motivates Software Salespeople? It's More than Money, in *The Sales Manager's Survival Guide,* Atlanta Culpepper and Associates, pp. 82–85.

11. Alfie Kohn (1993), *Punished by Rewards,* New York: Houghton Mifflin, p. 182.

12. O.C. Walker, Jr., G.A. Churchill, Jr., and N.M. Ford, Motivation and Performance in Industrial Selling: Present Knowledge and Needed Research, *Journal of Marketing Research* 14, May, 1977, pp. 156–168.

13. G.A. Churchill, Jr., N.M. Ford, and O.C. Walker, Jr., Personal Characteristics of Salespeople and the Attractiveness of Alternative Rewards, *Journal of Business Research* 7, 1979, pp. 25–49.

14. William T. Ross, Jr. Performance Against Quota and the Call Selection Decision, *Journal of Marketing Research* 38, August, 1991, pp. 296–306.

15. Gordon J. Badovick, Emotional Reactions and Salesperson Motivation: An Attributional Approach Following Inadequate Sales Performance, *Journal of the Academy of Marketing Science* 18(2), Spring 1990, pp. 123–120.

16. J.H. Donnelly and J.M. Ivancevich, Role Clarity and the Salesman, *Journal of Marketing* 35, January, 1975, pp. 71–74. See also D.N. Behrman, W.J. Bigoness, and W.D. Perreault, Sources of Job Related Ambiguity and their Consequences upon Salespersons' Job Satisfaction and Performance, *Management Science* 27, November, 1981, pp. 1246–1260.

17. S.X. Doyle and B.P. Shapiro, What Counts Most in Motivating Your Sales Force? *Harvard Business Review,* May–June, 1980, pp. 123–140.

18. G.A. Churchill, Jr., N.M. Ford, and O.C. Walker, Measuring the Job Satisfaction of Industrial Salesmen, *Journal of Marketing Research* 11, August, 1974, pp. 254–260.

19. Richard P. Bagozzi, Performance and Satisfaction in an Industrial Sales Force: An Examination of their Antecedents and Simultaneity, *Journal of Marketing* 44, Spring 1980, p. 70.

20. *Ibid.,* p. 71.

21. Richard P. Bagozzi, The Nature and Causes of Self-Esteem, Performance, and Satisfaction in the Sales Force: A Structural Equation Approach, *Journal of Business* 53, 1980, pp. 315–331.

22. Daniel Yankelovich, Yankelovich on Today's Workers, *Industry Week,* August 6, 1979, pp. 67–72.

23. A.H. Dunn, Case of the Suspect Salesman, *Harvard Business Review,* November–December, 1979, pp. 38–52.

24. Stephen Silha, Putting Wind in Your Sales Efforts, *Creative Living,* Spring, 1993, pp. 12–17.

25. For a summary and re-analysis of the literature see Steven P. Brown and Robert A. Peterson, Antecedents and Consequences of Salesperson Job Satisfaction: Meta-Analysis and Assessment of Causal Effects, *Journal of Marketing Research* 30, February, 1993, pp. 63–77.

26. Sanjeev Agarwal and Sridhar N. Ramaswami, Affective Organizational Commitment of Salespeople: An Expanded Model, *Journal of Personal Selling & Sales Management,* 13(2), Spring, 1993, pp. 49–68.

27. Charles M. Futrell and A. Parasuraman, The Relationship of Satisfaction and Performance to Salesforce Turnover, *Journal of Marketing,* 48, Fall, 1984, pp. 33–40.

28. James A. Roberts and Lawrence B. Chonko, Pay Satisfaction and Sales Force Turnover: The Impact of Different Facets of Pay on Pay Satisfaction and Its Implications for Sales Force Management, *Journal of Managerial Issues,* 8(2), Summer, 1996, pp. 154–170.

29. *Ibid.*

30. James S. Boles, Mark W. Johnston, and Joseph F. Hair, Jr., Role Stress, Work-Family Conflict and Emotional Exhaustion: Inter-Relationships and Effects on Some Work-Related Consequences, *Journal of Personal Selling & Sales Management,* 12(1), Winter, 1997, pp. 17–28.

31. *Ibid.,* p. 25.

32. George H. Lucas, Jr., A. Parasuraman, Robert A. Davis, and Ben M. Enis, An Empirical Study of Salesforce Turnover, *Journal of Marketing,* 51, July, 1987, pp. 34–59.

33. Steven P. Brown, William L. Cron, and Thomas W. Leigh, Do Feelings of Success Mediate Sales Performance-Work Attitude Relationships?, *Journal of the Academy of Marketing Science,* 21(2), Spring 1993, pp. 91–100.

34. Vincent Alonzo, Recognition? Who Needs It?, *Sales & Marketing Management,* February, 1997, p. 26.

35. Steven P. Brown, William L. Cron, and John W. Slocum, Jr., Effects of Goal-Directed Emotions on Salesperson Volitions, Behavior, and Performance: A Longitudinal Study, *Journal of Marketing,* 61(1), January, 1997, pp. 39–50.

36. Edward E. Lawler III (1992), *The Ultimate Advantage: Creating the High-Involvement Organization,* San Francisco: Jossey-Bass Publishers.

37. Emin Babakus, David W. Cravens, Mark Johnston, and William C. Moncrief, Examining the Role of Organizational Variables in the Salesperson Job Satisfaction Model, *Journal of Personal Selling & Sales Management,* 16(3), Summer 1996, pp. 33–46.

38. Robert K. Merton (1957), *The Student-Physician,* Cambridge, MA: Harvard University Press, 1957.

39. E. Stephen Grant and Alan J. Bush, Salesforce Socialization Tactics: Building Organizational Value Congruence, *Journal of Personal Selling & Sales Management,* 16(3), Summer 1996, pp. 17–32.

40. Ellen Bolman Pullins, Leslie M. Fine, and Wendy L. Warren, Identifying Peer Mentors in the Sales Force: An Exploratory Investigation of Willingness and Ability, *Journal of the Academy of Marketing Science,* 24(2), Spring 1996, pp. 125–136.

41. Steven P. Brown and Robert A. Peterson, The Effect of Effort on Sales Performance and Job Satisfaction, *Journal of Marketing,* 58, April, 1994, pp. 70–80.

42. Jay B. Barney, Organizational Culture: Can It Be a Source of Competitive Advantage? *Academy of Management Review,* 11(3), 1986, pp. 656–665.

43. Michael R. Williams and Jill S. Attaway, Exploring Salespersons' Customer Orientation as a Mediator of Organizational Culture's Influence on Buyer-Seller Relationships, *Journal of Personal Selling & Sales Management,* 16(4), Fall 1996, pp. 33–52.

44. Donald W. Jackson, Jr., Stephen S. Tax, and John W. Barnes, Examining the Salesforce Culture: Managerial Applications and Research Propositions, *Journal of Personal Selling & Sales Management,* 14(4), Fall 1994, pp. 1–14.

45. Alan Farnham, Mary Kay's Lessons in Leadership, *Fortune,* September 20, 1993, pp. 68–77.

46. Douglas MacGregor (1960), *The Human Side of Enterprise,* New York: McGraw-Hill, p. 30.

47. What Does Sales Force Turnover Cost You? *Canadian Manager* 15(2), June, 1990, pp. 24–26.

48. Orville C. Walker, Gilbert A. Churchill, Jr., and Neil M. Ford, Motivation and Performance in Industrial Selling: Present Knowledge and Needed Research, *Journal of Marketing Research* 14, May, 1977, pp. 156–68.

49. Jeanne Greenberg and Herbert Greenberg, Money Isn't Everything, *Sales & Marketing Management* 143(5), May, 1991, pp. 10–14.

50. See Pradeep K. Tyagi, Perceived Organizational Climate and the Process of Salesperson Motivation, *Journal of Marketing Research,* 19, May, 1982, pp. 240–254; Pradeep K. Tyagi, Relative Importance of Key Job Dimensions and Leadership Behaviors in Motivating Salesperson Work Performance, *Journal of Marketing,* 49, Summer, 1985, pp. 76–86; and Pradeep K. Tyagi, Work Motivation Through the Design of Salesperson Jobs, *Journal of Personal Selling & Sales Management,* 5, May, 1985, pp. 41–51.

51. Albert E.N. Gray, *The Common Denominator of Success,* reprinted by The National Association of Life Underwriters, August, 1976.

52. Carl H. Giles, What Great Speakers Can Teach Us About Selling, *American Salesman* 35(12), December, 1990, pp. 3–9.

53. Anthony Robbins (1986), *Unlimited Power: The New Science of Personal Achievement,* New York: Simon & Schuster.

54. Stephen R. Covey (1989), *The Seven Habits of Highly Effective People,* New York: Simon & Schuster, p. 47.

55. Martin E.P. Seligman (1991), *Learned Optimism,* New York: Albert A. Knopf.

56. T.L. Quick, Helping Your Star Performers Shine Even Brighter, *Sales & Marketing Management,* April, 1991, pp. 96–99.

57. J. Falvey, For a Better Yield. Prime Your Sales Force, *Sales & Marketing Management,* August, 1989, pp. 55–56.

58. J. Greenberg and H. Greenberg, Money Isn't Everything, *Sales & Marketing Management,* May, 1991, pp. 10–14.

59. William L. Cron, Alan J. Dubinsky, and Ronald E. Michaels, The Influence of Career Stages on Components of Salesperson Motivation, *Journal of Marketing* 52, January, 1988, pp. 78–92; William L. Cron, and John Slocum, Jr., The Influence of Career Stages on Salespeople's Job Attitudes, Work Perceptions, and Performance, *Journal of Marketing Research,* 23 May, 1986, pp. 119–129.

60. J.A. Conger, Inspiring Others: The Language of Leadership, *Academy of Management Executive,* 5(1) 1991, pp. 31–45.

12

SALES QUALITY MANAGEMENT

LEARNING GOALS

1. To learn how quality management techniques apply to sales
2. To be able to apply quality measurement and diagnosis techniques to sales
3. To understand approaches available for redesigning and improving the sales process
4. To be able to relate sales training to sales quality management

"The quality program asks each and every salesman to rise above manipulative techniques and look upon the customer as a partner, not as an opponent. It requires nothing less than a compassionately intelligent approach to every customer's business. A salesman who relies on quality principles doesn't trick his customers into a deal. He works his way into a customer's confidence, but not to sell the customer something he doesn't need, not to force a customer to do something he wouldn't otherwise do. Once he establishes a relationship with that customer, he begins to learn, in great detail, how the customer does his business . . . He spends weeks gathering information . . . and, in the end, produces a report showing specific ways a customer can save money, reduce employment, raise productivity, even before purchasing a single product . . . Of course, the sales pitch eventually comes, but a genuine quality approach makes the sales pitch almost insignificant with the generous intelligence of the analysis that precedes it."
—David Dorsey, *The Force*[1]

Sales techniques have evolved over time. High-pressure selling has given way to "softer" persuasion-based approaches. High-pressure selling burned the bridge back to the customer, cutting off the path to repeat purchases. Persuasion-based approaches, in turn, were replaced by information-based selling. Increasingly well-informed and sophisticated customers were less susceptible to persuasion, they required documentation of value. Although selling in the most advanced organizations is still information-rich, the focus is on assuring quality throughout the sales process.

The increasingly competitive business environment has led many top firms to adopt total quality management (TQM). Total quality management is "a management process and set of disciplines that are coordinated to ensure that the organization consistently meets and exceeds customer requirements."[2]

217

Although this approach began in the manufacturing area, it is increasingly applied to service in general and sales in particular. This new focus has been marked by the extension of international quality standards into the service and sales areas.[3]

As applied to the sales-and-service process, the TQM approach includes:[4]

- Defining the quality of the sales-and-service effort in terms of customer satisfaction.
- Selling service- and quality-driven value—rather than price—to create loyal customers and long-term profits.
- Understanding sales and service as a system of interdependent subprocesses that link individuals, departments, suppliers, and buyers.
- Measuring sales-and-service processes and outcomes scientifically.
- Setting challenging but reasonable improvement targets for sales-and-service quality.
- Attaining quality improvement by innovation and continuous refinement of the sales-and-service process, rather than by pushing individuals.
- Developing individuals through training and communications.

Underlying the entire TQM philosophy is the importance of understanding business operations from the perspective of customer wants and needs. Often managers and salespeople have informal and unquestioned assumptions about customer expectations. By focusing on customer expectations and probing them with formal techniques, TQM discovers misconceptions and opportunities. For example, although managers at one Westinghouse division thought that customers were buying based on price and technology, a thorough survey of customers found that this was true for only a small percentage of buyers. Most customers were buying for delivery and immediate availability of applications advice.[5]

Implementation of TQM in the sales-and-service process involves process innovation, interfunctional integration, and continuous improvement throughout the organization.[6]

Sales quality has emerged as an important business issue. The increasing sophistication of buyers not only expanded their demand for information, it limited their tolerance for delays and errors in the buying process. However well a salesperson documents benefits in terms of buyer needs, this does not offset mistakes in order entry, slow delivery, poor service, and other problems.

Sales quality is a logical extension of the quality movement. *Product quality* centers around the manufacturing process. It focuses on controlling the quality of inputs and the conversion process itself in order to produce goods that conform to design specifications.

Service quality, in turn, focuses on the exchange process between buyer and seller. Service quality encompasses both the tangible elements of exchange, as well as intangible elements such as responsiveness to customer needs, empathy with customer concerns, reliable service performance, and assurance of service capabilities.[7] Because it typically requires participation of the customer in the exchange, service quality is often more difficult to management than product quality. The inherent difficulty in managing service quality makes it a potential source of competitive advantage for the firm that can provide consistently high-quality service.

Although the importance of product quality is reasonably well accepted by employees, the need for service quality—and its importance—have not been as widely accepted. This situation should change as more firms realize the potential gains from improvements in sales quality. Because sales force expenses comprise 10% of the typical firm's budget, versus less than 4% for research and development, sales quality improvements could yield valuable bottom-line benefits.[8]

As quality guru Kaoru Ishikawa notes, "People in the service sector or in the marketing and customer service divisions tend to think that quality belongs to . . . people who work in the manufacturing divisions. This is a mistaken assumption. As long as a person is selling a piece of merchandise or a service, he is responsible for its quality."[9] In fact, buyers reportedly are five times more likely to switch vendors because of service complaints than they are because of price or product quality.[10]

··

QUALITY MANAGEMENT PRINCIPLES: SALES APPLICATIONS

Dr. W. Edwards Deming popularized quality among business executives, first in Japan and then the United States. Deming had worked under Dr. Walter Shewhart, the Bell Laboratories scientist who developed statistical process control. After World War II Deming was influential in helping Japanese manufacturers adopt quality management. The success of the Japanese at producing quality goods finally turned U.S. manufacturers' attention toward Deming in the early 1980s.

Deming summarized his approach to quality management in 14 key points, interpreted below in terms of sales.[11]

1. *Create constancy of purpose toward product/service improvement.*
   In order to be financially successful in the long term, firms need a mission—a cause for being in business—that transcends short-term gain. The most secure basis for sales is a sincere conviction that the firm provides value to customers. Deming recommended that dedication toward this long-term mission replace devotion to the latest management fads and techniques.

2. *Adopt the new philosophy.*
   Customer orientation is the starting point of quality management. As a result, customer perceptions are seen as the appropriate yardstick of quality measurement. From a managerial standpoint, this principle is supported by results of studies that demonstrate that customer orientation is related to profitability.[12]

3. *Cease depending on inspection to achieve quality.*
   Before the adoption of Deming's philosophy, many firms used inspections by a "quality control" department to assure quality. Deming believed that the individual worker should be responsible for assuring quality. Each salesperson, telephone order taker, and all other members of the sales-and-service team are individually responsible for assuring the quality of their work in Deming's view.

4. *Stop awarding business on price; minimize total cost instead.*
   This element of Deming's philosophy has had a profound effect on selling. Instead of awarding contracts to firms with the lowest price (and usually lowest quality), Deming recommended certification of supplier quality and development of long-term relationships with qualified suppliers. This shifted emphasis from bid price to cost-in-use pricing, and from spot bids to long-term buyer–supplier relationships.

5. *Continuously improve the system of production and service to improve quality and lower cost.*
   Deming encouraged managers to view their work in terms of developing and improving systems. In this view, the sales manager is most likely to increase his or her organization's performance by improving the underlying sales-and-service system. This includes redesigning the system so that it can operate more efficiently as well as encouraging employee participation in system improvement.

6. *Institute on-the-job training.*
   This injunction replaces the manager-as-cop with the manager-as-coach, responsible for orienting new employees in their role in the system and coaching veteran employees on methods for improvement.

7. *Institute leadership.*

Sales managers should provide their salespeople and other subordinates with clear direction that is consistent with a value-focused organizational mission. This guideline appears to be supported by research. Evidence exists that job satisfaction improves, and turnover may decline, if sales managers provide salespeople with "compatible, consistent, and non-conflicting demands."[13] Although the value of "transformational leadership" is in dispute,[14] keeping to the moral high ground—without resorting to short-term quota pressures—appears to have long-term value.[15]

8. *Drive out fear among employees.*

In Arthur Miller's play *Death of a Salesman,* Willy Loman was driven by fear of being exposed to the tirades of his sales manager. In reality, salespeople who are pressured pass it on to customers. The result may be short-term sales and long-term customer dissatisfaction. In a quality selling environment, managers focus on fixing the system rather than pushing the players. Besides, Deming argues that most of the responsibility for problems is poor management: "Workers are responsible for only 15% of the problems, the system is responsible for the other 85%. The system is the responsibility of management."[16]

9. *Break down interdepartmental barriers.*

From the customer's perspective, the sale–production–delivery–service chain is as weak as its weakest link. Problems within this system may be the "fault" of another department, but the customer doesn't care; it's simply the supplier to the customer. There is a lot to be gained, and nothing to lose, by overcoming the normal structural and interpersonal barriers across departments. Focusing on an interdepartmental commitment to quality is the primary vehicle for this change.

10. *Eliminate slogans relating to quality.*

Attempting to promote quality with slogans and posters can have a boomerang effect; employees see the campaign as "just another management fad." Deming urges managers to replace the promotional atmosphere with quality-related data.

11. *Eliminate work standards and management by objectives.*

The primary focus of quality management should be processes, defects, and cycle time, not artificial quantitative goals. A characteristic of systems is that the elements are interrelated. Thus a problem with quantitative goals is that a goal in one area (for example, sales) can be forced higher only at the expense of other goals (such as service or on-time delivery).

12. *Remove barriers to job performance.*

The job of a sales manager is to set up a system in which salespeople can succeed and take pride in their success. Thus the sales manager should focus on such tasks as clarifying work roles, allocating optimal sales territories, and providing systems that support instead of interfering with work performance.

13. *Institute a program of education and self-improvement.*

Research indicates that salespeople who understand the strategy of the firm outperform those who do not. Although understanding corporate strategy does not tell a salesperson how to sell, it does set a context that directs the salesperson's activities and motivate his or her performance. Training about quality management works in the same way. In the end, the program of education and self-improvement is about internalizing quality—making it part of the salesperson's belief system and lifestyle.

14. *Engage everyone in the transformation to quality.*

If quality occurs only within a system, then all elements of the system must participate for quality improvement to occur. Systems are not compensatory; quality manufacturing will not overcome errors in order-taking, deliberate over-commitments, or other defects in selling. Nor will sales quality overcome poor after-sale service.

SALES QUALITY: PROCESS MEASUREMENT AND DIAGNOSIS

Adopting process (or systems) thinking requires a mind-shift for many sales managers. Traditional sales organizations have trained salespeople and managers alike to think in terms of short-term effort—"making the sale." In this world view, sales managers are once-successful salespeople who can teach the new salespeople the persuasive skills and techniques required to complete the sale. If quotas are missed, salespeople are pressured—and perhaps coached—to improve their numbers. If too many quotas are missed by too many salespeople, the sales manager is pressured, coached, or replaced.

Instead, process thinking breaks performance down into its component elements and the linkages between those elements. Inputs and outputs at each stage of the process are examined; productivity is simply the ratio of the two. Careful and objective measurement of productivity then forms a basis for process improvement.

The ultimate goal of business is to produce satisfied, loyal, and profitable customers. Customer satisfaction legitimates business. Without satisfied customers the business has no ethical reason to exist in society. Customer loyalty bridges satisfaction and profitability. Loyal customers repeat their business and buy new products and services, often at a price premium. They also refer new business to the firm. Profitability is simply a requirement for maintaining and growing the business.

The Business Process

Sales is a process within a larger process aimed at producing satisfied, loyal, and profitable customers. The general business process, shown in Exhibit 12.1, includes sales as a link in the chain of value delivery. The chain begins with customer research, because customer satisfaction depends on understanding customers' wants and needs. Research links directly into sales because a quality sales contact—from the customer's viewpoint—is one that is framed in terms of the customer's wants and needs.

Sales triggers production, delivery, and service. Completion of this entire chain leads to some level of customer-perceived value, which is the test of the firm's worth. For this reason, research on customer-perceived value should drive changes in the system. The ultimate goals: improve the system to increase customer-perceived value (earning satisfaction and loyalty) and/or to reduce operating costs (increasing profitability).

Improvement of this overall chain of quality engages the sales manager at the highest level of the organization. This role is exemplified by this comment from Barbara Riggs, man-

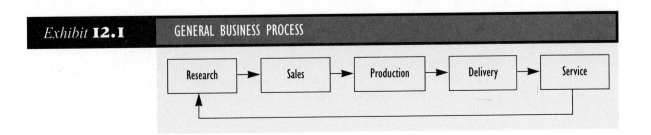

Exhibit **12.1**   GENERAL BUSINESS PROCESS

ager of National Sales Quality for Moore Business Forms: "Like many companies, we had initially focused on product quality, the quality of our manufacturing operations. It's been referred to as quality-in-a-box. We recognized, however, the critical need to move beyond that singular mindset to a holistic approach that encompassed all our business processes. A fundamental cornerstone was our belief that people inside the company build internal customer/supplier partnerships in order to satisfy and delight our external customers."[17]

Sales Process Elements

The sales system is nested within this overall business system. Identifying the elements and linkages within the sales process, as previously shown in Exhibit 4.1, forms the basis for improving it. When it is performed in a quality way, the sales process transforms prospects into satisfied and loyal customers at the lowest possible cost.

Analysis of the sales process element by element enables a manager to track productivity and to apply process improvements precisely. Sales reports may tell the manager that financial goals are not being met but they will not tell why, notes George Smith.[18] Breaking the sales process into its elements and developing productivity measures for each step will specify *where* problems are occurring. This enables the sales team to take directed and specific action to improve the situation.

Ongoing measurement of the selling process is an important part of the sales manager's job. Measures of the selling process provide the manager with the information needed to diagnose the cause of shortfalls in sales revenues. Knowing the causes of problems allows the manager to select the right quality improvement tools, which should result in improved bottom-line results.

Measurement of the selling process is a difficult task, which is why some sales managers do not do this well. Each step in the process is different. Although some steps lend themselves to objective quantification, others do not. For example, given a reasonably good accounting system, one can figure the cost per prospect—but the quality of a particular presentation or close is more subjective.

It is better to measure the right things poorly than the wrong things well. In particular, having identified the steps in the selling process, the sales manager is better off with rough measures of productivity at each step instead of using only the more precise (but less revealing) financial measures like cost per sales call. Although financial measures are sometimes important, they usually fail to point to the factors that cause them to change. Thus a given salesperson may be producing below quota, but the sales-to-quota figure will not tell the manager that the salesperson has poor presentation skills and needs appropriate training. By pinpointing the causes of problems through careful measurement on each step in the selling process, the sales manager can maximize the performance of the sales force. This approach also helps to minimize pain and suffering for everyone, including the manager, the salesperson, and the prospect.

Productivity is simply the desired results (output) divided by the resources consumed (input). Examples of key measures of the productivity of the overall selling process include sales revenue to the cost of selling or selling time to nonselling time.[19] Both measures are valuable indicators of productivity, either at the level of the individual salesperson or the sales force as a whole. Similar productivity measures can be developed to diagnose each step in the selling process.

Problems can occur at each stage in the selling process. The sales manager's responsibility is to help diagnose the problem in impersonal terms, pinpoint the cause of the problem, and help salespeople (as a group and individually) to identify potential solutions.

In the following section, suggested measures of productivity are provided and potential problems that can limit productivity are identified.

Prospecting for Leads   The purpose of prospecting is to generate valid leads. Thus the productivity of prospecting can be measured in terms of the cost per valid lead (total cost of lead-generating activity divided by number of valid leads). For example, if January lead-generating activity costs $1300 and yields 33 valid leads, the cost per lead is $39.39. If February lead-generating activity costs $1200 and yields 22 leads, the cost per lead increases to $54.54. Costs incurred to generate leads include both direct expenses (such as advertising and direct mail) as well as indirect expenses (such as salesperson time).

Potential problems in lead generation include lack of a lead-generation system, lack of information about potential lead sources, and reliance on outdated lead-generating mechanisms. Many sales managers and salespeople handle lead generation on a catch-as-catch-can basis. Yet the generation of leads is the starting point in the sales process. Without a dynamic lead-generating system, the sales force lacks the raw material it needs to move forward. Leads can come from industry trade publications, government data, response to advertising, client referrals, and other sources. Effective sales managers track the quality of leads by source and continuously scout out new sources of leads.

Lead sources can become outmoded as customers move to new communications and networking formats. The increasing convergence of consumers and business customers on the Internet is one example of this shift. Ralph Wilson, author of an Internet newsletter on web marketing, says that prospecting on the World Wide Web involves offering readers multiple opportunities to "sign in" and then qualifying them in terms of level of intent: Are they just browsing, contemplating a purchase, seriously planning a purchase, ready to buy as soon as possible, and so on.[20]

Classifying Leads   The purpose of classifying leads is to sort them into priorities. Just as emergency medical centers "triage" patients into groups that require immediate attention and those who can wait for care, sales organizations sort prospects into those with the most immediate potential.

Time-to-action is the pivotal issue in both cases. Prospects need immediate attention or they are likely to lose interest in a purchase. Given limited sales force time, the most promising prospects should receive the most immediate sales force attention.

A common approach to classifying leads is to measure the proportion of prospects based on revenue potential. A simple classification system is the ratio of high-revenue prospects to total "real" prospects.[21] For example, if January activity generates 4 high-revenue prospects out of 33 valid leads, the lead quality ratio is 4/33 or 0.12. If February activity generates 8 high-revenue prospects out of 22 leads, the lead quality ratio is 0.36. Although the total lead count has declined, the lead quality ratio has improved.

Problems that can occur in lead classification include prejudging of leads by salespeople and lack of intensive lead generation activity from appropriate sources. Lead classification is a critical task. For a promising lead to pass unnoticed is the sales equivalent of having a critically ill patient die from lack of attention. In order to classify leads accurately, sales managers and salespeople must agree on classification criteria and use them consistently. On the other hand, a poor ratio of high-to-low revenue prospects may indicate that the sales manager should reexamine the sources of leads in terms of the type of leads they are yielding. Shifting to richer prospect-generating mechanisms could improve the value of leads obtained.

Developing a Selling Strategy   The desired output of the time and information required to develop a prospect sales strategy is identification of valid reasons to purchase.[22] Although this is a subjective element in the sales process, it deserves careful analysis.

Sales strategies represent an attempt to match the customer's needs with the supplier organization's resources in a product–service package that offers superior value over packages offered by competitors. The customer's needs may be determined by background research and by interviews with the prospect. Presumably (but not necessarily) these needs will correspond to resources and capabilities offered by the supplier firm. The supplier hopes that these resources and capabilities can be assembled in a way that is superior to competitive offers.

Failure at this point can result from such problems as insufficient background information about prospects, lack of access to customers for pre-approach interviews, and poor interviewing skills on the part of the salesperson. Failure can also result from the salesperson's ignorance of the full capabilities of his or her own organization or of competitive products, services, and pricing.

Approach   The desired output of the approach stage is the customer allowing a presentation. One measure of productivity at this stage is the ratio of the number of presentations made to the total number of prospects in process.

Failure can occur at this point because of a negative or limited corporate image, problems with the salesperson's reputation with the buyer firm, domination of the prospect by a competitor, an inability to identify the appropriate decision-maker(s) within the prospect firm, or an inability to gain access to the decision-maker(s) in the prospect firm because of lack of time or other reasons.

Presentation   The desired output of the presentation is customer preference.[23] Preference is sometimes difficult to measure, because the prospect's decision process may be shielded from the salesperson. Further, the buyer firm may provide false signals on preference as a bargaining ploy, for example, suggesting that the offer is inferior to a competitor's offer in order to gain price or other concessions. Nonetheless, it is important that the quality of presentations—in relation to customer preferences—be evaluated.

Failure of the presentation may be a result of such factors as poor presentation skills, the absence of key decision-makers, or an inability to adapt the presentation to concerns expressed by the audience.[24] In some industries or selling environments, buyers have come to expect sophisticated multimedia displays as part of the presentation (such as computerized graphics or simulations of the final product) and the presentation can fail to meet these expectations.

Trial Close   The desired output of the trial close is a sale. In a sense, the trial close is an efficiency measure, in that it circumvents the need for handling objections if the customer is ready to purchase. The productivity of the trial close probably reflects that of the preceding steps. The effectiveness of prospecting, classifying, strategy development, approaching, and presenting is reflected in the percentage of sales completed at the trial close stage—that is, the percentage of sales closed without objections.

Handling Objections   The desired output of handling objections is a customer predisposed to purchase. Objections can include arguments by the prospect that the price is too high, product quality is inadequate (or unknown), the proposed delivery schedule is too late, or that the supplier has a poor (or unknown) reputation for post-sale service.

Closing the Sale   The desired output of closing the sale is the sale itself. Failure at this stage can result from the salesperson not asking for the sale, the salesperson not using an appropriate closing technique, or the prospect continuously postponing a purchase decision.

Follow-up   The desired output of sales follow-up is a satisfied customer. Failure to achieve a satisfied customer can result from problems with product quality, late delivery, poor post-sale service, or other factors.

It is important for the salesperson and his or her manager to keep in mind that the only criterion of customer satisfaction (or dissatisfaction) is the customer's own perceptions. Thus even if the promised product–service package is delivered on time as specified, any event (such as a competing product announcement) that causes the prospect to become less than satisfied is a potentially important issue.

Overall Sales Process Measures

Sales process elements that do not lend themselves to objective measurement can be measured through surveys of salespeople and customers. Surveys often are an appropriate measurement tool for these subjective elements in the selling process because the issue is perception. For example, a sales presentation is effective if the customer perceives that it is effective. There is no "higher" or more objectively correct criterion.

Sales Force Surveys   An in-house survey of salespeople is one means to diagnose productivity at each step of the selling process. This approach, as suggested by George Smith,[25] involves asking salespeople to evaluate their own performance at each stage of the selling process. A sample evaluation form is shown in Exhibit 12.2.

Smith suggests that selling process self-evaluations should be conducted anonymously. The results can be used in a process improvement workshop. In the workshop setting, salespeople can be divided into groups to identify the causes—and potential solutions—to problems at each step in the selling process. The results can also be used to help the sales manager identify training needs at the group level. By providing a menu of training options, dealing with the important needs suggested by the salesperson survey, individual salespeople can select specific training options that meet their own self-assessed deficiencies. Confidential one-on-one counseling by the sales manager may also help direct the salesperson into appropriate training channels.

Customer Surveys   In addition to internal surveys, sales managers can obtain direct measures of prospects' perceptions of the selling process. This may be done informally through direct contact or formally through a survey conducted by a third-party research

Exhibit **12.2**	SALES PROCESS EFFECTIVENESS SELF-EVALUATION FORM

Instructions: Circle the number that indicates your belief about your effectiveness at each of the following steps in the selling process. Your response is confidential.

Sales Process Step	Poor	Fair	Good	Very Good	Excellent
1. Prospect for leads	1	2	3	4	5
2. Classify leads	1	2	3	4	5
3. Develop selling strategy	1	2	3	4	5
4. Approach	1	2	3	4	5
5. Presentation	1	2	3	4	5
6. Trial close	1	2	3	4	5
7. Handle objections	1	2	3	4	5
8. Close sale	1	2	3	4	5
9. Follow-up	1	2	3	4	5
TOTAL SCORE					

SOURCE: Adapted from George A. Smith, Jr. (1995), *Sales Productivity Measurement*, Milwaukee: ASQC Quality Press.

firm. Informal contact can take the form of follow-up by the salesperson or sales manager to obtain the prospect's assessment of the selling effort, and whether or not the effort resulted in a sale. Formal contact through a third party can have the advantage that the survey is conducted anonymously and includes less bias.

The importance of customer surveys in the selling process is shown in an example from Cas Welch and Pete Geissler:[26]

> Marketing managers at one Westinghouse division knew for sure that their customers were buying on price and technology. An extensive survey demonstrated that this was true for only a small percentage of buyers. Delivery and immediate availability of applications advice were by far the most important buying criteria for over 90 percent of their customers. Knowing this, the entire sales and sales support functions were changed to absolutely guarantee the availability of a knowledgeable applications engineer at all times, and inventories were revised to absolutely guarantee availability of most products anywhere in the country.

Use of Time   Three major time-use issues affect sales: product development cycles, sales fulfillment cycles, and selling-to-nonselling time. Each of these issues is nested within the other, from product development cycles—which encompass the entire organization—down to the individual salesperson's selling time ratio.

Product development cycles continue to be compressed. Because product life cycles are getting shorter, the penalty for late market entry is higher. The international consulting firm McKinsey & Co. demonstrated that high technology products coming to market six months late—but on budget—will earn 33% less profit over five years, whereas those that come out on time—but 50% over budget—earn only 4% less.[27] Companies use concurrent engineering and other approaches to compress product development cycle time. Although product development extends across the organization, salespeople are a key element in the process, linking customers' needs and wants with product development plans.[28]

Sales fulfillment cycles are also being compressed, although the scale is more limited. The sales fulfillment cycle is the time that elapses from the time the salesperson takes an order until the order is fulfilled. Compressing this cycle reduces expensive work-in-process and inventory and increases the rate of product delivery. George Stalk reports that in the late 1970s the competition-minded engineers at Toyota Manufacturing were upset with their Toyota Motor Sales counterparts: it took 2 days to manufacture a car, but 15 to 26 days to close the sale, transmit the order, schedule and complete delivery. Sales and distribution costs were 20% to 30% of a car's cost—more than the manufacturing cost. By 1987 Toyota compressed the manufacturing-through-delivery process to 8 days.[29,30]

Salesperson time allocation refers to the amount of time devoted to selling versus nonselling activities. Selling time includes both face-to-face selling and telephone selling. Nonselling time includes all other activities, particularly travel, administrative work, and service work.[31] If a salesperson is involved in direct selling activities for 21 hours out of a 48 hour week, then 43.75% of his or her time is devoted to selling. This also means that 56.25% of his or her time is not producing an immediate return to the business.

Monitoring of selling time is a major sales management responsibility. When selling time is not directly measured, it tends to be ignored. Nonselling activities tend to expand and accumulate. New reporting and service activities are added, but existing activities are not reviewed and deleted. Waste creeps into the system.

A 1990 study by Dartnell Corporation, a supplier of training aids, reported results of a survey of 250 sales managers across a variety of industries. The average salesperson work week reported was 47 hours. The time allocation of these salespeople on average, is shown in Exhibit 12.3.

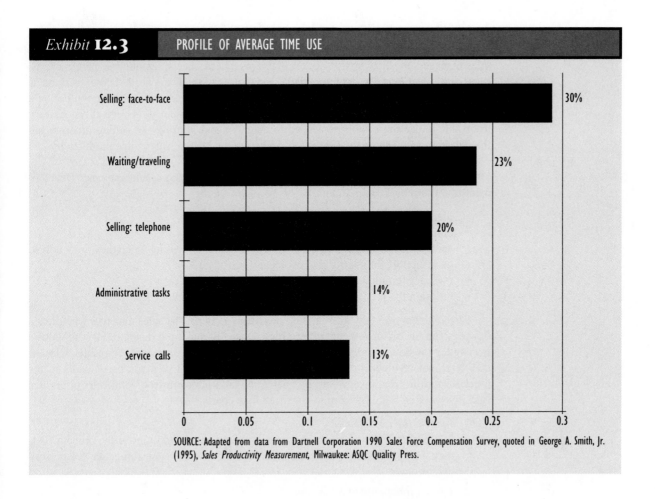

SOURCE: Adapted from data from Dartnell Corporation 1990 Sales Force Compensation Survey, quoted in George A. Smith, Jr. (1995), *Sales Productivity Measurement*, Milwaukee: ASQC Quality Press.

The cost of nonselling time is not a percentage of the salesperson's pay; it is the opportunity cost of lost sales. George Smith estimates the total cost of nonselling time for the average salesperson at $60,000 per year based on the following calculation:

$1,244,447 (the average annual sales volume per salesperson)
× 0.10 (annual selling cost as a percentage of sales)
× 0.50 (% nonselling time).

Smith estimates that nonselling time costs a company with 50 salespeople $3 million per year.[32]

PROCESS IMPROVEMENT TOOLS

Measuring quality is an important initial step toward controlling sales force performance. Unless it is measured, quality cannot be predictably improved—and the performance improvements resulting from quality improvement cannot be calculated. But measurement of quality is only the first step toward quality improvement: the next step is quality improvement itself.

Continuous quality improvement includes a set of methods for individuals, teams, and units to standardize and improve quality incrementally. Among the TQM tools available to sales managers are flow charts, scatter diagrams, check sheets, histograms, pareto charts, cause-and-effect diagrams, control charts, and "house of quality" charts. These instruments belong in the toolbox of a sales manager, just as they belong (and are) in the toolbox of a production manager. It is not necessary or productive to use them all at once. It is necessary to be able to use these tools as needed to diagnose and improve the selling process, and through improvements in the process to ratchet up the level of sales force productivity.

Flow Charts   Flow charts can be used to map the sales-and-service process. Development of a flow chart can help to:

- identify opportunities to streamline the process
- eliminate bottlenecks and other delays
- enable salespeople and others to understand the process in which they are involved
- gain support for quality improvement
- train new employees
- redesign the process from the customer's point of view

Development of a flow chart should be a team activity. The sales manager who plots a flow chart in the privacy of his or her office is usually making a mistake. The individuals involved in the flow of activities being charted are less likely to accept the results, because they were not involved in the charting process. More positively, the participants in the process can offer real insight into its operation—and improvement. John Burr offers five rules for working with the team to construct flow charts:[33]

1. *Involve the right people.*
   The people who are part of the system should chart and improve the process. This may include the salespeople, sales assistants, customers, customer service personnel, or others.

2. *Use an independent facilitator.*
   An independent facilitator can: (a) prevent problems of perceived interdepartmental bias; (b) offer candid suggestions about activities that should be eliminated; (c) assure equal participation in the process; and (d) handle the burden of administering the session.

3. *Keep all data visible to all participants.*
   Burr notes that using overhead transparencies or a whiteboard usually limits the group's view to a section of the process. He suggests using newsprint and masking tape to show all of the process across an entire wall. This allows participants to review and revise past steps; adding process elements that were omitted or revising elements that were incomplete.

4. *Budget enough time.*
   Like most activities, process charting usually takes more time than originally estimated. So budget enough time, and consider adding an additional session if necessary. The second session may be particularly useful if the group has not worked together before, and needs the initial session as a warm up.

5. *Encourage questions.*
   As Burr notes, "Questions are the key to the flowcharting process."[34] Some questions that might pertain in a selling process charting session:

   - Where does the order (or information request, etc.) come from?
   - How does the order (information request) enter the process?
   - Who makes the decision about price (or delivery, etc.)?

- Is there any other activity or decision that must occur in this process?
- Where does the product, (or service, information, etc.) go next?
- What tests are used to determine whether the product (or service, information, etc.) is ready to send?

The flow of activities involved in responding to a customer inquiry is charted in Exhibit 12.4. Note that there are a minimum of eight steps, with the possibility of eleven steps if a revision is required, and more with additional revisions. Each step introduces costs of time and materials. It is useful to estimate these costs—or at least elapsed time—at each step in the process.

A revision of this process, which switches from production of a paper document to transmission of a FAX, is shown in Exhibit 12.5. Note that the number of steps is reduced to four, the need for handoffs to other personnel is eliminated entirely, and paper is eliminated from the process.

Scatter Diagrams   Scatter diagrams are simple graphic plots of one variable against another. For example, a sales manager might plot the number of training hours against average weekly sales for his or her salespeople to see if the two are related (Exhibit 12.6).

Scatter diagrams are limited primarily by the sales manager's database; if the sales manager maintains accurate data on salespeople, the diagrams will be more informative. Some of this data may be collected from the salespeople about their own background, including years of selling experience, years of selling experience in the specific industry, and years of selling experience in the area. Other information should be collected on an ongoing basis,

---

Exhibit 12.4   PROCESS FOR RESPONDING TO CUSTOMER INQUIRY

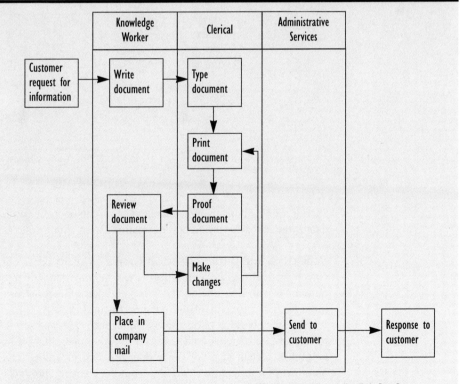

SOURCE: Adapted from Harry V. Roberts and Bernard F. Sergeskeette (1993), *Quality is Personal,* New York: Free Press.

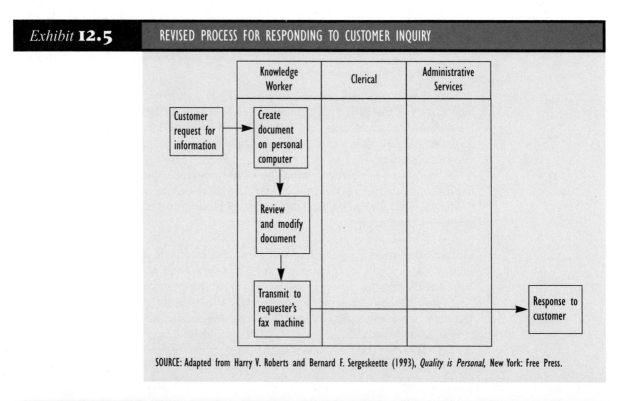

Exhibit 12.5   REVISED PROCESS FOR RESPONDING TO CUSTOMER INQUIRY

SOURCE: Adapted from Harry V. Roberts and Bernard F. Sergeskeette (1993), *Quality is Personal*, New York: Free Press.

Exhibit 12.6   SCATTER DIAGRAM

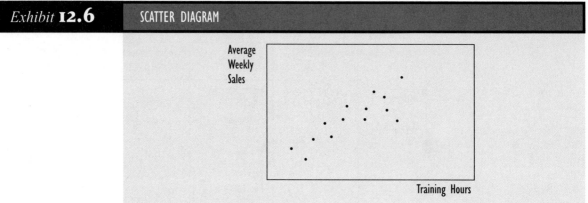

such as training hours completed per year, selling hours per week, and so on. Collecting this data is the first step toward an information-based approach to sales management.

Checklists and Data Collection Forms   Quality centers around data and consistency. Checklists and data collection forms can help to standardize both data input and quality output. As with flow charts, checklists and data collection forms should be prepared with input from everyone involved in the pertinent process.

Like the checklist pilots use before takeoff, sales and service checklists can be devised to improve consistency and quality in routine operations. Checklists can be particularly helpful in certain steps of the selling process, including developing a sales strategy (a checklist of information to collect about the prospect, products/services available to offer, benefits of each product or service, and so on), presentation (a checklist of presentation set-up needs or a proposal review checklist), and follow-up (a checklist of questions to ask the customer about product and service performance).

Data collection forms are required throughout the sales process. Sometimes they are instrumental to the process (for example, the sales order form) and sometimes they may be designed specifically for quality management purposes (for example, time use sheets). The Juran Institute has offered a number of suggestions for improvement of data collection forms, including the following:[35]

1. *Formulate precise questions.*
   Data collection guides quality improvement. Formulation of specific, well-targeted questions shows the salespeople, customer service representatives, and others who must use the forms that management knows what it wants to accomplish.

2. *Collect continuous variable data (when possible).*
   There are several types of data: categorical (for example, "male" and "female" are categories), ordinal (such as "small order" and "large order"), and continuous (for example, counts of number of service hours). The most mathematically useful is continuous data, because it can be converted into averages and other measures.

3. *Identify comprehensive data collection points.*
   Data collection takes time and thus costs money. It is not an end in itself, and should be minimized to the level required to measure and assure quality. It is helpful to identify a point in the system where multiple measures can be taken at once without interrupting the job flow.

4. *Use an unbiased data collector.*
   Numbers can be manipulated. The individual responsible for collecting data should not be provided with a motive for biasing it. Further, he or she should have direct access to the facts.

5. *Consider the data collection context.*
   Data collection occurs in an environment. The salesperson collecting data in the field may have many other responsibilities. Other activities may be going on and she or he may have other paperwork to handle. The data collection task itself may be unclear to the person collecting the data; training and practice may be required.

6. *Prepare simple forms.*
   Collect only useful data; always ask "What will we do with the results?" Make the collection form self-explanatory and the data requirements clear.

7. *Prepare data collection instructions.*
   Include a simple sheet of instructions for how to collect the data and what to do when special situations arise.

8. *Test the instructions and forms.*
   Exceptions or unanticipated situations usually come up during data collection. The best way to identify these is to test the data collection form. It is also helpful at this stage to test the use of the data in the analysis format (such as scatter chart or histogram) that it is to be used in.

9. *Train data collectors.*
   The people who collect the data should be told what it will be used for, how to properly complete the form, and why complete and unbiased information is needed. For example, data collection should be nonthreatening.
   If salespeople are collecting their own time use data, it should be made clear that the purpose is to improve performance (including perhaps commissions), and not to judge it.

10. *Audit the data collection process.*
     Review a random set of data collection forms periodically; look for missing or odd data entries.

Histograms   A histogram is a simple bar chart of the frequency with which something occurs. The histogram shows the amount of variance in a process. A normal distribution will tend to resemble the traditional bell-shaped curve, with the most frequent occurrences near the center of the distribution. Sometimes a distribution is skewed, with most of the occurrences at one end of the distribution. Such a situation might warrant more in-depth investigation. For example, a sales manager might prepare a histogram showing the number

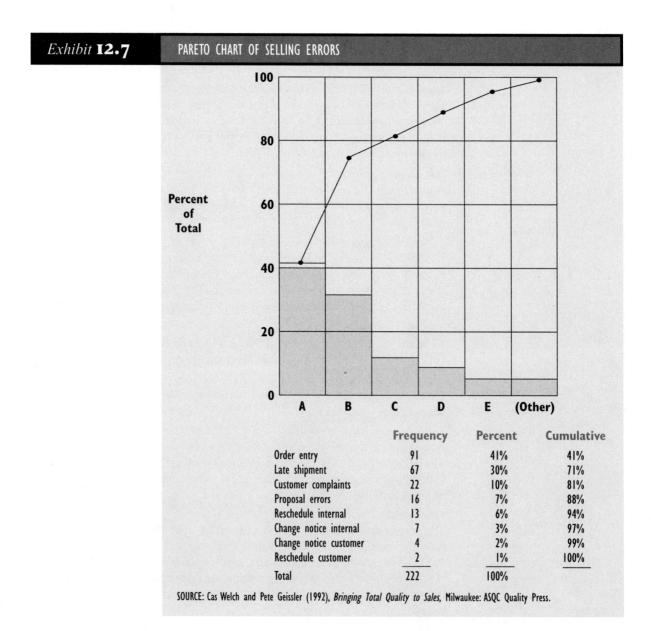

| *Exhibit* **12.7** | PARETO CHART OF SELLING ERRORS |

	Frequency	Percent	Cumulative
Order entry	91	41%	41%
Late shipment	67	30%	71%
Customer complaints	22	10%	81%
Proposal errors	16	7%	88%
Reschedule internal	13	6%	94%
Change notice internal	7	3%	97%
Change notice customer	4	2%	99%
Reschedule customer	2	1%	100%
Total	222	100%	

SOURCE: Cas Welch and Pete Geissler (1992), *Bringing Total Quality to Sales*, Milwaukee: ASQC Quality Press.

of customer contact hours per week by salespeople. If the distribution is highly skewed to the left (low) end of the distribution, it would mean that a few salespeople have found ways to maximize their time with customers, whereas most have not.

Pareto Charts   Most managers know that most of their problems come from only a few sources. This is the familiar "pareto" or "80-20" principle, which states that 80% of problems arise from 20% of available causes. The pareto chart is a portrait of causes and problems. For example, a sales manager might sort through a stack of customer complaints, group them by type of complaint and count the number in each group. If the count by group is converted into a simple bar chart, it is a pareto chart. The type of complaint that generates the most customer comments would be a candidate for the most immediate solution. Exhibit 12.7 provides an example of a pareto chart. It demonstrates that 71% of customer problems in this example are accounted for by two activities: order entry and late shipment.

Cause-and-Effect Diagrams   Once problems in the sales-and-service process have been identified, they are the focus of problem-solving efforts. One effective tool for solving problems is construction of a cause-and-effect diagram. This tool, also called the fishbone technique, can be used to identify causes of a problem, group the causes into related sets, and rank them in order of importance. Solutions to the individual underlying causes can then be identified. Exhibit 12.8 provides an example of a fishbone diagram focused on time-management problems.

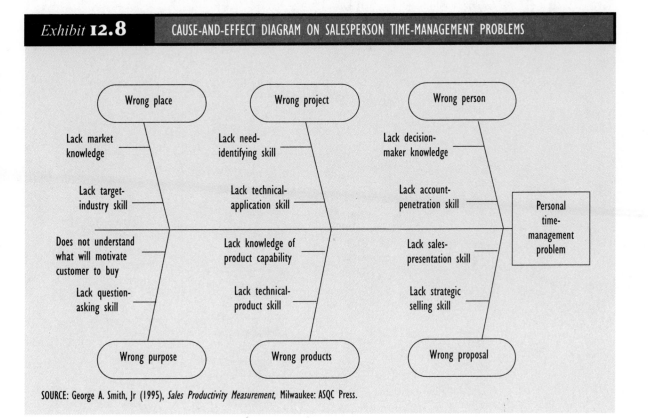

Exhibit **12.8**   CAUSE-AND-EFFECT DIAGRAM ON SALESPERSON TIME-MANAGEMENT PROBLEMS

SOURCE: George A. Smith, Jr (1995), *Sales Productivity Measurement*, Milwaukee: ASQC Press.

Control Charts   When key quality indicators have been identified, control charts can be used to monitor their variation over time. The purpose of this chart is to maintain statistical control of the system. Deviations from statistically determined upper and lower limits on this chart indicate lack of quality control. The goal of management is to limit these deviations and narrow the variation in the system. For example, a sales manager might chart the cost per sales call by week.

House of Quality   The "house of quality," also called a quality function deployment (QFD) matrix, is a tool that can be used to relate the "voice of the customer" to internal sales operations. This process begins by identifying and prioritizing customer requirements of the sales-and-service process, using the customers' own viewpoints. These requirements are then translated into internal "voice of the company" operational specifications, and examines how they interact (see Exhibit 12.9).

Wings to the house of quality are added by measuring both voices. The voice of the customer is measured externally and subjectively, usually using surveys of customer perceptions. The voice of the company is measured internally and objectively, using measures adapted to the specific operational variable.

Quality improvement tools are excellent for group decision-making. They allow members of the sales-and-service team to reach a shared understanding of the importance of customer orientation, the obstacles to customer satisfaction, and the means for improvement.

Exhibit **12.9**   BASIC HOUSE OF QUALITY

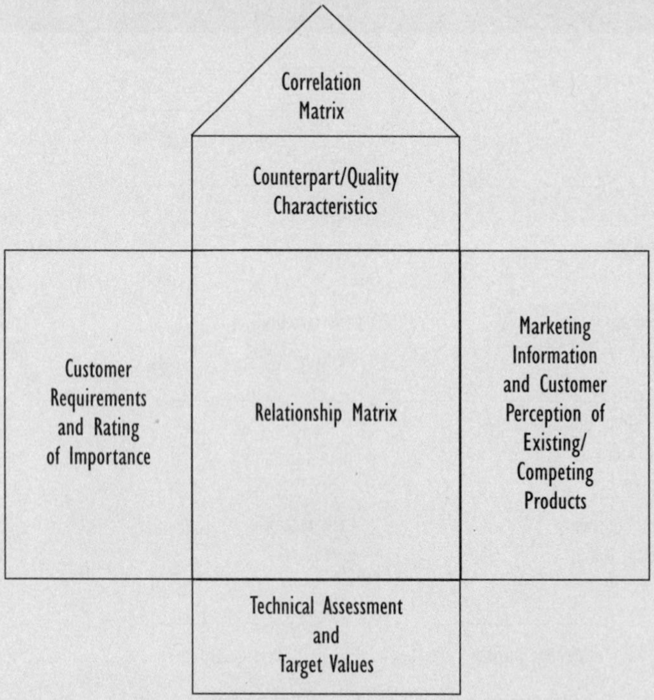

SOURCE: Harry Costin, editor (1994), *Readings in Total Quality Management,* Fort Worth: Dryden Press.

TRAINING FOR SALES QUALITY

Training is an area of great opportunity for sales managers, because training can lead to improved sales force performance—and because so many competing firms fail to train salespeople properly. In many firms, salespeople have not been told exactly what to do or how to do it. As a result, sales force training is a potential source of competitive advantage. Sales force training is imperative for the firm that intends to use a quality management approach. Without training, attempting to implement quality improvements just disrupts operations.[36]

By breaking the selling process into its component stages, and developing measures of productivity at each stage, the quality approach to sales management provides a method for identifying specific training needs. Training of salespeople is examined in more detail in Chapter 10; the following are training issues related directly to quality management.

Assessing Training Needs   The quality management philosophy suggests that training should be directed in terms of the selling process, and prioritized in terms of the steps in the process where training can have the greatest impact on productivity.

Developing a Training Strategy   Documented procedures should be developed for each function. These procedures should be the focus of training. In addition, all participants in the selling-and-service process, including all salespeople, should be trained in the use of quality management tools, including flow charts, scatter diagrams, check sheets, histograms, pareto charts, cause-and-effect diagrams, control charts, and house of quality charts. Learning objectives should be set in terms of each of both procedures and quality management tool use.

Producing Training Tools   Companies that use off-the-shelf technology to produce products gain no advantage on their competition. Similarly, sales managers who use off-the-shelf training gain no advantage; the result is usually a poor fit to the organization's specific selling process.

Training tools include lectures, workbooks, case studies, role playing exercises, videos, transparencies, and other materials. These should be developed to achieve specific training objectives, and integrated into a coherent training package.

Evaluating Training Results   Training is itself a program, and should be continuously assessed for quality. This includes the use of all tools described here, such as flow charting, checklists, and the like, to the training process.

SALES PROCESS REDESIGN

Process innovation means redesigning organizational work flows in order to improve performance. Increasingly rapid and radical process innovations have occurred among businesses in recent years because of advances in information technology. For example, IBM Credit used process innovation to cut the time needed to prepare a quote for buying or leasing a mainframe computer from seven days to one, while increasing the number of quotes prepared by a factor of ten.[37]

One expert on the subject notes that in the past U.S. firms have underinvested in process innovation in general and the marketing and sales processes in particular.[38] Sales management leadership can provide a catalyst for such innovation, both through leadership and training.[39] Examples of the powerful payoff from innovation of the sales process are shown in the Diagraph Corporation and Comcast Cable applications provided at the end of this chapter.

Phased Introduction

Although quality management offers the potential for substantial improvement in sales force performance, misapplication of quality management can lead to problems. By one report, as many as two-thirds of American managers think total quality management has failed in their companies.[40]

Problems with quality management often result from doing too much too soon. Notes Terrence R. Ozan, an Ernst & Young partner who conducted a study on quality management implementation with the American Quality Foundation: "A lot of companies read lots of books, did lots of training, formed teams, and tried to implement 9000 new practices simultaneously. But you don't get results that way. It's just too much."[41] The study identified three phases needed for quality management implementation:[42] fundamentals, best practices, and process innovation.

Quality Fundamentals   During this initial phase the organization should focus on training employees and involving them in resolving customer complaints, simplifying work processes, and reducing customer-response time.

Best Practices   During this phase organizations encourage employees to document and share best practices. Quality management ideas—collected from customers and employees—become more proactive. Innovations emerge beyond simple problem solving.

Process Innovation   In this phase, multidisciplinary teams work to establish world-class customer satisfaction. The teams focus on innovating processes that cut across departmental boundaries.

Case 12.1   QUALITY FOODS

Quality Foods (a fictitious name) was a large food distributor with an unusual problem: its selling success was causing problems. Quality's products were high in quality as the company's name implied, and its sales force was effective in moving the merchandise. The problem was that the company could not always deliver what was sold.

Each morning the distribution manager would provide the sales manager with inventory sheets. The inventory sheets identified the standing inventory. When Quality Foods salespeople called on customers, they would place orders based on availability indicated on the sheets.

Often the sales force sold products that were not available for delivery, because they did not know about sales made that day by other salespeople. Even when inventory was already low, the aggressive sales force tended to press against the out-of-inventory line. But the company was beginning to lose customers, who were increasingly complaining that they did not receive stock ordered on time—or at all.

CASE QUESTIONS

1. Form a team of four members, with one representing the sales manager, a salesperson, the distribution manager, and a customer.
   a. Flow-chart the selling-and-delivery process, as best you understand it in the case.
   b. Use a cause-and-effect (fishbone) diagram to identify the problems that you believe lead to selling unavailable stock.
   c. Brainstorm possible solutions to the most important problems identified in the step above.
   d. Based on the results of your cause-and-effect diagram and brainstorming session, develop an improved flow chart. What improvements have you introduced into the Quality Foods selling-and-delivery process?

Case 12.2   ABE'S CONSTRUCTION TOOLS

Abe Biswas and his father started their construction tool business 20 years ago, and still ran it as a hands-on operation. Recently, Abe realized that the firm was growing beyond the ability of the two owners to manage informally. The firm needed a clear direction, with strategies and tools to reach its goals. Many of his concerns had started after a recent conversation with Bill Black.

Bill Black, sales manager for the firm, provided examples of the problems encountered. After selling a good sized order, he was so uncertain about the availability of the tools that he had promised to deliver that he drove from the customer's construction site to Abe's warehouse to check. It took 2 hours, because he did not trust the firm's inventory control system.

In reflecting on this, Bill realized that the incident had cost the firm at least $150. If the other members of the sales force felt the same way, this mistrust of the inventory system was probably costing Abe $1000 to $1500 a week. Then there were also the sales lost be-

cause salespeople couldn't be checking inventory and making sales at the same time. This did not make the customers happy. The salespeople had no reason to be happy either, because they were paid on commission.

Bill recalled another problem. He had a phone call from a good customer who had called in three different times for the price of a tool, and gotten three different figures. He was confused and considering buying elsewhere. When Bill checked on the problem, there was little to go on: none of the price quotes were written down.

CASE QUESTIONS

1. What types of sales quality problems are occurring at Abe's Construction Tools?
2. What steps should Abe and Bill take to achieve control of the selling-and-service process?

Inter-unit Integration

Integration across units is a building block of total quality management that tends to be associated most strongly with process innovation. This approach involves focusing on the needs of the final customer and then building a chain of customers back throughout the organization and its suppliers. Glenda Shelby, a credit manager at Hammond Electronics in Orlando, Florida, used TQM techniques to build superior service for her customer: the sales department.[43] She began by determining what the sales department expected from the credit department. Next, using a survey, she determined how well Credit met Sales' expectations. Based on this, she established service standards to meet her customer's (the sales department's) expectations. Finally, she established a reward system within her own department for meeting those standards.

The chain of customers also extends to the final customer. One industrial sales organization uses an annual quality review as part of the selling process with each customer. First, the salesperson identifies any problems that have occurred with the customers' orders during the past year. Then he or she reviews the actions taken by the selling firm to correct the individual problems, as well as steps taken to change the process so that this type of problem is less likely to occur in the future. Finally, the salesperson identifies additional services the firm can provide to address needs that have shown up from the customer's side of the quality process. This annual quality review helps build both trust and business.

SUMMARY

Sales quality management is an approach that can build stable long-term performance. It is emerging as an important paradigm in selling. It follows the shift toward quality management initiated—and thoroughly implemented—in the manufacturing and operations side of business. The sales quality approach to selling is based on a philosophy that is focused on customer needs and process thinking. This approach uses tools that may be foreign to many sales managers as well as salespeople. If carefully implemented, it is an approach that should provide the sales manager with an increasing level of control over the selling process.

ASSIGNMENTS/DISCUSSION QUESTIONS

1. Identify barriers that would tend to keep sales managers from adopting the basic quality management principles. Suggest steps that could be taken to remove each of these barriers.

2. Working in teams, brainstorm the items that should be included in a quality-control pre-call checklist for salespeople working in a pharmaceutical firm.

3. Identify specific instances you have seen or read about on how technology has changed the sales process. In each instance, note the impact on the quality of the sales encounter.

4. Identify the types of barriers you believe a sales manager might encounter in trying to use total quality management tools with his sales force. Then note ways he or she might overcome those barriers.

5. Working with a team, create a data collection form to monitor quality as it occurs in a routine service situation (e.g., fast-food purchases). During the next week, have team members use the checklist each time they engage in that situation. At the next class period, compile the results as a pareto chart.

6. Brainstorm the benefits that a salesperson might enjoy in working for a firm that uses a quality management approach to sales, as opposed to a traditional approach. What impact do you expect these benefits to have on the salesperson, the sales force, and the firm, respectively?

ENDNOTES

1. David Dorsey (1994), *The Force,* N.Y.: Ballantine Books.
2. Peter Capezio and Debra Morehouse (1993), *Taking the Mystery Out of TQM: A Practical Guide to Total Quality Management,* Hawthorne, N.J.: Career Press, p. 1.
3. Bernd Jahnke, Michael Bachle, and Monika Simoneit, Modelling Sales Processes as Preparation for ISO 9001 Certification, *International Journal of Quality & Reliability Management,* 12(7), September-October, 1995, p. 76.
4. Adapted from Harry V. Roberts and Bernard F. Sergesketter (1993), *Quality is Personal: A Foundation for Total Quality Management,* New York: Free Press; Peter Capezio and Debra Morehouse (1993), *Taking the Mystery Out of TQM: A Practical Guide to Total Quality Management,* Hawthorne, N.J.: Career Press; and Cas Welch and Pete Geissler (1995), *Applying Total Quality to Sales,* Milwaukee: ASQC Press.
5. Cas Welch and Pete Geissler (1995), *Applying Total Quality to Sales,* Milwaukee: ASQC Press.
6. Harry Costin, Exploring the Concepts Underlying Total Quality Management, in *Readings in Total Quality Management,* Harry Costin, editor (1994), Fort Worth, TX: Dryden Press.
7. Valarie Zeithaml, A. Parasuraman and Leonard Berry (1990), *Delivering Service Quality: Balancing Customer Perceptions and Expectations,* New York: Free Press.
8. W. O'Connell (1990), *Sales Force Compensation,* Chicago: Dartnell and R. Buderi, A Tighter Focus for R&D, *Business Week,* October 25, 1991, p. 170.

9. Kaoru Ishikawa (1985), *What is Total Quality Control?* Englewood Cliffs, N.J: Prentice-Hall.

10. Cas Welch and Pete Geissler (1992), *Bringing Total Quality to Sales,* Milwaukee: ASQC Quality Press.

11. Adapted from Harry V. Roberts and Bernard F. Sergesketter (1993), *Quality is Personal: A Foundation for Total Quality Management,* New York: Free Press; Peter Capezio and Debra Morehouse (1993), *Taking the Mystery Out of TQM: A Practical Guide to Total Quality Management,* Hawthorne, N.J: Career Press.

12. John C. Narver and Stanley F. Slater, The Effect of Market Orientation on Business Profitability, *Journal of Marketing,* 54, October, 1990, pp. 20–35.

13. Eli Jones, Donna Massey Kantak, Charles M. Futrell, and Mark W. Johnson, Leader Behavior, Work-Attitudes, and Turnover of Salespeople: An Integrative Study, *Journal of Personal Selling & Sales Management,* 16(2), Spring, 1996, pp. 13–23.

14. Alan J. Dubinsky, Francis J. Yammarino, Marvin A. Jolson, and William D. Spanger, Transformational Leadership: An Initial Investigation in Sales Management, *Journal of Personal Selling & Sales Management,* 15(2), Spring, 1995, pp. 17–29; and Frederick A. Russ, Kevin M. McNeilly, and James M. Comer, Leadership, Decision Making and Performance of Sales Managers: A Multi-Level Approach, *Journal of Personal Selling & Sales Management,* 16(3), Summer 1996, pp. 1–15.

15. David Strutton, Lou E. Pelton, and James R. Lumpkin, The Relationship Between Psychological Climate and Salesperson-Sales Manager Trust in Sales Organizations, *Journal of Personal Selling & Sales Management,* 13(4), Fall 1993, pp. 1–14.

16. M. Walton (1986), *The Deming Management Method,* New York: Putnam Publishing Group.

17. Quoted in Cas Welch and Pete Geissler (1995), *Applying Total Quality to Sales,* Milwaukee: ASQC Quality Press pp. 44–45.

18. George A. Smith, Jr. (1995), *Sales Productivity Measurement,* Milwaukee: ASQC Quality Press, p. 8.

19. *Ibid.*

20. Ralph F. Wilson, Developing Sales Leads From Your Web Site, *Web Marketing Today,* http://www.wilsonweb.com>(September 1, 1997).

21. Smith, 1995.

22. *Ibid.*

23. *Ibid.*

24. Adapted from Smith, 1995.

25. Smith, 1995.

26. Welch and Geissler, 1995, p. 80.

27. Brian Dumaine, How Managers Can Succeed Through Speed, *Fortune,* February 13, 1989, pp. 54–59.

28. Welch and Geissler, 1992.

29. George Stalk, Jr., Time—The Next Source of Competitive Advantage, *Harvard Business Review,* July-August 1988, pp. 41–51.

30. Brian Dumaine, 1989.

31. Smith, 1995, p. 62.

32. Smith, 1995, p. 67.

33. John T. Burr, Going with the Flow(chart), in *Total Quality Management,* Harry Costin, editor (1994), Fort Worth: Dryden Press, pp. 171–175.

34. *Ibid.,* p. 172.

35. Material adapted from Juran Institute, Inc., Harry Ivan Costin (1994), Check Sheets, *Readings in Total Quality Management,* 1994, Fort Worth: Dryden Press.

36. Quality: Small and Midsize Companies Seize the Challenge—Not a Moment Too Soon, *Business Week,* November 30, 1992.

37. Thomas H. Davenport (1993), *Process Innovation: Reengineering Work through Information Technology,* Boston: *Harvard Business School Press.*

38. *Ibid.,* p. 6.

39. Judith J. Marshall and Harrie Vredenburg, An Empirical Study of Factors Influencing Innovation Implementation in Industrial Sales Organizations, *Journal of the Academy of Marketing Science,* 20(3), Summer, 1992, pp. 205–215.

40. Rahul Jacob, TQM: More Than a Dying Fad?, *Fortune,* October 18, 1993, pp. 66–72.
41. Gilbert Fuchsberg, Quality Programs Show Shoddy Results, *Wall Street Journal,* May 14, 1992, pp. B1,B7.
42. Smith, 1995, p. 13.
43. Glenda Shelby, Credit Versus Sales?: A Customer Service Approach, *Business Credit,* 98(3), March 1996, p. 29.

13

EVALUATING SALES PERFORMANCE

CONTROLLING SALESPERSON PERFORMANCE

In sales, the performance of each salesperson is important. Think of the sales team as a high-performance automobile engine. When an engine has compression problems in one cylinder, the performance of the entire vehicle is reduced. The car is not "firing on all cylinders." One of the sales manager's most important jobs is to assure that the sales team *is* firing on all cylinders.

The formal process involved in assuring optimal performance from each salesperson is straightforward. First, identify and communicate performance expectations. Second, measure whether the salesperson is performing according to those expectations. Third, communicate the gap between measured performance and expectations to the salesperson (a task known as performance appraisal). Finally, take corrective action when performance is below expectations. Corrective action can involve either helping the individual to identify and correct performance gaps or, in the event of repeated performance failures, firing the salesperson. This process is illustrated in Exhibit 13.1.

241

| Exhibit **13.1** | SALESPERSON CONTROL PROCESS |

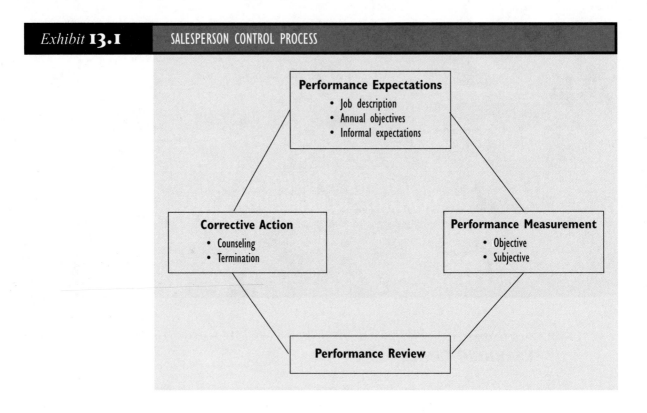

It is important that salespeople clearly understand the performance appraisal process. For example, the Gold Bond Building Products division of the National Gypsum Company has a six-step performance appraisal system that begins with an update of the job description and job accountability. This initial step recognizes that markets, technology, and competition can change what the salesperson must do to generate business. Step #2 requires mutual agreement on the definition of the measures to be used. Step #3 is a quarterly performance appraisal review. The salesperson submits performance records at this step. Step #4 requires the salesperson to file an annual report. In Step #5 the manager plans for the annual appraisal meeting. Step #6 is the annual performance meeting.[1]

The Salesperson Performance Control System

In order to understand the formal salesperson control process, it may be helpful to put it in context. Generally, there are two types of salesperson controls: informal and formal.[2]

Informal controls are the unwritten and typically employee-based mechanisms that guide behavior. There are three types of informal control: self-control, social control, and cultural control. *Self-control* involves the salesperson establishing personal objectives, monitoring their attainment, and adjusting behavior when it is off target. This is discussed in Chapter 5. *Social control* is the pattern of interpersonal behavior enforced informally within the firm. For example, salespeople as a group may establish norms (expected patterns of behavior) for filing expenses. *Cultural control* is the value-based pattern of behavior that guides employee behavior within the entire organization. Culture reflects "the way we do things around here" that makes the organization distinct. Sales managers often rely on social and cultural controls to shape salesperson performance, as described in Chapter 11.

Formal controls are the written guidelines developed by management. They are designed to increase the chances that employees will behave in such a way as to attain stated marketing objectives. There are three types of formal controls: input controls, process controls, and output controls.

Input controls are measurable actions taken by the firm before activity begins. Common input controls include selection and recruitment criteria and training. Careful management of input controls allows the sales manager to begin with "good material." Fine-tuning the salesperson selection and recruitment process, and following up with well-designed training programs, goes a long way to limiting problems and assuring sales success. These subjects are discussed in Chapters 9 and 10.

An example of input control is the employee-company value fit test used in Japanese companies. A person applying for a job in a Japanese company is given a test to see if his or her personality fits that of the company, rather than the immediate job sought. It is assumed that the individual will stay with the company and move through many assignments. A mismatch of individual-company values will result in an unproductive employee. The high turnover of U.S. employees in comparison with those in Japan is attributed to the U.S. recruiting processes.[3] There is a lack of good information in the U.S. about work applicants' habits, because former employees fear being sued if they give an unfavorable reference.

Process controls are used when the firm is trying to influence behaviors or activities. Common process controls used in sales management are sales calls per week and selling expenses. The sales manager monitors these types of measures for each salesperson so that problems can be identified and solved before they become critical. *Output controls* focus on results. The classical output control in sales management is a salesperson's sales. The present chapter focuses on process and output controls.

As you read this chapter think of the problem facing Tom Lewis, the district sales manager for Horrace Clark.

> Tom had been a district sales manager for 18 months and out of college for 5 years. Tom has a problem with Horrace but is uncertain how to most effectively handle the situation. In describing the problem to you he thought that it was a case of converting rapport into results.
>
> "Horace Clark is a young salesperson with two years of sales experience but he has worked for me for just two months. I like Horace, as do all of his accounts and people around our company. His customers like him because he is warm, friendly, and helpful, which can be explained by his strong need to be liked. He lacks the assertiveness and risk-taking behavior patterns of our highly successful salespeople! I have worked with him in many ways, but his performance is not acceptable to my boss. How should I handle this situation without destroying his good relationships with his accounts?"

PERFORMANCE EXPECTATIONS

Salespeople must meet three sets of performance expectations: the job description, objective performance criteria, and subjective performance criteria.

A salesperson's general duties are described in her job description. Sample job descriptions are included in Chapter 2, which focuses on the content of the salesperson's job. The job description is likely to focus on selling tasks, of course, but will probably also include providing selected services to buyers, gathering intelligence about competing products, filing reports on selling activities and expenses, keeping current on product changes and applications, and other similar tasks.

In addition, the sales manager is likely to set a number of benchmarks for the salesperson's objective performance. These may relate to either processes (for example, sales calls per day) or outcomes (for example, sales or return on assets managed). These objective performance expectations typically are subject to some negotiation between the sales manager and the individual salesperson. For example, performance standards may reflect the characteristics of the sales territory and projected market potential, as described in Chapter 16. In addition, the sales manager may take into account the salesperson's experience.

Some companies provide performance standards for inexperienced and experienced salespeople. For example, a regional office of Wallace, Inc., which sells information systems supplies, provides its representatives with the following list of minimum expectations.[4]

Salesperson Expectations at Wallace, Inc.

Activity	Experience	
	1–2 Year	Veteran
Sales calls/day	8	4
Set appointments	5	3
Phone calls to set appointments	40	15
Estimates/week	1	1
Written proposals/week	10	4
Designs/week	5	5
Entertainments/month	8	10
Orders/month	20	40
Letters/week	5	2
New samples/week	15	5
New business orders/month	3	6
Specialty product orders/month	1	1
New ribbon agreements/month	1	1
New DMS agreements/month	1	1

How would you explain the differences between the two columns?

Performance expectations are built on a job description and hiring criteria. Some companies combine the job description and appraisal form into a single document. Failure to link performance to the job description and hiring criteria is not only poor management, but it may be illegal under federal regulations regarding equal employment opportunities. The Equal Employment Opportunity Commission has extended its investigations from hiring and selection procedures to evaluation and promotion procedures. The characteristics of performance evaluation systems are now an important element in employment discrimination cases. One study of 66 cases found that the company had a better chance of winning if written instructions were provided to the evaluators, if behavior-oriented performance evaluations were used instead of trait-oriented appraisals, and if the results of the appraisals were reviewed with the employee.[5]

In addition to these objective performance expectations, the sales manager is also likely to have a number of informal, subjective expectations of the salesperson. These include development of certain skills and performance of certain selling and nonselling behaviors.

PERFORMANCE MEASUREMENT

There must be agreed-upon measures to assure progress toward both objective and subjective expectations. Further, these measures must be consistent with the goals of the sales department.

Sales-related measures vary by type and by subject, as illustrated in Exhibit 13.2. The types of measures include objective and subjective. *Objective measures* are those based on verifiable records. Typically, objective measures of salesperson performance are developed by linking existing accounting data to data generated by salespeople. *Subjective measures* are those that depend primarily on individual judgement. Typically, subjective measures of performance are developed based on the judgement of the sales manager and, increasingly, the salesperson's customers. Both objective and subjective measures can relate to the selling process and to its outcomes.

Objective Measures

The salesperson's activities and results generate extensive data that can be translated into both outcome and process performance measures. An advantage of such objective data is that they often relate directly to the firm's financial performance. The revenues and expenses generated by selling directly affect the bottom line.

When salespeople have personal computers or bar code scanning devices, they can quickly gather data and feed it to the home office computer, which then generates a *territory income statement.* This type of rapid objective feedback can benefit both the salesperson and the sales manager, who together can spot problems that require precise sales strategies. Such data systems have produced competitive advantages for companies in the grocery products, health care, and pharmaceutical industries.

Objective measures also provide salespeople with a means of self-regulation. If the manager and the salesperson agree on these objective measures, then corrective action can be taken by the salesperson when performance drops. The means for personal self-evaluation and correction by the salesperson are found in the job description, performance standards, specific objectives, required activities, call reports, expense accounts, quotas, computerized sales analyses, and compensation plans. These *automatic supervisors*—devices that provide feedback without a human supervisor's intervention—save the time of field sales managers.

Exhibit **13.2**	TYPES OF SELLING PERFORMANCE MEASURES

		Subject of Measurement	
		Selling Process	Selling Outcomes
Source of Measurement	Objective Data	Calls/day Cost/call Sales letters/week	Sales revenue Return on assets managed New accounts/lost accounts Repeat orders
	Subjective Data	Organizational citizenship behaviors Selling capabilities	Customer satisfaction

Objective Outcome Measures   A key objective outcome measure is *sales revenue*. Although this has been and continues to be one of the most widely used measures of salesperson performance, it has substantial limitations.[6] Sales volume in itself does not take into account differences in market potential or other external factors. Further, emphasis on sales revenue as a performance measure can encourage volume at the expense of profits. As a result, firms are increasingly emphasizing *profits* rather than gross sales. A study by Donald Jackson and his colleagues found that the percentage of sales managers using net profit as an output performance measure increased from 26% in 1983 to 69% in 1994.[7]

A variation on profits is *return-on-assets managed* (ROAM). Return-on-assets managed holds the salesperson accountable for the return on the territory assets which generally include accounts receivable, special inventories for an account, demonstration equipment, and an automobile. If two accounts generate $400,000 in sales and $40,000 in contribution, but the first account uses only $100,000 in territory assets and the second one requires special inventory and pays its accounts so slowly that it ties up $200,000 in assets, then the ROAM for the first account is 40% (($40,000/$100,000) × 100) whereas it is only 20% for the second account. Consequently, the higher ROAM, 40%, is more desirable than the lower, 20%. A salesperson who is evaluated according to the ROAM will be motivated to collect accounts and sell standard products instead of special items that require inventory.

While ROAM can be computed by the simple ratio of net contribution divided by the territory assets, this ratio conceals the sales level and the important concept of asset turnover, which is the number of times a dollar in assets is used per year. The detailed equation is as follows:

ROAM = (Territory Net Contribution/Territory sales) × (Territory Sales/Territory Assets)

Consider the situation illustrated in Exhibits 13.3 and 13.4. This analysis extends from the territory management discussion in Chapter 5. In that earlier analysis, it was determined that total contribution was $457,000 and direct costs (freight, technical services, advertising, and personal selling) were $142,000. This generated a net contribution of $315,000.

Exhibit **13.3**   RETURN-ON-ASSETS MANAGED

	CENTRAL	WESTERN	NORTHERN	OTHER	TOTAL
SALES FORECASTED (000)	285	262	203	1249	2000
ASSETS MANAGED ($000)					
ACCOUNTS (DIRECT)	[57.3]	[35.3]	[54]	253.4	[400]
INVENTORY (DIRECT)	[57.3]	[70]	[27.3]	145.4	[300]
DEMONSTRATION EQUIPMENT (% CALLS)	0.73	0.66	1.32	55.30	[58]
OFFICE EQUIPMENT (% CALLS)	0.13	0.11	0.23	9.53	[10]
AUTO (% CALLS)	0.09	0.08	0.23	6.67	[7]
TOTAL ASSETS ($000)	115.54	106.15	83.07	470.31	775
% ASSETS/ACCOUNT	14.91	13.70	10.72	60.68	100.00
ASSET TURNOVER (SALES/ASSETS)	2.47	2.47	2.45	2.66	2.58
NET CONTRIBUTION %	9.80	12.80	14.48	10.14	10.88
ADD: INTEREST ON INVENTORY	3.00	4.00	2.00	1.30	1.97
INTEREST: ACCOUNTS RECEIVABLE	3.00	2.00	4.00	3.00	2.97
TOTAL CONTRIBUTION	15.80	18.80	20.48	14.44	15.82
RETURN ON ASSETS	38.96	46.49	50.09	38.35	40.82

Data in brackets [ ] are supplied by the planner. The computer enters all other data.

The flow chart in Exhibit 13.3 shows how the territory data in Exhibit 13.4 computes the ROAM for each account. The net contribution ($315,000) divided by sales ($2,000,000) produces a contribution as a percent of sales of 15.8%.

The assets managed by salespeople total $775,000 (the sum of accounts receivable, inventory, and automobile and equipment). When sales is divided by this amount, it produces an annual asset turnover rate of 2.58.

The contribution as a percent of sales (15.8%) times the annual asset turnover rate (2.58%) yield a territory return-on-assets of 40.8%.

Using this approach on all four accounts, we see in Exhibit 13.2 that the rank of the accounts has changed again. Northern is the best account in terms of ROAM.

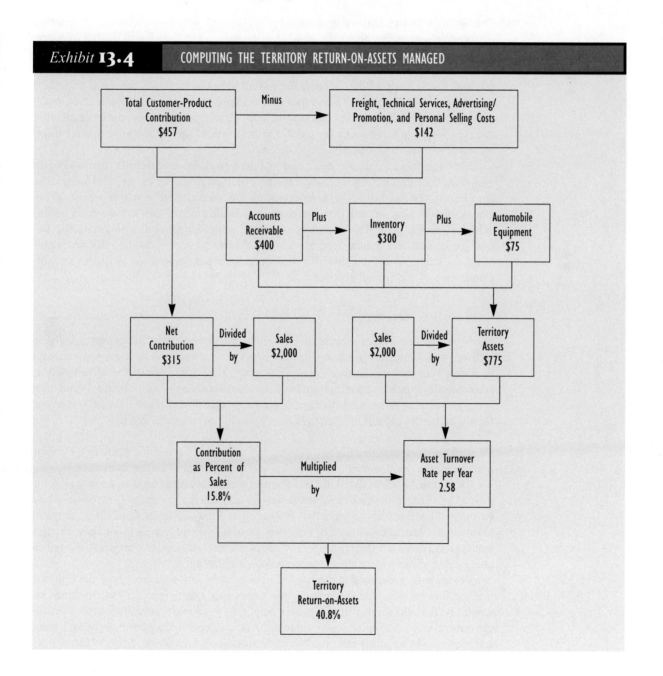

Exhibit 13.4 COMPUTING THE TERRITORY RETURN-ON-ASSETS MANAGED

Objective Process Measures   The same databases that offer salespeople and managers quick and clear feedback on outcomes can also measure certain aspects of the selling process. For example, call reports and orders can be converted into a ratio of the number of calls required to produce an order. This ratio can be examined over time for the salesperson and across salespeople. Other diagnostic ratios include expenses per call and the number of calls needed to make a presentation. The ratio of the number of presentations needed to produce an order will reveal any weakness in closing skills. The ratio of the number of orders to the number of presentations is known as the *hit ratio.* The number of repeat orders may reflect buyer satisfaction and the salesperson's follow-through. A high number of new accounts and few account losses show that the salesperson is contributing to the growth of the territory.

Cautions in Using Objective Measures   Although objective performance measures have certain advantages, they must be used with caution. The use of performance measures that are heavily dependent on a salesperson's records can be dangerous. First, many salespeople detest paperwork. If they are on commission they may refuse to file reports, which take time away from selling. Second, there is an incentive to falsify reports if they think that the data will determine their quota and, perhaps, their income. To gain compliance, management must demonstrate that reports help the salesperson to become more effective and therefore to achieve his or her goals. Job descriptions should also state that falsifying reports is a basis for dismissal with no defense.

Although these ratios are evaluated against agreed-upon standards, the job-related behaviors that produced these sales must be observed firsthand by the field sales manager during regular calls. These observations are documented in a *trip report,* a formal document that summarizes the manager's evaluation of the salesperson's selling behaviors in the field. This report is combined with statistical data to create the formal semiannual and annual reports. A *critical incident report,* which indicates something favorable or unfavorable that happened in the salesperson's territory, also becomes part of the formal reports.

Subjective Measures

Not all of the importance aspects of salesperson performance can be measured with objective, "hard" numbers generated by the firm's accounting system. Performance has a number of subjective elements—like developing skills, going above the call of duty to keep the sales group functioning, and keeping customers happy—that require special measures. Developing these subjective performance measures requires that the sales manager clearly define the capabilities and behaviors that the firm wants to instill.

Subjective Process Measures   Among the subjective factors that relate to the selling process are the development of capabilities and engagement in certain behaviors.

Capabilities include the skills and abilities that salespeople need to be successful in their roles. Research conducted by Challagalla and Shervani among salespeople at two Fortune 500 companies suggests that evaluating and rewarding for capabilities increases salespeople's intrinsic motivation, improves their selling aptitude, and builds a stronger manager-salesperson relationship.[8] This approach also reduces the salesperson's uncertainty about job requirements and increases job satisfaction.

Behaviorally based evaluations provide salespeople with guidance about the activities that are important to management. To the extent that salespeople are evaluated and rewarded on behaviors rather than objective output, they are more committed to the sales organization, more willing to accept direction and to cooperate as part of an overall team, and more accepting of the sales manager's evaluations and authority.[9] Salespeople also see managers who base evaluations on behavior as more innovative and supportive.[10]

Behaviors that are important in sales include both the activities directly involved in selling (described in Chapter 4) as well as organizational citizenship behaviors that help the sales group and the firm run more smoothly. It is important for the sales manager to explicitly identify and evaluate these citizenship behaviors, because research indicates that they are more heavily relied on than objective sales to evaluate salespeople.[11,12]

These citizenship behaviors include activities that are beyond the salesperson's job description, but that help the organization operate more smoothly. They include five categories:[13]

- *Altruism*—helping others with tasks that are important to the sales organization, like volunteering to help new salespeople.
- *Courtesy*—taking extra steps to avoid conflict with other people or departments, like checking with the service department before committing to a substantial delivery.
- *Sportsmanship*—tolerating inconvenient circumstances or work situations without complaining, like not making a major issue of it when office supplies are out of stock.
- *Civic virtue*—taking part in the rituals that are not required but that help the firm, like meeting with visitors to the firm.
- *Conscientiousness*—going beyond the minimum requirements of the sales job, like entertaining only when it is sales-related.

Research conducted by the Gallup Organization among a half million salespeople revealed that the best performers have a mix of capabilities and behaviors, including the ability to close a sale, intrinsic motivation, disciplined work habits, and the ability to build relationships.[14]

Great closers are salespeople who have a high ratio of closed sales to sales calls made, have self-confidence and are willing to risk failure. They recognize that increasing the number of successes can also increase the number of failures.

The ability to build relationships is a critical talent in team selling and partnering with the client. This individual is "empathetic, patient, caring, responsive, a good listener, and honest."[15] Relationship selling also requires that the salesperson focus on sales planning, sales support, and other customer-oriented activities.[16]

Subjective Outcome Measures   Sales and profit are not the only outcomes important to a firm. Sales may occur because of short-term considerations like price discounts or switching costs. Price discounts may generate sales, but they reduce profit and appeal to the customers that are most inclined to shop for a new supplier. Customers may also buy from a long-term supplier because of switching costs, which are the costs to the buyer of switching to a new vendor. For example, if a firm switches to a new accounting software, it must not only pay the cost of the software, but the time lost to train its employees on the new system and the time lost in converting to the new system. Eventually, customer dissatisfaction may overcome the cost of switching to a new vendor.

Long-term sales that result from repeat business with the same customers are important to business success. Repeat business tends to be more profitable than new accounts because repeat customers: (1) can be served more efficiently (for example, their requirements may be stored in the supplier's marketing information system); (2) are more likely to make cross purchases to other product/service lines offered by the supplier; (3) are more likely to increase the volume of their purchases; and (4) are more likely to refer new clients to the supplier. One of the best predictors of long-term sales is customer satisfaction.

Although customer satisfaction is not a numerical, objective measure, it is fundamentally important. For this reason, an increasing number of companies are tying customer satisfaction directly to the compensation of salespeople and customer service professionals.

Developing Subjective Performance Measures

The development of a form to measure salesperson performance can be a critical management activity. Crucial personnel decisions regarding compensation, training, promotion, and termination use data generated by these forms. A poorly designed form can result in legal action by an employee who thinks that it was the cause for not being promoted. Many companies have trained specialists or use consultants to develop these forms in order to avoid legal action.

A good performance measurement form has three characteristics. First, it must be relevant to the job being evaluated. In order to be relevant, the instrument must measure a result or an activity that is prescribed in the selling plan. Second, it must be valid; that is, it must truly measure the characteristic it claims to measure. Third, it must be reliable; that is, it must give the same results when it is used by a single rater over time and by different raters at a point in time. For example, if a measuring instrument were not reliable over time, you would not know if an observed change was caused by a change in the salesperson's behavior or because of an inconsistency in the measurement instrument. If it were not reliable across raters, two salespeople with similar performance would be rated differently because their managers interpreted the instruments differently.

Appraisal forms that are used in sales management include essay appraisals, behaviorally anchored rating scales (BARS), appraisals linked to job descriptions, weighted activity appraisals, paired comparisons of salespeople, and salesperson rankings according to critical criteria. Each of these methods will be explained and illustrated.

Essay Appraisal   The essay appraisal requires the manager to describe the main assignments of the salesperson and the results of his or her effort during the period covered by the evaluation. This description should cover strengths, weaknesses, and a program for improvement. Although the essay method is highly personalized, it is difficult to compare and combine the evaluations of separate reviewers. An example of how an essay should and should not be written appears in Exhibit 13.5.

Exhibit **13.5**   ESSAY APPRAISAL

Assignment/Results

(Describe the main assignment of this salesperson and the results of his or her efforts during the evaluation period.)

Jill's major objectives this year were to gain 80% distribution in her 15 major accounts, increase sales volume 7%, and develop her skills in overcoming objections. She increased her sales volume by 8%, so she met that goal, but she got product distribution through only nine major accounts for a 60% distribution rate. Her ability to overcome objections is still weak. This weakness contributes to the failure to sell major accounts.

Jill is enthusiastic about selling, but is slow to see the need for completing reports and requests for market information. She is eager to accept new responsibilities that are related to selling. For example, she volunteered to develop a sales presentation for a new product and to make a presentation at a district sales meeting. Her presentation was well received.

How *NOT* to Write an Essay Appraisal

Jill is an eager salesperson who is liked and respected by her peers and customers. She fits well into a variety of social situations, which will help her to sell the large accounts. She is quick-witted, learns rapidly, and listens carefully to advice. She is almost a workaholic and thrives on responsibility.

Behaviorally Anchored Rating Scales (BARS)   Some scaling techniques use a combination of verbal cues and numerical scales that provide more uniformity across raters. When the verbal cues describe desirable or undesirable behavior, they are known also as Behaviorally Anchored Rating Scales (BARS). The development of verbal cues with numerical ratings has a long history in the field of psychology known as *psychometrics*. To meet the requirements of the EEOC the scale must be developed by a psychologist who is trained in the field of psychological measurement. The BARS illustration in Exhibit 13.6 uses verbal cues, numbers, and provides space for open-ended comments.

A scale that is used in the grocery products industry is less difficult to develop. It uses what is known as the Semantic Differential Scale, where favorable and unfavorable adjectives are placed along a scale, as follows:

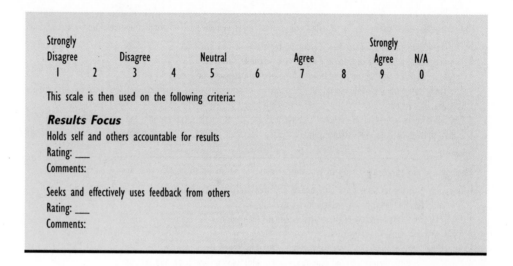

Strongly Disagree		Disagree		Neutral		Agree		Strongly Agree	N/A
1	2	3	4	5	6	7	8	9	0

This scale is then used on the following criteria:

Results Focus

Holds self and others accountable for results

Rating: ___

Comments:

Seeks and effectively uses feedback from others

Rating: ___

Comments:

This scale is used for questions in additional categories such as communication, business acumen, customer focus, entrepreneurial, skills/knowledge expertise, and team contributor.

Target Marketing Systems has a form that uses a four-point scale, with 1 equal to "performs consistently" and 4 equal to "cannot perform without significant supervision." It applies this scale to over 60 questions, divided into categories such as the following: strategic thinking, competitive awareness, political advantage, customer focus, and self management.[17]

Wallace, Inc., uses a straight line which is anchored only as low and high, with a dot to show the middle. To the left of this scale are the characteristics to be evaluated, such as communication, cooperation, creativity, leadership, planning, team player, and technical competence. To the right of the scale is space for comments.[18]

The complexity of computer software applications requires an extensive appraisal form. One company evaluates salesperson skills and knowledge of products and applications in four categories—trained, beginner, skilled, and expert.[19]

Relating Appraisals to Job Descriptions   The activities of the Equal Employment Opportunity Commission have drawn attention to the fact that many companies often use one set of criteria to recruit and select candidates and a different set for performance ap-

| *Exhibit* **13.6** | VERBAL AND NUMERICAL SCALES FOR EVALUATING SALESPEOPLE |

Check the number on the scale that describes this salesperson's performance for each dimension. Comment or give examples to explain your ratings. Write "Did not observe" where this statement applies.

*Performance Dimensions**

Sales Ability—ability to utilize appropriate interpersonal styles and methods to gain agreement or acceptance from customer.

1. No selling style. Just presents facts.
2. Uses same style with all customers, rarely listens or reacts to customer comments, and fails to ask for agreement.
3. Varies style and methods, but is reluctant to ask for agreement or acceptance from customers of ideas or proposal.
4. Reasonably effective in utilizing appropriate interpersonal and closing skills, but is unable to deal with certain customer types.
5. Utilizes interpersonal skills very effectively through intelligence and perseverance to gain customer agreement.
6. Combines natural sociability, intelligence, and persistence in exceptionally effective manner to gain customer agreement.

Comment: _____

Oral Communication Skills—ability to effectively express ideas in individual or group situations, preplanned or impromptu.

1. Oral presentations disorganized and inaccurate, replete with bad grammar.
2. Knowledgeable, but easily distracted, nervous, and becomes flustered.
3. Speaks reasonably well; uncomfortable with high-level professionals or groups.
4. Effectively communicates with individuals or groups in impromptu selling situations, but less effective with preplanned group presentations or complex interactions.
5. Very effective in variety of professional settings and groups, but style lacks warmth and sociability.
6. Tailors presentations to circumstances, interacts very well with audience, and uses personality to communicate effectively.

Comment: _____

Planning and Organization—ability to establish a course of action to accomplish goal; appropriating resources.

1. Does not plan ahead; waits until last minute and frequently misses deadline.
2. Does not establish priorities or adhere to plan.
3. Plans well, but responds too often to less essential "emergencies."
4. Plans well for normal circumstances.
5. Establishes realistic goals and sets contingency plans and schedules.
6. Establishes realistic immediate and long-range goals with contingency plans and schedules.

Comment: _____

*Note: These phrases should be scaled by a psychometric method on populations that are similar to those that are being evaluated. For a discussion, see J. C. Nunnally (1978), *Psychometric Theory*, ed 2, New York: McGraw Hill, pp. 77–80.

praisal. To prevent this inconsistency some companies use a form that combines the salespersons position description, performance standards, and performance appraisal. A combined form enables the applicant to see what is expected and how he or she will be evaluated if hired.

Weighted Activity Appraisals   Exhibit 13.7 illustrates how Hallmark Marketing (greeting cards) uses a weighted activity appraisal. In this example sales are weighted 50, retail sales development is weighted 35, and territory management is weighted 15. Weights are assigned based on the strategic goals of the sales unit. For example, in this case Hallmark is placing half of its emphasis on sales per se, but is also giving a separate 35% emphasis on new sales (i.e., sales development). Territory management—the routine activity of calling on and servicing clients—receives a 15% emphasis.

These weights are multiplied by the evaluations (the column to the left of the weights). The total rating of 465 can be compared over time to identify improvement and across salespeople to benchmark performance.

Exhibit **13·7**	WEIGHTED ACTIVITY APPRAISAL

HALLMARK MARKETING
ANNUAL PERFORMANCE REVIEW
1991 SALESPERSON

Name: Jan Hallmarker
Title: Salesperson
Start Date: 7/91 - Assignment
Date Hired: 7/90 - Hallmark
Sales Area: Region II - Southern Region
District: Jupiter

Employee: 999-99-9999-9

Review Period Covered:

Start: 7/8/91
End: 12/31/91

SECTION A: OBJECTIVE CRITERIA

1. Comb Curr Net Sales for '91 ED, '91 F/X, '92 Spring
2. Retail Sales Development
3. Territory Management

Objective	% Sold	Eval	Wt	Rating
	92.9%	4	50	200
		5	35	175
		6	15	90
Totals			100	465

Comments on Overall Performance (include any additional significant accomplishments or responsibilities not mentioned above):

SALES: Jan Hallmarker was given her first field sales assignment in July, 1991. Most of her sales objectives were prorated to correspond to the time she had to accomplish those objectives. On the surface, the last half of 1991 was a disappointing six months for Jan regarding achievement of her final sales objectives. It was an encouraging six months regarding her approach toward her job responsibilities.

Jan sold 89.1% of Everyday (last in the district), and 100.3% of Fall and Christmas (4th out of 8 in the district). Fall and Christmas were good for Jan! She sold 96.7% of Spring (7th out of 8), and 92.9% of Total (8th out of 8).

Comparing Representatives with Each Other   Rating scales attempt to evaluate a salesperson according to some absolute standard.

Another approach is to compare the performance of salespeople to each other. Exhibit 13.8 illustrates a paired-comparison method. Here, each salesperson in the column is compared with each salesperson in the row to the left. The sum of the X's received by each salesperson produces a ranking of salespeople. In this case, the ranking is Jones, Baker, Kerr, Thomas, and Wilson.

Although Exhibit 13.8 provides an overall comparison of salespeople, Exhibit 13.9 compares them along specific criteria. These criteria give the sales manager direction for coaching, counseling, and correcting behavior. For example, although Jones is the top salesperson, he could use improvement in planning, reporting, and territory management.

Because all salespeople in this example have scored low in reporting, the sales manager may want to have a special session on this topic. Wilson is strong in selling skills but weak in everything else. The manager must decide if Wilson should be terminated or a grand effort made to improve all of his major deficiencies. Some companies require sales managers to prepare these tables before making individual assessments. These simultaneous assessments have the advantage of reducing biases toward one person. They have the additional advantage of being completed at one point in time so that evaluations are not subject to changes in moods of the evaluator, whereas ratings take several days.

| Exhibit **13.8** | PAIRED COMPARISONS OF SALESPEOPLE'S OVERALL PERFORMANCE |

Salesperson	The Better Salesperson of the Pair*				
	Baker	Jones	Kerr	Thomas	Wilson
Baker		X			
Jones					
Kerr	X	X			
Thomas	X	X	X		
Wilson	X	X	X	X	
Totals	3	4	2	1	

*An X in the cell means that the salesperson in the column is superior to the one in the row. Thus Jones is better than Baker.

| Exhibit **13.9** | A COMPARISON OF SALESPEOPLE ACROSS CRITERIA SCALED 1 TO 5, WITH 5 THE MOST FAVORABLE |

	Salespeople				
Evaluation Criteria	Baker	Jones	Kerr	Thomas	Wilson
Product Knowledge	4	5	4	3	2
Planning	4	4	3	2	1
Reporting	3	3	3	2	1
Attitudes	4	5	4	3	2
Selling Skills	4	5	3	3	4
Territory Management	3	4	3	2	2
Totals	22	26	20	15	12

Developing an Appraisal Method   Designing and implementing effective performance evaluation measures is a critical sales management task. The measures used will vary with the nature of the industry, the company, and the sales tasks involved. No one measure is appropriate for all situations, and several measures—and types of measures—are more likely to provide better results in most situations. After reviewing results of behavior- and outcome-based control systems, Oliver and Anderson found that a hybrid system that mixes the two often worked best.[20] But they noted that management must find the system that works best in its own sales environment.

Team-Based Performance Measurement and Appraisal   Team-based selling is increasingly prevalent. For example, a survey of selling practices in the banking industry found that 60% of banks responding use team-based selling and corresponding team incentives; in large banks, the proportion is more than 80 percent.[21] Team-based selling involves engaging several members of the firm in the sales effort. For example, selling a complex industrial product may involve several specialists in the firm working together. Together these specialists work with their counterpart at the prospect firm. Although they may coordinate their efforts through the salesperson, the sale depends on their combined performance.

This approach to selling raises the issue of how to measure and appraise team-related performance. This is done at two levels: the individual and the team.

Individual Level The ability to work in teams is increasingly included as a measure of the individual salesperson's capabilities. Even in companies that are not organized into sales teams, the salesperson must develop strong working relationships with colleagues to assure proper account management.[22]

Peer evaluation is another powerful measure of an individual's teamwork. At Pittsburgh-based Mine Safety Appliances, which produces personal protective equipment like safety helmets and respirators, the 100-person sales force is divided into 28 teams. At the end of the year, team members evaluate each other on 12 competency issues using a questionnaire.[23]

The Basic Industry division of Nalco, a chemical company in Naperville, Illinois, uses 360-degree assessment: Employees are appraised by those who report to them, their peers, and their superiors. The company credits this process—which includes the district sales managers—with reducing turnover by pinpointing problems in sales management as well as selling.[24]

Team Level. When the sales force is organized into true teams, the team itself becomes an appropriate additional unit for evaluation. One method for accomplishing this is to develop subjective evaluation measures administered to team members. Scores are then averaged by team to look for problems that need to be addressed at the team level. Sales managers may develop subjective measures of such issues as.[25]

- Commitment to team (as opposed to individual) success
- Clarity of roles within the team
- Openness of communications within the team
- Clarity of team goals
- Other devices

Other approaches to evaluating teams include obtaining customer satisfaction ratings of team performance, conducting team-leader reviews, and management reviews of teams.[26]

Appraisal Pitfalls

Subjective evaluation of performance has many pitfalls. A brief discussion of these pitfalls will help the sales manager avoid them.

The manager must avoid letting personal feelings destroy the objectivity of the rating process. The evidence is clear that sales managers will tend to rate higher those whom they see as desirable work partners or friends and to attribute their performance problems to external causes; while rating lower those they see as less desirable, and attributing problems to the individual salesperson.[27] The evaluation of a salesperson should be limited to his or her proficiency on the job, not personal behavior outside the job or social desirability.

Personal biases in evaluations must be minimized through training for the evaluators. Controlled experiments have shown that biases occur in cases of age and gender.[28] A controlled experiment on the effect of the salesperson's height and weight on punishment for unethical behavior found that overweight salespeople were disciplined more harshly—more terminations and reprimands and fewer counseling sessions.[29]

There is also a danger of recency effects and dramatic incidents that may loom large in the mind of the rater, resulting in a favorable or unfavorable evaluation that does not reflect the salesperson's total performance. A halo effect may occur when a manager judges a salesperson as "good" on one activity and then continues this favorable evaluation for all activities. Similarly, a negative evaluation may carry over into all other activities. Because managers work closely with salespeople, there is a tendency to be lenient and rate no one below a scale value of "average." An experiment revealed that a salesperson's work history will bias an evaluation. Supervisors were likely to attribute poor performance to external sources if the salesperson had a good work history.[30]

There are also the problems of sales managers' dislike for paperwork and their preference for talking rather than writing. These conditions lead to performance reports that tend to evaluate everyone as average or above. They may be stilted and cryptic to the point of being useless in redirecting behavior. Yet, the application of good participative management practices and management communications mandates that every employee deserves a clear and accurate appraisal of performance. Furthermore, federal regulations require written evidence to prove a good-faith effort in compensation, upgrading or promoting, transferring, demotivating, or separating employees.

The comments section gives the evaluator an opportunity to vent some frustration. Selections from the fitness reports for officers in the British Royal Navy and Royal Marines illustrate this point.

"... His men would follow him anywhere, but only out of curiosity.

"... When this officer opens her mouth, it seems that this is only to change whichever foot was previously in there.

"... He has carried out each and every one of his duties to his entire satisfaction.

"... She set low personal standards and then consistently fails."[31]

The validity of appraisals is affected by the psychological reluctance to put disparaging comments about performance in writing if the individual will receive a copy of the report. Yet, failure to note unfavorable performance will result in a continuation of that performance.

PERFORMANCE REVIEW

A plan does not guarantee compliance; a feedback system is needed to communicate the results of the performance measures back to the individual salesperson. Feedback loops help salespeople to allocate their time and company assets in ways that will achieve the company's objectives. Research results suggest that consistently basing rewards on performance-based measures—rather than tenure or political behavior—may be a key to creating an achievement value system within the sales force.[32]

A performance system that is built upon mutually agreed upon standards has two goals. The first goal is to improve the performance of the salesperson, his or her district, the entire sales force, and the company. The second goal occurs if the performance system is truly open and two-way: the salesperson representative can provide important feedback for refining the goals, strategies, and selling programs.

Formal performance reviews are usually held annually or semi-annually. More frequent performance reviews occur when the manager gives the representative a *trip report* after a working visit every two or three months. An informal review is known as *curbside counseling,* which is held immediately after a sales call and takes place on the sidewalk, in the car, or over a cup of coffee. The opportunity for this type of counseling is disappearing as the span of control is widened because sales managers have less time to devote to each individual salesperson.

A curbside conference could go like this: "Lee, I noticed on the last several calls that each time you mentioned the price of our product, the customer objected to the amount of money he'd have to invest. Let's talk about that. Why would that have triggered that reaction when you didn't get the same reaction this morning? Do you remember phrasing it differently then? Let's role-play that sequence for a minute before we make the next call that you have scheduled."

If the performance review is to modify behavior of the salesperson, then he or she must receive feedback. Poor feedback systems may aggravate an already negative situation.

Writing the performance appraisals for subordinates is a perennial problem for most field sales managers for a variety of reasons. It is made more difficult by wider spans of control, teaming, rapid reshuffling of salespeople, and need for global appraisal systems. As a result of these dynamics companies are investing heavily in overhauling their performance evaluation systems.[33]

One counseling method that avoids the psychological problem for the field sales manager is called "positive reinforcement." Instead of emphasizing the deficiency, it stresses methods for achieving the objectives. For example, if a salesperson has achieved only 75% of a sales goal, the sales manager would compliment him or her on achieving 75% of the sales and ask what methods were used and if these methods could be used to achieve the remaining 25%.

To make an evaluation more relevant to the salesperson, the sales manager should address the evaluation to the salesperson in the second person and report to the regional manager in the third person. This is the reverse of the usual procedure. The distinctions between these two approaches appear in Exhibit 13.10. The second person approach clearly has more impact.

Conducting an Effective Performance Review Interview   The appraisal interview can be a motivating experience when the interviewee is an above average performer, but it will probably be traumatic and demotivating to the person who is a below-average performer. In the latter case the manager should make a special effort to create an environment that will not intensify the negative atmosphere. Punishment can have detrimental effects on both a salesperson's performance and job satisfaction.[34]

A good interviewing environment should:

1. Be conducted by the person who knows the salesperson best, talks the language of the trade, and has personally observed the behavior.
2. Be free of interruptions so that the interviewee feels that this is the most important event to the interviewer, thereby encouraging the interviewee's participation.
3. Recognize achievements, positive behaviors, and strengths to create a supportive environment.
4. Limit criticism to behavior that has been expressed factually in writing, warning of the outcomes (probation or termination) if not corrected.
5. Keep the appraisal objective by noting that any deficiencies are based on mutually agreed upon performance standards.
6. Avoid surprises by scheduling appraisals frequently.
7. Review the sequence of evaluation that begins with the job description, moves through the performance standards and the appraisal stage, and finally reaches the consequences of the salesperson's behavior—rewards (compensation, awards, promotion), probation, or termination.
8. Provide the salesperson with a signed copy of the written appraisal.
9. Follow the company's Affirmative Action Program to judge all salespeople fairly. The program should require at least the following components:
   a. Measurable objectives and standards that are based on the job description.
   b. Written and dated documentation of evaluations, efforts to correct deficient behavior, and the consequences of continued deficient behavior. These documents should be signed by the manager and the salesperson.

Exhibit 13.10   WRITING EVALUATIONS IN THE SECOND PERSON

Salesperson Trip Report #3   (Third Person)

Selling Skills

"Mary needs to be more aggressive in asking for the business. I had to put in my two cents' worth on several calls to get a commitment from the physicians to use the product."

Planning

"She will have to get more specific on her individual call objectives. She will have to zero in on the main reason for the call. We discussed this at length and set up some objectives for the next several calls, and her second day was more meaningful in this respect."

(Second Person)

Selling Skills

"I graded your selling skills on this trip, Mary, as 'Needing Improvement.' As I mentioned, you seem to close, but not strongly enough. As an example, you said on several occasions, 'I'd appreciate your keeping our product in mind.' I think, Mary, that you would be more successful in getting him to use our product on his next several patients if you ask him directly, 'Will you use it or try it on your next three or six patients, Doctor?' I think you will agree that this is asking for the business and getting a commitment at the same time. In the area of using selling tools, I think you'll agree that on that physician in Athens who was a member of the AAFP, you should have planned this call a bit better in advance. The CEU credit he will receive certainly pays off in good will and future support. Let's work on this, OK?"

Planning

"I realize you don't get into this area very frequently, but I was glad to see you using their appointment system. This should improve your time utilization. I also noticed you're getting more information from your stores and hospitals about new physicians in this area. These should be your future calls."

Salesperson Trip Report #4   (Third Person)

Product Knowledge

"He has the product knowledge to handle most details, but I had to fill him in on several instances when he didn't have all the information he should have. Knowledge of literature and other sales aids is OK."

Selling Skills

"Joe comes on strong when asking for the business and gets the pharmacist to commit himself on each product. He doesn't waste time getting to the close. Makes good comparisons of our products to competition and knows the right time to get to the crux of the matter in signing the order."

(Second Person)

Product Knowledge

"Joe, I think your product knowledge on this trip was effective and that you used good sales points, current literature, and other sales aids. Although we didn't get into a lot of in-depth details, I felt that what you did present was adequate. However, as I pointed out on several occasions, your level of PK is not up to the same high level of expertise you show so very well in your selling skills. Improvement on several products should also pay off in increased sales."

Selling Skills

"It was good to see your continuing use of Personal Selling Skills. As an example, you continuously closed, and closed very strong. I don't believe anyone else in the District asks for the business as convincingly as you do! Keep it up."

c. Documented activities that are scheduled to overcome deficiencies.

d. If there is **any** doubt about the procedures check with the EEOC officer in the personnel department or the legal department.

A review of the literature on the performance appraisal interview concluded that three factors consistently contribute to effective appraisal interviews: the superior's support, the superior's welcoming participation, and the superior's knowledge of the interviewee's job and performance.[35]

CORRECTIVE ACTION

When performance is below expectations, it is up to the sales manager to take corrective action. Generally, there are two types of corrective action: counseling or termination. Counseling involves helping the salesperson to identify and correct the underlying causes of the performance deficiency. Termination involves removing the salesperson from sales employment, usually after repeated unsuccessful attempts at counseling.

Counseling

Counseling involves helping salespeople to diagnose their performance gaps and to identify potential solutions. When sales are below quota, it may be because of inadequate prospect qualification (resulting in calls to prospects who are unprepared or unable to purchase), poor time management, or a host of other potential problems. Appropriate solutions will depend on accurate diagnosis.

In *nondirective counseling* the sales manager encourages the salesperson to create his own alternative solutions. An advantage of this approach is that the salesperson tends to take ownership of the solution. Having taken ownership, he is more likely to implement the solution when he is out in the field. However, salespeople may lack the sales manager's insight into the causes of the problem, either because of inexperience, lack of training, or individual biases.

In *directive counseling* the sales manager actively participates in diagnosis of the problem and development of solutions. Using this approach, the manager runs a risk that the salesperson will fail to accept—and implement—the recommended advice.

Typically sales managers take an approach that balances their participation in problem identification and solution development with that of the salesperson, depending on the situation. Inexperienced salespeople are likely to understand and value the manager's involvement in the diagnosis-and-solution process. More experienced salespeople are likely to be more involved in solving their own problems, but under the sales manager's supervision.

Counseling focuses on career development. This type of counseling is part of the sales manager's job; personal counseling is not. The manager must be careful in counseling sessions when poor job performance is the result of personal problems. The manager must acknowledge the limits of his or her training in counseling and direct the individual to corporate counseling services.

The clarification of company, management, and the salesperson's values is the beginning of the development of positive attitudes that will help the salesperson feel good about himself or herself, the company, the industry, and careers in selling. Thus counseling is not a lecture or a transfer of knowledge. It should not have as its goal the dispensing of advice or "straightening out" a salesperson. Instead, it is a process for analysis and understanding that leads to the following outcomes: self-discovery by the salesperson, a commitment to mutually agreed-upon goals, and a plan of action for the salesperson's career.

Managers avoid counseling because it is a time-consuming activity. It requires accurate problem identification and mutual trust, neither of which can be accomplished quickly. Because each individual is unique, with different strengths and weaknesses, the balance between guidance and criticism is delicate. The manager must listen carefully to distinguish the difference between acceptance of a point and agreement with the point. Acceptance means that consensus has not taken place and the manager has had to resort to organizational power to bring about a change in behavior. Acceptance may not result in a lasting behavioral change.

Managers need to receive training in counseling. The company needs to make counseling a clear part of the manager's job description, recognize superior performance, and reward it. Some companies include in managers' evaluations the number of persons whom they have promoted.

Termination

Occasionally the most appropriate corrective action involves terminating the salesperson. This may result from a violation of company policy *(objective cause)* or after the failure of repeated attempts at performance improvement.

Termination for Objective Cause   Terminating a salesperson for cause is less subjective than other reasons for termination that are based on evaluations of behavior. The termination for cause is the result of the employee's violating clearly stated personnel, corporate, or legal policies. Examples include stealing, lying, and falsification of reports. These causes for termination will be stated clearly in job descriptions and policy manuals. For example, the following case represents a violation of a policy that would be made clear when the employee was hired.

> "What a mess," Tim Kebles thought as he reflected on his three years as a sales trainer. Karl Taylor, a trainee of two weeks, was bright and pleasant, but he was a fake. His resume reported a college degree and experience that he did not have. Yet, he seemed well qualified for job.

What would you do if you were Tim?

Termination for cause must be substantiated with solid evidence. Procter & Gamble fired a 41-year veteran after publicly accusing him of stealing a $35 company telephone. The plaintiff said that it was his phone and the company libeled him by posting notices on the company bulletin boards. The jury awarded the plaintiff $1.5 million in compensatory damages and $14 million in punitive damages.[36]

Termination Based on Evaluations   Because evaluations and counseling are subjective the manager cannot immediately terminate a salesperson for poor performance. If counseling does not improve behavior, there are three steps toward termination: (1) a warning; (2) probation for an agreed-upon time period, as documented by a probation statement signed by the manager and the salesperson; and, if the agreed-upon behavior has not been reached in the time agreed to, (3) termination.

Consider the following situation.

> Susan Myer was promoted to first-level field manager at Timmon's Consumer Products. She had been a salesperson for three years, having joined the company straight out of college. When Susan had been a manager for two months, John Chalmar was assigned to her district. He had just graduated from college. He seemed perfect for the job—he had sales experience, and he was confident and slightly cocky.
>
> Susan's main objective was to develop John's selling skills, but he did not take suggestions. He seemed to think that her suggestions were not relevant to his accounts. After observing him make presentation for which he was not prepared, Susan held a curbside conference in the car. She evaluated his performance and asked him to send the account some information in the next day's mail.
>
> A month later, they returned to the account to make a new product introduction. The appointment was a waste because John had not resolved the mistakes of the previous visit and had not sent the requested information. This put the account two months behind the planned strategy.
>
> When Susan confronted John about the situation, he said that he just hadn't realized that it would matter. He claimed that she had not made herself clear and that he was doing his best.

(How could this situation have been avoided? What steps should Susan take at this time?)

Probation should be part of the document that establishes a mutually agreed upon plan for improving performance. It should be made clear that failure to reach mutually agreed upon goals during a three- or six-month probation will end in termination.

Although firing someone is traumatic, the end result should benefit the individual as well as the manager and the company. Keeping an individual in a job for which he or she is ill suited drains the individual's energy and keeps him or her from more positive activities. Many firings have jolted the individual and led to success.

Perhaps the best way for a manager to begin the exit interview for a terminated employee is with the admission, "We have all made a mistake. I thought that you would be well suited for this kind of selling, but I was wrong. I have tried my best, but I am simply holding you back from opportunities that are better suited to you."

The importance of letting the unproductive salesperson move on is illustrated in the following actual case. "You've probably forgotten me," the voice said on the other end of the phone, "but 12 years ago you fired me. It was the best thing that ever happened to me. It kicked me into action. I just wanted you to know that I straightened out and was just promoted to vice president of sales at another company."[37]

The foundations for termination begin when the candidate is given a job description, performance standards, outlines for training programs, and a performance appraisal. Every effort should be made to rehabilitate the salesperson because of the expense of firing and rehiring as well as for humanistic reasons. Rarely recognized is the personal satisfaction of helping an individual turn from a failure to a success. But when termination is the only alternative, signed documentation is critical to eliminating future problems and possible suits. The documentation trail should include the following:

1. Get a written agreement on the performance standards to be met.
2. Write regularly scheduled performance appraisals.
3. Develop a written agreement on corrective actions and consequences if goals are not achieved.
4. Document improvement, compliance, or lack thereof.
5. If deadlines are not met, take disciplinary action and document consequences for a relapse, including termination.
6. Be prepared to prove in future months or years that you took the above steps.
7. Check company policies, get approval of superiors, check for possible discrimination of protected groups, and check company files for similar cases.
8. Conduct the termination interview and create a document of what happened.

This list should serve as a guideline for hiring and developing salespeople.

The manager must also handle the effects of a firing on salespeople who remain with the firm. At first the firing will be sobering, but the salespeople who remain probably knew of the person's shortcomings and appreciate being assured that the company's standards are being enforced.

Experienced managers have developed guides for a termination interview. Schedule the interviews early in the week so that the salesperson does not brood all weekend. Keep it brief—5 to 30 minutes. Conduct the interview in a private environment, free from interruptions. The private environment will spare the individual embarrassment if he or she reacts strongly. Have all facts documented and readily at hand. If the evaluations and probation have been handled properly, the termination will not be a surprise. Work with the personnel department regarding the timing of termination and accrued benefits. Emphasize the support of senior management in the decision. Provide a list of activities required before the salesperson receives the final paycheck. These could include turning over territory records, samples, and a car. Be fair, firm, direct, and honest. Immediately document this session for the record.

There are also some termination don'ts. Don't get emotional, vindictive, angry, critical, or sympathetic. Don't review criticisms; they should have been covered and documented during evaluations. Don't bargain or equivocate. Don't make comparisons with the performance of others. Don't respond to threats to sue. Don't promise "gilded" references. Don't touch the person physically—keep hands off.

No matter how explicit the manager has been about the ultimate consequences of continued unsatisfactory performance, the actual termination can be traumatic. The manager can anticipate one of several reactions. The most normal reaction is disbelief, anger, hurt, disappointment, or tears. If the reaction is a violent one, the manager should remain calm, not responding with violence. An initial smooth calm acceptance of the decision will probably later give way to blowing up. If the reaction is shock, the manager may try to quietly talk the employee into reality or seek professional help. The salesperson may also respond with a sense of relief by saying, "I knew it was coming. What took you so long?"

Case 13.1   SKOKIE TOOL COMPANY

Jim Kelly, age 34, was a five-year veteran of Skokie Tool Company, headquartered in Cleveland, Ohio. He had worked for the previous eight years with Cleveland Pump Company in the same city where he had a great reputation with his customers. According to Jim, he left Cleveland Pump because they "were too conservative and had an archaic bureaucratic management system." Although none of his customers was very specific, they did confirm that Jim was "a great guy, well liked, and well remembered." Cleveland Pump had a policy that they observed strictly about not giving out any information about previous employees. Before joining Cleveland Pump, Jim had spent a year with the Cleveland Browns as a fullback until injuring his knee. He had a great college career at the University of Pittsburgh.

Personally, Jim was an affable Irishman with a ready wit, "a way with customers," an ability to get to see important decision makers, some tendency to cut corners in ordering procedures and pricing, a continuing dislike for reports, a big entertainer, and "a born salesman." The personnel records indicated that he had been put on warning the previous year by his district manager for his repeated violation of the company's expense and pricing policies.

In an industry in which inventory control was important because of the high cost of finished goods, there were only minor seasonal variations in sales, with peaks in the summer months. Jim's territory had larger than average swings. For example, with an annual quota of $6,500,000 last year, his sales for the winter quarter were $1,800,000, for the spring quarter were $1,300,000, for the summer quarter were $1,200,000, and for the fall quarter were $2,005,000. In the previous four years, sales in Jim's territory had totaled 102%, 84%, 96%, and 92% of quota.

This was the situation that Susan McCullough had found when she took over as the district sales manager (DSM) a year ago. At the end of that fiscal year, Susan had received a complaint from the comptroller about the excess inventory that they were carrying as a result of the inventory on hand during the summer months, which had been produced against the forecast negotiated between Jim and the previous DSM. This complaint was followed by a letter from the production manager and the shipping manager who complained that because of the lengthy production time they couldn't adjust their production rapidly enough to respond to the high sales in Jim's territory in the fall quarter. Because Jim had promised delivery early in the fall, the result was shipping delays and customer complaints that had gone directly to the president.

This year Jim's sales were at 96% of quota as of April 1, and 83% on July 1. In a telephone conversation, Jim had told Susan, "Don't worry, I'll make it up by the end of the year."

At the end of last year, Susan had asked Jim to evaluate his performance using the company's standard four-page Salespersons' Performance Appraisal Report, which she wanted to compare with her evaluation during their annual performance review. Susan had felt the need to conduct her first annual appraisal with Jim on a thoroughly businesslike basis because, frankly, she felt ill at ease in the role. Jim

Case 13.1 — SKOKIE TOOL COMPANY—CONTINUED

tended to overwhelm her and she had the feeling that in his friendly, boisterous manner he was really laughing at her and certainly not taking her seriously.

As a result, when Jim met her, Susan wasn't prepared for the very sketchy comments he had scrawled over the Comments section of the first page: "I was hired to sell and I'm doing a very good job of it. My customers like me, and my sales are ahead of last year for every year I've worked for Skokie Tool."

When Susan challenged him on the quality and content of his report, Jim laughingly said, "Aw, come on, Susan, you know these reports are for new kids. You and I don't have to play these kinds of games, and nobody pays any attention to them anyway. We ought to be spending this time with customers creating sales instead of rehashing the past, which doesn't serve any useful purpose." Susan flushed and pointed out that he was being very selective in the facts he remembered because he had never made the sales forecast except the year he joined the company, even though each year he had been ahead of the prior year's sales each year. Jim laughed hard and countered, "Boy, you sure have a hard heart for such a pretty girl, and anyway I can't be held responsible for those unreasonable quotas established by the front office. Those guys don't know what it's like out in the cruel competitive world. My customers are giving me all their business on our type of products. If we'd bring out some new products once in a while, I'd be able to do better." Susan had a hard time maintaining her self-control for the balance of the interview, but she did manage to tell Jim she wasn't satisfied with his sales performance, his attitude, the advance planning reports which she rarely received, or his sales call summary reports which were frequently late or incomplete, and that she would confirm it in writing. This didn't seem to faze Jim who replied, "Susan, don't take your job so seriously. Can't we be friends?" which infuriated her all the more.

When Susan discussed her dissatisfaction with Jim Kelly's performance and attitude with John Freeman, the national sales manager to whom she reported, he told her that she'd have to figure out a way to solve the problem herself. He also mentioned that it was his understanding that Jim was well liked by his customers.

Susan decided to list in the annual report the specific deficiencies she had noted. She asked Jim to respond in writing regarding what he planned to do about them. When Susan worked with Jim in March, by which time she had not received his reply, he said that what she was asking of him was a difficult thing for him to do, that the previous DSM had not been as unreasonable in his demands, and that he was working on a set of plans that he hoped would satisfy her but that "weren't finished as yet."

When Jim's plans did not arrive by the end of June, Susan scheduled herself to work with him the second week in July, only to learn that his forward itinerary indicated he was working out of town about 200 miles away. She scheduled herself to work instead with Harry Wilkins, the other salesperson headquartered in Cleveland. As a result, Susan was shocked to see Jim's car parked in front of his home as she drove by at 10:00 AM en route to the location where she had agreed to meet Harry. On the spur of the moment, she circled the block and parked about a half block from Jim's house where she was able to keep his car in full view. At 1:00 PM her vigil was rewarded when Jim came out in casual attire, a picnic basket in hand, with his wife and two children, got in his car and drove off. For a moment Susan was afraid that Jim had spotted her.

After considerable thought, Susan continued on to work with Harry Wilkins. On returning home after her working trip with Harry, Susan decided to wait for Jim's sales call summary report for that week before doing anything. As luck would have it, Jim's report came in on time with full activities reported for the week that he was supposedly out of town.

CASE QUESTIONS

1. What was Jim Kelly's quarterly seasonal quota last year and what percentage was his sales ahead or behind for each individual quarter?
2. What is the immediate problem?
3. What are the long-term problems?
4. What additional unresolved problems have occurred since Susan became Jim's district sales manager?
5. What combination of clues provided some early warning signals?
6. What should Susan do?
7. If the company has no policy on falsification of reports, what should Susan do?
8. On what basis would Susan recommend termination (firing) of Jim Kelly if there is no specific policy on falsification of reporting?
9. If, for whatever reason, Susan were to decide or be told that she could not terminate Jim Kelly, how should she handle their subsequent working relationship?
10. If we assume that Jim Kelly had not falsified his reports, but instead had written Susan a letter that she had not received saying he was taking several days vacation, and had sent in daily call summary reports for the vacation days marked "Vacation," what plan could Susan devise to correct their working relationship and Jim's productivity?

Case 13.2   A CONTEMPORARY PROBLEM

As a new district manager for a pharmaceutical company, I was excited after I spent my first week of orientation with the former district manager who had been promoted. We reviewed the paper work, geography, and the ten salespeople in the district. Marie, a second year salesperson, was a member of a minority, a registered nurse, in her late 20s, and a native of the area.

The first two-day work trip that I spent with Marie was enjoyable because she is a casual talker. She talked with pride about her husband and his profession, but she seemed nervous in front of the doctor and her presentations seemed canned. I assumed that she was nervous because I was a new manager.

Two weeks later the company launched a new product. Each salesperson received a learning unit and sales materials to study before taking a written test on the product. Marie did poorly on the written test. Then salespeople role-played a call and Marie struggled because her product knowledge and presentation were weaker than those of new trainees. Two experienced salespeople who were training for field sales management assisted with the role-plays. Neither seemed surprised at her role-play performance. One of them volunteered that Marie had been held back an extra six months from advanced training class to help her catch up.

A few weeks later on our next work trip, Marie's presentations showed little improvement so we went back to the basics of planning a simple introductory call. She memorized our role-plays and presented them to her doctors. The presentations went well until they asked a question. She answered only the simple questions and ignored objections. The next day at lunch she thanked me for all my help and told me how poorly the former manager worked with her. I changed the subject.

Six weeks later Marie informed me that she was pregnant. She had full intentions of returning to work after the baby was born. One of the other salespeople held a shower for her.

Marie's mind was certainly not on the job, for she was having problems with asthma and weight gain. She was trying to carry a detail bag with 30 pounds of reprints and materials, most of which were never used on the calls. I encouraged her to lighten the load but she didn't. It was over 90° and I was worried about her health as she struggled up stairs with the detail bag. Finally, to her astonishment, I dumped the contents of the bag into the trunk of her car and put in only the pieces she actually planned to use on calls. After that she seemed physically secure and emotionally relieved and her calls were more spontaneous. At lunch she said that the former manager had required her to carry all product materials, but I felt that her problem was not knowing how to use the materials.

Her doctor sent a note to the company saying that complications prevented her working after the seventh month of pregnancy. Later the baby was delivered normally and she was in great spirits.

Marie returned to work eight weeks after the baby was born and we both thought that this was a new beginning for her career. She seemed enthusiastic and I tried to help her gradually get back into the flow of the job.

Soon after the new beginning, Marie's paperwork, which was never perfect, greatly deteriorated. Her expense reports were not only inaccurate but late. When we discussed this on later work trips, Marie said that she could not do the paperwork until the baby was asleep, which was late into the night. I offered suggestions of how homework could be minimized by doing the work in the field.

Shortly before her annual salary review, my regional manager and I noticed that Marie was sending in call cards once a week, instead of the daily requirement because of prescription sample guidelines. When I confronted her with this possible terminating offense, she emphatically claimed that the calls were made as stated but that she did not understand the importance of daily reports. She promised to improve.

We then reviewed her overall sales and reported call activity, which were average in the district. She then proceeded to tell me that I was really only looking for a reason not to give her a good raise like the other salespeople always received. She wanted opportunities to earn extra money by working conventions and wholesalers. I attempted to communicate to her that salary and bonus are based primarily on performance in her territory on a day-to-day basis. Convention assignment decisions are based on geographic location and expertise and have little impact on compensation.

An ongoing pattern developed after that annual review. Paperwork continued to be late and inaccurate and doctor presentations were illogical with shallow or no technical proof. Usually, on the second day, she would bring up the issue of her low pay and limited opportunities for extra compensation. My repeated explanations were not accepted. All trust was gone.

Marie began the next year's annual review with a negative blast and a repeat of issues discussed numerous times. Once again, sales and reported activity were average and paperwork continued to be weak. Based on facts, I informed her that I would submit her for a competent or average salary increase again.

She is now a three-year salesperson who is unhappy with her "unfair" raises and low bonuses, which are at the national average for salespeople. Yesterday, she told me that she is unexpectedly pregnant again. What direction do I take now and in the future?

CASE QUESTIONS

1. What is the immediate problem?
2. How should the immediate problem be handled?
3. What are the long-term problems?
4. What caused the long-term problems?
5. What steps need to be taken to resolve the long-term problems?

SUMMARY

The sales manager controls the sales force with a system of appraisals, counseling, and correcting behavior, or with termination if correction is not possible. The process builds on the previous management steps of recruiting, selecting, training, coaching, and motivating salespeople.

The prerequisite to an effective appraisal system is a set of performance standards based on the salesperson's job description. Because these standards are not always measurable, they require subjective observations, such as a good attitude, as well as objective ones, such as sales or the number of presentations. Much of the data for objective evaluations are derived from activity reports. Subjective evaluations require the personal observations of the manager.

Counseling is a time-consuming activity because it requires the development of mutual respect and understanding in order to clarify values and goals. Ideally, counseling will lead to a process of self-discovery and self-development for salespeople that will minimize the future need for counseling. Because counseling takes time and because few managers have been trained in it, the quality of this important management activity varies greatly across districts. Companies that have given managers counseling training have found that sales productivity increases.

Correction ranges from slight behavioral modifications to probation and finally, if all efforts fail, to termination. If all previous steps, including evaluation, counseling, and correction, have been completed properly, along with documentation, then termination of a salesperson will be a logical conclusion for the salesperson and the manager. In many cases termination has been the shock that focuses the individual into positive action.

ASSIGNMENTS/DISCUSSION QUESTIONS

1. Define a performance standard and give an example for a field salesperson.
2. What is the overall purpose of the function of controlling?
3. Although performance is influenced by many variables not under his or her control, what will enable the salesperson to accept these variables?
4. What conclusions would you draw from data that indicate an experienced salesperson is making the required number of calls but whose productivity is significantly below average?
5. Explain the differences between the two types of essay appraisal in Exhibit 13.10.
6. Compare the advantages and disadvantages of Exhibits 13.8 and 13.9.
7. What is the purpose of a performance appraisal?
8. What are the benefits to the company and to the salesperson of an effective performance appraisal system?
9. Discuss the role of the manager during the performance appraisal interview in identifying and defining performance deficiencies.
10. What can the field manager do if "the extent the salesperson is able and willing to recognize his or her deficiencies is less than acceptable to the manager"?
11. Why do managers view coaching negatively?
12. What are the relationships among the position description, specific objectives (MBO), and sales results? Which should be used as the basis for the annual formal performance review?

ENDNOTES

1. Building Excellent Performance, Performance Appraisal System, Gold Bond Building Products Division, The National Gypsum Company, n.d.

2. Much of this discussion is based on Bernard J. Jaworski, Toward a Theory of Marketing Control: Environmental Context, Control Types, and Consequences, *Journal of Marketing,* 52, July, 1988, pp. 23–29.

3. Louis S. Richman, The Dark Side of Job Churn, *Fortune,* August 9, 1993, p. 24, quoting a study by Cornell University labor economist John Bishop.

4. Supplied by the Charlotte, NC office of Wallace Computer Services, September, 1993.

5. Hubert S. Field and William H. Holley, The Relationship of Performance Appraisal System Characteristics to Verdicts in Selected Employment Discrimination Cases, *Academy of Management Journal* 25(2), 1982, pp. 392–406.

6. Donald W. Jackson, Jr., John L. Schlacter, and William G. Wolfe, Examining the Bases Utilized for Evaluating Salespeoples' Performance, *Journal of Personal Selling and Sales Management,* 15(4), Fall 1995, pp. 57–65.

7. *Ibid.*

8. Goutam N. Challagalla and Tasadduq A. Shervani, Dimensions and Types of Supervisory Control: Effects on Salesperson Performance and Satisfaction, *Journal of Marketing,* 60(1), January, 1996, pp. 89–105.

9. Erin Anderson and Richard L. Oliver, Perspectives on Behavior-Based Versus Outcome-Based Salesforce Control Systems, *Journal of Marketing,* 51, October, 1987, pp. 76–88.

10. Richard L. Oliver and Erin Anderson, An Empirical Test of the Consequences of Behavior- and Outcome-Based Sales Controls, *Journal of Marketing,* 58, October, 1994, pp. 53–67.

11. Scott B. MacKenzie, Philip M. Podsakoff, & Richard Fetter, The Impact of Organizational Citizenship Behavior on Evaluations of Salesperson Performance, *Journal of Marketing,* 57(1), January, 1993, pp. 70–80.

12. Michael Levy and Arun Sharma, Relationships Among Measures of Retail Salesperson Performance, *Journal of the Academy of Marketing Science,* 21(3), Summer, 1993, pp. 231–238.

13. Scott B. MacKenzie, Philip M. Podsakoff, Richard Fetter, and Dennis Organ (1988), *Organizational Citizenship Behavior: The Good Soldier Syndrome,* Lexington, MA: Lexington Books.

14. Geoffrey Brewer, Mind Reading: What Drives Top Salespeople to Greatness? *Sales & Marketing Management,* May, 1994, p. 84.

15. *Ibid.,* pp. 84–88.

16. David W. Cravens, Thomas N. Ingram, Raymond W. LaForge, and Clifford E. Young, Behavior-Based and Outcome-Based Salesforce Control Systems, *Journal of Marketing,* 57, October, 1993, pp. 47–95.

17. Target Marketing Systems, Individual Skills Assessment, October, 1995.

18. Wallace Computer Services, Performance Review Record.

19. Confidential source.

20. Richard L. Oliver and Erin Anderson, Behavior- and Outcome-Based Sales Control Systems: Evidence and Consequences of Pure-Form and Hybrid Governance, *Journal of Personal Selling & Sales Management,* 15(4), Fall, 1995, pp. 1–15.

21. Paul Kalamaras, Carolyn LaPenta, Vicki Elliott, and Kim Dabrowski, Using Team Incentives to Achieve Business Growth, *Journal of Retail Banking Services,* 17(4), Winter, 1995, pp. 11–20.

22. Judith Oliver, New, Improved Salesforce, *Management Today,* December, 1996, pp. 82–85.

23. Michele Marchetti, Rewarding Team Players, *Sales and Marketing Management,* 148(4), April, 1996, pp. 35–37.

24. Ian P. Murphy, Firm Uses Feedback to Cut Turnover, Save Millions, *Marketing News,* July 7, 1997.

25. Based in part on John F. Monoky, How Does Your Team Rate?

26. Deborah Harrington-Mackin (1994), *The Team-Building Tool Kit,* New York: AMACOM.

27. Thomas E. DeCarlo and Thomas W. Leigh, "Impact of Salesperson Attraction on Sales Managers' Attributions and Feedback," *Journal of Marketing,* 60, 2 April, 1996, 47–66.

28. Benson Rosen and Thomas H. Jerdee (1985), *Older Employees: New Roles for Valued Resources,* Chicago: Dow Jones, Irwin. Ben Rosen and Thomas H. Jerdee, Sex Stereotyping in the Executive Suite, *Harvard Business Review,* March-April, 1974, pp. 45–58.

29. Joseph A. Bellizzi and D. Wayne Norvell, Personal Characteristics and Salespersons' Justifications as Moderators of Supervisory Discipline in Cases Involving Unethical Salesforce Behavior, *Journal of the Academy of Marketing Science,* 19(1), Winter, 1991, pp. 11–16.

30. Alan J. Dubninsky, Steven J. Skinner, and Tommy E. Whittler, Evaluation of Sales Personnel: An Attribution Theory Perspective, *Journal of Personal Selling & Sales Management,* 9(1), Spring, 1989, pp. 9–21.

31. Mary Rowe, Performance Evaluation Excerpts, *Innovation Network,* 3(113), November 8, 1996.

32. Michael J. Swenson and Joel Herche, Social Values and Salesperson Performance, *Journal of the Academy of Marketing Science,* 22(3), Summer 1994, pp. 283–289.

33. Timothy D. Schellhardt, It's time to evaluate your work, and all involved are groaning, *The Wall Street Journal,* November 19, 1996, p. 1.

34. Goutam N. Challagalla and Tasadduq A. Shervani, Dimensions and Types of Supervisory Control: Effects on Salesperson Performance and Satisfaction, *Journal of Marketing,* 60(1), January, 1996, pp. 89–105.

35. Douglas Cederblom, The Performance Appraisal Interview: A Review, Implications, and Suggestions, *Academy of Management Review,* 7(2), 1982, pp. 219–227.

36. Gabrriella Stern, Some Companies Discover that some Firings Backfire into Costly Defamation Suits, *The Wall Street Journal,* May 5, 1993, B1.

37. Personal communication with a general sales manager for a pharmaceutical company.

14

COMPENSATION AND OTHER REWARD SYSTEMS

LEARNING GOALS

1. To understand why the development of a compensation plan must come late in the management process
2. To appreciate why the reward systems must be kept current
3. To understand the links between the rewards and the needs of critical participants in the selling process—the customer, the salesperson, and the selling company
4. To be able to recommend incentive plans given different objectives
5. To be able to evaluate existing incentive plans

THE CHALLENGE OF SETTING SALES FORCE REWARDS

Developing a sales force compensation plan can be difficult. Changing an existing one can be extremely difficult and will challenge a manager's ability to manage change. A compensation plan is a critical part of a sales management strategy, but it must be built on a good definition of the sales force objectives and all of the other sales management functions must have been done well. A compensation plan cannot overcome recruiting and selecting the wrong candidates, a poor training program, the lack of performance standards and evaluation systems, weak field management, a demotivating environment, or poor communications. Without these basics, a compensation plan with many incentives will elicit only short-run changes in behavior. Salespeople will quickly say, "But what have you done for me lately?" Compensation plans must also consider the motivating effects of benefits such as health plans, vacations, retirement plans, profit sharing, use of a company car, and reimbursed expenses. Developing a compensation plan, therefore, must come after all other sales management decisions have been made. It can be an important element in recruiting and retaining the best salespeople. We will see in this chapter that a compensation plan is more likely to be a demotivator than a motivator.

269

To appreciate the difficulty of changing a compensation plan consider the task facing a young sales manager.

My company, a pharmaceutical wholesale company, paid commissions for achieving dollar quotas for four product lines. This system had been used for 5 years and it worked well, but currently company profitability has eroded as marketing expenses have increased. Now my boss wants to introduce a new concept—expense sharing—with customers and salespeople. He has data to prove that we retain 28% more customers every year when they buy three or more product lines from us. He also says that it is much less expensive for the order department to service an order of three or more product lines rather than one or two. He proposes to give the customer a discount if it buys three or more product lines on a single order, thereby sharing the savings in expense with the customer. This expense sharing would be reflected in future price lists. He plans to pay higher commissions on orders for three or more product lines and lower commissions for orders with only one or two product lines.

When I tried to explain this plan to my salespeople you would have thought my name was Captain Bligh. I think that expense sharing will soon be company policy. What can I do to get this plan accepted?"

THE ROLE OF COMPENSATION PLANS

The role of a sales force compensation plan is to meet the needs of the customer, the company, and the salesperson.

Customer Needs

Customer needs are met when the plan assures that the salesperson will spend time with the customers to understand their needs and to provide service. A plan based solely on salary would meet a customer's needs, whereas one based only on commission would probably not. A company strategy that requires partnering with an account is more concerned with *relationship selling* for a long-term relationship than for a quick volume sale, so its plan would be weighted toward salary. Highly technical equipment, such as computer installations, production lines, or a new hospital building will require close relationships and therefore will require a large salary component in the compensation package.

After-sale service, and particularly responsiveness to problems, has been ranked by customers as one of the most important salesperson attributes.[1] As a result, firms like IBM, Xerox, Digital Equipment Company, and the dealerships for Saturn, Infiniti, and Chrysler have developed compensation systems based on surveys of customer satisfaction.[2,3,4]

Thus a critical nonfinancial goal has been added to many compensation plans—customer satisfaction. Customer satisfaction directly affects the bottom line. The consulting firm of Bain & Co. showed that a 5% increase in a firm's customer retention rate increases profits from 25% to 85%, depending on the industry.[5] The gains in profitability come from more efficient operations (because of lower customer turnover, reduced advertising costs per customer, etc.), increased purchases per customer, cross-sales, etc., and increased referrals.

A traditional commission on sales or bonus for quota can destroy customer relations, as the Sears Auto Service Centers found in 1992. Commissions and bonuses encouraged their service consultants to sell unneeded services and parts, which led to lawsuits on behalf of consumers by the states of California and New Jersey. Sears quickly changed its compensation plan, but not until its image had been tarnished.

In contrast, a major portion of the Xerox salesperson's compensation is based on a customer satisfaction survey after each sale. The Xerox salesperson has a high incentive to be certain that the equipment performs as promised. "The No. 1 trend in sales compensation is building customer satisfaction into pay plans," according to Craig Ulrich, a consultant with William & Mercer.[6] Some car dealers have put salespeople on salary and General Electric's power generation business uses a team bonus to encourage a collective approach.[7]

Company Needs

A compensation plan must meet the needs of the company in a changing environment. The company's needs will change because of changes in the marketplace, such as new technology, domestic and global competition, and the changing tastes of consumers. Unfortunately, changes in corporate strategies may occur more frequently than changes in compensation plans.

For example, rapid introduction of new products by competitors may lead the firm to increase its own emphasis on new product development. However, the sales force compensation system may reward repeat sales, which are usually more efficient for a salesperson to complete than new product sales. Thus the old compensation scheme may leave the sales force out of synchronization with corporate objectives.

When the necessary changes do occur they must be substantial. For example, putting a higher commission on new product sales and reducing the commission on repeat sales may lead to a substantial short-term drop in total personal income for the salesperson.

This type of strategy-compensation shift can lead to substantial frustration at all levels. As one executive noted:

"It's an all-too-familiar scenario: the new sales compensation program you labored so hard to implement hasn't brought about the desired results. In fact, it created more problems than it solved—your sales force became dissatisfied with the new program; management was unhappy with the program's inability to motivate salespeople to perform with the company's best interest at heart; and anticipated gains in productivity and efficiency didn't materialize.

If left untreated, such problems may further manifest themselves in declining motivation, increased complacency, and high levels of turnover among your salespeople . . ."[8]

Salespeople will do what the system rewards. If commissions or bonuses are based on sales dollars, they will sell those products and to those customers that are easy to sell. They will not sell the products with high margins if the products require more effort and they will not engage in the time-consuming process of developing new accounts. In short, they will not manage their territories as businesses (Chapter 5).

If the corporate goal is growth in profits, then the compensation plan must be linked to growth and profits. For example, if the corporate goal is to increase the earnings per share by 10% each of the next three years, the sales management translation of this goal would be expressed in terms of selling higher margin products, selling more to present customers, opening new accounts, and reducing costs. To synchronize the corporate goals and the salesperson's behavior, commissions or bonuses should be based on each salesperson's contribution to profit, which would reflect selling higher margin products and reducing costs. The compensation plan should also reward opening new accounts. To reflect growth a bonus could be the percent improvement in contributions over last year.

The compensation plan must be flexible so that the company can respond to market dynamics, but it must give some security and stability to the sales force. The plan must be built on a clear understanding of the role of compensation in motivation, territory designs, quota systems, programs for career planning, and information systems that will make it possible to implement it.

A well-designed incentive system can provide a sales manager with an automatic control device. It also gives the salesperson a means for diagnosing his or her performance and taking corrective action. A good compensation plan will be fair to the company, its customers, and its salespeople.

Salespeople's Needs

Needs will change as salespeople move along their career and family life cycles. Behavior on the job is determined by how needs are met on the job. Many of these needs are met by nonfinancial incentives, such as opportunities for advancement and responsibility. A stimulating work environment will help meet the need for self-actualization. But financial compensation is needed to meet physiological needs, security needs, and social needs such as recognition, prestige, and personal self worth, as discussed in Chapter 11.

The compensation plan must consider the life cycle of the salesperson. After meeting physiological needs, the young salesperson may be more concerned with social recognition, whereas the older salesperson with family obligations is more concerned with security. Thus the compensation plan must have components for salespeople along the entire life cycle. The plan should also consider the personality of the typical salesperson. Risk-averse salespeople prefer compensation plans that have fewer incentive components.[9]

The plan must be based on activities that are challenging and yet within the salesperson's control. Research indicates that salespeople are motivated based on challenges that correspond to their own self-perceived selling skills. Salespeople with low self-perceived skills respond better to sales goals (such as quotas) set at lower levels, whereas salespeople with high self-perceived skills are motivated by goals set at higher levels.[10]

The compensation plan must be competitive within the industry. It must be understandable, which does not necessarily mean that it must be simplistic. Too often plans are selected because they are easy to explain and to administer, but they do not meet the needs of the company and the salespeople. Once the needs of the company and salesperson are clearly in mind, the manager may move to the steps in developing a compensation plan.

STEPS IN DEVELOPING A COMPENSATION PLAN

The first step in developing a compensation plan is to define the objectives in terms of the role of personal selling in the marketing plan. This role will be clearly defined in the job description, performance standards, and appraisal forms. Next, the level of compensation must be established for salespeople in different categories. At this point the compensation planner must determine the proportion of compensation that will be an incentive. Having identified this proportion the planner must decide on the mix of salary, bonus, commission, and contests. Expense plans must be considered because some companies require salespeople to pay their own expenses out of the commission. Implementing the compensation plan requires pretesting using data from prior years, introducing it to the sales force, and evaluating it. By now it is obvious that developing the salespeoples' compensation scheme is not an easy task. Each of these points is discussed below.

Define the Objectives

Corporate objectives are translated into sales objectives, which require incentive plans. Appropriate sales objectives and possible incentive plans are illustrated in Exhibit 14.1.

The selling objectives become the basis for specific sales quotas. Quotas are expressed in terms of results such as dollar volume, unit volume, profit margin, and the number of new accounts opened. Quotas may also be expressed in terms of activities to be performed. These activities often are steps in the selling process, such as the number of new prospects

Exhibit 14.1	LINKING OBJECTIVES TO COMPENSATION

Corporate Objective	Selling Objectives	Possible Incentive Plans
Growth business	Sell present accounts ⟶	Commission on new
	New products ⟶	Higher commission for new products
	New accounts ⟶	New account bonus
Hold present business	Build partnerships with major accounts ⟶	Salary, plus a bonus based on client satisfaction measures, plus commission on profit contribution
Open new business/territory	Open new accounts ⟶	Salary plus all expenses
Reduce working capital	Clear slow moving inventory ⟶	Contest on selected products
Maximize short-term profits	Maintain margins by not cutting prices ⟶ _or_ ⟶	Commission on gross margin / Mostly salary plus a bonus on high margin items[13]
Strong channel support	Maintain loyalty and motivation of independent salespeople ⟶	$750 training certificate at a resort for reaching quota[14]

identified, presentations made, closes, and follow-up services performed. To stimulate higher levels of performance rolling quotas may be used. These quotas pay higher commissions for higher levels of quota attainment. For example, up to 70% of quota could pay a 5% commission, 70% to 89% could pay 6.5%, 90% to 100% would pay 10%, up to a cap of 12% at 120% of quota or higher.[11]

Linking Job Description-Performance Appraisal-Salesperson Capabilities

The compensation plan should be based on activities that the salesperson is expected to perform, as outlined in the job description. These activities, in turn, should be reflected in the performance appraisal forms (Chapter 13). These forms specify the importance of each activity and how accomplishment will be measured.

Establish Compensation Levels

Compensation levels must be established for the different levels of a salesperson. A good starting point is the average in the industry or the national averages. For example, a sales trainee's may be $39,000, a mid-level salesperson's $50,000, a top-level salesperson's $68,000, and a regional sales manager's at $92,000.[12] These averages include salaries, commissions, bonuses, and other cash incentives. Within each level a company may specify a range, to allow for room to recognize improvement before promotion to the next level. Compensation ranges will exist for key account salespeople and for salespeople who call on specific industries, such as hospitals or insurance companies.

The upper limit of compensation for salespeople will often be below the lower limit for managers, thereby providing an incentive to become a manager. But not everyone is suited for management. Some companies, such as duPont, have established the position of professional salesperson, which is a career category that carries the respect and benefits (pay, automobile, club memberships, etc.) formerly available only to managers. The manager is generally compensated with a salary and a bonus based on the district's or region's performance. Sometimes there will be an executive bonus which is based on higher level corporate goals, such as profits.

Anticipated compensation levels can create some difficult decisions for a young salesperson.

Consider, for example, the case of Jonathan Strong, who graduated from the University of Vermont, near where he was born. Jonathan has been a salesperson for two years, working the state of Maine out of Portland. His girlfriend lives in Portland and has a good job as a programmer. He has been offered a territory in Washington, D.C., to call on government accounts. His increase in salary will not quite cover the higher cost-of-living, but the commission portion could be substantial. Those who have held this territory have had major promotions in two years, with considerable financial gains. Should Jonathan take the promotion?

Territory location is a critical issue in attracting and retaining top salespeople. To enhance the attraction of a move, companies are including cost-of-living allowances for cities such as New York, Los Angeles, and San Francisco. They are also reporting commission expectations so that the salesperson can decide if the move is worthwhile.[15]

Determine the Incentive Portion

The portion of incentive in the total compensation depends on many factors such as the maturing of the market growth rates, support mechanisms provided, programs for generating leads, advertising programs, brand awareness, the dollar volume per sale, and the buying cycle (i.e., the number of purchases per year). These factors balance against the efforts of the salesperson, as depicted in the balances in Exhibit 14.2. The upper balance puts most of the risk and uncertainty on the salesperson with an 80% commission because so much of the work has been done for him or her. The lower balance places more of the risk on the company because the brand is unknown, in a new market, with no lead generation program.

Sales managers should remember that the purpose of the compensation plan is to direct the salesperson's behavior toward the achievement of corporate goals. If the salesperson should be more aggressive, then the incentive should be the larger portion. If service and "care and feeding" of a client are vital, then salary should be the larger share.

If the incentive portion is increased to 60%, it is difficult to motivate salespeople to perform nonselling activities, such as gathering market information, collecting slow ac-

Exhibit **14.2**	THE INCENTIVE PORTION

Largely Commission

Strong Brand Awareness
Mature Market
Good Lead Generation
High $/Sale
Moderate Sales Cycle   Salesperson

20% Salary   △   80% Commission

Largely Salary

Brand Unknown
New Market
No Lead Program   Salesperson

75% Salary   △   25% Commission

The incentive balances the task and the reward

counts, and providing account service. The manager will need to spend more time following up on salespeople who do not complete their paperwork, which adds to administrative costs. Reducing the incentive portion to 10% could solve this problem but the incentive may be too small to be effective. Thus finding the right balance requires a careful analysis of the needs and resources of the company and the salespeople.

When the proportion of incentive has been decided, the next decision is the form that these incentives will take and the frequency of payment. The typical forms include commissions, bonuses, and contests. Contests are short-term motivators. Commissions tend to be paid more frequently than bonuses or contests.

CHOOSING COMPENSATION METHODS

Each of the compensation methods has advantages and disadvantages that must be evaluated when developing a plan. After reviewing these advantages and disadvantages, we will consider recent trends in compensation plans.

Straight Salary

A 100% salary plan is used when nonselling tasks are required (such as setting up displays and taking inventory), when team selling is appropriate, when the sale takes a long time so that it is difficult to relate the results to the effort, and when a consulting relationship exists, so that an incentive might cloud the objectivity of the advice, as in the Sears Auto Service Center legal case discussed on p. 270. The straight salary has the *advantages* of being easy to administer, making selling costs predictable, providing control over nonselling activities, and providing security for the salespeople during extended negotiations. Its *disadvantages* include: it discourages achievement, fixed costs are high during a sales decline, there are income inequities (poor performers are overpaid and outstanding ones are underpaid), it is inflexible as conditions change, and it tends to reward length of employment rather than productivity. In 1990, only 7% of salespeople received only a salary, down from 21% in 1981.[16]

Commission Only

A 100% commission plan is used when one or more of the following conditions exist: the company has limited working capital, few nonselling activities are needed, the salesperson is very experienced, the salesperson is self-motivated, and selling efforts and results are clearly linked. The *advantages* of this plan include the following: it conserves capital and avoids fixed costs, it maximizes the incentive to develop the market, it attracts high achievers, it requires little supervision, and it is easy to understand and administer. The *disadvantages* are as follows: there is little control over the salesperson to perform nonselling activities; the salespeople tend to overstock customers and avoid small accounts; salespeople in high growth territories receive easy windfall commissions, which causes resentment among other salespeople; unearned income occurs from price increases; salespeople assume ownership of accounts and resist territory cuts; there are difficulties in crediting phone and mail orders; and there are difficulties in crediting return goods and bad debts.

Combination Plans

Most plans are combination ones. The most common plans are salary plus a bonus for achieving a quota and salary plus a commission on sales volume. These plans are used when the salesperson needs some security and incentive and the company needs some control over their activities. The *advantage* of these combination plans is their greater flexibility to meet the changing needs of the salesperson and the company. The bonus has the advantage of limiting the amount that is paid when a goal is achieved. Bonuses are often used to reward the entire selling team for achieving a goal. These combination plans have several *disadvantages:* their complexity makes understanding by the salesperson and administration by the company difficult, the incentives may not be high enough for high achievers, and it is difficult to set the bonus for each member of a team, because it is unlikely that all persons contributed equally to the sale.

The base used for computing the commission can be dollar sales, gross margin, or dollar contribution. An example of a combination plan that uses a salary, two commission levels, a bonus, and an upper limit is shown in Exhibit 14.3 in tabular and graphic form. The base salary is $15,000. When sales reach $100,000 a commission of 5% of sales becomes active. At $200,000 in sales a $2,000 bonus is paid. When $300,000 in sales is reached, an additional 7% commission becomes effective. There is an upper limit of $34,000, so sales above $380,000 generate no additional compensation. This example also shows how a spreadsheet can be used to test the effects of changes in commission and bonuses.

Recent salary and incentive averages for selected selling and sales management positions are shown in Exhibit 14.4.[17] Across these positions, incentives average 26% of total pay, ranging from 22% for national or major account managers to 34% for senior salespeople.

Fine-Tuning the Plan

Once the basic salary, commission, and other compensation plan elements have been designed, the overall package should be adjusted to reflect the specific selling situation.

One issue that must be addressed in fine-tuning the commission element is the level of centralization that is applied. A highly centralized incentive program is one that allocates incentives to specific products and/or customers. Such a program limits the amount of latitude allowed to the salesperson.

A decentralized incentive program is one that allocates incentives based on general categories, such as general levels of sales or profits. Such programs maximize the salesperson's latitude. For example, if only a total quota and bonus are assigned, the salesperson can decide which customers and product lines to emphasize.

Centralized incentive programs are appropriate when the sales manager wants to motivate and channel salesperson activities while minimizing the direct supervision required. Decentralized incentive programs are appropriate when the sales manager is willing to monitor individual salesperson activities, when a sales manager wants to provide salespeople with greater income security and job satisfaction.[18]

Other adjustments may be seen as necessary because of the specific selling cycle. For example, Infomix Software establishes multi-year goals—and incentive packages—for its salespeople. During the initial year that a salesperson has a relationship with a client, only 25% of compensation is based on achieving sales revenue targets and the remaining 75% relates to achievement of non-revenue goals like identifying key decision makers and major projects in the client company. In the second year of the relationship, there is a 50:50 ratio of revenue-to-non-revenue objectives. In the third year, the salesperson's entire commission is based on sales revenue.[19]

TRENDS IN COMPENSATION PLANS

The trends in compensation plans include movement away from straight commissions and advances against future commissions. Movement is toward the inclusion of measures of customer satisfaction and incentives based on margin contribution and growth.

Exhibit **14.3**	AN EXAMPLE OF A COMBINATION COMPENSATION PLAN WITH AN UPPER LIMIT

	Commission Rates				Commission Income		Potential Total Compensation	Paid Subject to Limit
Sales ($000)	5%	7%	Salary	Bonus	At 5%	At 7%		
0	0		$15,000				$15,000	$15,000
20	0		$15,000				$15,000	$15,000
40	0		$15,000				$15,000	$15,000
60	0		$15,000				$15,000	$15,000
80	0		$15,000				$15,000	$15,000
100	5%		$15,000		0		$15,000	$15,000
120	5%		$15,000		$ 1,000		$16,000	$16,000
140	5%		$15,000		$ 2,000		$17,000	$17,000
160	5%		$15,000		$ 3,000		$18,000	$18,000
180	5%		$15,000		$ 4,000		$19,000	$19,000
200	5%		$15,000	$2,000	$ 5,000		$22,000	$22,000
220	5%		$15,000	$2,000	$ 6,000		$23,000	$23,000
240	5%		$15,000	$2,000	$ 7,000		$24,000	$24,000
260	5%		$15,000	$2,000	$ 8,000		$25,000	$25,000
280	5%		$15,000	$2,000	$ 9,000		$26,000	$26,000
300	5%	7%	$15,000	$2,000	$10,000	0	$27,000	$27,000
320	5%	7%	$15,000	$2,000	$11,000	$1,400	$29,400	$29,400
340	5%	7%	$15,000	$2,000	$12,000	$2,800	$31,800	$31,800
360	5%	7%	$15,000	$2,000	$13,000	$4,200	$34,200	$34,000
380	5%	7%	$15,000	$2,000	$14,000	$5,600	$36,600	$34,000
400	5%	7%	$15,000	$2,000	$15,000	$7,000	$39,000	$34,000

A Graph of the Combined Plan

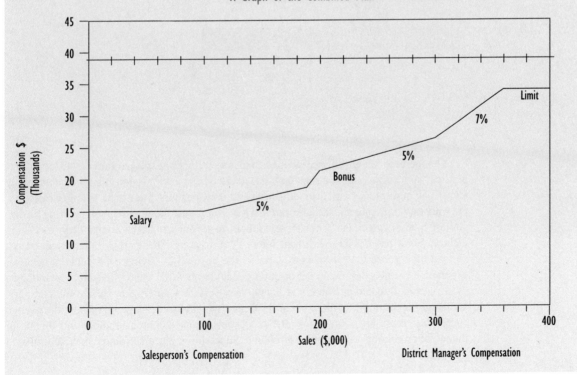

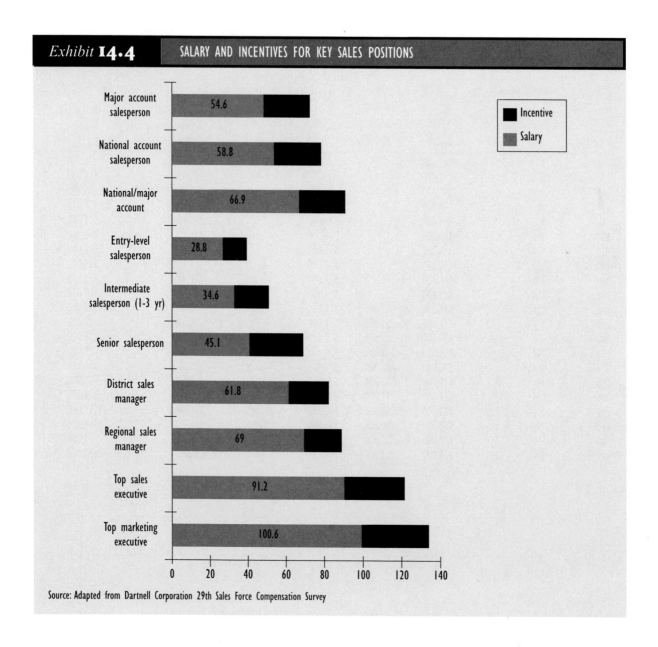

Exhibit 14.4   SALARY AND INCENTIVES FOR KEY SALES POSITIONS

Source: Adapted from Dartnell Corporation 29th Sales Force Compensation Survey

The increase in nonselling activities, such as setting up displays, training customer employees, and partnering relationships, has reduced the commission component in many plans. The movement away from advances and draws occurs among the younger salespeople whose compensation is largely commission. To provide them with income during the beginning of their career, the company gives them an advance or a draw so that they have some income, but it has to be repaid from future commissions. These arrangements can be demotivating because the salesperson is put in the position of paying off a debt—a negative experience. Some salespeople get discouraged and quit while owing the company money.

It was dissatisfied customers at Sears Auto Service Centers that caused the company to change its commission plan, but at the department stores of Dayton Hudson, the change agent was customers' distaste of pushy salespeople and declining morale and threats of unionization among salespeople. Highland Superstores, an electronics store, eliminated commissions. The problem is one of getting the right balance of incentives so that the needs of the customer, the salesperson, and the company are all optimized. Once the balance is identified, the next step is implementing the plan so that salespeople buy into the compensation change, seeing it as an advantage to them.

Incentives based on *contribution* to profit encourage salespeople to sell the higher margin products, to maintain price levels, and to control costs. Commissions based on *growth in contribution* require continued performance and do not continually reward a windfall sale. Baxter International, which sells a wide range of products to hospitals, introduced such a plan in 1991.

Assume that Bridgewater Office Supplies wanted an incentive plan that would reflect gross profit and sales growth. The commission could be based on a share of the contribution and sales growth and could be expressed by the following equation:

$$\text{Commission } \$ = (\text{Salesperson's Share}) \times (\text{Contribution}) \times (\text{Sales Growth Rate})$$

Because the business is very competitive, the salesperson has the authority to set prices within a specified margin range in order to get the business and maintain growth, but a lower margin will reduce the salesperson's contribution in the above equation. Thus the salesperson must balance between contribution and growth strategies.

This equation is illustrated for two salespeople in Exhibit 14.5. Each salesperson's share is 8%. Andrew Albright has higher sales than the district average ($1,885,000 vs. $1,617,000) and than Jennifer Dunlop ($1,380,000), but his commission is lower than Ms. Dunlop's ($29,810 vs. $30,300). Closer examination reveals that he is not maintaining the levels of margins and he has not maintained the growth rate for the second category of products. This compensation system should automatically motivate him to improve his margins and growth rate. Perhaps the district manager should have Ms. Dunlop run the next sales meeting to explain how she maintains margins and improves growth.

When this plan was introduced to the salespeople Andrew Albright thought he would be treated unfairly because his increases in sales volume are harder to achieve in his territory. He thinks that total volume should be part of the equation. His larger customers demand discounts. He argues that because his sales are 16.5% above the national average and many territories are below average, it would be easier for those territories to increase sales. How would you respond to his complaints? How would you modify the equation to meet his objection?

Bridgewater Office Supply concluded that slow paying customers were getting a free loan and that collection was the responsibility of the salespeople. To solve this problem it added two variables to the compensation plan. A salesperson who made a cash sale (defined as payment in 10 days) received 0.5% of the sale. The salesperson could retain this amount or pass along part of it as a discount to the customer. Similarly, 0.5% of overdue balances were charged against the salesperson's commission. The equation would appear as follows:

$$\text{Commission } \$ = (\text{Salesperson's Share}) \times (\text{Contribution} \times (\text{Sales Growth Rate}) + 0.005 \times (\text{Cash Sales } \$) - 0.005 \times (\text{Overdue Balances})$$

Additional columns can be added to Exhibit 14.5 to reflect these new variables.

Plans such as these become difficult to implement fairly. First, this type of program may be difficult for the salesperson to understand. Second, cost data are often not sufficiently detailed to evaluate an individual salesperson's performance. Any means for allocating costs is always subject to debate.

To simultaneously meet sales force needs and company objectives, some companies are introducing flexible plans from which a salesperson may choose. A Canadian holding company offers salespeople a plan in which they can choose among options

Exhibit **14.5**	A COMPENSATION PLAN THAT ENCOURAGES GROWING PROFITABLE BUSINESS

Bridgewater Office Supplies
Month: June
Salesperson's Income = Salesperson's Share × (Gross Margin × Growth Rate × Sales)
Salesperson's Share of Margin = 8.00%

Andrew Albright

Sales Year-To-Date

Products	Margin Range	Margin % Achieved	This Year ($000)	Last Year ($000)	Growth Rate	Salesperson's Commission ($000)
PAPER, SHIPPING ENVELOPES, SCHOOL SUPPLIES, PENCILS	10–15%	11.00%	$ 810	$ 720	1.13	$ 8.02
STANDARD FORMS, FAX MACHINES, TELEPHONES, COMPUTER SUPPLIES	16–25%	19.00%	$ 525	$ 617	0.85	$ 6.79
CREATIVE SERVICES-DESIGN FORMS, STATIONERY, LABELS COMPUTER SERVICES	26–40%	31.00%	$ 550	$ 500	1.10	$15.00
TOTALS			$1,885	$1,837	1.03	$29.81

Jennifer Dunlop

Products	Margin Range	Margin % Achieved	This Year ($000)	Last Year ($000)	Growth Rate	Salesperson's Commission ($000)
PAPER, SHIPPING ENVELOPES, SCHOOL SUPPLIES, PENCILS	10–15%	14.00%	$ 630	$ 490	1.29	$ 9.07
STANDARD FORMS, FAX MACHINES, TELEPHONES, COMPUTER SUPPLIES	16–25%	23.00%	$ 475	$ 390	1.22	$10.64
CREATIVE SERVICES-DESIGN FORMS, STATIONERY, LABELS COMPUTER SERVICES	26–40%	35.00%	$ 275	$ 200	1.38	$10.59
TOTALS			$1,380	$1,080	1.28	$30.30

District Averages

Products	Margin Range	Margin % Achieved	This Year ($000)	Last Year ($000)	Growth Rate	Salesperson's Commission ($000)
PAPER, SHIPPING ENVELOPES, SCHOOL SUPPLIES, PENCILS	10–15%	12.50%	$ 700	$ 650	1.08	$ 7.54
STANDARD FORMS, FAX MACHINES, TELEPHONES, COMPUTER SUPPLIES	16–25%	20.00%	$ 502	$ 475	1.06	$ 8.49
CREATIVE SERVICES-DESIGN FORMS, STATIONERY, LABELS COMPUTER SERVICES	26–40%	35.30%	$ 415	$ 390	1.06	$12.47
TOTALS			$1,617	$1,515	1.07	$28.50

where the commission portion ranges from 100% to 25% with the balance a base salary. Another company allows salespeople to stretch the goals in selected product categories.[20]

Contests

Contests are short-term motivators with an economic component. Many sales managers know that a highly visible prize, such as a camcorder, a cruise, or a ski trip, will be more motivating than the dollar value of the prize had it been given directly to the salesperson as a financial bonus. Incentive travel plans have been found to give $16 in added sales for each $1 of incentive.[21]

A contest, however, must be designed carefully to avoid its becoming a disaster and therefore a demotivator. Goals such as opening new accounts must be defined carefully. Is an old account that has been revived counted? There should be a reasonable probability of rewards for all individuals. If the top salesperson wins his third television, the others become demotivated. Rewards must be attractive to salespeople to motivate them. Sometimes rewards are expressed in terms of trading stamps so that the salesperson can choose from a catalog. There must be proper follow-through after the contest to assure that all winners receive their prizes.

Contests, probably more than any other compensation plan, tend to be abused. They should not be used too often because salespeople will regard them as part of their compensation. Furthermore, they do not solve basic problems in motivation and management. They are a short-run type that wears off with repeated use.

Expense Plans

Expense accounts are compensation plans that reimburse salespeople for expenses incurred on the job. The philosophy of an expense account plan is that it should not be a source of income for the salesperson, but rather a company investment for the benefit of the company, the salesperson, and the customer. Underspending can be more unprofitable than overspending, if, for example, the salesperson failed to buy a client's lunch and the missed conversation would have closed the sale. The plan should be fair to the company and the salesperson. The salesperson should not cheat and the company should pay promptly with the minimum amount of paper work by the salesperson.

Most companies have policies regarding reimbursement of personal expenses while traveling on company business. These policies cover laundry, cleaning, telephone calls home, entertainment of clients, and gifts. Some clients will have policies regarding entertainment and gifts. For example, Proctor & Gamble requires that it alternate with the vendor on buying meals and that gifts must not exceed $20 in value. The least controversial expenses are transportation (automobiles, taxis, and airfare) and communications (telephone, FAX, postage, and FedEx).

Expense plans include unlimited expenses and per diem (that is, standard per day) expense payments. Unlimited expenses are used with very senior salespeople engaged in long-term negotiations. Per diem expenses limit the amount that can be spent per day on food and lodging. If the salesperson decides to indulge in a special dinner to celebrate an event, then the amount in excess of the per diem rate is a personal expense. Some companies that have a 100% commission plan pay no expenses; the commission is set at a level to include the average expenses. In this situation, the salesperson is highly motivated to keep expenses low and the company has no administrative costs in implementing an expense plan. The salesperson, however, must keep detailed expense records for tax purposes.

Expenses can add from 23% to 34% of compensation to selling costs, depending on the industry and the level of the salesperson.[22] Thus there is an incentive for the company to control these expenses as tightly as possible. Some plans provide an upper limit on expenses that can be a fixed amount or a percent of sales.

Automobile expenses present a particularly complex problem for the general sales manager. Should the company supply the car or reimburse the salesperson for his or her car? If the company supplies the car, may it be used for personal travel? Should the type of automobile be part of the incentive? Some companies have several levels of luxury in cars. The luxury of the car for the year depends on whether the salesperson did not make quota, made quota, or exceeded quota. Should the senior salesperson get the most prestigious car? All of these questions must be answered by company policies.

Changes in the expense plan should be pretested on historical data, reviewed by managers, and then presented to salespeople for their recommendations before being implemented. The manager will need to call upon her or his skills in managing change throughout this process.

Team-Based Compensation

The increased focus on customer satisfaction has led to two changes in the way salespeople are compensated. First, as noted earlier, an increasing number of companies relate the salesperson's pay to the satisfaction of his or her customers.

Customer satisfaction is usually the result of more than a salesperson-customer contact. It also includes the delivery, service, and other functions within the organization that deal directly with customers or that provide resources to those who do. Thus a second change in compensation is that companies are placing increasing emphasis on the salesperson's ability to work in a team and to the team's impact on the customer. A sales force effectiveness study conducted by the Hay Group among 26 leading corporations found that the ability to work on a team is a key skill for successful salespeople. As the study noted: "The 'Lone Ranger' individual contributor is disappearing."[23]

Firms vary widely on how they compensate for team-based performance, ranging from those that pay all team members equally to those who pay based on contribution to the team effort. For example, Michigan-based Monroe Auto Equipment uses a 100% team plan where all team members are paid equally based on the team's performance.[24] At Mine Safety Appliances, on the other hand, salespeople are rated at one of seven different competency levels.[25] The levels are set by corporate and regional managers, but team members are assigned to levels based in part on the evaluation of their peers. Team incentives are distributed based on one's level. There are additional individual incentives for bringing in team orders.

MBO-Based Compensation

Commission-based compensation plans encourage short-term sales, but not the activities—like relationship building and after-sale service—that lead to long-term sales. In order to encourage specific activities, many firms have turned increasingly to compensation systems that reward the accomplishment of specific objectives. This ties directly into management-by-objectives (MBO) programs used in many companies.

At Texas Instruments (TI), for example, the selling cycle—from the discovery of a sales opportunity to closing a sale—is typically 18 to 40 months.[26] TI serves a niche market with customized products manufactured for original equipment manufacturer (OEM) customers. To sell to this market, TI defined a selling process with rewards for achieving milestones over multiple years.

Specific objectives are defined for each salesperson, using the forms shown in Exhibit 14.6. These objectives are prioritized based on the distribution of 150 potential points. A salesperson must earn 45 points (threshold level) to earn any bonus. An average salesperson must earn 100 points to earn an expected level bonus. To earn a target level maximum bonus, a salesperson much earn 150 points.

These objectives are broken down into specific actions that the salesperson must accomplish in order to make the long-term sale. Each action is translated into specific accomplishments—milestones—that earn the salesperson points (Exhibit 14.6b). The degree of difficulty increases for milestones from the threshold, to the average, to the target level.

Finally, the milestones can be assigned to expected achievement dates that specify what the salesperson should accomplish when (Exhibit 14.6c).

Exhibit 14.6a   STAR FORM 1: WEIGHTING OBJECTIVES THROUGH POINT VALUES

Plan Participant: _____   Date: _____

Objectives	Prioritized by Target Points
1.	
2.	
3.	
4.	
5.	

Target Point Totals of All Objectives   150

Exhibit **14.6b**	STAR FORM 2: DIVISION OF OBJECTIVE POINT VALUES FOR MILESTONES

Plan Participant:_____ Date: _____

Objective Number	Performance Level	Cumulative Points	Milestones Accounts/Opportunities	Individual Milestone Points
1	Threshold		• • •	
	Average		• • •	
	Target	*	• • •	
2	Threshold		• • •	
	Average		• • •	
	Target	*	• • •	
3	Threshold		• • •	
	Average		• • •	
	Target	*	• • •	

Total _____

Total _____

Total _____

•Total of Milestone Points must equal objective point value at Target

IMPLEMENTING THE PLAN

Implementing the plan consists of three steps—pretesting, presenting to the salespeople, and evaluating it continuously to see if it achieves the objectives.

Pretesting the Plan

The plan should be pretested in several ways. First a simulation of several different plans can be run. Creating a spreadsheet on a microcomputer provides a simple means to ask what-if questions regarding different levels of commissions and break points for bonuses. This desktop pretest could use historical data, managers' subjective estimates of impacts on sales, and their estimates of how salespeople would respond to the changes. The next

Exhibit **14.6c**	STAR FORM 3: DATES FOR MILESTONE ACHIEVEMENTS

Plan Participant:_____ Date: _____

Objective Number	Milestones—Accounts/Opportunities	Points	Expected Achievement Date			
			Qtr 1	Qtr 2	Qtr 3	Qtr 4
1						
2						
3						
4						
5						

TOTAL POINTS BY QUARTER _____ _____ _____ _____
TOTAL POINTS   150

Note: Points should be distributed as evenly as possible over all four quarters.

step is to have a small group of salespeople respond to a desktop run of the plan. The plan could be introduced to a pilot district before rolling it out to the entire sales force. At this point it should be clear whether or not the plan is fair, competitive, understandable, meets the objectives, and can be implemented with available data and accounting systems.

Presenting the Plan to the Salespeople

The program for introducing the new compensation plan to salespeople should give the reasons for change, the objectives of the plan, and the benefits to the salespeople. Any new documents, such as monthly compensation statements, should be explained at this time. This introduction will require managers' skills in managing change (Chapter 15).

When Greg Coleman introduced a change in the sales compensation plan at Reader's Digest, he wanted it to have a dramatic impact.[27] As the new publisher, Coleman wanted to increase Digest advertising sales. To accomplish this, he redesigned the sales force compensation plan from one that was 90 percent base salary and 10 percent incentive to one that was 65 percent base and 35 percent incentive. Further, the incentives were tied to profits rather than just revenue as before.

Coleman introduced the new plan at his first Digest national sales meeting. To start the meeting, he played an excerpt from the movie Glengarry Glen Ross, a 1992 movie about high pressure salespeople. The clip he played showed the hard-driving sales manager, portrayed by Alec Baldwin, telling his salespeople that they must make quota or lose their jobs. Noted

Coleman: "I wanted to give them a sense that change was imminent." Coleman then described the new compensation plan. Within a year, ten salespeople were fired and several others reportedly quit over the plan.

The longer-term result was increased sales and empowerment of salespeople. Under the new plan, salespeople took a harder look at expenses: The client dinner party that once came out of corporate's budget now came out of the salesperson's budget. Regional sales managers and individual salespeople became skilled at assessing the profitability of sales—to themselves and the company. During the 1993–97 period Reader's Digest advertising revenue increased 90% and the Digest contributed a higher share of profits to the parent company's bottom line. Further, not a single salesperson resigned during the 1995–97 period.

Evaluating the Plan

The dynamics of the marketplace require that the compensation plan, as all major sales management decisions, must be evaluated on a continuous basis. It is extremely important during the installation of a new plan to monitor whether it is achieving its goals, such as increases in sales, contributions, and new accounts. Any problems that develop must be immediately followed up. Later, the review can be lengthened to quarterly and then annually to determine if further fine tuning is needed.

This continuous evaluation of the plan should provide positive answers to the following questions:

1. Does it provide a realistic incentive?
2. Are payments made quickly so that the salesperson senses the link between effort and rewards?
3. Is the plan based on activities over which the salesperson has control?
4. Are performance goals measurable or based on agreed-upon subjective evaluations?
5. Are performance goals specified in terms of magnitude and time (e.g., 5 more calls per week)?

· ·

OTHER REWARDS

Indirect Monetary Rewards

Salespeople, like other employees, expect indirect monetary benefits such as health and life insurance, paid vacations, a pension plan, credit union membership, and expenses for moving. Sick and accident policies may also include disability plans that provide up to 60% of the compensation during disability. Retirement plans can allow the employee to tax shelter a portion of income. Some companies provide stock options, country club memberships, and airline club memberships when flying. A salesperson who works from home may be provided with a fax, a personal computer, and a copy machine. Salespeople who travel frequently are often given cellular phones. To keep them current in industry developments, they are sent to conventions and given subscriptions to trade magazines. High achievers receive awards, are presented at ceremonies, and are sometimes sent with their spouses to luxury resorts.

Hewlett-Packard has a "Must-Win" award that spotlights the salesperson who has the best approach and attitude each quarter in each region. In addition to a plaque, prizes, and $500, the salesperson appears with the director of sales on an interactive telecommunications network so that he or she can discuss achievements with people in 80 sales offices.[28]

These other monetary benefits can add 35% to 50% to the compensation of a sales-person. Such costs must be considered in the budget when planning additions to the sales force.

Nonmonetary Rewards

Nonmonetary rewards help to meet the social and self-actualization needs of salespeople. As noted in Chapter 11, motivation comes from providing an environment that allows the salespeople to use their talents, develop new ones, be accepted by the group, and be a part of decision processes. An important part of developing self-worth is the recognition of achievements. An important part of developing self-worth is the recognition of achievements. An organization with opportunities for future development provides an important reward.

EXAMPLES OF REWARD SYSTEMS

Examples from three different companies will illustrate the variety in compensation plans that are required to meet the needs of different companies, customers, and salespeople.

A grocery products company has a high base salary to compensate for working closely with accounts plus a year-end bonus that averages up to 20% of the base salary. There are also contests, awards, and prizes.[29]

During their first year the Wallace salespeople have a base salary plus a training bonus plus a commission. (Wallace is a supplier of information systems products). In the following years they have a salary and a commission.[30]

Nationwide Insurance outlines its benefit package as follows: time off for vacation, holidays, personal days, sick leave, and family illness; financial benefits that include a performance-based salary system, educational assistance of 50% to 100% reimbursement, credit union with free checking, flexible deposit account for medical expenses not covered by health care, retirement, and a matching savings plan; and group insurance that covers disability income, life insurance, dental, and medical care.[31]

REWARD SYSTEMS CAN DEMOTIVATE

Alfie Kohn has examined over 600 studies of the relationship between rewards and performance and has come to the startling conclusion ". . . that competition holds us back from doing our best work."[32] Furthermore, he concludes that extrinsic rewards based on quotas are effective only for a short time period and then only for simple, routine tasks.[33]

Incentives can be detrimental to performance when they trivialize a task that the individual finds interesting and challenging because it is without an obvious solution. In such cases the individual is more driven by intrinsic motivation than by extrinsic financial motivation.

He identifies five reasons for rewards failing. First, they punish the individuals who did not receive them. Second, they rupture relationships among team members and with the manager who is deciding who will get the reward. Third, rewards ignore the reasons for nonperformance by those who did not get the reward. Fourth, rewards discourage risk-taking and exploration. Fifth, and most critical, they have a long-term negative effect on intrinsic motivation.[34] He found that these findings apply to performance in industry, the classroom, and the family.

Kohn concludes that the stimulus-response model of B.F. Skinner has taken us down the wrong path. Although it may apply to laboratory rats and dogs it does not fit the complex behavior of humans who are driven by intrinsic motivation, which may be unique to the human brain. Where do Kohn's findings leave the manager who is creating an incentive program? He provides no easy answer. These findings suggest, however, the importance of understanding the needs of the individual, the company, and the customer, which is the starting point for developing a compensation plan. It also raises doubt about the use of competition among individuals who work in selling teams. Perhaps rewards to individuals should be given individually, as criticism should be individual. Finally, the manager must find the intrinsic motivators and create an environment that will allow the individual to use them.

| *Case* **14.1** | THE SOUTHWEST FOODS COMPANY |

You have been asked to design a compensation package for Southwest Foods. This four-year old company sells to restaurants in the mid-price range. Its sales are presently $5 million and have been growing at 15% per year. Seven of its 12 salespeople have 5 or more years experience in the industry, three have been with Southwest for three or fewer years, and two just joined the company after graduating from college. These new recruits worked their way through college with various jobs in local restaurants. The home office and one warehouse are in Phoenix, Arizona, with another warehouse in Albuquerque, New Mexico. The company's growth in a tight market has been achieved through a computerized inventory system that enables the salesperson to inform the buyer immediately what can be delivered the next day. Southwest has maintained a 97% fulfillment rate on all orders.

A time-and-duty study of salespeople indicated that they spent 25% of their time in face-to-face contact with the customer, 20% on the phone with present customers, 15% on paperwork and planning calls, 15% on the telephone and on visits to prospects, and 25% traveling.

CASE QUESTIONS

1. To learn the needs of salespeople in this industry, talk with local restaurant owners and food wholesaler salespeople. What are the needs of the customers and the salespeople?
2. What are the needs of the company?
3. Talk with classmates to determine what would motivate them to consider this competitive industry. Note especially the differences in personal needs for single and married students. How would you reflect this difference in designing a compensation plan?
4. What other facts do you need to design a compensation plan? Make reasonable assumptions and make them clear.
5. Develop several alternative combination plans and pretest them with a spreadsheet.

SUMMARY

The development of compensation programs begins with a translation of company and marketing objectives into sales objectives. These sales objectives are the company's needs for the plan. The salespeoples' needs are identified in the motivation plan (Chapter 11).

The prerequisites to developing a plan include a clear definition of the sales objectives, the job description, performance standards, evaluation systems, recruiting, selecting, training, motivating, and communication. These basics must be in place for a compensation plan to be successful. No compensation plan can overcome bad sales management practices.

A compensation plan should allow for various grades of salespeople, such as trainees senior salespeople, and salespeople who have been assigned to special tasks. The next step is to determine what portion of the compensation should be assigned to an incentive system. The most commonly used incentive plans are commissions, bonuses, contests, and some combination of salary and incentives. The plan should be pretested using historical data and feedback from managers and salespeople. A program for implementing the plan will require skills to manage change, because compensation is so important to salespeople.

Expense plans attempt to reimburse salespeople for expenditures that should benefit the company, the customer, and the salesperson. Expense plans include unlimited reimbursement, per diem limits, fixed upper limits as a percent of sales and no expenses reimbursed where salespeople are expected to pay expenses from commissions.

Indirect monetary benefits can add another 35% to 50% to the direct monetary compensation of a salesperson. Nonmonetary rewards are often the most important part of the reward system after the salesperson's basic needs have been met.

ASSIGNMENTS/DISCUSSION QUESTIONS

1. Why is compensation often a short-term motivator?

2. If a company has 500 field staff members, provides benefits that add an additional 25% to the total compensation package, and plans to increase salaries $100 per month, how much must be added to the budget to cover these costs? Why should the sales manager keep such calculations in mind?

3. What are the pros and cons of cost-of-living allowances for major cities?

4. When would a compensation plan based on dollar sales be unfair?

5. Why does an increase in the incentive portion of compensation add to the cost of management?

6. Review the advantages and disadvantages of different incentive systems.

7. What are the advantages and disadvantages of contests where the prize appeals to the family?

8. Discuss a plan that gives a larger inflation increase to the younger salespeople.

ENDNOTES

1. Alvin J. Williams and John Seminerio, What Buyers Like from Salespeople, *Industrial Marketing Management,* 14(1), pp. 75–78.

2. Arun Sharma and Dan Sarel, The Impact of Customer Satisfaction Based Incentive Systems on Salespeople's Customer Service Response: An Empirical Study, *Journal of Personal Selling & Sales Management,* 15(3), Summer 1995, pp. 17–29.

3. Christopher Power, Lisa Driscoll, and Earl Bohn, Smart Selling: How Companies Are Winning Over Today's Tougher Customer, *Business Week,* August 3, 1992, p. 46.

4. Gary McWilliams, Reveille for DEC's Sleepy Sales Force, *Business Week,* August 30, 1993, p. 74.

5. Frederick F. Reichheld and W. Earl Sasser, Jr., Zero Defections: Quality Comes to Service, *Harvard Business Review,* September-October, 1990, 105–111.

6. Power, Driscoll, and Bohn 48.

7. Ibid.

8. Robert G. Head, Restoring Balance to Sales Compensation, *Sales & Marketing Management,* August, 1992, p. 48.

9. Richard L. Oliver and Barton A. Weitz, The Effects of Risk Preference, Uncertainty, and Incentive Compensation on Salesperson Motivation, Marketing Science Institute, Working Paper No. 91-104, February, 1991, pp. 12–14.

10. Jhinuk Chowdhury, The Motivational Impact of Sales Quotas on Effort, *Journal of Marketing Research* 30, February, 1993, pp. 28–41.

11. Steve Benfield, Rolling Quotas Gather No Moss, in *The Sales Manager's Survival Guide,* J. Brian Pope, editor, Atlanta: Culpepper and Associates, 1991, p. 102.

12. Salespeople's Average Annual Compensation, *Sales & Marketing Management,* June 17, 1991, p. 73.

13. Kate Bertrand, Sales Strategies Drive Pay Plans, *Business Marketing,* 73(12), December, 1988, pp. 30, 32.

14. Michael Gates, Independent Sales Reps: Keeping Them Happy, *Incentive,* 162(7), July, 1988, pp. 28–30, 71.

15. Richard Szathmary, Compensation: The Location Equation, *Sales & Marketing Management,* 143(6), June 1991, pp. 131–32.

16. Gregory A. Patterson, Distressed Shoppers, Disaffected Workers Prompt Stores to Alter Sales Commissions, *The Wall Street Journal,* July 1, 1992, p. B6.

17. Quoted in Andy Cohen, They're in the Money, *Sales & Marketing Management,* December, 1996, p. 15.

18. Rene Y. Darmon, Selecting Appropriate Sales Quota Plan Structures and Quota-Setting Procedures, *Journal of Personal Selling & Sales Management,* 17(1), Winter, 1997, pp. 1–16.

19. Geoffrey Brewer, Brain Power, *Sales & Marketing Management,* May, 1997, pp. 39–48.

20. Dean Walsh and Joanne Dahm, Going Flex—Four Adjustable Comp Plans That Work, *Sales & Marketing Management,* 141(11), September, 1989, pp. 16–21.

21. Jim Rauter, Performance Payoffs, *Insurance Review* 49(1), January, 1988, pp. 26–29.

22. Compensation and Expenses by Industry, *Sales & Marketing Management,* June 17, 1991, p. 72.

23. Hay Group study cited in Brewer, 1997, p. 40.

24. Wally Wood, Reinventing the Sales Force, *Across the Board,* 31(4), April, 1994, pp. 24–30.

25. Compensation: Rewarding Team Players, *Sales & Marketing Management,* April, 1996, pp. 35–36.

26. This section and the associated exhibits are based on personal correspondence with John Paster, manager for sales and marketing, worldwide control products, Texas Instruments, February 27, 1995.

27. This account is based on Michele Marchetti, Not So Easy to Digest, *Sales & Marketing Management,* February, 1997, pp. 55–65.

28. Melissa Campanelli, The Secrets of America's Best Sales Forces, *Sales & Marketing Management,* January, 1992, p. 92.

29. Confidential correspondence from managers in this industry.

30. Rich Campbell, District Manager, Wallace, in a letter to G. David Hughes, May 14, 1997.

31. Nationwide recruiting literature.

32. Alfie Kohn (1993), *Punished by Rewards,* New York: Houghton Mifflin, p. xii.

33. *Ibid.,* p. 46.

34. *Ibid.,* Chapters 4 and 5.

GENERAL SALES MANAGEMENT: THE VIEW FROM THE TOP

••

LEARNING GOALS

1. To learn how the functions and activities of a general sales manager differ from those of field sales managers
2. To understand the changes that will have major effects on general sales management
3. To appreciate the impact of global forces on sales management

••

ANOTHER SHIFT IN THINKING

Congratulations. You're now a general sales manager. You are earning about $130,000 per year, which is slightly more than the top marketing executive and more than the top persons in accounting, human resources, engineering, and production/operations.[1]

The functions you will now perform are the same as when you were first promoted as a district sales manager (Chapter 7), but their importance has changed. You now must regard planning and organizing as twice as important and staffing only one-third as important as when you were a first-line manager (Exhibit 7.3). Your time horizon must be extended to several years, not just one year. Your geographic domain is now national and global.

You also face dynamic changes in how a sales force is managed. Sales management at the end of the 1990s is quite different from what it was a decade ago. Changes in information technology, workforce diversity, and global competition have forced companies to respond with flatter organizational structures and more responsive strategies.

This responsiveness required going beyond consultation to relationships selling. The emphasis on productivity and downsizing has led to demands for more efficient sales systems—using direct marketing—instead of simple direct selling with a salesperson.

Sales executives who do not adapt to these changes will find themselves managing a weakened sales force. On the other hand, a sales manager who links the sales force to

291

changes such as just-in-time purchasing and production, sophisticated computer-based materials planning, and the growing concentration of buyers will find that sales are facilitated through partnering arrangements with major clients. Sales force efficiency is being increased by linking traditional personal selling approaches to newer methods such as database marketing, telemarketing, and automated reordering between buyer and vendor computers. As the new manager, you will be presiding over a more powerful sales force.[2]

Many of these changes have been driven by the heightened importance of customer satisfaction. As one Japanese executive has said, "The customer is not a king or queen, but a dictator."[3] Measuring customer satisfaction and linking these measures to business performance has become central to management. Customer satisfaction is being linked to financial success, compensation plans, and team-selling systems.[4]

New organizational designs are emerging. Human resource strategies that use teams and empowerment are increasing creativity and productivity and breaking down structured hierarchies in the sales force.

Changes in retailing are also having an impact on sales management. Competition among retail stores and sophisticated chain-store data bases developed with the use of bar codes have resulted in a new, sophisticated breed of retail buyer who quickly tracks changes in market trends and is evaluated according to his or her contribution to profit from the category of products managed. To sell to this new buyer, the general sales manager needs a sales force that is better trained and has the information to compete.

Michael Dell, the founder of Dell Computer, was a success because he discovered that computer retailers were not meeting the customers' needs. The retail sales clerks often knew less about computers than the customer. Thus the stores were charging for services that were not delivered. Dell went to direct marketing telephone sales where the telephone salesperson is highly trained and able to make precise recommendations. Furthermore, instead of selling a machine off the shelf, Dell builds one exactly to the customers specifications.[5]

FORCES OF CHANGE AND SALES MANAGEMENT RESPONSES

An examination of these forces and responses will help a general sales manager to prepare for the future.

Forces of Change

Information technology has been the major force that has driven the reorganization of the sales force. In earlier chapters we saw how the World Wide Web has become a major medium for the recruiting process. E-mail, voice mail, modems, and cellular phones have so revolutionized field managers' communications with salespeople that the span of control has increased from seven salespeople per manager to twelve or more.

Sales force automation has increased salespersons' effectiveness and efficiency. Salespeople for Gerber baby foods are more effective because they have information that is only 48 hours old rather than four weeks, which was the time delay before sales automation. Only 5% of their time is spent on administrative tasks, versus the industry standard of 12%. At headquarters only 10% of sales management's time is spent on administration, versus 22% for the industry.[6]

Wells Fargo Alarm Services provides an example of how technology can work in an industrial marketing situation. Before installing an expert system, which is a form of artificial intelligence, the salesperson would need to analyze customers' security needs and then search through product books and pricing literature for more than 12,000 items to build a system that could cost a million dollars. The result was a slow process and 80% of the systems were incorrectly designed. Now the sale can be completed in 20 minutes in front of the customer by answering questions posed by the computer. The system builds a bill of materials, prints a pricing proposal, and sets up the contract. Incorrectly designed systems have dropped to 5%. By increasing the closing rate from seven to eight sales per month extra revenue was $8 million, versus the $1.6 million cost for the system.[7]

Diversity is America's strength and good business. Companies such as Mobil, Chase, American Express, Hewlett-Packard, Chrysler, and Fannie Mae go beyond Equal Employment Opportunity Commission mandates by making diversity part of their strategic initiatives. Diversity is no longer limited to narrow definitions of gender, race, and age. It reflects differences in physical and mental abilities, lifestyle, and education. It has moved beyond the department of human resources to be part of the strategy of all functional areas. Aggressive training and development programs can produce dramatic results. For example, in Fannie over 50% of upper management are women and minorities. There has been a 75% increase in business with vendors who are minorities and women.[8] Diversity brings creativity and innovation to companies by providing fresh viewpoints. Sales managers must learn how to facilitate diversity to achieve corporate goals.

Competition can occur in many forms. Product life cycles are becoming shorter. For some personal computer products, they are less than 1 year. Further, competition is emerging from sources outside traditional industry boundaries. For example, telecommunications, computers, and cable entertainment are all moving into each other's markets. In addition, global competition is increasing, which requires firms to continuously scan the environment for potential new foreign competitors.

New demands of customers are a powerful force, as Procter & Gamble discovered. The average grocery shopper, generally a woman, has little time to browse and sort among the features of over 30,000 items in a supermarket. She will buy 18 items in 21 minutes from the time she leaves the car until she returns. This is a reduction in time of 25% in five years. She did not want a variety of brands, sizes, prices, and promotions. She wanted the product at the same price in the same place. She forced P&G to change its strategy to single pricing, reduced promotions, and few product line extensions. The strategy shift produced a major change in the sales force. The sales department was renamed Customer Business Development. It stopped pushing items on stores, a policy which created hatred in stores and a 25% error in orders. It reorganized its sales force to relationship selling by eliminating seven different product category salespeople calling on individual stores and created account executives who called on chain headquarters handling all P&G products.[9] This change in strategy had a dramatic effect on the sales force structure. It eliminated the traditional positions of the salesperson, the unit manager, and the district manager. All of these positions had been training grounds for managers.

The organization that holds information holds power and the information shifted from the grocery products manufacturers to the channel when the channel used computers to track inventories. The chains know better than the manufacturer what products are selling where. The use of bar codes facilitates just-in-time inventory delivery to the individual stores, reduces the chains' warehousing costs, and automatically reorders products from manufacturers. This computer-to-computer reordering eliminates a major function of the salesperson who called on stores. In eliminating one function the computer upgraded the requirements of the new salesperson. Manufacturers' representatives must be able to track information on their notebook computers and make sophisticated slide presentations to chain store buyers.

Sales Management Responses

One response to the new competitive environment has been a reduction in the number of organizational levels, resulting in a flatter organization. This flat organizational design requires new personal selling strategies at all levels of sales force management, from the job description, through recruiting, selecting, training, evaluating, and rewarding. Campbell Soup flattened its sales organization into 21 autonomous regional offices that could respond to regional differences in tastes. Salespeople were called brand sales managers to reflect the authority that they had to fit the product to the local markets.[10]

Another response to the fast-changing environment has been the development of a selling strategy that integrates multiple approaches. One study estimates that sales volume is now distributed among many different selling strategies as follows: direct sales 75%, telemarketing 5%, intermediaries (distributors, wholesalers, and value-added retailers) 11%, outside agencies 7%, and others 2%.[11]

The use of teams has also become a common strategy for responding to these dynamic changes in the marketplace. Teams focus on process rather than functions, thereby blurring the discrete functional boxes in the organization chart. Teams include people from sales, product development, market research, product management, operations, finance, and human resources. The use of teams makes the organization more open and adaptive, so that it sometimes is called a learning organization.

In addition, an increasing number of companies have managed environmental change by establishing long-term buyer-seller relationships. In the process, relationships between the salesperson and the customer have moved up a hierarchy from a vendor relationship to a partner relationship, as described by Trailer and Vavricka and illustrated in Exhibit 15.1.

These new partner relationships, and the accompanying new skills, require new measures of salespersons' performance. One approach to these new skills is suggested by a study conducted by the Gallup Organization. Based on their research, Gallup developed a client satisfaction hierarchy that consists of the following six dimensions:

Accuracy in details of client transaction.

Availability when needed.

Credibility as a resource person.

Partnership in sharing ideas and strategies to meet goals.

Trust in follow-through and keeping his/her word.

Discovery of really new ideas.[13]

To develop a selling strategy that will respond to these changes the general sales manager must ask and find answers to critical questions. These questions can focus on problems with the present system, such as missing goals, or the need to innovate with a new

---

Exhibit 15.1   RELATIONSHIP SKILL REQUIREMENTS

Relationship	Skills Required
Partner	Understand organizational issues
Contributor	Understand customer's industry
Consultant Preferred	Understand customer's business
Supplier	Understand applications/functions
Vendor	Have good product/service[12]

system to identify and tap new opportunities. We will examine both traditional problem-solving methods and creative problem-solving methods to meet these two different needs.

PROBLEM-SOLVING APPROACHES FOR SALES MANAGERS

Problem solving begins with asking the critical questions. The sales manager should develop a list of recurring questions such as the following:

1. What is our mission? What values are we adding for customers, employees, and stockholders? The Jack Morton Company, which is a communications consulting company, states its mission as " . . . Setting you apart by making your ideas and goals real to your customers, employees, franchisees, and dealers."[14]
2. What are our SMART goals? (Specific, Measurable, Agreed upon, Realistic, and Time related)
3. What external and internal forces work against our reaching our goals?

External forces are largely uncontrollable and include economic variables, demographic variables, public policy, and competition, all of which can be domestic and global. Internal variables include the company's financial status, organization (that is, leadership, structure, staffing, and motivation), and the marketing mix. Facts are needed to answer these questions or else reasonable assumptions must be stated clearly when facts are not available or are too expensive to collect. Analysis of these facts and assumptions should produce logical conclusions. SWOT is sometimes used as an acronym to remind the analyst to consider the company strengths, weaknesses, opportunities, and threats. For example, to examine the threats we can ask, "How do our products compare with the competitor's?" Opportunities may be discovered by asking, "How can we make our products better than our competitor's?"

A competitive analysis identifies key factors that determine success in a given industry and then rates the firm's position relative to competitors on those factors. Exhibit 15.2 illustrates a competitive analysis for a hypothetical automobile manufacturer. Its competitive advantages are in product benefits; its weaknesses are in finance and management.

4. What new problems or opportunities did the analysis uncover?

What are the causes of the problems? Are the causes events that we can change (such as a product deficiency) or must we adapt to uncontrollable events (like a slow economy)? To tap new opportunities, what skills and resources must we have? How can we rank these problems and opportunities so that we focus on the most important ones first?

5. What alternative strategies can we take to meet our goals by solving our problems and tapping opportunities?
6. What resources will each alternative require? How long will it take to implement each alternative? How do we measure the outcome?
7. How can we motivate salespeople to take the action that is necessary to make the strategy a success for them and the company?
8. How will we know if we are tracking along a path that will lead to the goal?

If we have applied the SMART criteria when defining the goal we anticipated this evaluation and control question. Feedback loops (Exhibit 15.3) to each phase of the planning process will identify the strengths and weaknesses of the plan as well as indicate the kind of action needed to bring the system back in control.

Exhibit 15.2 — ANALYSIS OF OUR COMPETITIVE POSITION IN EACH BUSINESS

Our Relative Position on Competitive Success Factors in this Business

	Competitive Disadvantage		Par	Competitive Advantage		Comments
PRODUCT BENEFITS	−2	−1	0	+1	+2	
Styling			▬▬▬			
Mileage			▪			
Space			▬▬▬			
Repair Costs	▬▬▬▬▬▬					
Speed		▬▬▬				
Comfort				▬▬▬▬▬		
Trunk Space			▬▬▬			
PRICE						
Initial Price			▪			
Life-Cycle Costs	▬▬▬▬▬▬					
COST COMPONENTS						
Experience Curves		▬▬▬				
Position		▬▬▬				
Raw Material Costs			▪			
Raw Material Availability			▪			
Superior Purchasing			▪			
MANUFACTURING						
Production Facilities				▬▬		
Engineering Expertise				▬▬▬▬▬		
Labor Conditions			▪			
DISTRIBUTION						
Logistics			▪			
Selling		▬▬▬				
Servicing			▪			
FINANCE						
Working Capital		▬▬▬				
Credit Position		▬▬▬				
ADVERTISING						
Creativity				▬▬▬▬▬		
Effectiveness				▬▬▬▬▬		
SALES MANAGEMENT						
Cost			▪			
Effectiveness		▬▬▬				
MANAGEMENT						
Capacity for New Ventures		▬▬▬				
Effectiveness		▬▬▬				
RESEARCH & DEVELOPMENT						
Innovative			▪			
Personnel		▬▬▬				

Exhibit **15.3**	THE PLANNING PROCESS

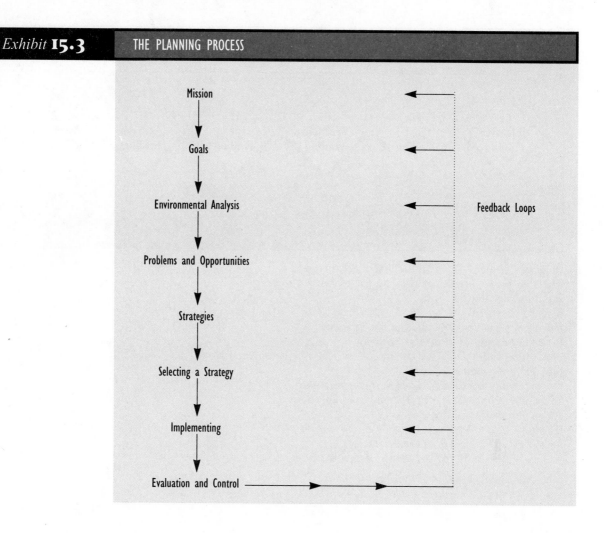

Mission

Goals

Environmental Analysis

Problems and Opportunities

Strategies

Selecting a Strategy

Implementing

Evaluation and Control

Feedback Loops

Creative Problem Solving To meet the competition and take advantage of new technology the general sales manager will need to think innovatively. This will require out-of-the box thinking. A procedure known as creative problem solving has been developed to take a team through the six steps of the process. This process, which is outlined in Exhibit 15.4, has roots in industry practice and has been verified with academic studies.[15]

The creative problem-solving method shown here has two important new elements. First, two steps are included before problem definition: (1) identification of the objective sought; and (2) creation of an exhaustive list of facts about what caused the mess or what drives reaching the objective.

Second, the approach shown in Exhibit 15.4 forces divergence before convergence at each step, as shown in the arrows for the first step in Exhibit 15.4. Traditional problem solving methods converge immediately on a limited number of alternatives, thereby missing the point that there are better alternatives.

Companies that use creative problem solving methods are amazed to learn that they were converging with a set of alternatives that would have created more problems later.

Exhibit **15.4**	OSBORN-PARNES CREATIVE PROBLEM SOLVING MODEL

OF Objective Finding	FF Fact Finding	PF Problem Finding	IF Idea Finding	SF Solution Finding	AF Acceptance Finding
Identify Goal/Wish/ Challenge	Gather Data	Clarify the Problem	Generate Ideas	Select and Strengthen Solutions	Plan for Action

Objective Finding—Identify Goal/Wish/Challenge
What is the goal/wish/challenge upon which you want to work?

Fact Finding—Gather Data
What's the situation/background?
What are all the facts/questions/data/feelings that are involved?

Problem Finding—Clarify the Problem
What is the problem that really needs to be focused on? What is the concern that really needs to be addressed?

Idea Finding—Generate Ideas
What are all of the possible solutions for how to solve the problem?

Solution Finding—Select and Strengthen Solutions
How can you strengthen the solution(s)?
How can you select the solutions to know which one will work best?

Acceptance Finding—Plan for Action
What are all of the action steps that need to take place in order to implement your solution?

Creative Problem Solving Institute, Transformation: Moving from Dreams to Action, Brochure for 43rd Annual session, June 22–27, 1997, p. 9.

One company was going to take strong action against the salespeople for accounts that were slow in paying. After a creative problem-solving session they realized that the problem was in not training the salespeople in communicating the payment terms clearly to the client.

Developing alternatives is the most creative activity in management. Ackoff, a leading strategy scholar, states that the most essential properties of good management are competence, communicativeness, concern, courage, and creativity, and that the greatest of these is creativity. "Without creativity a manager may do a good job, but he cannot do a great one. At best he can preside over the progressive evolution of the organization he manages, he cannot lead it to a quantum jump—a radical leap forward."[16]

Creativity is now an important topic in corporate training programs. "Nearly one of every three companies now offers some sort of creativity training to its employees, stressing problem solving, creative thinking, and a host of other mental skill-building activities. Just five short years ago, that figure was only one company in 25. A hotel supply company added 12 hours of creativity training to its 120-hour sales training program. Sales for the 150 persons who graduated from this course increased about 30%."[17]

HUMAN RESOURCE STRATEGIES

Boxes in organizational charts have been crumbling for decades, but translation of this change into formal human resource strategies has been recent. A sales manager for a leading grocery products company once said, "The organization chart does not say what really is happening. Create an organizational chart of how the company really operates, put it in your desk drawer, and look at it every morning."[18] This general sales manager was acknowledging the fact that market conditions change faster than organization charts.

The sales manager can anticipate how sales management will change. The sales manager may turn to production where the pressure to increase productivity occurred early. Production teams are *empowered* to make strategic decisions. For example, a line-worker team at a General Motors Saturn plant hires workers, approves parts from suppliers, chooses its equipment, and handles its budget. Labor and management work as partners to lower costs.[19] In the dealerships, service managers sit down with the customer over a cup of coffee to discuss automotive problems. Salespeople are paid a salary, which reduces the pressure to reach a quota. The result has been a customer satisfaction level that ranks only slightly lower than the luxury cars of Lexus and Infiniti and above Mercedes and Lincoln.[20]

Customer satisfaction has become a key competitive strategy. The consulting firm of Bain & Co. has shown that boosting customer-retention rate by 2% has the same effect on profits as cutting costs by 10%.[21]

Hallmark Cards focuses on business process redesign (BPR) in which teams share ideas, skills, and experiences across department and division boundaries. Participants enjoy learning new skills and "thinking outside their box." This approach has had many benefits, including lowering production costs and reducing the development of a new product from several years to a matter of months.[22]

Taco Bell Corporation's change in human resource strategy began with a new mission statement. Instead of focusing on making food they shifted to feeding people. When they focused on people they found that customers value food, service, and the physical appearance of the restaurant. They realized that they could not execute the strategy with their seven-layer organization. Furthermore, they needed talented, motivated people with timely information to track the performance of restaurants. By empowering store managers they were able in three years to extend the span of control from one supervisor for five restaurants to 20 or more restaurants per supervisor. The role of the supervisor changed from directing and controlling managers to coaching and supporting them.

The major change in each restaurant was shifting the focus of local personnel from preparing food to serving customers. Food preparation, such as chopping lettuce, was contracted outside the restaurant. Meat arrived chopped, spiced, and in a boil-in plastic bag. The ratio of 70% kitchen and 30% seating area was reversed, so that 70% of the restaurant was a seating, revenue-generating area instead of a cost area.

To implement this strategy, Taco Bell changed its human resource strategy. It worked with The Gallup Organization to develop an interviewing procedure that identified prospective managers who were responsible, were team players, and had life themes that predicted success in service work. Manager training included skills in communication, team building, coaching, and worker empowerment. The base salaries for managers were raised and bonuses were paid for performance in hospitality, quality of surroundings, labor management, and financial targets.

The strategy of focusing on customer service and implementing the strategy with a new human resource strategy produced impressive results. Turnover among restaurant general managers declined from 45% to 22% and among frontline workers from 223% to 160%. Given the costs of recruiting, training, and separating employees, lowering turnover translates directly to profit. Kitchen labor was reduced 15 hours per day. Peak-hour capacity was increased by 54% and customer waiting was reduced by 71%. The financial impact was dramatic. In a market that was flat or declining, sales growth of company-owned Taco Bells exceeded 60% and profits increased by over 25%. McDonald's profit growth during this period was less than 6% annually. During this period Taco Bell also cut core menu prices by over 25%. Thus the customers benefited in many ways.[23]

EVALUATION

Strategy begins with evaluation. This statement has a double meaning. First, it is rare to start a strategy from scratch. For an established company, feedback loops reveal a problem or opportunity that requires a change in strategy. Feedback loops make it possible to evaluate every step in the planning process (Exhibit 15.3). The second meaning underscores the fact that if the results from the strategy cannot be evaluated, then it is impossible to know if the goal was achieved. The Taco Bell strategy could be evaluated because goals were set in measurable terms—employee satisfaction, reductions in turnover, sales growth, profit growth, peak-time capacity, and customer waiting time.

The sales force is only one part of the marketing mix, so changes in market share, sales, and profit cannot always be linked to changes in selling strategies. Thus intermediate goals must be set for the sales force. These goals could be percent of quota achieved, the number of new accounts opened, the hit ratio (number of sales divided by the number of calls), or ratios that are related to the selling process, such as the number of proposals divided by the number of calls. Communication goals can provide an important basis for evaluating the sales force. Exhibit 15.5 illustrates an actual problem faced by a pharmaceutical company: there was a communication gap between the physicians' perception and the company's perception, which was determined by scientific studies. Clearly, the sales force had not met its communication goal.

How can the general sales manager be evaluated? *Sales & Marketing Management* magazine gives annual Best Sales Force awards that are based on surveys of persons in six industries, which include beverages, food products, life insurance, metal manufacturing, scientific and photographic equipment, and shipping and delivery. The criteria can be useful when developing a system to evaluate a general sales manager. The criteria include the following activities: (1) recruiting top salespeople, (2) the ability to keep salespeople, (3) the quality of training, (4) opening new accounts, (5) holding accounts, (6) the product and technical knowledge of the sales force, and, (7) reputation among customers.[24]

TOP MANAGEMENT SALES PLANNING TOOLS

The general sales manager has a variety of tools for controlling the sales force effort at all levels. To manage the entire selling effort the general sales manager will use the selling plan, the productivity analysis, the budget, and policies and procedures.

The Selling Plan

The selling plan translates marketing goals into sales force quotas, which are further divided into regional, district, and territory quotas. Quotas may be expressed in dollar or unit

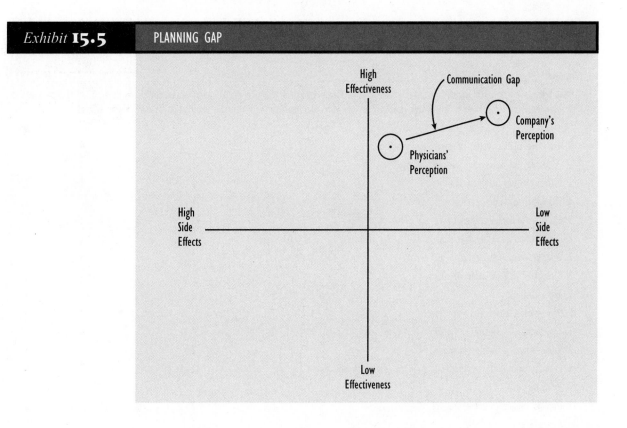

Exhibit **15.5**   PLANNING GAP

sales, market share, activities (calls, presentations, etc.), or contribution to profit. The plan supplies customer and competitive information so that the salesperson can anticipate objections and develop a strategy. The plan includes promotional literature and videotapes that the salesperson can send before the presentation or use during the presentation.

The selling plan includes specific short-term objectives for products and accounts. Some companies pretest a plan with salespeople to make certain that they buy into it. If they don't, they will not use it and a uniform selling strategy will be lost. Plans need to be adjusted to local economic and competitive conditions, which is an important activity for the district manager. District sales managers also need to coordinate all plans for national accounts with national account managers.

The creation of the selling plan requires internal and external input. Product managers provide benefit statements, competitive analysis, and goals. The sales promotion department seeks input from salespeople regarding the success of previous plans before creating new promotional materials. Outside consultants are hired to provide additional capacity and special knowledge for a major new product launch. For example, these external firms assume the responsibility for coordinating the production of selling aids, special equipment, display material, launch programs, display booths for conventions, training materials, video programs, films, and contracting with actors and other outside professionals.

Productivity Analysis

Continuous control of the selling effort is accomplished by productivity analysis, which consists of performance standards and measures designed to determine if the selling plan is producing the desired results. Productivity analysis includes analysis of historical data

Exhibit **15.6**	EVALUATE YOUR MANAGER

Manager: _____   Date: _____

Listed below are a series of statements about your manager. Please take some time to evaluate each statement (1 = Never, 5 = Always). Space has been provided for comments. Your honest feedback will provide your manager with valuable information. This evaluation is confidential.

	Never				Always
1. Goals are communicated effectively to the entire team	1	2	3	4	5
2. Organizes and directs the work of employees	1	2	3	4	5
3. Possesses strong technical skills	1	2	3	4	5
4. Sets high standards	1	2	3	4	5
5. Evaluates performance frequently	1	2	3	4	5
6. Demonstrates flexibility and explains reasons for change	1	2	3	4	5
7. Delegates responsibilities	1	2	3	4	5
8. Recognizes staff for achievements	1	2	3	4	5
9. Approachable	1	2	3	4	5
10. Demonstrates openness to new ideas	1	2	3	4	5
11. Communicates regularly with staff	1	2	3	4	5
12. Supports and promotes teamwork	1	2	3	4	5
13. Ensures that sufficient authority is given to accomplish objectives	1	2	3	4	5
14. Promotes trust	1	2	3	4	5
15. Displays confidence under pressure	1	2	3	4	5
16. Possesses positive attitude	1	2	3	4	5
17. Acts decisively	1	2	3	4	5
18. Resourceful	1	2	3	4	5
19. Easy to talk to about work problems	1	2	3	4	5
20. Asks for employee input	1	2	3	4	5
21. Demonstrates consistency with procedures	1	2	3	4	5
22. Handles staff professionally	1	2	3	4	5
23. Consistently provides positive and negative feedback	1	2	3	4	5
24. Treats exempts and non-exempts equally	1	2	3	4	5
25. Is available to staff	1	2	3	4	5
26. Serves as a role model	1	2	3	4	5
27. Communicates issues to staff, i.e. keeps them in the loop	1	2	3	4	5
28. Results oriented	1	2	3	4	5
29. Concerned about staff development and training	1	2	3	4	5
30. Explains to staff why decisions were made	1	2	3	4	5

and experiments to confirm or reject the hypotheses regarding the links between selling effort and changes in sales.

Historical Analysis   A comparison of sales data with the selling plan reveals three possible outcomes—on target, below target, or above target. The last case is a happy one. The manager may want to reallocate resources from this part of the plan to other parts that are below target levels. When the plan is not achieved the manager must identify the problem by answering the following question: Is the total plan faulty or are there only isolated problems in a territory or region?

Answering this question has become easier with the development of new information processing technology. Sophisticated databases provide daily analysis. Sales managers who have access to bar code data from retail stores can quickly detect when results are not on track. Companies that provide their salespeople with lap or notebook computers can also have daily data. Sales analysis can also come from more traditional sources such as order forms, invoices, call reports, expense accounts, customer and prospect records, warranty cards, reports from distributors and dealers, store audit reports, and customer surveys.

Once the basic data have been gathered, many useful ratios can be computed, such as the number and average size of orders for each salesperson, the number of new accounts opened, the number of calls needed to make a presentation or a sale, selling expenses per call or sale, and the number of accounts lost. Because the analysis problem is often one of information inundation, the manager must devise a means for using information effectively. To eliminate useless data churning the manager should ask, "Will this information help me to manage more effectively?"

Controlled Experiments Correlation is not causation. To be certain that a selling plan produced the increase in sales, it is necessary to conduct an experiment that uses at least one test and one control group. Such experiments can be expensive, but the results can be very rewarding.

An experiment begins with an analysis of historical data, which leads to hypotheses that must be tested with an experiment. For example, a manufacturer with 12 products found that 81% of the total profit was contributed by three products and that two products lost 15% of the company's total profit. This analysis led to the hypothesis that a reallocation of selling effort from the unprofitable to the profitable products would increase total profit contribution. This hypothesis was tested in a controlled experiment. The contribution from the profitable products increased from 16% to 31%.[25]

The Budget

Budgets direct the allocation of resources to a product, activity, territory, or account. These resources include people, working capital, and information. Field sales managers are given expense budgets. Salespeople must budget their time, promotional materials, and travel and entertainment expenses. Budgets force specificity in planning and provide a basis for accountability. They are an important tool for controlling and coordinating the selling effort, but they must be flexible so that they can be adapted to local conditions.

Budgets must be sold downward to the field staff and upward to management. To sell the budget to upper management, the sales forecast should be realistic and the benefits to the company should be demonstrable.[26]

Policies and Procedures

Policies are standing decisions regarding recurring strategic matters, whereas procedures are standardized programs of action regarding recurring tactical matters. These automatic decision-makers free managers from rethinking responses to routine events. They provide uniformity across territories, fairness, and efficiency, and they simplify communications. A few items from the policy and procedures manual of a pharmaceutical company will illustrate the areas that are often covered by policies and procedures.

1. Advertising—product request forms, literature and stationery order form, and professional services mailing list

2. Automobile—operating instructions, reporting expenses, insurance and accident reports
3. Conventions—convention reporting, hospitality suites, and shipping, setting up and dismantling exhibits
4. Expenses—general information, instructions for completing reports, and audit adjustments
5. Marketing—product complaints, shipping and receiving specimens, and working with product planners
6. Recruiting—recruiting policies and guidelines
7. Territory management—call-reporting forms, due dates, supervisor's activity reporting procedure, and consignment of equipment

MANAGING GLOBALLY

Today's sales manager must think in terms of global management. Cultural differences across countries will be reflected in processes for recruiting, selecting, and evaluating salespeople in other countries. Different cultures will also require changes in strategies and business practices, such as gift giving. The need for thinking and managing globally is reflected in the fact that the following U.S. companies have more than one-half of their sales revenue and assets overseas: Alfax, Exxon, Manpower, Coca-Cola, Gillette, Avon Products, Citicorp, McDonald's, and Procter & Gamble.[27]

Global strategies are more than just correct translations. Everyone is familiar with the old example of General Motors naming a car Nova, which in Spanish means it does not go. A general sales manager will need to understand more than the language. He or she will need to understand current world events, such as the impact of free trade agreements and local cultures.

Experiences of U.S. companies in Mexico provide examples of the need to be sensitive to local cultures. Managing in Mexico requires personal relationships. A manager needs to be more of an instructor, teacher, or father figure than a boss.[28] Fernando Duenas, manager of Federal Express in Mexico, found that his late deliveries were reduced from 20% to 1% when he converted a plush conference room next to his office into an employee cafeteria. "In Mexico, people will work harder for you if they can see you, if work becomes a personal thing between you and them," he said.[29]

A Mexican manager will want to spend more time recruiting and screening candidates because severance can be for only the most grievous display of negligence and requires a payment of three months' salary plus 20 days' wages for each year worked.

Although there are concerns about Mexican environmental laws not being strict, a manager may be surprised to learn that Mexican regulators can close a polluting plant immediately, whereas the U.S. Environmental Protection Agency requires a court order.

Achieving a Global Perspective

The first step in global sales management is self-evaluation. In order to be effective, the general sales manager must reach a truly global perspective.

The difficulty in achieving a global perspective is underscored by a series of studies conducted by the Center for International Business Studies in Amstelveen, the Netherlands, among 15,000 managers from around the world.[30]

Consider how you would answer the following questions:
1. You run a department of a division of a large company. One of your subordinates, who you know has trouble at home, is frequently coming in significantly late. What right has this

colleague to be protected by you from others in the department? (a) A definite right? (b) Some right? (c) No right?[31]

2. Which of the following is the best description of a company? (a) A company is a system designed to perform functions and tasks in an efficient way. People are hired to fulfill these functions with the help of machines and other equipment. They are paid for the tasks they perform; or (b) A company is a group of people working together. The people have social relations with other people and with the organization. The functioning is dependent on these relations.[32]

3. A meeting is called to make a decision about the dismissal of an employee. He has worked 15 years for the company, and has performed his job in a satisfactory way. For various reasons, last year the results of his work dropped to an unsatisfactory level. There are no reasons to believe that this situation will improve. Members at the meeting are divided.
(a) Part of the group says that job performance should remain the criterion for dismissal, regardless of the age of the person and his previous records. (b) The other part of the group argues that it is wrong to disregard the 15 years the employee has been working for the company. One has to take into account the company's responsibility for his life. Which one of these two ways of reasoning is more appropriate?[33]

Managers from seven different cultures were asked to respond to these questions. The results are reflected in Exhibit 15.7. For example, on question #1, about 94% of U.S. managers felt the friend had no right to expect protection, whereas only 53% of the French managers said he had no right. On question #2, about 74% of U.S. managers thought of a company as a "set of tasks," versus 29% of Japanese managers and 35% of French managers who thought of a company that way. Finally, 77% of U.S. managers said they would tend to fire the ineffective veteran, whereas most of the managers from the rest of the world said they would tend not to do so.

The general sales manager who must manage with salespeople from a variety of other cultures, or who must send domestic salespeople into foreign environments, must learn to understand these differences in perspective. Failure to do so is likely to lead to unexpected, and probably disappointing, results.

Types of Sales Forces An initial decision the general sales manager must make is what type of sales force to use abroad. Among the options: (1) independent sales agents; (2) company salespeople hired from within the host country; or (3) domestic salespeople who are sent abroad.

Sales Agents Independent sales agents in foreign countries are used by about 72% of multinational companies in their operations outside the United States.[34] Sales agents are appropriate when: markets are geographically dispersed, demand levels are limited or uncertain, the product is new, the firm lacks international experience, and/or the firm is seeking to simplify its activities.[35] Although this is a low-cost option, it can lead to problems of company loyalty, particularly if the agents also represent local competitors.

Host-Country Salespeople Another option is to hire salespeople locally (that is, in the foreign or host country). Among the advantages of hiring host-country salespeople is that they have the advantages as local agents—market and cultural knowledge, language skills, and business contacts—but are loyal by employment.

Although more expensive as an option than agents, host-country employees are usually less expensive than sending home-country salespeople abroad. (Not all labor is cheaper. A Mexican brand manager may cost $73,000 per year, but only $53,000 in the United States because in Mexico there is great demand for the relatively small pool of such people). Some countries require firms to hire their citizens.[36] On the other hand, host-country employees often need extensive training about the company and its products.

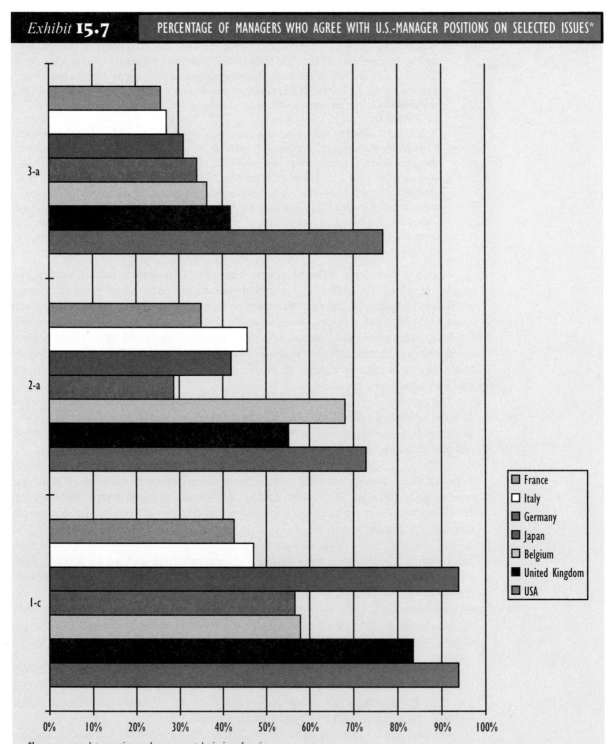

Exhibit 15.7   PERCENTAGE OF MANAGERS WHO AGREE WITH U.S.-MANAGER POSITIONS ON SELECTED ISSUES*

*Issues correspond to questions and responses at beginning of section.
SOURCE: Adapted from Charles Hampden-Turner and Fons Trompenaars, (1993) *The Seven Cultures of Capitalism: Value Systems for Creating Wealth in the United States, Britain, Japan, Germany, France, Sweden, and the Netherlands,* New York: Piatkus.

Recruiting internationally will generate a smaller pool of applicants because of fewer persons attending college and the low perception of selling careers for those with an adequate education.

Recruiting across countries will be further complicated by ethnic composition, religion, and class systems. None of these elements has a dominant effect on daily living in the United States, but they do in most other countries. Canada has 25% French speaking citizens, Belgium is split along Flemish and French origins, and India has between 300 and 1000 dialects and subcultures.

Although the United States is largely Protestant, religion does not have a major influence on life or business. In contrast, Catholicism does influence daily life in Latin American countries. In Asian and Middle Eastern countries, "traditional religions such as Hinduism (800 million followers) Buddhists (350 million) and Muslims (900 million adherents) not only dwarf Protestantism in numbers but also essentially dominate the behavior of their followers."[37]

Social class in the United States is largely income based and movement among classes is based on the ability to accumulate wealth. In contrast, classes in other countries are based on factors that cannot be changed. "Other countries however, most with longer social histories than the U.S., base their social class distinctions on seniority criteria (Japan) hereditary criteria (India, and to a lesser extent, Western Europe), or ethnic criteria (South America for example). All societies with social distinctions have one thing in common—they are taken seriously by enough people to affect individual and group behavior in business."[38]

Home-Country Salespeople Abroad (Expatriates) Because of the emphasis on product knowledge and service, expatriate salespeople are often used in technical industries.[39] This is a problematic decision for the general sales manager, because: (1) there is a 1-in-4 chance that the expatriate salesperson will fail to complete his or her international tour;[40] (2) about 2 in 5 expatriate salespeople are marginally effective or ineffective as a result of poor selection;[41] and (3) about 1 in 4 leave their companies within a year of returning to the United States.[42]

Many of the problems are attributed to culture shock, which refers to the loss of control and frustration people often feel in a foreign culture. Initial enthusiasm for the novelty of a foreign assignment often gives way to frustration over inability to understand the language and culture of the new setting.

With experience, people often adapt to the foreign assignment, but then face a "reverse culture shock" on returning home.[43] The initial pleasure of returning home diminishes as the salesperson discovers that his/her friends have gone on with their careers, key contacts have changed in buyer companies, and his/her role in the organization may have shifted.

These problems, and the fact that an expatriate salesperson costs 2.5 to 3 times as much as the local equivalent, makes management of an expatriate sales force a critical issue.[44]

Managing Expatriate Salespeople

The low success rate in expatriate salesperson placements calls for careful management, both for the sake of the firm and the salesperson. The odds of success can be improved by careful selection and training of salespeople for the international assignment, proper support for the salesperson while abroad, and attention to repatriation upon his or her return.[45]

Selection The general sales manager who selects a salesperson for assignment abroad must understand the host environment, the salesperson, and the degree of fit between the two. Traditional criteria, like technical competence or interviewing skills, have little value in this decision process. Among the factors to consider important are: (1) intercultural attitude; (2) host country knowledge; (3) adaptability; and (4) personal constraints.

Intercultural Attitude Some people tend to evaluate other cultures based on their own. This tendency, called ethnocentrism, limits one's ability to accept and relate to the other culture on its own terms. For example, an American salesperson who is highly efficient might consider two-hours of casual conversation over lunch a waste of time. But if the salesperson is working in France, an inability to adapt to this style—which a French counterpart might consider an important social occasion—might limit the salesperson's effectiveness.

Openness to foreign cultures is a key criterion in placing a salesperson abroad. Ethnocentrism, lack of empathy (that is, an inability to identify with another person's viewpoint), and a tendency to avoid interaction with people from other cultures are all indicators that the placement will be ineffective.

Host Country Knowledge   Host country knowledge is important at two levels: first, because personal factors may prevent a salesperson from being effective in a particular culture; and second, because the salesperson's knowledge of the culture is likely to improve his performance in that culture.

The importance of personal factors is seen in the example of Malaysia, as noted by researchers Earl Honeycutt and John Ford.[46] They note that tensions exist in Malaysia between the Malay and the Chinese, as well as between the Muslims and the Buddhists. On top of this, Malays are uncomfortable with ambiguous social positions. So sending a Chinese-American salesperson to Malaysia may pose problems.

In general, the more a salesperson knows about the host country, the more effective his/her performance. Skill in the language, and knowledge of the culture and its social traditions and customs, are key issues in selection. Researchers Victoria Bush and Thomas Ingram summarize this dimension in terms of "attributional confidence": that is, the extent to which one can explain and predict the behavior of others.[47]

Adaptability   Another set of traits that are important in a salesperson who is to be assigned abroad is a generalized ability to adapt. Foreign assignments require individuals to go through substantial change. Their effectiveness will depend on their ability to adjust to these changes effectively. This generalized adaptability may be assessed through psychological tests, assessment centers, and/or interviews with co-workers.[48]

Personal Constraints   Finally, a general manager—and the salesperson under consideration—may want to consider personal factors that may limit a candidate's ability to function in a foreign assignment. These issues might include family obligations, personal health, career plans, and related concerns.

Training   The purpose of training a salesperson for foreign assignment is to improve the fit between the salesperson and the host country environment. This purpose implies that weaknesses identified in the selection process should be addressed in training before assignment. Often this training is not conducted but it is likely to improve the effectiveness of the expatriate salesperson.[49]

Candidates who are oblivious to intercultural differences require training that the differences are real and important to job performance abroad. This training might include watching videotapes about the country, reading detailed descriptions of the culture, and dining on indigenous foods.

Candidates who are open to other cultures but lack specific coping skills might be exposed to expected behaviors. An example is to arrange a meeting for a specific time but arrive a half-hour late.[50] The point of the training is then to explore one's values and how to cope with the behavior of others who do not share them.

Training in specific cultural issues that salespeople are likely to encounter, like gift giving customs, can be particularly important. Gift giving can backfire in most cultures. For example, in the Arab world one must never give alcoholic beverages, send a card with a picture of one's family, or offer anything with the left hand.

A variety of resources are available for managers of international sales forces. The International Society for Intercultural Education, Training, and Research (SIETAR) offers publications and seminars useful for training salespeople for international positions.[51] Colleges also offer international programs designed for businesspeople assigned abroad. For example, Williams College reportedly conducts five-week seminars for companies like GE, IBM, Polaroid and others.[52]

Support   The home office can limit the effects of culture shock by providing ongoing support. Researchers Guy and Patton suggest that this support should include:[53]

- adequate monetary support
- social support in the host country
- a mentor in the host country
- language and cultural assistance
- a work environment that is as familiar as possible
- on-going communications with, and regular return trips to, the home office

Repatriation   Guy and Patton also note that it is useful to begin planning the salesperson's re-entry into the home office six months to a year in advance.[54] This can be expedited by naming an internal sponsor for the salesperson. A person who has previously had a foreign assignment may be particularly well suited to this task. The returning salesperson may need assistance with family issues (e.g., help finding a job for the salesperson's spouse, school enrollment for children, etc.) as well as work-related issues.

Administration and Control

Managing an international sales organization raises complex issues of administration and control. Commissions are customary as motivators in the United States, but are not as common in Japan and the Middle East, where increased responsibilities and job security are more accepted.[55] Using both expatriates and host country salespeople in the same country can cause problems, because the former are often paid much more than the latter—leading to pay equity difficulties.[56]

The need to adjust criteria for performance evaluation to local conditions has been noted in Chapter 16, but comparisons across cultures become even more difficult. For example, recognizing, rewarding, or praising employees is almost unheard of in most Japanese companies. Corporate strategies focus on manufacturing, not marketing. The group approach to planning means that no one takes responsibility for the marketing plan.[57] A Team Evaluation Consensus approach has been suggested by Edwards, Cummings, and Schlacter.[58] This approach uses international team members to evaluate pairs of salespeople from different countries.

....

TRAINING SALES MANAGERS

While the sales managers' job is getting more complicated, few receive adequate training in management. A survey of managers in the computer software industry revealed that only 50% had management training and they rated the training as a 6 on a 9-point scale. Although hiring, interviewing, maintaining customer satisfaction, and motivation are critical, only about 50% of the training programs covered these skills.[59] Too often it is assumed that a high-performing salesperson would be a good manager, which explains why on-the-job training is the most common means for training managers.[60]

Many lists of leadership skills exist. John Rau, a banker, then a business school dean, and then a banker suggests the following list of seven lessons that he learned in his careers.

1. Learn the defining issues of the time. Presently they are technology and people.
2. Attach yourself to the right people.
3. Learn to manage people who know more than you do.
4. Look for positions where you can make a difference.
5. Don't hire managers to run the organization you have; hire those who can run the organization you want to create.
6. Some time off can help you define what you really want out of life.[61]

The elimination of positions that provided training has created a need for management training programs for outside consultants. The Gallup Organization has created a school of management. Its Leadership Institute is based on 25 years of studying the profiles of 40,000 successful executives. It focuses on seven demands of leadership—visioning, mentoring, knowing one's self, making sense of workplace experiences, seeking challenging assignments, building a constituency, and stabilizing values.[62] Before the program, participants' self-evaluations of leadership skills are compared with their subordinates' evaluations. This comparison is repeated 9 to 12 months after the program. An improvement in leadership is noted as a result of the program.

Case 15.1 — A GENERAL SALES MANAGER'S JOB DESCRIPTION

The following job description for the general manager was used by a large pharmaceutical firm. What are its strengths and weaknesses? What changes would you make?
· A General Sales Manager's Job Description

OBJECTIVE

To plan, organize, lead, and control the activities and personnel of the sales staff to achieve the planned level of sales within the approved levels of expenses.

MANAGEMENT SKILLS

Analyzing information to identify opportunities, problems, and their causes.

Decision making by identifying alternative courses of action, estimating the costs and benefits associated with each alternative, and selecting the best alternative.

Communicating effectively downward through the sales organization and upward to top management.

FUNCTIONS/ACTIVITIES

PLAN

Forecast
- Sales, expenses, competition, environmental, technological, and regulatory changes
- Personnel needs
- Space and equipment needs
- Sales promotion and staff support needs
- Training needs
- Management succession needs
- Nonselling responsibilities, such as committees

Set Objectives
- Translate corporate objectives into sales objectives.
- Establish goals for market penetration, changes in personnel, programs, procedures, and training.
- Establish priorities for various dimensions of the job.
- Make objectives behavioral, individual, specific, measurable, achievable, and time-oriented.

Case 15.1   A GENERAL SALES MANAGER'S JOB DESCRIPTION—CONTINUED

- Establish personal goals.

Develop Strategies
- Create sales force strategies.
- Participate in developing strategies for products, services, advertising, promotion, price, and channels.
- Evaluate the effectiveness of selling strategies.

Develop Policies
- Monitor policies (company and statutory) for sales force compliance.
- Evaluate present policies.
- Develop or suggest new policies as circumstances change or in anticipation of changes in the environment, competition, or regulation.
- Interact with the company compliance officer and government inspector.

Develop Programs
- Select the best mix of selling activities to achieve the sales goals.
- Make strategic decisions regarding the deployment of resources.
- Evaluate existing programs.
- Develop new programs and promotions.

Set Procedures
- Monitor compliance with procedures.
- Evaluate present procedures.
- Develop new procedures.

Budget
- Deploy resources to achieve financial goals, such as sales levels, expense ratios, and return-on-assets managed.
- Monitor field sales manager's efforts in controlling salespersons' expenses.
- Monitor field sales manager's expenses.
- Anticipate expense trends and suggest alternatives.
- Create annual estimates of needs for compensation, expenses, promotional materials, equipment, automobiles, office space, and public relations.

ORGANIZE

Establish Organizational Structure
- Determine the size and structure (e.g., product or geographic specialization) of the sales force.
- Consider alternative personal selling methods, such as brokers, manufacturers' representatives, direct mail, and telephone selling.

Create Position Descriptions
- Evaluate current position descriptions in the light of changes in marketing strategies, the environment, and competition.
- Work with field sales managers, salespeople, and the personnel department to revise position descriptions.
- Evaluate and revise own position description.

Establish Position Qualifications
- Evaluate current qualifications for salespeople and field managers in light of the present flow of applications, federal regulations regard-

ing equal .employment opportunities, marketing strategies, competition, turnover, and performance levels.
- Revise position qualifications as necessary.

STAFF

Recruit and Select
- Develop programs for recruiting and selecting to maintain an adequate sales staff, given objectives and strategies.
- Evaluate turnover, pirating, and terminations to determine future needs and deficiencies in policies, programs, and procedures.
- Evaluate competitive recruiting schemes.
- Comply with Affirmative Action Plans to assure applicant flow from protected groups and minorities.
- Evaluate recruiting sources.
- Cultivate minority applicant sources.
- Comply with federal and state regulations regarding interviewing.
- Anticipate future skills that are required.

Orient and Train
- Develop programs for orienting new salespeople and relocated salespeople into the company, territory, and community.
- Develop training programs for new and present salespeople to improve their knowledge, attitudes, skills, and habits.
- Be aware of the changing values, qualifications, and needs of the applicants.
- Be aware of the changing expertise required because of new products, strategies, competition, and regulations.
- Keep informed of new training methods and equipment.
- Update company training programs.
- Provide management training for field sales managers.

Develop Personnel
- Be aware of the effect of turnover and training on sales productivity and market share.
- Develop team spirit.
- Recognize the "dead wood" and "walking wounded" and take appropriate action.
- Anticipate future needs.
- Identify changing behavioral and technical requirements.
- Identify potential promotables.
- Provide growth and educational and training opportunities.
- Monitor developmental activities of field sales managers.
- Provide rotation for experience.
- Approve transfers and reassignments consistent with future needs, growth, and promotability.
- Create a pool of qualified managers.
- Develop your replacement.

DIRECT

Delegate (assign responsibility and accountability)
- Train sales staff and distributors' salespeople.

continued

Case 15.1   A GENERAL SALES MANAGER'S JOB DESCRIPTION—CONTINUED

- Recruit, select, and hire salespeople.
- Evaluate, counsel, and coach salespeople.
- Customer service.
- Distributor selection.

Motivate
- Provide charismatic (emotional) and intellectual leadership.
- Develop pride, self-esteem, loyalty, willingness to work.
- Monitor the results of field managers' motivation efforts.
- Provide opportunities for field managers to meet their individual needs.

Coordinate
- Coordinate the activities of field sales managers.
- Coordinate the activities of salespeople through field sales managers.
- Encourage time management.
- Manage the technical work of the sales force.

Manage change
- Create flexibility in the systems and organizations so change is possible.
- Encourage innovation and criticism by others.
- Create early warning systems that will monitor the environment, competition, technology, and regulation for opportunities and problems.
- React appropriately to emergencies and recover quickly.
- Inform top management immediately when conditions indicate that an approved plan will not be achieved.

CONTROL

Establish Reporting Systems
- Collect and present field marketing data in actionable form.
- Provide field managers, appropriate departments, and higher management with appropriate information in actionable form.
- Develop information systems to evaluate policies, procedures, and programs.
- Be aware of new technology in information development.
- Be aware of new information sources that will signal changes in the environment, competition, technology, and regulation.
- Understand the limitations of information systems and market research.

- Detect early any unsatisfactory trends and deviations from plans.

Develop Standards
- Establish performance standards for salespeople and field sales managers.
- Challenge job descriptions and performance standards on a regular basis.
- Assure that standards comply with federal and state regulations for equal opportunities for compensation and promotion.
- Assure that standards are observable, measurable, and mutually agreed upon.

Measure Performance
- Develop measuring instruments that are valid, reliable, and acceptable under federal regulations for equal opportunities in employment
- Appraise field managers regularly, accurately, and fairly.
- Monitor the appraisals of salespeople as conducted by field managers.
- Evaluate changes in performance since last evaluation and the resulting consequences from success or failure in performance.
- Evaluate field sales managers' performance in management skills and activity performance.

Take Corrective Action
- Take prompt, corrective action when unsatisfactory trends in behavior are noted.
- Counsel and coach field sales managers in management skills.
- Monitor the counseling and coaching of field sales managers.
- Identify problems and alternative solutions, including training.
- Take negative actions such as reassignment, demotion, or separation.

Reward
- Reward favorable behavior in accordance with individual needs.
- Keep compensation schemes competitive with industry.
- Anticipate necessary changes in the compensation levels and methods.
- Assure that compensation is consistent with performance.
- Identify disparate impact of compensation schemes on protected groups and minorities.
- Regularly review compensation schemes for field managers and salespeople.

Case 15.2   SUPERIOR PUBLISHING COMPANY

When Harry Bunting, the Northeast District Sales Manager for Superior Publishing, learned that Nancy Cunningham was pregnant but planned to continue working her field sales territory as long as possible, Harry had the feeling that his supervisory responsibilities were going to become considerably more complex.

Harry had been reviewing the current sales figures for the territories in his district and was troubled by the continuing flat-dollar trends. The Northeast District was running at 94% of forecast with only four months remaining in the fiscal year. This compared with sales of 101% of forecast for the Eastern Region, and 99.7% nationally. Six of the 10 territories in Harry's district were at or very close to their quotas. Of the remaining four, Nancy Cunningham's territory was the one most significantly behind, at 76% of quota. Mr. Shepherd, Harry's Regional Manager, had recently questioned him about Nancy's performance, and had remarked about the fact that the Northeast District was the only one in the Region behind quota. This would affect the share of the year-end bonus that Harry and his salespeople would receive. He reminded Harry that he had asked previously for a program or plan of action to turn Nancy's performance around.

Nancy had been difficult for Harry to supervise ever since she was hired four years ago. She was friendly, very well spoken, vivacious, and energetic. As a result, she was very well liked by her accounts. However, in spite of her ability to make friends easily, Nancy failed to make quota in any of the four years she was employed, with her year-end sales at 96%, 94%, 89%, and currently 76%. Although Harry had personally participated in Nancy's field training and had selected the other salespeople to round out her training schedule, he had not been totally satisfied with her early progress. Although his own observations and the reports from the trainers indicated her satisfactory performance during the training period, Nancy's use of methods and tactics outlined in the Selling Plan and of the selling tools provided by the company was too inconsistent and too awkward to suit Harry. He had the feeling that she followed the Plan only when he worked with her. His analysis was that she relied too heavily on her personality to do her selling for her.

In considering what he might do to help Nancy improve her performance, Harry's major concern was to be fair and to avoid the label of being prejudiced. (Nancy was the first female salesperson in Harry's district and, at the time she was hired, Harry's wife Virginia voiced her concern about Harry's working with Nancy on out-of-town trips.) Although he recognized that one's selling style was individualistic and that Nancy's personality was an asset, Harry believed that her unconventional methods, for whatever reason, were behind her less-than-satisfactory productivity. Unfortunately, Nancy's personality and degree in business administration from UCLA, together with Harry's manner, did not make it easy for her to accept Harry's appraisal and counseling.

Nancy's response to Harry's efforts was an alternating defense of her individuality, with repeated references to the acknowledged warm relationships she had with her customers, and a friendly tolerance of his suggestions, all of which Harry found difficult to deal with. With little improvement, the status quo was maintained until less than a year ago when Nancy married. Her husband, a successful lawyer, supported Nancy's ambition to develop her own career. Unfortunately, Nancy's performance was anything but enhanced by her marriage. In addition to a continued slow decline in sales, Nancy's correspondence and reporting fell behind on more than one occasion, and she failed to make at least two scheduled out-of-town trips in compliance with her itinerary. When pressed for an explanation, Nancy admitted that her marriage was probably responsible, but insisted that it was a temporary lapse and that she would work out a better system to prevent any recurrence.

When Nancy telephoned Harry last weekend to announce her pregnancy, she told him that she was due to deliver in approximately six months, that she planned to work as long as possible, and that she planned to return to work after the birth of her child. To put it mildly, Harry was upset. Although he did not communicate his concern to her at that time, Harry calculated that Nancy would probably stop working six to eight weeks before her delivery date, would take another six to eight weeks personal leave of absence (without pay), and then she might decide that she didn't want to return to work. This would mean that her territory would be open for as long as four months—on top of the last eight months of declining sales—a set of circumstances he was certain his regional sales manager, Mr. Shepherd, would consider intolerable. Summarizing the situation in a lengthy memorandum to Mr. Shepherd, Harry reviewed the alternatives and made a number of recommendations for his approval.

CASE QUESTIONS

1. If we assume that the three other territories in the Northeast District that are behind forecast (in addition to Nancy Cunningham's) are equally so, what are their current sales as a percent of forecast or quota?
2. How might Nancy's "too heavy reliance on her personality" have interfered with her productivity?
3. For this case:
   a. Define the problem(s).
   b. Identify the causes.
   c. Determine the contribution of each cause to the problem.
   d. Determine the control over each cause for Nancy and Harry.
   e. Prioritize the causes for Nancy and Harry.
   f. Establish decision-making criteria.
   g. Create alternative programs.
   h. Make a decision.
   i. Implement the decision.
   j. Follow through.

Case 15.3   THE INFLATED APPRAISAL

After an in-depth analysis of the productivity of the salespeople in the six districts of his region, Jack Hunter was convinced that the relative productivity in terms of dollar sales versus potential in two of his districts did not match the individual performance appraisals submitted by the district sales managers. This seemed particularly true in the case of Carol Thompson's district. Judging by the annual performance appraisals submitted by Carol, the overall performances of her 10 representatives ranged from a "high satisfactory" to an "outstanding" rating. By contrast, the total sales productivity of Carol's district was significantly below the regional average, three of her representatives were at the bottom of the regional list and none was in the top quartile when compared on sales versus potential.

At the last district sales managers' quarterly conference, Jack conducted a workshop with a series of case studies on the importance of realistic performance appraisal reports, and stressed the fact that he had contributed to this problem in the region by accepting annual appraisals, which his better judgment had told him were inflated. At the same time, he served notice that he planned to tighten up this procedure on the appraisals that were due during the next quarter.

As a result, he was annoyed a month later to receive an envelope from Carol Thompson containing five annual appraisals, all of which, in Jack's opinion, were inconsistent with the comparative sales data. In checking further into his files, Jack dug out copies of correspondence from Carol to her salespeople, and a series of trip reports that Carol completed following each working visit with her salespeople, all of which provided documentation to support Jack's conclusion that the appraisals were inflated.

After agonizing over the situation for a day and feeling that the problem had existed far too long and had to be solved, Jack telephoned Carol and told her that three of the five reports were unacceptable and would have to be resubmitted. As expected, Carol protested, contending that the appraisals reflected her best judgment of the activities ratings of these salespeople. Jack's rejoinder was that if the sales results were inconsistent with the ratings of the activities that produced these results, then the ratings were inflated. He added that if Carol could not provide evidence to justify the higher ratings, then he'd reduce them. Although Carol conceded the logic of Jack's position, she argued that she couldn't recall and change the appraisals because she had already held the performance appraisal and counseling sessions with these salespeople, had them sign the appraisals, and had given them their copies. At this point Jack insisted, saying that he had made his position clear at the last managers' conference and that the problem was Carol's to resolve. Jack would not accept the reports as originally submitted.

CASE QUESTIONS

1. What is Jack Hunter's problem?
2. What is Carol Thompson's problem?
3. What are the possible reasons for Carol's inconsistency in appraising her salespeople?
4. What options are available to Carol?
5. If Jack will not yield, how could Carol conduct the reappraisals in an effort to minimize the trauma?
6. What harm is done by inflated appraisals?

SUMMARY

The management functions for a general sales manager are the same as for the first-line manager, but the general manager focuses more on planning than staffing, has a longer time horizon, and has a view of opportunities and problems that are corporate-wide, national, and global. Planning can focus on the present system by asking critical questions regarding the mission and goals of the company and the environment in which it operates. Answers to these questions lead to the identification of problems and opportunities. Strategic alternatives are created to solve the problems and tap the opportunities. An alternative is selected and a plan is developed for its implementation. The plan must include a system for its evaluation and the control over the resources used to implement it. Creative problem-solving approaches can be used to go beyond the present system to innovate new ones.

To assure that the sales force is moving toward the sales goals, the general sales manager needs control systems. These systems consist of the selling plan, productivity analysis, the budget, and policies and procedures.

In many companies the general sales manager must think globally. Managing globally requires an understanding of the nuances in other cultures that will affect recruitment of salespeople, managing and terminating them, and giving gifts to clients.

ASSIGNMENTS/DISCUSSION QUESTIONS

1. Role-play with a classmate the case of the salesperson whose call reports reflect calls mainly on customers with moderate potential and product sales analysis reveals that only the old and less complex products have been sold. Switch roles so that each person has an opportunity to be the salesperson and the manager.

2. Give five possible causes why a 55-year-old salesperson is 20% below average in sales while the district average is 15% above average.

3. When should a general sales manager become involved in a salesperson's personal problems?

4. What should a field manager do if a salesperson wants to take a problem to the general manager? What should the general manager do?

5. Who should announce a salesperson's promotion to the salesperson and to the entire sales force? Why?

6. Why would a salesperson promote a company's product that was not featured in the current selling plan?

7. What conclusion would you draw if historical analysis shows the salesperson is on target with the number of calls and promotes the assigned products, but dollar sales are below quota?

ENDNOTES

1. Kenneth Labich, The new pay game . . . and how you measure up, *Fortune,* October 19, 1992, p. 117.
2. William A. O'Connell and William Keenan, Jr., The Shape of Things to Come, *Sales & Marketing Management 142(1),* January, 1990, pp. 36–41.
3. Tatsuo Shoda, *in personal correspondence with the authors, 1992.*
4. The Conference Board, *Customer Satisfaction: The Mandate for Business Success,* November 4–5, 1993.
5. L.B Gschwandtner, Who is Michael Dell? *Personal Selling Power,* March, 1993, p. 16.
6. Thayer C. Taylor, Information-based Selling, *Sales & Marketing Management,* Part 2, December, 1994, p. 38.
7. Melissa Campanelli, Sound the Alarm, *Sales & Marketing Management,* Part 2, December, 1994, pp. 20–25.
8. Diversity: America's Strength, *Fortune,* Special Section, June 23, 1997.
9. Raju Narisetti, P&G, Seeing shoppers were being confused overhauls marketing, *The Wall Street Journal,* January 15, 1997, pp. A1, and A8.
10. Barbara Hetzer, Pushing decisions down the line at Campbell Soup, *Business Month,* July, 1989, pp. 62–63.
11. William A. O'Connell and William Keenan, Jr., The Shape of Things to Come, *Sales & Marketing Management,* January, 1990, p. 38.
12. Barry Trailer and Joe Vavricka, SFA, OMS and Other Mysteries, www.salesmastery.com (June 13, 1997).
13. Mick Zangari, Measure your sales traits, *International Newspaper Marketing Association,* December, 1995, p. 27.
14. The Jack Morton Company, Our Mission, www.jackmorton.com, (March 3, 24, 1997).

15. For a summary see G. David Hughes, Innovate to be admired (grow, be profitable, and survive), working paper, June 12, 1997; Roger L. Firestein, (1996) *Leading on the Creative Edge,* Colorado Springs: Pinion, and Sidney J. Parnes (1997), *Optimize the Magic of Your Mind,* Buffalo, NY: Creative Education Foundation.

16. Russell L. Ackoff (1978), *The Art of Problem Solving,* New York: John Wiley, p. 1.

17. Bristol Voss, What's the Big Idea? *Sales & Marketing Management,* July, 1991, p. 36.

18. Confidential statement to the author.

19. David Woodruff, James B. Treece, Sunita Wadekar Bhargava, and Karen Lowry Miller, Saturn, GM Finally has a Real Winner, *Business Week,* August 17, 1992, pp. 86–91.

20. David Woodruff, May We Help You Kick the Tires? *Business Week,* August 3, 1992, pp. 49–50.

21. Cristopher Power, Lisa Driscoll, and Earl Bohn, Smart Selling, *Business Week,* August 3, 1992, p. 47.

22. *Crown,* July, 1991, pp. 6–7.

23. This discussion is based on Leonard A. Schlesinger and Roger Hallowell, Taco Bell Corp, Harvard Business School Case No. 9-692-058; Leonard A. Schlesinger and James L. Heskett, The Service-Driven Service Company, *Harvard Business Review,* September-October, 1991, pp. 71–81;. James L. Heskett, W. Earl Sasser, Jr., and Leonard A. Schlesinger, Achieving Breakthrough Service, *Participant's Guide,* Harvard Business School, Video Series): n.d.

24. William Keenan, Jr., America's Best Sales Forces, *Sales & Marketing Management,* September, 1992, pp. 46–64.

25. Charles H. Sevin (1965), *Marketing Productivity Analysis,* New York: McGraw-Hill.

26. Jack Falvey, The Battle of the Budget, *Sales & Marketing Management,* 143(14), November, 1991, pp. 10, 12.

27. Murray Weidenbaum, Neoisolationism and Global Realities, Center for the Study of American Business, Policy Study No. 130, May 1996, pp. 3–5.

28. Matt Moffett, Culture Shock, *The Wall Street Journal Reports,* September 24, 1992, p. R14.

29. *Ibid.,* p. R13.

30. Charles Hampden-Turner and Fons Trompenaars (1993), *The Seven Cultures of Capitalism: Value Systems for Creating Wealth in the United States, Britain, Japan, Germany, France, Sweden, and the Netherlands,* New York: Piatkus.

31. *Ibid.,* p. 22.

32. *Ibid.,* p. 32.

33. *Ibid.,* p. 112.

34. John S. Hill and Richard R. Still, Organizing the Overseas Sales Force: How Multinationals Do It, *Journal of Personal Selling & Sales Management,* 9(2), Spring, 1990, pp. 57–66.

35. Earl D. Honeycutt, Jr. and John B. Ford, Guidelines for Managing an International Sales Force, *Industrial Marketing Management,* 24(2), March, 1995, pp. 135–144.

36. *Ibid.*

37. John S. Hill and Meg Birdseye, Salesperson Selection In Multinational Corporations: An Empirical Study, *Journal of Personal Selling & Sales Management* 9, Summer, 1989, p. 39.

38. *Ibid.*

39. Honeycutt and Ford, 1995.

40. Rosalle L. Tung, Selection and Training Procedures of U.S., European, and Japanese Multinationals, *California Management Review,* 25(1), 1982, pp. 57–71.

41. L. Copeland and L. Griggs (1985), *Going International,* New York: Random House.

42. H.B. Gregersen and J.S. Black, Antecedents to Commitment to a Parent Company and a Foreign Operation, *Academy of Management Journal,* 35, 1992, pp. 65–90.

43. Bonnie S. Guy and W.E. "Pat" Patton, Managing the Effects of Culture Shock and Sojourner Adjustment on the Expatriate Industrial Sales Force, *Industrial Marketing Management,* 25(5), September, 1996, pp. 385–393.

44. Subhash C. Jain (1990), *International Marketing Management,* Boston: PWS-Kent Publishing.

45. Bonnie S. Guy and W. E. "Pat" Patton, Managing the Effects of Culture Shock and Sojourner Adjustment on the Expatriate Industrial Sales Force, *Industrial Marketing Management,* 25(5), September, 1996, pp. 385–393.

46. Earl D. Honeycutt, Jr. and John B. Ford, Guidelines for Managing an International Sales Force, *Industrial Marketing Management,* 24(2), March, 1995, pp. 135–144.

47. Victoria Davies Bush and Thomas Ingram, Adapting to Diverse Customers: A Training Matrix for International Marketers, *Industrial Marketing Management,* 25(5), September, 1996, pp. 373–383.
48. Guy and Patton, 1996.
49. Rosalie Tung, Selection and Training Procedures of U.S., European, and Japanese Multinationals, *California Management Review,* 25, 1982, 57–71.
50. G. Trifonovitch, On Cross-Cultural Orientation Techniques, in *Cultural Learning: Concepts, Applications, and Research,* R. Brislin, editor (1997), University Press of Hawaii, pp. 213–222.
51. SIETAR can be contacted on the Internet at http://aspin.asu.edu/~sietar/info/whatis/indext.html
52. Rosaelie Tung, Language Training and Beyond: The Case of Japanese Multinationals, *Annals of APPSS* 511, 1990, pp. 97–108.
53. Bonnie S. Guy and W.E. "Pat" Patton, Managing the Effects of Culture Shock and Sojourner Adjustment on the Expatriate Sales Force, *Industrial Marketing Management,* 25(5), September, 1996, pp. 385–393.
54. *Ibid.*
55. Edward Cundiff and Marye Tharp Hilger (1988), *Marketing in the International Environment,* Englewood Cliffs, NJ: Prentice-Hall.
56. Honeycutt and Ford, 1995.
57. Bill Kelley, Culture Clash: West Meets East, *Sales & Marketing Management* 143(8), July, 1991, pp. 28–34.
58. Mark R. Edwards, W. Theodore Cummings, and John L. Schlacter, The Paris-Peoria Solution: Innovations in Appraising Regional and International Sales Personnel, *Journal of Personal Selling & Sales Management,* November, 1984, pp. 27–38.
59. Brian Pope, Sink or Swim: How companies train their sales managers, in J. Brian Pope, editor (1991), *The Sales Manager's Survival Guide,* Atlanta: Culpepper and Associates, p. 7.
60. C. David Shepherd and Rick E. Ridnour, The training of sales managers, *Journal of Personal Selling & Sales Management,* Winter, 1995, p. 71.
61. Hal Lancaster, John Rau learns from his staff, then finds a way to guide, *The Wall Street Journal,* May 6, 1997, p. B1.
62. Leadership Institute: Leveraging Individual Talent for Organizational Excellence, Brochure, The Gallup Organization, 1997.

16

CREATING A SALES INFORMATION SYSTEM

LEARNING GOALS

1. To understand the different roles that information management plays in effective sales force management
2. To identify important sources of data that are useful in sales management and to learn how to assess data quality
3. To understand the diverse techniques available for analysis of sales-related data, including their uses and limitations
4. To learn the different methods of conducting a forecast and the advantages and disadvantages of each method
5. To learn the basic methods for sales territory analysis
6. To understand the dynamics of information dissemination in an organizational environment

MARKETING INFORMATION SYSTEMS

In the late 18th and early 19th centuries economists stated that value was created only by land and labor. Capital was added as a factor of production in the 19th century. Management skills and entrepreneurship were added in the early 20th century. At the end of the 20th century information was finally recognized as a factor that added value. The information revolution that was driven by microelectronics made it possible to collect, store, process, and distribute massive amounts of information in fractions of a second. The information revolution is changing selling processes, as was seen in earlier chapters, and it is changing how the sales function is organized, which will be seen in the next chapter.

Information Is an Asset

Information is an asset, but it rarely appears on the balance sheet. It has unusual properties. When information is used it does not depreciate. In fact, analysis can improve its value. Although information does not wear from use, it can be outdated very quickly and lose value as more people have it. It can make marketing more efficient by moving information instead of goods (for example, musical recordings shipped via the Internet) or people (such as shopping on the television network).

Rapid information feedback from the point of sale to the operations/production functions increases an organization's ability to adapt to unpredictable conditions. Thus instead of predicting the computer configurations that will sell, and stocking up expensive inventories—which become a burden if the prediction is wrong—Dell Computers builds computers based on orders. Similarly, Frito Lay's huge force of salespeople—each armed with computers linked to headquarters—helps the company detect and counteract competitive inroads from local competitors. In both cases, the direct information linkage between the point of sale and base operations enables large national firms to act like small local ones.

Because information is a valuable asset it must be protected. AT&T established an information policy. First, it defined information as "an aggregation of data that is used for decision making; data is the representation of discrete facts."[1] Then it established a policy based on the following points:

1. Data will be safeguarded as a corporate asset, protecting it from alteration, destruction, or inappropriate disclosure.
2. Data will be shared according to policies because it does not belong to one person or function.
3. Data will be managed as a resource, to be planned for at all corporate levels.
4. Data will be defined according to standards that assure completeness, accuracy, and reduce redundancy.
5. Information quality will be managed actively for accuracy, availability, accessibility, and ease of use.
6. Information will be used to maintain present and create new markets and products.[2]

Evolution of Sales Information Management

Companies appear to progress through four stages of sales information management, as illustrated in Exhibit 16.1: (1) passive, (2) sales-focused, (3) customer-focused, and (4) strategic. These stages do not happen on their own. For a company to progress from one stage to another, management must design and implement specific organizational changes. These changes are not simple or easy. They must be adapted to the company's specific situation. They must also overcome inertia and resistance. But they can move the firm to a stronger competitive position.

Passive Information Management   occurs because of the lack of focus or discipline. At this level, managers simply react to environmental events that are brought to their attention. Aside from basic accounting information on actual sales, passive information management includes no systematic review of customers, competitors, or environmental trends.

Information that is brought to management's attention, by customers, salespeople, or others, is either random or accompanied by a motive other than the organization's. For example, customers may lobby the supplier company for more frequent and generous sales promotions. This move may fit the customer's needs, but not necessarily the suppliers or the entire chain of distribution's. By passively reacting to information provided by others, management gives up control of the firm's destiny. This approach to sales information

Exhibit **16.1**	EVOLUTION OF SALES INFORMATION MANAGEMENT			
	Sales Information Management Stage			
Value-Added Issue	**Passive**	**Sales-focused**	**Customer-focused**	**Strategic**
What data is collected?	Internal transaction records	Sales leads and salesperson performance	Customer needs	Synergy across functions
How is data assimilated?	Accounting system	Salesperson evaluation process	Cooperative buyer-seller relationship	Cross-functional teams
How is data analyzed?	Gross sales per salesperson	Performance ratios	Benefit-cost analysis for customers	Both quantitative and qualitative
What is basis for data interpretation?	Absolute differences in sales by salesperson	Standardized differences in sales by salesperson	Customer perceptions of value	Competitive advantage
How is information disseminated?	Financial statements	Internal performance appraisals	Customer presentations	Strategic planning process

management is increasingly rare because such firms eventually find it impossible to survive in competitive industries.

Sales-focused Information Management is probably the most common stage in use today. Under this approach, the organization actively develops information on potential customers, qualifies and prioritizes sales leads, and monitors the rate of conversion from lead to customer by territory, type of customer, and other critical factors. Similarly, the sales manager may monitor salespeople in terms of calls per week, sales per call, or other pertinent measures.

By all visible signs, this can be an effective information-based approach to managing sales. The problems with this approach are less visible. New sales are five times more expensive than repeat sales, more in industrial firms. But the lack of repeat sales is less obvious. Firms operating at this stage of the information-evolutionary scale may not even account for sales based on new and repeat business, or track the time lag since clients' last purchases, or monitor customer satisfaction.

Customer-focused Information Management is both rare and valuable to customers, so it should presently constitute a source of competitive advantage to the firms that have evolved to this point. Firms that practice customer-focused information management continue to actively manage the flow of prospect-qualification-conversion information. However, these firms are different in two important ways: (1) information used in selling is framed from the customer's viewpoint; and (2) the firm systematically monitors customer satisfaction, retention, and recovery.

Customer-focused selling is the information-based identification of customer needs and presentation of solutions. It requires that the selling firm actively acquire information about the customer's product/service usage situation, analyze that situation from the viewpoint of customer benefits, and present potential solutions. This approach to selling is more than providing the customer with product information; it is actively consultative.

The customer-focused selling approach requires that:

- the selling firm develop an extensive database of product/service applications
- salespeople engage in significant field research to diagnose customer problems
- solutions are presented in terms of quantitatively documented benefits

Firms that have adopted a customer-focused sales information system also systematically monitor customer satisfaction, retention, and recovery. Customer satisfaction is a leading indicator of future sales performance. Satisfied customers tell others about the company; dissatisfied customers do the same, but even more actively. Even if a fairly high proportion of customers say they are satisfied, a firm can have more negative word-of-mouth than positive, because of a small but energetic group of dissatisfied customers. Thus it is important to monitor customer satisfaction and to pinpoint causes of dissatisfaction.

Customer retention and defection are also monitored in customer-focused firms. For example, one long-distance telephone company monitors the proportion of subscribers in each of its sales territories that switch to other carriers. If the switch rate exceeds a control level, local competition is examined and a counterattack launched.[3] Statistical models using the multiple regression or discriminant analysis techniques described later in this chapter can also be used to identify the types of customers likely to defect. This allows the firm to take preemptive action.

Specific customers can be recovered, even after they have decided to switch to a competitor. Customer recovery requires that information structures be developed that:

- inform the selling firm about the defection (or the plan to defect)
- provide solutions to the defectors' problems (or responses to competitive offers)

Further, this recovery system must be in place and ready to respond rapidly. The odds of service recovery decrease over time. So firms that are not actively soliciting customer complaints and watching for defectors, and do not have the potential to act swiftly when dissatisfaction or defection is identified, are more likely to lose firms to those that do.

Strategic Sales Information Management   places customer-focused selling in a long-term context. *Strategic selling* aligns the elements of the sales effort into a mutually reinforcing pattern. Firms that sell strategically:

- carefully identify their target markets
- develop products that can be adapted to meet the needs of individual customers within those markets
- integrate communications-and-selling efforts to communicate with those customers in terms of their solutions to their problems
- develop delivery and service systems that fit with those individualized solutions
- cultivate a sales force culture that supports the strategy of the firm

The identifying characteristic of a strategic selling organization is the *fit* among these elements: target markets, products, marketing communications, delivery and service, and sales force culture. The marketing elements are mutually reinforcing.

Achieving this level of fit among marketing elements requires a more complex sales information management system. This includes: (1) target market profiles with a battery of adaptive selling techniques appropriate to each segment; (2) an integration of sales and operations for flexible production; (3) integrated communications programs that orchestrate marketing and selling activities over time; (4) systematic cross-functional planning sessions to coordinate selling and service; and (5) feedback from salespeople and other customer-contact personnel, through employee attitude surveys and less formal mechanisms, to monitor the selling environment.

Advancing to a high level of sales information management is difficult. It requires designing systems to gather data and develop information on complex subjects, and then implementing these systems across a sales force that may not welcome the change. On the other hand, the difficulty inherent in this implies that the manager is finding a path that competitors are less likely to follow.

The Sales Information Value Chain

Information management requires collecting and adding value to data. This basic process, illustrated in Exhibit 16.2, fuels any selling system, whether it is sales-focused, customer-focused, or strategic. Although the content of the data is different for firms operating at different levels of selling, the dynamics of the process remain the same: data must be collected, assimilated, analyzed, interpreted, and disseminated.

Data Collection involves identifying specific types of data required and developing mechanisms to collect it. The data to be collected aligns with the focus of the firm, whether it is sales-focused, customer-focused, or strategic. Thus sales-focused firms must put in place systems to identify new prospects as well as internal record keeping that helps to qualify those most likely to purchase. Customer-focused firms require these systems, as well as systems to gather problem-related data from the customer's viewpoint.

Strategic selling organizations gather a wider variety of both internal and external data. For example, Searle Laboratories developed a special 800-number hotline to quickly absorb sales force feedback and special forms for conveying information on competitors.[4] The close alignment between organizational strategy and sales force culture in a strategic selling organization should lead to greater salesperson involvement in data-gathering.

Data is gathered from a variety of sources in a variety of formats. Data sources include people (such as salespeople and customers), published information (such as industry periodicals and competitor promotional materials), and electronic systems (such as Census data on the internet). Data formats range from informal (such as notes on conversations) to formal (such as the electronic Census data). Each format and source has advantages and disadvantages. Informal personal data may be of questionable reliability, but it is often more timely than formal published data. For example, the first indications that a competitor is planning a new product may come from a supplier's comment to a salesperson. Although the trade newspaper announcement may be more reliable, it may come too late for an effective countermeasure. Thus company executives rely more on the sales force than any other internal or external source for competitive intelligence.[5]

Although published data sources are low-cost and often readily available, they typically do not quite fit the problem at hand precisely and are sometimes out-of-date. For example, to compute the number of people in a geographic market segment we can use the *U.S. Census of Population,* but it is conducted only every 10 years, it takes at least a year for the first data to be available, and it is subject to frequent revision.

Exhibit **16.2** | SALES INFORMATION VALUE CHAIN

| Data Collection | Data Assimilation | Data Analysis | Data Interpretation | Information Dissemination |

A more up-to-date source is the "Survey of Buying Power," by *Sales & Marketing Management magazine* (S&MM). Each August it publishes its estimates of population by age groups, income, and retail sales by major categories for all major U.S. markets, states, cities, counties, and towns. It has been in existence for 60 years and it has tracked closely with the total estimate by the U.S. census. For example, the S&MM estimate for 1990 was 249.8 million persons. The final 1990 Census count was 248.7 million, which makes S&MM only 0.4% high.[6] When the S&MM data are used at the disaggregate level they are less accurate. Estimates at the state and regional levels are generally within $+/- 10\%$ for demographic data but are less accurate for economic variables such as the effective buying income and retail sales.[7] The S&MM data should be used along with other data.

A variety of other privately developed data sources are available. For example, Weight Watchers uses consumer-confidence indexes from the Conference Board and the University of Michigan to plan for leasing space for its 20,000 meetings per week. Ford Motor Company monitors traffic in dealer showrooms.[8] The Conference Board Survey of Consumer Expectations has an impressive history of predicting swings in the Gross Domestic Product.[9] Consumer attitudes toward the economic outlook are important because consumer expenditures account for two-thirds of the gross domestic product.

For business-to-business marketers, the *County Business Patterns,* published by the Census Bureau, provides data on the number of establishments, payroll, total employment, and the number of establishments by employment size. This data is provided by Standard Industrial Classification (SIC) by county and state. As explained in Appendix 16.1, this information can be downloaded directly from the Internet and incorporated directly into widely used spreadsheet software to evaluate business markets.

Subscription research bridges the primary and secondary categories. These data are collected by a research company and sold to marketers. Nielsen Marketing Research is familiar to marketers in the package goods industry as well as television networks. It sells national and regional projections of purchase and viewing behavior. Consumers in a panel of 40,000 persons use a hand-held scanner to record UPC-coded purchases. In this way manufacturers can track purchases by demographic categories. These purchase patterns are linked to media usage to estimate the effect of advertising and promotions.

The number of subscription sources for data are extensive. *American Demographics Magazine* publishes a directory of companies that sell marketing information. These companies sell demographic data including population and income estimates. The direct marketing companies sell lists and databases of persons who fit a specific profile. Some companies sell data for ethnic markets or international markets, whereas others focus on teenagers or college students.

In business-to-business marketing, companies such as American Business Lists will sell lists of businesses in SIC codes, giving information such as the owner, the address, and the phone number for 10 million businesses. These lists can be ordered on mailing labels, magnetic tape, PC diskettes, or cards.

Databases are combined with PC mapping software to help managers create territories. Using a mouse the manager can shift a city or county into a different territory and immediately see the impact on the new territory in terms of the number of people and potential sales. The computerized maps show highway and physical characteristics such as a lake or mountain that would make it impossible to have one salesperson serve two markets. Dictaphone used such a system with dramatic results. Productivity and morale increased while sales force turnover decreased because there was a more realistic link between territory potentials and quotas.[10]

The Conference Board, which is funded by industry, has a Consumer Research Center that continuously updates data on population, marriages, births, households, children, education, labor force, occupation, employment, earnings, income, expenditures, housing, retailing, advertising, prices, and production rates.[11] These are key variables used by forecasters.

Data Assimilation   involves assessing the quality of the data and then incorporating the data into a framework that allows for further processing and/or for interdepartmental use (that is, a traditional database). Bits of data can result in the commitment of substantial organizational resources. Thus the quality of the data is important. Data can be assessed in terms of timeliness, reliability, validity, clarity, and scope.[12]

These address the following questions:

- Is the data going to be received in time for appropriate action to be taken? (Timeliness)
- Is the data representative of the true population? (Reliability)
- Is the correct issue measured? (Validity)
- Is the data understandable? (Clarity)
- Does the data cover the whole situation at issue? (Scope)

Data Analysis   involves identifying patterns in the data that relate to a particular issue or outcome. Generally, managers who develop statistical models make better decisions than those who do not.[13] Although data analysis was left to professional researchers a generation ago, the widespread availability of personal computers and user-friendly statistical software (like SPSS, SAS, NCSS, and others) has made data analysis a powerful tool for sales managers.

The key to effective management is to develop an accurate mental model of how the competitive market works. Astute sales managers use data analysis tools to build such a model for themselves. These tools allow sales managers to develop and refine their models over time. In the process, their understanding of the factors that improve performance in their specific industry and company becomes clearer, and their decisions become more effective.

Among the types of analyses used in sales management are the following:

Graphical summaries: techniques for summarizing data graphically. Two commonly used graphical summaries are bar charts (such as the number of sales calls by customer type) and x-y plots (such as a plot of average monthly sales by years of salesperson experience).

Descriptive statistics: numerical summaries of the central tendency (for example, mean, median, and mode) or variation (for example, standard deviation, range, and interquartile range) in data. For example, a sales manager might examine the mean monthly sales per salesperson and the range in sales per salesperson.

Multiple regression: a statistical technique for estimating the impact of selected variables on some outcome. For example, sales management could use multiple regression to estimate the impact that (1) years of selling experience; (2) years with the company; (3) hours of training; and (4) personality have on sales by each individual salesperson. Multiple regression analysis provides an estimate of how much change in sales is a result of these independent variables, both collectively and individually.

Discriminant analysis: a statistical technique for classifying people or objects into categories. For example, a sales manager could use discriminant analysis on the sales database, drawing on key demographic and behavioral variables to predict those who will buy and those who will not buy. (The IRS reportedly uses discriminant analysis to predict tax evaders from legitimate taxpayers).

Factor analysis: a statistical technique for identifying underlying dimensions in a set of variables. This analysis tool is often used in questionnaire design, to determine which questions in a survey "go together" as part of a larger issue. A sales manager might use factor analysis to identify which sets of features customers consider part of the same package.

Cluster analysis: a statistical technique for grouping people or objects. A sales manager might use cluster analysis to identify market segments, so that presentations can be developed for the different clusters.

Data Interpretation is the process of inferring meaning from perceived patterns in the data. This is a critical judgment stage in adding value to the data. Whereas statistical techniques can help an astute sales manager build his/her judgments, less astute managers tend to accept statistics uncritically and fail to understand their full meaning.

Most statistical studies adhere closely to the "garbage in, garbage out" rule. The sales manager's participation in designing the analysis (if he/she does not actually conduct the research and analysis) will help assure its quality and relevance. In conducting these studies, the sales manager should be calibrating his/her mental model of how the company's marketplace works. Relegating this study design task entirely to staff researchers will not accomplish this goal. Participation in design also provides a perspective for interpretation of results.

In interpreting the results, understanding the logic of the marketplace is usually more important than the specific quantitative data. The manager should think through this logic in terms of the study. Surveys of industries often find that advertising is strongly related to sales, but the astute manager may be cautious in interpreting this finding. Because many firms use a percentage of sales approach to set advertising budgets, the reality may be that sales causes advertising, rather than the other way around.

Information Dissemination involves providing information (interpreted data) to appropriate individuals and departments in the organization and in allied organizations. There has been a major trend during the 1990s toward more open communication of information within and between organizations. The widespread use of personal computers, and increasing friendliness of analytical software, has tended to decentralize the entire information management and sharing process. There is evidence that this leads to more effective information use and decision making.

The test of research value is its use in making business decisions. Research conducted by Rohit Despande suggests that managers are more likely to use market research when they feel that they have greater control over marketing tasks.[14] Research by Christine Moorman found that market research is more likely to be shared and believed in organizations whose members are close-knit and mutually trusting.[15] An ability to use market research findings to create a shared strategic direction may be important to organizational performance.[16]

. . . .

SALES FORECASTS

The Need for a Sales Forecast

"BUSINESS STUDENTS BEWARE! If you hoped that the statistics course would be the last time you would ever have to think about statistics, you better sit down. In researching this paper I discovered that just about everyone in a typical business organization deals with statistics in the form of forecasting," wrote a student in a sales management report.[17]

The sales forecast is a critical part of the strategic planning process for all functions of the business. Exhibit 16.3 summarizes how the short-run sales forecast is used for marketing and operations/production strategies. The long-run sales forecast is used to plan new products, personnel needs, equipment changes, plant improvements, and capital and cash budgeting.

Although forecasting can be a complex and highly quantitative process, it reduces to a concept that is now familiar—understanding the needs of the customers. Forecasters refer to these needs as the capacity (C) of the market to absorb a product or service. The measurement of market capacity (C) can be reduced to three variables—the number (N) of people in the market segment, the proportion (P) of this group who use the product, and the rate *(R)* at which they use it. The formula for computing capacity is as follows:

$$C = N \times P \times R.$$

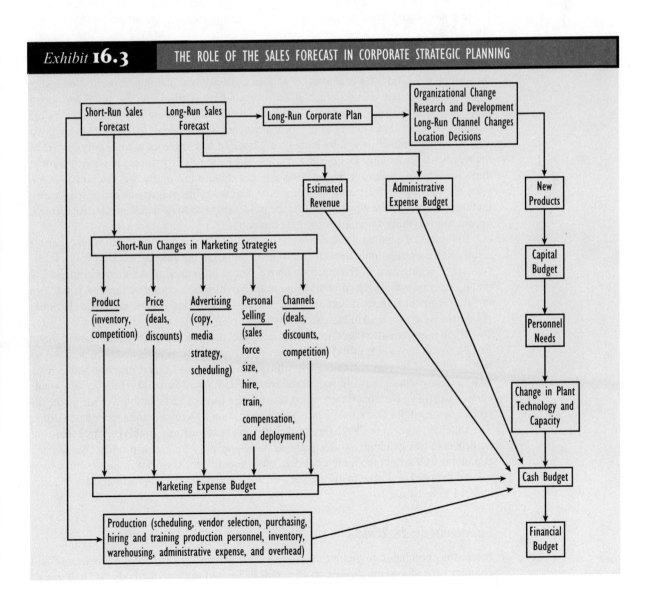

Exhibit **16.3** THE ROLE OF THE SALES FORECAST IN CORPORATE STRATEGIC PLANNING

If you wanted to compute the soft drink capacity of 50,000 fans at a football game and 20% bought about 2.25 soft drinks during a game, then the best estimate of capacity is 22,500 soft drinks.

Suppose that you wanted to know how much Coke and Pepsi to have in inventory. Now you need to know an additional variable, market share (S). A brand's market share will be the result of all of the marketing effort that has led to brand preference until the time of the game. To introduce the effect of the marketing effort (the marketing mix), we simply add S to the above equation, thus:

$$C = N \times P \times R \times S.$$

If Coke had a 60% share in this stadium (market segment), then the estimate of brand sales would be .60 × 22,500, or 13,500 Cokes. Selling strategies that attempt to increase P and R focus on industry demand and would be appropriate when the company is the innovator for a new product. Locating new *users* would increase P. Identifying new *uses* would increase R. Developing *brand preference* would increase S. Finding new users, new uses, and increasing brand preference are all part of sales force strategies.

This equation does not produce a forecast because it measures only one point in time, the Saturday game. If we were forecasting for each of the future games we would need to forecast N, P, R, and S for each date. *N* will vary according to the importance of the game. *P* will generally not change much if the mix of fans is the same for large and small turnouts. *S* will probably not change much in a few weeks because it is determined by the cumulative effect of marketing effort for many years. *R*, the rate of usage, could change as a result of the weather. It will be higher for a hot day and lower for a cold rainy day. Thus the weather forecast must be considered when estimating R. To estimate N we will want to know the attendance during the last few years that these teams met at this stadium and consider the ranking of the teams then and now. Considerable judgement is needed in estimating N. Although the equation makes the process appear to be mechanical, management experience is required to implement the equation.

To forecast the national soft drink sales at football games the general sales manager for a soft drink company must consider all football games in the country. This brings us to the concept of segmentation. The equation above should be applied to weather conditions and brand preferences for each football game in the country. The company forecast is the sum of these segment forecasts. Forecasts that are based on adding segments tend to be more valid because errors tend to be offset.

Brand maps are often used to link the concepts of needs, segments, and market share. People do not buy a soft drink. Instead *they buy a bundle of benefits* that they perceive as best meeting their needs. Exhibit 16.4 illustrates a perceived brand map for soft drinks. Two needs are shown in two-dimensional space. The vertical dimension reflects taste—tart versus sweet. The horizontal dimension conveys the level of carbonation. We see by the diameter of the circles that most people, segment B, want a sweet, medium carbonated drink. The smallest segment prefers a tart drink with lower carbonation. In this example there are no drinks in this quadrant, so this presents an opportunity for a new product. We see that Brand a is well within the preference area of segment A drinkers, but Brands b and c have missed the market. These maps are very useful for product development and for the creation of advertising.

Forecasting Methods

Forecasting combines qualitative and quantitative methods. While there are extensive and complex procedures, the discussion here will be limited to those methods that will gener-

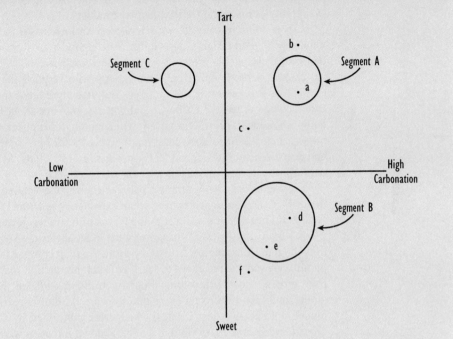

Exhibit 16.4   A BRAND MAP OF SOFT DRINKS

Note: The size of the circle reflects the number of persons in the segment. The small letters represent consumers' perception of the available brands.

ally be used by a sales manager.[18] We will examine judgment, time series, and causal modeling techniques.

Judgement Methods   All forecasting methods use some judgement, but some methods are largely judgement, including estimates by salespeople, case history analogies, expert opinions, Delphi, consensus opinions, surveys of users, and consumer intentions and confidence surveys.

Estimates by the salespeople are evaluated and modified as they are passed up through the levels of sales management. Two food wholesalers, Sexton and Biggers Brothers, rely mainly on their salespeople to do the short-run forecasts. Salespeople refer to historical territory data. Management makes the long-run forecasts and forecasts for special promotions, seasonal products, and new products. But even these management forecasts depend on customer surveys administered by salespeople. The free upward and downward flow of information creates a "buy-in" by the salespeople and management for the forecast.[19] When the individual forecasts are summed to form region, division, and corporate forecasts this is referred to as the *buildup approach*.

Sales estimates by salespeople can have limitations, so they should be part of a system that includes other forecasting methods. Salespeople tend to have a short time horizon, generally a 1-year maximum. They also tend to be optimistic, hate paper work, and they may be inclined to make an estimate that will give them a favorable quota for next year. To assure good estimates from the salespeople, forecasting must be made part of their job description and they should be rewarded for good forecasts.

Case history analogies simply compare new products with the growth curves of existing products. The resulting forecasts can be classified as fair to good after the initial three months, which are very difficult to forecast. The cost and development time depend on the availability of historical data for similar products.

Expert opinions can produce fair short-term forecasts if there are knowledgeable individuals with good insights, good judgement, a good track record, and few biases. Costs can be low if these people presently work for the company.

Delphi methods use a panel of experts who respond anonymously to estimates of events that will determine future sales. The procedure feeds the group results back to the experts who discuss the estimates and vote again. After about four iterations there is generally a consensus on when an event will occur and its impact on the forecast.[20] This technique develops fair to good long-range forecasts for new product development. The cost and development time depend on the availability of experts. Microcomputers and individual response devices speed this process and lower its cost.

Consensus opinion is simply a panel of informed executives or salespeople who know the market. This approach is used when expediency is critical. The quality of the forecast is doubtful because it is subject to the biases of the power structure of the organization.

A *survey of users* is often part of a business-to-business forecast. For example, Cummins Engine Company used a survey in the *buildup* component of its forecast. Salespeople interviewed each account to learn its truck production plans, its engine inventory, its back orders, and its marketing program. Cummins totaled these estimates by account, model, and month to reach an engine forecast. At the same time it used an econometric model to forecast industry sales, which were multiplied by Cummins' share to reach a *breakdown* forecast. The buildup and breakdown forecasts were then reconciled using executive judgement to create a final forecast. Cummins found that the buildup method, which was closer to the marketplace, was better for shorter periods whereas the breakdown method was more reliable for periods of six months or more.[21]

Consumer intentions and confidence surveys are important because consumer expenditures account for over 60% of the gross domestic product (GDP) in the United States. Consumers' concerns over unemployment or inflation are reflected quickly in GDP. The Conference Board's Consumer Confidence Index is used as a leading economic indicator by the U.S. Department of Commerce. Some industries respond very quickly to a lack of confidence in the economy. For example, men's clothes decline early in a recession and recover late in the upswing. It appears that dad can wait for a new outfit longer than anyone else in the family. The Conference Board began its survey in 1967 whereas the Survey Research Center at the University of Michigan began its consumer survey in 1946. Because of their aggregate nature these surveys are most appropriate when using the breakdown approach.

Time Series Analysis Time series analysis assumes that the patterns in a series of sales data will be repeated. Time series data can be reduced to four components— trend, seasonal, cycle, and random. A *trend* is a long-term component that remains constant across many years. The *seasonal* component has monthly patterns that are related to the weather, holidays, and others. Clothes, for example, will have two to five seasons. A *cycle* is a wave-like pattern that is repeated over many years. Some sales cycles are only a few years long whereas some business economic cycles are 20 years long. Cycles are difficult to estimate because the patterns do not repeat well. We will see this problem in an example below. *Random* components do not occur in any predictable pattern. A natural disaster, such as the worst flood in 100 years, will influence the sale of some products, but it cannot be forecasted. To understand time series analysis we will walk through an example.

Assume that you are a general sales manager for a pharmaceutical company that has a prescription product for upper respiratory illnesses. You are planning a call strategy for the salespeople who call on pediatricians and other specialists who see children. The liquid form in the 4-ounce size will be the focus of your strategy. You have asked for a forecast based on the number of prescriptions that have been written during a 10-year period so that you can forecast for the next two years. To establish the model the marketing analyst used data that were generated by a panel of 7000 physicians who created an extra copy of their prescriptions and supplied them to IMS, a pharmaceutical research firm. The analyst gave you the graphs shown in Exhibits 16.5 through 16.7. How can these graphs help you to understand what is going on in this market? How do you explain the trends, seasonal patterns, and cycles shown? Given the forecast, what strategies would you recommend to marketing management? How would these patterns affect your sales force strategies? How will this forecast affect other functions in the company? To answer some of these questions we will examine the patterns in each of these exhibits.

Exhibit 16.5 illustrates the first step in a time-series analysis, the smoothing of the data. There are various methods for smoothing data. Because he had 10 years of monthly data the analyst used a 12-month moving average approach, which uses the present month

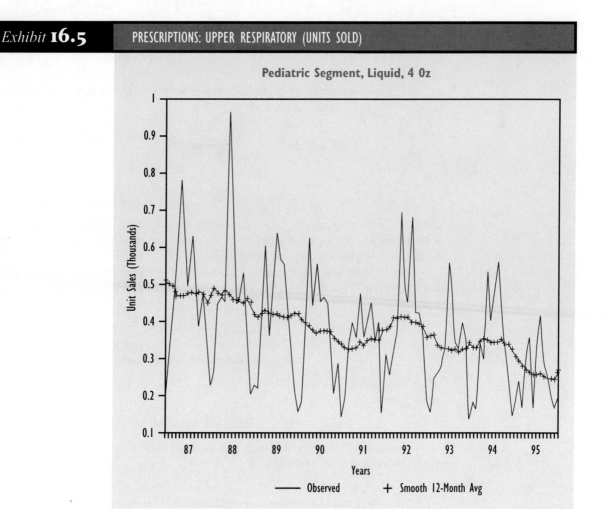

Exhibit **16.5**   PRESCRIPTIONS: UPPER RESPIRATORY (UNITS SOLD)

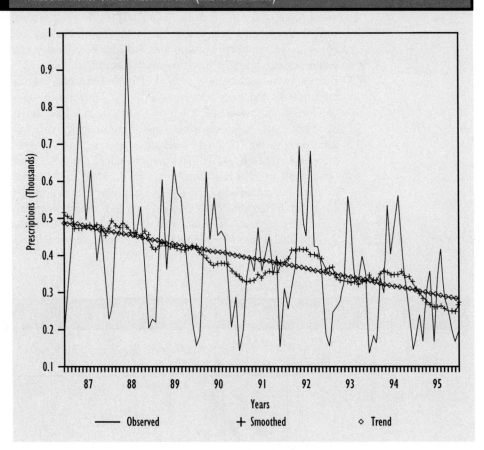

Exhibit 16.6   PRESCRIPTIONS: UPPER RESPIRATORY (TREND ANALYSIS)

and the 11 preceding months. Some forecasters use only a smoothing procedure to make a short-term forecast for a few years. Looking at this smoothed curve we note a downward trend, which is shown in the next exhibit.

A straight line, least-squares model was fitted to the smoothed data, yielding the downward trend line (T) in Exhibit 16.6. The shape of this curve is described by the following equation:

$$\text{Trend T} = a - b \times M,$$
where b is the slope of the line downward and
M is cumulative number of months.

A new product rate would have a curve that took on the following form for an upward sloping curve:

$$\text{Sales} = a + b \times M.$$

If the adoption rate were very high sales could be increasing exponentially, so the trend model would appear as follows:

$$\text{Sales} = a + B \times M^e,$$
where e is an exponent that determines the rate that the curve bends upward.

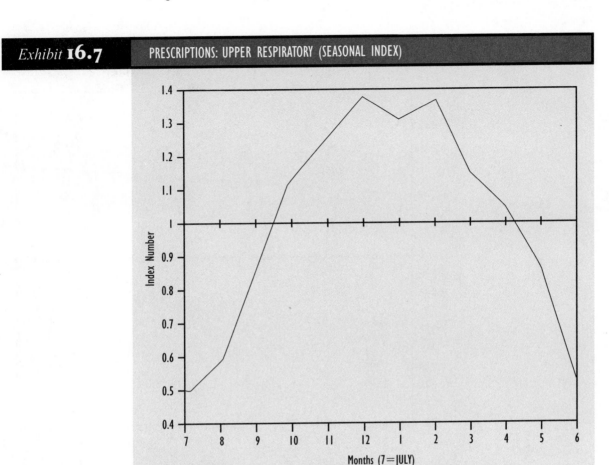

Exhibit 16.7 — PRESCRIPTIONS: UPPER RESPIRATORY (SEASONAL INDEX)

A long-term trend line could reflect the familiar S-shaped curve that describes the product life cycle. A variety of models exist for estimating the underlying trend,[22] but the importance of Exhibit 16.8 is understanding the forces that created this downward trend. Why would prescriptions for upper respiratory illnesses (including colds and flu) be on a downward trend? Possible explanations focus on the age of the population. During the period from 1971 to 1981 the baby boom was moving into the teens, who get fewer colds than younger children. Other explanations include the high cost of doctor visits, the availability of more self medication products in the drug stores, and a population that takes better care of itself by exercising and eating well. Can you think of additional explanations? What are the implications of this trend for marketing and sales management?

It seems reasonable to assume that there will be a seasonal component to a product for respiratory illnesses. This assumption is confirmed by the seasonal index that is plotted in Exhibit 16.9. It will be noted in month 7 (July) that prescriptions for this illness were 0.5, or half the average for the year. December (#12) and February (#2) were the high points with an index over 1.3. But why is there a dip in January? Perhaps the public spent so much on Christmas gifts that they could not afford to go to the doctor. There could also be a problem with the collection of the data. Perhaps the physicians failed to send the forms during the holiday.

The seasonal pattern in Exhibit 16.9 requires a product and sales strategy to offset the summer lows. New products could be developed or acquired that have highs in the sum-

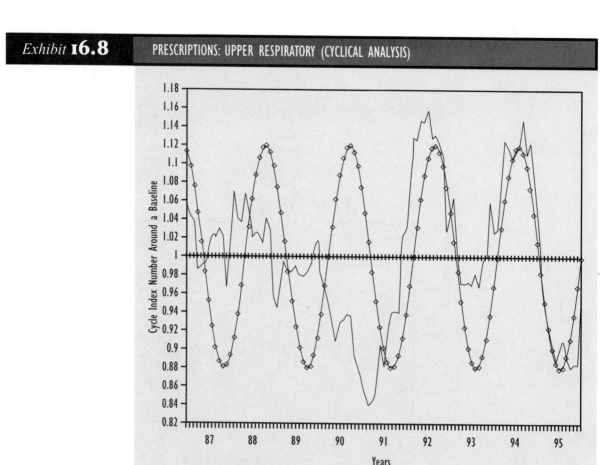

Exhibit 16.8 **PRESCRIPTIONS: UPPER RESPIRATORY (CYCLICAL ANALYSIS)**

mer and lows in the winter, such as a suntan product. To level sales and production the company could use aggressive summer sales programs to have drug stores stock up on cold remedies, but delay billing until the winter months. One such program used college students as temporary summer salespeople, thereby giving students an opportunity to experience sales and keeping the company selling costs low.

Analysts in the pharmaceutical industry hypothesized that there is a three-year flu cycle. They thought that every third year will be a large flu year. The cycle estimates in Exhibit 16.8 do not support the analysts' hypothesis. The period from 1991 to 1995 reveals a two-year cycle with a high on alternate years. The period from 1987 to 1991 has a very irregular pattern of such low amplitude that it can hardly be called a cycle. The pattern during this period, however, is a two-year one.

Although the cycle is difficult to estimate, it is important in the pharmaceutical industry because many of the products are biological which have a long production cycle and a short shelf life. Thus if the market were underestimated it would not be possible to have a new production run to catch the cycle peak. If the market were overestimated, the short shelf life of 2 years or less would prevent carrying the product over to the next big cycle.

A forecast of the prescriptions written by the 7,000 physicians in this sample would be computed each month using the following equation:

$$Rx = (T \times S \times C),$$

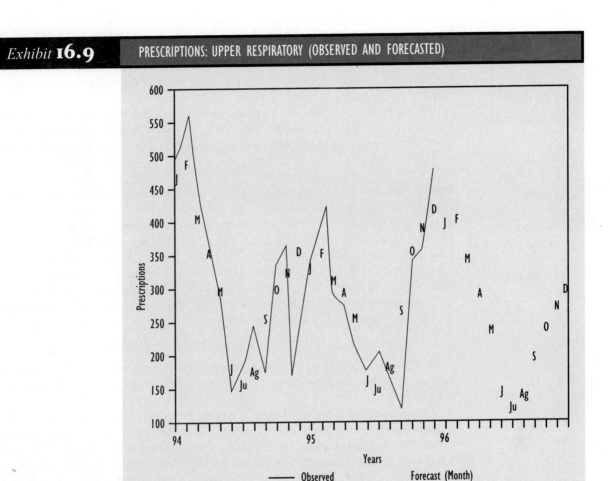

Exhibit 16.9   PRESCRIPTIONS: UPPER RESPIRATORY (OBSERVED AND FORECASTED)

which simply multiplies the value of the trend projected for that month times the seasonal and cycle indices for that month. If there is reason to think that an irregular random effect will occur, executive judgement can be added. Exhibit 16.9 graphs the forecast for the sample data. If the 7,000 physicians represent the 140,000 physicians in the United States, then a U.S. forecast for prescriptions for this segment can be computed simply by multiplying the sample forecasts by 20.

To compute your company forecast you must *break down* this industry forecast into a company forecast by multiplying the industry forecast by the market share (S). Your estimate of share will be based on your knowledge of your company marketing strategies for the period and your estimates of those of competition. The company forecast is then broken down further into regional, district, and territory sales quotas. Sales quotas are generally slightly higher than the forecasted figures to provide salespeople with incentives.

Forecasting a new product is difficult because there are no historical patterns to model. One approach for a new ethical drug started with physicians' perceptions of the drug along attributes such as effectiveness, the range of illnesses that the Food and Drug Administration approved for the drug, and physician prescribing rates for drugs in this category. A repeat purchase diffusion model was used when sales were a function of the drug's marketing effort versus competitive effort and word-of-mouth information among physicians.

Initially, sales were forecasted without sales data, but the forecasts were refined as sales data became available, which improved the forecast.[23]

Some new product models are designed to eliminate the need for a test market. These models simulate the buyer adoption process which includes the trial and repeat-purchase rates.[24]

A prelaunch forecast for a new automobile was developed using the rate of active information search by prospects, dealer visits, word-of-mouth communication, magazine reviews, and production constraints. Consumer clinics provided test and control group measures for the model.[25]

Causal Models   Some models attempt to establish a cause and effect relationship between independent variables and sales. The simpler models weight independent variables according to judgement or statistical estimates. *Sales & Marketing Management Magazine* uses judgement weights to create a buying power index (BPI) for major markets, cities, and counties in the United States. This index gives effective buying income (EBI) the largest weight, 0.5, because it assumes that people must have money in order to buy. Retail sales (RS) in the geographic area are weighted 0.3 because they represent channels of distribution in the area and the success of these retailers. The number of people (N) in the area are weighted 0.2. The model is then as follows:

$$BPI = 0.5 \times EBI + 0.3 \times RS + 0.2 \times N$$

These weights could vary by region, so forecasters will want to use multiple regression to compute weights for their regions. The BPI is used frequently as one input for building territory quotas.

Multiple regression and the Survey of Buying Power data in *Sales & Marketing Management* can be used to identify the importance of market segments, in this case age categories. The number of persons in each of four age categories in 30 counties in Minnesota were used as independent variables and the dependent variable was the dollar sales in eating or drinking establishments and auto expenditures. Eating and drinking place sales included establishments selling prepared foods and drinks for consumption on the premises or takeout, institutional food services, fast-food restaurants, and pizzerias. Auto sales included automobile sales, auto supplies, boat dealers, recreational vehicles, and motorcycles.[26] Using ordinary least squares we see that the annual expenditures for each age category were as follows:

Product Category	By Age Category Annual Expenditures Per Person			
	18–24	25–34	35–49	50+
Eating/Drinking	$2,341	$2,174	$919	Not Significant
Auto	3,527	4,851	2,144	Not Significant

It comes as no surprise that the youngest category, 18–24, spent the most per year in eating and drinking restaurants, takeouts, and institutional facilities, such as at colleges. The 35–49 group was in the family stage that would eat at home, hence the per capita expenditure was only $919. The 50 and above group presented such a mixed pattern that the coefficient was not significant. The 25–35 category spent the most on autos, the 18–24 category was second, and the 35–49 group was third. Why do you think this 35–49 group was the lowest of these three categories? The oldest category again was not significant. This category requires further study using variables other than age to understand what is driving it.

Using *S&MM Buying Power Data* for the same 30 counties and multiple regression, a causal model was built using four independent variables—population (head count), median age, number of households, and effective buying income (EBI). The dependent variable was one of the following product categories: food (for home consumption), eating/drinking, general merchandise (dry goods, apparel, housewares, hardware), furniture and appliances (floor covering, drapery, bedding, lamps, household appliances), auto, and drugs (prescriptions, proprietary drugs, and nonprescription medicines). The statistically significant coefficients are as follows:

Product Category	Population	Median Age	No. of Households	EBI
Food	1.29			
Eating/Drinking	.67		−.63	.03
General Merchandise	10.97		−13.87	−.27
Furniture/Appliances		−.97		.02
Auto				.07
Drugs	.93			−.02

We see that median age is not a good variable for eating/drinking and auto sales, so we must focus on the two specific age categories that were important earlier, which were the 18–24 and 25–34 year old groups. Because the number of households and EBI were significant in the previous regressions, these will be included in this model. The significant variables are as follows:

Product Category	Households	EBI	18–24	25–34
Eating/Drinking		.04	1.55	
Autos		.09		8.07

In this model households drop out of the significant range. We see that effective buying income is significant for both categories. The 18–24 category is significant for the eating/drinking category and the 25–34 age group is significant for auto sales. This finding has considerable *face validity,* which means that this is what you would expect. The younger people eat in fast food restaurants and the 25–34 group are into cars.

This last regression could be helpful in forecasting sales and establishing territories. It shows how autos are more sensitive to EBI than eating/drinking. Economists refer to this as *income elasticity,* which is like *price elasticity,* but the denominator is the percentage change in income instead of price. The sales manager for products in the auto category will want to track economic factors such as unemployment levels and changes in income. Sales managers in both categories will want accurate head counts in these two age groups.

(A technical note. If you want to compare coefficients across different models you will need to standardize the coefficients by dividing by the standard error of the coefficient.)

These regression models used a single equation. Many product categories are influenced by a system of variables that must be modeled with a system of equations. Such a system is known as an econometric model.

Econometric Modeling   The communication highway will combine the telephone, television, and computers, to provide homes and businesses with data sets, entertainment, interactive capability, news, information, and services not presently invented. How does one forecast for such an event? Measuring this capacity will require a system of models, each one of which will have individual modules or equations. One way to begin would be to examine the model that was used by AT&T. This model appears in graphic form in Exhibit 16.10. It consists of an environment model (the economy, regulation, and wage levels), a corporate model (pricing, demand, finance, capital market, and production), a management model (finance strategies and the mix of labor and equipment), and finally the output module that shows the rate of return on investment and the earnings per share. But this model is now out of date because of the Supreme Court's decision to break up AT&T. There are now regional Bell companies, three major long distance suppliers, AT&T, Sprint, and MCI, and smaller wholesalers of long distance services. Thus a module for competitive phone services must be added to the environment model. The market becomes more difficult to estimate when we see that IBM is getting into the telecommunications business, AT&T bought NCR, a computer company, and then spun it off as Lucent Technologies, and a regional Bell company struck a deal with a cable entertainment company. Measuring the impact of competition will be extremely difficult in the dynamic fields of communications and computers. (What other difficulties do you anticipate in measuring the market capacity in these industries?)

Models are also used to determine what makes a salesperson productive. One sales response model used factors such as the company marketing strategy, the sales force organization, characteristics of the field sales manager, characteristics of the salesperson, competition, and customer characteristics.[27]

A Combination of Methods   The judgment, time series, and causal techniques are summarized in Exhibit 16.11 according to their accuracy, costs, development time, data requirements, and applications. The sales manager must still use judgement when forecasting. In practice a combination of methods should be used to improve accuracy and different methods may be appropriate over the product life cycle.[28] For example, Howmedica, a division of Pfizer Hospital Products Group, uses simulation to forecast new products and simple moving averages to forecast demand for declining products.[29] The Corporate Marketing Research Department at Coca-Cola also uses various methods. It forecasts 137 time series data for soft drink unit volume using a 10-year database. It uses six bivariate regression models. Forecasts for six consecutive years have been within 3% of actual sales, averaging a 1% error.[30]

Many companies reconcile buildup and breakdown methods, as we saw in the Cummins Engine example. In the consumer field the Rubbermaid Home Products Division of Rubbermaid uses forecasts from Group Product Managers for the buildup method. Members of the operating committee independently formulate their forecasts. These two forecasts are then reconciled.[31]

Instead of asking salespeople to forecast the final sales for a product line, some companies require them to estimate where these sales are at the several points in the selling

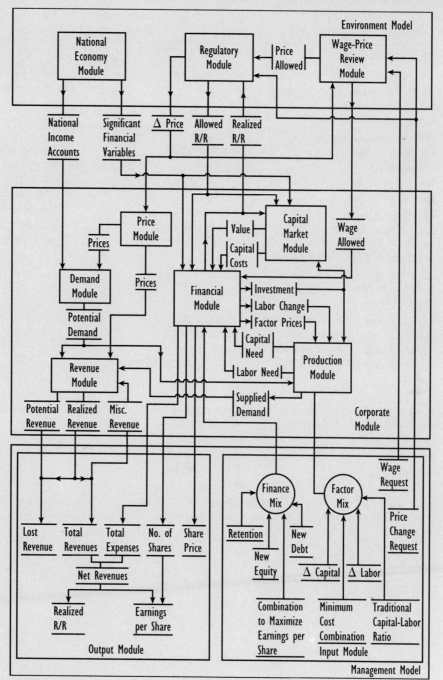

Exhibit **16.10**   AT&T FORECASTING MODEL FOR CORPORATE POLICY ANALYSIS

B. E. Davis, G. J. Caccappolo, and M. A. Chaudry, An Econometric Planning Model for American Telephone and Telegraph Company. Copyright 1973, The American Telephone and Telegraph Company. Reprinted with permission from *The Bell Journal of Economics*, Spring 1973.

Exhibit 16.11		**A COMPARISON OF FORECASTING TECHNIQUES**			
Technique	**Accuracy**	**Costs**	**Development Time**	**Data Required**	**Illustrative Applications**
Judgmental					
Case History/Analogy: Compare new product with growth of similar existing products.	Fair to good after initial three months.	Variable, depends on data availability.	At least one month.	Several years of history for similar products.	New products and profit forecast.
Expert Opinion: Estimates by knowledgeable persons who have good records for judgment and insight.	Fair for short term.	Minimal, if current staff is used.	Several weeks.	Experts give several future scenarios.	New product and margin forecast.
Delphi: Panel of experts are surveyed anonymously and results are fed back so experts may revise opinions in the light of new information.	Fair to good in medium and long term; fair to good in identifying turning points.	Panel members' time is the major cost. Cooperation is required.	Two months.	Coordinator develops, edits, and reissues questionnaires.	Long-range product development.
Consensus Opinion: Panel of key executives or the sales force makes estimates.	Good for short-range planning. Subject to organizational biases and quota effects; poor to fair identifying turning points.	Major cost is time of executives and sales force.	One month or less.	Two sets of reports over time.	New product sales and margin forecasts.
Survey of Users: Users' estimates of needs, especially in industrial marketing.	Good for periods less than one year.	Varies according to complexity and size of the market. Using the sales force may not be the least expensive.	Three months.	Two sets of reports over time.	New product sales and margin forecasts.

Sources: John C. Chambers, Satinder K. Mullick, and Donald D. Smith (1974). *An Executive's Guide to Forecasting,* New York: Wiley Interscience. George C. Michael, (1979). *Sales Forecasting,* Chicago: American Marketing Association, Monograph Series #10; Vithala R. Rao and James E. Cox, Jr., (1978). *Sales Forecasting Methods: Recent Developments,* Cambridge, Mass.: Marketing Science Institute, Report No. 78-119.

| Exhibit 16.11 | A COMPARISON OF FORECASTING TECHNIQUES—CONTINUED |

Technique	Accuracy	Costs	Development Time	Data Required	Illustrative Applications
Learning Curves: Developed in the aircraft industry to forecast technological development and estimate future production costs. The learning curve is a logarithmic function that reflects the fact that when the cumulative number of units produced doubles, the cumulative average costs and the unit costs are reduced by a constant learning percentage. The learning rate may change over the life cycle of the product.	Very good forecasting short-, intermediate-, and long-term production costs.	Inexpensive, using manual techniques or log-log graph paper.	One day.	Production costs two points in time and cumulative units produced.	Forecasting new product production costs; competitive pricing decisions.

Causal

Technique	Accuracy	Costs	Development Time	Data Required	Illustrative Applications
Regression: An equation that relates sales to independent predictor variables such as advertising effort, number of sales calls, product quality, etc. Leading indicators may be used in regression equations.	Good to very good for periods up to two years; very good in identifying turning points.	Less than $100 if data is unavailable and relationships known.	Depends on knowledge of relationships.	At least two years of monthly data.	Forecasts of sales by product class, forecast margin.
Consumer Intentions and Confidence Surveys: Measure intentions regarding durable purchases and the public's opinion about economic conditions.	Better for aggregate events, such as GNP, than disaggregates such as product purchases.	Low if secondary sources are used.	At least several weeks if surveys are conducted.	Primary or secondary opinion data. Surveys are conducted by U. of Mich., Survey Res. Center, Sindlinger Corp., and the Conference Board.	Sales forecasts of product classes.

Time Series

Technique	Accuracy	Costs	Development Time	Data Required	Illustrative Applications
Trend Fitting: Trend line is fitted to historical data for projection to the future.	Very good for periods less than one year. Good for longer periods; poor in identifying turning points.	Costs depend on data availability.	One day if data available.	Five years if annual data.	New product forecasts.

continued

Exhibit 16.11	A COMPARISON OF FORECASTING TECHNIQUES—CONTINUED

Technique	Accuracy	Costs	Development Time	Data Required	Illustrative Applications
Moving Average: Data are averaged for a fixed number of months, dropping the oldest month as the new month is added to smooth the series and identify seasons.	Good for one year forecasts; poor in identifying turning points.	Inexpensive if computer program available.	One day.	At least two years of monthly data.	Inventory control for standard items and financial projections.
Exponential Smoothing: A smoothing procedure where more recent data points are given more weight. Adaptive control techniques use iterative procedures to determine weights.	Very good in the short term, poor for longer projections; poor in identifying turning points.	Inexpensive if computer available.	One day.	At least two years of monthly data.	Inventory control for standard products and financial projections.
Box-Jenkins: A mathematical technique that enables the computer to select the model that best fits the time series data.	Excellent for three months, poor to good for longer periods; fair in identifying turning points.	Low, if computer is available. High expertise required.	One day.	At least 50 historical data points.	Production and inventory control financial projections.
Econometric: A system of interdependent regression equations that describe some sales or profit activity.	Good to excellent for short-, medium-, and long-term forecasts; excellent for identifying turning points.	Expensive. High expertise required.	At least two months.	At least two years of monthly data.	Prediction of market potential, company or division.
Input-Output Models: A matrix of industries or departments showing the flow of inputs required for certain outputs.	Good intermediate and long-range forecasts for aggregated data, especially commodities. Fair in identifying turning points.	Very expensive, $100,000 or more. High expertise required.	At least six months.	15 years of data in considerable detail.	Forecast sales for division or company.
Brand Switching Models: These models use patterns of past brand switching and brand shares at equilibrium.	Users report highly accurate. The models predict but do not explain brand behavior.	The costs and developmental time are not available because the most widely used model, the Hendry model, is proprietary.	Consumer panel purchase data.		Market share, competitive analysis, and optimal marketing expenditures for frequently purchased consumer brands.
Attribute Models: Various models are used to relate buyers' perceptions of product attributes to brand choice.	Limited accuracy in predicting brand behavior. These models help to explain brand behavior better than switching models.	Moderately expensive and time consuming because survey or laboratory methods are needed.			Product developments; promotional strategy.

Sources: John C. Chambers, Satinder K. Mullick, and Donald D. Smith (1974). *An Executive's Guide to Forecasting,* New York: Wiley Interscience. George C. Michael, (1979). *Sales Forecasting,* Chicago: American Marketing Association, Monograph Series #10; Vithala R. Rao and James E. Cox, Jr., (1978). *Sales Forecasting Methods: Recent Developments,* Cambridge, Mass.: Marketing Science Institute, Report No. 78-119.

process. For example, a company that sells computer software requires estimates at the stages of qualified prospects, prospects who have received proposals, and prospects who are at the closing stage.[32] Attaching probabilities to each of these stages produces an expected sales volume at that point in time. It also provides a diagnostic for salespeople who may have difficulty moving to the later stage in the selling process.

The Dangers and Politics of Forecasting

Forecasting is associated with both dangers and politics. Companies are now suing forecasters when the product does not meet the forecasted numbers.[33] There can be great pressure on the forecaster when the forecast will affect the stock price or financing plans, both internal and external. The most common ways for influencing the forecast are as follows: management requests adjustments in revenue and cost projections, management provides "appropriate" estimates and requests forecasts to support these estimates, qualitative estimates are used instead of appropriate quantitative ones, and departments withhold critical information or provide misleading information.[34]

Developing Territories

Territories are formed by *breakdown* and *buildup* methods. Both methods require judgement and analytical skills.

The *breakdown* method begins with an estimate of the company's market potential and an estimate of the average productivity of a salesperson. The number of salespeople needed is computed by dividing the potential by the productivity. For example, if the market potential is $50 million and the average salesperson produces $1 million per year, there should be 50 salespeople in the sales force, plus managers and staff. Although this method is simple it suffers from the use of averages, which ignore the fact that some accounts are more difficult to sell than others and some accounts require more travel time. Like the breakdown method in forecasting sales, the breakdown method for territory formation is often part of a system of methods that are reconciled to form territories.

The buildup method consists of five steps, as follows:

1. Select the smallest market unit for which market potential data are available. This unit could be a state, a trading area, counties, cities, zip codes, Standard Industrial Classifications, or a specific account.
2. Estimate the market potential for each unit.
3. Estimate the workload required to tap this potential. The workload can be expressed in terms of hours or calls. The estimates are made by the salespeople and the managers. The workload will differ according to brand loyalty, competitive advantages, the newness of the product or salesperson, promotional support, and the desired level of service. Compute the workload (hours or calls) for each unit. For example, if a unit requires 2 calls per month, that would be 24 calls per year.
4. Build up to the total number of calls needed by the company by adding the calls required for each unit.
5. Compute the total number of salespeople needed by dividing the total calls needed by the average calls per salesperson. If the total calls needed are 250,000 and the average salesperson makes 2000 calls per year, the company needs 125 salespeople.

The buildup method is generally better because it estimates for smaller units and errors tend to be offsetting, but it still suffers from using averages, such as the average number of calls per salesperson. A better approach is to combine the breakdown and buildup methods using the best judgment of the salespeople and the managers. Personal computers and mapping software make this possible. The computer will have a database of market potential by geographic units. The manager and the salespeople sit together at the computer with a map on the screen. Using the computer mouse they can point and click on a geographic unit, such as a city. Relevant data for that city will be in the data bank, so the manager can immediately see the impact of adding that city to a territory. For a pharmaceutical company the number of physicians by specialty and their prescribing rates for specific products would appear. By pointing and pressing on geographic units with the computer mouse a territory can be built. The computer screen shows mountains, lakes, and highways that could affect efficient territory coverage. The district sales manager would review the possible territories with a regional manager before making the assignment final. This approach to territory building involves the salespeople and links their quotas to market potential, all of which improves sales force morale.

Case 16.1 THE SIERRA HOTEL

The Sierra Hotel is an upscale, small hotel, located in California near two large universities. It asks you to provide a time-series analysis of its occupancy rates, the occupancy rate for other hotels in its market, its average total revenue per day, and its average daily revenue per customer. (See Exhibit 16.12 for data.) Based on your analysis what strategies do you recommend?

Exhibit 16.12 THE SIERRA HOTEL

Month/Year	Ave. Daily Occupancy (SH)	Ave. Daily Occupancy (OC)	Ave. TR/Day (SH)	Ave. Daily Revenue per Customer (SH)
January-94	50%	55%	$ 3,428.00	$ 86.00
February-94	65%	70%	$ 4,876.00	$ 94.00
March-94	75%	75%	$ 5,530.00	$ 92.00
April-94	84%	82%	$ 6,289.00	$ 94.00
May-94	74%	59%	$ 6,036.00	$ 103.00
June-94	74%	79%	$ 5,447.00	$ 92.00
July-94	57%	63%	$ 3,696.00	$ 81.00
August-94	73%	73%	$ 5,110.00	$ 88.00
September-94	73%	72%	$ 5,913.00	$ 101.00
October-94	81%	80%	$ 7,436.00	$ 115.00
November-94	78%	81%	$ 7,098.00	$ 114.00
December-94	57%	46%	$ 4,806.00	$ 105.00
January-95	68%	50%	$ 5,386.00	$ 99.00
February-95	75%	60%	$ 5,970.00	$ 100.00
March-95	78%	66%	$ 6,365.00	$ 102.00
April-95	90%	68%	$ 7,920.00	$ 110.00
May-95	88%	67%	$ 8,029.00	$ 114.00
June-95	83%	65%	$ 7,237.00	$ 110.00
July-95	67%	62%	$ 6,189.00	$ 115.00
August-95	71%	64%	$ 6,698.00	$ 118.00
September-95	83%	82%	$ 8,398.00	$ 126.00
October-95	82%	82%	$ 8,640.00	$ 132.00
November-95	73%	71%	$ 7,638.00	$ 131.00
December-95	50%	52%	$ 4,804.00	$ 121.00

(SH)-Siena Hotel
(OC)-Orange County

Case **16.2**   HARTLINE INDUSTRIAL PRODUCTS

Meggan Hartline had worked as an operations manager for a Little Rock, Arkansas wholesaler for five years before she decided to venture out on her own. As operations manager, one of her responsibilities was assuring the rapid and safe movement of products. She was also responsible for procuring the supplies and equipment needed to handle those products.

One of her problems was wood pallets. Wholesalers and manufacturers use wood pallets in handling shipments. Products arrived by train and truck at the wholesale warehouse, where they were broken down into smaller quantities. These smaller batches were covered in shrink-wrap and moved around the warehouse by fork-lift on wood pallets.

Meggan purchased pallets directly from manufacturers in the region. Sometimes shipments arrived later than expected. The pallets would also break occasionally during handling of product loads, causing product damage. Although this was a problem for Meggan as operations manager, she began to see it as a business opportunity, as well.

Late in 1997 she left the wholesale firm and formed Hartline Industrial Products. During her five years in wholesaling, she had formed friendships with other wholesale operations managers. In addition to meeting regularly with other wholesale operations managers in the Little Rock area, she had become active in the state wholesalers association. Through her work with the state association, she had formed contacts throughout the state. She felt those contacts, and her MBA, would serve as a base for her company.

Hartline Industrial Products was created to manufacture and ship wood pallets to wholesalers and distributors. Meggan wanted to focus initially on the Arkansas market, because of her contact network. Based on backing from a bank, and her family, she initially employed 10 persons in the business, somewhat smaller than the average pallet manufacturer, which employed 15 persons.

According to Census of Manufacturer statistics, the industry average shipments per employee in pallet manufacturing were about $73,300. Meggan figured she would need to increase her production and sales

to at least $733,000. Although she was president, she also intended to plan and direct sales for the small firm.

Based on figures she obtained from the *Benchmark Input-Accounts for the U.S. Economy* at the local library, she found that 71% of wood pallet shipments were purchased by wholesalers, with the remaining sales fragmented across a variety of manufacturing and service firms. These included manufacturers of refrigeration and heating equipment (2.2%), aircraft and missile equipment (1.7%), motor vehicle parts manufacturers (1.6%), freight forwarders (1.6%), canned fruit and vegetable manufacturers (1.3%), motor freight transportation and warehousing firms (1.2%), metal can manufacturers (1.1%), and paperboard mills (1.1%). Each of the remaining industries using wood pallets consumed less than 1% of the supply.

Given this data, her spreadsheet software, and her Internet account, Meggan began to assemble a sales plan for her new firm.

1. Using the instructions in Appendix 16-1 to access SIC-related data:
   (a) Develop a table for all Arkansas counties (as row headings) and the SIC codes for the industries described above (as column headings). Complete the table (Table 1) using number of employees per SIC per county.
   (b) Link Table 1 to a second table (Table 2), in which each cell is a percent of the table total employment times the total Hartline Industrial Products sales target.
   (c) Using the results of Table 2, create a list of Arkansas counties, in order of targeted sales.
2. If wood pallet shipments totaled $33.1 million in Arkansas, what percent of shipments (market share) would Meggan need to attain?
3. Conduct a search on the Internet to identify information pertaining to the wood pallet industry (SIC 2448). Provide a summary of your findings as well as a copy of the most pertinent materials.
4. Assume that Meggan not only met her goal, but that her sales have tripled. As a result, she has decided to hire three salespeople to cover the state. Allocate sales territories for the three, using a county map of Arkansas with the data in Table 2. Explain your rationale for the territory divisions.

··

SUMMARY

The sales forecast is a critical input for all of the short-run functional strategic plans and the long-run capital plans of a company. The concept behind measuring a market's capacity to absorb a product or service is simple: understand the market's needs. Actual measurement of these needs is difficult. The most common methods depend heavily on judgement by informed individuals, but self serving biases occur when the judges are in the company. Time series analysis is based on the assumption that patterns in sales will be repeated. Sales often contain trends, seasonal patterns, cycles, and difficult to predict random components. Causal models attempt to identify independent variables that seem to result in sales. The causal relationship is generally inferred from statistical methods rather than field experiments because of the high cost of these experiments. Multiple regression, single-equation models are often used. More complicated systems require econometric models which use a system of equations to forecast. Sophisticated researchers use more than one technique, often reconciling the buildup and breakdown approaches. To implement these models requires information, which is now recognized as an important factor of production and as an asset. Primary, secondary, and subscription data sources must be evaluated carefully because the vast amount of information available can make the purchase of subscription information expensive and information inundation can generate more heat than light.

Given all of the difficulties of forecasting, perhaps the best advice is from Peter Drucker, who said, "The best way to predict the future is to invent it."[35]

ASSIGNMENTS/DISCUSSION QUESTIONS

1. You have been assigned as the sales management representative to the product committee for the prescription product that was analyzed in Exhibits 16.5 through 16.9. Write a two-page executive brief on the product's current position and your recommended strategy.

2. Interview a local company regarding its sales forecasting procedure. What recommendations would you make for improvement?

3. Use data from the *Sales & Marketing Management Survey of Buying Power* and multiple regression to create a model of the retail sales of eating and drinking establishments for counties in your state. PC spreadsheets such as Lotus 1-2-3 and Excel have convenient least-squares regression routines.

4. As the new vice president for marketing at a mid-sized machine tool manufacturer, you have been told by the CEO that your first task is to dramatically improve the company's relationship with its buyers. After reviewing the company information systems, it seems clear that past focus has been on selling activities, with little regard for customer needs. Although the company has extensive data relating to sales potential and salesperson performance, there is little if any data about customer needs. What actions could you take to move the firm up to the next level of information management?

5. Identify the statistical techniques or tools that you would be most likely to use to: (a) identify market segments; (b) differentiate between viable and nonviable prospects; (c) determine the effect that number of salespeople, amount of promotional advertising, and number of mailings have on company sales; (d) group questions on the sales job application questionnaire in terms of common underlying themes.

6. As sales manager for an industrial pump manufacturer, what information would you want salespeople to gather and communicate back to you? Design a form for the salespeople to collect and submit this information.

7. Describe step-by-step how the information gathered by the salespeople in question #6 should be processed in a firm's sales information value chain.

8. The CEO of your firm, which sells industrial lighting fixtures to architects and builders throughout the Northeastern United States, has complained that the sales forecasts prepared in the past, based on polling salespeople, have been biased downward. He suspects that the salespeople simply want to understate goals so they can make quota. But he is concerned that production won't be sufficient to meet demand if he uses the forecasts based on the salespeople. So he has turned to you, the new VP-Sales, for advice on how to forecast sales. What do you recommend?

Appendix 16.1 USING COUNTY BUSINESS PATTERNS ON THE INTERNET

County Business Patterns (CBP) is an annual data series that includes data on state and county-level employment, payrolls, total number of establishments, and number of establishments by employment size class (e.g., number of firms with 0–19 employees, 20–99 employees, and so on). This data is reported by industry, as reported in the *Standard Industrial Classification Manual: 1987*. The data is obtained from various survey programs that the Bureau of Census conducts with business.

In order to access and use the County Business Patterns data, one must understand the SIC Code system for classifying industry, the FIPS Code system for classifying geographic places (like states and counties), and specific procedures for downloading the County Business Patterns data from the Internet.

The SIC Code System

The Standard Industrial Classification (SIC) code classifies firms by primary product or service produced, within the major categories of agricultural services, forestry, and fishing; mining; construction; manufacturing; transportation and public utilities; wholesale trade; retail trade; services; and unclassified establishments. Establishments within these major categories are classified using a hierarchical system of two-, three-, and four-digit subcategories. For example, one classification set within the manufacturing category includes:

   24 Lumber and wood products
     244 Wood containers
       2448 Wood pallets and skids

Each two-digit category includes all three-digit subcategories. Thus 24 includes 241 (logging), 242 (sawmills and planing), 243 (millwork, plywood, and structural members), 244 (wood containers), etc. Similarly, each three-digit category includes all the four-digit (and more detailed) subcategories. Thus, 244 includes 2441 (nailed wood boxes), 2448 (wood pallets and skids), 2449 (wood containers, not elsewhere classified).

Although not particularly exciting, the SIC Code system serves industrial marketers as a reference system that is widely used across diverse governmental and private databases. This classification system has occasionally changed as new types of industries developed. The 1987 system is scheduled to be replaced by the North American Industry Classification System (NAICS), which will be used by the U.S., Canada, and Mexico under the North American Free Trade Agreement. The first NAICS-based system was scheduled to go into effect with data for 1997.

The FIPS Code System

Another classification system, important both to industrial and consumer marketers, is the FIPS Code System. The FIPS Codes classifies states based on two-digit codes (for example, Arkansas is 05) and counties based on five-digit codes (for example, Ashley County in Arkansas is 05003, where the first two digits signify the state and the last three the specific county within the state).

The increasing power and sophistication of personal computer software allows an increasing number of sales managers to map their own data using FIPS Codes. Using software like BusinessMAP, a program that retailed for about $100 in 1997, a sales manager could link spreadsheet data to a map. This could be used to display geographically-based data visually.

Downloading CBP Data

In order to download County Business Patterns data from the internet, one must:

- go to the Census Bureau home page at http://www.census.gov,
- select "A–Z,"
- select "C" and then "County Business Patterns" within the C section,
- select "Download County, State, and U.S. to use with your favorite spreadsheet or database software" from the "County Business Patterns" page,
- select the appropriate data from the "CBP Download Page."

Tabular data from the "CBP Download Page" can be downloaded as text files and converted in a popular spreadsheet. For example, "1994" data (the latest available in 1997) can be opened in Excel (using the "all files" setting), and opened into an Excel spreadsheet (using delimited, comma, and general default settings). Column headings can be added using information from the "Record Layout for County Files" information, also available on the CBP Download Page. Row headings can be obtained from the "Industry Definitions" file available through the same Download page.

ENDNOTES

1. AT&T Information Policy, *What it Means for You,* a brochure, n.d.
2. *Ibid.*
3. John Deighton, Don Peppers, and Martha Rogers, Consumer Transaction Databases: Present Status and Prospects, in *The Marketing Information Revolution,* Robert C. Blattberg, Rashi Glazer, and John D.C. Little, editors (1994), Boston: Harvard Business School Press.
4. Conference Board, *Competitive Intelligence,* 1988.
5. *Ibid.*
6. Demographics, *Sales & Marketing Management Magazine,* May 1991, p. 42.
7. W.E. Patton, III, How Accurate are the "Survey of Buying Power" Projections? in *Enhancing Knowledge Development in Marketing,* Robert P. Leone and V. Kumar, editors, (1992), Chicago: Proceedings: American Marketing Association, pp. 415–422.
8. Paul Magnusson, Need an Economic Forecast? Maybe the I Ching Can Help, *Business Week,* September 13, 1993, p. 38.
9. The Consumer as Forecaster, Conference Board Promotional material, 1997.
10. Bob Attansio, How PC-Based Sales Quotas Boost Productivity, Morale, *Sales & Marketing Management,* September, 1991, pp. 148–150.
11. A special service for marketing executives from The Conference Board, promotional literature, 1997.
12. Adapted from Francis Joseph Aguilar, 1967. *Scanning the Business Environment,* New York: Macmillan Company.
13. J. Edward Russo and Paul J.H. Schoemaker (1990), *Decision Traps: The Ten Barriers to Brilliant Decision-Making and How to Overcome Them,* New York: Fireside Book.
14. Rohit Deshpande, A Comparison of Factors Affecting Use of Marketing Information in Consumer and Industrial Firms, *Journal of Marketing Research,* February 24(1) 1987, pp. 114–119.
15. Christine Moorman, Organizational Market Information Processes: Cultural Antecedents and New Product Outcomes, *Journal of Market Research,* 32, August, 1995, pp. 318–325.
16. Christine Moorman and James M. Sinkula, Market Information Processing and Organizational Learning, *Journal of Marketing,* 58, January, (1995), pp. 35–54.
17. Debbie Cassidy, University of North Carolina student, 1983, in a paper for a course in sales management.
18. For a nontechnical review of forecasting methods for managers see Spyros Makridakis and Steven C. Wheelwright, editors, (1987), *The Handbook of Forecasting: A Manager's Guide,* 2nd. ed., John Wiley.

19. Cassidy, 1983.
20. Haiyang Chen and Michael Y. Hu, How Managers Can Forecast Sales of New Products, *Journal of Business Forecasting,* 10(2), Summer, 1991, pp. 26–28.
21. David L. Hurwood, E.S. Grossman, and Earl L. Bailey, *Sales Forecasting,* Report No. 730, New York: The Conference Board, 1978, pp. 110–112.
22. For a discussion of smoothing and trend models see Everette S. Gardner, Jr., Smoothing Methods for Short-Term Planning and Control, Makridakis and Wheelwright, pp. 173–195. For a discussion of the ARIMA and Box-Jenkins models see David J. Pack, A Practical Overview of ARIMA Models for Time Series Forecasting, pp. 196–218.
23. Ambar G. Rao and Masataka Yamada, Forecasting with a Repeat Purchase Diffusion Model, *Management Science,* 34(6), June, 1988, pp. 734–752.
24. William S. Sachs, Forecasting New Product Outcomes in Packaged Goods, *Journal of Business Forecasting,* 6(4), Winter, 1987/1988, pp. 20–23.
25. Glen L. Urban, John R. Hauser, and John H. Roberts, Prelaunch Forecasting of New Automobiles, *Management Science,* 36(4), April, 1990, pp. 401–421.
26. Definition of Terms in the Survey of Buying Power, *Sales & Marketing Management, 1993 Survey of Buying Power,* August 30, 1993, pp. A16–A17. Data for Minnesota may be found on C88.
27. Adrian B. Ryans and Charles B. Weinberg, Territory Sales Response Models: Stability over Time, *Journal of Marketing Research,* 24(2), May, 1987, pp. 229–233.
28. Essam Mahmoud, Gillian Rice, and Naresh Malhotra, Emerging Issues in Sales Forecasting and Decision Support Systems, *Journal of the Academy of Marketing Science,* Fall, 1988, pp. 47–61.
29. Terry Anderson, Demand Forecasting at Howmedica, *Journal of Business Forecasting,* 10(2), Summer, 1991, pp. 2–4.
30. N. Carroll Mohn, Forecasting Sales with Trend Models—Coca-Cola's Experience, *Journal of Business Forecasting,* 8(3), Fall, 1989, pp. 6–8.
31. Richard B. Barrett and David J. Kitska, Forecasting System at Rubbermaid, *Journal of Business Forecasting,* 6(1), Spring, 1987, pp. 7–9.
32. Confidential correspondence to G. David Hughes, April, 1997.
33. Craig S. Galbraith and Gregory B. Merrill, The Politics of Forecasting, *California Management Review,* 38(2), Winter, 1996, pp. 29–43.
34. *Ibid.*
35. Peter Drucker (1985), *Innovation and Entrepreneurship: Practice and Principles,* New York: Harper & Row.

17

ORGANIZING AND INNOVATING
THE SELLING PROCESS

LEARNING GOALS

1. To understand the traditional organizational designs for managing the selling effort
2. To understand the technological, competitive, and other changes that have led to changes in the sales organization
3. To learn ways that the selling effort is being redesigned
4. To learn the limitations of some of the new designs

The adoption of a process view of business is a revolutionary change that is occurring among managers.[1] This change toward viewing the business as a system of interrelated activities has driven the reengineering and quality improvement movements. It has caused managers to shift their emphasis from static hierarchical structure to the dynamics of workflow.

At the heart of this change is the process: a "structured, measured set of activities designed to produce a specific output."[2] Companies have multiple processes that interlink to form a value-production system. Even large and complex companies can be defined in terms of 20 or fewer major processes, suggests Thomas Davenport, a leading researcher in the field.[3] For example, IBM has identified 18 processes in its organization, Xerox has 14, and Dow Chemical has 9.[4]

Whereas hierarchical structures provide information about formal reporting relationships, processes add the measurable dynamics focusing on cost, time, product/service quality, and customer satisfaction. These elements are measurable and can be improved through radical redesign or incremental change. To be successful, a customer viewpoint must pervade these process improvements.[5]

Selling is a key process that has received little investment in most organizations.[6] This represents an opportunity for most organizations and for their sales managers. The opportunity is to identify the selling process within one's organization, to redesign the selling organization and its processes toward more effective and efficient performance, and to incrementally improve the new selling process continuously over time.

The issue of continuous quality improvement is addressed in Chapter 12. This chapter addresses the organization and innovation of the selling process. The chapter begins with

351

an overview of traditional sales force designs from the perspective of formal hierarchical structures. The environmental forces that are driving changes in these structures—and leading to the more dynamic process view of sales organizations—are then described. Finally, new emerging organizational designs—and reemerging older designs—are examined.

....

TRADITIONAL SALES FORCE ORGANIZATIONAL DESIGNS

The traditional sales force designs are illustrated in Exhibit 17.1. Horizontal arrangements enable specialization, whereas vertical ones add capacity to the organization. In this exhibit horizontal positions on the chart enable geographic and product specialization. Vertical levels with divisions, regions, and districts, add capacity for managing. Adding a staff function for training takes this function from managers, which allows them to specialize in managing.

Two critical questions must be answered when designing the sales organization: What is the appropriate span of control? How many layers of management should be used? Until recently the ideal span of control was often stated as five to seven persons per manager.

| Exhibit **17.1** | VARIOUS SALES FORCE DESIGNS |

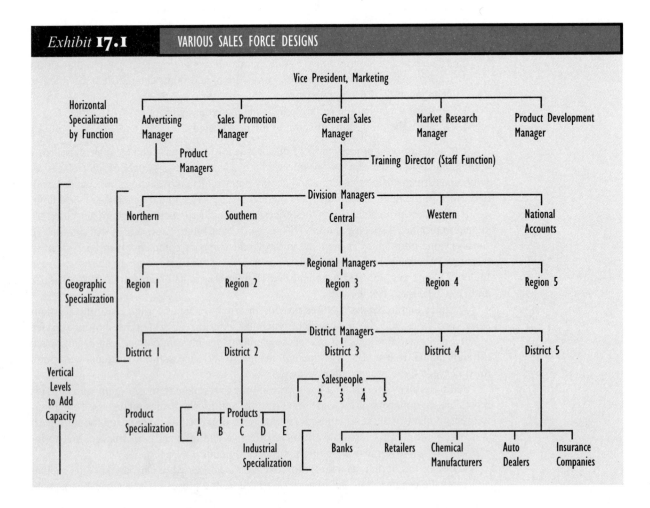

This will vary, of course, according to the experience of the sales force. An inexperienced sales force with high turnover will require fewer salespeople per manager. In contrast, an experienced salesperson will require less supervision, so 10 salespeople could be supervised by each manager. Today managers in many companies use e-mail and voice mail to communicate with salespeople, so that the span of control is 15 or more salespeople per manager.

Adding layers of management can increase the capacity of the sales force, but it can distance management from the marketplace. Many companies, such as Campbell Soup, have eliminated layers of management so that top management is closer to the customer. Shorter communication lines also make the salesperson feel like an important part of the company.

The tradeoffs between span of control and number of organizational levels are illustrated in Exhibit 17.2. For example, assume that there are 64 people in the sales force. There could be two levels with eight salespeople per manager or three levels with four salespeople per manager. *What conditions would determine choosing one design over the other? Which design would you use in a growing company? Which design would you want as a salesperson?*

Account management is becoming an important assignment for a young salesperson. A salesperson with 2 years of sales experience in the grocery products industry will typically be assigned a small, local chain of stores, with an annual quota of $2 million. Large accounts will be assigned to experienced salespeople. For instance, Xerox will assign an experienced salesperson to one or two universities. Account executives are accountable for the profitable development of these accounts.

A study of the sales organization charts for many companies illustrates how the product line and corporate strategies will determine the sales force organizational design. For example, Wallace Systems sells customized business forms and supplies, which requires close supervision of its sales force. It has many layers of management, as follows:

Vice President Corporate Sales
Geographic Division Vice Presidents
Regional Managers
District Managers
Salespeople[7]

Exhibit **17.2**	TRADEOFFS BETWEEN SPAN OF CONTROL AND ORGANIZATIONAL LEVELS FOR SALES FORCES OF VARIOUS SIZES

	Total Number of Salespeople at Each Organizational Level				
Span of Control	One Level	Two Levels	Three Levels	Four Levels	Five Levels
4	4	16	64	256	1,024
5	5	25	125	625	3,125
6	6	36	216	1,296	7,776
7	7	49	343	2,401	16,807
8	8	64	512	4,096	32,768
9	9	81	729	6,561	59,049
10	10	100	1,000	10,000	100,000

A paint company that sells through paint dealers has a flatter organization, as follows:

Vice President Sales & Marketing
    Corporate Dealer Relations Manager
        Product Information Center Supervisor
        Promotion and Merchandising Manager
        Director Color Marketing
        Corporate Interior Designer
    Corporate Sales Manager
        Order Processing Manager
        Corporate Sales Administrator
    Corporate Marketing Manager[8]

A company that sells swimming pools has a geographic design, as follows:

Vice President, Sales
    Vice President Sales—Western Region
    Regional Manager, Northeast Region
    Regional Manager, Southeastern Region
    Export Sales Manager[9]

Bethlehem Steel Corporation has a general sales manager for automotive sales, reflecting the importance of this industry.[10] Nestle, an international food company, has two major strategic business groups that include major product categories, along with five zones reflecting continents.[11] After a major reengineering of the marketing and sales organization a grocery products company developed the following team design:

Executive Vice President, Major Product Category
    Vice President, Customer Development Group
        Team Vice Presidents
            Team Leaders, Geographic
                Account Executives
                Business Development Managers
                Logistics Manager
            Team Leaders, Major Account[12]

This design reflects the need for closer relationships with the grocery chains.

When the general manager has decided on the number of account executives, the span of control, and the layers of management, the next decision is whether to have territories.

Assigning territories to individual salespeople is done for very good reasons. Sales territories result in better coverage of the market through better planning, efficient call patterns, better understanding of the customer, improved customer service, clear responsibility, and a clearer matching of salespeople to market potential. Furthermore, territories link the selling effort to sales promotion and the total marketing strategy. They also permit the control of expenses.

Although the reasons for territories are important, some conditions make them inappropriate. A small company may find that the benefits are less than the cost of managing territories. A rapidly growing company may not have sufficient salespeople to cover new territories, but this lack of territories permits salespeople to concentrate on the lucrative accounts until the company develops broad distribution, when it switches to penetration coverage with territories. Some services, such as insurance, stocks, and mutual funds, are sold on the basis of social contacts, so territories are not appropriate.

Sales force organizations may be the last function in the company to feel the pressure to improve productivity. In the past there were few alternatives to traditional sales organizations, but domestic and global competition, maturing product lines, new technology, and very sophisticated channels of distribution have led to the need to rethink the role of the sales force. These environmental forces and companies' responses will be examined. Finally, some of the limitations of the new approaches will be considered.

FORCES OF CHANGE IN THE ORGANIZATION AND PROCESS OF SELLING

Major forces affecting organizations—as identified by the International Association for Product Development, an association of high-technology manufacturers—align along the following dichotomies:

FROM	TO
Top down/command and control	Horizontal/customer driven
Information processing	Knowledge creation
Compartmentalized knowledge	Shared knowledge
Functions retain power	Core process team has power
Function "owns" skills	Core competencies "supply" skills
Dominant function leads	Leader represents team
Narrow *results* focus (sub-optimization)	Broad *process* focus (optimization)
Rewards are within chimneys (i.e., functions)	Rewards are based on overall performance of the organization
Slow/bureaucratic	Quick/empowered

Reading down the *TO* column we can see how these changes have resulted in the following changes in the sales force: customer driven, team designs rather than individuals, rewards based on group performance, and quick responses to market changes.

The *information revolution* has shattered traditional, hierarchical structures. Reduced costs of storing and processing information and increased capabilities for distributing information to the field have enabled many organizations to radically redesign their selling efforts. Information can now be shared by persons throughout the organization, and informed decisions made by empowered employees in the field.

New technology, such as telecommunications and the personal computer, provide low-cost alternatives to personal sales calls. A trained telephone salesperson can make 5000 to 7500 contacts per year.[13] These can be persons who are fully responsible for the account or who serve on a team with an outside salesperson. Dell Computers runs a $2 billion business using only telephone salespeople. Air Products and Chemicals has a telemarketing program that generates $35 million in sales per year with sales costs 65% lower than with a sales force.[14] Signal Thread, a privately owned manufacturer and distributor of commercial sewing threads, had nine salespeople, but they could not cover all of the accounts, especially the small ones. It added six trained phone salespeople and a toll-free number for orders. Signal rapidly reached a small market that it had not reached before.[15] Computerized geographic mapping routines can do more than design territories, as noted above. Windshields of America, an auto glass repair company, created a mapping service that shows insurance companies the districts and policyholder zip code locations where claims are occurring. This value-added service established a partnering relationship with key buyers.[16] I.M.S. International, recently acquired by Dunn & Bradstreet, dominates the pharmaceutical market research field. Its sophisticated communications links include 16 data processing centers, public networks, software to allow pharmaceutical salespeople to access data from their homes, and a satellite link is planned.[17]

A second major force is the ***maturing of industries,*** which means that products are becoming commodities that are bought on price. This situation dramatically reduces the need for a sales force. For example, manufacturers of office equipment face dwindling margins per unit (under $100) and increasing costs per sales call ($250). To remain profitable, alternative selling methods must be developed. The salesperson can be eliminated completely by teleprospecting, telequalifying, telephone ordering, or by the buyer's computer contacting the seller's computer directly.

When PPG Industries' Fiber Glass Reinforcement Products division faced a maturing market, it took a customer-driven strategy to meet this challenge. The sales force was developed into a creative, proactive department that involved the research and development department in identifying customers' present and future needs.[18] Thus selling was turned into creating opportunities, not taking orders.

There is a subtle difference between being market driven and being customer driven. A ***market-driven*** strategy tries to find a common set of needs among many customers. A ***customer-driven strategy*** focuses on the unique needs of a single customer. The former is a ***market segmentation*** strategy whereas the latter is a ***partnering*** strategy. Thus in many markets we are witnessing the demise of the popular concept of market segmentation.

The ***speed of market change,*** a third major force in the environment, requires that market decisions be made closer to the marketplace. Campbell Soup created 21 mostly autonomous regional operations, with each accountable for local market planning and spending. This regionalization of critical decisions increased revenues and profits.[19]

Reduction in the number of suppliers per buyer, a fourth major force, has key implications for obtaining and retaining customers. Because firms buy from fewer sources, with which they maintain long-term relationships, new customer acquisition opportunities are rarer. Buyers are under increasing pressure to create a competitive advantage for their firm through strategic purchasing.[20] This has led to increasingly sophisticated information requirements—which translates into the need for more sophisticated selling.

The reduction in the number of suppliers per buyer also increases the importance of existing customers. Buyers want a salesperson who understands their needs and helps them to achieve their goals, including minimizing order costs. Wal-Mart stores have vendors tied into the Wal-Mart computer so the vendor can track sales and plan production runs. In addition, ". . . the customer is demanding more attention just when many companies—including such stalwarts as Apple Computer, IBM, Merck, and Procter & Gamble—are ***reducing*** their sales forces."[21]

Closer customer relationships, a fifth major force acting on selling organizations, has led to greater customer access to suppliers and greater commitment to helping customers.[22] Many functions from organizations increasingly interact with customers, with broader responsibility for meeting their needs. This means that many more positions need the customer-contact skills traditionally associated with sales. It also means that many more employees affect the initial purchase and the potential for a repurchase.

Changing federal regulations, a sixth major force, have continued to restructure entire industries to become more customer-responsive. For example, changing regulations are affecting the role of salespeople in the pharmaceutical industry. Pharmaceutical firms spend about 20% of their revenue on sales and marketing. The concern for managing the growing costs of healthcare has raised criticisms from physicians and the government.[23] Pharmaceutical firms are searching for alternative ways of communicating with physicians, such as a physician television network.

The Conference Board summarized the forces driving a need to reinvent the sales organization as follows: "Customers demand more for less. Markets are more fragmented. Constrained resources must serve increasingly demanding customers."[24] Reinventing the selling process involves roles for the sales force in developing marketing strategy, strategies for the sales force to create competitive advantage by adding value to products and services, quick and effective responses to new market opportunities, and working with the operations/production functions for Total Quality Management.[25] *How have companies responded to these environmental forces?*

INNOVATING THE SELLING PROCESS

Process innovation means redesigning organizational work flows in order to improve performance. Increasingly radical process innovations have occurred among businesses in recent years as a result of advances in information technology. These changes usually involve improvements in both efficiency and effectiveness. For example, IBM Credit used process innovation to cut the time needed to prepare a quote for buying or leasing a mainframe computer from seven days to 1, while increasing the number of quotes prepared by a factor of ten.[26]

Instead of the term reengineering, The Alexander Group, a sales consulting firm, uses the term reinventing the sales force. It states that, ". . . while re-engineering often focuses on taking costs out of the sales and services process, reinventing means making the right investment in the sales function at the right point in its life cycle."[27] This approach requires putting a cost on a sales call, so the salesperson can decide if the call is worth the profit generated, and it holds the account executive responsible for the profit of the account.

Successful innovation of the selling process begins with top-management support. For the innovation to be successful, this support must also pervade the entire selling organization—from sales managers, to salespeople, to staff assistants. Fostering this level of support requires visible commitment from top managers and sales managers, involvement of all levels in the planning process, and training in process design and implementation.[28]

For example, Hallmark Cards focuses on business process redesign (BPR), in which teams share ideas, skills, and experiences across department and division boundaries. Participants enjoy learning new skills and "thinking outside their box." This approach has had many benefits, including lowering production costs and reducing the development of a new product from several years to a matter of months.[29]

Innovating the selling process of a firm focuses on three major issues: (1) identification of the key process elements; (2) evaluation of technology available for improving the process; and (3) reformulation of the process to achieve a competitive advantage, by increasing customer-perceived value or reducing internal operating costs for the supplier firm.

Process Identification

Processes cut across traditional functions. They involve activities that are linked to achieve a specific outcome. Thomas Davenport identifies three processes that relate the business directly to the customer: marketing, selling, and service.[30] He notes that "in some organizations, these activities are best considered as one interlinked process; in others they can reasonably be broken down into three or more related processes."[31]

The decision of whether to link the marketing-selling-service functions into one process, or to treat them as separate processes, depends on the extent to which the elements of each function require information and action from the other functions. Even when the marketing, selling, and service functions are treated as separate processes, they must be connected through specific information flows.

Davenport identifies the order management process, shown in Exhibit 17.3, as the "heart of sales processes."[32] It begins with the customer's placement of an order through to the receipt of payment by the firm. Although it may occur quickly, it involves complex co-ordination of materials and information across several traditional functions. Because of the cross-functional nature of order management, there are many opportunities for the customer order to "fall through the cracks" of the organization. These potential gaps in the processes are key points for process redesign.

Application of Technology

The reason for the recent focus on process innovation among firms is that advances in information technology have enabled them—and their competitors—to improve efficiency and effectiveness. Firms that do not take advantage of these capabilities to rationalize their selling processes soon find themselves outdistanced—or acquired—by more competitive rivals.

These technological "enablers of innovation" in the selling process include systems that:[33]

- Track and manage prospects and order processing.
- Automate tasks traditionally performed by salespeople.
- Integrate direct mail, telemarketing, and sales actions.
- Allow salespeople to communicate information from the field.
- Allow customers to enter and check their own orders.
- Increase product information and service available to customers.
- Match products and services to customer needs.
- Exchange data between firms.
- Configure products to customer specifications, then price and ship them.
- Predict demand and continuously restock.
- Transfer order information needed across functions.
- Provide customer, product, and production data.
- Integrate voice, graphics, and data.
- Empower customer-contact workers with information and action capabilities.

Exhibit **17.3**	THE ORDER MANAGEMENT PROCESS

Source: Thomas H. Davenport (1993), *Process Innovation: Reengineering Work through Information Technology*, Boston: Harvard Business School Press, p. 248.

Competitive Advantage

In the rush to technologically enabled innovation of the selling process, it is important to maintain a focus on the object of the effort: competitive advantage. Generally, this is achieved in one of two ways: increasing revenue and/or decreasing costs. Process innovation increases revenue by offering unique product-service configurations that are valued by customers and difficult for competitors to imitate. Innovation of the selling process can also decrease the firm's operating costs, with a corresponding improvement in profit margins. Strategies for achieving sales-focused competitive advantage are shown in Exhibit 17.4.

Selling Process Improvements that Increase Revenue   The central issue in improving the selling process to increase revenue is customer-perceived value. The selling process can deliver value by:

- Reminding the customer of the need to place an order
- Providing information—available when and where the customer requires—that reduces the financial or performance risks inherent in placing an order
- Identifying opportunities for the customer to use the firm's products and services to improve performance or reduce costs

| *Exhibit* **17.4** | MULTIPLE PATHS TO COMPETITIVE ADVANTAGE IN SALES |

Approach	Objectives	Tactics
Downsizing	• Radical costs reduction	• Employee termination • Outsourcing
Process innovation (reengineering)	• Quantum improvements in efficiency and effectiveness	• Mapping of sales process • Identification of critical points and weaknesses • Redesign of sales process
Sales force automation	• Reduce costs • Reduce sales cycle time (i.e., time to complete sale)	• Computer support for individual salespeople and sales managers (word processing, multimedia presentation, etc.) • Integrate sales team via intranet, groupware, and enterprise software • Automate selling alliances via electronic data interchanges (EDI) and extranets
Integrated (database) marketing	• Reduce cost of selling • Increase responsiveness to individual customers • Link sales to other marketing communications activities	• Sorting prospects based on potential • Substitution of telemarketing and/or direct mail for personal contacts with selected prospects • Careful linkage between timing and content of direct mail, telemarketing, and personal sales calls • Systematic management of long-term prospect and customer follow-up
Re-organization of sales	• Closer alignment of sales with customer needs	• Team selling • Industry accounts • National and international account management • Agency and distribution selling • Shared sales forces
Alliance formation	• Reposition firm vis-à-vis buyers and competitors	• Buyer-seller integration • Sole-sourcing • Customer participation in marketing planning • Horizontal selling alliances

- Increasing the product and service options available to a customer
- Providing product and service options that are not available elsewhere
- Reducing the time and effort required to place an order
- Allowing the customer to order anytime, anywhere
- Assuring that the order is processed according to the customer's specifications
- Increasing orders-per-customer through information-based cross-selling
- Providing rapid delivery of the product/service
- Providing followup service when and where the customer requires
- Maintaining contact with the customer to assure him/her of continued service

Selling Process Improvements that Reduce Costs   If two firms are equally valued by customers, but one has lower operating costs that are difficult for competitors to imitate, then the latter firm has higher margins—and a competitive advantage. The selling process can be redesigned to reduce operating costs by:

- Enabling customers to place orders (such as through catalogs, the Internet)
- Substituting low-cost outbound customer contact methods (telemarketing) for higher-cost methods (direct sales)
- Increasing sales-per-contact (decreasing selling costs/sales revenue) through more precise prospect identification and more complete prospect information
- Applying customer contact and service based on the requirements of the prospect or account
- Reducing errors in order acquisition and processing
- Decreasing the communications costs involved in order processing
- Enabling customers to provide self-service through customer-friendly support manuals, FAX-on-demand or Internet service information
- Reducing service costs through on-line service

It is important to maintain a customer focus throughout selling process innovation efforts. This can be attained by involving customers in the planning process, reviewing proposed changes with customers through interviews or focus groups, developing and conducting simulations of the new process to identify unintended negative consequences for customers, and conducting test runs of the process with a group of "leading edge" customers (similar to a "beta test" of new software).

Customer focus should be maintained on both the value-creation and cost-reduction elements of the proposed new selling process. The customer defines value, not the sales manager. Many times the manager's perception of what customers want is inaccurate, because of lack of adequate customer-based research.[34] This can include believing that customers value elements of the selling process that they do not, as well as missing elements that customers truly value.

On the other hand, it is important to assure that cost-reduction elements do not reduce customer-perceived value. Some efforts to increase internal operating efficiency can benefit both the customer and the supplier firm. Other efforts can reduce internal costs without affecting the customer directly. But it is critical that cost-reducing moves be examined carefully in terms of unintended erosion of customer-perceived quality, either through individual changes or through the collective impact of several changes in the selling process.

IBM provides an example of the process issues in sales force organization. In 1992, it established specialized fields which included the following activities: consultant, information technology architect, project manager, client executive, opportunity manager, marketing/sales, and information systems availability manager. Each of these fields had at least three levels of expertise. This design was very difficult to communicate to the sales force. In the spring of 1993, Louis V. Gerstner became president of IBM and said that the organization of the sales force was the major reason for IBM's problems. He planned to reverse the concept of a generalist salesperson. By the summer of 1993, he had changed his mind and decided not to change the sales force because the customers told him that they wanted to see one face from IBM.[36] The difficulty in having a generalized sales force is that no single person can fully understand all of the high-tech products and applications that IBM sells. Most companies faced with this problem use team selling.

Selling process innovations have had substantial impact on traditional sales force roles. The role of the district sales manager is questioned in some organizations as team selling takes over and the sales management hierarchy breaks down. Functions formerly performed by the manager are now performed by outside specialists. For example, recruiting and selection are being done by specialist companies such as Gallup and Target Market Systems. Training is done by consulting firms that specialize in industries. Communication functions are being replaced by voice mail, e-mail, and teleconferencing.

The district sales manager title has been dropped in some companies, such as Procter & Gamble. Former district managers are now team leaders for major accounts. One major grocery products firm looked at the IBM problems and decided to make changes before market conditions forced it to make them. This grocery chain is organizing the selling function along the lines that the customer is organized. If the local store manager has no authority to make a decision then the salesperson does not call on this account.[37]

Other examples of the powerful payoff from innovation of the sales process are shown in the Diagraph Corporation and Comcast Cable applications provided at the end of this chapter. How do all of these changes affect sales management? In the words of Alston Gardner, CEO of Target Market Systems, "Managers no longer manager people, they manage systems."[38]

. . . .

EMERGING SALES ORGANIZATION DESIGNS

Vertical (Supplier-Buyer) Integration

Selling is one of the few business processes that inherently extends outside of the firm. The supplier-buyer linkage is fundamental to the survival of the supplier firm. Increasingly, this linkage has been formalized through processes shared by both supplier and buyer. Barbara Bund Jackson notes that these close supplier-buyer relationships have several important characteristics.[39]

Increased Buyer Loyalty   Jackson characterizes strong supplier-buyer relationships as "lost-for-good" to competitors. The increase in the number of these types of relationships implies that new accounts will be harder to win, and that retention of existing relationships is a key success factor for the firm.

Higher Switching Costs   Switching costs are the buyer's costs for adopting a new product or service, aside from the cost of the product or service itself. They may include the cost of establishing new interpersonal relationships, the cost of order processing infrastructure (such as electronic data interchange), the costs associated with identifying purchasing requirements and specifications, the costs of learning procedures involved with using the new product or service, and so on. For example, most sales forces use contact management computer software. Although competing companies may introduce new software with superior features in any given year, a sales manager may decide not to switch to the new products because of the cost of retraining the sales force on the new software. This retraining is a switching cost.

Astute sales managers can increase switching costs by building unique linkages with buyers through such elements as: (1) construction of databases that anticipate customer needs; (2) building unique and efficient order-processing systems for the customer to use; (3) earning the customer's long-term trust; (4) creating multiple linkages with the customer through cross-selling; and (5) training the customer to use the product and services.

Substantial Investments   Long-term relationships often involve substantial investments for both the supplier and buyer. Process partnerships are sometimes more expensive for the supplier than the buyer, and can create a situation in which each buyer is a source of nonstandard order handling.[40]

High Perceived Risk Exposure   Accompanying the higher switching and sunk costs in a long-term supplier-buyer relationship is a higher perceived risk exposure. Buyers deliberately considering a purchase in terms of entering a long-term relationship are likely to engage in more thorough and sophisticated evaluation of potential suppliers. This calls for more complete information and sophisticated selling on the supplier side. The buyer in this situation will tend to consider not only the initial purchase price but also long-term operating costs, service availability, and product/service technology. This shifts the focus of selling from price to value.

Focus on Technology or Vendor   Long-term supplier-buyer relationships tend to emphasize an underlying technology or a vendor that can be counted on to keep the buyer up-to-date on new advances.[41] Short-term relationships tend to focus more on the particular salesperson or a product. Because of turnover and advancement, the salesperson is an insubstantial basis for a long-term supplier-seller relationship. Similarly, because of technological advances, specific products also lack this capability.

Long-term supplier-buyer relationships tend to range from sole-source purchasing agreements to less formal arrangements that still include high buyer involvement in the relationship.

Sole-Source Alliances   Limiting the number of suppliers allows firms to reduce the costs associated with obtaining and reviewing bids, and fluctuations in product/service quality variations among suppliers. Further, sole-sourcing allows firms to reduce the cost of routine transactions by streamlining order processing, automatic reordering, and joint inventory planning.

Customer Participation   Buyer participation in the order management process offers the seller a number of advantages. It shifts work responsibilities from the seller to the buyer. It can also increase buyer loyalty through increased control and involvement. For example, Federal Express' Powership customer-premise terminals allow customers sophisticated roles in service order placement and monitoring. American President Lines "customer managed" shipment systems allow customers to reserve space on ships, figure shipping prices, and monitor shipment status.[42]

Horizontal Selling Alliances   The increasingly sophisticated and interrelated technological components of products and services have led many firms to form horizontal selling alliances. In these alliances, providers of complimentary products and services sell together. Although most often found in the computer and telecommunications industries, selling alliances are also found in advertising, insurance, consulting, and other industries that emphasize "turn-key" customer solutions.[43]

Trust is a critical variable in selling alliances, as it is in many high-involvement business relationships. In background interviews conducted for their study of selling alliances, Smith and Barclay found that **trust** was "*the* critical factor differentiating effective from ineffective selling partnership arrangements."[44] They found that trust eroded when partners had different motivations, goals, or ways of doing business. They suggested that both "micro" behaviors (such as reps returning phone calls) and "macro" behaviors (such as joint planning) are needed to create successful selling alliances.

For example, the recent sale of more than 8500 personal computers by Compaq Computers to Electronic Data Systems (EDS) was assisted by an alliance with Microsoft.[45] Mike Clark, Compaq's VP for regional sales, said the Compaq-Microsoft selling alliance was a key success factor in beating out competitors for the deal. Because the new Compaq PC's would use Microsoft Windows NT, "They wanted to see how we work together," said Clark. So salespeople from both firms planned their presentation together.

Thomas Ingram identified the following seven drivers of the move to relationship selling: intensified competition, controlling market information through technology, time compression in product development, continuous improvement by the buyer requires closer vendor relationships, reduction of legal and ethical problems created by the sales force, demand for improved sales productivity, and the elevated status of the purchasing function. He notes that these forces have brought about the following changes in the selling function: team selling, salespeople shift from producing revenue to producing profits by managing their key assets—customers, and salespeople developing listening and questioning skills.[46]

Team-Based Selling

The increasing complexity and technological sophistication of products and services has also led to an increase in team selling arrangements. Team development consultants say that teams provide superior results in situations where "real-time" combinations of skills must be used.[47] In team selling, a group of sales and non-sales personnel work under the direction of a team leader to develop selling strategies and coordinate information flows.[48]

Team-based selling tends to be used when: (1) a team is created to provide sales and service to a single national or international account; (2) national account executives work with geographically dispersed field salespeople; and (3) salespeople work as a team, without a national account representative, to coordinate sales for a single national account that cuts across their respective territories.[49]

For example, when 3M surveyed its industrial customers in the early 1990s, it found that customers wanted information that salespeople lacked, and that industrial customers wanted to consolidate their purchasing activities. As it was a purchasing manager might have to deal with different 3M salespeople for products like sandpaper, safety masks, masking tape, computer disks, and more. 3M responded with its Integrated Solutions program, wherein salespeople sold in teams. Jack Tencza, 3M manager of sales and marketing learning and development, notes that "we're adding a lot more value to customers by coming in as a team of consultants."[50]

Teams can also be used to enhance the traditional salesperson's time. For example, at Hewlett-Packard every eight to ten salespeople are assigned a field support specialist (FSS), who handles follow-up activities.[51] If a customer has a question or a problem, the FSS can field it for the salesperson leveraging the salesperson's time and keeping the customer satisfied. FSS's often move up into salesperson positions.

Selling teams can be structured to operate through a single contact or through role-linkages.[52] In a single-contact arrangement, the salesperson acts as the customer contact, who accesses technical, production, service and other team members on the client's behalf.

In a role-based linkage arrangement, selling team members work with their opposite number in the buying firm. An advantage of the former is that it simplifies working relationships. An advantage of the latter is that it minimizes the possibility that technical information will be distorted in the communications process. Hybrid arrangements would allow for team-leader contact with supplemental technical contacts as required by the complexity of the information being conveyed.

Although teams are an increasingly popular format for organizing selling processes, they cannot be left unmanaged. Katzenbach and Smith suggest that team management has three major elements: accountability, commitment, and skills.[53] They note that both individual and team-level accountability must be built into the team organization, as well as mutual accountability of members to the team. Further, they suggest that effective teams have a common approach to work that focuses on a shared and meaningful purpose. This purpose should include specific goals that motivate team action. Finally, the teams should be trained in group problem-solving and interpersonal skills, as well as the technical/functional skills that normally constitute team members.

Teams also require time to become effective. Margaret Sears, an organizational development specialist, says that teams go through four stages: forming, storming, norming, and performing.[54] After the *forming* stage, during which team members get to know one another, they pass through a *storming* stage of contention over team roles, into a *norming* stage where an agreed way of doing things is established, and into a *performing* stage of effective operations.

Industry- and Account-Focused Selling

The growing importance of industry-specific technologies and the advent of long-term customer relationships have led to increasing use of industry- and even account-specific selling organizations.

Industry accounts allow salespeople to become experts on a particular type of client. For example, CEO Louis Gertsner and Ned Laurenbach, senior WP and group executive for worldwide sales, have moved IBM from a geographic focus to an industry-and account-centered focus. "The primary reason for our success is simple: We are listening to our customers," said Lautenbach. "We reorganized our sales force around customers' key industries, which has enabled our client executives to think like customers and offer solutions faster."[55]

National and international account management take focus to a new level. The goal of national account management is to build a profitable long-term relationship with a single firm by a focused effort "across multiple levels, functions, and operating units in both the buying and selling organization".[56] In national accounts, long-term contracts on pricing, delivery, and service are developed at the top-management level, with field salespeople servicing the accounts in their areas.

For example, Unisource, a distribution company based in Valley Forge, Pennsylvania, created a national account relationship with its key customer Cargill, a food processing firm in Minneapolis. "With six hundred locations nationwide, it was hard for us to monitor what everyone was buying," said Gary Kelso, director of corporate procurement at Cargill. "Now there is one contract for the whole company and each location is serviced by those guidelines."[57]

Similarly, in 1995 Procter & Gamble eliminated up to 500 jobs in its sales representative organization to form a new sales force that would respond to the consolidation of retail channels. P&G's 500 largest customers will have a single account manager instead of individual salespeople handling product categories such as paper, soap, food, and beverages.[58] Other grocery manufacturers are expected to follow this shift to match the increased power of the larger chains, which requires relationship selling.

National account programs tend to move salespeople to a salaried basis, for servicing the accounts at the local level, with a salary-plus-bonus structure for the national account manager.[59] The national account manager must be able to operate at the top management level of the customer organization, creating long-term relationships with executives and negotiating strategically developed contracts. "A national account manager should be used to deal with customer's executives, not just customers," noted Herb Burnap, a national account manager at Moore Business Forms in St. Louis.[60]

Sales Process Automation

The development of low-cost, high-capacity computing and communications systems has allowed leading firms to automate much of the selling process. This development has included automatic order placement over electronic data interchanges; handling of routine transactions through electronic "expert systems;" substitution of e-mail, computer conferencing, and other electronic communications for expensive on-site visits; shifting salespeople from the home office into the field through the creation of mobile "virtual offices;" allowing customers to place and monitor orders directly over the Internet; and more.

The capabilities of advanced computerized information systems continue to be explored. Because the capabilities are new, they enable and challenge firms to identify the optimal new designs for combining direct person-to-person selling with computerized enhancements.

For example, telemarketing is used to identify and screen prospects in business-to-business, in insurance, and in financial selling. The cost of office space can be eliminated with telecommuting, a virtual office consisting of a computer, a cell phone, and a fax. IBM representatives do not even have a personal desk when in their office. They are assigned one in a large room for the period that they are in the office. Procter & Gamble wanted to supply personal advice for customers considering their beauty-care products. Putting an advisor in the grocery store was too expensive so they experimented with a telephone consultant by placing a telephone in the aisle near their products.[61]

Mobile virtual selling arrangements offer significant advantages for in-the-field real-time order configuration and placement. Davenport describes a major food distribution company whose salespeople use laptop computers to confirm price and product availability, and to guarantee next-day delivery. The arrangement was potentially valuable to customers because it allowed them to plan menus without the fear that ingredients will not be available, while also maintaining low inventories.[62]

During 1996 Xerox began sending its salespeople home to virtual offices, outfitted with laptops, printers, fax machines, and phone lines. The result has been increased flexibility for salespeople and clients. As one salesperson noted: "I handle clients in the entertainment business, and these are energetic and extremely demanding people who tend to work all different hours, and they usually need equipment immediately."[63]

In business-to-business marketing Copperweld Corporation closed its district offices, moving the customer service function to the home office for faster service. Salespeople are linked to the home office via personal computers and voice mail. Customers liked the change.[64]

REEMERGING COST-SAVING DESIGNS

Increased competition and maturing markets have pressured most organizations to reduce operating costs. Because of the high costs involved in maintaining a direct selling force, this pressure has led to reemergence of some traditional selling structures, including agency selling and shared sales forces.

Agency and Distributor Selling

Managers often must reevaluate whether to use their own salespeople or external ones. Distributors and manufacturers' agents represent several suppliers simultaneously. They are independent private businesses, subject only to their contractual agreement with the supplier. As such, they are less directly accountable to the sales manager. For example, they do not tend to provide the sales manager with formal call reports.[65] Because of this arm's length arrangement, they require a certain amount of diplomacy from sales management. On the other hand, agents and distributors offer a number of advantages, including:[66]

- Knowledge of their territories and customers
- Long-term relationships with customers
- An ability to react quickly to situations in the field
- Extensive geographic coverage
- Generally older and more experienced salespeople
- Professional office setups with support staff in place

A new variation on the theme of using distributors and manufacturers' representative is sometimes called "rent-a-rep." MMD specializes in providing detail salespeople for pharmaceutical companies. Similar companies represent firms in the meat packing and grocery industries. The rent-a-rep sales forces are used by small companies that cannot afford to have their own sales force, by large companies with a short capacity need for an event such as launching a new product, and by large companies for whom it would be costly to place a salesperson in a remote area.

A sales manager who has used a distributor or agent will want to evaluate the costs and benefits of creating a company sales force. The manager must determine if the incremental gross profit would be more than the added costs, whether sales would increase because of tighter control of the salespeople, and whether the terminated distributors or agents would take customers with them. One study has shown that there is considerable inertia in switching from independent sales forces provided by distributors and agents to a direct one developed by the company.[67]

Shared Sales Forces

Another approach that some companies use to reduce operating costs is sharing a sales force among a number of divisions or product lines. The intention behind this approach is usually to lower costs, increase efficiency, achieve "synergy" or "economies of scope."

A difficulty that top management must consider in deciding whether to share a sales force is whether the added stress on salespeople will lead to poorer selling performance. The basic duties of a salesperson—monitoring customer and competitor trends, learning product capabilities, interacting with other organizational members to coordinate order processing and service—become increasingly more complex as more products are added to his or her list. This complexity becomes even more pronounced if the products are diverse.

Researchers Ravipreet Sohi, Daniel Smith, and Neil Ford found evidence that the more a shared sales force is used, the more role stress salespeople encounter.[68] In particular, they found that in shared sales forces, salespeople were more likely to face conflicting duties and unclear job responsibilities. These outcomes were lessened somewhat if the organization had a more formalized and decentralized structure. But the bottom-line results—sales per salesperson—were not improved by sharing a sales force.

Overall, Sohi and his colleagues concluded: "Whereas sharing a salesforce neither helps nor hinders salespeople in achieving their sales, profit, and market-share objectives, it certainly impairs their ability to develop new accounts and serve existing customers."[69]

Some Limitations of New Designs

A careful evaluation of new organizational designs suggests caution. Many theories and technologies have not lived up to their expectations. A few examples will stress the need to study the downside as well as the upside.

Digital Equipment downsized its sales force in its health-industries group, which improved profits in the short run, but it disrupted longstanding relationships with major customers. Resellers of Digital computers dropped their exclusivity with Digital and added other suppliers. Customers turned to IBM and Hewlett-Packard equipment. Laid-off workers went to Hewlett-Packard and took clients with them. Thus downsizing, in the name of reengineering, considered only the immediate cost saving, not the impact on revenue generation.[70] RJR Nabisco merged sales forces, only to learn that groceries and candy went through different channels and that salespeople could not handle such a broad line.[71] Thus

---

Case 17.1 — WHICH WAY TO GO?

The Phillips Corporation, which manufacturers components and sub-assemblies for original equipment manufacturers, is acquiring the Central Appliance Co., a manufacturer of industrial appliances. Phillips located in St. Louis, has a national sales force of 16 salespeople. Central is located in Milwaukee and services the central states with six salespeople, but it plans to go national with 14 salespeople in the next three years. Although there is some overlap in potential industrial customers, the decision makers for both product lines are different.

Discuss the advantages and disadvantages of alternative sales management structures for the merged sales organizations. What do you recommend?

Case 17.2 — SALES SYSTEMS INTEGRATION AT DIAGRAPH CORPORATION

James Brigham faced a problem.[76] As owner of Diagraph Corporation, a St. Louis manufacturer of industrial labeling, coding, and marking equipment, he had watched profits decline for four years, despite increasing sales. The sales process that the company had used for years, based on cold calls, trade shows, and passive referrals, wasn't working any more. The label-printing division, Diagraph's fastest-growing unit, had the lowest margins. And the marking-equipment division, its cash cow, was beginning to run dry.

Investigation of the problems showed inefficiencies in the sales process. Marking-equipment salespeople would go out on calls, which experts estimate to cost an average of $250 each, and return with only a $200 order for heavy-duty pens, inks for stencil machines, and similar supplies.

Brigham solved his problem by redesigning the sales process. He added a telemarketing program and created a catalog, which he mailed to all customers and prospects. Customers could now place routine orders themselves by calling a toll-free number, which cut Brigham's cost per order from $250 to $10.

To remotivate the salespeople, Brigham restructured his commission program to focus on generating new business. He cut the commission on his traditional marking-equipment line from 10% to 3.5%, but boosted the commission on newer company lines up to 10%.

Diagraph also uses the telemarketing subsystem for lead qualification. When prospects respond to company ads, telemarketers call for more information, including buying intentions and qualifications. Prioritized leads are then routed to the salespeople.

1. What types of technological systems could be used to enhance the operations of Diagraph Company?

2. What resistance might the sales manager expect in this situation? How should that resistance be managed?

it appears that reengineering works when the task is routine, like handling information or order processing, but it does not apply in relationships, a nonhomogeneous activity.

The team approach is commonly accepted as a means for selling a highly technical product or when making a complex presentation. But a team approach can cause problems. Procter & Gamble found that it was difficult to get the marketing, finance, distribution, and operations people to work with each other.[72] To be effective functional areas must overcome thinking in functional "silos" and work together as a team.[73]

Companies are sometimes at opposite ends of an adoption cycle for a new idea. While AT&T is eliminating its branch sales offices by giving salespeople notebook personal computers, Hewlett-Packard (HP), one of the first companies to furnish salespeople with laptops, has pulled back from sales force automation. It concluded that something more than computerization is needed to increase sales productivity. One insider at HP said, "We were naive. We thought we knew what the sales process involved and how to automate it. We didn't. Because we didn't understand the process, the tools we pushed on the reps didn't help."[74]

Recent remedies for management ills have carried names such as process reengineering, benchmarking, total quality management, broad-banding, worker empowerment, and skill-based pay. Implementing these approaches involves financial, performance, and social costs, as well as potential benefits. The result sometimes demoralizes the employees and leads to conflict, leading to abandonment or substantial revision of the new selling process design.

For example, Compaq Computer tried to change its strategy in order to get closer to its customer. After failing to acquire the direct telephone sales competitor Gateway 2000, it decided to hire 2000 salespeople. This move threatened Compaq's traditional distributor system and led to unexpected conflict.[75] Changing a sales force strategy can be difficult.

··

SUMMARY

The information revolution is changing the sales organization from a pyramid to a flat organization that uses a team approach. The traditional hierarchical sales management design uses horizontal structures to enable specialization and vertical structures to increase the capacity of the selling function. This design requires the general manager to decide on the span of control, the levels of management, and the role of staff functions that relieve managers of tasks such as training. The need for district managers is reduced when a time-consuming activity like training is moved to the home office and when recruiting and selection are handled by an external specialized consulting firm. In some companies the district sales manager function is being replaced by the role of a team leader who focuses on a few key accounts.

Assigning salespeople to territories is appropriate in some industries. Managing territories adds to selling costs, but in many cases it is more than offset by an increase in productivity. Personal computers with mapping software enable the manager and the salesperson to build up a territory. This computer approach improves morale because it provides a better match of territories and potential, in addition to involving the salesperson.

The sales force is under pressure to increase its productivity. Some of the pressures for change are the result of the information revolution that has introduced alternatives such as telemarketing, the maturing of industries so that products are bought on price, greater demands from customers for sales service, the speed of market change, and federal concerns for healthcare costs.

Companies such as IBM and Procter & Gamble have redesigned their sales forces, but the experiment continues. There is no ideal design. Even the team design, which is becoming popular, has limitations when strong-willed functional members fail to cooperate.

ASSIGNMENTS/DISCUSSION QUESTIONS

1. Think about a company that you would like to work for and design its sales force organization for five years from now. What environmental changes stimulated this design?

2. List what you consider the top five new technologies that have been introduced into the selling process in the past decade. Identify the advantages and disadvantages of each, from the company's perspective, the salesperson's perspective, and the customer's perspective.

3. In which company would you prefer to work, A or B? Why?

Position Title	Number of Persons In:	
	Company A	Company B
General Sales Manager	I	I
Regional Sales Manager	0	2
District Sales Manager	12	16
Salespeople	144	144

4. Southwest Airlines has become known as a classic example of a firm that combines differentiation (through its customer-friendly culture, efficient service, and low prices) with low operating costs. An example of its process innovation is ticketless travel: Corporate customers pay for tickets with a credit card and receive a confirmation by FAX; no ticket is issued. Although this program saves time, paperwork, and money, many customers are uncomfortable without tickets.

   Southwest's 90-person field marketing team has been asked to promote the "ticketless program" to the corporations, travel agencies, and associations that they call on. If you were in charge of the team's effort to promote the "ticketless program," what elements would you include in your plan?

5. AT&T has begun to reorganize its selling efforts, moving away from allowing several salespeople to call on different contacts within a company toward appointing a "client business manager" to act as the customer liaison. The client business manager is responsible for managing a team of technical specialists from a number of "knowledge communities" within AT&T. During 1996 about 10% of the AT&T sales force was working under the new customer-focused structure, but the proportion was to increase to about 90% within a year.

   What difficulties would you expect a "client business manager" to encounter? How could these difficulties be overcome?

6. Kraft Foods recently organized its U.S. operations into 21 regions, with customer business teams in each region. Each team consists of a customer business manager

and five to eight customer category managers (CCMs). The CCMs sell all of Kraft's brands in their assigned regions. Under this arrangement, a buyer from Wal-Mart would deal with one customer business manager from Kraft, as opposed to the nine different salespeople that would be required to represent the nine company divisions.

What advantages do you see in the new system? What disadvantages? How could Kraft overcome the disadvantages?

7. Blake Williams sat listening to a focus group session he had commissioned for his wholesale building supply firm. The building contractors in the focus group complained that they wanted to be able to obtain pricing and inventory availability information any time of the day or night. They wanted to be able to place orders without waiting for the "inside salespeople" to open at 7:30 AM. They also considered the "outside salespeople" who called on the individual project worksites to be less than useful; "too late with too little," as one contractor put it.

Williams reflected that new technology might be an answer to his problems. But he knew that the contractors were mostly small businesses, with wide ranging variation in their own technical capabilities.

How might Mr. Williams reorganize his sales and information systems to accommodate his customers?

ENDNOTES

1. Thomas H. Davenport (1993), *Process Innovation: Reengineering Work through Information Technology,* Boston: Harvard Business School Press.
2. *Ibid.*
3. *Ibid.*
4. *Ibid.,* p. 7.
5. *Ibid.,* p. 7.
6. *Ibid.,* p. 6.
7. Personal communication with Wallace, Inc.
8. The Conference Board, Organization Chart Collection, 1997.
9. *Ibid.*
10. John G. Maurer, Judith M. Nixon, and Terrance W. Peck (1996), *Organization Charts,* 2nd ed., Detroit: Gale, p. 33.
11. *Ibid.,* p. 150.
12. Confidential communication.
13. Rudy Getting and Geri Bantman, Telemarketing: Dial "M" for Maximize, *Sales & Marketing Management* 143(6), June, 1991, pp. 100–106.
14. Ellen Goldbaum, Telemarketing Rings up More Chemical Sales, *Chemical Week* 142(23), June 8, 1988, pp. 32–33.
15. M. Daniel Rosen, Expanding Your Sales Operation? Just Dial 1-800. . . , *Sales & Marketing Management,* July, 1990, p. 82.
16. Richard Lewis, Putting Sales on the Map, *Sales & Marketing Management,* August, 1992, p. 76.
17. John T. Mulqueen, Research House Crosses Oceans and Continents to Track Drug Sales, *Data Communications* 17(6), June, 1988, pp. 92–96.
18. Kevin F. Sullivan, Richard A. Bobbe, and Martin R. Strassmore, Transforming the Salesforce in a Maturing Industry, *Management Review* 77(6), June, 1988, pp. 46–49.
19. Barbara Hetzer, Pushing Decisions Down the Line at Campbell Soup, *Business Month* 134(1), July, 1989, pp. 62–63.
20. Mark Blessington and Bill O'Connell (1995), *Sales Reengineering from the Outside In,* New York: McGraw-Hill.
21. Patricia Sellers, How to remake your sales force, *Fortune,* May, 1992, p. 90.
22. Blessington and O'Connell, 1995.

23. George Anders, Managed Health Care Jeopardizes Outlook for Drug 'Detailer', *Wall Street Journal,* September 10, 1993, pp. 1, 6.

24. The Conference Board, Reinventing The Sales Organization, Conference, Booud, New York, September 28, 1993.

25. *Ibid.*

26. Thomas H. Davenport (1993), *Process Innovation: Reengineering Work through Information Technology,* Boston: Harvard Business School Press.

27. Wally Wood, Reinventing the sales force, *Across The Board,* April, 1994, New York.

28. Judith J. Marshall and Harriet Vredenburg, An Empirical Study of Factors Influencing Innovation Implementation in Industrial Sales Organizations, *Journal of the Academy of Marketing Science* 20(3), Summer 1992, pp. 205–215.

29. Davenport, 1993, p. 240.

30. *Ibid.,* p. 243.

31. *Ibid.*

32. *Ibid.,* p. 247.

33. Adapted from Davenport 1993, p. 247, and James W. Cortada, Reading the Tea Leaves, in *Reinventing the Sales Organization,* Elizabeth Miranda, Editor (1990), Report Number 1102-95-CH, New York: The Conference Board.

34. Valarie A. Zeithaml, A. Parasuraman, and Leonard L. Berry (1990), *Delivering Service Quality: Balancing Customer Perceptions and Expectations,* New York: Free Press.

35. This discussion is based on Leonard A. Schlesinger and Roger Hallowell, Taco Bell Corp, Harvard Business School Case No. 9-692-058; Leonard A. Schlesinger and James L. Heskett, The Service-Driven Service Company, *Harvard Business Review,* September–October, 1991, pp. 71–81; James L. Heskett, W. Earl Sasser, Jr., and Leonard A. Schlesinger, Achieving Breakthrough Service, *Participant's Guide,* Harvard Business School, Video Series, n.d.

36. Laurie Hays, IBM's Gerstner Holds Back From Sales Force Shake-up, *Wall Street Journal,* July 7, 1993, p. 31; Catherine Arnst, At IBM, More of the Same—Only Better? *Business Week,* July 26, 1993, pp. 78–79.

37. Confidential conversations between one of the authors and persons in the grocery products industry.

38. Personal communication, March 25, 1997.

39. Barbara Bund Jackson (1985), *Winning and Keeping Industrial Customers: The Dynamics of Customer Relationships,* New York: Lexington Books.

40. Davenport, 1993, p. 250.

41. Jackson, 1985.

42. Davenport, 1993, p. 249.

43. J. Brock Smith and Donald W. Barclay, The Effects of Organizational Differences and Trust on the Effectiveness of Selling Partner Relationships, *Journal of Marketing* 61(1), January, 1997, pp. 3–21.

44. *Ibid.,* p. 4.

45. Geoffrey Brewer, Ginger Conlon, John F. Yarbrough, Andy Cohen, Michele Marchetti, Tom Dellecave Jr., Chad Kaydo, and Allison Lucas, The Top, *Sales & Marketing Management* 148(11), November, 1996, pp. 38–56.

46. Thomas N. Ingram, Relationship Selling: Moving from Rhetoric to Reality, *Mid-America Journal of Business* 11(1), (Spring, 1996), 5–13.

47. Jon R. Katzenbach and Douglas K. Smith (1993), *The Wisdom of Teams: Creating the High-Performance Organization,* Boston: Harvard Business School Press.

48. Mark Blessington, Five Ways to Make Team Selling Work (Really!), *Business Month* 134(2), pp. 71–72.

49. Frank V. Cespedes, Stephen X. Doyle, and Robert J. Freedman, Teamwork for Today's Selling, *Harvard Business Review* 67, March/April, pp. 44–58.

50. Brewer et. al, 1996.

51. Brewer et. al, 1996.

52. Jim Rapp, Team Selling is Changing the Sales Trainer's Role, *Training,* May, pp. 6–10.

53. Katzenbach and Smith, 1993.

54. Timothy D. Schellhardt, To Be a Star Among Equals, Be a Team Player, *The Wall Street Journal*, April 20, 1994.

55. Brewer et. al 1996.

56. Benson P. Shapiro and Rowland T. Moriarty (1982), *National Account Management: Emerging Insights,* Cambridge, MA: Marketing Science Institute Report, p. 8.

57. Andy Cohen, A National Footing, *Sales & Marketing Management* 148(4), 1996, pp. 76–81.

58. Raju Narisetti, Procter & Gamble is restructuring U.S. sales force, *The Wall Street Journal,* October 20, 1997, p. B5.

59. Cohen, 1996.

60. Cohen, p. 196.

61. Jennifer Kent, P&G tests beauty hot lines, *The Post,* September 14, 1994, p. 5D.

62. Davenport 1993, p. 249.

63. Brewer et. al, 1996.

64. Martin Everett, Who Needs District Sales Managers, *Sales & Marketing Management,* 139(8), December, 1987, pp. 54–56.

65. Key Issues in Territory Management, *Sales Agency Magazine,* 26(5), May, 1996, pp. 4–8.

66. Expanding Sales and Profits in a Downsizing Environment, *Sales Agency Magazine* 27(3), March, 1997, pp 25–27.

67. Allen M. Weiss and Erin Anderson, Converting from Independent to Employee Salesforces: The Role of Perceived Switching Costs, *Journal of Marketing Research,* 29, February, 1992, pp. 101–115.

68. Ravipreet S. Sohi, Daniel C. Smith, and Neil M. Ford, How Does Sharing A Sales Force Between Multiple Divisions Affect Salespeople?, *Journal of the Academy of Marketing Science* 24(3), Summer 1996, pp. 195–207.

69. *Ibid.,* p. 203.

70. Alex Markels and Matt Murray, Call it dumbsizing: Why some companies regret cost-cutting, *The Wall Street Journal,* May 14, 1995, p. 1.

71. *Ibid.*

72. Patricia Sellers, How to remake your sales force, *Fortune,* May 4, 1992, p. 100.

73. Edward A. Morash, Cornelia Droge, and Sahwnee Vickery, Boundary spanning interfaces between logistics, production, marketing, and product development, *International Journal of Physical Distribution & Logistics,* 26(8), 1996, pp. 43–62.

74. Thayer C. Taylor, The Future, *Sales & Marketing Management,* June, 1992, pp. 47–60.

75. Evan Ramstad, Compaq to hire 2,000 sales people in '97, *The Wall Street Journal,* May 14, 1997.

76. Adapted from Paul B. Brown, Opportunity Rings Once, *INC.,* November, 1990, p. 152.

18

SALES FORCE AUTOMATION

LEARNING GOALS

1. To learn to identify the general benefits and costs of sales force automation
2. To understand the different levels of sales force automation
3. To learn the constraints and benefits of group-level sales force automation
4. To understand the steps involved in planning for sales force automation

INTRODUCTION

The information revolution that is sweeping through society is changing the nature of selling. Initially the changes were shallow. Information once kept on index cards was computerized. Contacts made by telephone (after repeated rounds of "phone tag") or letter were replaced by more efficient e-mail exchanges. But gradually the depth of the changes have increased. Industrial buyers have become "hard wired" to their suppliers for automatic reorders. Salespeople equipped with laptops are designing and pricing products, checking availability, and offering printed contracts, all during one visit in the field. Automated selling systems rank leads, forward them to salespeople, and monitor field performance, all without human intervention. And this appears to be only the threshold of changes to come.

THE AUTOMATED SELLING ENVIRONMENT

Things have changed in sales. The rapid and continuous drop in the price of computing, coupled with advances in communications technology, have altered the competitive

373

environment—and the structure and process of selling. Businesses are increasingly global. Firms in an increasing number of industries are reaching new worldwide economies of scale and scope. Efficient global communications systems bring international competitors into local markets. Organizational structures are increasingly flattened as middle managers, the information gatekeepers of yesteryear, are pressed out. Company operations are pared down to their essential materials, processes, and people; and then these are reviewed again for waste.

Sales have gone out the door, literally. The salesperson of the information age is a virtual office on the move. A one-person mobile telecomputation system, the salesperson of the information age carries global telecommunications access and more computational power than rode in the Apollo 18 spacecraft. This space-age setup equips the salesperson for the complexities of selling through information. It is required to meet the needs—and challenges—of the increasingly "information affluent" customer.[1] The officeless-but-automated salesperson on the street helps reduce overhead while increasing selling time.

Change is difficult for everyone. The change to sales force automation poses difficulties for the sales manager and salesperson alike. The sales manager must balance the costs and benefits of the sales automation options that continuously arise. Failing to automate sales is less and less an option, as more and more competitors push forward to make sales force automation a basis for both cost leadership and differentiation with customers. Yet moving forward with sales force automation often involves an irrevocable commitment to uncertain technologies. The difficulties imposed on the salesperson—learning to use new technologies and operating increasingly on his or her own—amplify the problems of the sales manager. One writer offers a sales force automation checklist (Exhibit 18.1).

Sales Force Automation Costs and Benefits

Estimating the costs and benefits of sales force automation options is a perilous process. The Gartner Group, a sales force automation consulting firm, estimates that 60% of all sales force automation projects fail.[2] Other estimates are as high as 80%. "I've found more tombstones in the backyards of companies in honor of sales force automation than I have in honor of total quality management programs," Jim Cecil, a sales and marketing consultant, told *INC.* magazine.[3] Many problems are possible. The selling system may be poorly defined, the wrong system may be chosen for automation, key managers could be excluded from the automation process, an inappropriate hardware-software configuration might be selected, salespeople could balk at using the system, it might add more work (and thus cost) to the selling process, or it might not fit customer's needs. Yet, when used correctly, sales force automation can increase sales from 15% to 85%, notes Pentech Corporation, a sales force automation consulting firm in Atlanta. Among the benefits are improvements in both selling efficiency and effectiveness.

Efficiency   Sales automation systems allow salespeople to do their standard work in less time. A Dartnell Corporation survey of salespeople found that 81% said that technology has simplified their work.[4] A major reason for the salesperson's approval of technology, according to the study, is that they could do more work in less time. Among the efficiency advantages of sales force automation are the following:

Less Paperwork   Even the simplest sales force automation systems usually replace work done manually, such as writing call reports, placing orders, invoice preparation, and data collection, entry, and transmission. In so doing, these systems typically accelerate routine work, freeing additional salesperson time for selling.

Exhibit **18.1**	OFFICE AUTOMATION CHECKLIST

Place a check mark (✓) beside each question that is true for your organization. Scores of 5 or higher are said to indicate office automation may not be at desirable levels.

ITEM

1. Are handwritten notes in use?
2. Are letters and documents dictated?
3. Are proposals prepared by secretaries?
4. Do people go to file drawers to retrieve documents?
5. Is there a typewriter in the office that is used?
6. Is a card file in use to keep track of names and addresses?
7. Would you be OK without your notebook computer?
8. Do you leave your desk to send a FAX?
9. Do you find faxing printed material difficult?
10. Do you lack an e-mail address?
11. Does it take more than an hour to send out 500 personalized letters?
12. Is each salesperson managing the same number of prospects as she or he was three years ago, or fewer?
13. Is publishing a newsletter a problem?
14. Do documents have to be entered manually (that is, by keystrokes)?
15. Has the support staff-to-salespeople ratio stayed the same (or increased) in the past five years?
16. Are pink paper message notes still in use?
17. Is there often a line at the copy machine?
18. Has the computer system stayed the same any year for the past five years?
19. Do you seldom hear the terms "uploaded" and "downloaded" commonly used?
20. Is assembling a mailing list a problem?

TOTAL ✓ MARKS ———

SOURCE: Adapted from John R. Graham, Test Your Office Productivity: You Are Not Automated If . . ., *Agency Sales Magazine*, 26(3), March, 1996, pp. 28–29.

More Clients Seen   Additional selling time available equates to more clients seen. In addition, the information processing capability of automated systems increases a salesperson's ability to handle an expanded number of clients, in terms of keeping track of information about buyers and their orders.

Decreased Call Preparation Time   Centralized customer databases make visit preparation more efficient.[5] The salesperson is able to call up client data as well as background data about the firm and the industry. Further, integrated presentation packages make it possible for salespeople to assemble high-quality, customized presentations in the field.

Decreased Proposal Development Time   Electronic price lists, product specifications, and standardized proposal formats provide salespeople with an ability to draft proposals immediately during presentations. This not only increases the salesperson's efficiency by eliminating the need for a repeat visit, it improves the chances for successful closing of the sale by producing the offer during the time of the buyer's peak interest.

Effectiveness   In addition to improving the efficiency of standard selling tasks, automation allows the sales force to accomplish several tasks—and provide customer benefits—that were not possible with manual systems. Among these are the following:

Increased Information Access   Thomas Siebel and Michael Malone, authors of *Virtual Selling,* argue that sales force automation enables the development of knowledgeable sales professionals.[6] The defining characteristics of this individual—whom they say is rare—include a thorough understanding of his or her company's and competitor's products and services, a strategic perspective on the marketplace, immediate access to follow up information, and an aptitude for assuring delivery and service.

Improved Prospecting   Selling is a numbers game; the number of sales closed is related to the number of clients seen. Higher quality of the prospects increases the "close ratio," and sales force automation can provide sales managers and salespeople with more accurate and comprehensive systems for evaluating prospects. Thus not only does sales force automation enable the salesperson to see more clients, but the potential inherent in the clients he or she sees can be increased by the same process.

Improved Offers   The offer in most business settings is a complex combination of products and services that varies in relation to price. In some situations, there can be thousands of potential combinations that the salesperson and client can consider. Sales force automation can enable the salesperson to guide the client through this decision process, often providing graphic models or displays of possible offers for the client to consider.

More Rapid Fulfillment   Speed of business cycles has become a critical success factor in many industries. The cycle time of a company is related to that of its suppliers. Firms that seek to improve their cycle time as a source of competitive advantage require suppliers that can fulfill orders rapidly. Sales force automation enables salespeople to expedite orders by checking inventory and delivery dates in the field, as the order is being taken. These orders can then be posted from the field immediately on closing of the sale.

Because of these advantages, sales force automation software alone was estimated to be a $700 million industry in 1995, with expected sales in the year 2000 reaching to $10 billion.[7] In 1996 it was estimated that about 2.5 million of the 9 million salespeople in the United States (about 28%) were involved in use of automated sales tools.[8] There is also evidence that sales management dominates corporate information technology issues. A Computerworld survey of information service executives found that 58% said sales and marketing receive most of their attention, compared with 3% who identified research and development or corporate administration as focal areas.[9]

LEVELS OF SALES FORCE AUTOMATION

Movement toward sales force automation has not been a "before-and-after" experience for firms. Automating sales is not like flipping a switch. Firms move, sometimes unsteadily, toward "higher" levels of sales force automation, as shown in Exhibit 18.2. The phases of sales force automation described in this exhibit are only approximately sequential. Firms sometimes move forward to a new phase, while also investing in improvement of automation at an earlier phase.

Individual Sales Roles

Initial efforts at sales force automation have focused on the individual salesperson and sales manager. Efforts aimed at the individual salesperson have focused first on documentation and presentation of sales information, and then on various aspects of salesperson-

Exhibit 18.2   PHASES OF SALESFORCE AUTOMATION

Potential Benefits (and Challenges)

	Documents and Presentations	Contact Management	Sales Management	Sales Team Automation	Business Automation	Sales Alliance Automation
Level	Individual salesperson	Individual salesperson	Individual sales manager	Sales department	Interdepartmental	Interorganizational
Challenges	Individual change and training	Individual change and training	Individual change and training	Team change and training	Organizational change and training	Interorganizational change and training
Benefits	Improved presentations, product/offer configuration	More rapid and systematic client contact and access to client information	More accurate and efficient decision making	Improved customer-focused coordination across functions	Improved customer-focused coordination across departments	Improved customer-focused coordination across firms
Technology	Laptop computer Word processing Presentationware Multimedia	E-mail contact and opportunity management software	Lead and territory management Order entry Call reporting Sales analysis	Intranets Groupware	Intranets Groupware Enterprise software	Electronic data Extranets Groupware

customer contact management. Beyond the level of the salesperson, sales managers have benefited from a variety of sales force automation devices that help in decision making or salesperson management. Eventually the return on additional investments in sales automation at the individual level diminishes.

Group Sales Automation

Another level of complexity—and potential performance improvement—is found when information technology is focused on coordination within and between groups. As firms search for new methods to improve sales through technology, they begin to redesign selling itself around expanding information processing and communications capabilities. This includes: (a) linking members of the sales team to focus on customer sales and service; (b) coordinating across business departments; and (c) creating automated business alliances.

The phases in the evolution of sales force automation are described in more detail later in this chapter.[10]

AUTOMATING INDIVIDUAL SALES ROLES

In the early stages of automation firms tend to focus on making the salesperson more efficient, first by improving his or her document handling and then by improving his or her contact management and communications. As Michael Malone, an author of Virtual Selling, notes: "Most of the SFA software that has been installed to date uses automation to supercharge existing processes."[11] Gradually these gains in efficiency move into the sales management area, with improvements in management of territories, orders, and calls.

Documents and Presentations

The early gains in selling efficiency produced by technology were from document management applications such as word processing and spreadsheets. These tools allowed the salesperson to manage documents more efficiently by storing "canned" proposal components, quickly adapting selling materials to meet clients' perceived needs, "scanning" in graphic materials (such as photographs of products, illustrations of service processes, the prospect's company logo), recalculating prices based on spreadsheet templates, and otherwise accelerating and improving the flow of paperwork.

Document processing merged into, and grew with, another type of application: presentation software. Initial versions of this type of software made it easy to prepare transparencies for use with overhead projectors (first in black print and then in color) or 35-millimeter slides. Later versions of presentation software grew to include on-screen computerized presentations. Using this approach, a salesperson with a laptop computer could prepare and offer a presentation in the field. Special projectors could be linked to the computer for presentations to groups. Advances in computer memory capabilities expanded the capabilities of this type of presentation. It became possible to include other types of media to achieve a more powerful, but still usually portable, impact.

A logical extension of the early days of printed documents has been the use of multiple media ("multimedia") to present product information. These formats, delivered on floppy computer disks, CD-ROM, or on-line, combine color, animation, video clips, and sound. This range of media allows a firm to provide information about itself and competitors, price data, delivery schedules, and research statistics. Prospects can take a plant tour, see a product demonstration, or view "live" testimonials through video clips delivered on a laptop computer screen through multimedia.

The multimedia format can move beyond presentation to capture the prospect through involvement. Multimedia can be structured to allow the prospect to control elements of the presentation, exploring his or her own questions or test complex "what if" scenarios involving product features and price. Multimedia can also allow the salesperson-as-consultant to design products or services at the point of sale.

> Bill Burg, senior area sales manager with the air compressor group of Ingersoll-Rand was making his first computer-based presentation to a customer. The presentation had been prepared by a leading advertising agency for $50,000. The chief engineer for an Iowa manufacturing plant and one of his lieutenants huddled around Burg's laptop computer. The feature of Burg's demonstration: A $100,000 air compressor. He was allowed 20 minutes, which was not a good sign. As Burg clicked through the presentation, the chief engineer began to ask "what if" questions about operating and power costs. Soon the engineers were nudging Burg out of the way, and running their own numbers. They stayed at it for two hours.[12]

Due to its impact with prospects, multimedia use has continued to grow. A 1994 survey of senior managers found that about 70% of respondents use multimedia for business and sales presentations, and about 60% of those surveyed plan to increase the use of multimedia for these purposes.[13] Multimedia has been particularly useful in presenting technical or complex products and services.

Advantages of Multimedia[14]   Growth in the use of multimedia has been the result of a number of key advantages; including the following:

Easy to Update   Because multimedia are essentially digital data, presentations can be quickly changed. New product images can be scanned into a presentation or additional data added without replacing the entire presentation, as one might have to do with a self-contained video.

Visualization   Video capabilities allow multimedia to bring the company, the product, and/or the service to the prospect. Computer graphic capabilities allow the presenter to create visual prototypes of products, or show products or services as they would appear in use.

Sound   Audio capabilities add dramatic impact to multimedia presentations. They also allow key participants—such as company executives and satisfied customers—to literally voice their views in the presentation.

Corporate Image   A professional multimedia presentation demonstrates technological leadership and capability to the prospect, who may not know the seller's firm or its reputation. Multimedia can serve as the representation of the company in the field.

Interactivity   Involvement is a powerful device for growing a prospect's interest. By allowing the presentation to be guided by the prospect's questions, multimedia adapts the selling process to his or her interests. In addition, participation dramatically increases information retention. It has been reported that people retain 20% of information they hear, 40% of information they see, and 60% to 70% of information they participate in creating.[15]

"What If" Applications   The time lapse between interest and information can be fatal to a sale. If the salesperson's visit generates interest, but the complexity of the project requires substantial time to respond with a detailed product design and pricing, the sale may be lost to new and pressing issues that arise in the meantime. Multimedia applications that allow prospects to test the pricing or long-term cost of various product-service configurations on the spot collapse the sales cycle and increase the probability of an order.

Electronic Transfer   Because it is based on digital data, multimedia can be transferred inexpensively to client locations by disk, CD-ROM, or through the Internet. This allows the members of the prospect firm to share the information with other decision makers.

Multimedia Delivery Vehicles   A critical issue that must be considered in designing a multimedia support for a sales force is the delivery vehicle: How will the multimedia content be delivered to the prospect? Three dominant delivery vehicles include on-site presentations, distributed media, and use of "decision centers." Each has unique advantages.

On-Site Presentations   One dominant approach to delivery of multimedia content is through on-site presentations by a salesperson using a laptop computer. The computer monitor can be sufficient as a visual presentation vehicle for one or two prospects. A computer screen can be supplemented by computer projection equipment for use when several participants are involved. Advantages of this approach include increased control in the quality of the presentation, adaptation of the presentation to the prospect's interests, and the involvement of the salesperson to assure use of and attention to the presentation.

Distributed Media   Because multimedia can be distributed electronically, as previously noted, the presentation can be offered directly to the prospect in disk or CD-ROM format or via the Internet. An advantage of this approach is that it broadens the potential for distributing the presentation, because it does not require a salesperson's presence.

> In launching its Post-It Easel Pads, 3M commissioned production of a diskette that included a description of the product, tips on how to run better meetings, and a fax-back form for free office suppliers. This "electronic brochure" was sent to 10,000 buyers. A followup survey commissioned by 3M found that 90% favored the diskette over printed advertising, catalogs, or sales reps.[16]

Decision Centers   Certain types of presentations often involve visits by the prospect or a prospect team to the seller's site. For example, prospects involved in selecting industrial locations often need to visit the sites under consideration as part of the purchase decision process. In these situations, sellers (such as economic development organizations and industrial real estate firms) often develop "decision centers" that provide powerful multimedia support. An advantage of this approach is that it allows the seller to engage a full range of multimedia resources in a stationary setting. Typically decision centers include corporate conferencing facilities together with multimedia computerization and projection equipment. These centers can often achieve multimedia effects that would be difficult to accomplish in the field or on a distributed basis, because of equipment limitations.

> Alternate Realities Corporation (ARC) offers interactivity in a 360-degree video. The Raleigh, North Carolina, firm's VisionDome is a virtual reality ampitheater. In this setting, the prospect can "enter" a computer-generated product simulation—whether it is an automobile, a building, or a manufacturing facility—and "try it out" as though it were real.[17]

Multimedia Training   Sales managers who commission development of multimedia support to be used in the field or through decision centers should also train salespeople in the appropriate use of these presentation platforms. Salespeople can place too much emphasis on multimedia or assume a passive role, essentially reducing the personal selling effort to that of equipment operator. It is important to convey to salespeople that multimedia is one of several selling tools at their disposal, but that the salesperson has the responsibility for using these tools to sell and to build customer relationships.

Bob Cooper, president of Frontier Media and a veteran trainer in using sales-oriented multimedia, notes that salespeople must learn to: (1) prepare the multimedia equipment for presentations (checking power supplies, projection equipment, seating, and other arrangements); (2) handle the physical elements of multimedia presentations (such as learning where to stand, how to use the mouse while presenting, how to deal with clients while also closing up the equipment, and so on); (3) maintain control of the presentation by developing an active presentation that links to the multimedia display and by prompting prospects with questions to drive the direction of the presentation; and (4) continuously improve the presentations.[18]

Contact Management

The next stage in making selling more efficient through technology grew out of applications focusing on contacting prospects. "Contact management" software began as computerized client files. In addition to containing all of a client's history, the systems typically keep the salesperson's schedule, allow him or her to produce and store client-related documents, and remind the salesperson when additional contact is required. When linked through a computer network, these applications can be shared across multiple salespeople for groupwide scheduling, open database access, and other joint information functions.

> Greg Eaton, a sales rep for Farmland Industries, kept a black book of customer information for 15 years. His notes showed the type of grain storage facilities used, purchase history, the last order placed, the last quote provided, delivery instructions, and other customer information. Then the regional sales office announced that all reps would use a computerized contact management system called Goldmine. Greg was reluctant, but each rep attended a day-long class. Then the reps entered information about their customers into their computers. As a result, Greg has grown to rely on the system, which has enabled him to record all the information he needs. The system has helped Farmland's reps all work together as a team, provided documented records when reps or service staff left, and helped coordinate handling of customer-accounts across departments.[19]

E-mail An increasing number of salespeople and prospects use electronic mail ("e-mail") in place of voice communications. E-mail often reduces the number of contacts required to complete an information exchange. Whereas salespeople might play "phone tag" with a prospect for days before both were available simultaneously, e-mail allows completed exchanges at the convenience of each party. Later contact management applications combine prospect record management with telecommunications capabilities, allowing the salesperson to pull up a prospect's file, automatically dial the appropriate telephone listing or transmit to the e-mail address, and then log the communications in the database.

> Danny Turano's workday as Oracle System Corporation's regional vice president for sales in New York began at home office on the computer, reading through his e-mail. An early start helped him work through the 80-to-100 e-messages he received each day. When he left the house for the city, he carried a Hewlett-Packard 100LX, a wireless e-mail and message device. It connected to Radiomail, a national network, that allowed him to send and receive e-mail wherever he is throughout the day. The HP 100LX connected by cable to his home computer so that he could upload and download data. From this mobile center, Turano managed 42 salespeople that sold $80 million in Oracle software.[20]

Managing E-mail Communications   As e-mail grows in use within the sales force, sales managers must direct the positive development of this tool—and prevent negative developments from occurring. In particular, the sales manager must assure that: (1) e-mail is properly balanced with direct personal communications, (2) time is not wasted due to trivial e-mail traffic; and (3) salespeople are properly advised about ethical issues and/or company policy on e-mail messages. One author suggests a checklist of e-mail do's and don'ts (Exhibit 18.3).[21]

Encouraging Balanced Communications   E-mail can supplement personal communications, but it cannot replace the value of regular face-to-face encounters. E-mail should not be allowed to replace personal communications, either between the sales manager and his or her salespeople, or between salespeople and clients.

Manager-salesperson relationships are built on face-to-face encounters. Sales managers should reserve time to meet in person with salespeople for training and coaching. Similarly, reprimands or termination should not be handled by e-mail. CompuServe, the on-line computer service, had a policy that no employee was to be dismissed by e-mail.[22] On the other hand, e-mail can be used to motivate salespeople or offer a note of congratulations. E-mail can also provide documentation of a salesperson's non-performance issues. For example, a series of three or more e-mail notices about failure to perform certain duties or reach sales goals can help substantiate a manager's claim that the employee was warned of a problem.

Salesperson-customer relationships are also built on personal encounters. Mary Boone, a technology consultant, advises that problems with clients should not be resolved by e-mail; problems should prompt a phone call or visit. But e-mail can be used to develop a consultative salesperson-client relationship. Especially when a salesperson cannot visit a customer regularly, use of e-mail can help to create a stronger bond, notes Boone.[23]

Avoiding E-mail Abuse   Time management is critical in sales, and e-mail is an opportunity to waste time as well as save it. A joint UCLA-Arthur Anderson study among 1500 employees found that their primary use of e-mail was to "chat with other employees."[24] Only about 22% indicated use of e-mail to communicate with clients.

Some companies have taken steps to limit e-mail use. For example, SmithKline Beecham in Philadelphia reportedly charges its business divisions a user fee based on the number of messages sent and the length of those messages. Similarly, *Sales & Marketing Management* reports that Computer Associates in Islandia, New York, shuts down its e-mail system for four hours every day to keep employees from spending too much time on e-mail.

Exhibit **18.3**   **E-MAIL DO'S AND DON'TS**

DO communicate regularly with salespeople via e-mail.
DO send congratulatory notes to salespeople via e-mail (and copy their colleagues).
DO regularly consult with clients via e-mail, and encourage salespeople to do the same.
DO set clear guidelines for e-mail use.
DO proofread e-mail messages carefully for misspellings and other errors.
DON'T substitute e-mail when a personal touch is required.
DON'T reprimand or fire salespeople via e-mail.
DON'T send offensive or suggestive e-mail messages.
DON'T send trivial e-mail.
DON'T assume that deleted e-mails are gone from company records.

Source: Adapted from Michael Adams, Mixed Messages, *Sales & Marketing* Management, June, 1997.

Ethical and Policy Issues   Sales managers should make it clear to salespeople that offensive or discriminatory communications should be avoided on e-mail as in other communications. Copies of e-mail communications are arising in a number of discrimination lawsuits. In a lawsuit filed against a major investment banking firm, the employees contend that they were subjected to racist jokes via e-mail. Another suit at a major printing firm is using e-mail messages to demonstrate a pattern of racial bias and harassment.[25]

Employees should also be told whether the firm monitors e-mail and whether specific e-mail policies exist. About a third of the firms included in a 1996 study by the Society for Human Resource Management had written policies stating that the company had the right to access e-mail communications. Epson America in Torrance, California required employees to sign an acknowledgement of the company's policy on this issue. Intel and Kmart both regularly monitored employee e-mail communications. Salespeople should also be told that e-mail messages—even deleted messages—can be stored by companies for subsequent review and action.

Opportunity Management

Combining contact management and multimedia also allows the sales force to reshape the selling effort, making it more effective by doing new kinds of things. As with the earlier evolution of automated selling efficiency, this approach begins at the level of the individual salesperson and the individual transaction. The focus is a shift from the "prospect management" approach to what the Gartner Group, a sales automation consulting firm, calls an "opportunity management system."[26] The focus of contact management software on individual prospects has been both a strength and a weakness. Prospects are potential customers, and use of contact management software may have strengthened a customer-orientation—and strong customer relationships—among salespeople. On the other hand, contact management strategy lacks a direct link to organizational strategy. Sales opportunity management systems (OMS) link sales projects (such as, "gain acceptance for a new service") directly to organizational objectives. Ken Dulaney with The Gartner Group calls OMSs the backbone of future sales force automation efforts.[27] Related developments help salespeople and managers respond to opportunities that were previously unavailable.

Marketing encyclopedia systems (**MESs**) compile product and pricing information into centralized databases that can be accessed conveniently by salespeople, and that are consistent with requirements of other departments. MESs include audio, video, text, and graphic information, allowing the salesperson to prepare customized presentations that provide prospects with a clear image of their planned purchase. *Sales configuration systems* quickly assemble complex product-service-pricing bundles. For example:

> Lou Adler, Jr., district sales manager for Chevrolet in Atlanta, helped car dealers figure out what cars local markets want, and then price and orders. To do this, he carried three heavy binders: one for standard models, another for options, and a third with price data. A typical dealer might need about 300 cars, and Adler would spend about 20 minutes figuring out the model-option-price combination for each. After these were submitted, the factory tended to reject about 25% as unbuildable. A laptop computer and proprietary software program changed all this. Using the new system, Adler could configure buildable vehicles and price them, all in less than two minutes each.[28]

Sales Management Automation

The third phase of sales automation led to improvements in the efficiency of sales management. As with the salesperson, these early-phase sales management automation efforts are aimed at improving the performance of existing tasks, rather than doing new types of tasks. Computer applications in this phase include:

- **Lead Management**—computerized systems for identifying and qualifying prospects and communicating them to the field sales force.
- **Territory Management**—systems that allow sales managers to allocate sales territories and to monitor performance across territories.
- **Order Entry**—telecommunications systems that channel salesperson or customer orders directly into production and/or fulfillment centers.
- **Call Reporting**—telecomputation systems that allow salespeople to automatically transmit their call reports to a central computer, where numerous reports are compiled for review by the sales manager.
- **Sales Analysis**—analytic software that converts raw sales call report data (e.g., number of calls, expense reports, etc.) into data that can be compared meaningfully across salespeople (e.g., cost per call).

When Jim Jobin was hired as a marketing consultant to Fisher SpacePen Co., sales leads were tracked in a notebook, there was no historical sales data, and no sales automation. Fisher's product, ironically, was a pressurized pen that could write under zero gravity. It had gained fame in the 1970s due to use in the NASA space program. Jobin, who later became the firm's vice president of sales and customer support, set about automating sales. First he set up a networked system of personal computers. Then he obtained an 800 number that allowed sales reps to link into the office. Jobin used D&B MarketPlace, a database on CD-ROM, to identify the leads that he routed to salespeople. The average number of contacts-to-sales decreased from five to two. This allowed Jobin to add 53 sales reps to the firm, including international account managers. Finally, he set up a Web site (http://www.fisherpen.com/spacepen). The result: a 67% increase in sales in one year.[29]

The sales management automation phase used technology to handle individual tasks more efficiently. Yet this phase, like most of the sales management automation accomplished during the early-to-mid 1990s, tended to apply technology to existing salesperson or manager functions. The more substantial benefits from sales force automation appear to be linked to changing the sales process to take advantage of advanced computing and communications technology.

. . . .

AUTOMATING THE SALES PROCESS WITHIN AND BETWEEN GROUPS

Shifting the focus of sales automation from individuals to groups raises the level of difficulty and the potential rewards. Once the focus of sales force automation shifts from the individual sales manager or salesperson to groups—from sales teams, to departments within the organization, to organizations engaged in an alliance—the level of difficulty progressively increases.

Constraints and Benefits of Group-Level Sales Automation

At each level—the sales team, the firm, and between firms—a variety of factors constrain sales and service integration. Individuals, departments, and firms each tend to develop self-serving goals. These sub unit goals may also be suboptimal, in that they do not contribute as much as they could to the entire organization. Further, like individual salespeople, groups tend to develop operating styles that they collectively consider satisfactory. Changing group operating styles is even more difficult than it is for individual salespeople because it includes changing individual work patterns as well as the interactions between individuals.

Yet automation of the sales-and-service process within and across groups offers a number of potential sources of competitive advantage. Indeed, the difficulty of managing the change to group-level sales automation, and of operating such a system efficiently and effectively, is one of the barriers to competitive implementation that makes this a potential source of advantage. Another reason group-level sales and service automation is a potential source of advantage is the value it adds through increased customer revenue and reduced operating costs. These advantages accrue through such factors as reduced cycle time, increased adaptive capability, increased efficiency, and higher quality.

It is important to understand these benefits. They are not automatic by-products of sales force automation. Instead, the sales manager must plan the automation effort based on the specific strategic benefits sought. The quality of the planning effort will determine the benefits realized by the firm. This requires selection and targeting benefits that are important to the firm and its customers, and focusing development and implementation of the sales force automation system on the benefits targeted. Because of their importance, several of the more prominent sales and service automation benefits are reviewed below.

Reduced Cycle Time   Cycle time is the time required to complete a process. For example, the life cycles of products are getting shorter. Each new brand has a shorter and shorter "lifespan," particularly in high-technology industries. According to a McKinsey & Company consulting study, it is more profitable to develop such products on time but substantially over budget, rather than to stay within budget but come out with the product somewhat later.[30] Just as it is becoming increasingly profitable to compress product development cycles, it is also increasingly attractive to compress sales and service cycles. Automation of sales and service accelerates the process by eliminating duplication and standardizing operations. Accelerating the sales and service cycle, in turn, has several critical advantages. It accelerates revenue flow, much like stock turnover increases the profitability of a discount firm. It increases response time to leads, which typically will increase closure rates, because prospects are called on while their interest is still strong. Accelerate order fulfillment and service also increases customer satisfaction, which increases referrals and repeat business.

Increased Adaptive Capability   Increasing globalization, competition, and technological advances are also increasing the need for firms to adapt to change. Adaptive capability refers to an organization's ability to anticipate and adapt to customers' changing needs and wants. Adaptive capability within the sales and service process involves the ability to change elements of this process, beginning with prospecting and ending with delivering and servicing the completed sale. Separation of functions within an organization are a primary factor that inhibit the ability to adapt. Using information technology to automate these functions can increase the firm's ability to adapt how it sells to environmental change. Examples include identifying prospects on the Internet, integrating personal and direct selling, and using electronic devices on the customer site to detect service requirements.

Increased Efficiency   Automating sales activities that occur within and between groups can increase efficiency by: (1) substituting machine for higher-cost human labor, for example, automatic computerized reorders when stock is low; (2) eliminating duplication, such as by consolidation of sales and service databases; (3) on-site configuration of product and pricing configurations, as with computerized proposal preparation; (4) reducing waiting time; and (5) increasing the speed of information exchange.

Higher Quality   Quality is conformance to customer expectations. Quality is important in sales as well as products and services. Quality in the sales and service process includes calling on the right prospects, making information-rich presentations that document customer benefits, configuring the product and pricing package precisely to fit customer needs, delivering at the correct time and place, and servicing promptly and professionally. Integration of the sales function within and between groups helps to improve its quality by improving the reliability of these functions and increasing their responsiveness to customer needs and wants.

Levels of Sales Group Automation

There are unique challenges—and potential rewards—associated with shifting from automation of the individual salesperson to automating exchanges between people. At the group level the technological emphasis shifts as well from computation to connectivity. This shift involves use of toll-free telephone numbers, file-transfer protocols, electronic data interchange, electronic mail, group-support software like Lotus Notes, videoconferencing, and the Internet. The technological combinations vary with the size and scope of people united through automated selling.

Automating the Sales Team   Automating the sales team involves integrating the roles of the sales manager, sales support staff, telemarketers, and salespeople through computer information systems that focus on the buyer. Automated sales teams integrate individual work roles around selling opportunities.

> Aetna Life & Casualty Co. re-engineered its process for issuing policies, cutting the time it took to issue a basic policy from 15 to 5 days, its operations staff from 3,000 to 700 employees, and the number of people needed to handle a policy from as many as 60 down to 1—the sales rep. Leveraged by a personal computer, and linked to the firm's actuarial and other databases, the rep can now perform all the steps needed to process a life insurance application. Once the rep has gathered all the needed information, the policy is transmitted to the company's Hartford headquarters, and the policy is printed and mailed within one day.[31]

As Ken Dulaney notes: "We predict that by the year 2000, 50% of the revenues of the 1000 largest companies in the world will be sold through sales teams that are tightly integrated around customers."[32] Integration of such work roles requires complex information management and scheduling.

> The 8-person sales crew at Livingston Trade Technologies was automated within three months. The goals: Link the reps with one another and their clients, develop proposals in the field, and reduce non-selling time. The equipment: IBM Thinkpads with contact management and word processing software, portable printers, and portable telephones for each rep. The firm also obtained 800-numbers for each rep that routed inbound calls to them at any location. Given this setup, the reps send new data to an electronic mailbox. Later a system at headquarters automatically dials the mailbox, retrieves the uploaded information, combines the rep data, prepares a consolidated report, and routes it to the mailboxes. Each morning, the reps download the fresh data.[33]

Automating the Sales Process across Organizational Functions   Automating the sales process across departments involves integrating *organizational functions* through computer information systems that focus on the buyer. The integration of functions around selling opportunities expands the level of challenges and opportunities.

Expanding automation of the sales process across functions can be a challenge because of differences in culture and goals. A culture is a shared set of beliefs, values, and norms.[34] Cultural differences in people may be based on national origin (for example, Asian and Western cultures) and on place of employment (for example, some firms are seen as more aggressive whereas others are more collegial). There are also cultures within firms, typically aligning within departmental boundaries. People within departments often share the same professional training, the same friendships, and other interlocking communications. They also tend to develop a common language around the unique aspects of their work. The structure of organizational goal and reward systems also contribute to differences between departments; for example, production is often rewarded for cost management, whereas sales is often rewarded for revenue generation. Automating across functions can help bridge these differences for more effective performance.

Texas Instruments links worldwide business functions around sales through its "Design-Win" system.[35] Design-Win is a computer-based system that leads the sales group and other TI departments through the sales process. It goes into effect when a rep identifies a sales opportunity. Data on the prospect and their requirements are automatically shared throughout the organization. For example, a TI rep in Oklahoma City identified an opportunity for business with Seagate, a San Jose, California-based manufacturer of disk drives. Using the Design-Win system, the product was designed for Seagate at TI offices in Houston, manufactured in plants in Houston and Dallas, assembled in the Philippines, and built into Seagate's disk drives at the firm's Singapore manufacturing plant. "It's like everybody was in the same office," said Gene McFarland, vice president of TI's semiconductor group and head of worldwide marketing.

Facilitating integration of sales with other organizational functions is enterprise software. This new type of software replaces individual programs used in accounting, finance, marketing, inventory management, and other functions with one system and one database. Changes made in sales under an enterprise software system are posted to all users commonly. The advantage is elimination of duplication and communications barriers. The disadvantage may be expense (some enterprise software costs $1 million or more) and loss of some department-specific functionality.[36]

A dominant worldwide vendor of enterprise software is SAP, which was founded in 1974 by four IBM executives. An example of the scope of SAP-type applications is seen in the aggressive business-wide reengineering of Toledo, Ohio-based Owens Corning. Central to the firm's growth strategy is integration through SAP. David L. Johns, director of global development for Owens Corning, said that "The underlying principle in our reengineering effort . . . is to make our systems global, common, and simple."[37] The program began by a business process redesign, conducted by five teams totalling 150, and covering all the firm's operations in the world, including Europe, Latin America, Asia, Canada, and the United States. The firm uses SAP to link sales, accounting, human resource, manufacturing, distribution, and other functions worldwide. SAP add-on applications allow SAP users to upload and download information on pricing to a remote sales force using the Internet.[38]

Automating the Selling Process across Organizations   Selling alliances that automate relationships across entire organizations offer a variety of potential sources of competitive advantage, depending on the types of organizations linked and the nature of the linkage. Generally, these linkages include use of information technology to automate buyer-seller alliances and joint marketing alliances.[39]

Automated Buyer-Seller Alliance   The most common form of inter-organizational automation is a buyer-seller alliance facilitated by information technology like electronic data interchange. *Electronic data interchange* (EDI) is electronic transfer of common sales-related information such as purchase orders, invoices, and funds. Used mostly by large manufacturers, distributors, and retailers, it has been estimated that about half of all interorganizational business documents were sent via EDI by the mid-1990s.[40] Large retailers such as Wal-Mart and Sears expect suppliers to include EDI in their marketing mix, so sales managers who lack EDI support often must lobby management for such systems.[41]

Recent buyer-seller alliances have evolved around intranet systems, which are Internet-based connections that limit or exclude access from outsiders.

Buyer-seller alliances have fundamental advantages, including reducing costs associated with: obtaining and evaluating bids from a variety of potential suppliers, rework and/or lost business because of variations in quality, inefficiencies in buyer-seller coordination, and downtime or inventory holding costs caused by inconsistent delivery schedules. Automating these relationships amplifies the benefits of buyer-seller alliances and adds new ones, such as reduced costs and faster cycle time.[42] For example, EDI has been estimated to reduce order-management cycle time by 40%.[43] Because salespeople are freed from routine order processing, it has been estimated that EDI also increases selling time by 40%.[44] It also increases the buyer's costs of switching to a new supplier, which is beneficial to the supplier's long-term position in the relationship.

In summarizing the impacts of EDI systems on the sales function, Ned Hill and Michael Swenson note that these systems: (1) allow salespeople to spend more time on consultative selling, rather than order taking and paperwork; (2) forced managers to redesign information flows; (3) added computer literacy as a requirement for salesperson competence; (4) increased the potential information value added provided by the salesperson to the client; (5) provided firms with a potential competitive weapon; and (6) forced sales managers and salespeople to become familiar with the collateral technology of the information age, such as bar coding, light pens, satellite communications, image processing, and laptop computers.[45]

Automated buyer-seller relationships work at multiple levels. Several large retail grocery and discount chains have negotiated automated relationships with suppliers. When shipments leave the retailer's warehouse, notice is automatically sent to the supplier. Labor costs that would have been involved in ordering, quoting, and similar steps in the selling process are eliminated, inventory holding is minimized, production schedules are optimized, and both allies reduce operating costs.

Baxter Healthcare has extended this buyer-seller alliance by positioning itself as a platform for several suppliers to reach several buyers.[46] Baxter distributes equipment, supplies, and information to the healthcare industry, but it also serves as a single platform through which its buyers can reach a variety of suppliers. In addition to distributing medical supplies, it offers its customers office supplies and even the medical supplies of a competitor. The service has developed as a major new revenue stream for Baxter.

Automated Joint-Marketing Alliances   Firms with complementary product lines can sometimes achieve a strategic advantage by forming a selling alliance. For example, an alliance between Compaq computer and Microsoft enabled the two firms, bidding together, to win contracts against rivals acting alone. Buyers were attracted to the mutually held responsibility for software-hardware system functionality. Automating such marketing alliances can improve their efficiency and institutionalize the benefits. Indeed, automation can serve as the facilitating agency for joint marketing alliances. For example, credit card companies, airlines, and hotels have created marketing alliances such that use of one medium automatically accrues benefits on the others.

PLANNING AND IMPLEMENTING SALES FORCE AUTOMATION

Automating a sales force costs between $8,000 and $17,000 per employee initially, and an additional $2,100 to $2,500 per year per user to maintain the system, according to research compiled by *Forbes* magazine.[47] Despite the fact that automation is estimated to increase each user's revenue by 20% to 30%, *Forbes* also reports estimates that about 80% of initial sales automation projects fail.

Introducing Sales Force Automation into the Firm

There are a number of hurdles along the path to sales force automation (Exhibit 18.4). Based on a survey of 402 firms conducted by International Data Corporation, the top two barriers to effective sales force automation were lack of top management support (reported in 32% of projects) and salesforce resistance (30%). In other words, the sales manager is caught in the middle on this issue. Top management is likely to be skeptical because of the project cost and because of the frequent failure of information technology investments to pay off in business. The sales force is likely to resist because automation is a change, and typically one that is seen as a threat to their power and their job security.

Both of these problems lead to a third cause of problems in automating the sales force: Lack of sales management support. Even when the project is mandated by upper management, 19% of projects suffer from sales management resistance, according to the IDC survey. Other problems: complexity of organizational change (19%), the need to keep upgrading hardware (11%), the costs of internal software development (11%), and the lack of packaged software that meet the firm's individual needs (11%).

Avoiding these problems requires careful sales force automation planning.

Planning Stages

Careful planning is a key to successful sales force automation. Among the steps in this planning process are the following: (1) obtain top management support, (2) involve those affected by the system, (3) identify objectives, (4) design the system, (5) select a project vendor, (6) develop and test a system prototype, (7) train salespeople, (8) reinforce salesperson use, and (9) monitor system performance and benefits. Each step is described in detail below.[48]

Obtain Top Management Support   Top management support for sales force automation is needed for at least two reasons. First, sales force automation can involve a significant organizational investment, and the return on that investment can be delayed by years. Top management must develop a clear understanding of the reason for this investment, in terms of the role sales force automation can play in the execution of organization strategy. In addition, top management must have a realistic view of the financial commitments involved, and the length of time required for sales automation to pay back the investment. Lacking this level of commitment, the sales executive who champions sales force automation could find himself or herself without support—and the project abandoned—when implementation problems arise or costs mount without immediate return.

Second, many people in the selling process—from sales representatives to service personnel—may resist sales force automation. Sales force automation involves change. People do things the way they do because they believe it works best for them. Changing their work pattern involves risk: that they won't be able to perform the new tasks, that they will lose power—or their jobs—under the new routine, that they won't like their new work roles, or that the new system will reduce their performance (particularly if their pay is tied to performance). The more the employee is a veteran of the old system, the more likely he or she is to see any new system as a fad that can be safely ignored. Visible top management commitment to a program like sales force automation may be an important factor in gaining the attention and involvement of reluctant employees.

Involve Those Affected by the System   Involving the people who will be affected by the sales force automation system in its design has both functional and psychological

| Exhibit **18.4** | SALES AUTOMATION IMPLEMENTATION PROBLEMS |

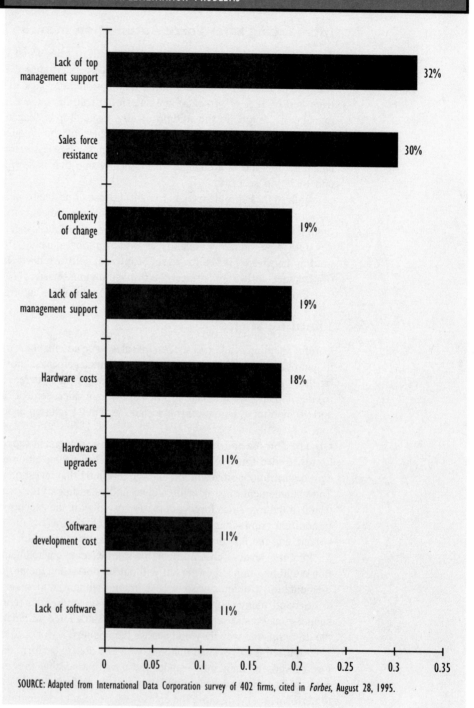

SOURCE: Adapted from International Data Corporation survey of 402 firms, cited in *Forbes*, August 28, 1995.

benefits. At the functional level, using cross-functional teams to design a process usually leads to gains in effectiveness and efficiency. This has been shown in product design as well as process innovation programs. Effectiveness gains occur when team members contribute to the usability of the new system. A sales force automation system can affect many constituents: customers, service personnel, information systems technicians, sales associates, salespeople, sales managers, and others. A system designed from any one perspective, for example, from that of the information systems technician, or the salesperson is likely to be biased toward the needs of that role. Developing the most effective system possible requires optimizing customer benefits from across the remaining roles, at the lowest possible cost to the organization. The participants in those roles, including the customers, are most likely to be able to suggest most precisely how the system can be optimized. Cross-functional teams are also more likely to be able to work out inter-role conflicts.

Involving the various parties who will be affected by the sales force automation system in its design also has psychological benefits. It provides them with symbolic acknowledgement of their importance as members of the sales and service system. Providing those affected with input is likely to be seen by them (and others in the organization) as a more just approach to process design. Finally, involvement enlists commitment. If parties affected by sales force automation are involved, or represented by others, in the design stage they are more likely to be committed to the use and success of the system when it is implemented.

Identify Objectives   Sales force automation is not an end in itself. Many different types of sales automation tools are available that will accomplish a variety of tasks. It is critical to begin sales force automation by clearly identifying the desired outcomes. These outcomes should be described in terms of specific and meaningful objectives. These objectives, in turn, should drive subsequent planning, implementation, and evaluation of the system.

To be effective, sales force automation must fit within the framework of the business' overall strategy. This necessarily includes a clear definition of the firm's target markets, the products and services to be provided, and the technology to be used—including sales force automation—to provide those products and services.

Beyond these basics, it is important to identify the critical elements of the firm's sales and service process, to rate the importance of these elements, and to rate the firm's effectiveness on each. The first two tasks can be performed by the cross-functional team. Ratings of the firm's effectiveness on each process element should be based, where feasible, on a customer perspective.

The most meaningful company ratings are "blind," meaning that customers rate multiple firms and do not know which firm is requesting the ratings. This usually requires use of an independent research firm, but it eliminates response biases from "friendly" customers. The features that affect "internal customers" (when services or information are provided by one department to another) should be rated by those customers as well. This composite profile of sales and service system elements, their relative importance, and effectiveness ratings, can help the cross-functional team determine, and focus on, appropriate sales force automation goals.

When one distribution company automated its sales force, they conducted brainstorming sessions with all the salespeople to identify what they wanted out of the system.[49] The brainstorming process provided everyone affected with a voice in the design of the new system and an opportunity to contribute their perspective. The objectives they targeted included:
- *The ability to spend more time with customers*
- *Enhancement of the perceived value of the company and its salespeople*
- *Reduction of sales process cycle time, including quoting and ordering*

• An increased number of closed orders
• Improved communications throughout the sales channel

Design the System   The purpose of this step is to develop a clear map of the process to be automated. System design includes identifying the activities in the process that is to be automated, linking those activities in sequence, and identifying opportunities for improving the system of elements and linkages.

One approach to process mapping is to conduct a brainstorming session with the cross-functional team to map the flow of an order from prospect identification to product delivery. A simple way to do this is with 5×7-inch index cards, marker pens, and colored tape.

"Is" Process Map   First, have team members take turns identifying a step in the process and posting it on a wall (using tape or pins) in its place in the sequence of events, left to right. Events that can occur at the same time can be placed above one another. Then have team members take turns identifying action linkages with the colored tape. A team secretary can then convert the wall display to a drawing.

"Should" Process Map   Next, ask team members to identify ideas in which automation could be used to streamline the process. Begin by conducting a group decision process to develop a list of sales force automation ideas and to reach a consensus about which ideas are most important. Redesign the "Is" map into a "Should" map based on use of the top-rated ideas.

The results of the system mapping process should provide outside vendors and/or consultants with a clearer view of the selling systems involved and the appropriate technology to apply. Selection of such a vendor/consultant is the next step in the planning process.

Select a Vendor/Consultant   A critical decision in sales force automation is the selection of an experienced outside firm to provide consultation in the project and to provide direction on the selection of computer hardware and software. Depending on the project requirements, this outside vendor might be a consulting firm, a hardware supplier, or a software provider. The general process for selecting such a firm should include the following steps.

Develop Vendor/Consultant Selection Criteria   Hundreds of firms exist that provide sales force automation consulting, computer equipment, and software. It is important that the team narrow the field of firms under consideration. This should be done by developing project-focused selection criteria. Vendor criteria might include experience with comparable projects, industry-specific experience, technological capabilities, and so on. Appropriate selection criteria can be developed by the team using appropriate group decision processes.

Indentify Candidate Vendors   Given criteria specific to its needs, the cross-functional team can narrow the field of potential vendors. Candidate vendors can be obtained through contact with other sales managers, trade or professional association executives, the annual technology issue of *Sales & Marketing Management* magazine, and similar sources. From these and other sources, the team should develop a list of four to seven vendors whose characteristics and capabilities suggest that they are most likely to meet the vendor criteria.

Prepare an RFP   A Request for Proposals (RFP) is a formal statement specifying what is needed and requesting proposals by a stated deadline. The RFP should provide sufficient information about the background and operations of the firm to provide potential vendors with a clear understanding of the context of the project. It should also include project specifications and a request for at least three references on recent comparable projects from each vendor, including names, contact information, and project descriptions.

Review Proposals   The purpose of reviewing proposals is to identify the top candidate vendors. An effective method for reviewing proposals is to convert the vendor criteria into a rating sheet. Using this sheet, cross-functional team members can rate each proposed vendor on all criteria. Evaluation scores can then be adjusted by the relative importance of each criterion, and a weighted rating for each vendor can be calculated.

View Vendor Presentations   The cross-functional team should request presentations from the three top-rated vendors. These presentations should be limited to a specified time period (such as 30 minutes), but should include additional time for questions from the team. The purpose of these presentations is to obtain "live" demonstrations of the vendor's capabilities, particularly as they pertain to the firm's specific project.

Check Vendor References   Before making a final vendor selection, it is important to check references. The cross-functional team should develop a list of open-ended questions about the vendors (such as: "Was their project for you completed on time and on budget?"). Team members should contact at least two references from each of the top three vendors.

Make Final Selection   The final selection of a vendor includes subjective as well as objective considerations. The vendor-firm relationship is likely to be long-term, as additional support or expansion of the system is required. Thus the final selection should be similar to the selection of an employee that the team will be required to work with on an ongoing basis.

Develop and Test a Prototype   Experimentation is a basic approach to learning. In planning a sales force automation system, the sales manager can learn how to optimize the system by using it on an experimental basis. This involves developing a prototype system that is scaled down to a limited number of users. A trial run of the prototype system, along with careful observation and discussion with the users, can identify opportunities for improvement. This is the equivalent to a "beta" test that software vendors conduct when they allow "lead" users to try out new program versions. A sales manager can continue the trial runs, and make adjustments in the system along the way, until he/she believes it is ready for general introduction. This approach reduces the waste and increased salesperson resistance that could occur if an untested system were implemented across the sales force. It also provides information that can be used in training salespeople to use the new system.

Train Salespeople   It is easy for sales managers to neglect sales force automation training. The equipment and software involve substantial expenses, which may prompt top management resistance. At least the equipment and software are tangible, whereas the value of an intangible like training is difficult to visualize. And training can cost between one and three times as much as the automation system itself.[50] Because training of salespeople may take them out of the field, this adds an opportunity cost of lost sales to the project.

Yet carefully developed training is a key to sales force automation success. Training clarifies the new post-automation job responsibilities of salespeople. Lack of proper training leaves salespeople unclear about their new duties, which is likely to lead to dissatisfaction with the automation program and perhaps the job itself. As with planning for sales force automation, training to use it should begin with the end in mind: What do salespeople need to know in order to use the new system effectively? Given these goals, the sales manager should direct the production of corresponding learning tools and training applications. He or she should also direct the development of measures to determine whether each salesperson has learned what he or she needs to know in order to use the system properly.

Reinforce Salesperson Use   People tend to continue their prior behaviors, and only repeat new behavior if it is rewarded. Simply installing a sales force automation system and training salespeople to use it will not ensure long-term use. The old way of doing things is more comfortable—and seems more productive—for many salespeople. Although the benefits of change, and the required behaviors, may be demonstrated in the training phase, the "refreezing" of the desired new behavior will not occur without a carefully designed program of reinforcement.

Use of the sales force automation system can be rewarded through recognition, promotions, or formal performance evaluations. Recognition can be provided for salespeople

---

Case 18.1   GULF INDUSTRIES[51]

Michael Hays was a regional sales manager with Gulf Industries, a sign-making firm in Torrance, California. His job involved meeting with prospects and attempting to develop appealing signs. He would spend an hour or so cutting and pasting graphics and type, asking the prospects to imagine different fonts and colors. If the response was positive, he would have to ask for time to check with Gulf's production department about whether the design was feasible, and, if it was, when it could be produced, and at what cost. This created a gap through which sales were lost.

When Gulf equipped Hays with a laptop and multimedia software, he could design a sign with customized graphics—scanning in the

company logo and perhaps a featured product—in 15 minutes. Because the program had been developed with Gulf's production department, designs were automatically authorized. Contracts were printed out on the spot.

1. Identify the benefits of Gulf Industries' sales force automation system, from the perspective of the company itself, Michael Hays' role as a sales manager salesperson, and the customer.
2. Suggest additional ways that sales force automation could be used to improve performance of Gulf Industries, its salespeople, or its customer service.

Case 18.2   MULTICOM COMMUNICATIONS[52]

Multicom Communications is a $5-million firm in St. Louis that manages data and communications systems for clients. The company's initial move into sales force automation was through use of contact management software. Although the contact management information helped the firm increase sales five times over, it also helped the CEO Michael Koenig to see that communications was sometimes poor across Multicom departments.

As a result the company formed an intranet system, linking every department, including those in the field, through a company-wide Internet site. Using this system, every department worked from one electronic document per job, which the salesperson begins at the start of a new client relationship. Each week CEO Koenig pulls leads from the Dodge Report (downloaded directly into the firm's database through a

program written by the chief engineer), rates them on potential, and divides them among the firm's four salespeople. When a prospect becomes a client, an electronic job form is completed on the intranet, providing project details and scheduling to all departments. Scheduled authorizations are forwarded across departments—from accounting, to production, to fabrication—by e-mail. The system has helped Multicom collapse the sale to service cycle in its business.

1. Identify the benefits that this group-level sales force automation system has provided to Multicomm, its individual salespeople, and its customers.
2. List the types of training that were probably needed before this system could be effectively implemented.

who most effectively use the new system during sales force meetings and in the sales division's newsletter.

Promotional events could also be designed incorporating use of the new technology.

MCI Telecommunications Corporation conducted a sales contest on the company intranet to encourage its 5000 business sales and service salespeople to use it.[53] The salespeople could earn points for achieving selected sales revenue objectives by product line. The points were redeemable for more than 300 prizes—trips to Monte Carlo, home fitness centers, and the like—which were posted in an on-line catalog. Salespeople had to use the intranet to track their performance, read program announcements, and select prizes. No paper was used in the entire contest.

Use of the sales automation system could also be made part of the salesperson's formal performance evaluation. This addition to the evaluation criteria would need to be announced in advance and the basis for evaluation clearly specified. The sales manager should also provide ongoing feedback to salespeople regarding their performance on this new job role.

Monitor System Performance and Benefits   A final step in implementing sales force automation is to develop a system to monitor performance of the system, including benefits that accrue from use of the system. Sales force automation is a continuous process, not a one-time event. The sales manager can be assured that there will be a recurring need to upgrade equipment and software, to enhance the system with new features, and even to redesign it to take advantage of emerging technological capabilities. Documenting and communicating the benefits of automation from the beginning can help in the sales manager's effort to grow support from the two key constituencies involved: salespeople and top management.

It is also important to monitor and regularly adjust sales force automation system operations. This will involve use of the quality management tools described in Chapter 12, including identification of the key system elements, development of performance measures for those elements, and then using quality diagnostic tools to improve the system.

SUMMARY

Recent advances in information technology have changed the way business is conducted. Sales managers can use these new technologies to improve the performance of individual salespeople and the sales force as a whole. At the level of individual work roles, sales automation can improve documentation and presentations, contact management, and sales management functions. At the group level, sales automation can improve coordination between members of the sales team, between departments within the firm, and between organizations. Because an estimated 60% to 80% of sales automation projects initially fail, it is important that the sales manager use appropriate sales automation planning.

ASSIGNMENTS/DISCUSSION QUESTIONS

The following assignments can be assigned individually or as in-class team exercises.

1. Brainstorm a list of potential advantages and disadvantages of sales force automation from the perspective of a: (a) salesperson; (2) sales manager; (3) company president; and (4) customer.

2. Prepare a list of "worst case" sales force automation scenarios; things that could go wrong when the sales force is automated at each level, including: (a) independent salespeople on laptop computers; (b) sales teams connected by automated systems; (c) interdepartmental systems; and (d) interorganizational systems. Then identify ways that the worst-case scenarios could be prevented.

3. Identify negative things a sales manager could do to automate the salesforce, if she or he were determined to do it *wrong*.

4. Assume the role of an expert, and develop a prioritized list of tips on sales force automation.

5. Design a contact management program for you to keep in touch with your friends and business contacts. What would be the key elements of the program or system? What features is it likely to have that are in typical sales-oriented contact-management software? What features would it have that are lacking in such software?

6. Based on your own experiences with e-mail, identify what you consider to be the advantages and disadvantages of this medium of communications. What could be done to improve e-mail as a communications medium?

7. List the computerized communications and presentation systems (software, hardware, and other) that are available today that were not commonly available 10 years ago. Brainstorm a list of systems that might be available 10 years from now, that are not now commonly available. How might they be used to improve selling and sales management?

8. Many of the sales force automation systems limit or eliminate the role of the salesperson. Identify the advantages and disadvantages of limited or no salesperson contact from the standpoint of: (a) the business; and (b) the customer.

9. Develop a list of automated joint marketing alliances with which you are familiar. Then develop a list of alliances that you consider plausible, identifying the strategic advantage(s) of each.

10. Given your knowledge of the steps involved in sales force automation, identify what you expect would be the three most critical steps and explain why you believe they are top priority.

ENDNOTES

1. Louis A. Wallis, Changing Sales Roles with CSS, in Wallis (1994), *Computer-Based Sales Force Support,* New York: The Conference Board, Report No. 953, p. 11.
2. Sarah Schafer, Supercharged Selling, *INC.,* Special Technology Issue, No. 2, 1997, pp. 42–51.
3. *Ibid.,* p. 44.
4. Christen P. Heide, *'Thumbs Up' for Technology, Sales Reps Say.* <http://www.dartrd/corp.com/press8.html> (August 1, 1997).
5. George A. Smith, Jr. (1995), *Sales Productivity Measurement,* Milwaukee: ASQC Quality Press.
6. Thomas M. Siebel and Michael S. Malone (1996), *Virtual Selling,* New York: Free Press.
7. MIRC USA, New Developments in Sales Automation Software Markets, MIRC USA, I-1, 1993.
8. *Ibid.*
9. Michael Sullivan-Trainor, It's All in the Numbers, *Computerworld,* September 13, 1993, p. 9.
10. Much of the description of the evolution in sales force automation found in this subsection is adapted from material developed by The Gartner Group, a sales and marketing consulting firm in Stamford, Connecticut, although certain elements of that material have been modified here and other elements have been added. An interesting presentation of the Gartner Group's work in this area can be found in "The Automated Sales Force," *Marketing Tools,* October, 1996, pp. 57–63, an article written by Ken Dulaney, vice president and product director for platform and operating system technology for The Gartner Group.

11. Shari Caudron, Sales-Force Automation Comes of Age, *Industry Week,* 245(10), May 20, 1996, pp. 146–150.

12. Ginger Trumfio, The Future is Now, *Sales & Marketing Management,* November, 1994, pp. 74–80.

13. OmniTech Consulting Group survey results reported by Ginger Trumfio, The Future is Now, *Sales & Marketing Management,* November, 1994, pp. 74–80.

14. Much of this subsection is adapted from Bob Alexander with Malcolm Fleschner, Revolutionize Your Presentations, *Personal Selling Power,* May/June, 1995, pp. 26–31.

15. *Ibid.,* p. 31.

16. Brian Silverman, Get'em While They're Hot, *Sales & Marketing Management* 149(2), February, 1997, pp. 47–50.

17. *Ibid.*

18. Trumfio, 1994.

19. Based on Marc Semanoff, Meeting the Challenge of Contact Management, *Industrial Distribution,* 85(11), November, 1996, pp. T16–T18.

20. Jeffrey Young, On the Day On the Wire: A Road Warrior's Journal, *Forbes,* August 18, 1995, pp. 102–106.

21. Based on Michael Adams, Mixed Messages, *Sales & Marketing Management,* June, 1997, pp. 72–76.

22. *Ibid.*

23. *Ibid.,* p. 74.

24. *Ibid.*

25. *Ibid.,* p. 76.

26. Ken Dulaney, The Automated Sales Force, *Marketing Tools,* October, 1996, pp. 57–63.

27. *Ibid.,* p. 59.

28. Shari Caudron, Sales Force Automation Comes of Age, *Industry Week* 245, May 20, 1996, pp. 146–150.

29. Based on Julia King and Mindy Blodgett, Sales Tools Will Get Integrated Face-Lift, *Computerworld,* 30(27), July 1, 1997, pp. 1–16.

30. Brian Dumaine, How Managers Can Succeed Through Speed, *Fortune,* February 13, 1989, pp. 54–59.

31. Howard Gleckman, The Technology Payoff, *Business Week,* June 14, 1993, pp. 57–68.

32. Dulaney, 1996, p. 61.

33. Melissa Campanelli, Starting From Scratch, *Sales & Marketing Management,* November, 1994, pp. 55–56.

34. Harrison M. Trice and Janice M. Beyer (1993), *The Cultures of Work Organizations,* Upper Saddle River, Prentice Hall.

35. Tom Dellecave, Jr., Chipping In, *Sales & Marketing Technology,* June, 1996, pp. 35–37.

36. David S. Fondiller, Client Serving, *Forbes,* 14(1), July 4, 1994, pp. 130–131.

37. Laura K. Romei and Ron Billie, New Technologies Strengthens New Commitment, *Managing Office Technology,* 41(7), July, 1996, pp. 18–20.

38. Jim Kerstetter, Trilogy Links Pricing Software to SAP's R/3 for Remote Sales, *PC Week,* 1997, 14(8), February 24, pp. 8–9.

39. Benn R. Konsynski and F. Warren McFarlan, Information Partnerships—Shared Data, Shared Scale, *Harvard Business Review,* September–October, 1990, pp. 114–120.

40. Ned C. Hill and Michael J. Swenson, The Impact of Electronic Data Interchange on the Sales Function, *Journal of Personal Selling & Sales Management,* 14(3), Summer 1994, pp. 79–87.

41. Thomas J. Wall, The ABCs of EDI, *Sales & Marketing Management,* Sales Management Technology Supplement, June 1996, pp. 30–33.

42. G. Premkumar, K. Ramamurthy, and Sree Nilakanta, Implementation of Electronic Data Interchange: An Innovation Diffusion Perspective, *Journal of Management Information Systems,* 11(2) Fall 1994, pp. 157–186.

43. Wall, 1996.

44. Michael E. Leeman and Peter J. Sevcik, All for One, *Communications Week* 585, November 20, 1995, pp. 38–41.

45. Hill and Swenson, 1994.

46. Konsynski and McFarlan, 1990.

47. Jeffrey Young, Can Computers Really Boost Sales?, *Forbes,* ASAP Supplement, August 28, 1995, pp. 84–94.

48. Adapted from Melissa Campanelli, Taking the Next Step, *Sales & Marketing Management,* December, 1994, pp. 43–48; George W. Colombo (1994), *Sales Force Automation,* New York: McGraw-Hill; Jeffrey Young, Can Computers Really Boost Sales, *Forbes,* August 28, 1995, pp. 84–94; Bob Alexander with Malcolm Fleschner, How IBM Solves the Automation Puzzle, *Personal Selling Power,* September, 1994, pp. 30–36.

49. Dave Witwer, Investing in Sales Automation, *Industrial Distribution,* 85(10), October, 1996, pp. 92–93.

50. Jeffrey Young, Can Computers Really Boost Sales?, *Forbes,* August 28, 1995, pp. 84–94, based on recommendations from The Guide to Sales, Customer Service, and Marketing Automation, published by Barton Goldenberg Information Systems Marketing, Inc.

51. Based on Schafer, 1997.

52. Schafer, 1997.

53. Andy Cohen, Sales Contests Go Interactive, *Sales & Marketing Management* 148(7), July, 1996, pp. 45–46.

Appendix 1

INTEGRATIVE CASES

Case A-1. The Regional Manager's Dilemma[1]

Jessica Mueller, a salesperson with 10 years experience, received a phone call from Dan Freedman, a former customer that she had successfully worked with about three years earlier. Dan said that he was back in Chicago with an electronic funds verification company and wanted Jessica to come by so they could establish a new account. Jessica determined that Dan had the authority to buy at his new company. Upon asking directions, Jessica quickly realized that the account was not only in another salesperson's territory, but in another district. She immediately approached her regional manager, explained the situation, and strongly requested that she be allowed to pursue the account. The regional manager met with the district manager responsible for the area the account was in to learn if anyone was calling on the account. The district manager responded by saying the district's newest hire had just cold called the account and she was very excited about it, as was the district manager herself. The regional manager reflected on several relevant facts. Jessica writes a tremendous amount of business and, as is true of most successful salespeople, has a big ego. The account in question would constitute a top opportunity for the new salesperson, both district managers, who were somewhat inexperienced, and the regional manager, all of whom are paid on incremental sales increases.

What should the regional manager do?

Case A-2. Motivate or Reassign?

It is inevitable that in any sales organization, veteran salespeople retain accounts that they are not actively developing. Typically these are accounts with a large potential but the veteran salesperson sees them as low maintenance money makers that they have earned through relationship building and solution selling a long time ago. The district manager sees the account as a huge untapped source of sales volume and a fantastic opportunity for a young, aggressive salesperson. One young salesperson has a "starter territory" with three or four of these underdeveloped accounts in it. If the account in this case was reassigned, the veteran salesperson would lose his second largest account. The manager's pay is based on increased sales and meeting profit objectives.

What should the manager do? Should he/she attempt to motivate the veteran salesperson to expand the position? Should he/she take the account and reassign it to a younger salesperson? Or should the manager take some entirely different action? What would that action be?

Case A-3. Reassigning a Salesperson[2]

Grocery Products, Inc., uses a team approach to call on accounts. Tim Kemp was assigned to the southwestern team as its new manager. After examining the data for Family Fare, one of his leading chains, he decided that Jeff was underperforming. He replaced Jeff with Susan. Ralph, the Family Fare buyer, complained and said that the business would suffer because Jeff was no longer on the account. Tim, knowing Susan's capabilities, stood firm on his decision. After several months Ralph started to make personal advances toward Susan. What should Tim do? Should he reassign Jeff and try to motivate him? Should he transfer Susan and put another man on the account? Or should he do something else? What would that be?

---

[1]Cases A-1 and A-2 were supplied by Rich Campbell, District Manager, Wallace, May 1997.
[2]This case was supplied by a manager in the grocery products industry.

Case A-4.   Hiring for Latin America[3]

Alexander Frelier is in charge of sales for Burlington Industries in Latin America. When interviewing for salesperson positions he uses the following criteria:

1. Fully bilingual in English and Spanish
2. Bicultural—the ability to deal with different, and sometimes conflicting, cultures
3. The ability to perform in complex situations and changing environments, to have a flexible mindset, and to work under pressure
4. The ability to learn and to change
5. Motivation to learn, to have a positive attitude, and to stay with the company for a long time
6. Demonstration of maturity
7. Experience with international trade and computer literacy are helpful
8. To have entrepreneurial energy but be effective in a large organization

Relationship selling is practiced. The salesperson is trained to listen to the customer, communicate issues to company management and staff, make an action plan that will address customer needs, and present the plan effectively to the customer. A targeted return on an account is used to achieve an overall ROI. There can be important tradeoffs between production capacity, inventory, margins, new products, sales quotas, and reducing process complexity. There is a six-month review of performance versus objectives. Forecasting is a critical part of the salesperson's job because customers want delivery in 45 days although production can take three times longer.

Write a job description for this representative.

Case A-5.   Sick Leave[4]

Pillar Cat Food gave all of its salespeople a fleet car. The job demanded extensive travel during each week. Because the company was very safety-conscious it rewarded employees for accident-free driving. Its goal was fewer than eight accidents per one million miles.

Doug injured his foot playing baseball, so his right foot was put in a bubble cast. He claimed that he could not drive safely with his left foot so his manager put him on short-term disability leave. In return Doug agreed to complete some special projects at home.

The manager checked in a month and found that Doug had not completed any of his special projects. Furthermore, Doug was driving the company car for personal business, such as grocery shopping.

What should the manager have done to avoid this problem? What should she do now?

Case A-6.   Hiring Documentation

Tim Kebles sighed as he sat down at his desk. "What a mess!" he thought. Tim had been a sales trainer for almost three years, but today was unique. He had been training James Taylor for two weeks and found that he was bright and caught on quickly. Tim enjoyed working with James. This morning James' manager called Tim with the shocking news that "James is a fake. He lied about almost everything on his resume. He does not have a college degree and none of his listed past experiences are real. He wrote his own letters of recommendation and asked others to sign and mail them for him."

Design a procedure that will prevent this faking of hiring documentation again.

---

[3]Material for this case was supplied by Alexander Frelier of Burlington Industries.
[4]Case A-5 and A-6 were written by a pharmaceutical representative.

Case A-7.   The Decision To Enter the Japanese Cosmetic Market

MARKETING IN JAPAN[5]

Selling in Japan requires a long-range commitment from top management. This commitment must include extensive preparation; long-range planning; an integrated marketing plan that includes products that have been modified for the local markets, the right advertising, and good distribution; a service center; and quality local staff. Relationships and partnering are important in developing a Japanese marketing strategy. In addition to understanding the local culture, the new entrant to Japan must never forget that the Japanese consumer is king or queen, perhaps even a dictator.

PLANNING TO SELL IN JAPAN

Taking a Long-Range View

Preparing for selling in the Japanese market requires a top management commitment, extensive preparation, and patient planning.

Top Management Commitment

Successful selling in Japan begins with a commitment that includes long hours of senior management and quick cooperation from the following departments—corporate planning, marketing research, research and development, technical service, personnel, finance, production, logistics, and marketing.

Extensive Preparation

Before making a business contact, extensive preparation should include a feasibility study using market research to answer the following critical marketing questions:

1. Do you have better products than Japanese competitors? Do you have patented technology or know-how that Japanese companies do not have?
2. Is your price at the customer's door competitive?
3. Do the estimated sales volume and profits make it worthwhile to invest manpower and capital?

Top management must then answer questions regarding staffing the project and the management philosophy:

1. As the president of a corporation, are you willing to—

    - be the leader of the Japanese project?
    - visit prospective customers, stores, and channels in person?
    - assign the best senior management to Japan?

2. Are you willing to be flexible, adjusting your business conduct to satisfy demanding Japanese customers who think that the customer is king or queen?
3. Are you willing to delegate the authority of marketing decision making to those people who you have assigned to live in Japan?
4. Are you patient and consistent in your behavior? Will you wait several years to reach break-even? (Many American companies failed because they sought a short-term return on investment or changed policies when top management changed.)

---

[5]This material was supplied by Professor Tatsuo Shoda, who, at the time, was General Manager, Hathaway Division, Kanebo Co., Ltd. He was formerly with Snow Brand Milk Products Co., Ltd as a brand manager, sales manager, advertising manager of the international department, and Senior Manager of the corporate marketing division. He had also been the business manager of the biscuit division of Campbell, Japan, Inc.

Be Patient

Reaching break-even could easily take four years. The research and negotiation with a partner will take at least one year. Patience is required to get answers from a partner because the decision-making process in Japan is so different. In a Japanese company, a plan to start a new business is considered by middle management, general managers, and finally top management who formally decide whether to accept the plan. This slow process can be frustrating early in the project, but once the plan is accepted it is implemented quickly because everyone is familiar with the details. Once the plan is implemented, reaching break-even can take two or three years.

Developing a Local Organization

The development of a local organization begins with finding a good partner, establishing relationships with suppliers and channels, and finally selecting quality people for sales management.

Selecting a Good Partner

Attacking the fiercest competitive market requires a good guide who knows the territory. A partner may be a local manufacturer, a distributor, or an agent who understands your company philosophy, products, and strategies. A good partner will give strong advice, even when it is not welcome. This partner will help to recruit key staff, such as a sales manager.

Selecting the Best Channel of Distribution

The distribution system must be able to deliver the right product, in the right quantity, on time because many supermarkets do not have their own warehouses. Thus Japanese retailers use just-in-time logistics just like manufacturing.

Establishing Relationships

Japanese companies want to do business with a reliable supplier, so it is important to establish good relationships with channels of distribution and customers. The prospective buyer in a company needs to know that you are dependable so that he can recommend you with confidence to his colleagues and upper management. To succeed you must have more than a better product at a lower price. Customers want to know your company history, technical standards, quality assurance system, distribution systems that enable you to deliver the product on time, and post-sales service, and they want know about top management as individuals.

Selecting Quality Local Staff

It is critical to select quality local staff, but the task is not an easy one. The general manager must understand your company goals and strategies as well as have leadership skills to deal with Japanese employees. Finding someone with these skills and a working knowledge of English can be a difficult assignment.

Implementing a Marketing Strategy

Implementation in Japan begins with an integrated marketing plan based on research, target customers, clearly identified product benefits, competitive analysis, a channels strategy, and communications strategies for advertising and personal selling. In short, implementation in Japan requires the same basics as in the U.S. market, but the differences in the culture and competition leave little room for error in Japan, so each component of the plan must be developed with care.

It is unlikely that products that are successful in other markets will succeed in Japan because of differences in preferences and cultures. Many U.S. companies have struggled because they failed to do the research that was necessary to develop a product that was right for the Japanese market and better than competitive ones.

A technical service center will be needed in most cases during the product development phase to answer quickly the questions from potential customers and channels of distribution. After the product is introduced post-sales service systems must be established to assure customer satisfaction. Service after the sale is the best way to build and maintain the critical good customer relationships that will ensure repeat business.

Japanese attitudes, likes, beliefs, systems of thinking, and methods of expression are so different from other markets that new advertisements must be created for Japanese markets. It is rarely possible to simply adapt existing ones to the Japanese markets. Companies must be willing to invest in research to determine those characteristics of commercials that make them effective in Japan. Key managers of the company must study the Japanese culture.

SALES MANAGEMENT IN JAPAN

High Technology

In Japan over 42,000 supermarkets and convenience stores are equipped with scanning systems. These systems provide the manufacturer with data on the movement of each item for the previous week. The data are used for production planning and to measure the success of new products, advertisements, and in-store merchandising. Many chain stores have electronic ordering systems, which means that the old-style salesperson is dead.

Some advanced companies supply salespeople with hand-held computers that communicate store inventories and orders directly to the manufacturer. Manufacturers use computers to help retailers develop a schematic plan for a shelf allocation strategy.

Developing Sales Managers

In Japan sales managers come from two sources. A manager may be promoted from chief of a sales section or as part of a company rotational policy. In the second case a chief marketing planner becomes a local sales manager and, after a few years, is promoted to a product manager position at the head office. This rotation develops future executives who know the field and who have experience leading people in the battlefield of the marketplace. Product managers are promoted to branch manager and then to general manager at headquarters.

An excellent sales manager should be able to understand marketing strategies. Headquarters will give him a time schedule, a goal for the year, a marketing plan, and a budget. The sales manager will then develop the marketing and sales plan for his territory.

Once territory goals are set in terms of sales volume, store coverage, and market share, many Japanese sales managers use a team of salespeople to develop sales goals and merchandising strategies for each store. These small teams function like quality circles in production, which have been so successful in improving the quality of products.

Training Salespeople

The typical training for a Japanese salesperson is as follows:

1. The new recruit training begins at the company training center with the company history, product knowledge, the accounting system, the computer system, and training in the plant to learn the production process. This training can last from one month to several years. (A person who is new to marketing will be assigned as a sales clerk for a year to handle orders and physical distribution.)
2. After the initial training, the field sales trainee will call on retail stores, checking the inventory of his or her company's product, the date of the product, and assist the salesperson.
3. The trainee is promoted to salesperson for a small chain store, taking orders, introducing new products, and promoting in-store merchandising for his or her stores.

4. When the salesperson is promoted to sales manager or sales chief, he or she directs young sales colleagues to achieve their annual goals and serves as an account manager for a large regional chain. The account manager role includes presenting an annual in-store-promotion plan for the chain.

During each of these phases there are many training programs. On-the-job training is given by senior people. Off-the-job courses are prepared by the training department at headquarters. These courses include introductory selling, advanced selling, in-store merchandising, sales consulting, and sales strategies. Some companies require sales managers to take a correspondence course from Cornell University that has been translated into Japanese.

Motivation and Compensation

Human relations and recognition are very important in Japan. Many companies have an annual convention to celebrate the best salespeople. A good sales manager always is careful not to put his people in a shameful position. In most Japanese companies older salesmen are given the honorary name of "Kachou-taiguu," which means that they are treated as managers even though they do not have any subordinates.

In Japan, a good sales manager tries to be a paternal leader who takes good care of his subordinates and is willing to be a consultant for their private problems. People work for his company from their youth to retirement. They say, "I work for so-and-so company," not "I am a salesman." His company is his whole society or community. For example, many salary men play golf on the weekends only with a boss or company friends. In recent years this company orientation is weakening among the younger generation.

Salespeople for most Japanese manufacturers are paid only a straight salary. Generally speaking, salaries and promotion are based on seniority. Within the same seniority group increases will depend on individual differences in abilities and results for the last year. The proportion based on evaluation of ability has been increasing in recent years.

INVESTIGATING THE JAPANESE COSMETIC MARKET[6]

A First-Hand Investigation of the Market

Rex Clark, the general sales manager of Amcom, Inc., a U.S. cosmetics company, was considering the introduction of the AsianGlo cosmetics line to the Japanese market. AsianGlo had been very successful in the Asian-American market in the United States. He decided to investigate the market firsthand. His investigation began by studying the *Osaka English Business Directory* to locate a trading company. He selected the Mizuho Trading Company and contacted its president Mr. Tomio Masuda. Mr. Masuda, who spoke fluent English and German, dealt frequently with foreign cosmetics companies. He indicated that he would be happy to meet with Rex.

Rex had not been in Japan before so leaving his hotel and heading for the subway station was an adventure. He bought a ticket to Yodoyabashi and then switched to the Keihan train headed for Kyoto. After the 40 minute ride he got off at the Tambashi station, where he was met by a company secretary who guided him for the 10 minute walk to the company. He was served Japanese tea while he awaited Mr. Yamada, Mr. Masuda's assistant.

The Initial Briefing

Before meeting Mr. Masuda, Mr. Yamada gave a brief profile of the company and explained its functions as follows:

1. Maintain long-term relationships with current suppliers.
2. Visit and select potential foreign manufacturers based on the quality and price of their products and their willingness to cope with the Japanese culture.

[6]These materials were supplied by Alice Lee, who has lived in Taiwan, the United States, and Japan.

3. Test the imported cosmetic products according to the guidelines from the Japanese Ministry of Health and report all findings.
4. Maintain a close relationship with wholesalers and retailers.
5. Promote the foreign products because the foreign manufacturers do not know how to promote or advertise in Japan. Once a product is proven to be successful, the first-level wholesalers will start to help with advertising.
6. Be responsible for storage.

He also pointed out two aspects of the Japanese cosmetics industry that are difficult for foreign companies to comprehend.

1. The Japanese Ministry of Health requires all cosmetics companies to submit the formula for each product that it plans to sell in Japan. Many foreign companies are reluctant to reveal their secret formulae.
2. The retail price in Japan is about 4 times the manufacturer's list price. The margins for most cosmetics products are as follows:

Manufacturer	25%
Trading Company	25%
Wholesaler 1	15–20%
Wholesaler 2	15–20%
Retailer	10–15%

Even though the trading company explains the products and marketing strategies to wholesaler 2 directly, the products must still pass through wholesaler 1. Although wholesaler 1 performs no initial functions, once the product has been proven successful in trial markets it will take over the promotion and utilize its full network. Some Japanese companies have tried to simplify their distribution systems. Several manufacturers were brought to court by their wholesalers for skipping them in the distribution of products. The court ruled in favor of the wholesalers. It concluded that even though there was no written contract, the companies had been doing business together for years and this unwritten agreement is binding forever. Thus it is illegal for the manufacturer to terminate a wholesaler.

Mr. Yamada explained different types of rebates that suppliers and wholesalers use to promote sales through retailers. In one rebate form, the trading company sets a one-month quantity goal for the retailer. If the goal is accomplished, a percentage of sales is rebated to the retailer. The trading company does not pay the rebate until two months after the sale, thereby eliminating revenues that are later offset by returned goods. The trading company salesperson receives 2 or 3% of the net sales during this promotion.

Rex wanted to consider direct salespeople who would call directly on customers. Mr. Yamada said that such a form of distribution was very minor in the cosmetics industry. He noted that, "Because there were problems with the door-to-door network, about 7 years ago this concept was virtually destroyed in Japan."

The Next Step

Mr. Yamada then took Rex to meet the president, Mr. Masuda. After a brief tea ceremony Mr. Masuda said, "I think that Mr. Yamada has answered your initial questions. Before we proceed further we need a strategic plan from you that will be consistent with the Japanese methods for foreign sales in Japan."

Rex has asked you to draft such a plan. Indicate clearly any assumptions that you make and additional data that are needed. Where could you get such data? If critical data are missing make a range of assumptions so that a first draft of the plan will help Rex to decide if he wants to market AsianGlo in Japan. After you make this plan, what is your recommendation? Should Rex proceed or drop the idea to move into Japan and instead explore other Asian countries?

Case A-8.   InTek[7] Corporation Considers a New Compensation Plan

In 1997, Glen Godwin was assigned the task of evaluating the compensation plan for the InTek sales force in the United States. InTek, located in San Jose, California, manufactures electronic chips, components, and subassemblies for other manufacturers of personal computers, fax machines, printers, and telecommunication equipment. The company has a sales force of 200 salespeople who call on value-added manufacturers. Before 1992 InTek had a compensation system that included a base salary and a bonus incentive that was 40% of the salesperson's total compensation. The total bonus was determined by the company achieving certain goals. The allocation to salespeople was based on their performance evaluation by managers. Salespeople found this system demotivating because they thought it was subjective and did not always reflect their effort.

In 1992 the company developed the following point system:

Product	Assigned Points	Assigned Quota (000)	Quota Achieved	Percent Achieved	Earned Points
A	50	$ 300	$ 210	70%	35
B	150	200	280	140%	210
C	100	400	400	100%	100
D	200	100	150	150%	300
Total	500	$1,000	$1,040		645

Points were assigned according to the importance of the product and the relative difficulty in selling it. For example, product A could be an old product that was largely a re-order sale. Product B was a product that was facing competition and it was important for retaining a customer who would buy other related products. Product C was average in technology and competition. Product D was a new product that required the salesperson to know the new technology and to do an extensive systems analysis of the customer's needs. The assigned dollar quotas reflected the market potential of the customers in the salesperson's territory. In this example we see that the salesperson exceeded the assigned total quota by only 4%, but exceeded the assigned points by 29% (645/500) by focusing on the more difficult products with the higher assigned points. The earned points for all salespeople in a district would be added. Each salesperson's share of the district bonus would be based on his or her share of these total points. The district bonus, it was reasoned, encouraged salespeople to help each other, to build the district bonus pool. In addition, a district bonus pool tended to be fairer than a corporate pool because economic conditions could vary across industries and geographic areas. Some industries tended to be concentrated in geographic areas.

By 1997 the fast paced electronics industry required a reexamination of the compensation system. One company-wide system no longer fit the needs of each of InTek's business units (IBU). It did not recognize the needs of specialist sales forces for managing major accounts and developing markets that would not realize sales for many years. It did not reflect the importance of customer satisfaction for repeat business. It did not sufficiently reward over achievers. Additional skills are needed for account management, relationship selling, network selling, and the leadership of an account team. These skills must be developed and rewarded. Glen formed a team to examine what was needed to make InTek's sales coverage effective and efficient. It began with a market assessment of each customer

[7]The case is real but the name and some numbers are modified to assure confidentiality. Cases are presented as a basis for class discussion and are not examples of good or bad sales management.

segment and major accounts to determine the buying processes, the breadth of products purchased, historical buying patterns, maturity and growth patterns, competition, and benefits sought in the products. This analysis showed common building blocks that could be varied across IBUs to meet specific needs for sales coverage. New titles were created, each having a different compensation plan, as follows:

Title	Role	Salary/ Incentive	Incentive Components			
			Quota	Strategic Products	New Accounts	Critical Objective
Account Executive	Multiple products to major account	75/25	70	15		15
Named Account Executive	Multiple products to multiple accounts	75/25	50	25		25
Strategic Specialist	Single product to single account	60/40	25			75
Program Development Manager	New solution & trial	80/20	40			60
Business Development Representative	Multiple products in prospective territory	65/35	60			40
Product Specialist	Product focus in geographic territory	50/50	50	30		20
District Manager	Generalists	40/60	60			40
International Manager	International sales/ HQ assistance	85/15	75			25
Sales Engineer	Technical support on team	90/10	50			50
Regional Manager	Manage multiple territories	40/60	60			40

The roles are outlined in detailed job descriptions. The salary/incentive mix was determined by Glen's team, subject to executive approval. The quota was a multiple quota that included a general product quota and an attack brands quota. Strategic products could be products that were critical to retaining accounts from moving to competition or products that were being cleared from inventory. New account quotas were based on volume. Critical objectives were valuable to the company but may not generate profits within the year because of long sales cycles. Examples of goals for these objectives could include the following: improve customer satisfaction 10% in the next 18 months, initiate a product trial in account X in the next 6 months, and standardize new products in 10% of the accounts each quarter.

These components can be used to compare the performance of a salesperson with all salespeople as well as being used to calculate the incentive portion of income. For example, a named account executive could have the following pattern, which indicates that his total performance was only 1.25% above what was expected. He underperformed in the lower weighted areas and overperformed in the highest one.

	Performance		Weight Adjusted Performance	
Quota	110%	$\times$	50% =	55.00%
Strategic Products	90%	$\times$	25% =	22.50%
Critical Objectives	95%	$\times$	25% =	23.75%
Annual Weighted Average Achievement				101.25%

The computation of the incentive pay and total income is outlined in Exhibit A-8.1. Each salesperson is given an Excel spreadsheet for his or her compensation plan. This spreadsheet allows the salesperson to test the effect of different personal strategies on his or her total income.

A bonus can come from either the salesperson's sales executive who will set a goal to meet an immediate need, or the president of an IBU who needs salespeople to take specific action, such as promoting a new product. A salesperson can sell products across all business units.

Which of the InTek needs will this plan meet? What are its limitations? Are there any features of the old plan that you would like to see in the new plan? What changes would you make in the plan to meet the InTek needs in the rapidly changing market in which it operates?

EXHIBIT A-8.1.   InTek SALES COMPENSATION REPORT

FOR THE YEAR ENDING DECEMBER 31, 1998
PERSON: Chris Hernandez
POSITION: Named Account Executive

TOTAL INCOME CALCULATION

Salary	$ 75,000
Total Incentive (calculated below)	$ 79,400
Bonuses: Sales Executive for special quota achievement	$ 5,000
IBU President for introducing new product	$ 10,000
Total annual income for year	$ 169,400
Variable pay at risk (target incentive base determined by policy)	$ 25,000

INCENTIVE CALCULATION

Annual Sales Quota

	Assigned	Achieved	% Achieved	Weight	Wt. × Ach.
Total Orders:	$ 4,000	$ 5,200	130%	40%	52%
Total Revenue:	$ 3,500	$ 4,200	120%	60%	72%
Total Weighted % of Annual Quota Achieved					124%

CALCULATION OF QUOTA COMPONENT

Proportion of Incentive Assigned to Quota	50%
Variable Pay × Proportion Assigned	$12,500

Sales Quota Achievement Table

If total weighted % of annual quota achieved is between:			
0.0% and 100.0% multiply each % achieved by 1	100%	100%	$ 12,500
100.1% and 115.0% multiply each % achieved by 3	15%	45.0%	$ 5,625
115.1% or higher multiply each % achieved by 6	9%	54.0%	$ 6,750
TOTALS	124%		$ 24,875
Total Annual Sales Quota Achievement			$ 24,875

CALCULATION OF STRATEGIC PRODUCTS COMPONENT

Proportion of Incentive Assigned to Strategic Products	25%
Variable Pay × Proportion Assigned	$6,250

This section contains all orders OR all revenue, not a mix.
Which to use will be a decision by the salesperson and manager at the beginning of the year.
The maximum achievement is 140%.

If strategic orders or revenue % achieved is between:	Achieved	Applies	Mult. Rate	Earned*
0.0% and 100.0% multiply each % achieved by 1	100%	100%	100%	$ 24,875
100.1% and 140.0% multiply each % achieved by 2	60%	40%	80%	$ 19,900
	160%	140%		$ 44,775

*Amount Earned = Mult. Rate × Total Annuals Sales Quota Achieved, above.

Total Annual Strategic Sales Achievement $ 44,775

CALCULATION OF CRITICAL OBJECTIVES (CO) COMPONENT

Proportion of Incentive Assigned to Critical Objectives	25%
CO Component = Variable Pay × Proportion Assigned	$ 6,250

Each critical objective (CO) weight must be at least 10%
Each CO maximum achievement is 150%

Critical Objective	Weight%	Achieved%	Max. Allow	Wt. × Max.
Improve Customer Satisfaction	30%	170%	150%	45%
Product Trial in X	50%	130%	130%	65%
Standardize 10%	20%	90%	90%	18%
	100%			128% CO Achievement %

If CO % achieved is between:	Achieved	Applies	Mult. Rate	Earned*
0.0% and 100.0% multiply each % achieved by 1	100%	100%	100%	$ 6,250
100.1% and 150.0% multiply each % achieved by 2	28%	28%	56%	$ 3,500
	128%	128%		$ 9,750

*Earned = Mult. Rate × Critical Component Amount (above)

Total Annual Critical Objective Achievement $ 9,750

TOTAL INCENTIVE INCOME $ 79,400

Case A-9. Westmont Business Forms

At the end of December 1997, Drew Westmont, President of Westmont Business Forms, Inc., was examining the sales data for the year. He was wondering why his sales were flat, while the industry seemed to be growing. (See Exhibits A-9.1, A-9.2, and A-9.3.)

The Business Forms Industry

The business forms industry supplies business with a variety of standard and custom forms, such as invoices, checks, computer continuous forms, and sales orders. It is characterized by many national and regional firms that sell directly and through independent distributors. Westmont Business Forms, Inc., is an Atlanta-based company that serves the Southeastern United States.

The business forms industry enjoyed a healthy growth during the period of the early 1990s, with its highest growth rate between 1995 and 1997, reaching 11.7% per year. Due to alternatives such as computer graphics, scanners, and high-speed printers, the rate after

1997 is expected to drop to 8.3% per year. The rate of profitability may not follow this growth in sales because increased competition will reduce margins. In 1992 many forms companies had large inventories of standardized forms and paper, which turned out to be an advantage when there was a shortage of paper. They had lower inventories in 1997.

EXHIBIT A-9.1.   WESTMONT BUSINESS FORMS CO. INCOME STATEMENT 1996

SALES	$6,320,000
Materials	2,281,520
Labor	2,009,760
Variable Factory Expenses	214,880
Costs of Goods Sold	4,506,160
GROSS PROFIT	1,813,840
Depreciation	347,600
Selling & Administrative Expenses*	1,068,712
	3,230,152
OPERATING PROFIT BEFORE TAXES AND INTEREST	397,528
Interest	632
NET PROFIT BEFORE TAXES	$ 396,896

*Includes advertising, personal selling, market research, administrative, and R&D expenses

EXHIBIT A-9.2.   WESTMONT BUSINESS FORMS CO. BALANCE SHEET 1996

ASSETS		
Fixed Assets	$1,500,000	
Cash Assets	270,000	
Receivables	765,000	
Inventory (LIFO)	891,000	
Other		36,000
Total Assets	$3,462,000	
EQUITY		
Accounts Payable	$ 234,000	
Debt Due	72,000	
Other		333,000
Current Liabilities	$ 639,000	
Owners' Equity	2,823,000	
Total Equity	$3,462,000	

EXHIBIT A-9.3. WESTMONT SALES ($ MILLIONS) AND EXPENSE PERCENTAGES

	1998*	1997	1996	1995	1994	1993	1992	1991	1990	1989
SALES	$ 6.73	$ 7.16	$ 6.32	$ 6.17	$ 5.68	$ 5.62	$ 4.98	$ 5.30	$ 4.47	$ 3.74
Variable Costs:										
Material		36.6%	36.1%	36.4%	36.5%	36.6%	36.2%	35.8%	36.2%	36.6%
Labor		32.0%	31.8%	31.9%	32.3%	32.5%	32.1%	31.5%	32.0%	32.5%
Factory		3.4%	3.4%	3.4%	3.5%	3.6%	3.5%	3.4%	3.5%	3.7%
Total C.G.S.		72.0%	71.3%	71.7%	72.3%	72.7%	71.8%	70.7%	71.7%	72.8%
MARKETING COSTS										
Advertising		1.5%	1.3%	1.5%	1.6%	1.7%	1.5%	1.4%	1.6%	1.8%
Personal Selling		5.5%	5.5%	5.5%	5.5%	5.5%	5.5%	5.5%	5.5%	5.5%
Market Research		1.0%	1.0%	1.0%	1.0%	1.0%	1.0%	0.9%	1.1%	1.2%
Distribution		2.0%	2.0%	2.0%	2.0%	2.4%	2.0%	2.2%	2.1%	2.2%
Total Marketing Costs	10.0%	9.8%	10.0%	10.1%	10.6%	10.0%	10.0%	10.3%	10.7%	
Total Variable Costs		82.0%	81.1%	81.7%	82.4%	83.3%	81.8%	80.7%	82.0%	83.5%
FIXED COSTS										
Administrative		7.00%	7.00%	7.00%	7.00%	7.50%	7.50%	7.50%	7.50%	7.50%
Depreciation		5.50%	5.50%	5.50%	5.50%	5.50%	5.50%	5.50%	5.50%	5.50%
Interest		0.01%	0.01%	0.01%	0.01%	0.01%	0.01%	0.01%	0.01%	0.01%
R&D		0.13%	0.11%	0.10%	0.18%	0.16%	0.13%	0.18%	0.16%	0.12%
Total Fixed Cost		12.64%	12.62%	12.61%	12.69%	13.17%	13.14%	13.19%	13.17%	13.13%
PROFIT		5.36%	6.28%	5.69%	4.91%	3.53%	5.06%	6.11%	4.83%	3.37%

Years

During 1996, the industry passed cost increases, averaging 11.5%, along to its customers as price increases. This strategy may not be possible in the future for several reasons. If there is a recession, customers may switch from the showy, customized forms, to stock forms that are very competitive and have a lower margin. Customers who have purchasing agents are tending to ask for bids, thereby reducing price and increasing the cost of getting a job.

Competition in the forms industry is strong and may become more so if bidding becomes an industry trend. There has also been a proliferation of small printers in the industry. Products are diverse, so competition depends more on what product lines are carried than on where one competes. Thus some companies compete on many levels, whereas others do not compete at all.

Westmont Business Forms, Inc.

Westmont Business Forms is a relatively small company for the forms industry, but competes successfully in the southeast. It is based in Atlanta, but sells from Virginia to Florida and westward to Alabama and Tennessee. At present, it has 144 employees, seven of whom are salespeople. Westmont has no plans for expansion that would increase company size. Its production facilities can handle a 30% expansion in present markets or the addition of new ones without an increase in labor or equipment.

Westmont Business Forms was founded nearly a century ago by George S. Westmont. Since that time, it has had a reputation for producing top-quality forms and, thus a somewhat expensive line. Westmont also tries to offer service of the highest standard. The company works with its customers in such a way that it has many longstanding customers, generally handled by the vice president.

Westmont carries standard forms in inventory and makes custom forms to customer specifications. Standard forms include sales and purchase orders, receiving reports, invoices, credit memos, reply message forms, bills of lading, delivery and packing tickets, repair order forms, requests for quotations, ledger cards, journals, labels, hospital bills, and mortgage loan sheets. Westmont imprints the customer's name on the blank form.

Custom forms may include special customized formats to reflect a customer's artwork and colors. These forms include payroll, accounts payable, dividend checks, magnetic striped ledgers, computer continuous forms for bank trust tax summaries, stock certificates, restaurant customer checks, invoices, and letter sets.

Westmont sells directly to several thousand customers and indirectly through approximately 150 distributors. Standard and customized products are sold through distributors. These distributor accounts are handled by the sales manager and one new salesperson. Most of the business of Westmont is in the custom line, which is more consistent with its policy of providing service and quality at a fair price. Forms are usually purchases in order sizes of about $700. Delivery time is three to four weeks for all forms.

Since its founding, the company has stayed within the family. At present, Drew Westmont, the great-grandson of the founder, is president and has been for seven years. The Westmont family controls stock ownership with 51%; the remaining stock is held by Carter Price, the vice president. Both men have worked in sales, but Westmont also spent some time in production; thus top management has a complete picture of the workings of the company.

Westmont and Price are joint decision makers, but Westmont oversees production while Price is in charge of sales with the assistance of the sales manager, Cathy Umstead. She and Price are both involved in selling, as well as in managerial activities. Westmont wants to keep the organizational structure informal because he feels it allows for more communication within the company.

Drew Westmont presents the company as one that is "very close-knit and tightly run, yet informal. Our staff is competent and company-minded, wages are high with good benefits; thus we have no union to deal with. Carter and I make decisions together. We grew up in the business so we feel that basically two heads are better than one. Even when we disagree, I don't use my position to override him. Eventually, we compromise."

"This may not seem to be a sophisticated management style, but we are small, we don't really need fancy techniques. We're doing fine without them. With a recession a possibility, we may have a few tight years coming up, but we can handle it. Lately, our growth has been somewhat slower than the industry's, but that's probably because we're smaller."

Carter Price backs up Westmont's views of the company. He adds, "Company growth has almost come to a halt and I can find no clear-cut reason for it. We're known and have a good reputation—maybe a little expensive, but our customers have always been willing to pay for our quality. We need to increase our sales. I guess we could use a larger sales force, but we have no training program, so we have to hire the experienced salesperson who knows accounting and computers. Right now, they aren't easy to find. Cathy, the sales manager, is still selling, but not as much as a full salesperson. One trend that bothers me is the move toward bidding for a job. We are more expensive than some of our competitors, so often our bids are higher and we don't get the job. Maybe two out of five jobs are lost on bids. Our salespeople don't want to cut the price too much and who blames them? The company wants a profit and they want their commission. We've a few problems, such as sales and production rarely being balanced. There are frequent bottlenecks in order writing, composition, and shipping. But this type of thing is common in the forms business. I'd like to see us add about a million and a half in sales in the next year so that we could absorb some of our unused capacity. I think that we could do it with a little effort on everyone's part."

Management sees the future of Westmont Business Forms as strong. The trend toward competitive bidding is seen as temporary, and as the economy grows stronger, companies will return to the customized form. Management feels any problems in the company will correct themselves with growth. No changes are needed from inside; as Westmont puts it, "It's been working like this for almost 100 years. Why make changes now?"

Westmont's Sales Force

Westmont's sales force (Exhibit A-9.4) is directed by Carter Price with the assistance of a part-time sales manager, Cathy Umstead. Price continues to handle a few of his old accounts because he feels they're extremely important to the company. As the company has grown, Price feels he has less and less time to spend on these accounts and is considering turning them over to Umstead. He hesitates because he is afraid of the customers' reactions to such a move.

EXHIBIT A-9.4. THE WESTMONT SALES FORCE

Salesperson	Territory	Years with Company	Age	Experience/Education
Cathy Umstead	Distributors in Florida, Alabama, Georgia	6	29	Sales, administrative work (manager)
Ron Emerson	1/2 North Carolina, South Carolina	15	46	Work in production, then sales
Cliff Styres	Tennessee, 1/2 Alabama	4	31	Administrative work with some selling
David Whitaker	Atlanta, Georgia	4	35	Sales in another business forms company
Rick Hackney	1/2 Alabama, Florida	3	30	MBA
Margaret Linden	1/2 North Carolina, Virginia	2	26	College graduate, one year selling experience
Jeff Cobb	Distributors in North Carolina, South Carolina, Tennessee	1	24	College graduate

Cathy Umstead, the sales manager for the past year, has been with Westmont for 6 years. Along with her managerial duties, she is responsible for 65 distributor accounts. She took over these when she became manager because she thought that they required less time than her industry customers. At present, Cliff Styres is in charge of Umstead's old accounts.

Umstead tries to work most of the week at the Atlanta office on her managerial activities, but does travel each week in Florida, Georgia, and Alabama. Time away from the office varies between one and three days a week. Her administrative duties include all reports on salespeople, including recruiting, selecting, training, and evaluating them. Her job could easily be full-time without the selling activities. Umstead also tries to be available to the salespeople for assistance with any special problems they may encounter. With so many duties, Umstead neglects some that she feels are unimportant, such as the weekly call reports of the salespeople. She believes she gets more out of direct contact with salespeople.

Umstead describes her job as being a salesperson with some administrative duties. "I could actually spend all my time on my accounts, but instead divide it up to include my managerial duties. Right now I'm most concerned about getting a couple of new salespeople. There is a large untapped market in our area that needs reaching. I feel this should be our top priority, but Price thinks with new salespeople we can go into new territories. Then none of our problems would be solved. Getting new salespeople is going to be hard because we have no training program. We need people who can sell and, at the same time, know the industry. Jeff Cobb, our newest salesperson, is handling the other distributor accounts because they are the easiest way to learn something about the forms industry. He isn't ready to take on industry customers, so I can't move him out to let a new inexperienced salesperson take over Cobb's distributors. He has potential, so I don't want to push too hard. I doubt we'll be able to get experienced salespeople immediately. As soon as I get new salespeople though, some changes on the force will be made."

Ron Emerson, Westmont's senior salesperson, has been with the company for 15 years. Emerson was considered the top candidate for the manager's job, but turned it down. He believes he is better off with his sales commission of 5.5% than with the manager's salary. Emerson has been in sales with Westmont for 10 years and has a strong group of established customers. He no longer does much prospecting because he is satisfied with the income that his present customers allow him to make. He travels most of the week, but the majority of his work consists of checking on his customers and taking new orders.

Emerson described his selling style as follows: "I check on each account every six weeks and spend three or four nights a week on the road. Occasionally I check in on a potential customer recommended by one of my accounts, but otherwise I really don't look for new accounts. I'm making an adequate salary with my commission—better than if I'd taken the manager's job, so I'm satisfied. Plus, management doesn't push me to do more prospecting so why bother? Another reason I didn't take the manager's job is its structure. It should be full-time. Umstead doesn't have time to fulfill all her duties. Knowing this, I don't even turn in all the required reports and sometimes she doesn't even notice. I'm not blaming her though. The top people need to put some structure into the company. The sales force can't do it all."

The five remaining members of the sales force (Exhibit A-9.4) have all been with the company for under five years. Umstead believes that Whitaker, Styres, and Linden are doing well with their territories, but could use some help in covering such large areas. Umstead is having problems with Hackney and feels that his work should be better after three years. If she can get new salespeople, Umstead is considering firing Hackney.

Cobb, the newest salesperson, has been with Westmont for one year and handles distributorships in North Carolina, South Carolina, and Tennessee. These accounts are the easiest to handle, so Umstead put Cobb on them to aid in his training.

Cobb sees his job as an ". . order taker. I do very little, if any, real selling. Umstead tells me to look after all the old customers and don't worry about getting new accounts; yet, at the few sales meetings we have, she continually talks about the need to reach more of the market. Half the time, I don't think management knows what they want, and even if they did set goals, they wouldn't have any plans on how to reach them. The company pays well and could be great to work for, but I have my complaints. After a year, I still have no real selling experience and I wasn't even trained to start with. Sure, college gave me an idea of what to expect, but it really is a lot different out there. I probably should be out looking for a new job. Maybe it's me, but I don't know what the company expects of a salesperson, and as a new member of the force, I feel I need some guidance."

Price and Umstead both see the need for some new salespeople. Price believes that once the sales force is larger, the problems in this area will work themselves out. Umstead, on the other hand, feels some changes are needed, especially some structure added to the work of the company.

With the expansion of the sales force, Price is considering making the manager's job full-time, but isn't sure the job really requires that much effort. Another area he is considering changing is the size of the territories. He has discussed with Westmont the possibility of going into some new states. Price feels that "we're doing great where we are; why not branch out?"

Competition

The strongest competitors of Westmont sell customized forms. (See Exhibit A-9.5.) Cobb Corp., Inc., sells nationally; Johnston Forms Co. sells in the eastern United States; and American Paper Products sells in the South and Gulf regions. American is noted for its excellent quality, service, and delivery commitments, so it is Westmont's closest competitor in the minds of forms buyers. Johnston uses some of the newer high-speed presses, so its prices tend to be lower, in the long run, than Westmont, but its quality is not always good. Because of its size, Cobb offers the largest line of forms. It can be very price competitive and does very good work. Westmont worries that Cobb may expand its sales force in the southeast. The sales for these companies appear in Exhibit A-9.6.

EXHIBIT A-9.5.   WESTMONT BUSINESS FORMS, 1997 TOP COMPETITORS* ($ MILLIONS)

Company	Sales	Region	Products
Cobb Corp. Inc.	$137.70	National	Business forms, custom packaging
Johnston Forms Co.	$ 23.85	Eastern U.S.	Customized forms, standard forms, data systems equipment
American Paper Products	$ 10.30	South and Gulf	Forms for computers and business machines, printing, catalogs, textbooks

*Most competition is in the area of customized forms. These companies are larger than Westmont with a broader range of products.

EXHIBIT A-9.6.   SALES FOR WESTMONT'S COMPETITORS ($ MILLION)

	Years								
	1997	*1996*	*1995*	*1994*	*1993*	*1992*	*1991*	*1990*	*1989*
COBB	$ 153.00	$ 137.30	$ 119.10	$ 106.60	$ 94.80	$ 90.50	$ 92.90	$ 52.80	$ 44.90
JOHNSTON	$ 24.75	$ 23.85	$ 19.49	$ 17.06	$ 15.22	$ 13.84	$ 15.04	$ 11.50	$ 9.71
AMERICAN	$ 11.70	$ 10.30	$ 8.59	$ 7.40	$ 6.62	$ 5.90	$ 5.01	$ 3.68	$ 3.25
	$ 189.45	$ 171.45	$ 147.18	$ 131.06	$ 116.64	$ 110.24	$ 112.95	$ 67.98	$ 57.86

ASSIGNMENTS/DISCUSSION QUESTIONS

1. What are the problems Westmont has that are contributing to the reduced growth of sales?

2. What changes in marketing and sales strategy do you recommend? Relate your recommendations to the anticipated demographic, economic, and technical trends for the next decade.

3. Develop a retraining program for *existing* salespeople.

4. Develop a training program for three new salespeople who will be hired out of college with no industry experience.

5. Assume that Cathy Umstead will be a full-time sales manager. Write a job description for her, noting any organizational changes that you recommend.

6. Develop a control process for the salespeople. Distinguish between those controls that are automatic and those that are not automatic.

7. What are the problems with the compensation plan? Design a new compensation plan and include the objectives of your recommendation.

8. What are the motivational problems in this case? What do you recommend to motivate the salespeople toward greater activity?

Appendix 2   ## THE JEFFERSON-PILOT CORPORATION CASE[1]

JEFFERSON-PILOT: 1993

On February 28, 1993, Roger Soles, Jefferson-Pilot's (J-P) President, Chairman of the Board, and Chief Executive Officer for the last 25 years, retired. J-P Corporation had 1992 revenues of $1.2 billion from its four business segments (individual, group, casualty and title insurance; and a communications group) and from investment income.

Soles had used a strong leadership style to guide J-P during his tenure. Decision-making and management had a top-down focus, and Soles exercised a high level of control. Despite J-P's success under Soles' leadership, however, revenues had been basically flat for the last five years (1988–92). Low interest rates, which affected investment earnings, and declining life insurance sales contributed to the sluggish revenues and earnings. The corporate culture also seemed resistant to change and fixed on retaining the status quo—the traditional way of doing things.

J-P's Board of Directors felt the company needed aggressive new leadership if the company were to be a market leader. In order to provide for a smooth transition following Soles' retirement, the Board selected David A. Stonecipher to become President-elect and brought him on board in September 1992. Stonecipher had been with president and CEO of Life of Georgia, an Atlanta-based insurance company. He also served as President of Southland Life Insurance Company and had recently become President of GeorgiaUS Corporation, the parent company of both Life of Georgia and Southland Life.

Stonecipher had a reputation as an aggressive, outgoing leader who was willing to change and try new things. He realized that increased sales would be the key to J-P's revenue growth and that he needed a strong management team if he were going to make the necessary changes. With that in mind, one of his first acts was to appoint Kenneth Mlekush as Executive Vice President of Individual Insurance. Mlekush, who had previously served as President and CEO of Southland Life, brought over 30 years of experience to the position and specialized in marketing individual life and annuity products. Mlekush later asked Ron Ridlehuber, who had worked with him at Southland, to join J-P as Senior Vice President for Independent Marketing. Ridlehuber had 18 years of experience in marketing and field sales management. Stonecipher also promoted Bill Seawell from his position as an agency manager in J-P's career sales force to serve as Senior Vice President for Ordinary Marketing. Seawell had been with J-P since 1976 and had managed the Greensboro agency since 1981. During that time, the Greensboro agency had consistently been among J-P's leading agencies.

A Strategic Review

After assembling his management team, Stonecipher asked a major consulting firm that specialized in working with life insurance companies to conduct a strategic marketing review of the firm. Now, in early 1993, Stonecipher had assembled the new team in a conference room in the firm's corporate offices in Greensboro, North Carolina, to hear the consultant's report. He knew this report would provide a basis for the strategic decisions the group would have to make if the company were going to meet the Board's and the shareholders' expectations. The managers knew that a key focus of the report and of the decisions facing them would be how J-P should structure and manage its sales force because

[1]Dr. Lew G. Brown, Associate Professor, and Michael Cook, MBA, Joseph M. Bryan School of Business and Economics, University of North Carolina at Greensboro. The authors express their appreciation to Jefferson-Pilot Corporation for its cooperation in development of this case. Case is for classroom discussion purposes only.

life and annuity sales would need to grow dramatically in order to increase revenues significantly.

J-P's Sales Force

J-P distributed its individual insurance products through three separate systems: career agents, **independent producing general agents (PGAs),** and financial institutions. J-P hired **career agents** and provided them with extensive training, an office, and full staff support. The company paid the agents a salary subsidy during their training year and then changed them to a commission-only basis. The agents earned a commission on the premiums each policy generated. The agent earned a higher commission rate on the first-year premium and then earned a lower commission rate on renewal premiums thereafter as the policyholder renewed the policy year after year. The career agents were very loyal. In fact, the company was very selective in choosing career agents. Becoming one was difficult, and those who were successful were very proud of their position. But growth based on a career system was slow, and the costs of maintaining the sales force were high.

In early 1993, J-P had approximately 800 career agents. They sold about 90 percent of its life insurance policies. Agents on average during 1992 wrote about 30 policies and earned about $26,000 in first-year commissions (the commissions paid on the policy's first-year premium). The first-year commission rate averaged 50 percent of the first-year's premium. The average career agent earned total income, including commissions on renewal policies, in the high $40,000 range. Bill Seawell was responsible for managing the career sales force.

At the beginning of 1993, there were approximately 1,400 independent personal producing agents (PGAs) distributing J-P's life and annuity products. Twelve salaried regional directors recruited about 15 to 20 PGAs each year, seeking agents who were already established in the insurance business. Although the independent agents did not work directly for J-P, the company provided extensive training and support. The PGAs allowed J-P to extend its marketing operations (in a limited way) beyond its core geographic distribution areas. Although there were more PGAs than career agents, many of them sold few J-P policies each year. They had contracts with J-P as well as with other insurance companies and could sell policies offered by any company they represented. First-year commission rates on policies PGAs sold by were in the 80–85% range. These rates were higher than those for career agents because J-P did not pay any of the PGAs' expenses, as it did for career agents. Ron Ridlehuber was responsible for managing the independent sales force.

J-P also used an additional distribution channel consisting of 19 relatively small community banks and savings **institutions** that contracted to distribute life and annuity products. J-P designed the annuity products for these institutions and controlled pricing.

(Exhibits 2.1 and 2.2 present financial data on Jefferson-Pilot, and the second part of Appendix II presents additional information on J-P and its history.)

The Consultants' Presentation

David Stonecipher glanced around the conference room to make sure everyone was ready. "Well, gentlemen, let's begin." Aaron Sherman and Larry Richardson, who directed the project for the consulting firm, began the presentation.

"Gentlemen, I have given each of you a detailed report summarizing our findings. We wanted to meet with you today to present an overview of the key points and to answer any questions you have," Aaron Sherman began. "As you are aware, we began this process by holding a workshop with J-P's executives at which we asked them to rate issues the company faces. The number one issue they identified was the fact that your total annualized premium income has declined during the past five years while most of your major competitors' revenues have grown. Although J-P has an excellent core of field and home-office people and is in excellent financial condition, our analysis highlights areas where you need to take action.

EXHIBIT 2.1. CONSOLIDATED STATEMENTS OF INCOME
JEFFERSON-PILOT CORPORATION AND SUBSIDIARIES

(Dollar Amounts in Thousands Except Per Share Information)	Year Ended December 31		
	1990	1991	1992
REVENUE			
Life premiums and other considerations	$238,326	$230,369	$230,034
Accident and health premiums	375,872	382,624	383,552
Casualty and title premiums earned	47,078	45,270	44,815
Total premiums and other considerations	661,276	658,263	$658,401
Net investment income	342,053	352,772	360,882
Realized investment gains.	28,201	33,963	48,170
Communications operations	127,330	125,045	129,734
Other	3,753	3,433	5,142
	1,162,613	1,173,476	1,202,329
BENEFITS AND EXPENSES			
Death Benefits	111,444	104,131	105,013
Matured endowments	5,223	4,455	4,576
Annuity benefits.	13,903	14,912	15,054
Disability benefits.	1,224	1,151	1,185
Surrender benefits.	59,297	47,174	38,485
Accident and health benefits.	322,922	318,876	317,350
Casualty benefits	34,605	36,657	30,025
Interest on policy or contract funds.	89,651	93,995	94,106
Supplementary contracts with life contingencies. . . .	4,997	5,346	5,637
(Decrease) in benefit liabilities	(10,050)	(764)	(1,292)
Total benefits	633,216	625,933	610,139
Dividends to policyholders	16,950	16,598	16,997
Insurance commissions.	63,396	57,237	54,382
General and administrative	125,101	124,470	128,501
Net (deferral) of policy acquisition costs	(15,745)	(12,214)	(11,536)
Insurance taxes, licenses and fees	22,750	24,351	24,668
Communications operations	95,356	92,334	93,568
	941,024	928,709	916,783
Income before income taxes	221,589	244,767	285,626
Income taxes (benefits):			
Current.	68,031	77,839	88,889
Deferred.	(4,079)	(8,759)	(6,501)
	63,952	69,080	83,388
Net Income.	$157,637	$175,687	$203,238
Net Income Per Share of Common Stock	$2.94	$3.42	$3.99

Source: Jefferson-Pilot 1992 Annual Report

EXHIBIT 2.2.   **JEFFERSON-PILOT SEGMENT INFORMATION (DOLLARS IN THOUSANDS)**

	1990	1991	1992
REVENUE			
Life insurance	$ 946,262	$ 956,426	$ 965,862
Other insurance	55,164	53,472	53,907
Communications	127,330	125,045	129,734
Other, net	33,857	38,533	52,826
Consolidated	$1,162,613	$1,173,476	$1,202,329
INCOME BEFORE INCOME TAXES			
Life insurance	$179,725	$202,349	$217,635
Other insurance	6,575	919	7,820
Communications	16,902	18,023	24,262
Other, net	18,387	23,476	35,909
Consolidated	$221,589	$244,767	$285,626
IDENTIFIABLE ASSETS AT DECEMBER 31			
Life insurance	$4,132,811	$4,535,398	$4,817,482
Other insurance	136,449	147,309	158,741
Communications	111,130	102,836	99,938
Other, net	74,518	139,677	159,676
Consolidated	$4,454,908	$4,925,220	$5,235,837
DEPRECIATION AND AMORTIZATION			
Life insurance	$ 5,031	$ 5,741	$ 6,055
Other insurance	155	209	194
Communications	9,980	10,013	8,425
Other, net	324	327	172
Consolidated	$ 15,490	$ 16,290	$ 14,846

Source: Jefferson-Pilot 1992 Annual Report

Target and Managerial Peer Companies
"In conducting our analysis, we looked at a group of 13 companies, seven of which we call "managerial peers" and six of which we call "target companies." The **target companies** are those you face on a day-to-day basis in competing for policyholders and new agents. Some of these operate using a "general agent," that is an independent agent who is not an company employee. The **managerial peer companies** are those you compete with when you sell policies or recruit agents, but all of them use a career system like J-P, with agency managers who are responsible for the agents who work out of their offices. J-P has the highest rating in terms of claims-paying ability from both A.M. Best and Standard and Poor's rating services. Only five of the 13 peer companies have similar ratings. Some of your agents see the company's financial strength as a competitive weapon, while some others question whether the company has been too conservative.

EXHIBIT 2.3. JEFFERSON-PILOT'S SUMMARY OF OPERATIONS 1987–1991

(DOLLAR AMOUNTS IN MILLIONS)

	1987	1988	1989	1990	1991
Premiums and annuity considerations	$648.1	$718.0	$716.3	$727.2	$768.9
Net investment income	250.1	295.3	313.0	326.6	338.7
Other income	32.0	25.8	24.1	28.0	26.8
Total income	930.2	1,039.1	1,053.4	1,081.8	1,134.4
Total expenses	802.3	916.8	890.0	896.9	930.6
Net gain before dividends	127.9	122.3	163.4	184.9	203.8
Dividends to policyholders	18.8	25.3	24.7	23.8	22.5
Net gain after dividends	109.1	96.9	138.7	161.1	181.3

(DOLLAR AMOUNTS IN MILLIONS)

	Change from 1987–1991			Average Annual Percent Change		
	JP	Target Group Average	Managerial Peers Average	JP	Target Group Average	Managerial Peers Average
Premiums and annuity considerations	$120.8	$850.9	$3,182.0	4.4%	7.5%	11.7%
Net investment income	88.6	371.7	723.4	7.9%	9.1%	6.2%
Total income	204.2	796.5	3,590.1	5.1%	4.7%	8.6%
Deductions	(128.3)	(528.9)	(3,337.8)	(3.8)%	(3.5)%	(8.8)%
Net gain before dividends	75.9	267.6	252.3	12.4%	14.4%	6.3%

Source: Jefferson-Pilot

Performance Analysis

"This overhead (Exhibit 2.3) presents a summary of your operating performance over the 1987–91 period as compared with the 13 target and managerial peer companies. As you can see, premium income and net gain before dividends have grown more slowly than the target group's average but faster than the managerial peers' average. Over this same period, the number of J-P's career-ordinary life agents has shrunk from 1,186 to 546. As a result, you have seen a decline in the percentage of your total premium income coming from life insurance. This results also from a decline in the number of policies written and in the face amount per policy. It also appears that the productivity of your agents has lagged behind competitors. You also rely heavily on the business you develop in North and South Carolina and Virginia, as this overhead indicates (Exhibit 2.4).

Customer Analysis

"Next, we looked at your customers. This overhead (Exhibit 2.5) first compares J-P and the peer groups on the basis of premium per policy and average size per policy. Then, we break down your customers into male, female, and juvenile groups. As you can see, J-P has a lower premium per policy, average size policy, and premium per $1,000 coverage than do the peer companies. Like the peers, however, your typical customer is a male, under 35

EXHIBIT 2.4.   JEFFERSON-PILOT 1991 MARKET SHARE FOR SELECTED STATES

	JP Share of Ordinary Life Insurance			JP's Ordinary Life Premiums
	% Premium	*% Issues*	*% In-Force*	*(000)*
CORE SOUTHEASTERN STATES				
North Carolina	3.97%	2.86%	3.57%	$ 63,794
South Carolina	2.08	1.62	1.86	15,884
Virginia	0.94	0.54	0.88	13,017
OTHER MAJOR SOUTHERN STATES				
Texas	0.58	0.36	0.50	19,368
Florida	0.37	0.19	0.35	10,268
Georgia	0.59	0.39	0.55	8,785
Tennessee	0.57	0.30	0.52	5,865
Louisiana	0.51	0.52	0.55	4,352
Alabama	0.36	0.07	0.28	3,108
Mississippi	0.63	0.29	0.68	2,794
Kentucky	0.33	0.35	0.31	2,181
OUTSIDE THE SOUTH				
Virgin Islands	3.73	0.60	3.28	433
Puerto Rico	2.58	1.15	1.89	3,853
California	0.07	0.03	0.05	3,738
U.S. Total	0.32%	0.20%	0.29%	$175,446

Source: Jefferson-Pilot

EXHIBIT 2.5.   COMPARISON OF PREMIUMS AND AVERAGE SIZE PER POLICY

Premium/Policy Size:

	Jefferson-Pilot	*Target Group*	*Managerial Peers*
Premium per policy	$889	$1,211	$966
Average size policy	$101,470	$126,940	$91,580
Premium per $1,000	$8.76	$9.54	$10.55

Percent of Policies (Premium Per Policy)

Customer Demographics:

	Jefferson-Pilot	*Target Group*	*Managerial Peers*
Male	51%	57%	53%
	($1,213)	($1,567)	($1,257)
Female	38%	33%	36%
	($ 639)	($ 879)	($ 744)
Juvenile	11%	10%	11%
	($ 233)	($ 255)	($ 303)

By Whom Sold:

	Full-Time Agents	PGAs
Percent of policies	91%	9%
Premium of policy	$837	$1,439
Average size policy	$100,920	$127,580
Premium per $1,000	$8.29	$11.28

Source: Jefferson-Pilot

EXHIBIT 2.6.   ANALYSIS OF ADULT MALE CONSUMER BY OCCUPATION, INCOME, AND AGE

Adult Males Percent of Policies (Premium Per Policy)

OCCUPATION	Jefferson-Pilot	Target Group	Managerial Peers
Executive	37%	36%	28%
	($1,756)	($2,003)	($1,728)
Professional	33%	41%	28%
	($1,234)	($1,651)	($1,492)
Blue Collar	21%	18%	38%
	($ 710)	($ 884)	($ 772)
Clerical	9%	5%	6%
	($ 866)	($1,664)	($ 734)
INCOME			
Under $25K	26%	14%	24%
	($ 625)	($ 582)	($ 603)
$25K–49.9K	45%	41%	51%
	($ 841)	($ 811)	($ 956)
$50K or over	29%	45%	25%
	($2,421)	($2,400)	($2,541)
AGE			
Under 35	39%	47%	47%
	($ 561)	($ 671)	($ 688)
35–44	31%	32%	27%
	($1,169)	($1,647)	($1,034)
45 or over	30%	21%	26%
	($2,056)	($3,536)	($2,494)

Source: Jefferson-Pilot

years old who is employed in a professional or executive position. Your career agents sell 91 percent of your policies, but the policies they sell are smaller in terms of size and premium than those sold by your PGAs.

"Because adult males account for a little over half of your policies and 70 percent of your premiums, we wanted to look more closely at this group. This overhead (Exhibit 2.6) shows the occupation, age, and income distribution for your male customers and those of the peer companies. Although we saw earlier that your typical customer is under 35 years old, you will note that the peer companies have larger percentages of their customers in this group and that you have a higher percentage of your customers over 45 years old. This would suggest that you should have higher premiums per policy, yet your premiums per policy are lower in both the younger and older groups and overall. Our analysis indicates that your typical male customer has a median income of $37,500."

"Why do you think our premiums are typically lower than those of the peer companies?" Ken Mlekush asked.

"That's a good question, Ken," Larry Richardson responded. "Our feeling is that the lower premiums are the result of your company's concentration in the Southeast, where incomes are generally lower than in the Northeast. A number of the peer companies have a major presence in the Northeast. Also, some of your agents may not be capitalizing on the opportunities in their markets, but we believe the regional difference is the key factor."

Product Comparison

"If that answers your question, Ken, we'll move on to our discussion of your products," Aaron Sherman resumed. "Our next overhead (Exhibit 2.7) presents an analysis of J-P's product mix, based on first-year commissions, as compared with the peer companies. As the exhibit shows, J-P has been steadily selling less life insurance, down from 76 percent of first-year commissions to 63%, just since 1989. The other companies' life insurance shares have held relatively constant over this time. Your salespeople are selling considerably more disability income and health insurance and annuities than are the other companies."

"Why do you think our agents are selling more annuities and disability income policies?" David Stonecipher asked.

"Our experience indicates that agents find it easier to sell disability income and annuities as compared to life insurance," Aaron Sherman answered. "Consumers can understand these policies better and salespeople find them easier to explain. Thus, the salespeople go for the easy sale. What is more important to understand, however, is that it is unusual for a company with a large career sales force to stress universal life. Whole life policies provide more support for the field sales force because consumers tend to keep the policies in force longer and the renewal premiums are higher."

Sales Force Comparison

"How do our salespeople feel about the products we give them to sell?" Bill Seawell asked.

Larry Richardson responded by presenting an overhead (Exhibit 2.8). "This overhead summarizes our findings on that question. As you can see, relative to the norm for other companies we have surveyed, your agents were less pleased with the variety of products and were significantly less pleased with new product development. They also seemed to feel that the company is not as market driven as it should be."

"Larry, while we are on the subject of how the salespeople feel, how did we stack up relative to recruitment and retention of the sales force?" Ron Ridlehuber wondered.

"That's an important question, Ron. Our study shows that only 35% of J-P's new agents made it through the first year, 15 percentage points below the industry average, and only 24% made it through the first two years. Moreover, only 7 percent stay more than four years.

"This overhead (Exhibit 2.9) summarizes your situation pretty well. The first part of the overhead shows that in 1991, recruits represented 48% of your base sales force, as compared with 29% and 38% for the two peer groups. Further, as we've noted, your base sales force has been declining while your peers' sales groups have been stable or increasing. Likewise, your turnover rates have been consistently higher than your peers. Finally, the overhead shows that only 35% of your sales force has been with you more than five years as compared with 40% and 46% for the two comparison groups. And after five years, we expect agents to be in their most productive period."

EXHIBIT 2.7. PRODUCT MIX TRENDS (PERCENT OF FIRST-YEAR COMMISSION)

	1989	1990	1991
JEFFERSON-PILOT			
Life	76%	70%	63%
DI/health	9	12	12
Annuities	11	13	17
Investment Products	4	5	7
Group	0	0	0
Total	100%	100%	100%
TARGET GROUP			
Life	78%	75%	75%
DI/health	7	6	6
Annuities	4	6	7
Investment Products	5	6	8
Group	7	7	5
Total	100%	100%	100%
MANAGERIAL AGENCY PEERS			
Life	76%	78%	77%
DI/health	5	5	5
Annuities	8	9	9
Investment Products	3	3	4
Group	7	6	4
Total	100%	·100%	100%

Source: Jefferson-Pilot

EXHIBIT 2.8. SALES FORCE'S RATINGS OF JP'S PRODUCTS (PERCENT OF AGENTS AGREEING)

Agents' Overall Assessment of Companies' Products	Jefferson-Pilot	Norm
I am pleased with the variety of products our company offers.	66%	78%
I am satisfied with our company's development of new products.	33	65
Our company is market driven, responding to the needs of its target market with appropriate products and services.	25	66

Source: Jefferson-Pilot

EXHIBIT 2.9.   SALES FORCE RECRUITMENT AND RETENTION

Recruits as a Percent of Base Force

Jefferson-Pilot

	Rate	*No. of Recruits*	*Target Group*	*Managerial Peers*
1991	48%	280	29%	38%
1990	58	378	31	41
1989	34	316	30	40
1988	40	459	30	45
1987	42	501	33	41

Percent Change in Base Force

	Jefferson-Pilot*	*Target Group*	*Managerial Peers*
1991	−6%	−1%	−1%
1990	−11	+	2
1989	−31	+	1
1988	−2	+	9
1987	−2	1	6

*The field force has declined from 1,161 to 546 full-time agents
 + = Less than 1/2 of 1 percent

Turnover Rate			
1991	36%	24%	28%
1990	44	24	28
1989	48	23	28
1988	30	23	25
1987	31	24	25

Distribution of Sales Agents by Years of Service

Years of Service			
1	35%	24%	29%
2	15	14	15
3	10	9	9
4	5	7	7
5+	35	46	40

Source: Jefferson-Pilot

"Larry, what did you determine about our agents' productivity versus the peer groups?" David Stonecipher asked.

"We looked closely at the issue of productivity. We found that J-P agents earned on average lower first-year commissions (not including renewal commissions) in each year as compared with the peers. Your base sales force had average first-year commissions of about $22,000 versus $31,000 for the target group and almost $25,000 for the managerial

---

EXHIBIT 2.10. RESULTS OF AGENT SURVEY - PRODUCTION GOALS

In Our Agency, A Good Job Is Done Of Helping Agents Set Challenging But Attainable Production Objectives:

	Percent Agreement
Agency Manager	88%
Sales Manager	73
Agent	49
Norm for FT agent	52%

If Validation Requirements Were A Production Level Goal Toward Which I Was Working, I Would See It As:

	Jefferson-Pilot	*Target Group*	*Managerial Peers*
Challenging	30%	40%	48%
Modest	51	35	33
Too low	18	23	14
Too high	1	2	5

In The Past Month, How Many:

	Jefferson-Pilot	*Target Group*	*Managerial Peers*
Prospects have you mailed to	99	231	278
Prospects have you phoned	113	211	147
Cold calls have you made	41	74	63
Appointments have you had	29	49	41
Fact-finders have you completed	22	17	17
Closing interviews have you done	17	18	18

Source: Jefferson-Pilot

---

peer group. When we looked at number of policies sold, we also found that your agents sold fewer individual life policies."

"Do you have any ideas as to why our productivity is lower, Larry?"

"Yes, David. Although there are many factors that affect productivity, it seems to the project team that J-P's production standards are low compared to the peers' standards. This may cause more experienced agents to place less business with J-P. They may meet their performance goals with you and then place other business with other firms in order to meet goals there.

"There is also evidence that the agents feel that the production levels are too low. As this overhead (Exhibit 2.10) shows, your managers believe that they help agents set high but attainable goals, yet slightly less than half of the agents feel that way. In looking at the validation requirements, the performance standards that first-year agents must meet, 69 percent of the agents believed they were modest or too low. Finally, your agents had considerably less activities in direct mail, telephone prospecting, etc., than did agents from the peer companies. Many salespeople don't like to perform these activities, but experience shows that the activities are a key part of building a clientele.

EXHIBIT 2.11.   RESULTS OF AGENT SURVEY—PRE-CONTRACT

In Our Agency, New Agents Are Given A Realistic Picture of the Agent's Career:

	Percent Agreement
Agency Manager	100%
Sales Manager	93
Agent	32
Norm for FT agent	39%

Managers: Which Activities Do You Typically Require of Producers Prior to Contract?

	Jefferson-Pilot	Target Group	Managerial Peers
Learn a sales talk	100%	63%	83%
Make joint calls	93	57	60
Market opinion surveys	93	74	78
Complete sales	81	57	53
Basic insurance knowledge	70	79	77
Become licensed	59	82	93

Agents: Which Of The Following Activities Were You Required To Complete Prior to Being Contracted?

	Jefferson-Pilot	Target Group	Managerial Peers
Market opinion surveys	64%	24%	39%
Basic insurance knowledge	51	54	51
Become licensed	49	62	66
Complete sales	47	28	27
Learn a sales talk	39	36	40
Make joint calls	30	19	18
None	8	17	12

Source: Jefferson-Pilot

"Your managers and agents also seem to have different perspectives on what is required of new agents. This overhead (Exhibit 2.11) indicates that over 90% of your managers felt they give a realistic picture of an agent's career to an agent they are recruiting, yet only 32% of the agents felt that way. Moreover, when we asked the managers which activities they required of a new agent prior to signing a contract with them, we got a very different set of responses than we got when we asked the new agents the same question. Seventy-three percent of your new hires have not been full-time life agents previously, so it is not hard to understand that they might not fully understand what being a career agent requires."

Marketing Costs

"How did we compare as far as marketing costs, Aaron?"

"Ken, our analysis indicates that your marketing costs are generally in line with the managerial peer group. As you know, because of the one-time cost of issuing a policy and the high first-year sales commission, it costs J-P about $1.65 for each $1.00 of premium

EXHIBIT 2.12. **COMPONENTS OF MARKETING COSTS; 1991 (PER $100 OF WEIGHTED NEW PREMIUMS)**

	Jefferson-Pilot	Target Group	Peer Group
Producer Compensation[1]	$ 61	$55	$ 62
Management Compensation[2]	26	23	19
Field Expenses Paid by Company[3]	37	36	43
Field Benefits	17	17	24
Sub-Total	141	131	148
Home Office Marketing Expenses	24	14	18
Total	$165	145	$166

[1]Includes all compensation *other than* renewal commissions; Includes first-year commissions on management personal production
[2]Includes compensation paid to agency managers and second-line supervisors
[3]Includes all operating expenses paid by Company (e.g., clerical salary, rent, postage, telephone, etc.)
Source: Jefferson-Pilot

income in the first year. In other words, you lose $.65 for every dollar of premium income in the first year. That's why it is so important to keep policies on the books. It takes into the second or third year before the company makes any money on the policy.

"Your $1.65 figure compares with $1.66 for the managerial group, but it is higher than the target group's average of $1.45. We think that comes from your having more smaller offices. When we controlled for office size, your costs seemed to be in line. This overhead (Exhibit 2.12) shows the elements of your costs as compared with the peer companies. Your costs are higher for both producer (agent) compensation and management compensation due to your competitive bonus structure and your agent financing plan. Your home office expenses are probably higher simply because you are a smaller company than some of the peers, and there are certain fixed costs you have to bear. You should be able to grow and spread those fixed costs. To help you compare your agencies' costs with the peer group's, I prepared this overhead (Exhibit 2.13). It shows that your agencies are on average about one-third the size of the average peer agency."

"How do our agents feel about their compensation, Larry?"

"Bill, I prepared this overhead to summarize our findings on that point (Exhibit 2.14). As you can see, your full-time agents are below the norm in every category for all agents in our survey. On the other hand, your managers are above the norm in each category except for how secure they feel about their income.

"David, I think that about covers the points we wanted to present at this time. We will, of course, be available to answer additional questions you have as you proceed with your planning," Larry concluded.

"Thank you, Larry and Aaron. Your work will be very helpful. We'll let you go now while we continue our discussion."

Options

"Well, I don't know that any of the consultants' findings surprised us, but hearing them all together is certainly sobering," David began. "We've got our work cut out for us if we are going to achieve the growth and profitability goals the Board has set. It wants us to grow earnings per share by 10% per year and achieve above average returns on capital. Ken, what do you think our options are?"

"David, even if we choose the option of continuing to have the same kind of company we've had, that is one focused primarily on using the career agent to sell our products,

EXHIBIT 2.13.   1991 AVERAGE AGENCY CHARACTERISTICS

	Jefferson-Pilot	*Peers*
Manager income*	$100,913	$150,145
Agency first-year commission revenue	$247,941	$778,431
Managers' years of service	9.9	6.1
Number of agents	11.1	32.9
Number of recruits	5.7	11.2
Number of 2nd-line managers	1.5	2.2
2nd-line manager income*	$ 23,489	$ 52,075
Number of agencies	35	473

*Excludes personal production
Source: Jefferson-Pilot

EXHIBIT 2.14.   ATTITUDES TOWARDS COMPENSATION

Full-Time Agent Responses (Percent Agreement)

	Jefferson-Pilot	*Norm*
I have a secure income.	39%	46%
I have a good compensation plan.	46	58
My compensation plan is competitive.	38	49
My compensation plan is clear and understandable.	51	53
I have good fringe benefits.	51	64

Manager's Responses(Percent Agreement)

	Jefferson-Pilot	*Norm*
I have a secure income.	33%	58%
I have a good compensation plan.	67	65
My compensation plan is competitive.	56	55
My compensation plan is clear and understandable.	66	57
I have good fringe benefits.	44	73

Source: Jefferson-Pilot

we've got to make a number of changes to address the issues in the report. We seem to be in a cycle of declining performance. Fewer agents lead to less new business. This causes an expense problem. Due to that problem, we don't do the things we need to do to develop competitive products. It's a vicious cycle. Don't you agree, Bill?"

"Yes, Ken. But I think it is important for us to remember that our career-agent system is our key strength. We are known as a company because of that system. We have many long-term, loyal agents. As you know, my father worked here and was in charge of our career agents. We need to improve the quality of our recruits, train them better, and keep them with us. If we can do those things, we will grow faster and be more profitable."

"That's true, Bill," Ron joined in, "but it seems to me that we need to look more closely at complementing the career system by increasing our emphasis on the independent agent. We have many independent agents now, and the report shows that they are very productive. But they have never been the focus of our system. Under a new system we would contract with existing insurance agents, allowing them to offer our products. This avoids the problem of having to hire and train new recruits, and it would allow us to expand our geographic coverage more quickly. Further, we would not have to pay the office costs and associated salaries. We could pay these independent agents on a commission-only basis. Instead of using our 12 regional directors to recruit, we could license independent marketing organizations to recruit for us, with them earning an override commission on sales their agents made."

"Ron, I know you used this kind of system at Southland, but it would be such a radical change for J-P," Bill responded. "If you increased the size of our sales force substantially by using independent agents, I'm not sure how our career force would react. I'm afraid they'd be terribly threatened. And the folks in the home office are used to working with career agents. The independents would not be loyal to the company. We would have less control over what they sell and over the quality of their work with policyholders. And can you imagine what will happen the first time one of our career agents runs into an independent agent trying to sell the same product to the same customer!"

"David, you asked about options," Ken continued. "I guess this exchange points out that we could continue with a predominantly career-based system, move to a predominantly independent system, or have a combination of the two approaches. We're going to have to make significant changes under any of the options, and I'm sure there will be problems we'll have to address. A final growth option, of course, is to acquire other insurance companies. We certainly have the financial strength to do that, but even then we are going to have to address the issue of how we distribute, how we sell, our products to our policyholders."

"Yes, Ken, distribution is a key issue. I can see that there are many issues we need to think carefully about before we make a decision. Here's what I'd like for you to do. I'd like for each of you independently to consider our situation and develop recommendations as to how we should proceed. I'd like to meet again in two weeks to hear your presentations. I'll call you to set up a specific time once I check my calendar."

HISTORY OF JEFFERSON-PILOT CORPORATION

J-P had its origins in the Worth-Wharton Real Estate & Investment Company, which was incorporated in Greensboro in 1890. In 1905, the owners changed the name to Southern Life and Trust Company; and in 1924, the company reorganized as Pilot Life Insurance Company. A separate company, The Jefferson Standard Life Insurance Company began operations in 1907 in Greensboro. The North Carolina business and civic leaders who founded these companies believed they could meet the needs of the region better than existing competitors. They wished to keep capital in the area to support economic development.

Both companies succeeded and rapidly extended their initial reach, eventually achieving national significance. Jefferson Standard's equity interest in Pilot dated to 1931, and, in 1945, Jefferson Standard acquired all of Pilot's stock. Both companies accelerated their expansion after World War II.

The two companies were complementary. Jefferson Standard focused on a single product line, individual ordinary life insurance, while Pilot, which began as an ordinary life company, entered the home service business in 1945, thus becoming a multiple-line company. The companies' distinctiveness lay in marketing. Jefferson Standard sold through company-owned regional agencies staffed with career agents, while Pilot's primary marketing channel was through independent general agencies.

With the formation in 1968 of J-P Corporation, both Jefferson Standard and Pilot became wholly-owned subsidiaries of that company. Following that, the two companies drew closer together, and, through a joint planning process, coordinated their business strategies closely. The companies jointly developed products, and each company's agents began selling the other's products. Their common interests led to the formation of subsidiaries providing services to both in investment management, data processing, pension plan sales and administration, and investor services.

As the positive aspects of the dual marketing system became evident, the owners decided to merge the two companies. On January 1, 1987, Jefferson Standard Life Insurance Company and Pilot Life Insurance Company combined to form the Jefferson-Pilot Life Insurance Corporation.

The J-P Corporation had four major business segments at year-end 1992:

Individual Insurance—This segment offered life insurance, annuities, disability income, mutual funds, and 401-Ks. The primary markets were estate planning, income protection, retirement planning, and investment. Individual insurance accounted for 68.1% of J-P's operating profits in 1992. Over 2,200 Career Agents, Personal Producing Agents, Independent Brokers, and Managers; along with 470 Home Service Agents and Managers; 12 Individual Health Regional Sales and Service offices; and 19 Financial Institutions distributed J-P's individual insurance products.

Group Insurance—This segment offered many products and services, including employee and dependent term life, mass-marketed payroll deduction universal life, short-term and long-term disability income, dental benefits, vision benefits, accidental death and dismemberment, prescription drug benefits, and managed care. Group insurance has its primary markets in employee groups with more than 10 people, with the greatest concentration on companies with 25 to 1,000 employees. Group insurance products and services were distributed by 85 sales and service representatives, 22 regional sales and service offices and the company's agents and independent brokers. The group insurance segment accounted for 23.3% of J-P's 1992 total operating profits.

Casualty & Title Insurance—This segment offered commercial insurance lines such as workers compensation, commercial property, commercial auto and general liability. This segment also marketed personal insurance lines such as automobile, homeowners insurance, and title insurance. Six regional sales offices and 303 professional independent agents distributed the products. The segment contributed 4.1% of J-P's total operating profits in 1992.

Communications—This segment contained three elements: broadcasting properties, Jefferson-Pilot Sports, and J-P Data Services. J-P owned two television stations and six radio stations. Jefferson-Pilot Sports produced broadcasts of Atlantic Coast Conference and Southeastern Conference football and basketball games. J-P Data Services provided information to television and radio broadcasters, cable networks, and advertising agencies and representatives. The communications segment provided 8.3% of J-P's operating profits in 1992.

Investments—Although this segment did not directly produce or deliver a product or service, its objective was to invest premium income. The net investment income was $361 million in 1992, despite a low interest rate.

As of December 31, 1992, J-P had approximately 3,900 employees with revenues of $1.2 billion. The average number of outstanding shares in 1992 was 51 million, which were held by 9,881 stockholders. Besides its executive offices in Greensboro, NC, it also owned facilities in Colorado, Florida, Georgia, California and Virginia.

J-P held licenses to operate in 39 states, the District of Columbia, Puerto Rico, and the Virgin Islands.

J-P's summary financials are presented below:

Operating Income Per Share	Stockholders' Equity Per Share
1988 - $1.66	1988 - $22.81
1989 - $2.23	1989 - $26.31
1990 - $2.59	1990 - $26.13
1991 - $2.98	1991 - $30.47
1992 - $3.56	1992 - $33.44

Dividends Per Share	Year-end Stock Price
1988 - $0.83	1988 - $20.00
1989 - $0.90	1989 - $28.33
1990 - $0.98	1990 - $24.67
1991 - $1.09	1991 - $37.67
1992 - $1.30	1992 - $48.13

Appendix 3

THE LIFE INSURANCE INDUSTRY

Life Insurance

People buy life insurance for many reasons, but mainly to provide financial protection for their families if the policyholder should die prematurely. Life insurance provides support for the insured's survivors and pays any estate obligations at the time of death; accumulates funds for retirement, emergencies, and business use; and defers or avoids income taxes. A person can use life insurance to create or add to an estate and then can protect that estate by maintaining the policy.

Historical Background

Ancient Babylonians and the early Greeks developed the concept of insurance. Under Babylonian law, a person could adopt a son, raise him, and then depend on him for support in later years, thereby providing a type of retirement insurance. The Greeks belonged to various religious sects to which they paid monthly dues. As a benefit, the sect promised a decent burial according its rites, as well as money to pay the deceased's obligations. If members fell behind in their monthly premiums, they had to pay fines.

The Romans furthered the concepts of burial insurance and settlement of obligations. They began to place less emphasis on the religious aspects and opened membership to the general public. They created a special society for soldiers that provided death benefits and pensions for disability or old age.

However, the development of modern insurance did not begin until the early 14th century. In 1310, the first insurance company was chartered in Flanders. Life insurance first appeared in the United States in 1759, with the formation of "The Corporation for Relief of Poor and Distressed Widows and Children of Presbyterian Ministers." This company, now Covenant Life Insurance Company, is the oldest life insurance company in continued existence in the world. In 1794, the Insurance Company of North America became the first chartered general life insurance company in the United States. In 1840, the New York State Legislature enacted a law that protected a widow's life insurance proceeds from creditors' claims, strengthening a life insurance policy's protective power. In 1859, New York State established the first state government insurance department; and, in 1869, the U.S. Supreme Court upheld states' rights to regulate insurance companies. In 1911, companies introduced the first group life insurance policies for purchase by companies for their employees. In 1944, the U.S. Supreme court held that life insurance companies were subject to Federal laws because they were engaged in interstate commerce.

Classes of Life Insurance

Companies offer several different classes of life insurance. The classes differ in type of customers, policy amounts, cash values, methods of computing and collecting premiums, underwriting standards, and marketing methods.

Ordinary Life Insurance—Companies usually issue life insurance in amounts of $1,000 or more with premiums payable annually, semiannually, quarterly, or monthly. The ordinary department of most life insurers is their largest department, and many insurers write only ordinary life insurance. Ordinary insurance accounts for 51 percent of life insurance in force in the United States and about 76% of the insurance purchased annually. Term, whole life and universal life were all types of ordinary life insurance.

Term Insurance. Term insurance is the most basic type of life insurance. Term insurance provides only temporary protection, for a specified time period, such as one, five, or ten years, or until the insured reaches a specified age, such as sixty-five. Term insurance policies provide pure protection and do not accumulate cash values or offer any savings element. Most term insurance is both renewable and convertible. "Renewable" means that the policyholder can renew the policy for additional periods without evidence of insurability. "Convertible" means that the policyholder can exchange the policy for some type of cash value life insurance with no evidence of insurability. Term life insurance premiums increase as the policyholder ages. Purchasers use term insurance for three general situations: if their income is limited, if they have temporary needs, or if they want to guarantee future insurance availability.

Term insurance has two major limitations. First, because term insurance premiums increase with age, premiums often became unaffordable at older ages. Second, because term insurance has no cash value or savings element they do not help the insured save money for certain purposes, such as for retirement or for their children's education.

Whole Life Insurance. Whole life insurance has fixed premiums and provides lifetime protection. The most common types of whole life insurance are called ordinary life and universal life.

Ordinary life insurance has level premiums and lifetime protection to age 100. If the insured is still alive at age 100, the insurance company pays the policyowner the policy's face amount. Under an ordinary life policy, the premiums paid during the early years of the policy are higher than necessary to pay death claims, while the premiums paid during the later years were lower than necessary for paying death claims. Because of the higher-than-necessary early premiums, an ordinary life policy develops a legal reserve. The legal reserve becomes a liability item on the insurance company's balance sheet that formally recognizes the overpayment of premiums. The life insurer then has to accumulate assets to offset the legal reserve's liability.

Because the policyholder pays premiums that are larger than necessary, his/her policy develops a "cash value." Insurance companies use the cash value from their policies to make investments so they will be able to pay policy claims and also pay interest on the policyowners' savings. If the policyowner no longer wants the insurance, the policyowner can surrender the policy for its cash value. Although the cash surrender values are relatively low during the early years, they can accumulate to sizable amounts over time. Thus, an ordinary life policy allows the insured to provide for insurance and saving needs all in one policy.

Ordinary life policies also have disadvantages. Because ordinary life insurance is relatively expensive in the early years, some policyowners can still be underinsured. Additionally, ordinary life policies have some disadvantages as savings vehicles. Insurance companies do not have to state the rate of return on the cash value specifically when they issue the policy. Rates of return are relatively low on some policies. Finally, cash values are not legally required until the end of the third year. Thus, the amount of saving during the early years is relatively small, and the policyholder can incur a substantial loss if he/she allows the policy to lapse or if he/she surrenders the policy during the early years.

Universal Life Insurance. Universal life insurance is a relatively new, rapidly growing form of whole life insurance. Companies often sell universal life policies as investments that combine insurance protection with savings. Universal life insurance is a flexible premium deposit fund combined with monthly renewable term insurance. The policyowner pays a specified initial premium. The company credits the gross premium less expenses to the policy's initial cash value and deducts a monthly mortality charge for the pure insurance protection. The company then pays interest at a specified rate on the remaining cash value. Fundamentally, universal life insurance serves as a combination of a savings account and monthly renewable term insurance.

Universal life policies are very flexible. Policyholders can increase or decrease the premiums, skip premium payments as long as the cash value is sufficient to cover mortality costs and expenses, increase or decrease death benefits, add to the cash value at any time, and borrow money based on the cash value.

Special Purpose Policies and Riders

In addition to the basic policy types, life insurance companies offer several special policies. These policies are usually combinations of policies designed to meet specific life insurance needs. Many policies are designed as inflation-era products to help policyowners cope with the need for increasing death protection and savings as the value of the dollar declines. Many of these special policies provided coverage for more than one person, usually entire families. Others provided for payment of mortgages, etc.

Insurance companies often add supplemental agreements, called riders, to life insurance policies. Some riders add more life insurance, such as level, increasing, or decreasing term, to a basic whole life policy. Others deal with the waiver of premium payments in the event of disability, accidental death and dismemberment benefits, and the guaranteed right to purchase additional insurance. Some riders even increase or decrease the amount of insurance to reflect cost-of-living changes measured by the consumer price index.

Annuities

Annuities are another form of insurance that consumers can use to provide income. An annuity represents an investment that provides regular periodic payments for the owner's life or for a specified period. An annuity providing lifetime income is called a life annuity. A life annuity is true life insurance because it insures against outliving financial resources. Life annuities are important instruments in planning for financial security during retirement.

A consumer purchasing an annuity commits to make a specified payment each month for a specified period. Each payment adds to the annuity's cash value, and the account earns interest on that value. The owner can structure an annuity so that, at retirement, the annuity will be sufficient to make a certain monthly payment to the owner for the remainder of his/her life. Each payment has three components: interest, principle, and an insurance benefit. The interest earned declines each year as the principal is gradually liquidated through payments. Therefore, as years go by, more of the payment comes from principal and less from interest. If the owner's principal runs out before he/she dies, the payments then consist of an insurance benefit. When the owner dies, the remaining principal and accrued interest become part of his/her estate.

Life Insurance in the 1990s

Consumers purchased $1.6 trillion in life insurance in 1991, up 5.7% from 1990. Sales of ordinary life insurance accounted for nearly two-thirds of that amount. Purchases of whole life were 56%, down from 61% three years earlier. Universal and variable life insurance accounted for 21% of ordinary sales, down from a high of 40% in 1985.

In 1991, life insurance in force reached an all-time high, $9.98 trillion, up 6.3% from 1990. The average amount of life insurance per U.S. household was $102,700, some $4,300 more than in 1990. Eighty-one percent of American households owned life insurance. Approximately 70% of adult Americans owned some form of life insurance.

In 1991, benefit payments, excluding health insurance, reached a record $91.6 billion, up 3.6%. Payments to beneficiaries in 1991 totaled $25.4 billion. Companies paid about $29.6 billion to life insurance policyholders and $36.6 billion to annuity owners.

U.S. life insurance companies' assets were $1.6 trillion at year-end 1991. This was an increase of $143.0 billion, or 10.2%, from 1990 year end. Policy loans outstanding rose slightly in 1991, and totaled $66.4 billion. They accounted for 4.3% of assets - the lowest proportion since 1965. Life insurance companies' largest percentage increase in investments was in stocks, up 28.0% over year end 1990. The net rate of investment earnings before federal taxes (excluding separate accounts) continued to decline, to 9.09%, the lowest since 1983.

Life Insurance Purchases in 1991

Of the nearly 30 million new life insurance policies and certificates issued during 1991, 13.5 million were ordinary policies, 112,000 were industrial policies, and 16.2 million were group certificates. The average size of the ordinary policies continued to increase. In 1981, for example, the average new ordinary policy was $30,430; by 1986, the amount has increased to $55,540; in 1990, to $76,050; and in 1991 to $77,320. A sample survey of ordinary life insurance purchased by Americans in 1991 showed that 50 percent of all new policies sold were for people between the ages of 25 and 44.

In terms of the number of policies sold, term insurance accounted for 20% in 1991, down from 25 percent in 1987. Variable and universal policies dropped from 26% of sales in 1987 to 16% in 1991. Traditional whole life and combination sales continued to increase, to 64% of policies in 1991, but were still below the 69% share of 1982.

Life Insurance Companies' Earnings

Life insurance companies produce revenue from two main sources: premiums paid by policyholders and earnings on investments. There is a close relationship between these income elements. Part of each premium payment becomes available for investment. In calculating premiums, companies take into account the anticipated investment earnings, thereby reducing the price of life insurance.

In 1991, total income of all U.S. life companies was $411 billion with 64.2% from premium receipts and 28.9% from investment earnings. The remaining 6.9% came from other sources, including payments for supplementary contracts.

Premium receipts and annuity considerations totaled $263.8 billion. Americans spent the equivalent of 4.81 percent of total disposable income in 1991 for life insurance and annuities, compared with 5.07 percent during 1990.

Life insurance accounted for about 30% of all premium receipts in 1991. This proportion had declined in relation to the income received from annuities. In 1971, the proportion was 56.3%; by 1981 the proportion had dropped to 43.8%.

Ordinary policy premiums accounted for $62.8 billion, or 79.2% of the life insurance premiums in 1991. Most ordinary premiums were renewals. Group insurance premiums amounted to $14.3 billion, or 18% of all life insurance premiums, while industrial premiums accounted for $527 million, or 0.7%. Annuity considerations totaled $123.6 billion in 1991, down from $129.1 billion in 1990.

U.S. life insurance companies' policy reserves totaled $1.3 trillion at the end of 1991. These reserves represented the funds set aside to meet the companies' future obligations to policyholders and their beneficiaries. State laws required each company to maintain its policy reserves at a level that would assure payment of all policy obligations. Regulators calculated the reserve amount based on actuarial tables that took into account the funds from future premium payments, interest earnings, and expected mortality experience.

Life insurance companies' total reserves at the end of 1991 included $372.1 billion for life insurance policies, $38.3 billion for health insurance policies and $894.5 billion for annuities and supplementary contracts.

Life Insurance Company Assets

In 1991, U.S. life insurance companies' assets, including those held in separate accounts, totaled $1.55 trillion, an increase of 10.2 percent during the year, compared to an increase of 8.3% in the previous year. Net investments in U.S. capital markets by life insurance companies totaled $90.2 billion in 1991. Life insurance ranked second among private domestic institutional sources of funds, supplying 18.1% of the total funds flowing into financial markets. Companies' investments were primarily in corporate debt issues, government securities, mortgages, and preferred and common stocks.

Life Insurance Companies

In 1991, there were 2,105 U.S. life insurance companies and an estimated 50,000 life insurance agents. The number of companies reached an all-time high in 1988 but had been declining steadily. Most companies that discontinued operations did so by merging with other insurers or had all their outstanding business reinsured in other life insurance companies. The remaining companies terminated for various reasons, including conversion to nonlife company status.

The majority of new companies formed in recent years remained in business. By specializing in meeting the needs of families in specific regions, many had been able to compete successfully with older and larger companies whose operations encompassed larger areas.

Trends

In the late 1970s and early 1980s, the industry had to contend with high inflation and rising interest rates. New money market funds were paying 17% interest compared to only 5% for conventional whole life policies. Consumers shifted their insurance purchases to less expensive term insurance and invested the premiums they saved at higher rates elsewhere. Policyholders terminated their policies and took out low-rate policy loans. This aggravated insurers' liquidity problems and undermined profitability.

On the other hand, the high interest rates allowed the industry to realize higher returns on investments. As interest rates began to drop in the late 1980s, the industry once again faced financial difficulties. These problems were magnified by the real estate market's decline in the early 1990s. Many life insurance companies began increasing their real estate holdings in the early 1980s in order to improve investment returns. Unfortunately, the market slowed considerably, and commercial vacancy rates rose to the 20 percent level. Many companies were stuck holding non-performing assets.

Analysts expected competition in the life insurance segment to increase. Aging "baby boomers" would increase the demand for products that provided retirement income and health care financing. Additionally, life insurance companies would have to face competition from banks, mutual funds, and other financial institutions that were able to offer products that competed with life insurance products.

Name Index

Company Index

443

Subject Index